Principal Si
CITY OF SAN FRA
D0206999
4 ★★NOB HILL
Principal sectio
★★★ Highly recomm
★★ Recommended
★ Interesting
8 ★★★ ALCATRAZ
★Treasure Island
10 ★★★ FISHERMAN'S WHARF
★★★ LOMBARD STREET
★★★ COIT TOWER
5 ★★NORTH BEACH
6 ★RUSSIAN HILL
9 ★THE EMBARCADERO
★★ Transamerica Pyramid
COW HOLLOW
4 ★★NOB HILL
3 ★★FINANCIAL DISTRICT
1 ★★★CHINATOWN
7 ★UNION SQUARE AREA
17 JAPANTOWN
★★San Francisco Museum of Modern Art
22 ★★SOUTH OF MARKET
2 ★CIVIC CENTER
SAN FRANCISCO BAY
China Basin
Central Basin
Basic Brown Bear Factory
Anchor Brewing
21 ★MISSION DISTRICT
20 CASTRO DISTRICT & NOE VALLEY
India Basin
South Basin
McLaren Park
3Com Park
Candlestick Point

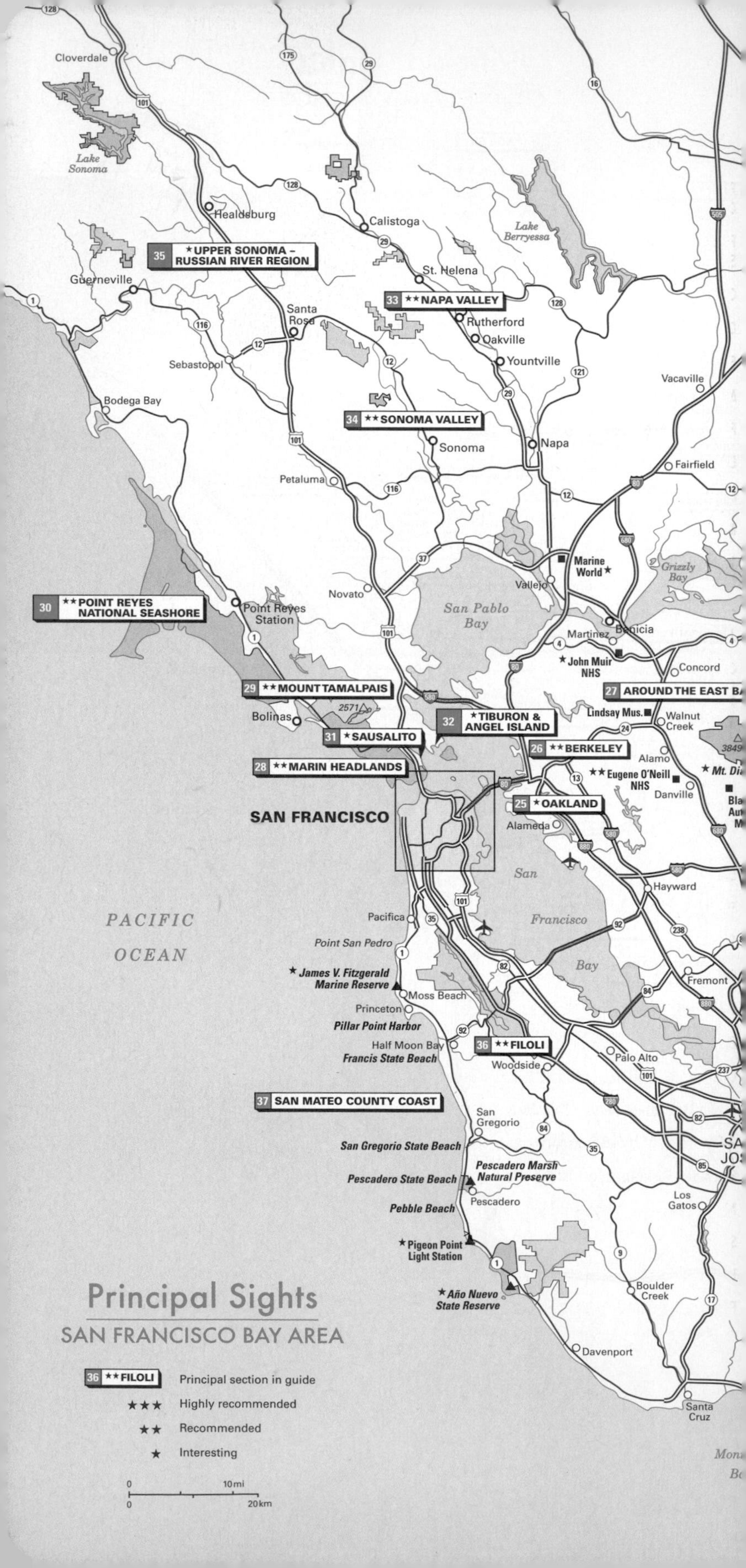

Principal Sights
SAN FRANCISCO BAY AREA
36 ★★FILOLI Principal section in guide
★★★ Highly recommended
★★ Recommended
★ Interesting
35 ★UPPER SONOMA – RUSSIAN RIVER REGION
33 ★★NAPA VALLEY
34 ★★SONOMA VALLEY
30 ★★POINT REYES NATIONAL SEASHORE
29 ★★MOUNT TAMALPAIS
32 ★TIBURON & ANGEL ISLAND
31 ★SAUSALITO
28 ★★MARIN HEADLANDS
27 AROUND THE EAST BA
26 ★★BERKELEY
25 ★OAKLAND
36 ★★FILOLI
37 SAN MATEO COUNTY COAST
SAN FRANCISCO
PACIFIC OCEAN
San Francisco Bay
San Pablo Bay
Grizzly Bay
Lake Sonoma
Lake Berryessa
Cloverdale
Healdsburg
Calistoga
St. Helena
Rutherford
Oakville
Yountville
Guerneville
Santa Rosa
Sebastopol
Bodega Bay
Vacaville
Napa
Sonoma
Fairfield
Petaluma
Novato
Point Reyes Station
Vallejo
Marine World ★
Benicia
Martinez
★ John Muir NHS
Concord
Lindsay Mus.
Walnut Creek
Bolinas
2571
Alamo
★★ Eugene O'Neill NHS
Danville
★ Mt. Di
Alameda
Hayward
Pacifica
Point San Pedro
★ James V. Fitzgerald Marine Reserve
Moss Beach
Princeton
Pillar Point Harbor
Half Moon Bay
Francis State Beach
Woodside
Palo Alto
Fremont
San Gregorio
San Gregorio State Beach
Pescadero Marsh Natural Preserve
Pescadero State Beach
Pescadero
Pebble Beach
★ Pigeon Point Light Station
★ Año Nuevo State Reserve
Los Gatos
Boulder Creek
Davenport
Santa Cruz
0 10mi
0 20km

List of Maps

Introduction

"We sailed down the magnificent bay with a light wind, the tide, which was running out, carrying us at the rate of four or five knots. It was a fine day; the first of entire sunshine we had had for more than a month. We passed directly under the high cliff on which the presidio is built, and stood into the middle of the bay, from whence we could see small bays, making up into the interior, on every side; large and beautifully wooded islands; and the mouths of several small rivers. If California ever becomes a prosperous country, this bay will be the centre of its prosperity. The abundance of wood and water, the extreme fertility of its shores, the excellence of its climate, which is as near to being perfect as any in the world, and its facilities for navigation, affording the best anchoring-grounds in the whole west coast of America, all fit it for a place of great importance ... "

Richard Henry Dana,
Two Years Before the Mast (1835)

© Brenda Tharp

Geographical Notes

Situated atop a peninsula that forms the western boundary of a 496sq mi bay, the city of San Francisco boasts an incomparable setting of mountains, hills and water. Its dramatic topography, agreeable climate and pervasive presence of sea and bay have invited exploration and enjoyment for centuries. The bay itself played an immensely important role in San Francisco's early development as the commercial and cultural hub of the western US.

Working Against Nature – The hills and valleys that characterize San Francisco and the Bay Area (as the region surrounding the city is known) form part of the **Coast Ranges**, a low, but rugged belt of mountains extending from Santa Barbara County to Oregon. Prominent summits in the Bay Area include **Mt. Tamalpais** (2,571ft), which

SPOT Satellite Image, July 8, 1985, 10:30am–Nigel Press/Tony Stone Images

looms over MARIN COUNTY to the north; **Mt. Diablo** (3,849ft), which backdrops the hills of OAKLAND to the east; and **Mt. Hamilton** (4,213ft), which lies southeast of the city in the South Bay area. Peaks within the city include Mt. Davidson (929ft), twin peaks (922ft and 904ft) and Mt. Sutro (908ft).

San Francisco's famed steep streets came of an early planner's unwillingness to depart from the strict, perpendicular street grids that were the standard of the day. In 1847, on the bare hills of the infant city, surveyor Jasper O'Farrell imposed a resolutely rectangular grid. The result: a host of streets that abruptly ascend the side of a hill, crest, then plummet vertiginously down the other side. Several commanding hilltops remained squatter settlements and goat pastures until the invention of the cable car made it possible for the well-to-do to get up and down. Later development in the city and its environs took the topography into account, so that in the hills of Berkeley, Oakland and other Bay Area towns, most streets sensibly follow the natural contours of the land.

Not all of San Francisco's original hills exist today, nor does much of its natural bay shoreline. In the course of the post-Gold Rush construction boom, small prominences were leveled or terraced to create building sites, and steam shovels removed the unstable sand hills that occupied large areas south of present-day Market Street. Sand and other excavated rubble were dumped into the shallows and mud flats along the bay shore. Near the present-day FINANCIAL DISTRICT, the spaces between piers were filled, extending the shore from its natural line around Montgomery Street to that traced today by the EMBARCADERO. The early sand beach that gave NORTH BEACH its name was obliterated with fill material in the mid-19C, and the houses of the MARINA DISTRICT sit atop shallows that were filled in with rubble from the 1906 earthquake and fire. Today, the bluffs of FORT MASON remain San Francisco's only original shoreline inside the Golden Gate.

The Mighty Bay – The Coast Ranges are bisected by the great **San Francisco Bay**, which serves not only as a coastal inlet but also as an estuary, through which the rivers draining the western slope of the Sierra Nevada Range and the flat plains of the Central Valley join and pass to the sea. The bay itself submerges a large, northwest/southeast-running Coast Range valley that would have been visible some 20,000 years ago when vast amounts of water were frozen in continental glaciers. The ancestor of the Sacramento River flowed across this valley and out through the Golden Gate, which then was a gorge. As long-term climatic warming that marked the end of the Ice Age melted the glaciers, the sea rose and backed up into the valley, creating a large, protected bay.

An Unstable Foundation – The Bay Area lies atop a complex system of tectonic faults created by the motion of the Pacific and North American plates, giant solidified sections of the earth's crust that move about atop the molten material of the earth's mantle. The two plates slide past each other at an average speed of two inches per year. Movements along faults occur frequently and, under normal conditions, imperceptibly. Occasionally, however, the slide is impeded by rigid material, and pressure increases as the plates strain to move. When the obstruction gives way, the pent-up pressure is released in a sudden lurch, accompanied by shuddering and trembling known as an **earthquake**.

The most notorious California fault is the **San Andreas rift zone**, extending from the Imperial Valley in southeastern California to Cape Mendocino on the state's north coast, passing en route beneath the seabed west of San Francisco. Along the San Francisco Peninsula, the long, linear valley of the Crystal Springs reservoirs, just west of Interstate 280, is a surface expression of the zone, as is the valley that separates Point Reyes from the rest of Marin County. In the famous 1906 earthquake, more than 16ft of movement occurred along this fault in a matter of seconds. The San Andreas fault is only the most widely known among many others in this shear zone. Perhaps most ominous is the Hayward fault, which runs along the base of the Oakland and Berkeley hills, an area that has become densely populated since the last major earthquake.

Climate – San Francisco summers are cool and dry while winters are wet and mild, characteristic of a Mediterranean climate accentuated by the peculiarities of the city's location. The high mountains of the Sierra Nevada range to the east block the frigid air masses that sweep across the rest of the country, and the Pacific Ocean to the west has a regulating effect on temperature extremes, such that the city registers the lowest mean summer temperature of any city in the US outside of Alaska, and rarely sees a winter frost. Snow has accumulated in the downtown area only twice in the city's recorded history, both in the 1880s.

Though seasonal temperature variation is remarkably slight, weather within the city and throughout the Bay Area is greatly affected by microclimates that result from the region's hilly topography. The dip of a mountain ridge or change in proximity to the ocean can create pronounced variations in temperature from neighborhood to neighborhood; temperatures can vary by as much as 35 degrees between coastal and inland areas. The staggered ridges of the Coast Ranges confine the chilling effect of the Pacific Ocean to a rather narrow frontage along the coast and the East Bay shore lying directly opposite the Golden Gate, while a short distance east across the hills or south along the peninsula, towns broil under a brilliant sun.

One of the factors most responsible for San Francisco's cool summer temperatures is the city's renowned **fog**, created when westerly winds, laden with moisture from the Pacific Ocean, cross the cold California current. The moisture condenses, creating dramatic rivers, fingers and banks of fog that suddenly flow over the city from the west, turning a brilliant day into a gloomy one within minutes. Such "advection fog" often forms a dense but shallow layer that hugs the ground and leaves higher elevations in the clear. In summer, fog typically builds during the day over the coast, then pours over the hills and through the Golden Gate, shrouding the Sunset District and other coastal neighborhoods in a dense gray mist while leaving other areas in the clear.

Rain generally falls between November and April. In summer, atmospheric circulation causes a cell of high-pressure air to settle towards the earth's surface, suppressing the upward convection that might form rain clouds, and deflecting fronts and storms into the Pacific Northwest. In winter, this high-pressure cell moves to more southerly latitudes and allows storms in, bringing rain, sometimes for days on end.

Historic Urban Plans

San Francisco (1868)

Immigrant Vegetation – As with the Bay Area's human population, much of the region's plant life originated elsewhere. The vast expanses of grass that shroud the "golden hills" of California are mostly European wild oats, seeds of which stowed away in the bags of wheat sent to Spanish missions; once rooted, they crowded out the indigenous bunch grasses. The eucalyptus trees that perfume many a park, campus and backyard were imported from Australia in the 1860s as a potential new source of construction timber, although the experiment proved a failure. California's one native species of palm is found only in the southern part of the state; most of the palms now visible in the Bay Area come from the Canary Islands and other places.
Indigenous features of the plant landscape include stately **live oaks**, which grow widely spaced on grassy hillsides in the warmer and drier parts of the Bay Area. Coast redwoods *(p 183)*, which live more than 2,000 years and grow to heights over 300ft, thrive in cooler and moister sites nearer the ocean.
Also typical of Bay Area landscapes are dense thickets of **chaparral**, formed not of a single plant but of an association of native species (including poison oak). The shrubby plants grow during wet winters, then survive the dry summers by minimizing water loss through leathery leaves and concentrated sap. As the chaparral dries in late summer, it becomes highly flammable, a perfect fuel for brush fires that periodically sweep over the hills, destroying houses and sometimes entire neighborhoods. The plants themselves are adapted to grow back quickly after a fire from burls below ground level.

San Francisco on Camera

San Francisco's quirky film history began in 1872 when Eadweard Muybridge, a Bay Area photographer, put together (at the request of Leland Stanford) a rapid succession of still photographs to prove that a running horse at one period of his stride has all four feet off the ground. Since then, directors from Erich von Stroheim to John Huston to Alfred Hitchcock to Francis Ford Coppola have used San Francisco's glorious cityscapes as the backdrop for numerous productions, from big-budget Hollywood blockbusters to smaller, independent films.

A selection of movies starring San Francisco:

After the Thin Man (1936)
The Maltese Falcon (1941)
Dark Passage (1947)
I Remember Mama (1948)
The Glenn Miller Story (1954)
Vertigo (1958)
The Birdman of Alcatraz (1962)
Guess Who's Coming to Dinner (1967)
The Graduate (1967)
Bullitt (1968)
They Call Me Mister Tibbs (1970)
Dirty Harry (1971)
Harold and Maude (1971)
Butterflies are Free (1972)
The Towering Inferno (1974)
High Anxiety (1977)
Nine to Five (1980)
48 Hours (1982)
Jagged Edge (1985)
The Presidio (1988)
Pacific Heights (1990)
Basic Instinct (1992)
The Joy Luck Club (1993)
Mrs. Doubtfire (1993)
When a Man Loves a Woman (1994)
The Rock (1996)

Historical Notes

Discoveries and Near Misses – Native Americans began settling the Bay Area around the 11C BC, building small villages of brush and tule bulrush. They enjoyed a rich and varied diet of shellfish, seeds, ground acorn meal, deer and other game. Although regional residents spoke different dialects and distinguished themselves by different tribal names, historians group them into three distinct peoples: the **Coast Miwok**, who dwelled north of the city (in present-day Marin and western Sonoma counties); the **Wintun**, who lived north of the Carquinez Straits (Solano, Napa and eastern Sonoma counties); and the **Ohlone**, or Costanoans, who inhabited areas east of the bay, on the San Francisco Peninsula, and south to Big Sur. Though discussion of death was taboo among the Ohlone, they believed their dead souls transmigrated westward across the sea to the Farallon Islands, which they called the Islands of the Dead. Despite small-scale but merciless feuds between some villages, trade and intermarriage promoted a generally peaceful and prosperous existence, as did the region's remoteness from the more bellicose cultures of Mexico and the Great Plains, and from the sea lanes of Europe and Asia. By the time the Spanish arrived in the 18C, the Bay Area supported between 7,000 and 10,000 people, and was the most densely populated region on the continent north of Mexico.

After its conquest of Mexico in 1521, the Spanish Crown was eager to expand its influence over the New World, especially over territories that could supply gold and other readily transportable treasure to subsidize the further costs of colonization and war. In 1542 Spain dispatched a sea expedition commanded by **Juan Rodríguez Cabrillo** up the coast of Alta California in search of a passage connecting the Pacific to the Atlantic. Although he made the first documented visit by a European to California, Cabrillo failed to find either the fabled Northwest Passage or the very real passage into San Francisco Bay that John C. Frémont—almost three centuries later—would christen the Golden Gate.

In 1579 English privateer **Francis Drake** put in for repairs in some sheltered bay of northern California—possibly present-day Drakes Bay, in the lee of Point Reyes. He claimed the land for Queen Elizabeth I as Nova Albion, but the English did not follow up on their claims, leaving California to gradual conquest by Spain.

Not until 1769 did the colonial government in Mexico move to plant colonies in Alta California, dispatching the Sacred Expedition under command of **Gaspar de Portolá**, a stalwart soldier, with a religious contingent headed by a Franciscan friar, **Junípero Serra**. Their orders were to establish a string of mission settlements along the coast of Alta California, with a provincial capital at Monterey Bay. While searching for the latter, but having overshot their mark, a scouting party led by **Sgt. José Ortega** stumbled upon San Francisco Bay in November of that year. Mistaking it for Drakes Bay, which the Spanish had renamed for St. Francis, the great inlet was incorrectly—but permanently—called San Francisco.

Hispanic Roots – Commissioned by the colonial government in Mexico, an expedition led by **Juan Bautista de Anza** arrived at San Francisco Bay in 1776 and formally established the PRESIDIO on a hill overlooking the entrance to the bay. De Anza also selected a site for a mission church near a small lagoon in the sheltered valley to the south, naming the lagoon for Our Lady of Sorrows (*Nuestra Senora de los Dolores* in Spanish). On October 9, 1776, padre Junípero Serra officially dedicated the new mission to St. Francis of Assisi, although it wasn't completed until 1791. (Today it is known as MISSION DOLORES.)

The Spanish mandate was to colonize the land and pacify the natives, converting them to Catholicism and teaching them agriculture. Overawed by Spanish bravado and firepower, and initially believing that they were ancestors returned from the Islands of the Dead, the native Ohlone and Wintun allowed themselves to be pressed into mission society, where they labored in the fields, lived in barracks segregated by sex, and received religious instruction. Those who resisted fled to the remote hills and the marshes of the Solano delta, where they mounted raids against mission herds, and were in turn hunted by Spanish and native soldiery. The old ways of life quickly disappeared as the Church seized tracts of land around the bay for grazing, eventually establishing three Franciscan missions in Ohlone territory, and one each in the Miwok (at San Rafael) and Wintun (at SONOMA) homelands. Thousands of natives died of European diseases, especially after smallpox was contracted from a trading expedition to the Russian settlement at Fort Ross in 1837.

After Mexico declared independence from Spain in 1821, the missions were secularized by a government decree that half their lands should go to indigenous peoples, the remainder to be sold or doled out to soldiers and civilians as private land grants in lieu of pensions or payments. The demoralized and undercapitalized natives, however, failed to work their lands, which were readily absorbed by the private landholders while the natives either went to work for them or drifted into vagabondage. Among the largest landholders around the bay were the ranching families of **Noe**, **De Haro** and **Bernal** on the tip of the San Francisco Peninsula; **Peralta** and **Martinez** in the East Bay and—most powerful of all—**Mariano Vallejo** to the north of the bay. Another ambitious settler was **John Sutter**, a Swiss adventurer who built extensive workshops and a fort on his land grant in the Sacramento Valley. With virtually no interference from the

Courtesy San Francisco Public Library

Mission Dolores (1856)

Mexican government, the Californios, as they called themselves, lived autonomous, self-sufficient lives. Served by small armies of cheap, native labor, they prospered by selling hides and tallow to visiting ships, many of them Yankee traders who carried glowing reports of the harbor's size and excellence to the East Coast of the US.

The Yankee Village – Until 1835, most of the San Francisco Peninsula's residents lived near the mission. In June of that year, however, an English sailor named **William Richardson**, who had married the daughter of the Presidio *comandante*, erected a tent dwelling and trading post on a hill above the shore of Yerba Buena Cove. This inlet on the northeastern shore of the peninsula had long been a favorite anchorage for visiting ships, for it provided both sheltering hills and deep-water mooring close to shore. The Richardsons soon improved their homestead with adobe buildings and drew up simple plans for a village called **Yerba Buena** ("good herb" in Spanish). Attracted by the prospect of trade with American whalers and other vessels, more American settlers set up trading posts, hotels, shops and other services. Hides and tallow were the biggest commodities, but the Yankees also began stocking a wider supply of ships' provisions, including sailors' grog. Among the most prominent settlers were Ohio trapper-turned-shopkeeper Jacob Leese; Hawaiian traders Nathan Spear and William Heath; **Sam Brannan**, a business leader and renegade agent of Brigham Young's Church of Latter-day Saints; and **William Leidesdorff**, a mulatto entrepreneur from the West Indies, who served as the first US vice consul and was the town's largest landowner at the time of his death in 1848. The focus of the settlement was the sleepy town plaza, where goats were tethered and sailors and vaqueros from the neighboring ranches slept off their binges.

Covetous of the fine bay, and goaded by impending war with Mexico, politicians in Washington sent adventurer **John C. Frémont**, guided by Kit Carson, to assess (and encourage) local interest in joining the Union. Frémont's efforts bore fruit in 1846 when a party of Yankees in Sonoma declared California's independence from Mexico and established it as the **Bear Flag Republic**. Less than one month later, Commodore John Sloat claimed California as American territory at Monterey and on July 9, 1846, 70 US marines and sailors, commanded by Captain John Montgomery, raised the US flag above Yerba Buena plaza, renaming it Portsmouth Square.

As real-estate speculation boomed, other amenities quickly followed, including the town's first school and first newspaper. Washington A. Bartlett, the town's first American *alcalde* (mayor), changed Yerba Buena's name to San Francisco in 1847, a decision he rightly believed would associate the little town with the growing fame of this huge port. Bartlett also hired Irish engineer **Jasper O'Farrell** to draw up a new town plan. O'Farrell laid out rectangular street grids, cut diagonally by the broad thoroughfare of Market Street.

Boosters celebrated San Francisco's promising future, but none could have predicted the extraordinary kismet that was shortly to befall it. This fate was unwittingly set in motion by good-natured John Sutter, whose prospering empire in the Sacramento Valley required timber. Dispatched to build a sawmill on the American River in the Sierra Nevada foothills, Sutter's foreman, James Marshall, noticed a glitter of metal in the mill's tailrace on January 24, 1848: It was gold! Sutter tried to keep a tight lid on the discovery, fearful that a frantic rush of prospectors might overwhelm his well-planned enterprise. Rumors did leak out, but San Franciscans remained skeptical until May, when Sam Brannan displayed a bottle full of gold dust and nuggets in Portsmouth Square, crying "Gold! Gold from the American River!" Much of the city emptied as gold-seekers headed for the mines, and in 1849, the first wave of gold-seekers from the outside world—the **Forty-niners**—hit San Francisco.

Gold Rush Boomtown – As thousands of treasure-hungry prospectors stormed ashore, the town exploded within months from a population of 800 into a boomtown serving some 90,000 anxious transients. American shopkeepers and old-time Californios rubbed shoulders with a floating population of men from Mexico, Hawaii, Australia, China, Chile and all the countries of Europe. Tents crowded the slopes of Telegraph and Rincon Hills, and abandoned ships were winched ashore to serve as hotels and warehouses. New buildings rose daily and burned down with alarming frequency; the city center was virtually destroyed by fire six times in four years. After the great fire of May 1851 (the most destructive before 1906), the business district was rebuilt of masonry. By 1852, San Francisco had 30,000 permanent residents, a lending library, restaurants, hotels, churches and hundreds of saloons and gambling halls, and was the fourth largest harbor city in the US. Enthusiastic audiences filled new theaters to cheer stage companies and acts from thousands of miles away. New piers extending into the bay rapidly became obsolete as Yerba Buena Cove was filled to create a flat, new business district. A few speculators, including Sam Brannan, became millionaires by selling provisions to miners.

Crime bred furiously in the manic society as gangs robbed and extorted from the general public. Brannan mobilized vigilante action, prodding frustrated citizens to dole out exile and even lynching to brazen criminals. From their makeshift stronghold popularly known as Fort Gunnybags, a Committee of Vigilance lynched corrupt city councilman James Casey and seized control of the city, staging torchlight parades, secret trials and summary executions. Though the crime rate declined, the governor, mayor, legislature, responsible citizens and newspapers spoke out against the militia tactics, and the committee disbanded after two months.

The Silver Bonanza – As placer gold deposits were depleted, lone prospectors were increasingly displaced by hydraulic and hard-rock mining corporations and engineers. San Francisco rose to meet new demands, becoming the financial and manufacturing center of the Far West. The 1859 discovery of the **Comstock Lode**, a fabulously rich vein of silver at what would soon become Virginia City, Nevada, brought a new boom as investors' profits flooded San Francisco. Ostentatious and high-living new millionaires capitalized a wide range of civic improvements and private construction, including factories, offices, theaters, wharves, hotels and transport systems. Boosters pushed for a city park to rival New York's. Millionaires vied to build spectacular mansions on NOB HILL. To provide service to the precipitous slopes, engineer **Andrew Hallidie** developed the **cable car** *(p 59)*, which took the city by storm, opening new tracts of steep or remote land for development. (By 1890 San Francisco was crisscrossed by eight different cable car lines and more than 100 miles of track.) The city expanded south to the slopes of POTRERO HILL and west over RUSSIAN HILL to PACIFIC HEIGHTS and the Western Addition.

Foremost among city boosters was **William Ralston**, founder and president of the Bank of California, who resurrected the profitability of the Comstock mines at a point when their fortunes seemed to be failing. With the help of his ambitious agent in Virginia City, William Sharon, Ralston earned millions and used his boundless capital to elevate San Francisco into a world-class city of economic dynamism and cultural refinement. Among the projects that Ralston helped capitalize were GOLDEN GATE PARK, the Spring Valley Water Company, the PALACE HOTEL (largest in the world in its day) and **Adolph Sutro**'s famous tunnel in the Comstock *(p 151)*.

San Francisco investors were almost universally convinced that a plan to link the city to the Eastern seaboard by a transcontinental railway would enrich California. In 1861 an ambitious route was plotted across the treacherous Sierra Nevada by engineer **Theodore Judah** and heroically constructed under arduous conditions by an army of laborers, including thousands of Chinese men. Driving eastward to meet the Union Pacific Railway at Promontory Point, Utah, the Central Pacific Railway was financed by a quartet of ambitious and cunning small businessmen in Sacramento: **Leland Stanford**, **Mark Hopkins**, **Collis P. Huntington** and **Charles Crocker**. Known as "the Big Four," they leveraged federal railroad right-of-way grants into a vast empire of real-estate holdings under the auspices of the Southern Pacific Corporation. Reaping vast personal fortunes, the Big Four turned Southern Pacific into the most powerful political and economic force in the West. Their power and reach, likened to the inexorable tentacles of an octopus, excited popular, passionate hatred and inspired the well-known proletarian novel by Frank Norris, *The Octopus*.

Courtesy San Francisco Public Library

Huntington

Courtesy San Francisco Public Library

Crocker

Dark Clouds with Silver Linings – Rather than a boon to the state, the transcontinental railway, which was completed in 1869, proved a bust. Cheap goods from eastern factories flooded California, causing factory closures, unemployment and widespread financial ruin in the 1870s. Overextended by $5 million, William Ralston was forced to close the Bank of California; he was found dead the same day, a probable suicide. Factory owners cut production costs by hiring Chinese workers at reduced wages, bestowing upon them the brunt of resentment from unemployed workers. As militant labor grew stronger, strikes became a common occurrence. Anti-Chinese riots spread across the West, bringing violence to San Francisco's CHINATOWN. Political pressure resulted in the federal Chinese Exclusion Act of 1882, which severely limited Chinese immigration until the act was repealed in 1943. Closed off from protection by the broader society, Chinatown fell prey to the **Tong Wars**, violent power struggles between criminal gangs. Despite an undercurrent of unrest, San Francisco's restaurants, hotels and mansions set the style to which other Western towns of the Victorian period aspired, and fed its reputation as the Paris of the West. Ostentation gilded the lives of the wealthy and infiltrated the flamboyant character of a city that cultivated notoriety as well as distinction. Arts and entertainment flourished in this prosperous and stimulating climate. While the **Barbary Coast**, a rough and licentious neighborhood of gambling clubs, saloons and brothels, thrived at the southern foot of TELEGRAPH HILL, great European opera companies and world-famous stage performers routinely played in the glittering footlights of downtown theaters. Distinguished writers like Mark Twain, Rudyard Kipling, Robert Louis Stevenson and Oscar Wilde celebrated its unique and rambunctious character in novel and essay. A fledgling bohemian movement, nurtured by Ina Coolbrith, Charles Stoddard, Gellet Burgess and Joaquin Miller, cultivated artistic tastes from ramshackle cottages on Telegraph and Russian hills, and at Miller's retreat in the OAKLAND hills. Architects A. Page Brown, Bernard Maybeck and Willis Polk cut their teeth on Bay Area projects. Photographer Arnold Genthe set up his studio in the city and began taking pictures of old Chinatown. Home from the mountains, John Muir scribbled the essays that would spark the early American conservation movement.

Courtesy San Francisco Public Library

Hopkins

Stanford

Rampant corruption crept into San Francisco politics, climaxing under Mayor **Eugene Schmitz**, candidate of the Union Labor party in 1901. Under the pernicious influence of his advisor, **"Boss" Abe Ruef**, the administration granted favors in exchange for bribes. Led by the *San Francisco Chronicle*, a reform party called for change.

The Great Earthquake and Fire of 1906 – On the morning of April 18, 1906, San Franciscans were jolted awake by a massive earthquake on the San Andreas fault. Residents of most neighborhoods were relieved and even bemused to find the most extensive damage to be fallen chimneys, broken water and gas mains, shattered windows, cracked plaster and smashed crockery. Downtown, however, and in the shoddily built neighborhood south of Market Street, the devastation was frightening. Although the modern skyscrapers had withstood the tremor with flying colors, fissures gaped in the streets and wooden tenement row houses listed dangerously, or lay in ruins. The colonnaded walls of City Hall had fallen away, leaving its magnificent dome hovering on a weakened steel frame, the most prominent victim of Abe Ruef's reckless fund-siphoning. The Central Emergency Hospital had collapsed, crushing medical staff and patients. Scores of people were hurt or killed by falling bricks. By noon, 52 fires were burning with impunity around the city. Unable to restore the water supply, firefighters watched helplessly as the conflagration spread alarmingly through the tenements south of Market Street. Hundreds evacuated by ferry to Oakland, which had survived relatively unscathed. By night, the flames of the burning city lit up the skies around the Bay Area.

Mayor Schmitz hastened to the newly finished FAIRMONT HOTEL atop Nob Hill to form disaster plans. Coordinating with Brigadier General **Frederick Funston**, army troops from the Presidio began patrolling for looters (seven of whom were indeed shot) and dynamiting broad fire lines along Van Ness Avenue. By dawn on April 19, the fire crested Nob Hill, destroying the "hill of palaces" and gutting the Fairmont. Prisoners were moved from the city jail to Alcatraz, and thousands of refugees streamed westward to makeshift tent camps on the Presidio grounds and in Golden Gate Park.

By the third day, the fire had burned south into the MISSION DISTRICT and clear to the northern wharves. Then the wind changed, pushing the flames back onto themselves. The holocaust was stopped at Van Ness Avenue, sparing the western half of the city. Some 250,000 people were left homeless and 674 persons were dead or missing. Virtually the entire center of the city was destroyed, some 514 blocks of offices, homes, warehouses, factories, saloons, churches and public buildings. Yet a plucky holiday atmosphere prevailed in the refugee camps.

California Street West to Nob Hill and Fairmont Hotel After 1906 Earthquake and Fire

Relief funds began pouring in from around the world and reconstruction proceeded with phenomenal speed. By 1915, the city was ready to celebrate its miraculous recovery. Building an enchanting "city" lit by electrical lights on newly filled land in what is now the MARINA DISTRICT, San Francisco hosted the **Panama-Pacific International Exposition**, the most highly regarded of the city's three world fairs.

A Grand Burst of Growth – The momentum of reconstruction culminated in an era of epic civil-engineering projects. CIVIC CENTER was rebuilt on a grand scale in the Beaux Arts style. Mayor **James "Sunny Jim" Rolph** cleared the way for residential development of the Richmond District by ordering the city's many cemeteries closed and all human remains removed to Colma, south of the city limits. Electric streetcars began replacing the cable car as the premier form of public transport. San Francisco's financial institutions—particularly A.P. Giannini's Bank of Italy—regained the central role in a new California "rush" that outstripped the gold and silver bonanzas of the previous century by capitalizing new farms and agricultural towns and building the state's role as the nation's fruit and vegetable garden. To secure a dependable source of good water, the city dammed the Tuolumne River at Hetch Hetchy canyon, 150mi east in Yosemite National Park, carrying the river water by aqueduct to the Crystal Springs reservoirs on the peninsula. Most spectacularly, in spite of the Great Depression, the city simultaneously built two of the largest bridges in the world, connecting the long-isolated city eastward across the bay to Oakland and north across the Golden Gate to Marin County. To again celebrate its vigor in flamboyant San Francisco style, the city threw another world's fair, the **Golden Gate International Exposition**, which rose on newly completed TREASURE ISLAND, the largest artificial island in the world.

Labor problems beset the city throughout these decades. Springing from resentment against the "robber barons" of the 19C, the 20C labor movement reorganized into an effective, if sometimes corrupt, political force, winning an eight-hour work day and turning San Francisco into a "union town." Labor strikes became a fixture in

PROCLAMATION
BY THE MAYOR

The Federal Troops, the members of the Regular Police Force, and all Special Police Officers have been authorized to KILL any and all persons found engaged in looting or in the commission of any other crime.

I have directed all the Gas and Electric Lighting Companies not to turn on Gas or Electricity until I order them to do so; you may therefor expect the city to remain in darkness for an indefinite time.

I request all citizens to remain at home from darkness until daylight of every night until order is restored.

I Warn all citizens of the danger of fire from damaged or destroyed chimneys, broken or leaking gas pipes or fixtures, or any like cause.

E. E. SCHMITZ, Mayor.
Dated, April 18, 1906.

ALTVATER PRINT MISSION AND 22ND STS.

California Historical Society, San Francisco. FN-21108

Handbill (1906)

local politics. Longshoremen staged the largest strike in American history in 1930, eventually winning better pay after strikebreakers stormed their lines, sparking riots that injured scores and left two dead. The century's most notorious unionist court case, however, was the **Mooney Trial**, when a rabble-rousing socialist named Tom Mooney was railroaded through court for a bombing that left 10 dead at a Preparedness Day Parade on the eve of World War I. Mooney was found guilty but was pardoned in 1939 after witnesses admitted they lied under oath.

War and Uneasy Peace – World War II brought another boom to the Bay Area as shipyards at Hunters Point and SAUSALITO tooled up for wartime production. Many of the workers were women and black newcomers from Southern states. Thousands of Japanese-American citizens were rounded up from Bay Area cities and expelled to internment camps. While the army built bunkers and batteries in the MARIN HEADLANDS to fend off a Japanese invasion that never came, 1.5 million soldiers, sailors and marines embarked for the Pacific theater from San Francisco, most of them from piers at Fort Mason.

The population continued to grow after the war, but with most of the new residents settling in Bay Area suburbs, the city began to lose its luster as the region's business hub. When Los Angeles surpassed San Francisco as the premier manufacturing center of the West Coast, tourism became the city's most important business. Its grand flamboyance and eccentric character San Francisco never surrendered. NORTH BEACH became the national focus of a bohemian movement, the Beat Generation, during the 1950s, when nonconformist writers like Jack Kerouac, Allen Ginsberg and Lawrence Ferlinghetti, encouraged by modest rents, cheap food and drink, and a society tolerant of unconventional behavior, frequented the Italian coffee houses, wrote poetry and "dug the scene." Curious tourists eventually drove the Beats from North Beach but the city generated another internationally celebrated bohemian movement in the 1960s, this time in HAIGHT-ASHBURY: Thousands of young people—hippies and "flower children"—gathered to experiment with drugs, music and libertine society. By the 1970s, however, that neighborhood was degenerating into a haven of drug pushers. Partly because of these widely renowned social movements, the Bay Area acquired a national reputation for what some would call political and social idealism, and others would label left-wing radicalism. As Huey Newton founded the Black Panther Party in Oakland, Berkeley—home of the University of California—became a national center of student protest over the Vietnam War and other issues. When thousands of gay men and women moved to San Francisco, the CASTRO DISTRICT became the "capital" of the American gay community. Relaxed immigration laws permitted an influx of larger numbers of Asian and Hispanic immigrants, greatly changing the ethnic makeup of the city.

Urban problems like homelessness, crime and blight compounded in San Francisco during the 1980s, yet single-issue politics constricted the government's ability to form a consensus for dealing with them. The 1990s, however, have witnessed a welcome renaissance in many city institutions, most spectacularly in the building of the new SAN FRANCISCO MUSEUM OF MODERN ART and a new main library, the birth and growth of a new arts center at YERBA BUENA GARDENS, and the refurbishment of City Hall, the opera house, the Geary Theater and the CALIFORNIA PALACE OF THE LEGION OF HONOR. Although San Francisco has acquired many of the trappings that serve its important role as one of the world's foremost tourist destinations, it remains a lively, creative, livable city, true to its unconventional and radiant past.

San Francisco Firsts

c.10,000 BC	Native Americans first settle in the Bay Area.
1769	Sgt. **José Ortega** and his scouting party are the first Europeans to sight San Francisco Bay.
1775	**Lt. Juan Manuel de Ayala** and his crew are the first Europeans to explore and map the bay.
1776	First mass is celebrated near the site of Mission Dolores. The first building on the PRESIDIO IS completed on September 17.
1791	Mission San Francisco de Asís (Mission Dolores) is completed.
1834	First town council is organized near Mission Dolores, with **Francisco de Haro** appointed as *alcalde*, or mayor.
1835	William Richardson and his wife build the first structure in Yerba Buena. Richard Henry Dana makes his first visit to San Francisco Bay as a sailor—a visit later described in *Two Years Before the Mast (p 6).*
1847	California's first newspaper, *The California Star*, is published by **Sam Brannan**. Yerba Buena is renamed San Francisco.
1848	First commercial bank and first American public school begin operating.
1849	California **Gold Rush** begins.
1852	**Wells Fargo** begins stage service for passengers and freight.
1857	California's first commercial winery, Buena Vista, is founded in Sonoma by Hungarian **Agoston Haraszthy**.
1859	The **Comstock Lode** silver deposits are discovered in Nevada.
1860	Pony Express begins carrying letters between San Francisco and St. Joseph, Missouri, ending with completion of first **transcontinental telegraph** line in 1861.
1865	Charles and Michael de Young found the *San Francisco Dramatic Chronicle*, later dropping the word *dramatic*.
1869	The Central Pacific and Union Pacific railroads are joined at Promontory, Utah, creating the first **transcontinental railway** link between San Francisco and the East Coast.
1873	Andrew Hallidie successfully tests the first **cable car** on Clay Street. **Levi Strauss** patents riveted blue jeans. Pacific Coast Stock Exchange is founded.
1892	**Sierra Club** is founded with John Muir as president.
1895	World's first three-reel slot machine is invented by Charles August Fey at his Market Street workshop.
1904	Produce wholesaler A.P. Giannini, an Italian immigrant, founds the Bank of Italy, later renamed **Bank of America**, thus pioneering branch banking in California.
1917	Architect Willis Polk completes **Hallidie Building**, the world's first skyscraper clad in a glass curtain wall.
1919	Ina Coolbrith becomes California's first Poet Laureate.
1927	Philo Taylor Farnsworth invents first all-electronic television in San Francisco.
1936	Pan Am begins scheduled passenger air service between San Francisco and Honolulu on the "China Clipper."
1945	United Nations charter is drafted at the Fairmont Hotel and signed at the Civic Center.
1958	The New York Giants move to San Francisco, establishing the first major league baseball team in the Bay Area.
1965	Promoter Bill Graham opens the Fillmore Auditorium, staging legendary rock-and-roll concerts.
1971	Alice Waters opens Chez Panisse restaurant in Berkeley, beginning the rage for **California Cuisine**.
1973	First BART train travels through the transbay tube from the East Bay to the Montgomery Street station.
1978	Mayor George Moscone and San Francisco's first openly gay city supervisor, Harvey Milk, are assassinated by ex-supervisor Dan White.
1993	When Bay Area politicians Dianne Feinstein and Barbara Boxer are elected to the US Senate, California is the first state to have two women senators simultaneously in office.
1995	San Francisco 49ers win an unprecedented fifth Super Bowl title.
1998	Bank of America merges with NationsBank, thus becoming the largest US bank, with headquarters in North Carolina.

Economy

San Francisco's early economy was shaped by its location. Isolated on the western edge of the continent, without easy access to other US cities until the transcontinental railroad was completed in 1869, mid-19C San Franciscans built their own economy from scratch. The discovery of gold at Coloma in 1848 transformed the settlement from the sleepy center of an active trade in cattle hides and tallow to a boomtown of commerce and manufacturing. Guarding the mouth of the largest bay along California's coastline, San Francisco also became the premier West Coast shipping hub, a bustling commercial outpost that benefited greatly from the millions of dollars worth of gold, silver and grain ("green gold") that flowed down two inland rivers and out through the Golden Gate.

In the 150 years that have passed since the Gold Rush, San Francisco has made the slow, sometimes painful transition from small working-class boomtown to large international center for business. In recent decades OAKLAND has assumed most of San Francisco's port activity, and heavy industry and factories have relocated to Alameda and Contra Costa Counties, while San Francisco has fashioned itself as a business-and-finance headquarters. Voted "the No. 1 Best City for Business in the US" by Fortune magazine in 1995, the San Francisco Bay Area now boasts one of the strongest urban economies in the nation, with retailing, banking, tourism, biomedical research, legal services, real estate and high technology heading the list of local industries. Home to more than 60 foreign consulates and trade offices, San Francisco is also the center of global marketing for the Bay Area, which has enjoyed a rise of 13 percent in international trade since 1993.

Business and Finance – Magnate and dynamo of corporate headquarters, financial institutions and businesses of every stripe, San Francisco's FINANCIAL DISTRICT has been called the "Wall Street of the West" since the mid-19C. Although its ability to generate capital remains as dynamic as ever, the city's ranking as the nation's third largest financial market was challenged in the late 1990s as mergers and acquisitions forced three of its largest banks (Bank of America, Montgomery Securities and Robertson Stephens) to move their headquarters to other cities. The Pacific Exchange, founded here in 1882, was the nation's fastest growing stock exchange—and a key player in the booming US-Asia trade—until it merged with the Chicago Board Options Exchange in 1998.

Today San Francisco has the headquarters of Wells Fargo, a bank with deep roots in the American West; Charles Schwab & Co., the nation's largest discount brokerage firm; Bechtel Engineering, Chevron Oil, and apparel makers such as the Gap, Esprit and Levi Strauss & Co. These and other downtown businesses employ more than 300,000 people—about 40 percent of the population of San Francisco. South of the city, Silicon Valley raised $3.66 billion in venture capital in 1997, fueling the continuing growth of its high-tech industries and boosting Bay Area merchandise exports to the highest level of any region in the US.

Robert Mizono/Courtesy The Pacific Exchange

Pacific Exchange

Conventions and Tourism – In 1997, San Francisco attracted more than 16 million tourists, business travelers and conventioneers, who together spent more than $5 billion on goods and services. Those dollars sustain more than 66,000 local jobs—about one in nine in the city. In 1998 San Francisco also hosted 84 major conventions of more than 1,000 attendees in such venues as the Civic Auditorium near CIVIC CENTER and Moscone Convention Center in SOUTH OF MARKET. The largest local facility, the Moscone Center contains 442,000sq ft of exhibit space and 160,000sq ft of meeting rooms, with plans for more in the works.

Retail and Restaurants – More than 10,000 retail establishments, employing upward of 76,000 workers, vie for San Franciscans' and visitors' dollars. Shoppers spend some $5.2 billion a year here, both in neighborhood shops and in UNION SQUARE AREA department stores. San Francisco's world-renowned restaurant industry, which employs 50,000 workers in 6,000 establishments, caters to foodies of every stripe.

Computers and Electronics – Silicon Valley, situated near the Bay Area city of San Jose, represents the epicenter of US high-tech growth. With about 7,000 electronics and software firms, exports of computers and related hardware from Silicon Valley grew by 81 percent from 1994 to 1997, hitting $29.3 billion in 1996. Some of the biggest names in computers, such as Apple, Hewlett-Packard, Intel and Sun Microsystems, got their starts here, while Bay Area start-ups such as Oracle, Adobe and Autodesk have become big players on the international software scene. As a region, the Bay Area ranks fourth in the world (after the US as a whole, Japan and Germany) for obtaining patents on new technologies and inventions.

In San Francisco, Multimedia Gulch, centered around South Park in the South of Market area, has grown into something of a technology hot spot in recent years, drawing firms such as Macromedia, which designs authoring tools for the Internet, and the magazines Wired and MacWeek, which chronicle trends in new technology.

Shipping and Transportation – Most of the shipping that goes on in San Francisco today consists of bits and bytes flowing over fiber-optic cables, but from the Gold Rush until well into the 20C, San Francisco's waterfront thrived. In its 1880s heyday, the San Francisco port, which employed thousands of longshoremen and sailors, handled 99 percent of all West Coast imports and 83 percent of all exports. Through the 19C the city was the whaling headquarters of the Pacific coast, but shipping declined with completion of the transcontinental railroad. Although the shipyards came alive briefly during World War II, in the 1960s San Francisco quietly ceded the bulk of its industrial shipping business to Oakland, which had made a sizable investment in up-to-date loading equipment and dredged its harbor to accommodate the latest generation of deep-draft ships.

Today San Francisco Bay maintains three major international ports: San Francisco, Oakland and Richmond, located north of Oakland in the East Bay. Asia accounts for two-thirds of the Bay Area's shipping trade, with the remainder split between Latin America; New Zealand and the South Pacific; British Columbia (Canada); and Europe. The Port of Oakland, third-largest in California (behind Los Angeles and Long Beach), handles 90 percent of the containerized cargo that passes through the Golden Gate. The Port of San Francisco is the nation's third coffee futures exchange port, handling more than 90,000 metric tons of coffee annually. Automobiles and newsprint are other major imports. The Port of Richmond primarily handles liquid petroleum and chemicals for East Bay refineries and factories.

Owned by the city and county of San Francisco, San Francisco International Airport (SFO) contributes $15 million per year to the city's General Fund. It hosts more than 39 million passengers every year, making it the fifth busiest nationwide. SFO also handles all of the Bay Area's international air-cargo trade, which now exceeds (in dollar volume) the combined total of all Bay Area ports by 16 percent. A $2.5 billion expansion currently in progress will make SFO one of the nation's largest international air terminals by the turn of the millennium.

Biotechnology – Home to some 500 bioscience companies generating $5 billion in annual revenues, the Bay Area is the world capital of biotech, a growing industry that concerns itself with finding marketplace applications for scientific innovations—from genetically engineering plants to provide higher crop yields, to manufacturing human insulin for diabetics. Beginning in 1976, when Genentech was founded just south of the city, biotech companies began flooding the region, complemented by some of the top health education and medical research facilities in the nation at UC San Francisco, UC BERKELEY and Stanford University.

Services – As in most densely populated cities, the service industry accounts for the lion's share of jobs in San Francisco. Government agencies employ more than 56,000 workers (125,000 in the three west Bay Area counties). Some 16,000 are employed at the University of California at San Francisco and San Francisco State University, including many of the nearly 35,000 health-care workers in the city. Real-estate, finance, and insurance firms provide 77,500 San Francisco jobs, and development projects such as Mission Bay and a new baseball stadium at China Basin promise to swell the ranks of local construction companies, which now support 14,000 workers.

Population

With a population of 735,315 (1996 estimate) inhabiting an area of only 46.38sq mi confined on the tip of a peninsula, San Francisco has the second highest population density (15,855 persons/sq mi) in the US after New York. Surprisingly small, it ranks as the fourth largest city in California after Los Angeles (3,553,638), San Diego (1,171,121) and San Jose (838,744). The city forms the cultural and financial hub of the San Francisco Bay Area, a nine-county region of more than 6.6 million (6,693,600) people.

Though eclipsed in size in the mid-20C by Los Angeles and other cities with room to expand, San Francisco led the state in population, culture and economic influence throughout the 19C and early 20C. Within months of the discovery of gold in 1848, the town's population of about 800 doubled, quadrupled and septupled with young men (who outnumbered women by 10 to 1) from every American state and European country, especially England and Ireland, France, the German states and Scandinavia. Great numbers came from China and Mexico, sizable minorities from Hawaii, Australia, Chile and other Latin American countries. The population rocketed to 34,776 within four years and exploded between 1860 and 1870 from 56,802 to 149,473.

Though the rate of growth slowed in the financial depression of the 1870s, by the turn of the century San Francisco was still the largest city west of St. Louis, with a population of 342,782. Population peaked at 775,357 in the mid-20C, after which a slow decline mirrored the city's loss of industry and port facilities to OAKLAND and other Bay Area cities. The region's population is nothing if not diverse, harboring a rich array of immigrants from Europe, the Americas and Asia. Currently, about 34 percent of San Franciscans are foreign-born.

Latinos – People of Spanish and Mexican ancestry have formed an important segment of the Bay Area's population since the arrival of Europeans in 1776. Politically dominant until the American conquest of 1846, the established Californio families contributed greatly to the founding and development of the village of Yerba Buena, though their political and economic power dwindled considerably with the influx of newcomers from the US. Even as generations of Hispanic families acculturate to American society, the continuing arrival of new immigrants, legal and illegal, keep Latino cultures robust over much of California. People of Hispanic ancestry today comprise about 13 percent of San Francisco's population.

Chinese – Forming about 18 percent of the city's population, the largest of any single ethnic group, the Chinese have constituted a substantial minority since the Gold Rush. Though historically persecuted, the Chinese were instrumental in countless enterprises that developed the West, not least in construction, agriculture and the fishing industry. The numbers of Chinese in San Francisco dwindled after passage of the Chinese Exclusion Act of 1882, reaching a low of 1.5 percent, or 7,744 people, in the 1920 census. Repeal of the act during World War II heralded a second wave of immigrants, greatly diversifying the Chinese community with wealthy families from Hong Kong and Taiwan, poorer families from China, refugees from Southeast Asia, and students. Although CHINATOWN has prospered from this influx, most Chinese Americans dwell in widely scattered and well-integrated neighborhoods of San Francisco (especially NORTH BEACH, RUSSIAN HILL, the RICHMOND DISTRICT and the SUNSET DISTRICT) and the Bay Area.

Edward Thomas

Schoolchildren at Play

Italians – People of Italian ancestry today constitute about 15 percent of the city's population. After the Chinese were expelled from the fishing wharves in the 1870s, FISHERMAN'S WHARF became known as a Genoese harbor, although currently Sicilians hold sway. The heart of North Beach has been known as Little Italy since the first decade of the 20C. With declining immigration rates, rapid acculturation and movement to the suburbs, the numbers of immigrants have since retrenched, but the influence of Italian Americans is still keenly felt in many aspects of city life.

Others – Many of the city's most prominent movers and shakers of the 19C and early 20C were of English, German and Scandinavian stock. Large numbers of working-class Irish families settled in the MISSION DISTRICT from the 1870s, becoming more than 23 percent of the population by 1910. Other ethnic enclaves around the turn of the century included the Maltese and the Japanese, who settled after the 1906 earthquake in the present neighborhood of Japantown. The African American population burgeoned during World War II, when thousands of Southern blacks came to work in Bay Area shipyards. Many settled along Fillmore Street (vacated by the incarcerated Japanese) in the Western Addition. Thousands of Filipinos have settled in the Bay Area since World War II, particularly in Daly City on San Francisco's southern border, and in the East Bay. The old Russian community in the Richmond District, which burgeoned after the 1917 Revolution, then dwindled through acculturation, is once again thriving under a new wave of immigrants.

An Eccentric, Enchanting Place – With much of its economy dependent on tourism and finance, San Francisco attracts and nurtures a diverse, largely well-educated population with strong interests in the arts, social experimentation and good living. Two-fifths of the city's residents are single, while nearly 60 percent have attended college. The arts thrive at all levels of society, from grand opera productions to neighborhood cultural centers. Eating well is a passion for San Franciscans, who are forever on a quest for new cuisines and creative restaurants, yet well-disposed toward traditional regional specialties. They enjoy working off their calories with outdoor exercise; weekends find them by the thousands jogging, hiking, biking and sailing, taking advantage of the waters and parklands surrounding their city.

San Franciscans actively guard their architectural heritage, willingly subsidizing the archaic cable car system and fiercely supporting zoning restrictions and retrofitting projects that preserve vintage buildings. They are also strong supporters of the conservation movement, and have preserved an unparalleled system of parklands in and around the city. Though a reputation for tolerance holds sway, San Franciscans value individualism over universality, and residents are notorious throughout the Bay Area for their stubborn political coalitions, special-interest groups that make consensus difficult, and neighborhoods that trenchantly guard their ethnic or cultural flavor.

Despite their preservationist attitudes, city denizens pride themselves for being at the forefront—though others might call it a sideline—of American social experimentation. Set in motion perhaps by its eccentric birth and history, the city's penchant for flamboyant eccentricity attracts an eclectic mix of people and ideas. Free-thinkers, poets, artists, counterculture gurus and revolutionaries have always thrived here. Following the same impulse, though on more established footing, are the many idealistic civic organizations that have taken root, such as the Sierra Club and Glide Memorial Church in the downtrodden Tenderloin district.

Architecture

The oldest major US city west of the Rockies, San Francisco revels in examples of many eras and styles of buildings. The city's built environment has been shaped by various entrepreneurial, artistic and political forces, all of which have contributed to its distinctive architectural legacy. San Francisco's role as a commercial and financial nexus continues to attract new and innovative forms of expression to its architectural landscape.

Native Americans and the Mission Period – In the days before the arrival of Europeans, many small communities of native Ohlone and Miwok peoples dotted the shores of the bay, living in cone-shaped structures made of reeds and trees lashed together. These natural building materials had a limited life span and no constructions remain from this era, although archeologists have recorded scores of shell mounds marking village sites around the shore of the bay, as well as acorn-grinding rocks in oak woodlands where the native peoples made seasonal camps.

The earliest extant structures in the Bay Area date from the mission period. The center of each mission community was a simple church and monastery, built of thick walls of whitewashed adobe capped by gabled red-tile roofs, supported upon heavy rough-hewn timbers. The Spanish friars designed the missions along classical lines, using elements such as pilasters, niches and arcades to embellish the exteriors, and ornate reredos, tiled floors and colorful frescoes to ornament the interior spaces. Much of the interest in mission decoration comes from the folk-art flavors imparted by the Native American laborers who did the construction work. San Francisco's oldest building, the chapel at MISSION DOLORES, remains the finest example of the architecture of this period, while the surrounding Bay Area holds a variety of others, most notably the well-preserved mission and town plaza of SONOMA.

Mexican influence on California's architectural style ended following American takeover of California in 1848. By the early 1850s, the immense wealth generated by the gold mines began to be channeled into increasingly substantial buildings, some of which still stand at the heart of the Jackson Square quarter of the FINANCIAL DISTRICT.

The Victorian Era – From 1860 to 1900, as wealth poured into the city from the gold mines and the silver deposits of Nevada's Comstock Lode, San Francisco's downtown commercial district grew in stature. Grand hotels were constructed to house visitors to the burgeoning metropolis, the most opulent of which was the Palace Hotel, completed in 1875. The US Mint (today the OLD MINT) was built nearby around the same time, and by the 1890s, Chicago School office towers such as the MILLS BUILDING and the Chronicle Building had begun to rise along the bustling streets. The landmark FERRY BUILDING was begun in 1894, and the Victorian era also saw the construction of elaborate resorts, most notably the second CLIFF HOUSE and the now-ruined SUTRO BATHS complex near Seal Rocks on the city's Pacific shoreline.

Italianate Style

The best-known and most enduring legacies of San Francisco's Victorian era remain the many blocks of homes erected in the distinctive substyles of this romantic period. Throughout PACIFIC HEIGHTS, HAIGHT-ASHBURY, the CASTRO DISTRICT and many other residential neighborhoods, streets are lined with abundantly decorated wooden houses, most of them built between 1870 and 1906. Using inexpensive redwood, fir and pine lumber produced from the dense forests of the northern California coast, contractors were able to produce homes quickly and inexpensively for the city's burgeoning middle class. Closely crowded on narrow lots and built to standardized floor plans, these houses were adorned with an almost endless catalog of decorative sidings, elaborately milled moldings and bay windows with intricately carved frames. The more elaborate of the homes were accentuated with fanciful turrets, false gables and intricate art-glass windows.

Most Victorian homes were designed not by architects but by home owners, builders and property developers. They often followed general principles laid down by "pattern books" that outlined design precepts of each of the main Victorian "styles." Most prevalent in San Francisco were the **Italianate** (1860-80), marked by Neoclassical ornament and pedimented false gables; the **Stick** or Eastlake (1870-90), epitomized by comparatively flat wall surfaces and more angular, geometric forms; and the **Queen Anne** (1870-1906), the most free-form and asymmetrical of the Victorian styles, often incorporating corner towers, turrets and a sometimes-frenzied variety of wall sidings, all on the same facade.

Stick Style

The free spirit of these "painted ladies"—so called because, though once mainly gray, they had flamboyant color schemes applied—has captured the fancy of visitors and locals alike. Thousands of Victorian homes march up and down San Francisco's streets, imposing a distinctive and colorful stamp on the city's architectural signature. One has been preserved for public viewing: the imposing Queen Anne-style HAAS-LILIENTHAL HOUSE in eastern Pacific Heights.

The latter part of the Victorian era saw the emergence of the **Arts and Crafts** movement, which in San Francisco brought together a loose grouping of artists and architects interested in the bohemian, "back-to-

Queen Anne

nature" teachings of a local preacher, Joseph Worcester. The SWEDENBORGIAN CHURCH epitomizes the movement's rustic approach to architecture adapted by such diverse and prolific San Francisco architects as A. Page Brown, Willis Polk, Ernest Coxhead and Bernard Maybeck, all of whom built numerous residences around the Bay Area. Using dark-stained shingles of redwood lumber and creating innovative spatial arrangements that took advantage of the region's picturesque topography and mild climate, these architects satisfied a Bay Area taste for cultivated rusticity.

The City Beautiful – At the turn of the 20C, San Francisco's civic government considered altering the city's layout along the lines of an ambitious plan proposed by Chicago architect Daniel Burnham. **The Burnham Plan** called for wide boulevards and Baroque public spaces like those of Paris or Washington DC, ideals at the forefront of the Beaux Arts-inspired "City Beautiful" movement *(p 43)*. The earthquake and fire of 1906 left a clean canvas upon which to implement Burnham's ideas, but commercial interests propelled the rebuilding of the city according to its previous layout. Some of San Francisco's most impressive commercial buildings, including the BANK OF CALIFORNIA and the grand FAIRMONT HOTEL, date from this period, as do many of the mansions of Pacific Heights. The city's main architectural gesture of recovery was the **Panama-Pacific International Exposition of 1915** *(p 92)*, which filled the reclaimed lands of the modern Marina District with a celebratory fairground of eclectic architecture. The sole survivor is Bernard Maybeck's stately PALACE OF FINE ARTS.

The only aspect of the Burnham Plan to be implemented after the earthquake was the new CIVIC CENTER. This monumental rectangle of libraries, theaters and other public buildings, centered upon the landmark Baroque-style dome of CITY HALL, forms a grand, dignified public space. Across the bay, the Neoclassical buildings of the UNIVERSITY OF CALIFORNIA, BERKELEY campus were constructed by John Galen Howard and others, including Julia Morgan.

The growing economy of the 1920s supported another building boom in the Financial District. The city's first skyscrapers sprouted at the end of that decade, including Timothy Pflueger's Art Deco-style PACIFIC TELEPHONE BUILDING, the Mayan-style tower at FOUR FIFTY SUTTER, and George Kelham's 31-story, Gothic-style RUSS BUILDING, then the tallest on the West Coast.

Depression and Postwar Era – Commercial construction slowed considerably during the Depression years, and during the postwar period San Francisco underwent a long period of suburbanization, at which time freeways were constructed to reach the new tract-house suburbs of the outlying Bay Area. Throughout the late 1950s and early 1960s urban-renewal projects caused the demolition of vast tracts of older buildings, which in turn inspired the origins of a movement to preserve San Francisco's historic architecture.

Clos Pegase Winery

Though by the 1960s some 30 years had passed with little change to San Francisco's downtown skyline, that decade and the one that followed saw it altered beyond recognition. The first distinctive new project was the 1959 Crown Zellerbach Building (today ONE BUSH STREET), an International-style glass box supported on piers above a paved plaza. More skyscrapers continued to be built, culminating at the end of the decade in the city's two tallest—Skidmore, Owings & Merrill's monolithic BANK OF AMERICA (1971) and William Pereira's unique TRANSAMERICA PYRAMID (1972).

Public outcry against the pace of growth, which critics claimed had "Manhattanized" the previously attractive city skyline, resulted in stringent planning controls, eventually encoded in the **Downtown Plan** of 1985. This put a cap on the amount of square footage of new construction permitted in the Financial District and effectively shifted future growth to the less densely developed area SOUTH OF MARKET.

Contemporary Architecture – Recent years have brought a number of internationally renowned architects to design projects in San Francisco and the Bay Area, among them Philip Johnson, Mario Botta, James Ingo Freed and Michael Graves, whose signature contemporary take on the Classical style may be seen at CLOS PEGASE WINERY in the NAPA VALLEY. San Francisco has witnessed a renaissance in public architecture through major projects like the expanded Moscone Convention Center and the adjacent YERBA BUENA GARDENS. In 1995, Botta's new home for the SAN FRANCISCO MUSEUM OF MODERN ART opened, followed in 1996 by Freed's striking new SAN FRANCISCO PUBLIC LIBRARY at Civic Center.

Visual Arts

The visual arts of San Francisco reflect the history, diversity and excitement of the entire Bay Area, making it one of the art capitals of the American West.

Early Artistic Landscape – San Francisco's rich, multilayered art history began with the Ohlone, Wintun and Coast Miwok Indians, who maintained a beautiful material and ceremonial culture. Today, baskets produced by native Californians are treasured for their dazzling geometric designs and precise weaving; many are on view at the Oakland Museum of California and other public collections.

The MISSION DOLORES stands as the primary reminder of the city's Mexican period—walls and ceilings of the old chapel reveal replicas of beautiful geometric patterns designed by native artisans. The population explosion during and after the Gold Rush introduced European values and aesthetics to the area's artistic activity. Important pioneer artists began visiting San Francisco, including landscape painters Albert Bierstadt and William Keith. Early photographers Carleton Watkins and Eadweard Muybridge (who helped settle a bet about horse racing with his groundbreaking photographic studies of animal locomotion) paved the way for one of the area's most enduring obsessions. The San Francisco Art Association, precursor of today's SAN FRANCISCO MUSEUM OF MODERN ART, was founded in 1871 by members Bierstadt, Keith, Muybridge and others to display art publicly and offer classes. "Robber baron" railroad magnates Leland Stanford and Mark Hopkins assembled major collections of European art in the late 19C.

Courtesy Maxwell Galleries, Ltd.

Chinatown by Dong Kingman

In the early 20C, important developments in the arts took root in San Francisco, including the California **Arts and Crafts** movement in painting, furniture and decorative arts, led by Arthur and Lucia Matthews; and **Tonalist** painting, which incorporated the colors of the city's distinctive foggy palette, exemplified by Gottardo Piazonni and Xavier Martinez. Following the influential Panama-Pacific International Exhibition of 1915, where works by European and New York modernists were displayed at the PALACE OF FINE ARTS, an explosion of color appeared in the work of Bay Area painters Clayton S. Price and Selden Gile. The latter was a member of the **Society of Six**, an informal association of artists who practiced a painterly, figurative style during the 1920s. During the 1920s and 1930s, a number of artists of Japanese and Chinese ancestry, including Chiura Obata and Dong Kingman, blended aspects of Asian art traditions with Western practices to create innovative Asian-American styles.

Photographers Ansel Adams, Edward Weston, Imogen Cunningham and others founded the **Group f.64** in 1932 and exhibited together the following year; reacting against the "pictorialist," blurred-focus work of their contemporaries, they embraced a sharp-focus, "precisionist" depiction of forms and textures. Social themes characteristic of the Great Depression are movingly rendered in the work of painter Maynard Dixon and his wife, photographer Dorothea Lange, as well as in pieces by African-American sculptor Sargent Johnson. Diego Rivera made repeated visits to the city with his wife, Frida Kahlo, during the 1930s; the Mexican muralist executed several works here, engendering a number of mural projects by other artists in public locations throughout the city *(p 140)*.

Abstract and Figurative – After World War II, SAN FRANCISCO ART INSTITUTE visiting faculty Clyfford Still and Mark Rothko inspired an explosion of abstract expressionist painting by their students, who included Sam Francis and Robert Motherwell. In response, painters Elmer Bischoff, Richard Diebenkorn and David Park created a painterly representational movement known as **Bay Area Figurative**, a motif that Berkeley-based painter Joan Brown and sculptor Manuel Neri later personalized. Beat culture and Zen philosophy helped inspire the work of individualists like Bruce Conner, William Wiley and Jay de Feo. Popular culture of the 1960s is recorded in the work of painters Wayne Thiebaud and Robert Bechtle. The latter counterculture movement also saw unique developments in poster art around HAIGHT-ASHBURY, as the cartoon art of R. Crumb and others gained worldwide exposure.

Artists working in craft media have continued to challenge the boundaries of their materials—ceramists Robert Arneson, Viola Frey and Peter Voulkos are known internationally, and textile-based sculptors Kay Sekimachi and Ruth Asawa have helped redefine the medium. Asawa is also the creator of some of San Francisco's most popular public works, including fountains at GHIRARDELLI SQUARE and at the Grand Hyatt Hotel near UNION SQUARE. Sculptor Beniamino Bufano created a menagerie of rounded and evocative animal forms and symbolic human figures which continue to populate the city's parks and public squares.

Courtesy of the artist/The Campbell-Thiebaud Gallery

Street Arrow (1974-76) by Wayne Thiebaud

The Contemporary Scene – Today, the SAN FRANCISCO MUSEUM OF MODERN ART, at home in its new building in the SOUTH OF MARKET area, honors its commitment to displaying pieces by Bay Area artists as well as cutting-edge works by international artists, while the Center for the Arts at YERBA BUENA GARDENS maintains an ambitious program of temporary exhibitions that keeps a continual flow of new art before the public eye. San Francisco's public and private galleries increase visitors' opportunities to see all kinds of visual art, most conveniently during the thrice-yearly San Francisco Open

Studios days *(p 219)* when galleries and artists' studios across the city hold open houses. College galleries at San Francisco State University and the San Francisco Art Institute mount exhibitions of national and international work.
The city remains the capital of the nation's alternative art centers with its concentration of nonprofit spaces and artist cooperatives, including S.F. Camerawork, New Langton Arts, Hunters Point Studios, GALERIA DE LA RAZA and the Headlands Center for the Arts in Marin County. Commercial galleries, many of them clustered in the UNION SQUARE AREA, present a range of exciting contemporary and historical art. Well worth looking into are Gallery Paule Anglim, John Berggruen and Bomani Gallery, located within a few blocks of one another. The work of performance and conceptual artists Guillermo Gomez-Pena, Karen Finley and collective SRL; painters Enrique Chagoya and Oliver Jackson; muralists Juana Alicia and Danel Galvez; and photographers Richard Misrach and Linda Connor, continue to infuse San Francisco visual arts with new ideas and vitality.

Performing Arts

Famed for its cultural diversity, San Francisco has always been a hotbed for the performing arts. A city of immigrants, it has nurtured the European traditions of opera, symphony and ballet while making room for Chinese opera, Latin jazz and ethnic dance. A haven for nonconformists, it has been the birthplace of new strains of rock-and-roll music and postmodern dance.

Opera – Of all the musical arts, opera is the one that has most enduringly won a place in San Francisco's heart. Even when the city was but a small, gritty mining outpost, luxuriant operas were staged on a regular basis in some of the most sumptuous theaters in the nation. Beginning with Bellini's *La Somnabula* in 1851, some 5,000 operatic performances were given by more than 20 companies prior to the 1906 earthquake. In 1923 the pianist and producer Gaetano Merola founded the **San Francisco Opera** with a production of *La Bohème*, but it was not until 1934 that the company christened the WAR MEMORIAL OPERA HOUSE, its permanent home, with a performance of Puccini's *Tosca*. Widely recognized as the preeminent operatic institution in the western US, the company has presented such greats as Luciano Pavarotti, Elisabeth Schwarzkopf and Birgit Nilsson. Smaller companies such as the Lamplighters, a Gilbert and Sullivan company formed in 1952, and Pocket Opera, a troupe that has performed classic works in English since 1968, illustrate opera's mass appeal with their inventive, accessible productions.

Classical Music – San Francisco's taste for orchestral music is well established. Founded in 1911, the **San Francisco Symphony Orchestra** hosted the adolescent debuts of violinists Yehudi Menuhin (1926) and Isaac Stern (1936) and developed a repertory rooted in the classical and romantic traditions. However, with the 1995 installation of Leonard Bernstein protégé Michael Tilson Thomas as its director, the symphony has undergone a renaissance. Tilson Thomas has challenged his musicians and his audiences with an array of difficult, under-recognized 20C masterpieces by Copland, Debussy, Varese and onetime Bay Area composers Lou Harrison and Darius Milhaud. Among chamber-music groups, the **Kronos Quartet**, founded in San Francisco in 1977, stands out for crystallizing the city's ethos of experimentation and fun with its original, often-playful arrangements of contemporary works. The male choir **Chanticleer**, the nation's only full-time classical a cappella group, has performed and recorded an eclectic array of new and ancient music since its inception in 1978, including rare Renaissance choral pieces, vocal jazz and gospel.

Jazz and Rock – It was not until the 1940s and '50s that San Francisco and Oakland enjoyed a brief flowering as jazz hubs. Breaking from the Dixieland tradition parlayed locally by Crescent City musicians, Bay Area native Dave Brubeck pioneered a new sound, characterized by syncopated rhythms, percussive piano playing and classical song structures. Brubeck's runaway success with his albums for Fantasy, a then-fledgling local label, made San Francisco one of the world centers for jazz recording. Today a critically acclaimed "new jazz" style, grounded in bebop but inflected by rock and funk, has been developed by a younger generation of San Franciscans, most notably guitarist Charlie Hunter.
San Francisco's place in the rock-and-roll canon was clinched in the 1960s when local bands the Grateful Dead, Jefferson Airplane and Big Brother and the Holding Company (featuring Janis Joplin) wrote the soundtrack for a decade of political protest and cultural revolution. Free concerts in GOLDEN GATE PARK and all-night jam sessions at the Family Dog, Fillmore, and Avalon ballrooms drew thousands to hear what became known as the **San Francisco Sound**. In the 1970s political folk singers like Joan Baez (from Carmel) and bands like Country Joe and the Fish emerged. Crooner Chris Isaak, whose stylish music has been described as rhythm-and-blues with roots in country and folk, burst onto the scene in the late 1980s. Around the same time, a hardcore punk scene coalesced around Jello Biafra's Dead Kennedys, preparing the way for a punk-pop explosion in the East Bay that hurtled the band Green Day from obscurity to platinum status in the '90s. Perhaps the most popular Bay Area band at the end of the century has been the mellow-toned R&B quartet Boys II Men.

Theater – Demonstrating its flair for the dramatic, San Francisco has always supported the theater. In the 1850s, 22 of the Bard's 38 plays were staged, but circus acts and minstrel shows were equally popular. In the 1860s some of the most sumptuous playhouses in the nation were built here—just as Barbary Coast melodeons were gaining a toehold. Audacious local stars like Lola Montez, Adah Isaacs Menken and Lotta Crabtree achieved near-mythic status in this crude yet sublime environment.
Once the transcontinental railroad was completed in 1869, San Francisco became a must-stop on the national touring circuit. It was not until the mid-20C, however, that the city regained a strong local theater community. In 1951 San Francisco State University professors Jules Irving and Herbert Blau founded the **Actors' Workshop**, introducing the work of Harold Pinter, Samuel Beckett and Edward Albee to local audiences. The **San Francisco Mime Troupe**, founded in 1959, today travels the world with its canny, self-styled political satires. In 1967 actor and director William Ball established the **American Conservatory Theater** (ACT), today considered one of the best regional theaters and drama schools in the US. In addition, a theater community of more than 100 professional companies mounts everything from the local camp classic *Beach Blanket Babylon* *(p 63)* to masterpieces by Shakespeare and Chekhov.

Dance – Second only to New York in the diversity, innovation and quality of its troupes, San Francisco stands at the forefront of classical and modern dance in the US. Founded in 1933, the **San Francisco Ballet** is the oldest resident classical ballet company in the country. The ballet presented the first full-length American productions of such 19C classics as *Swan Lake* and *The Nutcracker*, in addition to building a large repertoire of 20C works by George Balanchine, Jerome Robbins and various resident choreographers, including Lew Christensen and Michael Smuin. In the East Bay, the small but energetic Oakland Ballet has made its name by reviving classic ballets of the 20C, including the work of Vaslav Nijinsky.
Modern dance of every type is also well established in San Francisco. One of its foremothers, Isadora Duncan, was born here in 1877, though she spent most of her life abroad and performed in the city only twice. Anna Halprin emerged in the late 1950s as an influential teacher and choreographer; her explorations of ritual, physicality and the creative process sparked groundbreaking postmodern work in New York in the 1960s. Today, the Joe Goode Performance Group and Contraband have achieved stunning results by combining dance with theater and live music, and a wide array of ethnic dance companies explore and expand on everything from butoh and belly dancing to flamenco and capoeira.

Literature

Born in the wake of the Gold Rush, San Francisco's literary tradition began as a torrent of local magazines and newspapers that has since broadened and expanded into every genre and style. Today a host of renowned and up-and-coming journalists, novelists and poets make the city their home and source of inspiration.

The Golden Fifties and Silver Sixties – Legendary Mormon entrepreneur Sam Brannan founded San Francisco's first major newspaper, *The California Star*, in 1847. Soon the *Star* teamed up with *The Californian*, a Monterey-based publication, to form the *Alta California*, first daily newspaper in the West. By the mid-1850s San Francisco boasted a dozen dailies and nearly 40 weeklies—more publications than were produced in London at the time. While most of these were political organs or advertisers, they also encouraged some of the city's fresh young literary voices. Nearly every paper carved out room for a "poet's corner" on the front page, thereby nurturing the talents of miner-bards such as Alonzo Delano and John Rollin Ridge, who wrote under the *noms de plume* Old Block and Yellow Bird, respectively.
Through the 1860s, literary journals such as *The Pioneer*, the *Golden Era*, *The Californian* and the *Overland Monthly* flourished, as did the unconventional culture that aided and abetted them. Bret Harte *(The Luck of Roaring Camp and Other Sketches)* and Joaquin Miller *(Songs of the Sierras)* drew from their experiences working in mining towns for their early essays, short stories and poems. Others, like Ina Coolbrith and Charles Stoddard, found inspiration in nature and the emotions. Ambrose Bierce *(Occurrence at Owl Creek Bridge, The Devil's Dictionary)* and Mark Twain *(Roughing It, The Adventures of Huckleberry Finn)* made their reputations writing irreverent satires and burlesques. As the decade wore on, Bierce grew increasingly misanthropic and cynical, earning himself the nickname "Bitter Bierce" by becoming a vociferous champion of suicide and attacking progressive issues such as women's suffrage and the eight-hour workday. Twain, on the other hand, sharpened his skills and applied them to the picaresque fiction that would later assure his place in the American literary canon.
During the financial depression of the 1870s, many publications floundered and talents such as Harte, Miller, Twain, Bierce and Stoddard relocated elsewhere. A steady stream of writers came through the city in the next couple of decades, however. Poet Robert Frost was born in 1874 near the EMBARCADERO and lived there 11 years; Robert Louis Stevenson wrote in a flat near UNION SQUARE in 1879 and 1880; and in the late 1880s British Indian writer Rudyard Kipling tried, unsuccessfully, to publish his stories

in the city's major journals. Across the bay Gertrude Stein lived in OAKLAND from 1880 to 1891 before going to Radcliffe and then founding her salon in Paris. Of the 1860s bohemians, though, only Ina Coolbrith *(p 68)* stayed in San Francisco, hosting literary salons and encouraging the next generation of writers in their pursuits.

Social Realism – One of Coolbrith's many acolytes, Jack London *(Call of the Wild, The Sea Wolf)*, wrote in the tradition of Twain and Harte, using his many adventures to fuel his fiction. But like many writers of his time, London also addressed larger social and philosophical issues in his work. His story "South of the Slot" contains a sharp critique of class differences in San Francisco (the title refers to Market Street, which once sharply divided the rich from the poor). London's contemporary, Frank Norris, also saw contradictions in San Francisco society; his acclaimed naturalistic novel *McTeague* (1899), set in the Polk Gulch neighborhood, explores such themes as greed and social Darwinism from the point of view of a beleaguered dentist.

Taking a different tack, poet George Sterling wrote torrid romantic poems and famously described the city as a "cool, grey city of love." Other writers and artists of the era belonged to the fun-loving group Les Jeunes (the Young Ones), which published its work in *The Lark* (1895-97), "a magazine of humorous anarchy." The majority of Les Jeunes succeeded in doing their best-known work after the group's breakup, although founder Gelett Burgess remains famous for his frivolous poem "The Purple Cow," which appeared in *The Lark*.

Courtesy San Francisco Public Library

Jack London

From 1920 to 1929 Dashiell Hammett made San Francisco his home; the fog-cloaked slopes of Nob Hill provided a noir backdrop for the nighttime ramblings of Sam Spade, Hammett's hard-boiled detective hero of *The Maltese Falcon*. John Steinbeck also lived in the city in the late 1920s, although he drew from the environs of nearby Salinas and Monterey for his acclaimed novels *East of Eden* and *Cannery Row*.

Beat Happening – In the 1950s San Francisco underwent a literary renaissance as the Beat Generation came of age in North Beach. From the early to mid-1950s, Jack Kerouac churned out more than a dozen books about wanderlust, love and longing. Kerouac typed *On the Road* as one very long paragraph in 20 days of April 1951; upon publication in 1957, the book catapulted him and his Beat Generation cohorts to fame. According to poet and City Lights bookstore founder Lawrence Ferlinghetti, "The emergence of the Beat Generation made North Beach *the* literary center of SF—and it nurtured a new vision that would spread far beyond its bounds." Poet Allen Ginsberg, one of that vision's most articulate proponents, gave birth to the San Francisco poetry renaissance in 1955 when he read his poem "Howl" (first published by City Lights) to a standing-room-only audience in the Marina District.

In 1960 and 1961 Ken Kesey wrote *One Flew Over the Cuckoo's Nest*, his best-selling novel about a mental institution, from his home in Palo Alto. Journalist Tom Wolfe vividly captured the psychedelic counterculture in his 1969 book *The Electric Kool-Aid Acid Test*. In the 1970s Armistead Maupin followed the lives of young drifters in his long-running *San Francisco Chronicle* column, later published as the book *Tales of the City*. Before he died of AIDS in 1994, *Chronicle* journalist Randy Shilts *(And the Band Played On)*, gained renown writing about city politics, gay liberation and the AIDS epidemic in the 1970s and 1980s. For six decades until his death in 1997, Pulitzer Prize-winning *Chronicle* columnist Herb Caen entertained a huge and faithful following of avid readers with his witty blend of gossip and news about the city he loved. Today the city boasts a wide range of resident writers, including novelists Amy Tan *(The Joy Luck Club)* and Alice Walker *(The Color Purple)*, and British-born poet Thom Gunn—as well as a lively "spoken word" scene of public readings of new work by local novelists, essayists and poets.

Admission prices and hours published in this guide are accurate at press time.

Cuisine

San Franciscans are curious and demanding diners. Their adventurous willingness to experiment with new cuisines and with innovative interpretations of traditional favorites has earned the city a well-deserved reputation for fine dining. Fueled and sated by a dedicated legion of celebrity chefs, this passion has elevated Bay Area dining to the level of high art. The region's multiethnic heritage has created an environment in which international gourmet specialties happily coexist.

Locally Grown – Thanks to California's mild climate and fertile soil, a year-round abundance of locally grown fruits, vegetables, meats and dairy products flow into the city daily. They stock not only grocery stores and restaurant kitchens but also farmers markets at locations throughout the Bay Area. A stroll through one of these markets enables food-loving visitors, to behold, taste or purchase exotic seasonal delights such as juicy white peaches, sweet fresh apricots, fragrant herbs, young garlic and many varieties of tomatoes. Much of this produce is organically grown. Shoppers will also find fresh eggs, locally produced cheeses, and nuts from California's Central Valley agricultural region.

Dungeness Crabs on Ice

Although much of the city's seafood no longer comes from local waters, an enormous variety is flown or trucked in daily. Diners can select from a wide array—sea bass from Chile, salmon and oysters from Washington state, mussels from New Zealand, halibut from Canada—all absolutely fresh thanks to modern shipping techniques. From November through April, **Dungeness crab** appears on menus and in fish markets; this famed San Francisco treat is best consumed with sourdough bread and a glass of crisp white wine.

San Francisco's renowned **sourdough bread** remains a beloved local treasure. True devotees swear it cannot be produced anywhere but in the city. Dating from the 19C gold-mining days, the recipe for this tangy loaf calls for a yeast-like starter, no sugar, and microbes that apparently float only in San Francisco air.

California's phenomenally successful **wine** industry *(p 194)* produces an array of vintages to suit any palate or budget, from good, hearty table wines to world-class award-winners. Most San Francisco wine lists prominently feature vintages from the WINE COUNTRY to the northeast, though high-quality wines also come to the city from Mendocino County to the north, and from Monterey and the Central Coast to the south. Many restaurants also stock high-quality selections from Europe.

Locally brewed beers have experienced a popular resurgence in the past decade. Well worth sampling are brews from the San Francisco-based Anchor Brewing Company, whose Steam Beer traces its recipe back to the Gold Rush era, and such respected microbreweries as Sierra Nevada, Mendocino Brewing and Anderson Valley Brewing Company, whose Boont Amber is a rich, creamy ale.

Bay Area **mineral waters** tickle many a local palate. The most famous brand is Calistoga, bottled at the source near the eponymous Wine Country town.

International Flavors – Like many port cities, San Francisco's abundance of restaurants proffers cuisine from around the globe. In NORTH BEACH, a fragrant array of bakeries, trattorias, delicatessens and cafes dish up glorious **Italian** treats. Besides pasta, pizza and other Italian fare, look for the local specialty *cioppino*, a tomato-based seafood stew. **Chinese** restaurants are so abundant that there seems to be one on every street corner. A Cantonese specialty, favored at lunch or brunch, is *dim sum*,

■ A California Recipe: Risotto of Spring Vegetables

Traci Des Jardins, executive chef and co-owner of the Jardinière restaurant near the Civic Center, was born in California of French and Mexican ancestry, but apprenticed at several leading restaurants in France, including Lucas Carton and Arpège. Her culinary approach, as reflected by her background, is in some ways typical of San Francisco's legion of ambitious young chefs: combining fresh regional ingredients with continental styles.

Herewith a recipe for one of Des Jardin's favorite dishes, a risotto of spring vegetables:

Ingredients:

12	baby artichokes
2	lemons
6 tablespoons	olive oil
1 pound	peas, shucked
1/2 pound	fava beans, shucked
1 basket	cherry tomatoes, washed
6-8 cups	chicken stock
1	yellow onion, peeled and diced
2 cups	arborio rice
1 cup	white wine
1 bunch	basil, cut into thin strips
1/4 cup	Parmesan Reggiano cheese, grated
	salt and pepper, to taste

Directions:

Remove the tough outer green leaves from the baby artichokes; trim the bottom until only the heart remains. Cut the tough leaves off the top. Cut in half, remove fuzzy "choke" and place in water with the juice of two lemons. Remove from water and slice into 1/8-inch slices. Place 2 tablespoons of olive oil in a heavy-bottomed skillet on medium-high heat; sauté the artichokes for about 4 minutes or until cooked through. Season to taste with salt and pepper. Set aside.

Blanch the peas. Remove the husks from the fava beans and blanch them. Cut the cherry tomatoes in half. Season the chicken stock with salt and bring to a boil. In a heavy-bottomed pan, heat the olive oil slightly and add the onion; sweat until translucent, then add the rice. When the rice is heated, add the white wine. Let reduce completely. Begin adding the chicken stock a little at a time, stirring constantly for 20 minutes or until the rice is al dente. Add the peas, favas, artichokes, tomatoes and basil; grate the Parmesan on top. Season to taste.

a choice of many delicious sweet or savory dumplings filled with meat, seafood or vegetables. Lovers of other Asian cuisines can as easily sample sushi, peanut noodles or teriyaki dishes.

Mexican food may be found all over the city but particularly in the MISSION DISTRICT, where abundant Latino restaurants serve up large portions of tacos, burritos, enchiladas, tamales and *carne asada*. Other Central and South American specialties include *seviche*, a citrusy seafood soup.

California Cuisine – Drawing on California's polyglot heritage, and taking advantage of high-quality, readily available ingredients, a new approach to eating was introduced in 1971 when Alice Waters opened her Chez Panisse restaurant in BERKELEY. Reacting to the prepackaged, mass-marketed food that had come to dominate American menus, and drawing on her experiences in the French region of Provence, Waters developed a method of cooking based on seasonally varying, ultra-fresh, wild and locally grown produce presented in a visually appealing manner. **California Cuisine**, as it was called, transformed American gastronomy and reawakened the American palate.

Though very popular, California Cuisine gained a reputation for small portions at high prices. In the late 1980s, the "New American" spin-off took San Francisco by storm. Featuring hearty platefuls of traditional foods, prepared with the California Cuisine emphasis on fresh, locally grown produce, restaurants like the Fog City Diner drew packed houses for their deliciously unpretentious food and lighthearted, retro-Americana ambience. Since the late 1980s, Bay Area chefs have pioneered a New American approach to Asian cooking, resulting in what is often called "Asian fusion" cuisine.

Restaurants with Attitude – San Francisco's restaurant culture thrives on residents' fascination with the experience of dining out. Local newspapers exhaustively cover the restaurant scene. Chefs of trendy, successful eateries are feted as celebrities, their comings and goings altering the fates of restaurants almost overnight. In keeping with this heightened sense of importance, restaurateurs pay close attention to style and design. Interiors, table settings, waitstaff attire and music are carefully choreographed to complement the cuisine. Some restaurants feature "open kitchens" deliberately exposed to the dining rooms so that customers can keep an eye on the proceedings. Bold colors and soaring spaces are the order of the day. Diners generally dress the part, though dress codes are rare and casual clothing is welcomed in many places.

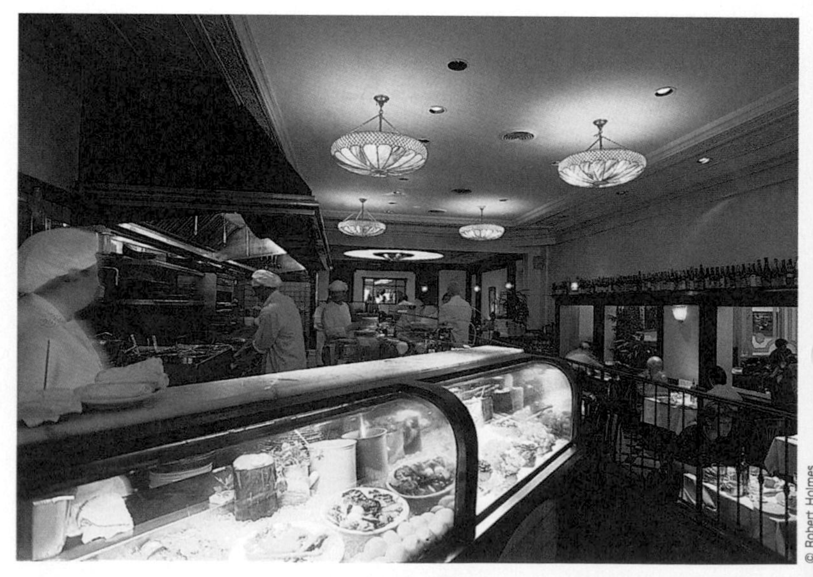

Open Kitchen, Kuleto's

Further Reading

Adventuring in the San Francisco Bay Area by Peggy Wayburn (1995, Sierra Club Books)

Berkeley Landmarks: An Illustrated Guide to Berkeley, California's Architectural Heritage by Susan Dinkelspiel Cerny (1994, Berkeley Architectural Heritage Assoc.)

The Best of Herb Caen: 1960–1975 (1991, Chronicle Books)

Big Alma: San Francisco's Alma Spreckels by Bernice Scarlach (1990, Scottwall Assoc.)

The Dashiell Hammett Tour by Don Herron (1991, City Lights Books)

The Earth Shook, the Sky Burned: A Moving Record of America's Great Earthquake and Fire: San Francisco April 18, 1906 by William Bronson (1996, Chronicle Books)

Golden Gate National Recreation Area (Golden Gate National Park Assoc.)

- **Guide to the Parks**
- **Alcatraz: Island of Change**
- **Cliff House & Lands End: San Francisco's Seaside Retreat**
- **Fort Point: Sentry at the Golden Gate**
- **Marin Headlands: Portals of Time**
- **Muir Woods: Redwood Refuge**

Post and Park: A Brief Illustrated History of the Presidio of San Francisco

Roughing It by Mark Twain (1871; reprint 1972, University of California Press)

San Francisco Almanac by Gladys Hansen (1995, Chronicle Books)

San Francisco Architecture by Sally B. Woodbridge and John M. Woodbridge (1992, Chronicle Books)

San Francisco Invites the World: The Panama-Pacific International Exposition of 1915 by Donna Ewals and Peter Clute (1991, Chronicle Books)

San Francisco Memoirs: Eyewitness Accounts of the Birth of the City compiled and introduced by Malcolm E. Barker (1994, Londonborn Publications)

San Francisco Stories: Great Writers on the City edited by John Miller (1990, Chronicle Books)

Tales of the City by Armistead Maupin (1994, HarperPerennial)

Tamalpais Trails by Barry Spitz (1995, Potrero Meadow Publishing Company)

This is San Francisco: A Classic Portrait of the City by Robert O'Brien (1994, Chronicle Books)

Two Years Before the Mast by Richard Henry Dana (1840) (1986, Penguin Books)

West from Home: Letters of Laura Ingalls Wilder, San Francisco, 1915 edited by Roger Lea MacBride (1995, HarperCollins Publishers)

Sights in San Francisco

Yerba Buena Gardens and San Francisco Museum of Modern Art/© Robert Holmes

1 • CHINATOWN★★★

Time: 1/2 day. all lines. MUNI bus 30–Stockton.
Map p 39

A teeming, colorful fusion of Cantonese market town and American Main Street, San Francisco's Chinatown spreads along the lower slope of NOB HILL overlooking the FINANCIAL DISTRICT. One of the four largest Chinese settlements outside Asia (the others are in New York City, Toronto and Vancouver), Chinatown ranks among the most densely populated neighborhoods on the North American continent. An estimated 30,000 people reside in the 24-block core bounded by Broadway, Montgomery, California and Powell Streets. Immigrants comprise the bulk of Chinatown residents, most of whom maintain their native dialects, customs, foods, festivals and religions. Chinatown is unique in that it also absorbs and refashions diverse American influences.

Historical Notes

The Chinese in the American West – Among the many thousands who flocked to California during the 1849 Gold Rush were Cantonese treasure-seekers, men who intended to return to China after striking their bonanzas. These expectations spurred few of them to learn English or assimilate Western culture, reinforcing their separation from American society. As China's ruling Manchu dynasty decayed through the 19C, however, and social and political conditions worsened in their homeland, ever-greater numbers of Chinese sought to remain and make their fortunes in the emerging American West.

By 1870 more than 63,000 Chinese, most of them men, were living in the US. In demand as laborers for large construction projects, they built much of the western half of the first transcontinental railroad, pioneered the fishing industry on San Francisco Bay and planted crops on California's new farmlands. In many Western towns, Chinese entrepreneurs opened small businesses such as laundries, retail shops and grocery stores.

As the premier point of entry for Asian immigrants, San Francisco harbored North America's oldest and largest Chinese community. Several Chinese settlements formed around the city and its bay, but by the late 1860s, most Chinese immigrants had consolidated their homes and businesses along Sacramento Street a block south of Portsmouth Square.

Surviving Troubled Times – Chinatown expanded during violent waves of anti-Chinese sentiment that swept the American West after the economic depression of 1872, when bankruptcies put thousands out of work and tycoons bolstered their profits by hiring Chinese workers at low wages. Riotous mobs of unemployed men stormed Chinese communities throughout the West, including San Francisco's Chinatown in 1877, beating (and sometimes killing) people and destroying property. Labor organizers pushed politicians to pass the Chinese Exclusion Act of 1882, which barred Chinese laborers (though not merchants or their families) from entering the US. The act effectively prevented thousands of men already in the US from sending for brides, thus preserving Chinatown's rough-and-tumble, male-dominated society until well into the 20C.

Chinese immigrants sought security in *tongs* (the word means "association" or "company"), whose membership was usually based on clan name or members' geographical origins. These organizations often sponsored new arrivals by paying their passage to San Francisco, assuming the roles of labor guild, insurance company, social club, legal advisor, protection agent and undertaker, in return for dues. A few were little more than criminal gangs. By the late 19C, Chinatown had acquired a villainous reputation as a haven for opium dens, gambling halls and brothels, and violent episodes known as tong wars erupted between different factions seeking to control profits. In an effort to restore order to Chinatown and to represent Chinese interests outside the neighborhood, men from the six most powerful tongs in 1882 agreed to form a confederation. Known as the **Chinese Six Companies**, the organization remains an active, if gradually diminishing, force in present-day Chinatown.

The repeal of the Chinese Exclusion Act in 1943 and a further relaxation of immigration laws in the 1960s heralded a new influx of immigrants from Hong Kong, China and Southeast Asia. As families became Americanized, many moved to other areas of the city. So many have settled in adjacent NORTH BEACH since the 1960s that section of that neighborhood between Broadway and WASHINGTON SQUARE, long known as "Little Italy," are now culturally an extension of Chinatown. Parts of the RICHMOND DISTRICT ar SUNSET DISTRICT in the western half of the city have also been transformed into "ne Chinatowns inhabited by wealthier, younger and better-educated Chinese.

Old Chinatown, however, remains the heart and soul of the now far-flung Chinese community. Its members flock here from around the city and the Bay Area to shop, eat and socialize in the lively markets, restaurants, bookstores and cultural centers. Tourists come by the thousands to wander Grant Avenue, Stockton Street and the warren of side streets between them, visiting the temples and herb shops, dining in the many restaurants, and shopping for Chinese groceries, embroidered linens, artwork, jewelry and souvenirs.

Chinatown Temples

Among the most illuminating and evocative manifestations of Chinatown life are its many religious temples. Conventional Western scholarship may categorize Chinese religion as either Confucianism, Taoism or Buddhism, but the truth is complex:

Confucianism is more a state doctrine than a religion. Its prescribed rites constitute a symbolic pact upholding an ideal of harmonious social order and stability, with a hierarchy headed by the emperor and each person happily ensconced in his or her appropriate niche.

Taoism, a more mystical religion, might be characterized as a way of organizing the enormous array of Chinese gods and natural forces into a formal system. Among the most popular Taoist deities worshipped in Chinatown temples are the god of warriors and poets, Guan Di, and the Queen of Heaven, Tin How, also known as Ma-Tsu.

Buddhism, imported into China from India more than 1700 years ago, has been shaped over the centuries into a distinctively Chinese belief system, in which a pantheon of different Buddhas and faithful disciples are worshiped. A less materialistic form of Chinese Buddhism is Ch'an, better known in the West by its Japanese name of Zen.

Since ancient times, the Chinese have paid reverence to their ancestors and propitiated the forces of nature through sacrifice and prayer. In every temple, worshippers can be seen offering sacrifices of fruit, rice wine, roast meats and flowers, burning incense to resident deities or to tablets inscribed with names of recently deceased relatives. After the spirits are thought to have consumed the essence of the sacrifice, the worshipper will remove the now-sanctified offering and freely partake of it at mealtime. Symbolic offerings of paper cars and houses, "cash" and even paper servants are sometimes burned in a temple furnace, by which means they are sent to deceased loved ones believed to be residing in the spirit world. The person sending the offering will often hit a drum announcing his or her sacrifice to the spirit.
Chinese temples usually contain figures of several deities, and although Buddhist temples normally house images only of the Buddha, many Taoist temples freely mix Buddhist statues among their deities. As long as beliefs do not interfere with social harmony—as long as the Confucian doctrine is upheld—the Chinese are very tolerant in matters of religion.
Visitors are welcome in most temples, though it may be necessary to ring a doorbell to gain admittance. Courtesy is expected; photography is not permitted. Contributions left in marked donation boxes will be appreciated.

Visiting Chinatown – To fully experience Chinatown's vibrant, intense character, visit the neighborhood on foot. Steep hills may present a challenge, but Grant Avenue and Stockton Street, the main thoroughfares, are nearly level. It's best to get to and from Chinatown by cable car or other public transportation, as street parking is very difficult. Underground garages are located at Portsmouth Square, the Holiday Inn and St. Mary's Square.

Temples and businesses typically open after 10am, but a visit to Chinatown can be interesting at any time of day. Arrive at Portsmouth Square before 8am to see neighborhood denizens practicing their morning *t'ai chi (p 63)*. In the early evening, local residents throng the streets for evening shopping, and delicious cooking aromas waft through the air. Saturday morning is probably the most crowded time of the week, particularly along Stockton Street; Sundays are barely less hectic. Note that temples may close for certain periods during the day; if one is closed when you arrive, try again later.

During Chinese New Year, which occurs between late January and late February depending on the lunar calendar, shops decorate with red and gold good-luck symbols and a festive air prevails. The popular **Chinese New Year Parade** *(p 219)* typically takes place on the fringe of Chinatown, ending near Portsmouth Square on Kearny Street at Columbus Avenue; check with the San Francisco Convention & Visitors Bureau *(p 220)* for the annual parade route.

Shop Window, Chinatown

WALKING TOUR *distance: .7mi.*

Begin at the intersection of Bush St. and Grant Ave. and walk north.

★★**Grant Avenue** – The eight blocks of Grant Avenue between Bush Street and Broadway comprise Chinatown's principal thoroughfare for visitors. The street abounds in architectural chinoiserie—painted balconies, curved tile rooflines, staggered towers and predominantly red, green and yellow color schemes—applied during the 1920s and '30s to otherwise-unremarkable buildings to give the neighborhood an exotic cachet. Ceramic carp and dragons on the roof of the **Chinatown Gate** *(Grant Ave. at Bush St.)* symbolize auspicious fortunes. Taiwan's government donated materials for construction of the gateway, which was designed in 1970 by Clayton Lee based upon ceremonial entrances of Chinese villages. North of the gate, shops selling curios, souvenirs, jewelry, artwork, furniture, cameras and electronics draw visitors in droves, while hardware stores, banks, poultry and fish markets, tea stores and small cafes cater to a mostly local clientele.

Numerous authentic Taoist, Buddhist and Confucianist temples are tucked away on upper floors behind unassuming doors throughout the neighborhood. Visitors are welcomed at the **Ching Chung Temple**★ *(615 Grant Ave., 4th floor; open year-round daily 11am–6pm; 20min guided tour available; ☎ 415-433-2623)*, where portraits of the founders of three Taoist sects distinguish the main altar, overlooking a host of ancillary gods.

★**Old St. Mary's Cathedral** – *660 California St., at Grant Ave. Open year-round Mon–Fri 7am–7pm, Sat 10am–7pm, Sun 7:30am–5pm. ♿ ☎ 415-288-3800.* The largest building in the state at the time of its dedication in 1854, this handsome Catholic church began as a cathedral, the first seat of the Archdiocese of San Francisco. The Gothic Revival structure was redesignated a church following construction of a new ST. MARY'S CATHEDRAL on Van Ness Avenue in 1891. Made of brick and iron on a foundation of

CHINATOWN
0 1/10mi
0 100m
★★NORTH BEACH
★★FINANCIAL DISTRICT
★★NOB HILL
★UNION SQUARE AREA
Broadway
City Lights
Columbus
Vesuvio Café
Chinese Historical Society
Pacific Ave.
★Golden Gate Fortune Cookie Company
Beckett St.
Ma-Tsu Temple★
Jackson
Sentinel Bldg.
Ave.
St.
Hotaling Warehouse
Golden Era Bldg.
★Stockton Street
Ross Alley
Old Chinese Telephone Exchange
Kearny
Washington
Transamerica Pyramid
St.
Holiday Inn
Tin How Temple
★Waverly Place
Chinese Culture Center
Portsmouth Square★
Bank of SF
Kong Chow Temple★
★Norras Temple
Clay St.
Pacific Heritage Museum
Commercial St.
Chinese Six Companies
★★Grant Avenue
Wells Fargo
Sacramento St.
★Ching Chung Temple
★Old St. Mary's Cathedral
580
California St.
STOCKTON TUNNEL
Montgomery St.
Line
St. Mary's Square
Bank of America
The Ritz-Carlton San Francisco
Pine St.
Russ Bldg.
Powell St.
Chinatown Gate
Bush
Hallidie Bldg.

granite quarried in China, the church was entirely gutted by the great conflagration of 1906, which melted its bell and marble statuary but left its stout walls intact. The somber inscription from Ecclesiastes on the exterior bell tower, "Son, observe the time and fly from evil," was reputedly aimed at the brothels that once flourished in the neighborhood. Historic photographs displayed in the vestibule offer fascinating views of 19C Chinatown.

The church serves as the venue for popular noontime concerts of classical music, featuring a variety of local and touring professional artists *(year-round Tue & Thu 12:30; for schedule ☎ 415-288-3861)*.

Across California Street from the cathedral lies St. Mary's Square, a small, serene park anchored by a steel and granite statue of **Sun Yat-sen (1)** (1938) by sculptor Beniamino Bufano. Sun visited San Francisco's Chinese community several times around the turn of the century to raise money and support to overthrow China's Manchu Dynasty and establish the Republic of China. The successful revolution took place in 1911.

Return to Grant Ave. and continue north, turning right on Clay St.

★**Portsmouth Square** – Formerly the central plaza of the Anglo-Mexican settlement of Yerba Buena *(p 13)*, this broad square is today Chinatown's most important outdoor gathering point. In 1846 Captain John Montgomery officially claimed Yerba Buena for the US by raising the American flag above the plaza, later renamed for his ship. California's first public school opened here in April 1848, and the square was the site of Sam Brannan's momentous announcement that gold had been discovered some 100mi east of San Francisco. During the ensuing Gold Rush,

© Michael S. Yamashita

Game of cards, Portsmouth Square

Portsmouth Square served as center of the rambunctious new boomtown and scene of many civic dramas. As commercial activity shifted to the landfilled flatlands around Montgomery Street in the 1860s, however, Portsmouth Square was left on the periphery.

Today elderly men congregate in the square to socialize and play cards or Chinese chess. On the square's south side stands a **statue (2)** of the Goddess of Democracy, a somber memorial to the 1989 Tiananmen Square massacre in Beijing. On the north side stands a sailing-ship **monument (3)** to Robert Louis Stevenson, who enjoyed sitting here watching the crowds during his extended visit of 1879-80. To the east, a pedestrian bridge leads across Kearny Street to the **Chinese Culture Center** *(Holiday Inn, 3rd floor; open year-round Tue–Sun 10am–4pm; www.c-c-c.org ☎ 415-986-1822)*, featuring temporary exhibitions of Chinese and Chinese-American art and a permanent display of Chinese musical instruments.

Leave the square and walk uphill on Washington St.

Old Chinese Telephone Exchange – *743 Washington St.* The neighborhood's most exuberant example of chinoiserie rises in three graceful pagoda-like tiers above a glossy, red-pillared pediment. Now a branch of the Bank of Canton, the one-story building was opened as the Chinatown Telephone Exchange in 1909 to serve the community's 800 telephones. Female operators working the switchboards had to know how to speak Cantonese, Sze Yup and three other Chinese dialects, as well as English.

Ten Ren Tea Co.

949 Grant Ave. ☎ 415-362-0656. The oldest and largest American outlet of a Taiwan-based tea empire, this purveyor of Chinatown's traditional beverage sells tea by the metal canister or painted box, and samples by the hot, steaming cup. It costs from $6 to $200 a pound—a pricey product, but it takes 70,000 young leaves to make a pound of top-grade tea.

Turn right on Grant Ave., walk one block and turn right on Jackson St. Walk half a block down the hill and turn left on Beckett St.

★**Ma-Tsu Temple of USA** – *30 Beckett St., 1st floor. Open Oct–Apr daily 9:30am–5:50pm. Rest of the year daily 10am–6pm. Contribution requested. ☎ 415-986-8818.* This brightly attractive and very accessible temple honors the Queen of Heaven (using her title as it is known in coastal regions of China's Fujian and Guangdong provinces and Taiwan). The central statue is guarded by figures of two ferocious warriors, Chien Li Yen (Thousand Li Eye) and Shun Feng Er (Favorable Wind Ear), noted respectively for their prodigious powers of seeing and hearing. (A *li* is a Chinese unit of distance; hence the guards can spot evil from 1,000 *li*.) Giant puppets of the pair can be seen striding the streets, arms swinging widely and rhythmically, in the annual Chinese New Year Parade.

Return to Jackson St. Turn right up the hill, across Grant Ave., to Ross Alley; turn left and continue to Washington St.

Jackson Street, Ross Alley and Washington Street traverse a densely populated warren of herbalists, jewelers, restaurants, small grocery stores and fragrant bakeries. Suspended between the main thoroughfares of Grant Avenue and Stockton Street, these side streets retain the dark, intriguing ambience of old Chinatown. Many turn-of-the-century tong war clashes occurred here, and **Ross Alley** is still known among old Chinatown residents as "Lu Song Hang" or "Spanish Lane," a reference to the Hispanic prostitutes in the alley's 19C brothels. Today the narrow lane supports a shop purveying shrines, lanterns and religious statuary, and a number of clothing factories humming behind closed doors. Especially popular with visitors is the **Golden Gate Fortune Cookie Company**★ *(56 Ross Alley; open year-round daily 10am–midnight; ☎ 415-781-3956)*, where passersby may step inside to see cookies being baked and stuffed with "fortunes" by workers seated at slowly rotating griddle-ovens.

Cross Washington St., walk a few steps downhill and turn right on Waverly Pl.

★**Waverly Place** – This two-block alley is often dubbed "the Street of Painted Balconies" in reference to the handsome touches of chinoiserie that grace its otherwise plain three- and four-story Edwardian brick buildings. The colors are symbolic: red stands for happiness, green for longevity, black for money, yellow for good fortune. Among older Chinatown residents, Waverly Place is known as "Tin How Miu Gai" or Tin How Temple Street. In addition to three temples, the street is home to a cluster of benevolent associations. From the street, pedestrians can often hear the sound of drums booming from upper floors as association youth groups practice lion dance drills and other festival activities.

Chinatown Herb Shops

Along Stockton Street and the side streets leading down to Grant, visitors can find many traditional Chinese herb shops. These shops are usually recognizable for the curious collections prominently displayed in the front windows: bottled snakes, preserved ginseng roots that parody almost-human shapes, medical charts of the human body, pieces of tree bark, elk horn, dried seahorse and other sundries. These are the stuff of an ancient Chinese system of pharmacology, a lore gathered by early Taoist monks and herbalists, chronicled, tested and refined over thousands of years.

Entering any shop, visitors will find a counter backed by wooden cabinets with drawers containing hundreds of dried herbs and other medicinals. Most by far are vegetable in origin: ginkgo for tuberculosis, mulberry leaves for cold and headache, sumac for laryngitis, loquat leaf for cough, climbing dogbane for rheumatoid arthritis, winter cherry leaf for diabetes, Job's tears for lobar pneumonia. Among the items most exotic to Western medicine might be dried centipedes, a remedy for infantile convulsions, spasms, cramps, and lockjaw; dead silkworm for sore throat and headache; snakeskin for abscesses; and decoction of silkworm cocoon to relieve exhaustion.

The herb most familiar to Westerners is ginseng, a root sliced and steeped to make a tea celebrated for its curative virtues. The finest examples of ginseng root grow wild in the mountains of north China and Korea, but these can be quite expensive and probably will not be casually displayed in the herbalist's shop. Less expensive grades of ginseng powders and teas, including a variety of American ginseng from Wisconsin, make popular gifts.

Tin How Temple – *125 Waverly Pl., 4th floor. Open year-round daily 9am–4pm. ☎ 415-421-3628.* Chinatown's oldest temple has operated since 1852, though the present building dates only from 1911. It is devoted to Tin How, a Chinese woman born in Fujian Province in AD 960 and now worshipped as the Queen of Heaven and protector of seafarers. Her miraculous rescues of sailors at sea inspired a cult upon her death in AD 987. The worship came to the US with Chinese immigrants—who fell under Tin How's care when they crossed the sea. Gold and red electric lanterns glimmer in the incense-smoked interior, above a wooden statue of Tin How carried to California from Guangdong during the Gold Rush.

★**Norras Temple** – *109 Waverly Pl., 3rd floor. Open year-round daily 9am–4pm. ☎ 415-362-1993.* A large, gilded statue of the Buddha surrounded by smaller, similar figures dominates this friendly hall of worship, the first purely Buddhist temple in the mainland US when it opened in 1960. As in most Chinese temples, visitors can cast their fortunes by shaking a tube of bamboo slips until one jogs loose, falling to the floor. Take the slip to a temple attendant, who will either interpret your fortune according to the number or hand you a printed interpretation to have translated.

Turn right on Sacramento St., walk uphill to Stockton St. and turn right.

Chinese Six Companies – *843 Stockton St. Open year-round Mon–Fri 2pm–5pm. Closed holidays. ☎ 415-982-6000.* Though its original function has changed, the Chinese Six Companies still wields considerable influence among Chinatown's business establishments. The building's colorful, eye-catching facade, best viewed from the east side of Stockton Street is one of the most elaborate in Chinatown. Inside is a reception hall evocative of an imperial throne room.

★**Kong Chow Temple** – *855 Stockton St., 4th floor (elevator; enter to left of post office). Open year-round Mon–Fri 9am–4pm. ☎ 415-434-2513.* The Kong Chow temple first opened on Pine Street in 1857. Among the original furnishings transferred to the present building (1977) are excellent examples of Chinese wood carving; note especially the altar closest to the balcony, which depicts in sharp relief a social gathering hosted by the mythical lord of the sea. At the main altar, the swarthy-faced statue with a black beard represents Guan Di, most popular deity for Chinese land-dwellers. The steadfast figure—typically depicted with a sword in one hand and a book in the other—can be seen all over Chinatown in small shrines and shop windows. Guan Di, a general during the Three Kingdoms period (AD 220-280), fought ferociously and loyally for his lord, a contender for the imperial throne. Killed by treachery, Guan Di was elevated into the Taoist pantheon, becoming the patron saint of a host of amazingly disparate professions, including soldiers, poets, prostitutes, police and gangsters. The figure of Guan Di is flanked at the altar by his bushy-bearded warrior "brother" Zhang Fei and by his gentler son, in courtly clothing, holding an imperial chop (stamp) with both hands. Together they symbolize Guan Di's balanced devotion to both the civil government and the military.

Continue north on the left side of Stockton St. to Broadway.

★**Stockton Street** – The four blocks of Stockton Street between Clay Street and Broadway feature Chinatown's greatest concentration of produce, poultry and fresh fish markets. The street draws enormous crowds of mostly Chinese-American shoppers from all over the city, especially on weekend mornings. Savory Chinese specialties like pressed or roast duck, barbecued pork and soy-sauce chickens hang in the windows of food shops. Mounds of fruits and vegetables displayed on sidewalk stands vie for space with vendors peddling live poultry or fresh-picked produce from curbside truck beds. Throngs of shoppers, market cries and vigorous bargaining contribute to the colorful but amiable havoc so characteristic of Chinatown.

Chinese Historical Society of America – *644 Broadway, 4th floor. Open year-round Mon 1:30pm–4pm, Tue–Fri 10:30am–4pm. Closed major holidays. Contribution requested. ☎ 415-391-1188.* A small, yet fascinating collection of photographs and artifacts housed in a temporary one-room gallery documents the role played by Chinese immigrants and their descendants in such important national ventures as the 1849 Gold Rush, the transcontinental railroad, the development of agriculture and the commercial fishing industry. *The museum is scheduled to move into larger, permanent quarters at 965 Clay Street by 2001.*

Imperial Tea Court

1411 Powell St. ☎ 415-788-6080. After plunging through bustling Chinatown, step into this tranquil teahouse, an oasis of dark woods and glowing lanterns. Beneath the soothing twitter of elegantly caged birds, a wide variety of rare teas is prepared and served in traditional fashion. Teapots, cups, canisters and kettles are offered for sale along with the tea.

ADDITIONAL SIGHT

Pacific Heritage Museum – *Description p 50.*

2 • CIVIC CENTER★

Time: 2 hours. MUNI bus 5–Fulton, 19–Polk, 42–Downtown Loop or 47–Van Ness; all streetcars Civic Center station. bart Civic Center station.
Map p 46

Contained within the triangle of Market Street, Van Ness Avenue and Golden Gate Avenue, San Francisco's center of government occupies one of the finest groups of Beaux Arts-style buildings in the US. Though today the area suffers from its proximity to the downtrodden Tenderloin district, the grandly designed complex still reflects the tenets of the turn-of-the-century "City Beautiful" urban planning movement, updated with sympathetic contemporary constructions.

Historical Notes

Political Heart of the City – San Francisco's present-day Civic Center did not materialize until the early 20C, fairly late in the city's life. In order to provide a proper home for the city's government, which through the mid-19C had occupied a series of buildings around Portsmouth Square *(p 39)*, a new city hall was planned in the vicinity of contemporary Civic Center in 1872. Endemic corruption, within both the construction industry and the city government, delayed completion of the building for more than 25 years and vastly inflated the cost of the structure. When the great earthquake struck in April 1906, this shoddy boondoggle of a building was damaged beyond repair.
In the aftermath of the fire, an idealistic group of businessmen and politicians embarked upon an ambitious scheme to create a suitable new center for the city's cultural and political life. Following the design guidelines recommended by the Burnham Plan *(below)*, the group of buildings that now form the core of Civic Center was erected over the course of 20 years, beginning in 1913. First completed was the Civic Auditorium, which opened in time for the Panama-Pacific International Exposition of 1915 *(p 92)*. The new City Hall opened to the public at the end of 1915, while a stately main library and federal office buildings followed soon after. The historic portion of the complex was effectively completed with the opening of the Veterans Building and the War Memorial Opera House in 1932.

United Nations Birthplace – From April to June of 1945, the United Nations Conference on International Organization convened in the War Memorial Opera House, focusing international attention on the area. The United Nations Charter was signed in the Veterans Building's Herbst Theatre on June 26 of that year. Throughout subsequent decades, Civic Center remained a locus of federal, state and civic administration, as well as home to such cultural institutions as the modern art museum, ballet and opera.
Completion of Davies Symphony Hall in 1980 as home base for the city's esteemed symphony orchestra expanded the Civic Center's position as a cultural center, a role that continues despite the relocation of the SAN FRANCISCO MUSEUM OF MODERN ART to YERBA BUENA GARDENS. Recently, the opening of the new Main Library and further plans for renovating buildings and public open spaces bring hope for reducing some of the urban tarnish that afflicts the area today.

■ The City Beautiful

Around the turn of the 20C, civic leaders across the country joined forces to improve the quality of life in American cities. This concerted effort, known as the City Beautiful movement, brought together business leaders, politicians and architects who worked to make urban areas better places to live and work. Their efforts included such seemingly mundane projects as widening streets, installing street lights and building sewer systems, but also encompassed more singularly aesthetic goals.
The most prominent designer associated with the City Beautiful movement was Chicago architect Daniel Burnham, who was hired by a group of San Francisco businessmen to develop a plan that would improve the image and efficiency of the city. Over the course of two years Burnham made many trips to the city, spending untold hours in a cabin on the slope of Twin Peaks, sketching and studying the topography and character of the city below. With help from local architect Willis Polk, in 1905 he presented what became known as the **Burnham Plan**, an ambitious proposal for wide boulevards, traffic circles with streets radiating outward, and public monuments much like those of Washington DC or Paris.
The Burnham Plan was adopted with strong support, and the leveling of the city by the great earthquake and fire of 1906 seemed to offer a clean slate on which to implement it. However, concerns for private property rights and the urgency of rebuilding homes and businesses outweighed civic altruism, and reconstruction of the city in the aftermath of the disaster occurred along the old street grid. Construction of Civic Center proceeded more slowly, and today the ensemble stands as San Francisco's only realization of Burnham's grand plan.

Visiting Civic Center – Civic Center is well served by BART and Muni subway trains, by the historic F-Market streetcar line, and by many bus lines. A large public parking garage lies beneath Civic Center Plaza, and street parking may be found along the plaza's perimeter. Office workers throng the streets at midday, the most cheerful time to visit, and performances at War Memorial Opera House and Davies Symphony Hall draw ballet, opera and symphony devotees by night. Visitors should be aware, however, that many homeless persons frequent the Civic Center area at all times of the day and night.

WALKING TOUR *distance: .8mi*

Begin at the intersection of Market, Jones and McAllister Sts.

★**Hibernia Bank** – *1 Jones St. Interior not open to the public.* Ornamenting the blighted Tenderloin neighborhood that surrounds it, this delightful Beaux Arts bank (1892, Albert Pissis) ranks among the city's most significant small buildings. Its design influenced many area architects to adopt the Classical idiom for commercial structures. Facing Market Street, the stately main entrance turns the corner of Jones and McAllister Streets with an ornate copper-domed vestibule supported atop Corinthian columns. Now used as a substation by the San Francisco Police Department, the interior was reconstructed following the 1906 fire; the elaborate banking hall remains unoccupied.

Walk southwest along Market St.

★**United Nations Plaza** – Linking Market Street with the Civic Center, this sleek, contemporary plaza (1980, Lawrence Halprin) commemorates the founding of the United Nations here in 1945. Brass inlays in the pavement mark the site's longitude and latitude, and a large fountain made of immense blocks of stone forms a striking centerpiece. In 1995, to celebrate the United Nations' 50th anniversary, the plaza was improved with additional stone markers. One of the blocks around the fountain is inscribed with extracts from President Franklin D. Roosevelt's speech to the US Congress proposing the United Nations, and a black, freestanding obelisk carries the full text of the Universal Declaration of Human Rights.

Heart of the City Farmers Market

UN Plaza. ☎ 415-558-9455. Wednesday and Sunday mornings, California's farm bounty finds its way to local kitchens via this cheerful, bustling market. The changing displays of fresh fruit and vegetables remind shoppers that beyond the hills of this cool, gray city lie places where seasons change.

Leading west from Market Street along the Fulton Street mall *(closed to vehicular traffic)*, the plaza is bordered by parallel rows of square columns carved with the names of United Nations member countries and the years in which they joined. Occurring in chronological order, the columns create, in effect, a passage through recent world history: the People's Republic of China in 1971, the two Germanies in 1973 and unified Germany in 1991, ending with Palau in 1994.

A large **sculpture (1)** of a rearing horse ridden by Simón Bolívar, the Venezuelan revolutionary who liberated South America from colonial rule, dominates the west end of Fulton Street mall.

Walk south on Hyde St. to Market St.

★**Orpheum Theater** – *1192 Market St. (at Hyde and Grove Sts.) ☎ 415-551-2000.* Originally designed (1926, B. Marcus Priteca) to showcase vaudeville acts, this theater evokes a glorified, pre-Reformation Spain. The intricate facade is patterned after a 13C Léon cathedral, the high vaulted lobby ceiling is reminiscent of the Alhambra, and the auditorium ceiling is ringed with full-bodied lions. The 2,200-seat theater became a movie house in the 1930s but returned to its live-theater roots with the 1970 production of *Hair*. Meticulously restored in 1997-98, the opulent Orpheum continues to stage such Broadway hits as *Lady Saigon* and *Stomp!*

Walk back to UN Plaza and cross Hyde St.

James Lick Memorial (2) – Among the city's most engaging monuments, this large-scale composition of sculptures (1894, Frank Happersberger) stands on an axis with City Hall, between the old and new library buildings. A gift of the James Lick Trust, the work depicts Eureka standing atop a 30ft central column. Around the base, a pair of allegorical female figures embody agriculture and commerce of the Golden State; two tableaux vividly depict scenes of a miner panning for gold and a friar preaching to a Native American. A series of plaques carry the names and portraits of important individuals such as Sir Francis Drake and Father Junípero Serra.

★**San Francisco Public Library** – *100 Larkin St. Open year-round Mon 10am–6pm, Tue–Thu 9am–8pm, Fri 11am–5pm, Sat 9am–5pm & Sun noon–5pm. Closed major holidays.* ✗ ♿ 🅿 *http://sfpl.lib.ca.us* ☎ *415-557-4400.* Opened in 1996, San Francisco's new Main Library (James Ingo Freed & Cathy Simon) blends a contemporary take on Civic Center's traditional architecture with the latest in high technology. The building's gleaming exterior, sheathed in granite from the same quarry that provided stone for early Civic Center structures, expresses this dual personality. The main facade, facing City Hall across Larkin Street, reveals an updated version of Beaux Arts classicism, while the Hyde Street elevation presents an angular, contemporary face. The interior, replete with catwalk bridges, shelves of books, artworks and an asymmetrical skylit atrium, boasts multimedia computers, specialized study centers and access to electronic databases as well as to books and magazines. But while the new library has won points for its user-friendly approach, it has come under fire for significantly reducing the number of volumes available for loan. Changing displays of art and literature are presented in the lower-level Jewett Exhibition Gallery.

The old library building (1917, George Kelham), which lies to the north of the new structure, is being renovated to the tune of $118 million and will become, in the fall of 2001, home to the ASIAN ART MUSEUM now in Golden Gate Park.

Exit library on Larkin St. and cross Grove St. to auditorium.

Bill Graham Civic Auditorium – *50 Grove St.* Originally completed for the 1915 Panama-Pacific International Exposition, Civic Auditorium (Arthur Brown, Jr.) has undergone many remodelings and name changes, most recently in memory of popular music promoter Bill Graham, who died in 1992. Banners and flags frequently bedeck the arcade of stone arches that form the Grove Street facade overlooking Civic Center Plaza. The auditorium has long been one of the city's prime performance and special-event venues.

Cross Grove and Polk Sts. to City Hall.

★★**City Hall** – *Bounded by Grove, McAllister and Polk Sts. and Van Ness Ave.* Testament to San Francisco's civic pride, this monumental Beaux Arts edifice, crowned by a magnificent dome, is considered by many to be San Francisco's most beautiful building. Designed by Arthur Brown, Jr., a graduate of the École des Beaux Arts in Paris, the building was completed in 1915 under the stewardship of populist mayor James Rolph, who had vowed to rid the city government of the corruption that contributed to the demise of the first City Hall.

The massive, four-story building occupies a rectangle covering two city blocks. Its splendid dome rises to a height of 307ft, about 13ft taller than the US Capitol Building in Washington DC. On the Van Ness Avenue facade, handsome Atlas-like telamones support the entrance. Doric pillars and colonnades along the porticoes, facades and dome reinforce the Classical idiom. Inside, a grand ceremonial staircase ascends to a 181ft open rotunda, flanked by city government offices arranged according to their relative importance. The office of the mayor occupies the space directly beneath the central pediment on the Polk Street facade, with a balcony facing east onto Civic Center Plaza.

The grand edifice was damaged in the Loma Prieta earthquake and closed in 1995 for repairs and seismic retrofitting *(expected completion 1999).*

To the east of City Hall lies **Civic Center Plaza**, once the site of rallies, demonstrations and fiery speeches. The broad, beautifully proportioned space retains its grand air, though children's playgrounds now share it with significant numbers of homeless individuals.

Continue west on Grove St. Cross Van Ness Ave. and walk north.

City Hall

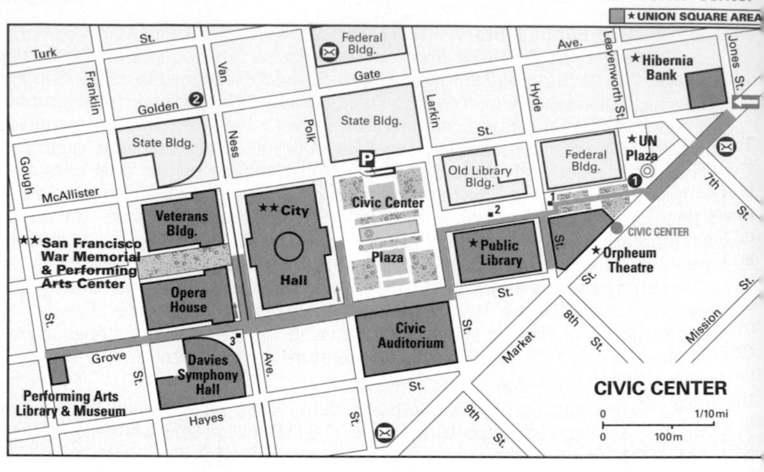

★★San Francisco War Memorial and Performing Arts Center – *Visit by guided tour (30min) only, year-round Mon 10am–2pm. Closed major holidays. $5 (includes tour of Davies Symphony Hall).* ☎ *415-552-8338 (ticket information p 234).* Flanking a formal courtyard designed by Thomas Church, these twin structures erected in memory of San Francisco's war dead served for decades as the city's center for the performing arts.

War Memorial Opera House – The first city-owned opera house in the country (1932, Arthur Brown, Jr.) hosted the plenary sessions that resulted in the establishment of the United Nations in 1945. The highly acclaimed San Francisco Opera and San Francisco Ballet perform here in an elegantly appointed 3,176-seat auditorium highlighted by a brilliant 27ft star chandelier. The proscenium, graced by Edgar Walter's gilded relief sculptures of two Amazons astride horses, is backed by a gold brocatelle curtain that weighs more than a ton. Gilt trim was reapplied to the auditorium and barrel-vaulted lobby ceiling during an 18-month, $88.5 million expansion and seismic retrofit, completed in 1997.

Veterans Building – Located north of the Opera House, this structure is home to city government offices and the intimate 928-seat **Herbst Theatre**, a venue for recitals, plays, lectures and public readings. It also contains the **San Francisco Art Commission Gallery** *(1st floor, open year-round Wed–Sat noon–5:30pm; Tue by appointment; 3rd & 4th floor corridors open Mon–Fri 8:30am–5:30pm;* ☎ *415-554-6080)*, which showcases community-oriented work by Bay Area artists.

Return to Grove St.

Across Grove Street, **Louise M. Davies Symphony Hall** (1980, Skidmore, Owings & Merrill) is home to the San Francisco Symphony Orchestra. In contrast to the Beaux Arts architecture of other Civic Center public buildings, this contemporary structure features a curving glass facade that reveals the lobby areas of the 2,743-seat hall. The elegant bronze sculpture *Four Piece Reclining Figure* **(3)** (1973) at the plaza entrance is by Henry Moore.

Continue west on Grove St.

A Clean Well-Lighted Place for Books

601 Van Ness Ave. ☎ *415-441-6670.* Well-lighted it is, and it never closes before 11pm. Wander in for a public reading or a private browse at the city's largest independent bookstore, located in Opera Plaza. The music, cooking, fiction, children's and travel sections are particularly strong; check out the "staff recommends" cards with handwritten reviews tucked beneath selections.

San Francisco Performing Arts Library and Museum – *399 Grove St. Open year-round Wed 1pm–7pm, Thu–Fri 11am–5pm, Sat noon–5pm. www.sfpalm.org* ☎ *415-255-4800.* This small nonprofit gallery and library presents exhibitions related to the city's rich performing arts heritage, from Barbary Coast bawdy houses to the present. A permanent research collection *(by appointment)* preserves news clippings, photographs, libretti, playbills, official records and other articles documenting the diverse history of Bay Area theater, music and dance, with particular focus on influential local artists such as Lew Christensen and Isadora Duncan. Changing displays are mounted three to four times a year in the small front gallery.

3 • FINANCIAL DISTRICT★★

Time: 6 hours. California Street. bus 1–California, 2–Clement, 3–Jackson, 4–Sutter, 12–Folsom, 15–Third, 41–Union, 42–Downtown Loop; all streetcars Embarcadero or Montgomery St. stations. Embarcadero or Montgomery St. stations. Map p 51

This cacophonous forest of skycraping steel, glass and stone, concentrated in a roughly triangular area north of Market Street along San Francisco's eastern bayshore, represents the heart of the city's financial community. Every large bank in the state maintains a presence here. Though modern in appearance, the district stands atop the city's historic core and counts among its structures some of San Francisco's oldest and most architecturally significant buildings.

Historical Notes

Gold Rush City – While San Francisco was born in 1776 at MISSION DOLORES and THE PRESIDIO, the roots of the modern downtown lie beneath the Financial District, where the village of Yerba Buena *(p 13)* grew up in the early 1840s along what was then a sheltered bayfront. In 1846 US forces occupied the town at the outbreak of the Mexican-American War, and the following year Yerba Buena's name was changed to San Francisco. Irish surveyor Jasper O'Farrell laid out a street grid, designating the muddy path along the waterfront as **Montgomery Street** in honor of Captain John Montgomery, commander of the US forces who took the village. O'Farrell traced Market Street at a diagonal to the already established downtown grid, then laid another grid at a competing angle south of Market Street.

Until 1848, the sleepy community of some 300 souls served as a trading and supply center for oceangoing vessels that sailed sporadically into the bay. The discovery of gold in the Sierra Nevada foothills changed everything. By late 1849, the waterfront buzzed with activity and San Francisco boomed as the principal communication and supply conduit between the mining camps and the rest of the world. Dozens of supply vessels that had sailed into the bay were abandoned as their crews jumped ship to head for the gold fields; many of the empty boats served as impromptu warehouses and hotels until more substantial buildings could be constructed. Wharves extended east from Montgomery Street to deep-water anchorage and the intervening mud flats were filled in with sand, dredgings and ship carcasses until the waterfront reached the line of the present-day EMBARCADERO. Today, with a few exceptions such as the area around Jackson Square *(p 55)*, very little remains of the Gold Rush city.

Wall Street of the West – Although San Francisco was molded by the Gold Rush, its role as financial center of the West Coast was cemented by silver. The immense fortunes engendered by Nevada's Comstock Lode during the 1860s brought stock exchanges, banks, the new transcontinental railroad and other commercial enterprises to the port city. Grand edifices arose in the Financial District, which quickly emerged as the commercial nexus of the West. By the 1890s, developments in construction technology made taller buildings possible, and Chicago-school skyscrapers such as the Mills Building and the Chronicle Building, both designed by Daniel Burnham, began to appear.

The great earthquake and fire of 1906 razed the Financial District, but within three years the area had been largely rebuilt. Many new buildings, such as the Bank of California, epitomized "City Beautiful" ideals *(p 43)*, employing Classical motifs on modern commercial structures to ensure a visual sense of order and substance. Another burst of new construction occurred during the 1920s: Three of the city's largest early-20C office towers—the Hunter-Dulin Building, the Russ Building and the Shell Building—were completed between 1927 and 1930. Though each of these structures expresses different historical motifs, they share features common to tall buildings of the early Art Deco period, such as setbacks on the upper stories, an emphasis on verticality, and ornamental tops that add interest to the city skyline.

The Great Depression and World War II put a temporary halt to growth, but the 1960s saw the start of another wave of construction. Dozens of skyscrapers rose, beginning with the influential Crown Zellerbach Building in 1959 and culminating in the early 1970s with two of the city's signature towers, the Bank of America Center and the Transamerica Pyramid. The swift pace of wholesale change led preservationists to lobby for protection of many older buildings and strict limitations on the height and bulk of new development, a movement that eventually resulted in the **Downtown Plan** of 1985. This series of mandatory guidelines put a cap on the square footage of new construction allowed per year in the Financial District; as a result, the bulk of new development has shifted to SOUTH OF MARKET. Nonetheless, the hallowed crossing of Montgomery and California Streets remains the heart of financial San Francisco.

Visiting the Financial District – The Financial District is very much a place of business, and its character changes completely at different times of day. Workers clog the streets during the morning and evening rush hours *(7–10am and 3–7pm)*. Garlicky aromas drift through the streets by mid-morning as restaurants prepare for lunchtime crowds; most eateries fill to capacity at noon. Streets can be very congested during rush hours and garage parking, though plentiful, is expensive; it's best to use the many buses, streetcars or cable cars that serve the area. Pay close attention to parking signs, as street parking is prohibited along certain thoroughfares during rush hours. The Financial District calms on weekends, particularly Sundays; note that many office buildings are closed outside of business hours.

When visiting the district, be sure to investigate office-building lobbies, many of which feature changing exhibitions of high-quality fine or decorative arts. Displays run the gamut from historic photographs to costume design and are well worth searching out. Some buildings boast rooftop or courtyard gardens, open to the public and ideal for taking a break or enjoying a picnic lunch.

WALKING TOUR *distance: 2.1mi*

Begin at the intersection of Post, Montgomery and Market Sts.

One Montgomery Street (A) – Standing at the symbolic entry to the "Wall Street of the West," this grand banking hall rose in the aftermath of the 1906 earthquake as the headquarters of First National Bank (later merged with Crocker Bank). The original section along Post Street was designed by Willis Polk; Charles Gottschalk completed the ornate interior hall in 1921. Originally a 14-story tower, the building was shortened in the early 1980s when it was incorporated into the Crocker Galleria complex that now fills most of the block. A Wells Fargo branch bank today occupies the cavernous **banking hall★**, replete with coffered ceiling and stately columns. On the Post Street facade, note the former main entrance to the office tower, sheltered by an ornate cast-iron canopy that is graced with figures flanking a shield inscribed with the words "Systematic Saving is the Key to Success."

© Robert Holmes

Crocker Galleria

From the corner, walk west on Post Street and enter the **Crocker Galleria★** (1983, Skidmore, Owings & Merrill), an elegant shopping center that cuts through the middle of the block, its three tiers of commercial spaces topped by a barrel-vaulted glass roof *(open year-round Mon–Fri 10am–6pm, Sat 10am–5pm;* ✗ ♿ 🅿 ☎ *415-393-1505)*. Pleasant cafes and deluxe boutiques such as Gianni Versace, Nicole Miller and Polo Ralph Lauren welcome tourists and workers from adjacent office towers.

From the upper level of the Crocker Galleria, a stairway leads to a tranquil **rooftop terrace** *(follow "Roof Terrace" sign to stairway or take elevator from bank entrance vestibule; open year-round Mon–Fri 7am–7pm)* atop One Montgomery. It overlooks the busy intersection of Market and Montgomery Streets fronted by the Palace Hotel *(p 54)*; the Hunter-Dulin building looms to the north.

Exit Crocker Galleria on Sutter St.

★★**Hallidie Building** – *130–50 Sutter St.* One of San Francisco's most noteworthy works of architecture, the seven-story office block opposite Crocker Galleria was designed by Willis Polk and completed in 1917 for the Regents of the University of California. It was named for one of their number: Andrew Hallidie, inventor of the cable car *(p 59)*. Because the facade is formed by a modular grid of glass panes hanging from a sturdy reinforced concrete frame, the building is widely considered to be the world's first glass-curtain-walled structure, a clear precursor of contemporary commercial architecture. A number of details on the facade make playful reference to its drapery qualities, such as the pelmet-like cornice made of sheet metal aged to look like wrought iron. The interior, however, is quite plain.

The Hallidie Building now houses the local headquarters of the American Institute of Architects, which operates a small **gallery** *(6th floor; open year-round Mon–Fri 9am–5pm; ♿ ☎ 415-362-7397)* offering changing displays of architectural drawings and photographs. A post office and a clothing store occupy the ground floor.

Walk east on Sutter St.

★**Hunter-Dulin Building** – *111 Sutter St.* Rising from the corner of Sutter and Montgomery Streets, this impressive, richly detailed building is an easily missed downtown gem. Completed in 1927 by the New York firm of Schultze and Weaver, designers of the Waldorf-Astoria Hotel, the building takes advantage of a freewheeling combination of historical styles. The main tower shaft, clad in terra-cotta panels colored to resemble granite, incorporates Romanesque-style arches and cast-iron spandrels embellished with medallions of mythical figures. Near the top, a slender central tower rises four floors to a chateauesque mansard roof complete with gabled dormers, adding visual interest to the downtown skyline while allowing sunlight to reach the ground. Step inside to see the richly detailed elevator lobby, replete with painted, beamed ceiling and inlaid marble floor.

Writer Dashiell Hammett set the office of his fictional hero, detective Sam Spade, in the Hunter-Dulin Building. The structure stands on the site of the Lick House, one of the premier hotels on the West Coast from the 1870s until it was destroyed in the 1906 earthquake and fire.

Walk to corner of Sutter and Montgomery Sts. and turn left.

Mills Building – *220 Montgomery St.* One of the few downtown structures to survive the earthquake and fire of 1906, this stately office building (1891) reflects the Chicago-school tenets espoused by its designer, Daniel Burnham. The first in the city to be clad in decorative terra-cotta panels, the building was reconstructed after the earthquake by Willis Polk. A richly ornamented, Romanesque-style archway forms the main entrance, leading to a comparatively plain lobby. The 22-story tower along the Bush Street facade was added in 1931 by Lewis Hobart. The environmental conservation group Sierra Club was established here in 1892.

★**Russ Building** – *235 Montgomery St.* Built toward the end of the "Roaring Twenties," this Gothic Revival landmark (1927, George Kelham) was the tallest tower on the West Coast until the 1960s. Rising to 31 stories and filling an entire block of Montgomery Street, it is still a prime business address. The main entrance, through a two-story ogive archway, leads to a striking **lobby**★ that features stone vaulting over the cloister-like corridors, inlaid mosaic floors and elaborate elevator panels. Three glass cases in the lobby display pieces from building owner Walter Shorenstein's collection of historic model ships. Another four ships are in the lobby of the Shorenstein-owned Bank of America Center *(see below)*.

Turn right at Pine St.

★**Pacific Exchange** – *301 Pine St. at Sansome St. Interior (illustration p 19) not open to the public.* Originally constructed in 1915 to house an office of the US Treasury Department, this proud structure was remodeled and enlarged with a tower in 1930 by Miller & Pflueger. The architects commissioned Ralph Stackpole, later one of the COIT TOWER muralists, to sculpt the remarkable pair of Social Realist-style monumental statues flanking the entrance. One of the granite figures depicts a trio of muscular men with a variety of tools, and a small boy with his right hand raised in a clenched fist; the other shows women harvesting grain and caring for children. *Now merged with the Chicago Board Options Exchange, the Pacific Exchange is scheduled to move its trading floor to South of Market in 2000.*

Backtrack to Montgomery St. and turn right.

★★**Bank of America Center** – *555 California St. (enter via Montgomery St. plaza).* San Francisco's largest building, this 52-story, dark-red behemoth (1971, Skidmore, Owings & Merrill) competes with the Transamerica Pyramid for dominance of San Francisco's downtown skyline. Occupying nearly an entire block at the heart of the Financial District, the tower serves as West Coast headquarters for the bank, founded in 1904 by A.P. Giannini as the Bank of Italy to serve the needs of Italian and other immigrants. (It merged with North Carolina-based NationsBank in 1998.) The building contains two million square feet of office space. Its distinctive color comes from the thick slabs of carnelian granite that wrap the faceted central shaft rising 780ft from street level. A grand, panoramic **view**★★★ extends from the top-floor **Carnelian Room** cocktail bar and restaurant *(take express elevator from Concourse Level; open to the public after 3pm)*; changing exhibits grace the Concourse Gallery and the main lobby, one floor above. The broad, open plaza along California Street is anchored by *Transcendence* **(1)** (1969, Masayuki Nagare), a dark, polished sculpture popularly dubbed "The Banker's Heart." From the plaza, glance north at the contentious post-Modern design of **580 California Street** (1987, Johnson & Burgee), incorporating 12 faceless, hooded human figures eerily encircling the 20th floor.

Cross Montgomery St. and walk east on California St.

★**Merchant's Exchange Building (B)** – *465 California St.* This 14-story office building (1903, Willis Polk) served as the focal point of commerce in turn-of-the-century San Francisco. Signals from its rooftop belvedere announced the arrival of ships through the Golden Gate. The edifice was badly damaged in the 1906 fire but was quickly restored. Prolific architect Julia Morgan maintained an office on the 11th floor for most of her 46-year career.
From the Ionic columns at the entrance, walk though the barrel-vaulted elevator lobby to the commodious **Grain Exchange Hall**★★. Here, beneath marble columns and gilt capitals, merchants and traders convened to transact business. Wall niches display a series of 13 nautical paintings by marine artist William Coulter, depicting the intricately rigged sailing vessels that once commanded San Francisco Bay. *(Though presently closed to the public, the hall may be included on some historical tours.)*

Return to Montgomery St. and turn right.

★**Wells Fargo History Museum (M¹)** – Kids *420 Montgomery St. Open year-round Mon–Fri 9am–5pm. Closed major holidays. ♿ www.wellsfargohistory.com ☎ 415-396-2619.* This modern gallery in the Wells Fargo corporate headquarters traces the colorful history of one of California's most prominent financial institutions. Concord coaches of Wells Fargo & Co. began transporting freight and passengers in 1852, and the company's gold shipping and storage services led naturally to its growth as a bank. The company's story and its inherent links to California history are told on two levels via photographs, documents, gold nuggets, bank notes and coins, while displays explore such topics as gold assaying, stagecoach robbery and telegraphing. Visitors can view a restored original coach and climb aboard a reconstructed one on the mezzanine to hear the recorded description of a harrowing cross-country stagecoach journey in the 1850s.

Continue north on Montgomery St. and turn left onto Commercial St.

Commercial Street – *Between Montgomery and Kearny Sts.* A stroll along this narrow alley offers intriguing glimpses of early commercial San Francisco. Before landfill extended the waterfront to its current line at the Embarcadero, this block formed the foot of Long Wharf, which ran across the mud flats along the line of present-day Commercial Street to deep-water anchorage. Look east to see the towers of Embarcadero Center *(p 53)* framing a fine view of the top of the historic FERRY BUILDING, which stands at what used to be the end of the wharf.
Tiny **Grabhorn Park** offers a quiet refuge for a break or a picnic; a plaque on the gate discusses the neighborhood's history as the center of San Francisco's publishing and printing industry. On the opposite side of Commercial Street *(no. 605)*, another plaque marks the location of the first building constructed on Yerba Buena Cove, a trading post built by the Hudson's Bay Company.

Pacific Heritage Museum (M²) – *608 Commercial St. Open year-round Tue–Sat 10am–4pm. Closed major holidays. ♿ ☎ 415-399-1124.* This elegant small museum displays changing exhibits of Asian art in an annex of the Bank of Canton. The bank building (1984, Skidmore, Owings & Merrill) incorporates the exterior walls and basement vaults of its predecessor, a US Subtreasury building (1877, William Appleton Potter), itself erected on the site of San Francisco's first mint. Interior windows on two floors reveal the original basement coin vaults from different perspectives.

Backtrack to Montgomery St. and turn left. Cross Montgomery at Clay St.

Bank of San Francisco – *550 Montgomery St. Open year-round Mon–Thu 9am–4pm, Fri 9am–5pm. ♿ www.banksf.com ☎ 415-781-7810.* Step inside this small building to see its gem of a **banking hall**★ clad in veined white marble. Note the egg-shaped, semi-precious stones embedded between window arches. The structure originally housed the main San Francisco office of the Bank of Italy, and was named a National Historic Landmark in 1982 in recognition of its role as the birthplace of branch banking. The hefty lock mechanism of the original vault is visible in the banking hall.

Cross Clay St.

★★**Transamerica Pyramid** – *600 Montgomery St.* In the years since its 1972 completion, this bold pyramid has come to symbolize San Francisco, playing a role similar to New York City's Empire State Building or Chicago's Sears Tower. Designed by William Pereira to house the corporate headquarters of Transamerica Corporation, a leasing and financial institution with roots in the Bank of America, the elegant 48-story spire is San Francisco's tallest building, rising 853ft from street level to the tip of its 212ft hollow lantern. The pyramid's slanted sides reduce the extent of its shadow on surrounding structures. The lobby-level gallery hosts high-quality changing exhibits of contemporary San Francisco art and design. Although the public is denied access to upper floors, a lobby-level **Virtual Observation Deck** Kids wired to rooftop monitors offers bird's-eye perspectives on the city in every direction. The site where the pyramid now stands was previously occupied by the Montgomery Block, built in 1853 as the premier office block on the West Coast and frequented by such diverse figures as Mark Twain and Sun Yat-Sen before it was razed in 1959. Construction

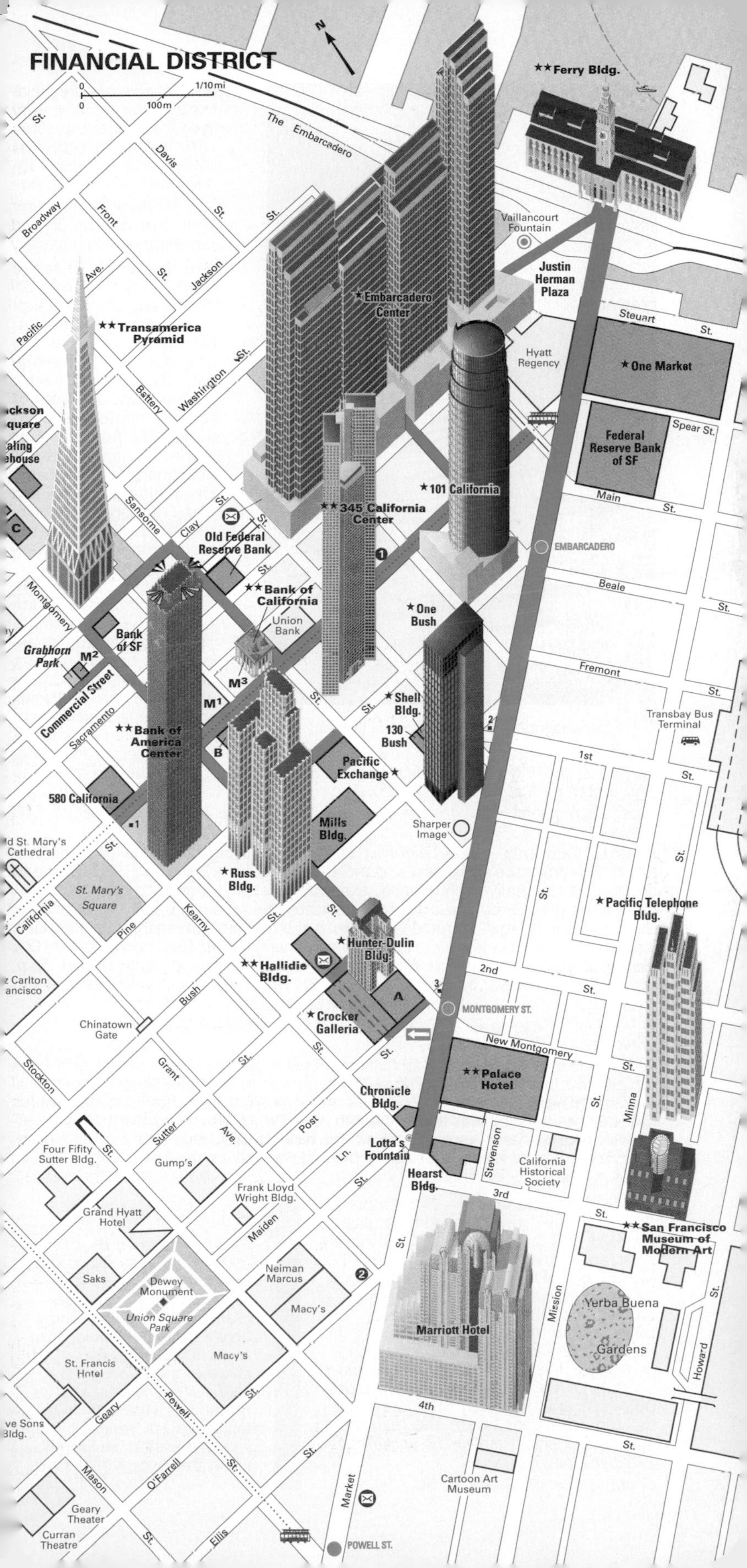
FINANCIAL DISTRICT
0 1/10 mi
0 100 m
N
★★ Ferry Bldg.
The Embarcadero
Vaillancourt Fountain
Justin Herman Plaza
★ Embarcadero Center
★★ Transamerica Pyramid
Hyatt Regency
★ One Market
Federal Reserve Bank of SF
★ 101 California
★★ 345 California Center
Old Federal Reserve Bank
★★ Bank of California
Union Bank
★ One Bush
EMBARCADERO
Bank of SF
Grabhorn Park
Commercial Street
★ Shell Bldg.
130 Bush
★★ Bank of America Center
Pacific Exchange ★
580 California
Mills Bldg.
Sharper Image
Transbay Bus Terminal
St. Mary's Cathedral
St. Mary's Square
★ Russ Bldg.
★ Hunter-Dulin Bldg.
★★ Hallidie Bldg.
★ Pacific Telephone Bldg.
★ Crocker Galleria
MONTGOMERY ST.
Chinatown Gate
★★ Palace Hotel
Chronicle Bldg.
Lotta's Fountain
Hearst Bldg.
Four Fifty Sutter Bldg.
Gump's
Frank Lloyd Wright Bldg.
California Historical Society
Grand Hyatt Hotel
★★ San Francisco Museum of Modern Art
Saks
Dewey Monument
Union Square Park
Neiman Marcus
Macy's
Yerba Buena Gardens
Marriott Hotel
St. Francis Hotel
Macy's
Cartoon Art Museum
Geary Theater
Curran Theatre
POWELL ST.
Broadway
Front
Davis
Jackson
Pacific
Battery
Washington
Sansome
Clay
Montgomery
Sacramento
Kearny
California
Pine
Bush
Grant
Stockton
Sutter
Post
Maiden
Geary
Powell
O'Farrell
Mason
Ellis
Market
Steuart
Spear St.
Main
Beale
Fremont
1st
2nd
New Montgomery
Minna
Stevenson
3rd
Mission
4th
Howard

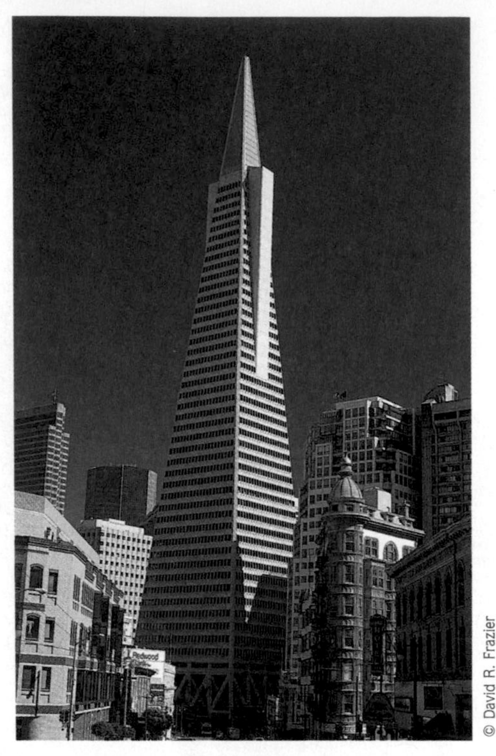
© David R. Frazier
Transamerica Pyramid and Sentinel Building

on the pyramid began a decade later. To the east, a peaceful grove planted with some 40 redwood trees forms a tranquil forest oasis beside the Vertigo restaurant.

Walk east on Clay St. and turn right onto Sansome St.

★**Old Federal Reserve Bank** – *400 Sansome St.* The facade of this classical Beaux Arts gem (1924, George Kelham) makes a dramatic first impression with its eight 25ft Ionic columns and the row of federal eagles perched above its portico. Designed to house district headquarters of the Fed, the building examplifies San Francisco's banking-temple tradition and the federal government's penchant for monumental architecture. Inside the lobby, walls and floors are finished in French and Italian marble, and doors are of solid bronze. Artist Jules Guerin, chief muralist for the Panama Pacific International Exposition of 1915, painted the impressive "Traders of the Adriatic" mural above the door leading to the banking hall. In 1984 the Fed moved to new offices on Market Street *(p 53)*. The upper floors today house a law firm.

Cross Sacramento St. and continue south on Sansome St. to the corner of California St.

★★**Bank of California** – *400 California St.* Today housing the Union Bank of California, San Francisco's grandest and most beautiful bank building (1907, Bliss and Faville) is a classically proportioned, exquisitely detailed temple to commerce that exemplifies the energy and resources dedicated to rebuilding San Francisco after the 1906 fire. A regal, coffered ceiling tops the magnificent, soaring banking hall, embellished with Corinthian pilasters. From here, stairs lead down to the tiny **Museum of Money of the American West (M³)** Kids *(open year-round Mon–Fri 9am–5pm; closed major holidays;* ♿ ☎ *415-765-3213)*, which displays the various forms of currency that circulated during the Gold Rush and Comstock Lode mining bonanzas of the mid-19C (and, by correlation, the mining and minting of gold and silver).

Walk east on California St.

Across California Street from 345 California Center *(below)*, the modern Union Bank of California building *(370 California St.)* replaced the landmark Alaska Commercial Building, of which all that remains is a series of whimsical, intricately carved walrus heads embedded on a wall above the entrance. Only a handful of these life-size, accurately detailed heads were saved from the more-than-50 that once formed a decorative frieze around the fourth floor of the building.

Cross California St.

★★**345 California Center** – *345 California St.* Two angular towers linked by a glass-enclosed "sky bridge" cap this futuristic skyscraper (1987, Skidmore, Owings & Merrill), one of the most striking facets of the downtown skyline. The building incorporated the California Street facades of earlier historic structures, including the J. Harold Dollar Building (1920) and the Robert Dollar Building (1919), former headquarters of the Dollar Lines steamships. Office spaces fill the lower 35 floors, while the top 11 stories house the luxurious Mandarin Oriental Hotel *(main entrance at 222 Sansome St.)*.

Continue east on California St.

1 Tadich Grill
240 California St. ☎ *415-391-1849.* Fresh fish is the fare, bulls and bears the topic of choice at this San Francisco institution, which began during the Gold Rush as a coffee stand. Go for the charcoal-grilled sole, the cold seafood salads, and for the no-nonsense service by long-aproned, white-jacketed waiters striding along the long, wooden bar.

★**101 California Street** – *101 California St.* This stepped-back glass silo (1982, Johnson & Burgee) occupies a prominent position at the foot of California Street. The three-story glass atrium slicing into the base of the building acts as the main entrance, while a triangular plaza runs south to Market Street.

Turn left on Davis St. Cross Sacramento St.

★**Embarcadero Center** – *Bounded by The Embarcadero and Clay, Sacramento and Battery Sts. Enter from Davis St. between buildings Two and Three and take the spiral stair to the Promenade (3rd) Level.* The largest office and commercial complex in the city, this series of four, slab-like office towers (1982, John Portman and Assoc.) plus the Hyatt Regency Hotel covers nearly 10 acres between The Embarcadero and the heart of the Financial District. Developed jointly by New York-based financier David Rockefeller and the San Francisco Redevelopment Agency, the center was constructed on the former site of San Francisco's low-rise Produce Market. An extensive, three-level shopping center occupies its lower floors, running along historic Commercial Street; pedestrian bridges traverse the cross streets to link the four structures. More than a dozen sculptures dot the center's public spaces, among them works by Jean Dubuffet and Louise Nevelson.

On the 41st floor of the westernmost tower (One Embarcadero Center), the **SkyDeck** *(open year-round daily 9:30am–dusk; closed Jan 1, Thanksgiving Day, Dec 25; $6; 40min guided tours available; ☎ 415-772-0555 or 888-737-5933)* offers sweeping views of the Financial District and San Francisco Bay. Televisions in the observation area broadcast short videos on historical topics. Linked to the easternmost tower (Four Embarcadero Center) by a pedestrian bridge on the Promenade Level, the Hyatt Regency (1973) boasts an asymmetrical 17-story **atrium**★, one of the more awe-inspiring of the city's interior spaces.

Opening onto The Embarcadero from the eastern end of the complex, brick-paved **Justin Herman Plaza** Kids was named for the former president of the city's redevelopment agency, who spearheaded controversial urban renewal efforts during the 1960s. The angular forms of the Vaillancourt Fountain (1971) invite exploration while enlivening the plaza's northeastern corner.

Cross The Embarcadero to the Ferry Building.

★★**Ferry Building** – *Description p. 78.*

Cross The Embarcadero to the south side of Market St.

★**One Market** – Filling an entire block at the foot of Market Street, this huge office complex was erected in stages, incorporating the facade of the Southern Pacific Railroad's original headquarters (1916, Bliss and Faville). Step inside to see an eye-catching, futuristically redesigned interior (1995, Cesar Pelli and Assoc.). The belvedere of the red brick fortress provides a focal point for California Street, which climbs NOB HILL to the west. Notice the view southwest along Market Street to the summits of TWIN PEAKS.

Walk southwest on Market St. and cross Spear St.

Federal Reserve Bank of San Francisco – Kids *101 Market St. Lobby open year-round Mon–Fri 9am–4:30pm. Closed major holidays.* ♿ *www.frbsf.com ☎ 415-974-3233.* This large, modern building (1982, Skidmore, Owings & Merrill) houses the administrative offices of the Federal Reserve Bank of San Francisco. A vaulted loggia covers the Market Street frontage, from which the bulk of the building steps back in a series of terraces. Be sure to visit the lobby, where interactive stations of **The World of Economics**★ exhibition offer entertaining but serious lessons in basic economics and the US economy. Computer simulators enable visitors (pretending to be legislators, the US President or Chairman of the Federal Reserve Bank system) to adjust the rate of money growth, set interest rates or raise and lower taxes, and to gauge the effect on the economy. The new **American Currency Exhibit**, showcasing paper money and coins from colonial times to the present, has its own room off the west side of the lobby.

Continue southwest on Market St. to Battery St.

One of the city's most energetic pieces of public sculpture, the **Mechanics Monument (2)** *(median at corner of Market and Battery Sts.)* vividly memorializes the craftsmen who built San Francisco. Created by Douglas Tilden in 1894, the sculpture was dedicated to the memory of Peter Donahue, owner of the city's first iron foundry. Set atop a granite pedestal, the work depicts a team of muscular workers straining to punch a hole through a steel plate.

Cross Bush St., then Battery St. to its south side.

★**Shell Building** – *100 Bush St., intersection of Bush and Battery Sts.* Clad in light brown terra-cotta, this graceful Art Deco tower (1929, George Kelham) was strongly influenced by Eliel Saarinen's second-place design for the Chicago Tribune Tower competition. The rather plain central shaft rises 20 stories, then steps back to form a slender, richly ornamented top. Decorative motifs, including a large gilt shell over the entrance and abstract shell forms covering the parapets, make clear reference to the Shell Oil Corporation, which developed the property as its Western headquarters.

■ The Historic Streetcars of the F-Market Line

San Francisco's cable cars are not the city's only bit of rolling history. Since September 1995, a colorful fleet of historic PCC (Presidents' Conference Committee) streetcars have glided up and down Market Street, a historical grace note amid the throngs of pedestrians, cars, buses and streetcars that swarm along the bustling thoroughfare. Elegantly streamlined and colorfully painted, PCC cars were manufactured in the US from 1936 to 1952 and put into service throughout North America and Europe. They served on San Francisco's streetcar lines from 1948 to 1982. The rehabilitated cars today reflect not only the Muni green-and-cream colors, but also the color schemes of other cities where these streetcars were used, including Boston (orange, cream and silver), Baltimore (yellow and gray), Los Angeles (red, orange and gray) and Kansas City (cream, black and silver). With the completion of new tracks sometime in 2000, these beloved antiques will traverse the shoreline on The Embarcadero from Market Street to Fisherman's Wharf.

Next door, at **130 Bush Street** (1910, McDonald and Applegarth), stands one of the city's narrowest office buildings. Gothic-style ornamentation covers the 10-story, bow-fronted tower that measures just 20ft wide.

Continue west on Bush St. one block and cross.

★**One Bush Street** – Originally known as the Crown Zellerbach Building, this distinctive tower represents San Francisco's best example of International Style architecture. Designed by Hertzka & Knowles/Skidmore, Owings & Merrill in 1959, and modeled after the latter firm's influential Lever House in New York City and Inland Steel Building in Chicago, the pale green glass box stands on concrete stilts above a broad plaza. At the base of the stilts lies a sunken plaza anchored by a small, freestanding circular structure once occupied by a bank; today it houses an outlet of the Sharper Image chain. The One Bush Street lobby presents temporary art exhibits, ranging from photography to folk crafts, that rotate quarterly.

Cross Sutter St., turn right on Market St. and walk southwest to Montgomery St.

An angelic female perched atop a stone shaft, above a miner waving an American flag, is the most prominent element of the **Native Sons of the Golden West Monument (3)**, which honors the establishment of California statehood in 1850. Sculpted by Douglas Tilden in 1897, the statue was originally erected farther down Market Street, then moved to GOLDEN GATE PARK before being placed at its present location in 1977.

Cross Market St.

★★**Palace Hotel** – *639 Market St.* This elegant hostelry on the border of the Financial District and the South of Market neighborhood figures prominently in San Francisco history. Constructed in 1875 by financier William Ralston as part of his plan to lure development south of Market Street, the Palace Hotel gained a reputation as the most opulent hotel in the West until it was gutted in the 1906 fire. Its owners immediately set about rebuilding it, reopening for business in 1909 with great fanfare. Rivaling the FAIRMONT HOTEL in sophistication and luxury, the new Palace

Garden Court, Palace Hotel

quickly became the focal point of San Francisco high society. The former Grand Court, where passengers once alighted from horse-drawn carriages, was transformed as an elegant, interior Garden Court where dignitaries and moneyed San Franciscans sipped tea and champagne beneath flourishing palm trees. The hotel has hosted many luminaries, including seven US Presidents (Warren G. Harding died here in 1923). After undergoing a complete restoration from 1989 to 1991, this long-standing landmark again ranks among the city's top hotels.

Enter from Market Street and stroll down the main corridor to the glorious **Garden Court★★**, capped by a stunning canopy of intricately leaded art glass. The corridor boasts several glass display cases containing fascinating mementoes from hotel history, including old photographs and scrapbooks, postcards, menus, china and wardrobe items. Also worth seeing is **Maxfield's**, an elegant bar and restaurant *(off corridor near Market St. entrance; open year-round daily 11:30am–2am; ♿ P ☎ 415-512-1111)* featuring an allegorical mural of the Pied Piper of Hamelin by Maxfield Parrish.

Armani Cafe

In Emporio Armani, 1 Grant Ave. ☎ 415-677-9010. At the long, oval lunch counter elegantly anchoring this stylish boutique, weary shoppers revive themselves with plates of antipasto, insalata, pasta and panini. Smokers head for the tables lining the sidewalk outside, while everyone is careful not to get an Italian stain on that new Italian dress or suit.

Cross Market St., turn left and continue to Kearny St.

A cast-iron column rising from a small fountain, beloved **Lotta's Fountain** *(northeast corner of Market and Kearny Sts.)* was given to the people of San Francisco by entertainer Lotta Crabtree in 1875. Every April 18, around 5am, San Franciscans congregate here to commemorate the anniversary of the great earthquake and fire of 1906.

The intersection surrounding Lotta's Fountain once represented the heart of San Francisco's newspaper industry. The former **Chronicle Building** *(690 Market St.)*, erected in 1889 by Burnham & Root, remains the city's oldest office tower, though a 1962 remodeling obscured its original facade. Across Market Street lies the terra-cotta-clad **Hearst Building** *(691 3rd St.)*, an exuberant, Spanish Revival-style structure that was the longtime home of the *San Francisco Examiner*.

ADDITIONAL SIGHT

★★ **Jackson Square** – *Bounded by Washington, Montgomery and Sansome Sts. and Pacific Ave.* Contrary to its name, San Francisco's oldest surviving commercial neighborhood is neither a "square" nor a park, but four blocks of well-preserved mid-19C structures between NORTH BEACH and the Financial District. The district formed the heart of the notorious **Barbary Coast**, the bawdy, Gold Rush-era district of saloons, theaters and burlesque houses that lined Pacific Avenue between Sansome Street and Columbus Avenue. The brick structures outlasted the great earthquake and fire of 1906, and since the 1960s many have been converted into upscale art galleries, design firms, law offices and antique stores.

Today the two- and three-story buildings, with brick, cast-iron or stucco facades, create a cozily uniform departure from the neighboring towers of the Financial District. The oldest buildings lie along Montgomery Street a block north of the Transamerica Pyramid. The **Belli Building (C)** *(no. 722)*, constructed in 1851 on a foundation of redwood that literally floats upon former tidelands, served as the law offices of famed attorney Melvin Belli, "the King of Torts," until it was damaged in the 1989 earthquake. The attached **Belli Annex** *(no. 726)*, a three-story brick Italianate built in 1852, marks the site of the first meeting (in 1849) of the California Freemasons. Next door, the two-story **Golden Era Building (D)** *(no. 732)* was built in 1852 as the home of the West's premier literary magazine. Indeed, the entire block dates from the early years after the Gold Rush.

Around the corner, the **Hotaling Warehouse** *(451-461 Jackson St.)* was constructed as a whiskey distillery and warehouse in 1866. The building was rescued from the flames of the 1906 conflagration thanks to the valiant efforts of local firefighters determined to keep its contents from going up in flames.

William K. Stout Architectural Books

804 Montgomery St. ☎ 415-391-6757. When books and magazines overflowed his apartment, architect Stout went into business as a bookseller. His space problem isn't solved: a huge selection of architectural titles, as well as art, photography, landscaping and other design-related books and magazines, now overflows this charming shop, where architects gather to browse and network.

4 • NOB HILL★★

Time: 2 hours. 🚌 all lines.
Map p 69

Nob Hill witnessed one of San Francisco's first infusions of wealth, and today remains a vivid example of the city's diverse urban community. Cable cars trundle up and down the hill's steep slopes, passing lovingly restored Edwardian homes and 1920s high-rise apartment buildings. Cozy bistros, flower shops and boutiques nestle together along the serene, tree-lined side streets. Sloping down to the southwest, Lower Nob Hill, bordered by Geary and Polk Streets, has a grittier feel, melding bustling theaters and restaurants with blockier residential buildings and quiet local taprooms.

Historical Notes

"Hill of Palaces" – Nob Hill acquired its reputation as home to San Francisco's wealthy elite during the city's earliest years. In 1856 Dr. Arthur Hayne, a well-to-do dentist, became the first to settle on the craggy hill, ambitiously cutting a path through the scrub to the 376ft summit and erecting a modest home where the Fairmont Hotel stands today. Hayne was joined soon after by William Walton, a merchant who built a grander residence at the present-day corner of Washington and Taylor Streets. By the late 1860s, a handful of millionaires had purchased property and built homes near the summit, establishing it as San Francisco's choice residential locale.

Nob Hill's exclusive cachet was ensured after 1873, when cable car lines were installed on its steep flanks. Capable of transporting people and materials easily and regularly, cable cars opened the door to development of the city's formerly inaccessible summits, and construction on the crest of Nob Hill boomed on a grandiose scale. As the rest of the city battled an economic depression prompted by the newly completed transcontinental railroad (which brought low-cost East Coast goods to compete with higher-priced West Coast products), Nob Hill quickly became what author Robert Louis Stevenson called "the hill of palaces," thanks in good part to a group of newly minted millionaires.

The Big Four – In 1859 four middle-class Sacramento merchants—**Leland Stanford**, **Charles Crocker**, **Mark Hopkins** and **Collis Huntington**—together purchased a modest number of shares in what seemed at the time an impossible venture: a railway across the western US *(p 14)*. A decade later the transcontinental railroad was completed and their small investments yielded millions of dollars in dividends. The four promptly moved to San Francisco, purchased lots on the summit of Nob Hill and built sprawling mansions where, according to Stevenson, they "gathered together, vying with each other in display, (and) looked down upon the business wards of the city." The hill was indirectly named for them: "Nob" is a contraction of "nabob," a term for European adventurers who made huge fortunes in India and the Far East.

In the 1880s the Big Four were joined on the hill by two of the four "Bonanza Kings," a quartet of Irish stock-market speculators who had extracted huge fortunes from Nevada's Comstock silver lode in 1873. **James Fair**, a former miner, bought Dr. Hayne's property, and **James Flood** erected his Italianate brownstone mansion, today the Pacific-Union Club *(p 57)*, across Mason Street.

Through the late 19C, large Victorian houses appeared on the flanks of the hill, near the cable car routes established along California and Powell Streets in 1878 and 1888 respectively. After the great earthquake and fire of 1906, the area was rebuilt with tall, narrow Edwardian homes and high-rise apartment buildings.

Today Nob Hill maintains much of its turn-of-the-century charm, though many of San Francisco's wealthiest residents live in neighborhoods to the northwest, where larger land plots accommodate palatial mansions in the spirit of the Big Four's legendary homes. Asian families populate the slopes to the north and east, near Chinatown, and a large singles population occupies studios and small apartments to the south and west.

Visiting Nob Hill – Any time of day is a good time to visit Nob Hill, although early-morning sun sometimes obscures the views to the east. As neighborhood denizens rush off to work, practitioners of *t'ai chi* congregate in Huntington Park. Traffic intensifies at the end of the work day, making street parking difficult to find, but cable car lines offer easy access from Union Square, the Financial District and Fisherman's Wharf. The Crown Room and the Top of the Mark, Nob Hill's skyscraping watering holes, open in early evening, a good time to stop for tea or a cocktail and drink in glorious city views.

WALKING TOUR *distance: .6mi*

Begin at the southwest corner of Powell and California Sts.

The first of the Big Four to build his mansion atop Nob Hill, Leland Stanford constructed an immense Italianate villa on this corner lot in 1876. Today it is the site of the **Stanford Court Hotel**, remodeled in 1972 from an elegant apartment building. The gray stone retaining wall encircling the block was built in the 1870s and was the only part of Stanford's mansion to survive the 1906 fire.

Walk west up California St.

Mark Hopkins Inter-Continental Hotel – *999 California St.* ✗ ♿ 🅿 ☎ *415-392-3434.* In 1877 Mark Hopkins began work on a sprawling Victorian mansion set to rival Stanford's in elegance and ostentation. Hopkins died in 1878 before it was completed; in 1893 his widow donated the residence to the California School of Design (later the SAN FRANCISCO ART INSTITUTE). The 1906 fire razed the structure, and in 1926 the Mark Hopkins Hotel rose on the site. Gracefully framing the corner of Mason and California Streets, the hotel is crowned by the **Top of the Mark** *(open year-round Mon–Thu 3pm–1am, Fri–Sat 3pm–1:30am, Sun 4pm–1am; evening cover charge $6 Sun–Thu, $10 Fri–Sat)*, a swank Art Deco-style bar designed by Timothy Pflueger and boasting panoramic **views**★★★ of the city and San Francisco Bay.

Cross California St.

★★ **Fairmont Hotel** – *Bounded by California, Mason, Powell and Sacramento Sts.* ☎ *415-772-5000.* With its opulent lobby, dignified facade and illustrious history, the Fairmont Hotel offers one of the best glimpses of turn-of-the-century Nob Hill. Construction began in 1902 on the dazzling building, designed by James and Merritt Reid under the stewardship of Tessie Fair Oelrichs, James Fair's daughter. Work was nearly complete when the 1906 quake struck and fire swept the hill, leaving only the hotel's granite outer walls intact. Architect Julia Morgan, then in the early stages of her career, oversaw the restoration and completion of the building in its original Italian Renaissance style.

On April 18, 1907, exactly a year after the earthquake, the Fairmont opened for business and quickly gained a reputation as the city's premier hotel. In 1945, the United Nations Charter was drafted in the elegant Garden Room; today, flags of UN-member countries above the hotel's main entrance commemorate the event. A modern tower was added in 1961.

In the ornate main lobby, massive marble pillars and wrought-iron balconies are all that remain of Morgan's 1906 design. Follow the northern hallway around to the rear of the hotel, where a glass-walled exterior elevator rises slowly to the **Crown Room** restaurant *(open year-round Mon–Sat 4pm–9pm, Sun 10am–2pm & 6pm–9pm)*, renowned for its glorious **views**★★★.

Walk west on California St.

★ **Pacific-Union Club** – *1000 California St. Not open to the public.* The only structure on Nob Hill to survive the 1906 blaze, silver baron James Flood's mansion was built in 1885 by English architect Augustus Laver at a cost of $1.5 million. Unlike other Nob Hill palaces, which were made of California redwood, Flood's 42-room Italianate home was built of Connecticut brownstone and withstood the 1906 earthquake, although the intense heat of the ensuing fire gutted the mansion's lavish interior. In 1908 renowned local architect Willis Polk shortened the central tower and added wings on two sides, softening the building's staunch vertical facade. The bronze fence surrounding it was patterned after a piece of lace favored by Flood's wife. Today the building is occupied by the private Pacific-Union Club, which traces its origins to 1852 and is considered the most exclusive men's club in the West.

1 The Tonga Room

Fairmont Hotel. ☎ *415-772-5278.* Order anything with an umbrella at the Fairmont's Polynesian-style restaurant and "hurricane bar." Thatched umbrellas hover over rustic tables, and every half-hour a sprinkler system simulates a tropical rainstorm above the indoor lagoon. Don't miss the happy-hour buffet, or the floating live band.

2 Swan Oyster Depot

1517 Polk St. ☎ *415-673-1101.* Displayed in the window, the catch of the day stops sidewalk traffic; inside, jokes fly along with the shucked shells. Six brothers, their youngest sister and a friend or two preside over the 20-stool lunch counter, bantering with regulars, cracking crab legs and serving up buttery clam chowder, fresh seafood cocktails and oysters on the half shell while making strangers feel at home.

Continue west on California St. and cross Taylor St.

★ **Grace Cathedral** – *California St. at Taylor St. Open year-round Mon–Fri & Sun 7am–6pm, Sat 8am–6pm, holidays 9am–4pm. Guided tours (1hr) available Mon–Fri 1pm–3pm, Sat 11:30am–1:30pm, Sun 12:30pm–2pm. www.gracecathedral.org* ☎ 415-749-6300. The third-largest Episcopal cathedral in the US anchors the crest of Nob Hill, its Gothic spires soaring majestically over the city. Consecrated in 1964, the edifice occupies the lot formerly owned by Charles Crocker, whose huge, Second Empire-style mansion stood side by side with a Victorian villa he commissioned for his son as a wedding present. After both homes were destroyed in the 1906 fire, the family donated the land to the Episcopal diocese. Grace's cornerstone was laid in 1910 but construction did not begin until 1928 for financial and technical reasons. Work was halted by the Great Depression and again by World War II. The Notre Dame-inspired design by Lewis P. Hobart was executed in steel-reinforced concrete to withstand the city's seismic tremors. Set in the Gothic eastern portal, the bronze **Gates of Paradise** are the cathedral's most prized architectural feature. Duplicates of a set cast by Florentine sculptor Lorenzo Ghiberti (the originals adorn the Santa Maria del Fiore Cathedral Baptistry in Florence), the 16ft doors are divided into 10 richly ornamented panels illustrating. scenes from

Gates of Paradise detail, Grace Cathedral

the Old Testament. Inside the cathedral, dozens of stained-glass windows and murals depict a diversity of figures from saints to modern historical figures, including Robert Frost, Franklin D. Roosevelt and Albert Einstein. A magnificent Aeolian-Skinner organ, built in 1934 in American Classic style, resounds with 7,286 pipes.

Exit cathedral on Taylor St. and cross to the park.

Huntington Park – Banked slightly above street level, Huntington Park gracefully crowns Nob Hill. Gardener John McLaren, who designed GOLDEN GATE PARK and other Bay Area public gardens, oversaw the design and cultivation of the 1.75-acre plot, which was donated to the city after Collis Huntington's opulent mansion on the adjacent lot was destroyed in the 1906 fire. Blackwood acacias and sycamores thrive here, framing the 20C replica of Rome's Tartarughe Fountain ("Tortoise Fountain") that forms the park's centerpiece. Purchased in Italy by William Crocker's wife to beautify the family estate, this replica was moved here in 1955.

Walk east on Sacramento St. and turn left on Mason St.

★★ **Cable Car Museum** – Kids *1201 Mason St. at Washington St. Open Apr–Sept daily 10am–6pm. Rest of the year daily 10am–5pm. Closed Jan 1, Thanksgiving Day, Dec 25. ☎ 415-474-1887.* The weathered brick building situated on the steep northern slope of Nob Hill offers an up-close look at the nerve center of San Francisco's renowned cable car system, the only one of its kind in the world. In addition to serving as a powerhouse and car storage barn, the structure houses a unique museum presenting the history of the cable car.

Begin on the upper level, where a balcony overlooks the cable car mechanism. Motors hum and giant wheels called "sheaves" rotate, powering the continuous loops of cable for the system's three lines. Instructive panels affixed to the balcony railings and a video presentation *(16min)* explain how the system works, while historical displays tell the story of the cable cars from their invention, through their late-19C heyday, to the present. Other exhibits include rudimentary hand tools, public transportation memorabilia and a fine collection of historic photographs. Among the museum's treasured pieces is **Car No. 8**, the only survivor of the Clay Street Hill Railroad, San Francisco's first cable car line, which began operation in 1873. The car had been shipped to Chicago for the 1893 World's Columbian Exhibition and not returned; it thus fortuitously escaped destruction in the 1906 fire.

On the lower level, a small viewing area offers a glimpse of the sheave room where the thick steel cables enter the building before being routed up to the main sheaves.

ADDITIONAL SIGHT

The Ritz-Carlton, San Francisco – *600 Stockton St. (between California and Pine Sts.)* ✗ ♿ 🅿 ☎ *415-296-7465.* Built on the Chinatown flank of Nob Hill (1909, Napoleon Le Brun & Sons) as the West Coast headquarters of the Metropolitan Life Insurance Co., the original 80ft cube was expanded in 1914 and 1920 with two symmetrical wings. A facade of 18 Ionic columns supports an entablature that features hourglasses and lions' heads, while an allegorical figure ("Insurance") spreads its wings over two symbolic families from the portico above the entrance. A pair of annexes and a central garden court were added later. Met Life sold the building in 1973; for 11 years, until The Ritz purchased the building, it housed Cogswell College. After a four-year renovation, the luxurious hotel opened in 1991.

Getting A Grip: San Francisco's Cable Cars

© PhotoDisc, Inc.

More than eight million visitors and San Franciscans annually ride the city's signature cable cars, a public transportation system invented and developed by Scotsman Andrew Smith Hallidie in 1873. Inspired by the work of his father, who had been awarded the world's first patent on iron-wire rope in 1835, 16-year-old Hallidie came to California in 1852, at the height of the Gold Rush, to build wire-rope transport systems for the mines. In his early 20s he moved to San Francisco, where he established a wire-rope manufacturing company and developed suspension bridges and cable tramways for the silver mines of Nevada's Comstock Lode. But it wasn't until 1869 that Hallidie first conceived of a similar system as a means of public transportation. Four years and $85,000 later, the idea that had been dubbed "Hallidie's Folly" took form as a primitive cable car line that ascended Clay Street between Kearny and Leavenworth at 6mph.

A testament to the quality of Hallidie's design, today's cable cars work in much the same way as those of 1873. The concept is simple: Just as a constantly moving tow-rope pulls a skier up a snowy slope, huge loops of steel cable run at a continuous 9.5mph underground along Powell, Hyde, Mason and California Streets, powered by electric motors at the Cable Car Barn. To start the car moving, the "gripman"—stationed in the middle of the car—operates a lever that extends down through a slot in the street. At the underground end of the lever, a "grip" closes and opens like a jaw on the moving cable. The tighter the grip closes, the faster the car goes. To reduce speed, the gripman opens the grip to release the cable; brakes are applied to stop. A conductor is stationed at the rear of the car to help with braking when necessary.

California Historical Society, San Francisco. FN-25322

Andrew Smith Hallidie

Because the soft metal dies, inside the jaws of the grip, are the only contact between the cables and the cars (which can weigh up to 10 tons), they must be replaced every four days. Likewise the cables, constructed of six strands of 19 wires twisted around a core of sisal rope, must be replaced every month or two through a labor-intensive process of cutting and splicing each individual strand. The track is inspected daily for imperfections, as are each car's three sets of brakes: wheel brakes, track brakes and emergency brakes. This is essential, considering the steep grades cars must negotiate.

Today the system, which was designated a National Historic Landmark in 1964, numbers 40 cable cars operating on three lines (Powell-Mason, Powell-Hyde and California Street). The entire system, including the powerhouse, was completely rehabilitated from 1982 to 1984, preserving this unique part of San Francisco's past.

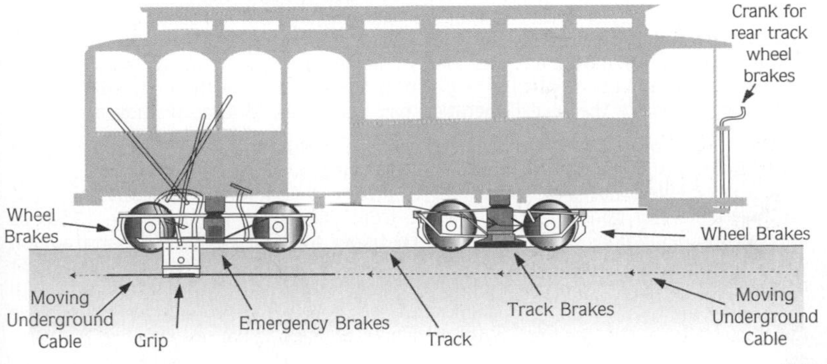

5 • NORTH BEACH★★

Time: 1/2 day. Powell-Mason. MUNI bus 15–Third, 30–Stockton, 45–Union-Stockton or 39–Coit.
Map p 66

The erstwhile heart of San Francisco's Italian community and one of the city's oldest neighborhoods, this sunny district nestled between bustling FISHERMAN'S WHARF and the steep slopes of Telegraph Hill and RUSSIAN HILL has become, in recent years, a prime residential haven for young professionals of diverse ethnic groups. Although shops and businesses from burgeoning CHINATOWN to the south slowly encroach across Broadway, the flavors (and enticing fragrances) of North Beach's Italian roots still predominate, as evidenced by the dozens of well-patronized trattorias, cafes and delicatessens found here. A onetime refuge for San Francisco's Beat counterculture, this historic district retains, to a certain degree, the close-knit character of a village.

Historical Notes

A Buried Beach – Only the name remains of the narrow stretch of sand that used to form the area's bayside border. As early as the 1850s, land-hungry speculators began dumping tons of fill material into the shallows that once lapped present-day Bay Street, eventually erecting a flourishing industrial zone atop the buried beach. Rough-and-tumble tent cities appeared on the sheltered southwestern slope of Telegraph Hill in the early Gold Rush years. **Little Chile**, populated by treasure-seeking Chileans and Peruvians, sprang up near Kearny Street. Directly to the east between Broadway and Union Street stood **Sydney Town**, home of a notorious group of former Australian convicts, many of whom regularly terrorized their South American neighbors. Ships' crews carved chunks from the side of Telegraph Hill to provide ballast for their homeward voyages, the vessels having been vacated by the argonauts *(p 14)*. The hillside scars remain visible today.

After the heady days of the Gold Rush, a polyglot mixture of newly arrived immigrants from Spain, France, Portugal, Germany and Italy moved into the valley, which subsequently became known as the **Latin Quarter**. Goats roamed the rocky crest of Telegraph Hill, where the working-class Irish had established an enclave on the eastern slope. Italian immigration, slow in the mid-19C, increased dramatically in the 1880s as successful émigrés brought their families from Europe. Newcomers, mostly from northern Italy, disembarked at the foot of Sansome Street and stayed put, attracted by North Beach's relatively warm microclimate, low rents and proximity to the wharves and canneries where many made their living. The Italian community gradually displaced other ethnic groups, and by 1900 the old Latin Quarter had given way to **Little Italy**.

The Best Minds of a Generation – As the children of the Italian immigrants grew up, they also moved out, seeking agricultural opportunities in the rich farmlands of Napa and Sonoma counties. In the mid-1950s, vacancies in North Beach had driven rents low enough to attract an anarchic assortment of poor and disillusioned—"beaten"—writers and artists bent on rejecting established societal and artistic norms. Calling themselves the **Beat Generation** but dubbed "beatniks" (by columnist Herb Caen), they and their hangers-on adopted bohemian, nonconformist lifestyles. They smoked marijuana, drank red wine and espresso, listened to jazz and bebop, and read poetry at favorite haunts like the Co-Existence Bagel Shop and The Place (both long since vanished). Of their principal gathering places, only City Lights Bookstore, Vesuvio Café and Caffé Trieste remain today.

The movement inspired an outpouring of creative activity by its leading lights: poets Lawrence Ferlinghetti, Kenneth Rexroth, Gregory Corso and Allen Ginsberg; novelist Jack Kerouac; and visual artists Jay DeFeo and Robert LaVigne. The 1955 reading of Ginsberg's raw, apocalyptic poem "Howl" gave birth to the San Francisco Poetry Renaissance and an enduring cultural legend. "I saw the best minds of my generation destroyed by madness," Ginsberg intoned, "starving, hysterical, naked, draggin themselves through negro streets at dawn lookin for an angry fix..."

Within a decade, the movement was over, ruined in part by busloads of "square" tourists who overran North Beach in their search for the cool. By the mid-1960s, many of the best minds of the Beat Generation had either passed away or moved on.

North Beach Today – Few in the counterculture could now afford the high rents of North Beach's surprisingly uniform, three- to four-story flats and apartment houses, built in a nine-year flurry of reconstruction after the 1906 earthquake and fire. The northward flow of families and businesses from Chinatown, begun in the 1960s as immigration restrictions on Asians eased, continues the neighborhood's long tradition of multiethnic coexistence. The area's Italian community, while diminished, has not disappeared. Many Italian Americans who live outside the city still consider North Beach home, returning often to shop, dine or gather at one of the many venerable Italian institutions still operated by descendants of the original owners.

Visiting North Beach – North Beach shows different faces at different times of the day. In the morning, a village atmosphere prevails as cafes fill with early-rising poets, eager job-seekers and neighborhood professionals stopping for a caffè latte before heading to work. The fragrances of baking bread and roasting coffee drift through the streets, and crowds gather to practice traditional *t'ai chi* exercises in Washington Square. In the evening, a young, international crowd takes over the bars, saloons and jazz clubs. Restaurants remain crowded until late at night, and floodlights illuminate several monuments, including Coit Tower and the Church of SS. Peter and Paul. The annual **Italian Heritage Day Parade** draws thousands of visitors to the streets of North Beach, as does the **North Beach Festival**, one of the oldest urban street fairs in the country *(p 218)*.

Use of public transportation, which serves all corners of North Beach, is strongly recommended. Parking spaces are scarce and nonresident street parking is usually limited to two hours. Read signs carefully; regulations are strictly enforced.

It's best to climb Telegraph Hill on foot or take the 39–Coit bus from the Union Street/Columbus Avenue stop on the south side of Washington Square. Cars often wait in line over an hour for one of the few parking spaces at the summit. The hill's flanks are steep; wear sturdy shoes and pause frequently to rest and admire the wonderful vistas that extend over city and bay.

WALKING TOUR *distance: 1.6mi*

Begin at the corner of Columbus Ave. and Broadway.

★**City Lights Bookstore** – *261 Columbus Ave. Open year-round daily 10am–midnight. Closed Thanksgiving Day & Dec 25. www.citylights.com ☎ 415-362-8193.* Founded in 1953 by poet and publisher Lawrence Ferlinghetti, this former beatnik hangout was the first all-paperback bookstore in America. It continues to be one of the best-known independent shops in the country, as much for its history as for its meandering layout, inviting atmosphere and unique titles, many released by City Lights Publishers. In the upstairs poetry and Beat Literature room, comfortable chairs encourage browsers to linger with their selections. Enlarged over the years, the store maintains its alternative reputation despite the presence on its shelves of clothbound books and other inevitable marks of changing times.

Across Jack Kerouac Alley from City Lights Bookstore lies **Vesuvio Café** *(255 Columbus Ave.; open year-round daily 6am–2am; ✗ ♿ www.vesuvio.com ☎ 415-362-3370)*, another popular landmark of North Beach's Beat heyday. It was here that a black-clad crowd of beatniks gathered on October 13, 1955, before attending Ginsberg's now-legendary reading of "Howl" at the Six Gallery (long gone from its former MARINA DISTRICT location). Vivid paintings and leaded glass enliven the cafe's wood-trimmed walls, which are crammed with photos and memorabilia from the beatnik era.

Walk north to Broadway, turn right and cross Columbus Ave.

As you cross, glance to your right for an impressive view of the TRANSAMERICA PYRAMID. The **Sentinel Building** *(916 Kearny St.)*, a green, copper-trimmed, flatiron-shaped office building (1905, Salfield and Kohlberg), rises in the foreground *(photograph p 50)*. Filmmaker Francis Ford Coppola purchased and restored the tower in the 1970s.

© Robert Holmes

Vesuvio Café

Broadway – *Broadway between Columbus Ave. and Montgomery St.* Though its reputation for danger, vice and sin has gentled in recent decades, the strip of sex shops and topless clubs along Broadway and Kearny Street harks back to San Francisco's less-than-savory past. Broadway's wicked renown originated in the waterfront dives of Sydney Town in the 1850s, when a notorious zone of dance halls, brothels, gambling dens and outlaw nests known as the **Barbary Coast** arose along lower Pacific Avenue, eventually extending to present-day Jackson Square *(p 55)* and parts of Chinatown. Sailors on shore leave enjoyed the strip's entertainments at great peril: "Shanghaiing" was an all-too-common practice (the verb, meaning "to recruit someone forcefully for maritime service," is said to have originated here). Civic pressure led to the cleanup of the Barbary Coast after the 1906 earthquake and fire, and bars offering exotic entertainment were restricted to Broadway where they have persisted, mostly undisturbed, for years.

During the topless-dancing craze of the 1960s and early 1970s, a number of new venues opened here. Among them was the once-racy Condor Club (now a sports bar) at the intersection of Broadway, Columbus and Grant Avenues. For several decades a neon figure of **Carol Doda**, the "queen of topless dancing," hung provocatively above the street, drawing scores of new visitors to the area. The cartoonish landmark was removed (and auctioned off piecemeal) in 1991, but several all-nude venues remain, catering mostly to curious college students and the occasional serviceman on shore leave during the Navy's annual Fleet Week visit to the Port of San Francisco in October.

Continue up Columbus Ave.

1 Molinari Delicatessen

373 Columbus Ave. ☎ *415-421-2337.* Heady whiffs of parmesan, basil, salami and olives waft from this century-old North Beach institution. Neighborhood denizens pop in early to pick up handmade ravioli, tortellini, cheeses, olive oils and vinegars from Italy. Later in the morning, meats and cheese appear on the chopping block for the sandwich-at-the-desk and picnic-in-Washington Square crowds.

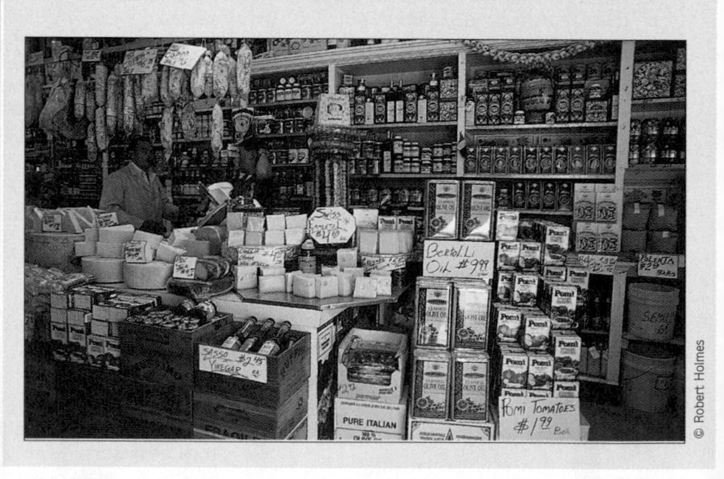

© Robert Holmes

Columbus Avenue – Designed in 1872 as a direct path from the FINANCIAL DISTRICT to the industrial zone growing along the northern waterfront, this broad, busy avenue traces the valley between Russian and Telegraph Hills, indiscriminately cutting across the city's square grid and creating several confusing six-way intersections. Called Montgomery Avenue at its construction, it was later renamed for Christopher Columbus to honor North Beach's Italian community. Today anchored by the Transamerica Pyramid, the thoroughfare extends through North Beach to THE CANNERY on FISHERMAN'S WHARF. The blocks between Broadway and Filbert Street, lined with fragrant bakeries, garlicky trattorias, pungent delicatessens and aromatic cafes, preserve the soul of Italian North Beach.

Continue to Stockton St. and turn left.

The melding of cultures that distinguishes present-day North Beach is clearly visible in the block of Stockton Street between Vallejo and Green Streets. Asian markets and Chinese street signs rub shoulders with old-fashioned Italian shops advertising fresh *tagliarini* and imported olive oil.

North Beach Museum – *1435 Stockton St. (Bayview Bank), mezzanine level. Open year-round Mon–Thu 9am–3:30pm, Fri 9am–5pm. Closed major holidays.* ☎ *415-626-7070.* This small, bank-sponsored museum highlights North Beach's multiethnic heritage through changing displays and photo exhibits of the Chinese and Italian communities in the late 19C and early 20C. The museum features an 11-panel photographic panorama of San Francisco in 1877 by Eadweard Muybridge, as well as an especially fine collection of photos of North Beach, Fisherman's Wharf and Telegraph Hill during and after the 1906 temblor. Especially worth noting is Lawrence Ferlinghetti's handwritten poem "The Old Italians Dying."

Return to Columbus Ave. and continue northwest.

★**Washington Square Park** – With a broad, sunny lawn and clusters of willow, cypress and sycamore trees, this pentagonal park occupies the heart of North Beach. The popular neighborhood gathering spot was donated to the city by its first mayor, John W. Geary, and set aside as a public park in 1847 by Jasper O'Farrell, surveyor of San Francisco's downtown street grid. After Columbus Avenue sliced off its southwest corner (now called Marini Plaza) in 1873, the park was landscaped to Victorian taste with shade trees and a broad, curving path for promenading. Hundreds of refugees camped here during the year following the 1906 earthquake and fire. Today, elderly Asians gather each morning to practice *t'ai chi*, a graceful form of martial arts *(below)*, and Italian retirees spend hours on the benches facing Union Street. Visitors and locals alike often picnic on the grassy lawn.

Situated on the western side of the park, the bronze monument honoring San Francisco's heroic **Volunteer Firemen (1)** (1933, Haig Patigian) was erected through a bequest of Lillie Hitchcock Coit, San Francisco's firefighter-loving eccentric *(p 65)*. A handsome bronze figure of **Benjamin Franklin (2)** stands at the center of the park; an inscription on its base refers to a time capsule buried in Washington Square Park in 1879 and opened a century later.

2 Caffeine and Conversation

For decades, North Beach denizens have stopped at the neighborhood's famed Italian coffeehouses to get that morning jolt. At **Caffé Trieste** *(601 Vallejo St.* ☎ *415-392-6739)*, or **Mario's Bohemian Cigar Store** *(566 Columbus Ave.* ☎ *415-362-0536)*, the price of a cup buys you a table for the day to work on your novel; the latter serves up the best focaccia sandwich going. Big windows at **Caffé Puccini** *(411 Columbus Ave.* ☎ *415-989-7033)* and **Caffè Greco** *(423 Columbus Ave.* ☎ *415-397-6261)* offer glimpses of daily life in North Beach. Is the coffee fresh at **Caffè Roma** *(526 Columbus Ave.* ☎ *415-298-7942)?* It comes right from the brass-trimmed roaster sitting in the window.

3 Beach Blanket Babylon

Club Fugazi, 678 Beach Blanket Babylon Blvd. (formerly Green St.). www.beachblanketbabylon.com ☎ *415-421-4222.* Where else could you find Elvis and Madonna, Bill Clinton and Monica Lewinsky, Louis XIV and Carmen Miranda, Mr. Peanut and Snow White together on the same stage? This outrageous spoof of current events and pop culture has played before packed houses eight times weekly at the same location for 24 years, and is acclaimed as the longest-running musical revue in theater history.

■ T'ai Chi

Early-rising visitors enjoying a morning trek through North Beach, Russian Hill, Nob Hill or other residential areas of the city are likely to spy individuals or groups of people dressed in everyday clothes performing what appears to be a slow-motion outdoor ballet. *T'ai chi ch'uan*, an ancient, noncompetitive martial art, is practiced by many city residents as a form of exercise. The slow, meditative transitions between specific stances and positions is believed to condition the body and relax the mind through a harmonizing of the passive and active principles of *yin* and *yang*. Almost any serene corner of the city can serve as a good place to perform this morning ritual, but groups tend to gather at Ina Coolbrith Park, Huntington Park, St. Mary's Square and especially Washington Square Park.

Coffee in North Beach

Black as night, strong as sin...

Long before every shopping mall and fast-food joint in America installed a coffee bar, before the Beats of the'50s were bolting shots of espresso in smoky cafés, the Italian-American residents of North Beach were drinking fine coffee. Today, with more than a dozen cafés and two traditional roasteries, North Beach is still a prime spot to enjoy some form of the bitter black liquid.

Espresso: Strong and black, made from finely ground, dark-roasted beans. Served in a demitasse, it is the base for all other coffee drinks. Called caffè romano when accompanied by a twist of lemon peel.

Caffè latté: Espresso with steamed milk, sometimes topped with foam. Often served in a tall glass.

Cappuccino: Espresso with a cap of milk foam. Served in a broad mug.

Mocha: Espresso with steamed milk and chocolate, topped with whipped cream. Also called "dessert."

Machiatto: Espresso "stained" with a drop of steamed milk. Served in a demitasse.

Caffè americano: Basic American-style coffee. In North Beach, even this is good.

Café au lait: American coffee with steamed milk.

★**SS. Peter and Paul Church** – *666 Filbert St., north side of Washington Sq. Open year-round Mon–Fri 6:30am–4pm, weekends 6:30am–7pm. ♿ ☎ 415-421-0809.* Erected in the Gothic Revival style with Italianate details, this handsome, twin-spired church (1924) is fondly known as San Francisco's "Italian Cathedral." Lawrence Ferlinghetti dubbed it "the marzipan church on the plaza," a description particularly true at night when floodlights bathe its cream-colored exterior. The imposing facade bears the opening line of Dante's *Paradiso:* "The glory of Him who moves all things penetrates and glows throughout the universe." The interior of the building is warm and inviting, enclosed by an unusual flat ceiling of dark wood and illuminated by banks of votive candles and richly colored stained-glass windows. Screen legend Marilyn Monroe and baseball great Joe DiMaggio took wedding photos on the front steps of SS. Peter and Paul, contributing to the myth that they married inside. The church reflects North Beach's multiethnic character, offering Mass in English, Italian and Cantonese.

4 Dining around the Square

Around Washington Square lie some of North Beach's best (and best-loved) restaurants. It's not unusual to start at one, dine at another and cap the night at a third. **Fior d'Italia** *(601 Union St. ☎ 415-986-1886)*, opened in 1886 and claims to be the oldest Italian restaurant in the US; the service, decor and menu are old-fashioned and courtly. At **Little City Antipasti Bar** *(Union at Powell St. ☎ 415-434-2900)*, starters circle the globe, from quesadillas to ahi tuna to gravlax. At both **Washington Square Bar and Grill** *(1707 Powell St. ☎ 415-982-8123)* and **Moose's** *(1652 Stockton St. ☎ 415-989-7800)*, deal-makers dine, writers circulate, "What's wrong with the Giants?" is an opening gambit, and the food is first-rate.

From the church, walk east up Filbert St. and climb the hill, following the "Stairs to Coit Tower" signs. To avoid the steep climb, take the 39–Coit bus from Washington Square.

★**Telegraph Hill** – The abrupt rise that punctuates the eastern edge of North Beach was named for a long-vanished semaphore erected atop its summit in 1849. A precursor to modern telegraph systems, the semaphore signaled the arrival of ships through the Golden Gate by the varicolored flags hoisted along its two arms, which were positioned according to the type and nationality of the vessel. The Gold Rush-era shacks and tent cities that dotted the hill's steep, rocky flanks developed into working-class neighborhoods that persisted until the early 20C, when the invention of the automobile opened the way for wealthier citizens. Most of the structures on the hill (and in surrounding North Beach) burned to the ground during the 1906 fire, but houses on the eastern slope were saved by determined Italian Americans, who beat back the flames with blankets soaked in red wine.

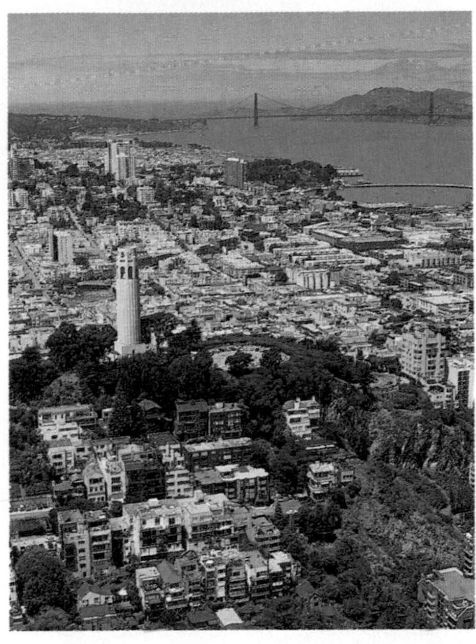

© David R. Frazier

Coit Tower and Telegraph Hill

The tree-filled expanse at the hill's 274ft summit, today known as **Pioneer Park**, was donated to the city in 1876 by a group of businessmen intent on preserving the open space for future generations. *(A park improvement project is currently underway.)* The bronze statue of **Christopher Columbus (3)** at the center of the Coit Tower parking area was erected by the local Italian-American community. Panoramic **views**★★ from the summit encompass major landmarks including LOMBARD STREET, the GOLDEN GATE BRIDGE, the BAY BRIDGE, ALCATRAZ and TWIN PEAKS. On clear days, the East Bay hills come into view. As you gaze, listen for the sounds of barking sea lioins drifting up from PIER 39.

★★★ **Coit Tower** – Kids *Summit of Telegraph Hill. Open May–Sept daily 10am–7:30pm. Rest of the year daily 10am–6pm.* P ☎ *415-362-0808.* Towering 180ft above a 32ft rectangular base, this fluted, concrete column (1934, Arthur Brown, Jr.) was an enduring gift to San Francisco's citizens from an unusual woman who wished to add "to the beauty of the city which I have always loved." Initially infamous for the heated social controversy incited by its lobby murals, Coit Tower ranks today among the city's best-known landmarks.

"Firebelle" Lillie – When **Lillie Hitchcock Coit** (1843-1929) was a child in San Francisco, daring teams of volunteers battled the many fires that regularly ravaged the city. It is said that one afternoon in the 1860s young Lillie, who had been saved from a fire during her childhood, came upon Knickerbocker Engine Company No. 5 struggling up Telegraph Hill en route to a blaze. Throwing down her schoolbooks, she rallied onlookers to help the firemen. In return, the company made her an honorary member. For the rest of her life, even as a wealthy widow in Paris, Coit wore a gold, diamond-studded fireman's badge everywhere she went; it was pinned to her clothing when her remains were cremated in 1929. In her will, she bequeathed $125,000 to the city, part of which paid for the statue of her beloved volunteer firemen in Washington Square Park *(p 63)*. The bulk of the gift provided funds for Coit Tower, which, despite persistent local lore, was not designed to resemble a firehose nozzle.

California Historical Society, San Francisco. FN-13122

Lillie Hitchcock Coit

The Murals – The first major commission of the Depression-era Public Works of Art Project (PWAP), a New Deal initiative that engaged artists to decorate public buildings, the 19 fresco **murals**★★ in the lobby of Coit Tower were created in 1934. Working for an average of $31.22 a

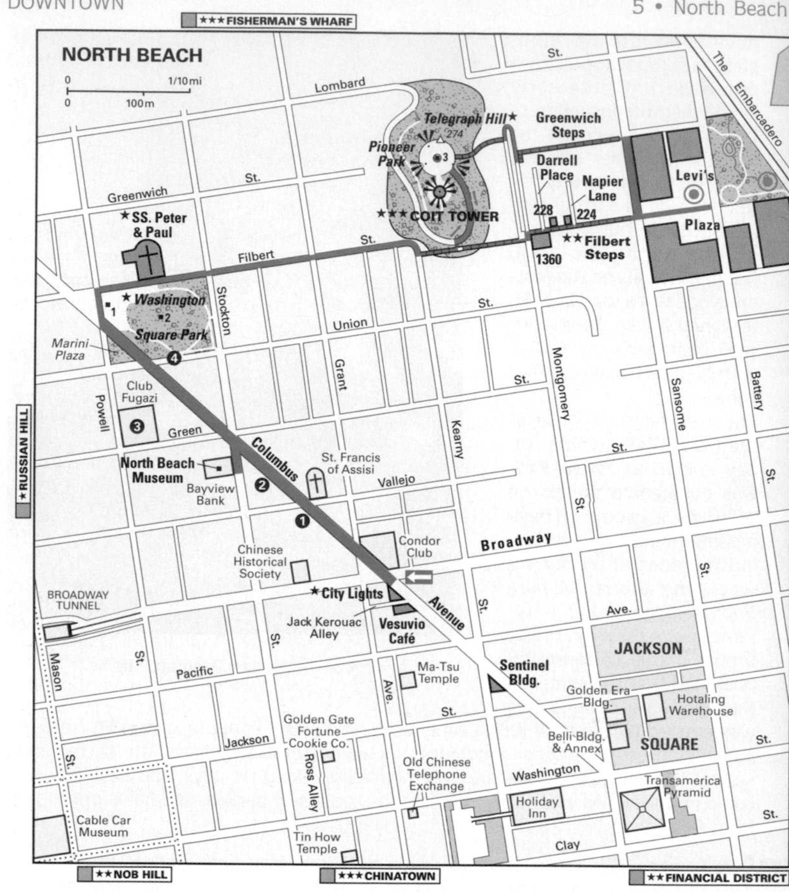

week, 26 local painters and numerous assistants labored for five months to produce a series of frescoes depicting contemporary life in California. While celebrating the state's abundance and diversity, the works contained powerful images that bluntly criticized the economic inequities of life during the Great Depression.

The murals' left-wing content raised the hackles of San Francisco's conservative elite. Fueling the controversy, a tense labor conflict smoldered along the waterfront at the base of Telegraph Hill, erupting into the longshoremen's Pacific Maritime Strike just as work on the murals drew to a close. The sometimes violent strike crippled the entire West Coast and caused some to view any form of social criticism as radical agitation. Responding to civic pressure, the San Francisco Art Commission delayed the opening of Coit Tower and considered destroying the murals. After vigorous debate on both sides of the issue, only the most blatant (hammer-and-sickle) symbols of left-wing sympathy in Clifford Wight's mural (no. 4) were effaced, and the building was finally opened to the public in October of 1934.

Visit – The murals display remarkable uniformity in both theme and style despite the fact that so many different artists created them. **California Industrial Scenes** (John Langley Howard) depicts the despair of the era through an image of a migrant family posing beside their disabled Model-T, while a group of well-to-do daytrippers gazes on them as if they were a tourist attraction. **The Library** (Bernard Zakheim) inspired controversy for its suggestion that the works of Karl Marx might offer a viable form of government. In **City Life** (Victor Arnautoff), perhaps the best-known mural, a bustling street scene none-too-subtly criticizes the indifference of urban dwellers to one another.

■ Jungle City

The relative warmth of Telegraph Hill and Washington Square attracts colonies of colorful parrots, descendants of household pets who escaped the confines of domestication. The parrots now form a curious and vocal part of North Beach's landscape, their loud screeches and brilliant colors enlivening Telegraph Hill's verdant flanks and the leafy canopies of Washington Square. Many of the birds also nest in the tall date palms that line Dolores Street in the MISSION DISTRICT.

A brief elevator ascent *($3; purchase tickets in gift shop)* and a short flight of stairs take visitors to the observation deck. From here, panoramic **views★★★** sweep ANGEL ISLAND and Marin County to the north, the Bay Bridge and TREASURE ISLAND to the east, downtown San Francisco to the south, and Russian Hill and the Golden Gate Bridge to the west.

From Coit Tower, descend the curving sidewalk along Telegraph Hill Ave. to the first corner and turn left at Filbert St.

★★ **Filbert Steps** – Concrete and wooden stairs descend this steep section of Filbert Street, one of the city's most charming and surprising pathways. The stairs pass a gleaming, Art Deco apartment house at **1360 Montgomery Street** (1937), a fine example of the Streamline Moderne style. The house appeared in the 1947 film *Dark Passage* as the place where the character played by Lauren Bacall hid an escaped convict (Humphrey Bogart).

Below Montgomery Street, continue down the wooden staircase alongside lushly landscaped terraces. These gardens bear the name of Grace Marchant, their original designer and a long-time resident of the neighborhood. Those who live along the steps today continue to cultivate her verdant legacy, and the gardens flourish year-round. Inhabitants of the treehouse-like neighborhood along the pedestrian streets of **Darrell Place** and **Napier Lane** occupy handsome, mid-19C wooden cottages in styles exemplifying the vernacular architecture of the post-Gold Rush period. Note especially the simple facade at **no. 228** (1869), a delicately restored example of the Carpenter Gothic style, and the cottage at **no. 224** (1859).

At the bottom of the steps, cross Sansome St.

Levi's Plaza – *Filbert St., between Sansome and Battery Sts.* Completed in 1982, this award-winning group of buildings (Hellmuth, Obata & Kassabaum) was designed to harmonize with the varying architectural styles of the surrounding neighborhood. Stand at the intersection of Battery and Filbert Streets and look west to appreciate the way its stacked-box profile mimics the houses marching down the steep backdrop of Telegraph Hill. Administrative headquarters of Levi Strauss & Co., the complex boasts inviting, beautifully landscaped open spaces that serve as a placid haven amid the bustle of the nearby Embarcadero *(p 77)*.

Walk north on Sansome St. to Greenwich St. and turn up the steps.

The **Greenwich Steps**, while not as lushly picturesque as the Filbert Street staircase, scale nasturtium-covered rocks and patches of fragrant anise along the ascent to the top of Telegraph Hill.

6 • RUSSIAN HILL★

Time: 2 hours. Powell-Hyde or Powell-Mason.
Map p 69

Bounded by Francisco, Taylor, Pacific and Polk Streets, Russian Hill rises abruptly from the landfill flats of FISHERMAN'S WHARF and NORTH BEACH. Its precipitous flanks harbor a number of pre-1906 architectural gems and a rich history of literary activity. Topping 360ft at Vallejo Street between Taylor and Jones, and 294ft at Lombard and Hyde, the hill's two summits offer splendid views of COIT TOWER, the FINANCIAL DISTRICT, ALCATRAZ and the bay. Several secluded pedestrian stairways and paths negotiate the dips between the two peaks, making for beautiful, if vigorous, walks. A smattering of pleasant sidewalk cafes, restaurants, bars and shops on nearby Hyde and Polk Streets provide welcome places to eat, relax or browse.

Historical Notes

According to San Francisco lore, Russian Hill was named in the mid-19C when the graves of Russian seal-hunters were discovered atop the crest of present-day Vallejo Street. Only after thousands of people turned out to see the city's first public hanging here in 1852 did Joseph Atkinson build the first house on the south side of Russian Hill. Others followed, mainly working-class families who built simple wooden residences and climbed the steep slopes on foot.

By the 1880s, cable car lines had crept up Russian Hill's flanks and San Francisco's burgeoning population began eyeing the newly accessible heights. Small Victorian flats were built side-by-side with simple shingled cottages. An active community of writers and artists moved in, securing Russian Hill's reputation as a bohemian enclave before upscale development took root. From 1856 through the 1890s, Catherine Atkinson kept her home at 1032 Broadway open to such literary lights as Mark Twain, Ambrose Bierce, Robert Louis Stevenson and a group known as Les Jeunes, which included architect Willis Polk and poet Gelett Burgess. From the late 1860s until 1906, local literary maven Ina Coolbrith *(below)* also hosted literary salons, inviting Twain, Bierce, Bret Harte, Charles Stoddard, George Sterling and others to her house at 1604 Taylor Street.

For more than two decades after the 1906 earthquake and fire, the California Literary Society met in Coolbrith's upstairs flat at 1067 Broadway. In the 1940s Russian Hill provided the setting for several locally written mystery novels, and in 1952 Beat writer Jack Kerouac spent six months on the hill, staying with friends Neal and Carolyn Cassady at 29 Russell Street and working on several novels, including *On the Road.* Unlike elite NOB HILL, Russian Hill continued to develop as a middle-class neighborhood, with small homes set relatively far apart and separated by gardens and wells. Although a few residential enclaves survived the 1906 fire, many homes were destroyed, and the ensuing architectural ferment of 1906-1920 continues to define Russian Hill's aesthetic. Two- to four-story Edwardian buildings flourished, as did a number of pueblo-style stuccoes and Spanish and Art Deco apartment towers. Several less attractive high-rises were erected in the 1960s and '70s, blocking views; a 40ft height limit was imposed in 1974. Today, Russian Hill is a living testament to the city's architectural ingenuity and diversity. Its lofty heights, well-tended homes, and tranquil parks and gardens make it one of San Francisco's most picturesque neighborhoods.

Visiting Russian Hill – It's best to begin and end a visit to Russian Hill with a cable car ride. Take the Powell-Mason line to the corner of Mason and Vallejo Streets to begin the walking tour, then pick up the Powell-Hyde line from the top of Lombard Street to finish. While not long, the route entails several steep climbs—be sure to wear sturdy shoes.

WALKING TOUR *distance: 1mi*

Begin at the intersection of Mason and Vallejo Sts. and walk west, climbing the left staircase.

Ina Coolbrith Park – A narrow plot of steep hillside bursting with Monterey pines, agave plants and hydrangea bushes along the Vallejo Street stairs, Ina Coolbrith Park was dedicated in 1931 as a memorial to the acclaimed poet and avatar of San Francisco's turn-of-the-century literary community.
The niece of Mormon prophet Joseph Smith, **Ina Donna Coolbrith** (1841-1928) moved west with her family as a child. After spending her teenage years in Los Angeles, she moved to San Francisco in 1861. During the 1860s Coolbrith wrote poetry for and helped edit *The Californian* and the *Overland Monthly,* both highly esteemed literary journals, while spearheading the vibrant local salon scene. Later, during her long tenure as a librarian, Coolbrith encouraged writer Jack London and dancer Isadora Duncan in their artistic pursuits. The state legislature named her California's poet laureate in 1919.
From the Taylor Street stairhead, Coit Tower, the BAY BRIDGE and Yerba Buena Island are visible to the east through the trees. Begonias, zinnias and other blooming flowers garnish the paths that zigzag across the tiny park, and benches provide a peaceful place to rest.

Cross Taylor St. and continue up the Vallejo St. stairs to the summit.

Take a moment to enjoy the **views★★** out over the bay to the east before turning to admire the charming historic residences along the summit of Vallejo Street. Tucked behind tall shrubbery and a redwood fence, the **Williams-Polk House★** *(1013-1019 Vallejo St.)* was designed in 1892 by Willis Polk for Mrs. Virgil Williams, whose husband was one of the founders of the California School of Design (now the San Francisco Art Institute, *p 70*). The house is seven stories high on the side facing Broadway *(not visible)*. Inspired by the Arts and Crafts aesthetic, Polk embellished his creation with indigenous materials. So pleased was he with his design and with the view from the house that the architect waived his fee in exchange for quarters in the eastern third of the building.

The large, shingled structure at 1020 Vallejo Street contains the **Hermitage Condominiums** (1982, Esherick, Homsey, Dodge & Davis). The building occupies the former site of a one-story cottage that was home to the Rev. Joseph Worcester, an early proponent of the Arts and Crafts movement in the West (Worcester himself had a hand in designing both his cottage and the SWEDENBORGIAN CHURCH). Many similar small cottages were demolished in the mid-20C to make way for large-scale building projects. Next door, two of Worcester's original designs, the three-story, gable-roofed **Marshall Houses** *(1034 and 1036 Vallejo St.),* both built in 1889, have survived the century largely unaltered.

Continue walking west to Florence Ln. on the left.

Screened by a charming, rose-covered fence, the shingled mansion at **40 Florence Lane** (1857) was remodeled by Willis Polk in 1891, and expanded nearly a century later by architect Robert A.M. Stern.

Cross the street to Russian Hill Pl.

Built in 1916 by Willis Polk, the houses at **1, 3, 5 & 7 Russian Hill Place** appear from the front as tiny Mediterranean-style cottages. The houses drop several stories at the back, however, presenting an imposing facade along Jones Street.

Turn right on Jones St. and walk north to Green St.

From the corner of Jones and Green Streets, fine **views★★** extend to the north over Alcatraz. The 1000 block of Green features a handful of beautifully restored, Victorian-era earthquake survivors. Note especially the **Feusier Octagon House** at no. 1067,

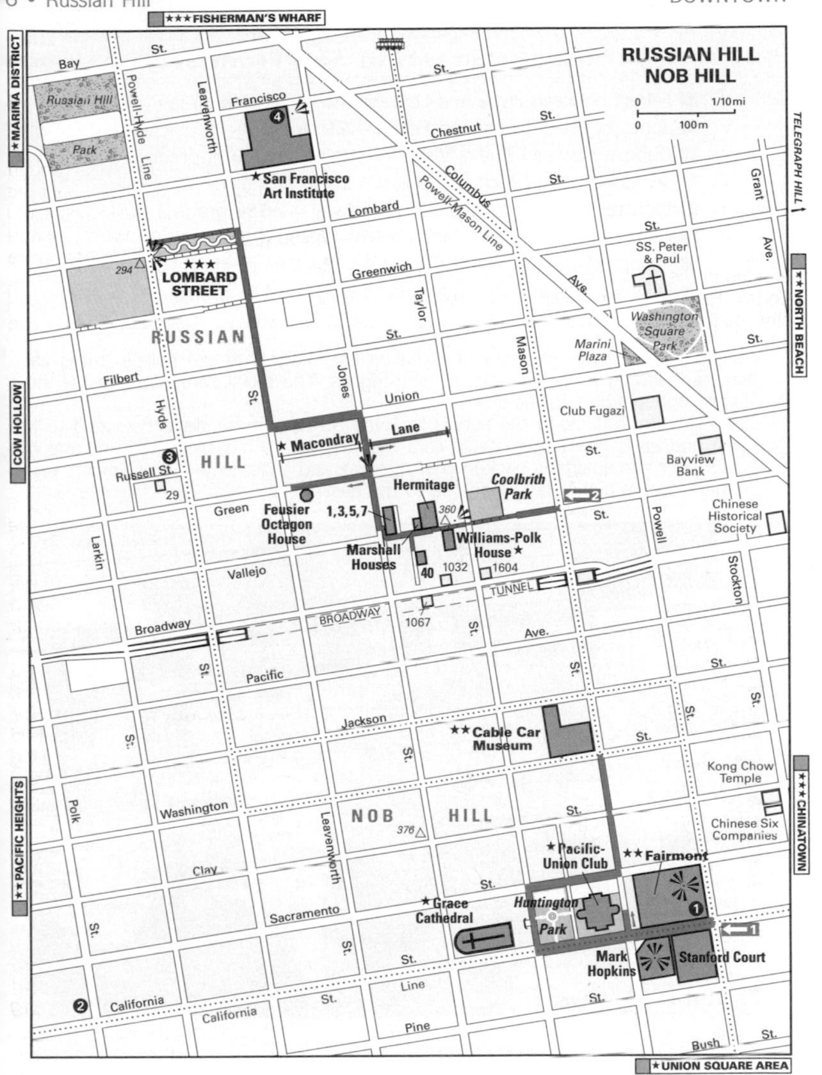

designed in 1857. The house was sold in 1870 to Louis Feusier, a friend of Leland Stanford and Mark Twain; the handsome mansard roof was added several years later.

Return to Jones St. and turn left, continuing to Macondray Ln. Turn right and stroll to the wooden staircase.

★ **Macondray Lane** – This enchanting little walking street, overhung by lush greenery, was one of Ina Coolbrith's favorite places to roam; it also appeared as "Barbary Lane" in author Armistead Maupin's serialized 1970s epic, *Tales of the City*. Turn-of-the-century clapboard houses and modern glass condominiums share the cozily private lane.

Return to Jones St. and continue north, turning left on Union St. Turn right on Leavenworth St. and continue to Lombard St.

★★★ **Lombard Street** – Kids One of San Francisco's most renowned tourist attractions, the 1000 block of Lombard Street boasts eight switchbacks in its one-block descent from Hyde to Leavenworth. The block's natural 27 percent grade was gentled to 16 percent in 1922, when cobblestones were used to pave the street.

3 Swensen's Ice Cream

Union St. at Hyde St. ☎ 415-775-6818. San Franciscans don't cope well with hot weather. When his troop ship sailed into the South Pacific, native son Earle Swensen, looking for the coldest place aboard, volunteered to make ice cream. Upon the war's conclusion, he opened shop here. The flagship in Swensen's fleet of 400 ice cream parlors holds only about a dozen customers, so most eat their cones out front while waiting for the cable car.

Steepest Streets of San Francisco

- Filbert between Hyde and Leavenworth – **31.5%** grade
- Jones between Union and Filbert – **29%** grade
- Duboce between Buena Vista and Alpine – **27.9%** grade
- Jones between Green and Union – **26%** grade
- Webster between Vallejo and Broadway – **26%** grade
- Duboce between Alpine and Castro – **25%** grade
- Jones between Pine and California – **24.8%** grade
- Fillmore between Vallejo and Broadway – **24%** grade

Today, roughly three-quarters of a million cars negotiate the hairpin turns each year, descending through banks of hydrangeas. The block ranks among the most photographed sights in the city.

Climb the stairs flanking the curves to Hyde Street, where **views★★** extend to the north and east. From here, cable cars coast down to GHIRARDELLI SQUARE and the HYDE STREET PIER against a backdrop of Alcatraz and ANGEL ISLAND. Coit Tower, Yerba Buena Island and the Bay Bridge lie to the east.

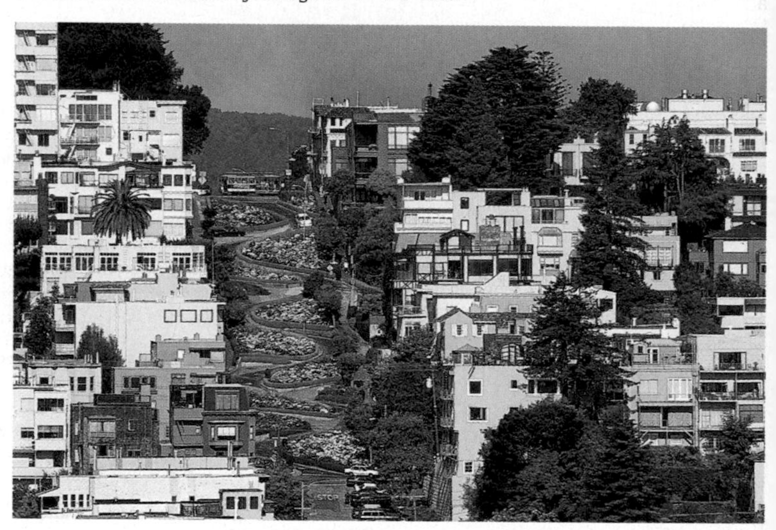

Switchbacks of Lombard Street

ADDITIONAL SIGHT

★**San Francisco Art Institute** – *800 Chestnut St. Open year-round Mon–Fri 9am–5pm.*  *415-771-7020.* Founded in 1871, this prestigious fine-arts college occupies a Spanish Colonial Revival-style building (1926, Arthur Brown, Jr.). A vibrant cultural center as well as a college, the institute welcomes the public to its exhibits, galleries and avant-garde film screenings. Displays of student work change regularly in its quiet, open-air courtyard, and temporary exhibits are mounted in the **Walter/McBean Gallery** *(open year-round Tue–Wed 10am–5pm, Thu 10am–8pm, Fri–Sat 10am–5pm, Sun 10am–noon)* and the chapel-like **Diego Rivera Gallery** *(open year-round daily 9am–9pm; closed major holidays)*, which features *The Making of a Fresco Showing the Building of a City* (1931), a two-story mural by the famed Mexican artist. Rivera himself appears in the work, along with his wife, Frida Kahlo. In 1969, English-born architect Paffard Keatinge Clay expanded the original structure in the béton brut style. Stroll out on the rooftop deck to see grand **views★★** extending over Telegraph Hill and the northern waterfront.

4 San Francisco Art Institute Cafe

San Francisco Art Institute, 800 Chestnut St. ☎ *415-749-4567.* Wind your way through the art- and handbill-lined hallways to the Art Institute's broad back deck. Grab a sandwich, a potato or a daily entree—guaranteed to fill a starving artist at rock-bottom prices—sit back, and relax. The foreground of congregating students against a stunning backdrop of city, bay and sky may inspire you to bring out your brushes.

7 • UNION SQUARE★

Time: 2 hours. Powell-Hyde or Powell-Mason. bus 2–Clement, 3–Jackson, 4–Sutter, 30–Stockton, 38–Geary, or 45–Union-Stockton; all streetcars Powell St. station. Powell St. station.
Map p 73

Roughly bounded by Sutter, Taylor, Kearny and O'Farrell Streets, the Union Square area bustles as San Francisco's most vibrant and prestigious urban shopping district. Dominating the square itself, major department stores stand shoulder-to-shoulder with upscale boutiques and a turn-of-the-century hotel. To the east, designer shops crowd in beside art galleries and specialty stores, and chichi cafes set up umbrella-shaded tables along secluded pedestrian lanes. To the west extends the city's theater district, where large and small venues mix with art galleries, hotels, all-night diners and exclusive social clubs.

Historical Notes

In 1850, San Francisco mayor John White Geary presented the city with Union Square Park, a precious gift during the height of the Gold Rush when land was at a premium. For the next two decades the neighborhood remained largely residential, staid Victorian homes and churches flanking the open square. Through the 1880s and '90s, the area grew increasingly commercial as merchants, attracted to the upscale, picturesque and central square, rented the homes of wealthy residents who had relocated west to the more spacious environs of PACIFIC HEIGHTS. Sutter Street became the area's first fashionable shopping artery, followed by the streets flanking the square itself.

Large retail establishments began appearing on the square in 1896 when the **City of Paris** department store took up residence at the corner of Geary and Stockton Streets. Across the park at Geary and Powell, white-gloved porters opened the doors of the St. Francis Hotel for the first time in 1904. With its grand lobby, luxurious guest rooms and fine restaurants, the St. Francis, along with City of Paris and **Gump's**, an esteemed interior-design gallery, ensured Union Square's elite cachet.

The 1906 earthquake and fire nearly razed the district, but determined entrepreneurs lost no time in rebuilding. In 1908 the City of Paris store rose anew; architects Bakewell & Brown preserved much of its original design and added a stained-glass rotunda reminiscent of one in Paris' Galeries Lafayette. The St. Francis Hotel was reconstructed and expanded that same year in its original Renaissance Revival style. In the blocks east of the square, Gump's was rebuilt, and new boutiques appeared along Maiden Lane. To the west, numerous theaters took root, many sporting Neoclassical facades. In the following decades, prestigious social clubs took root in the area, among them the Romanesque Revival-style **Olympic Club** *(524 Post St.)*, the Moderne-influenced **Bohemian Club** *(624 Taylor St.)* and the **Metropolitan Club** *(640 Sutter St.)* for women only.

Today this preponderance of theaters and stores, along with numerous hotels, makes Union Square one of the city's liveliest districts. During the day, shoppers mob the stores around the square, especially **Macy's**, **Saks Fifth Avenue** and **Neiman Marcus**, while flower vendors, shoeshine boys, buskers and panhandlers cram the sidewalks and traffic chokes the streets. At night, crowds shift west toward the Powell Street cable car lines and the theater district.

Visiting Union Square – Weekday mornings are the best time to shop in the Union Square area; crowds throng the stores and sidewalks during afternoons and weekends. Most stores open at 10am. Small boutiques and galleries close around 5pm or 6pm, although large department stores remain open until 9pm or 10pm during sales and before the winter holidays. Visit at night during the Christmas season to see creative window displays and the square's enormous and brightly lit tree.

Public transport through the area is plentiful; cable cars offer the best access to other downtown areas and Fisherman's Wharf. It's best to avoid driving here during the morning and evening rush hours. Street parking is hard to find and meter time is limited. Several parking garages dot the neighborhood; a large one lies beneath Union Square Park *(access from Geary St.)*.

The city sponsors a variety of public events at Union Square throughout the year, including free concerts and a Cable Car Bell-Ringing Competition in late July. For a schedule, call the San Francisco Convention & Visitors Bureau *(p 220)*. On the Stockton Street side of the park, a **Tix Bay Area** *(p 234)* booth sells advance tickets and same-day, half-price tickets to live performances around the city *(open year-round Tue–Thu 11am–6pm, Fri–Sat 11am–7pm; www.theatrebayarea.org ☎ 415-433-7827)*. Public restrooms are situated on either side of the ticket booth.

WALKING TOUR *distance: .5mi*

Begin at the center of Union Square Park.

★**Union Square Park** – *Bounded by Post, Stockton, Geary and Powell Sts.* One of the few designated public parks in Jasper O'Farrell's rigid street plan *(p 13)*, this 2.6-acre parcel was landscaped in the early 1850s. It was named on the eve of the Civil War when it hosted numerous rallies in support of the Union.

Union Square

In 1901 the elegant **Dewey Monument (1)**, commemorating Admiral George Dewey's 1898 defeat of Spanish naval forces in the Bay of Manila, was erected at the center of the square. Newton Tharp designed the slender, 97ft granite Corinthian column and Robert Aitken cast the bronze figure of Victory—armed with wreath and trident—surmounting it. In 1942 a five-story parking garage was constructed beneath the square, raising the park slightly above street level.

Union Square Park has hosted numerous heated demonstrations over the decades, but today its palm trees, Irish yews and boxwood hedges create a peaceful respite for workers, shoppers and passersby. Homeless people and street musicians frequently avail themselves of the park's benches and retaining walls, while adventurous skateboarders take over in the evenings. A $6 million redesign of the park is tentatively planned for early in the 21C.

Cross the square to the corner of Geary and Stockton Sts.

Neiman Marcus – *150 Stockton St. (at Geary St.). Open year-round Mon–Sat 10am–7pm (Thu 8pm), Sun noon–6pm. Closed Thanksgiving Day, Dec 25.* ☎ *415-362-3900.* With its rose-colored, harlequin-patterned granite exterior and rounded glass-and-aluminum entrance corner, this post-Modern department store (1982, Johnson & Burgee) marks a sharp architectural departure from the Renaissance-style, Baroque-ornamented City of Paris store that once stood here. The beloved City of Paris landmark was demolished in 1981, but its exuberant stained-glass **rotunda★** was preserved and today soars above the entrance foyer, framed by enameled, wrought-iron balconies. As befits its original surroundings, the rotunda depicts Paris' emblem, a sailing ship, and its motto, *Fluctuat nec Mergitur* ("He Floats but Does Not Sink").

Walk north up Stockton St. to Maiden Lane.

Art Galleries and Rare Book Shops

49 Geary St. Collectors of art and rare books know they have to penetrate the bland facade here to find the treasure trove within. The second floor contains five antiquarian and rare book shops, and on the floors above, cavernous spaces designed to house Western Union machinery have been converted into galleries. Several art dealers specialize in photography.

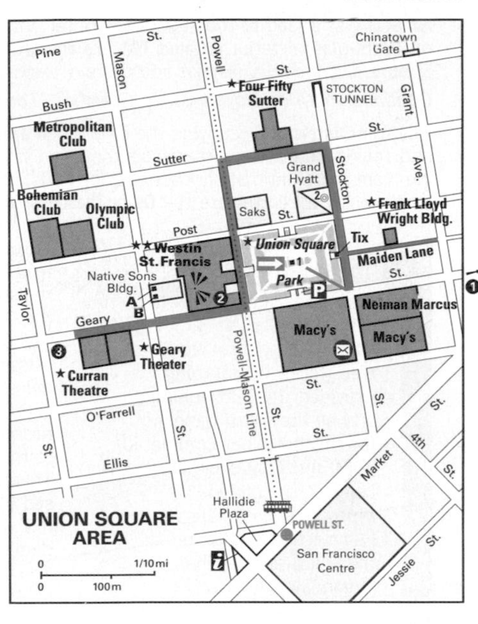

Maiden Lane – Previously flanked with Barbary Coast-style brothels, Maiden Lane was reincarnated after the 1906 fire as a quaint pedestrian street lined with maple trees, cafes, boutiques, salons and galleries. At no. 140 stands the **Frank Lloyd Wright Building**★ (1949), the only building in San Francisco designed by Wright and a forerunner to the famed architect's Guggenheim Museum in New York City. Now home to the museum-quality collection of Folk Art International, the skylit gallery boasts a curvaceous interior with many circular and spiral motifs, including small round porticoes used as display cases, cutout porthole-like windows, a huge hanging planter and a ramp spiraling up to the second floor.

Return to Stockton St. and continue north.

Ruth Asawa Fountain (2) – Kids *Stockton St. deck (at corner of Post St.) of the Grand Hyatt hotel.* This playful fountain (1972) by San Francisco sculptor Ruth Asawa represents a triumph of collective creativity. Asawa asked 250 city residents, ages 3 to 90, to sculpt city landmarks out of baker's dough. She cast the flour-and-water bas-reliefs in metal and arranged them around the fountain's cylindrical base in a maplike fashion. Look for whimsical depictions of the TRANSAMERICA PYRAMID and the SUTRO BATHS, juxtaposed with fantastical elements such as Superman in flight above Montgomery Street.

Continue north to Sutter St. and turn left.

★**Four Fifty Sutter** – *450 Sutter St. Open year-round Mon–Fri 8am–6pm. Weekends & holidays 9am–2pm.* ☎ *415-421-7221.* This 26-story tower (1929, Timothy Pflueger), housing medical and dental offices, is one of San Francisco's finest Art Deco skyscrapers. Elaborate Mayan motifs cover the spectacular gold-painted elevator lobby, adorn the plaster ceiling and decorate the undulating terra-cotta exterior all the way up to the top floor.

Continue west to Powell St. and turn left.

★★**Westin St. Francis Hotel** – *335 Powell St. Self-guided walking tour maps available at concierge desk.* ☎ *415-397-7000.* An internationally renowned San Francisco institution, this elegant Renaissance- and Baroque-Revival structure fronts the entire west side of Union Square. Opened in 1904 as the St. Francis Hotel, it was commissioned by millionaire Charles Crocker as a stylish accommodation for visitors to the city. After the 1906 fire, Bliss & Faville rebuilt and enlarged the structure, which had previously occupied only half the block; the hotel resumed business in 1907. In the decades since, celebrities and dignitaries have favored the St. Francis for its sumptuous interior, its central location and its emphasis on service, which extends to washing the coins given as change in the intimate Compass Rose bar and tearoom.

Today the hotel's turn-of-the-century grandeur is most evident in the beautiful entrance hall, where coffered ceilings, marble-sheathed Corinthian columns and ornate balconies create a luxurious ambience. A local icon, the "Magneta" grandfather clock, is a favorite rendezvous point for San Francisco socialites. In 1972 a 32-story tower (William L. Pereira

2 The Compass Rose

Westin St. Francis Hotel. ☎ *415-774-0167.* Step up from the St. Francis' main lobby to this elegant salon, faithfully recreated from its 1904 design. High tea is the afternoon specialty here, served with scones, berries in Grand Marnier cream, petits fours and tea sandwiches. Pay high, just for the pleasure of receiving your change in freshly washed coins.

Assoc.) was added to the rear of the hotel. Visitors who brave the vertiginous ride up in its glass exterior **elevators**  are rewarded with expansive **views★★** of Union Square, the FINANCIAL DISTRICT and the BAY BRIDGE.

Continue south on Powell St. to Geary St. Turn right.

Theater District – Occupying the four-block area bounded by Sutter, Powell, Geary and Taylor Streets, San Francisco's theater district comprises about 10 venues ranging from spare, intimate houses to enormous, ornate, multibalconied palaces. Grandest among the latter are the **Geary Theater★** *(415 Geary St.)*, designed by Bliss & Faville in 1909, and the adjacent **Curran Theatre★** *(445 Geary St.)*, designed by Alfred Henry Jacobs in 1922. Both of them registered National Historic Landmarks, the Geary and the Curran were constructed of reinforced concrete in the Neoclassical style, the Geary's fancifully embellished terra-cotta columns and stolid exterior setting off the Curran's Romanesque arches and mansard roof. Home to the celebrated American Conservatory Theater since 1967, the Geary was closed in 1989-96 for renovation and seismic retrofitting after suffering structural damage in the Loma Prieta earthquake. The Curran Theatre has staged long-running Broadway shows since it opened. Nearby are the **Cable Car Theater (A)** *(450 Mason St.)* and the **Stage Door Theatre (B)** *(420 Mason St.)*, housed in the Native Sons Building; look for the medallion portraits of prominent California-born persons embedded in the building's facade. *Consult the Practical Information section (p 233) for more San Francisco and Bay Area theater listings and ticket information.*

3 The Redwood Room

Geary St. at Taylor St. in the Clift Hotel. ☎ 415-775-4700. A single redwood tree (felled by lightning) provided the 22ft columns and all the wood paneling for this hotel bar completed in 1934. Sip a cocktail beneath the gilded reproductions of Gustav Klimt artworks that adorn the walls, and let the streamlined Art Deco fixtures soothe your senses.

We welcome corrections and suggestions that may assist us in preparing the next edition. Please send us your comments:

Michelin Travel Publications
Editorial Department
P. O. Box 19001
Greenville, SC 29602-9001

8 • ALCATRAZ***

Time: 3 hours. Blue & Gold Fleet ferry from Fisherman's Wharf.
Map p 3

A mere 1.5mi from the comforts of San Francisco, this infamous 12-acre island, now inhabited by scores of seabirds who nest among its crumbling ruins, once held scores of prisoners incarcerated atop its sheer cliffs. Aptly nicknamed "The Rock" and isolated from shore by the cold, treacherous currents that swirl through the bay, Alcatraz served variously as a fortress, military prison and US Federal Penitentiary until its conversion to a national park and museum in 1972. A visit to Alcatraz provides a haunting journey into one of the harshest chapters of American judicial history.

Historical Notes

Military Days – The first Europeans to sight the barren island were Spanish explorers José de Cañizares and Juan Manuel de Ayala *(p 188)* in 1775. Noticing the large number of cormorants nesting on the cliffs, they named the rocky spot *Isla de los alcatraces*, or "island of gannets," because the roosting birds reminded them of similar fowl that inhabited the waterways of Spain. With no fresh water and little natural vegetation, the island remained uninhabited until President Millard Fillmore designated it a military reservation in 1850 following the US takeover of California. Its location at the mouth of the bay made it a natural choice for a fortress, and construction on a garrison began in 1853. Though cannons were mounted on the island, advancing military technology soon rendered them obsolete; not one was ever fired in defense. In 1861 Confederate sympathizers and renegade US soldiers were incarcerated at the garrison, and in the 1870s its walls held Native American prisoners from various Indian wars in California and the West. In 1901 the last cannons were dismantled, and six years later regular troops abandoned the island, to be replaced by members of the US Military Guard.

A "Super Prison" – Mounting costs and increasing protest over conditions in the prison led to the 1933 transfer of the property to the US Department of Justice, which established a federal penitentiary on the island. Banishment to the maximum security facility on Alcatraz was reserved for the most "desperate and irredeemable criminals" in the federal system, including those designated "public enemies" and deemed a danger to society, even behind bars. The ratio of one guard to every three prisoners, a strict "no talking" rule, brutal isolation cells and a near-impenetrable security system quickly established Alcatraz's reputation as America's bleakest prison. Notorious inhabitants of "the Rock" included Al "Scarface" Capone, George "Machine Gun" Kelly, Alvin "Creepy" Karpis, and Robert "Birdman" Stroud (who, contrary to popular lore, never kept birds here).

Over the years, 36 men tried to escape from Alcatraz in 14 separate attempts, all of them apparently unsuccessful. Some of the escapees were captured, some were shot, and some disappeared forever in the cold, swift currents of the bay. The most notorious attempt, in which three inmates disappeared in 1962 and were presumed drowned or eaten by sharks (they were never seen again), raised serious questions about the prison's deteriorated condition. That, combined with the high cost of maintenance and the complaints of San Franciscans worried about the less-than-secure prison in their bay, led to the decision to close Alcatraz. After the last inmates were transferred in 1963, the island fell vacant until 1969, when a group of Native Americans occupied it. Citing an 1868 treaty granting them the right to claim uninhabited federal land, the group began efforts to establish a Native American cultural enclave. The occupation ended 19 months later, its goals unrealized. On October 12, 1972, Alcatraz was designated part of the Golden Gate National Recreation Area.

VISIT

Kids *Blue & Gold Fleet ferry departs from Pier 41 May–Sept daily 9:30am–4:15pm every 30–45min. Rest of the year daily 9:30am–2:15pm every 30–45min. Closed Jan 1 & Dec 25. $11 including audiocassette (highly recommended). Guided tours and ranger talks are frequently offered, hours vary and are posted daily on the island. Alcatraz After Hours tours are offered Apr–Oct Thu–Sun 6:15pm & 7pm. Oct–Nov 4:15pm & 5pm. Rest of the year 4:15pm. $18.50 including audiocassette. Reservations should be made at least one week in advance by calling ☎ 415-705-5555.*

Note: Cold sea spray and strong winds often buffet the island, and pathways are rough. Wear protective clothing and strong, comfortable shoes. An Easy Access Program is available for the physically impaired. See ranger at entrance to island.

The ferry trip *(15min)* to the dock at Alcatraz offers stunning **views**★★ of the San Francisco skyline, the GOLDEN GATE BRIDGE and the imposing cliffs of the island. Graffiti from the Indian occupation can be spotted on the bluffs and dock buildings. At the ferry wharf, rangers provide an informative orientation near the landing, after which visitors are free to inspect the exhibit area on the lower floor of the Barracks Building (1867), view an **orientation video** *(12min)* in the theater, or climb the steep, switchback road past the ruins of the Post Exchange and Officers' Quarters to the cellhouse. Ranger-led talks and guided strolls in otherwise inaccessible parts of the island are occasionally offered; a list of the day's topics is available at the landing dock. Alcatraz After Hours offers a darker view of prison life: A haunting view of the city skyline, sometimes as it becomes obscured by fog, contributes to the sense of isolation inmates must have felt.

★★ **Cellhouse** – *Self-guided audiocassette tour available at cellhouse entrance.* While most of the island's buildings have been reduced to ruins and turned over to raucous flocks of seabirds, the forbidding cellhouse is intact enough to provide a chilling glimpse into the bleak life of the federal prisoners who were sentenced here. Built by convicts in 1911, it was, for a time, the largest reinforced concrete structure in the world.

Visitors enter the building near the bunker-like control center, formerly an arsenal of arms and tear gas. Beyond the control center lies the Visitation Area, where prisoners were separated from visitors by thick plate glass, and spoke over a monitored telephone. Once inside the cavernous main room, visitors can stroll down "Broadway," the wide central passage between B and C Blocks leading to "Times Square," and step into a cramped, cold cell furnished with a regulation army cot, a folding table and chair and a squat, open toilet. Prisoners who violated the strict rules of Alcatraz were subjected to solitary confinement in the dank isolation rooms, or "dark holes," of D Block. The tear-gas canisters in the ceiling of the mess hall at the rear of the building were never used. Access to the recreation yard and library, now open for exploration, was a privilege awarded for good behavior.

Several concrete paths lead around the perimeter of the island where wild blackberry brambles, California poppies and coyote brush grow. Most of the land is not accessible to the public. The main road to the cellhouse and the western road from the cellhouse to the base of the recreation yard exit remain open year round.

Main Cell Block, Alcatraz Federal Prison (1956)

9 • THE EMBARCADERO★

Time: 3 hours. MUNI bus 6–Parnassus, 7–Haight, 8–Market, 9–San Bruno, 14–Mission, 21–Hayes, 31–Balboa, 32–Embarcadero or 71–Noriega; all streetcars Embarcadero station. BART Embarcadero station.
Map p 147

A waterfront promenade stretching some three miles from FISHERMAN'S WHARF to China Basin, the Embarcadero ("boarding place" in Spanish) combines expansive views of the bay with public artworks, educational installations and recently built or renovated office and residential complexes to form one of the city's newest and most engaging public spaces.

Historical Notes

Port of Call – The vibrant hub of San Francisco's shipping and transportation industries from the Gold Rush until the 1950s, the Embarcadero took shape in the 1850s when landfill extended the shore from its natural line along present-day Montgomery Street. As San Francisco boomed through the late 19C, sailors, longshoremen and warehouse workers frequented the increasingly rowdy area, patronizing a growing number of gambling dens and union halls. Steamships, schooners and whalers embarked from the docks on commercial runs for shipping enterprises such as the Pacific Mail Steamship Company and the Alaska Packers.

Ferries from points across the bay began docking here before the turn of the century, and the waterfront swarmed with daily commuters until 1936, when rail service and auto lanes over the San Francisco-Oakland Bay Bridge siphoned away ferry traffic. Through the mid-20C, the Embarcadero's piers, rail yards and warehouses fell into disuse as shippers gradually transferred their activities across the bay to the better-equipped Port of Oakland.

In the early 1950s work began on the controversial **Embarcadero Freeway**, planned as a link between the Bay Bridge and the GOLDEN GATE BRIDGE. Dominating the shoreline and blocking views of the Ferry Building and the bay, the elevated viaduct greatly diminished the waterfront's appeal, arousing San Franciscans' ire. Construction had reached Broadway before massive protest halted progress in 1959. By the late 1970s the Embarcadero south of Broadway had deteriorated in the shadow of the massive concrete roadbed. When the freeway was razed after being damaged in the 1989 Loma Prieta earthquake, revitalization efforts began in earnest.

A New Beginning – Ongoing redevelopment projects are now revitalizing this historic area with new public spaces, residential and commercial complexes and public art projects. Extending 3.2mi from Fisherman's Wharf to China Basin is **Herb Caen Way ...★**, a promenade named for the popular late *San Francisco Chronicle* columnist whose trademark ellipses punctuated many a morning read from 1938 to 1996. This long ribbon of sidewalk draws visitors, residents and swarms of joggers to enjoy glorious views of the bay, the Bay Bridge and the towers of the FINANCIAL DISTRICT and SOUTH OF MARKET. Placed at intervals along the walkway, attractive striped pylons bearing interpretive text and photographs draw visitors into colorful stories about aspects of local history. Fishermen gather at the end of **Pier 7** *(near Broadway)* with its old-fashioned wrought-iron railings and park benches, creaky wooden planking and expansive views of the bay and the city.

"What is this mysterious amalgam that keeps on working? There is no plan, certainly, and never was. It is almost in the realm of the metaphysical: a brew of gold rushes and silver bonanzas, sailing ships and shrouded dawns, overnight fortunes and brilliant disasters, bootleg gin, champagne suppers, minestrone and Peking Duck, new-old, beautiful-ugly—a city like no other, sea-girt, Bay-blocked and wide open to the winds and the wildest ideas, none so wild that an audience can't be found. Sometimes tacky, sometimes tawdry, often dirty and too often heedless——and yet, even in the current explosion of Plastic Inevitable, strong enough in personality to anthropomorphize: San Francisco lives!"

San Francisco Chronicle **columnist Herb Caen (1967)**

Other new additions include the **Promenade Ribbon**, a linear sculpture made of concrete and glass block, illuminated at night with a fiber-optic cable; Canary Island date-palm trees towering above the Embarcadero meridian; and elegant, double-torch street lamps. South of the Ferry Building, brick warehouses and factories of the onetime waterfront industrial belt are reborn as residential and office spaces, some with trendy eateries. **Hills Plaza**, with its distinctive brick tower, is a noteworthy example; erected in 1924, it originally housed the headquarters for Hills Brothers Coffee Company. New commercial and residential complexes enliven the west side of the Embarcadero from the Bay Bridge to attractive **South Beach Park**, anchored by Mark diSuvero's towering abstract sculpture **Sea Change (1)**.

A transit center is scheduled for completion in 2000 near the Ferry Building, where the historic F-Market trolley line *(p 54)* will turn northward along the Embarcadero toward Fisherman's Wharf. In addition, a new baseball stadium is slated to be ready that same spring at China Basin, the Embarcadero's southern boundary.

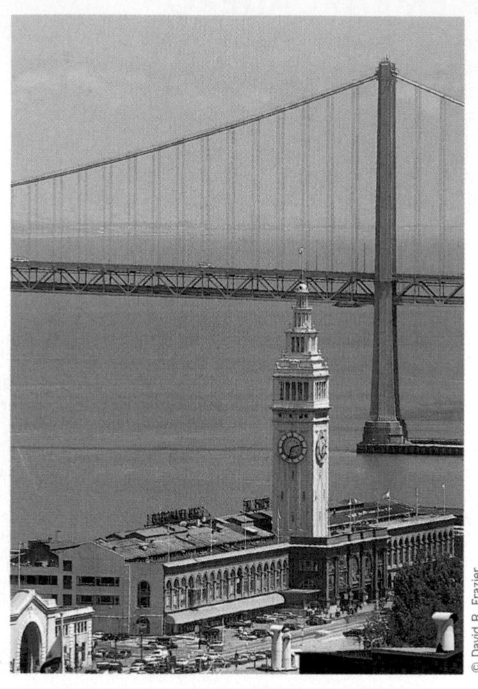
© David R. Frazier

Ferry Building and Bay Bridge

SIGHTS

★★ **Ferry Building** – *Embarcadero at Market St.* Though its status as San Francisco's signature landmark has been supplanted by the Golden Gate Bridge and other monuments, the handsome Ferry Building remains one of the city's beloved historical markers. Designed by A. Page Brown of Colusa sandstone and anchored on 111 steel-framed concrete piers, the building was hailed at its dedication in 1898 as the most solidly constructed edifice in California, a claim that was roundly proved when it survived the great earthquake of 1906 with only its exterior stones loosened. The Ferry Building's 235ft clock tower, designed by Willis Polk, was inspired by the Giralda Tower on the Cathedral of Seville and boasts four huge (and accurate) clock faces.

Until completion of the Golden Gate and Bay Bridges in the late 1930s, the Ferry Building served as San Francisco's main transportation hub. An estimated 50 million people passed through it annually, commuters from Marin County and the East Bay, long-distance travelers from the transcontinental railroad terminus in OAKLAND. In 1956, after ferry traffic declined, the northern half of the structure was converted into office space, and in 1962 the southern half was remodeled to house government agencies.

Today the World Trade Center occupies the north half of the Ferry Building. On its first floor is the small **International Children's Art Museum (M¹)** Kids *(open year-round Mon–Fri 11am–5pm, Sat 10am–4pm; closed major holidays; $1; ☎ 415-772-9977)*. From a permanent collection of more than 4,000 works by children 3 to 18 living in 100-plus countries, rotating exhibits display art with such subjects as fairy tales, foods, festivals, animals and environment. All of these themes were proposed by Paintbrush Diplomacy, an exchange of art and writing between American and foreign students that grew from the museum's seed, the Pribuss Collection of children's art. In the main gallery, a 6ft-by-7ft chalkboard and accompanying basket of chalk entice visiting children to record their own fleeting works of art.

Stroll behind the building to the wooden sundeck, where commuter ferries still depart for Sausalito and Larkspur in Marin County. Just north, another ferry offers service to Alameda, Oakland, Tiburon and Vallejo. The tranquil monument to Mohandas K. Gandhi **(2)** was donated to the city in 1988. The pier behind Gabbiano's restaurant offers sweeping **views★** of the Bay Bridge and Yerba Buena and Treasure Islands.

1 Farmers' Markets

Green St. at The Embarcadero. ☎ 415-981-3004. Every Saturday morning, rain or shine, Bay Area organic farmers, bakers, cheese makers, pasta makers, fishmongers and florists gather to sell their wares. Chef tours, live music and cooking demonstrations are regular fixtures on the scene, as are seasonal fruit festivals and holiday celebrations. A Tuesday Farmers Market *(11am-3pm)* is held opposite the Ferry Building in Justin Herman Plaza.

★ **Rincon Center** – *101 Spear St. Open daily year-round.* ✂ ♿ P ☎ *415-777-4100.* This multistory shopping and residential complex (1989), a block south and west of the Ferry Building, boasts a panoply of stores and cafes. The former Rincon Annex Post Office (1940, Gilbert S. Underwood), which now functions as the center's **lobby**, remains its most gripping feature. Especially worthy of note are Russian-born artist Anton Refregier's **murals★** depicting Northern California's rough-and-tumble history, beginning with the arrival of Sir Francis Drake in 1579 and ending with

World War II. Completed in 1948 and rendered in broad, muscular strokes and bold colors that underscore Refregier's thematic emphasis on labor, struggle and war, these 27 panels provide an unsparing view of the wild West. Adjacent display cases present historical artifacts and photographs that further address Refregier's themes. In the lofty atrium off the lobby, an 85ft **Rain Column** (1988, Doug Hollis) forms the eye-catching centerpiece of a spacious food court.

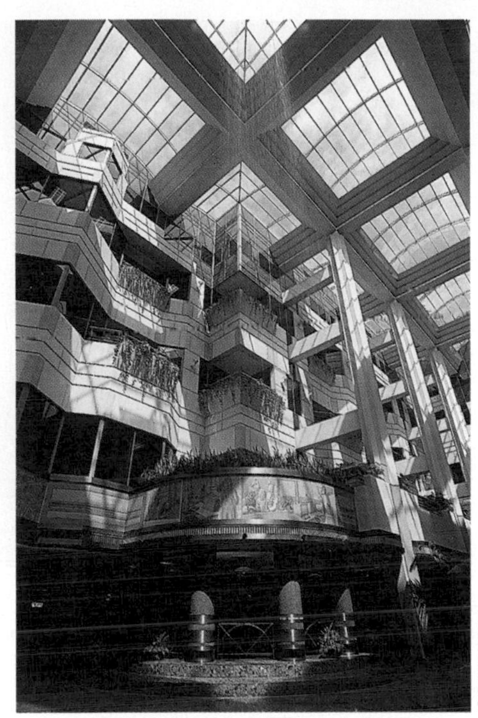
© Robert Holmes

Rain Column, Rincon Center

★ **SS Jeremiah O'Brien** – Kids *Pier 32. Open year-round daily 9am–4pm. Closed Jan 1, Thanksgiving Thu & Fri, Dec 24, 25 & 31. $5.* P *☎ 415-441-3101. From mid-June to mid-September, the O'Brien may berth next to the USS Pampanito at Pier 45, Fisherman's Wharf; call to confirm hours & location.* Occupying an isolated mooring south of the Bay Bridge, this noble gray vessel formed part of the 5,000-ship armada that stormed Normandy Beach on D-Day in 1944. Launched on June 19, 1943, she was one of a fleet of 2,751 Liberty Ships that served as the backbone of the supply line to US armed forces in Europe and the Pacific during World War II. Lovingly restored and maintained by a crew of volunteers, the ship remains unaltered and fully operational. Self-guided tours cover all areas of the vessel, including the wheelhouse, engine room, crew's quarters, deckside guns and ship's store. On "steaming weekends" *(3rd weekend Jan–Apr, Jun–Sept & Nov)*, the crew fires up her triple-expansion steam engines, used in the blockbuster movie *Titanic* to replicate the engines of that ill-fated luxury liner. The O'Brien also welcomes visitors on all-day cruises of San Francisco Bay several times a year.

2 **Red's Java House**

Pier 40, The Embarcadero (between Townsend & Berry Sts.) ☎ 415-495-7260. This tiny shack on the pier beside the South Beach yacht harbor recalls a time when longshoremen stopped in for burgers, beers and strong coffee. Pick up a tasty, dirt-cheap cheeseburger or tuna sandwich, settle down on a stool and get a taste of colorful, workaday San Francisco.

ADDITIONAL SIGHTS

★★ **San Francisco-Oakland Bay Bridge** – *Open daily year-round. $2 toll westbound only from Oakland. Nonvehicular crossing of the bridge prohibited. www.dot.ca.gov ☎ 510-286-4444.* Though often overshadowed by the celebrity of the Golden Gate Bridge, this double-deck engineering marvel is a distinctive and beloved landmark in its own right. Begun in 1933 to alleviate traffic on the transbay ferries, which shuttled some 6 million cars between San Francisco and the East Bay, the project was financed by a $77 million federal loan during the nadir of the Great Depression. Engineers Charles H. Purcell, Charles E. Andrew and Glenn B. Woodruff joined forces with architect Timothy Pflueger to design the bridge, which had to cross 8.4mi of water—Including approaches, its span is nearly eight times that of the Golden Gate.

To traverse the distance, the bridge was conceived as two structures meeting at Yerba Buena Island, a rocky promontory midway across the bay. The western section, comprising two 2,310ft suspension bridges, joins San Francisco and the island. The roadway hangs suspended from steel cables draped between four distinctive X-braced towers; a concrete pier rises 48 stories from the floor of the bay to anchor the two suspension bridges in the center. The eastern section, joining Yerba Buena Island and Oakland, is a cantilever-truss design—the roadway rests

Bay Bridge and Financial District from Yerba Buena Island

on steel-and-concrete piers joined by a network of steel beams. Between the two sections, a tunnel pierces Yerba Buena Island; 76ft wide and 58ft high, its diameter may be the largest of any vehicular tunnel in the world.

Completed in November 1936, the bridge carried trains on its lower level and cars on its upper level for two decades. Today each deck bears five lanes of automobile traffic. Travelers on the westbound upper deck enjoy glorious **views**★ of the Financial District and the Embarcadero as they approach the city.

★**Treasure Island** – *1hr. Take I-80 east across the Bay Bridge; exit at Treasure Island/Yerba Buena Island exit and proceed to main gate.* Lying in San Francisco Bay midway between San Francisco and Oakland, this flat, man-made terrain was constructed in 1938 to host a world fair. The 400-acre island offers stupendous panoramic views as well as charming insights into a sometimes-overlooked chapter of San Francisco history.

The Pageant of the Pacific – As work on the Bay Bridge and the Golden Gate Bridge drew to a close, San Francisco boosters began planning a world fair to celebrate and to advertise the city's emergence from the Great Depression. For the fair site, the Army Corps of Engineers set to work creating an artificial island north of Yerba Buena Island, constructing a rectangular seawall and filling the space with bay dredgings and rubble excavated from the Bay Bridge tunnel. The city intended to locate its new airport on the site after the fair closed.

Opened on February 18, 1939, the **Golden Gate International Exposition of 1939-1940** drew more than 17 million visitors during its two-year run. In all, 36 nations and 31 states participated in the fair, themed "The Pageant of the Pacific" to prompt awareness of trade potential with Pacific Basin nations. Pan American Airways moved its then-innovative **China Clipper** seaplanes—offering passenger flights to Asia—from nearby Alameda to Treasure Island between 1939 and 1944, and visitors reveled in an extravaganza of exotic, Asian-inspired, Art Deco buildings and sculptures designed by a team of architects including Timothy Pflueger, Arthur Brown, Jr. and Lewis P. Hobart.

World War II brought an abrupt end to the jubilant celebration of Pacific relations. Most of the fair structures were demolished and the island became a naval training center for the duration of the conflict. By 1945, aerospace technology had so advanced that new aircraft required runways longer than Treasure Island could provide, and the city leased the site to the US Navy in exchange for land on the peninsula (site of present-day San Francisco International Airport). Naval Station Treasure Island operated at this scenic location from World War II until it closed in September 1997.

Today, while the City of San Francisco and the US Navy haggle over the island's uncertain future, public access is limited. The causeway at the gated entry area still affords a sweeping **view**★★★ over the city, encompassing, from south to north, the suspension portion of the Bay Bridge, the San Francisco skyline and backdrop hills, the Golden Gate and ALCATRAZ, MOUNT TAMALPAIS and Marin County, ANGEL ISLAND and finally the North Bay with the Richmond-San Rafael Bridge. Officials express hope that the Art Deco-style **Treasure Island Museum** (1937, George Kelham) and visitors center, once intended to be the main San Francisco airport terminal, will reopen by 2001.

10 • FISHERMAN'S WHARF★★★

Time: 1 day. Powell-Hyde or Powell-Mason. Muni bus 19–Polk, 30–Stockton, 32–Embarcadero, 39–Coit or 44–Downtown Loop (Red Arrow).
Map pp 82–83

San Francisco's vibrant and colorful maritime legacy survives in this bustling and extremely popular district extending along the shoreline between TELEGRAPH HILL and FORT MASON. Amid the historic sailing ships and converted piers and factories are a working fleet of fishing boats, a pod of vociferous and amusing sea lions and scores of boutiques and souvenir shops. Street performers and sidewalk seafood stands add to the carnival atmosphere along Jefferson Street, while quiet piers and unobstructed views of Alcatraz Island, Marin County and the GOLDEN GATE BRIDGE make the wharf's western end one of the loveliest spots on San Francisco's waterfront.

Historical Notes

A Working Wharf – In 1853, **Henry "Honest Harry" Meiggs**, councilman, entrepreneur and later the most notorious embezzler of public funds in the city's early history, constructed a wharf extending 1,600ft from present-day Francisco and Powell Streets across North Point Cove into the bay. From its inception, Meiggs' wharf was an important center of industry. The ferry terminal to SAUSALITO was located at its far end, and a sawmill, a pipe works and a junk shop crowded its length. Shipbuilding flourished on the sands of NORTH BEACH, and visitors came down to the wharf to enjoy stunning bay views and the cheap beer, cracked crab and hot chowder at institutions like Paddy Gleason's Saloon and Abe Warner's Cobweb Palace.

Sidewalk Seafood

A stroll along the north side of Jefferson Street between Jones and Taylor Streets leads through a symphony of smells and tastes whose overriding note is fresh seafood. The tradition of eating outdoors on the wharf dates from the beginning of this century, when Italian fishermen returning from early morning runs grabbed steaming bowls of chowder from sidewalk stands before hurrying off to sell the day's catch. In 1916, Tomaso Castagnola began offering walkaway crab cocktails to tourists who came down to see the colorful fishing fleet. His success led Italian fishing families to set up their own steaming pots along the wharf from which they sold freshly cooked Dungeness crab. Even the opening of large, full-service restaurants in the 1930s could not diminish the popularity of the sidewalk stands. Today, a ladle of creamy clam chowder in a hollowed-out loaf of sourdough bread has become a mandatory part of the San Francisco experience. Fresh crab, flown in daily when it is out of season here, continues to be the major attraction, and many of the crab sellers make a rhythmic show of cracking the sweet crustacean's 10 legs. Although nontraditional items such as pizza have recently appeared, the best fare on the wharf still comes from the sea, including shrimp or crab salad sandwiches on crusty sourdough rolls, freshly steamed Pacific rock lobster, prawn and crab cocktails, oysters, crab cakes, and an assortment of fried squid, fish and clams.

In the 1860s, North Point Cove from Bay Street to the current shoreline was filled with rock blasted from the eastern face of Telegraph Hill, creating a flat stretch of land that became a manufacturing and industrial zone. A multitude of factories opened along the shore, including the Selby Lead and Smelting Works and the Pioneer Woolen Mill (later site of the Ghirardelli Chocolate Factory). Several railroads and piers were also built to serve the growing industries.

Home of the Pescatori – During the city's early years, fishermen tied up at several wharves along Vallejo, Green, Union and Filbert Streets. The 1872 legislation that authorized the construction of COLUMBUS AVENUE also directed the State Board of Harbor Commissioners to designate the Union Street Wharf "for the sole and exclusive use of the fishermen of the city." Development of downtown shipping zones, however, forced the fishermen to move twice: first in 1885 to the Filbert Street Wharf, and again in 1900 to their present home at the foot of Taylor Street.

Even before the fleet found its permanent mooring, Italians had established a virtual monopoly in all aspects of the fishing industry. After anti-Chinese legislation in the 1870s *(p 15)* restricted commercial opportunities for the Asians, who previously had dominated the fishing industry, Genoese immigrants took to the seas and became the largest ethnic group on the bay. Over time, the Genoese fishermen (*pescatori* in Italian) were outnumbered by their compatriots from Naples, Calabria and Sicily. Today descendants of Sicilians dominate Fisherman's Wharf, from the fishing boats that continue to depart from here to the wildly popular restaurants and sidewalk seafood stands that bear the names of their prominent Italian-American founders.

Through the first half of the 20C, fishing remained a major industry. As maritime technology became more efficient, however, the bay and surrounding waters were overfished, forcing the boats to move farther and farther beyond the Golden Gate or to relocate altogether. By the 1950s the fleet's numbers had been severely reduced, and large sections of the old industrial zone had become rundown or abandoned.

Tidal Wave of Tourism – The opening of the National Maritime Museum *(p 87)* in 1951 marked the beginning of the northern waterfront's rebirth as the city's most popular tourist destination. The area boomed in the 1960s when visionary developers began purchasing historic properties such as the California Fruit Canners Association building and the old Ghirardelli Chocolate Factory, converting them into architectural and commercial showpieces.

In years since, burgeoning tourism has sparked an explosion of related businesses, few of them linked to the maritime legacy that makes the wharf such an interesting place to visit. Brightly lit T-shirt shops and souvenir stands line the south side of Jefferson Street along with several novelty museums. Street performers often block the already-crowded sidewalks with their mime and magic shows, juggling acts and music. Large shopping complexes like The Anchorage and Cost Plus Imports share the once-industrial bayfill blocks with wharfside seafood establishments that, while not usually considered "fine dining," provide fun-filled and scenic settings for dinner.

Through the glitter and the glitz, much of the area retains its salty flavor of old. As the San Francisco Bay fishery has resurged in number and variety, the number of fishing boats has likewise grown. Visitors who step off the main path will discover a series of working, albeit less-active piers, fabulous views of the bay and several evocative monuments to the city's maritime past.

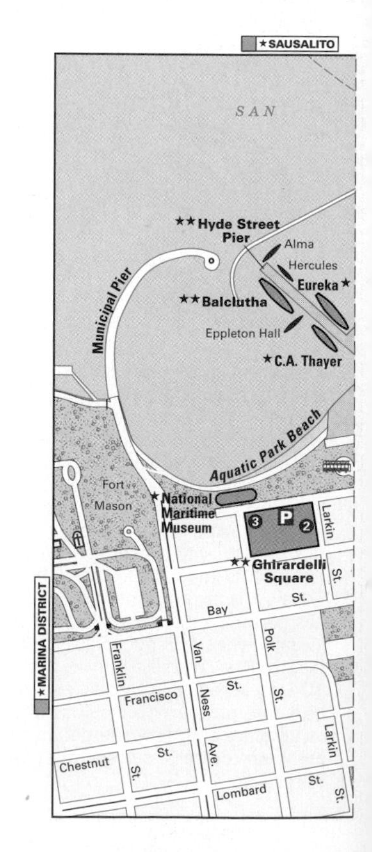

Visiting Fisherman's Wharf – In summer and on most weekends throughout the year, massive crowds make movement on the sidewalks difficult, especially on the south side of Jefferson Street. During peak tourist seasons, tours to Alcatraz are often booked as far in advance as a week; it's best to reserve as early as possible. In winter, when crab fishing is in full swing, the wharf is at its most interesting and least congested. Public transportation is the best way to get here. Traffic is especially congested during construction of the F-Market historic trolley line, scheduled for completion in early 2000 *(p 54)*. Street parking in the area is scarce and meters are limited to two hours;

regulations are enforced every day, including Sundays and holidays. Several well-marked lots along Jefferson between Taylor and Powell, and a large garage across from Pier 39 *(Beach St. between Stockton and Powell Sts.)* are expensive and often full. Other garages lie within the Anchorage Shopping Center *(Jones St. between Jefferson and Beach Sts.)*, Ghirardelli Square *(entrances from Beach St. or Larkin St.)* and Cost Plus Imports *(entrance on Taylor St.)*.

Ferries for SAUSALITO, TIBURON AND ANGEL ISLAND leave from Pier 43 1/2. Check the signs carefully, as ferry operators also offer scenic bay cruises *(p 84)* that depart from this pier. A $2 million public ferry terminal at Pier 43, slated to open in 2000, will serve commuters to Vallejo.

The Blessing of the Fleet takes place the first weekend of October each year with a solemn procession from the SS. Peter and Paul Church *(p 64)*.

SIGHTS

★**Pier 39** – Kids Built over a dilapidated turn-of-the-century pier, this festive, bi-level marketplace of shops and amusements ranks among the top tourist destinations in the state. On either side of its central passage lie rugged buildings covered with planks salvaged from Piers 3 and 34 prior to their reconstruction. After the Port of San Francisco lost its shipping supremacy to Oakland in the 1970s, Pier 39 was nearly demolished, but an ambitious redevelopment (1978) attracted all manner of shops from video arcades and novelty stores to confectioneries, clothing boutiques and seafood restaurants. A brightly painted, two-tiered carousel anchors the far end of the complex, and performers regularly take the stage behind it to entertain thousands of daily visitors.

A two-story, IMAX-style cinema mounts screenings of two **films:** *The Great San Francisco Adventure* and *The Living Sea (year-round daily 10am–9:15pm; $7.50 for one, $10 for two; shows every 45min;* ✂ ♿ P *$5.50/hr* ☎ *415-956-3456).* The former film *(30min, 15 times daily)* presents a humorous overview of the city's rough-and-tumble history featuring characters from its past and present, while *The Living Sea (40min, daily 10am only)* explores man's relationship with the marine environment.

Adding to Pier 39's carnival atmosphere, a group of wild California **sea lions**★ occupies the docks off its west side. Informal interpretive talks on the creatures are offered by volunteers from the **Marine Mammal Center** *(year-round weekends 11am–5pm;* ☎ *415-705-5500).* The reason for the sea lions' arrival here in 1990

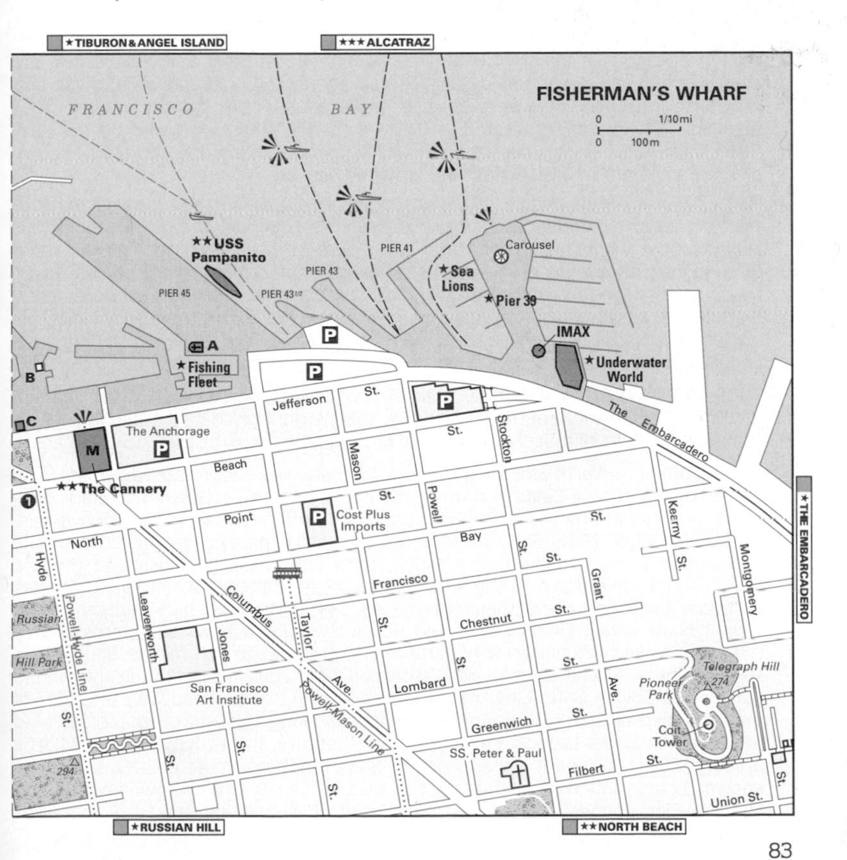

is a mystery, but it is thought that they are members of the same colony that inhabits Seal Rocks, near CLIFF HOUSE. Their raucous barking can be heard from as far away as the top of Telegraph Hill. A walk along the outer edge of the pier gives visitors a privileged view of the clowning sea lions, Alcatraz *(p 75)* and the BAY BRIDGE.

★**Underwater World** – Kids *Open Memorial Day–Labor Day daily 9am–9pm. Rest of the year daily 10am–8:30pm. Closed Dec 25. $12.95 ($15.95 includes IMAX movie).* ♿ *www.underwaterworld.com* ☎ *415-623-5300.* Visitors here may enter and view the undersea world up close. Following a short video presentation and stroll through a selection of Northern California marine habitats, visitors descend via an ersatz "diving bell" to traverse two main tanks by way of a 300ft acrylic **tunnel**. Audiocassette players provide narration as visitors stand on a slow-moving walkway or hop off to fully experience the gripping sensation of seeing a shark or ray glide overhead.

★**Bay Cruises** – Kids A scenic cruise on San Francisco Bay offers visitors a new perspective of the city, from a peek at the underside of the Golden Gate Bridge to wide, glorious **views**★ of steep hills and imposing skyline. From the vantage point of the bay, visitors can learn about the history of San Francisco and get a glimpse of the waterfront as a busy, working port. The Blue and Gold Fleet's **Bay Cruise** *(depart from Pier 39 May–Sept daily 10am–6:45pm; rest of the year daily 10am–4pm; round-trip 1hr; commentary; $17;* ✗ ♿ P *www.blueandgoldfleet.com* ☎ *415-705-5555)* travels west along the shoreline, circles beneath the Golden Gate Bridge and passes very close to the north side of Alcatraz on the return, accompanied by English-language narration.The Red and White Fleet's **Golden Gate Bridge Cruise** *(depart from Pier 43 1/2 Memorial Day–early Nov daily 10am–6:15pm; rest of the year daily 10am–5pm; round-trip 1hr; commentary; $16;* ✗ ♿ P *www.redandwhite.com* ☎ *415-447-0597)* follows a similar route; individual headsets broadcast a well-produced narrative (available in six languages) that uses a combination of historical and dramatic voices, plus authentic sound effects, to tell the story of the sights passed on the cruise.

★★**USS Pampanito** – Kids *Pier 45. Open Memorial Day–Labor Day daily 9am–8pm. Rest of the year daily 9am–6pm (Fri & Sat 8pm). $7. www.maritime.org* ☎ *415-775-1943.* A World War II, Balao-class submarine built in the Portsmouth naval shipyard in 1943, this deep-diving, 311ft vessel made a half-dozen patrols during her two years of service in the Pacific, sinking six Japanese ships and damaging four others. In September 1944, the *Pampanito* and two other submarines jointly attacked a convoy of Japanese ships in the South China Sea carrying oil, raw rubber and other war supplies. After sinking several ships, the three subs pursued the surviving vessels out of the area. When the *Pampanito* returned a few days later, the crew spotted men clinging to pieces of wreckage; the 73 rescued were British and Australian prisoners of war who had been aboard the sunken vessels. That number—73—is commemorated on the *Pampanito*'s flag, displayed on the pier. Other informative panels describe the workings of a submarine and tell the story of the *Pampanito*'s construction and wartime service.

Visit – *Note: a certain degree of physical agility is required to slip through the submarine's narrow corridors and small hatches.* The haunting, self-guided audio tour begins on the submarine's upper deck and moves from the rear (aft) torpedo room through the maneuvering room, engine rooms, galley, control room and officers' quarters to the cramped forward torpedo room, where members of the crew slept beside the massive weapons. A former commander of the sub narrates the audio tour, his matter-of-fact voice and understated descriptions effectively conveying the claustrophobia, fear and boredom that faced those who signed on for submarine duty.

★**SS Jeremiah O'Brien** – *Pier 45. Description p 79.* Moored most of the year on the Embarcadero south of the Bay Bridge, this World War II Liberty Ship may berth from mid-June to mid-September (as it did in 1998) next to the *USS Pampanito.*

★**Fishing Fleet** – *North side of Jefferson St. between Jones and Taylor Sts.* The small, colorful fishing boats tied up at the docks just off Jefferson Street are remnants of an active and successful fleet that once numbered more than 450 vessels. Names like *Pico, Nina, San Giuseppe* and *Angelina*, painted on the sides of the boats, bear witness to the Italian roots of the city's fishing industry. In the late 19C, visitors came down to the wharf (then located at the foot of Filbert Street) to watch fishermen mend their nets or set sail in their sky-blue feluccas, lightweight boats with triangular sails and delicately pointed bows and sterns. Today the boats leave their berths very early in the morning to fish for rex and petrale sole, sea bass, mackerel, sand dab, rock cod, ling cod and herring in the waters outside the Golden Gate. Early-morning visitors will be rewarded with the sight of the fishermen returning to unload their catches along this and other piers behind the Jefferson Street Lagoon. For more than a century, this activity was the wharf's primary attraction, and it remains one of San Francisco's more evocative, if lesser known, sights. Although most of the fish sold in the city is now flown and trucked in, 20 million pounds of seafood still come into this port annually.

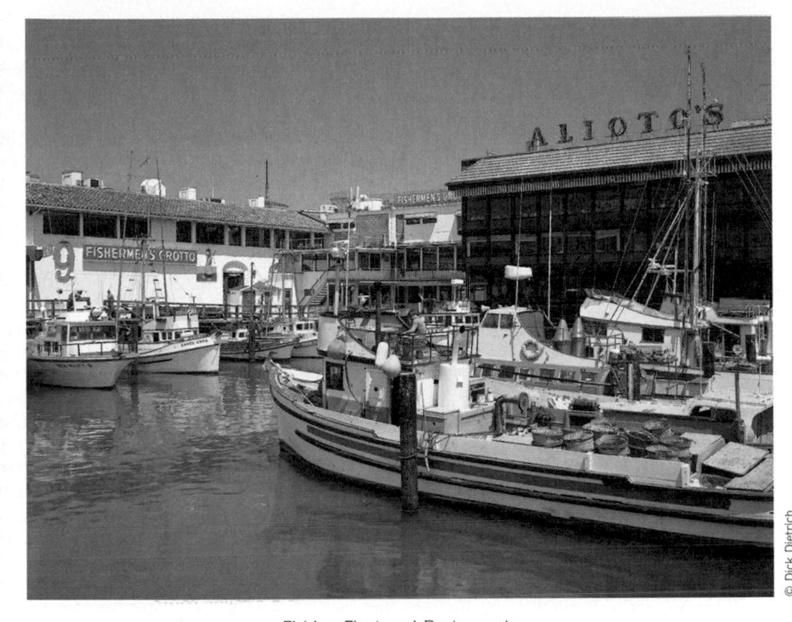

© Dick Dietrich

Fishing Fleet and Restaurants

A small, simple building of dark brown wood with a stained-glass ship's wheel over its door rests at the western foot of Pier 45. Erected in 1980 by the Fisherman's Wharf community, this **Fishermen's and Seamen's Memorial Chapel (A)** *(☎ 415-626-7070)* remains truly ecumenical, hosting christenings, bar mitzvahs, Latin masses, Buddhist memorials and weddings of all sorts.

★★**The Cannery** – *2801 Leavenworth St. at Jefferson St. Open year-round Mon–Wed 10am–6pm, Thu–Sat 10am–8:30pm, Sun & holidays 11am–6pm. ✗ ♿ www.thecannery.com ☎ 415-771-3112.* Anchoring the west end of Jefferson Street, this airy, light-filled shopping complex belies its industrial origins. Built in 1907 as a packing plant for the California Fruit Canners Association, the building housed the most productive peach-canning operation in the world from 1916 to 1937. Rough economic times during the Great Depression forced the owner, Del Monte, to close the plant, and for the next two decades the building was used mainly as a warehouse. The handsome brick structure was saved from demolition when a local developer purchased the property in 1963.

Today the four external brick walls are all that remain of the original structure. The interior, completed in 1967, reveals a seamless modern design of open stairwells, bridges, spacious courtyards and meandering passageways lined with more than three dozen boutiques, restaurants and gourmet shops. On sunny days, the courtyard on the west side is one of the most pleasant spots in the neighborhood to relax with a cold drink and listen to the various street musicians who perform here. Open-air escalators and a modern glass elevator take visitors to the top floor, where **views** sweep over the bay and the Marin County shoreline. The Jacobean carved fireplace, intricate plaster ceiling and oak paneling in **Jack's Cannery Bar** on the ground floor date from 1609, and once belonged to the estate of newspaper tycoon William Randolph Hearst.

Museum of the City of San Francisco (M) – *3rd floor. Open year-round Wed–Sun 10am–4pm. Closed Jan 1, Jul 4 & Dec 25. $2 contribution requested. ✗ ♿ www.sfmuseum.org ☎ 415-928-0289.* Opened in 1991 and named the official history museum of the city in 1995, this small but growing archive maintains a fine collection of photos and memorabilia of the 1906 earthquake and fire (pictures from the 1989 Loma Prieta temblor also are on view), along with changing displays of artifacts from various eras of the city's history. Glance up to see the hand-carved 13C Byzantine ceiling from the Palacio de Altamira in Toledo, Spain, acquired from the Hearst estate.

Across a passageway, the associated small **Museum of Motion Picture Technology** houses a fascinating assortment of vintage film projectors, the earliest dating from 1904. *(Open on an irregular schedule; inquire at the City Museum for tour arrangements.)*

★★**Hyde Street Pier** – Kids *Open year-round daily 9:30am–5pm. Closed Jan 1, Thanksgiving Day, Dec 25. $4. www.maritime.org/safrhome.shtml ☎ 415-556-3002.* The historic ships and maritime artifacts on display at this long wooden pier evoke the era when San Francisco was an active and bustling port, and the sea the city's most important avenue of trade and transportation. Built as a ferry terminal in the years before construction of the Golden Gate and Bay Bridges, the Hyde Street Pier eventually became the mooring for six historic ships purchased and restored by the San Francisco Maritime Museum. The pier is now part of the **San Francisco Maritime National Historical Park**, which maintains what may be the largest historic fleet afloat. In addition to its six ships—all but one of which may be boarded and explored—the pier houses a turn-of-the-century "ark" (a flat-bottomed houseboat that served as a summer retreat on the bay), the 1850s-era office of Tubbs Cordage, several old tug boats and a small **boat shop (B)** that offers lessons in boat building and restoration. Demonstrations of seafaring skills are occasionally presented. The **Maritime Store (C)** at the entrance provides information about the park, and offers a vast array of books on maritime subjects.

★**Eureka** – *Right side of pier.* This enormous sidewheel ferry, built in 1890 and still the world's largest wooden floating structure, could carry up to 2,300 commuters at a time. Originally named the *Ukiah*, the ship served as a railroad-car ferry until 1922, when she was rebuilt as the Eureka and launched as a passenger and auto ferry between Sausalito and San Francisco. After 1941 the *Eureka* plied the waters on the Oakland-San Francisco run until her giant walking-beam engine snapped in 1957. Today, visitors can sit on the restored commuter benches, wander the massive decks or operate a model walking-beam that stands beside the actual four-story, steam-powered engine. The ferry, which underwent a $2.7 million restoration in 1994, has since been used as a stage set (a floating police station) for the TV show *Nash Bridges*.

★**C.A. Thayer** – *Across from the Eureka.* Built in 1895 to haul logs of heavy Douglas fir between Washington and California, this venerable, three-masted wooden sailing schooner is one of only two such ships in the country (the other, the *Wawona*, is berthed in Seattle). Her single deck, open hold, shallow draft and relatively wide beam enabled her small crew to hold the 156ft craft steady in shallow, turbulent coves called "dogholes" as timber was loaded from the bluffs above. The *C.A. Thayer* served as a codfisher in 1925-31 and again 1946-50. In the intervening years, she was used by the army as a barge to store empty shells from target practice at sea. Visitors who now descend into the ship's hold find themselves in a dark cave, its walls worn smooth by many loads of rubbing logs. Just above are the handsome captain's quarters and adjacent formal dining room. In the forecastle, a video *(11min)* recounts the story of the ship's last voyage. Deckhands in period costume often introduce the boat to groups of schoolchildren; sea chanteys are sung on board the first Saturday night of each month.

★★**Balclutha** – *End of pier on the left.* Looming majestically over the pier, virtually sparkling after a $1.5 million overhaul completed in June 1998, this three-masted, steel-hulled square-rigger was launched in Glasgow in 1886, eventually rounding

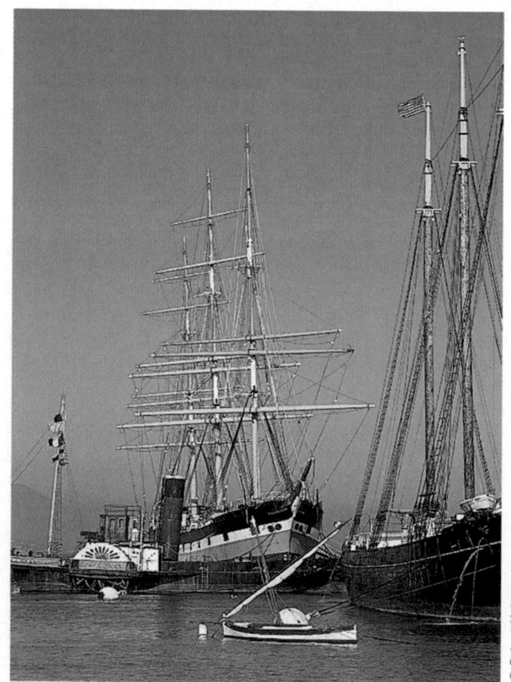

© Robert Holmes

Eppleton Hall, Balclutha and C.A. Thayer

Cape Horn 17 times on voyages between Europe and California. A deep-sea cargo vessel measuring 301ft, the *Balclutha* carried wine, spirits, hardware and coal from European ports to San Francisco, returning to the continent loaded with California wheat. In 1904 her owners based her in San Francisco and she began a long career in the salmon industry, running cannery supplies and workers between Alaska and California. A promoter bought the ship in 1933, renamed her the *Pacific Queen*, and displayed her in various West Coast ports as a "pirate" ship. Following this ignominious stage of her career, she came to rest on the Marin mud flats, a near wreck. In 1954 the National Maritime Museum purchased and refurbished her, restoring her original name.

Today visitors board to admire the views of San Francisco from the *Balclutha*'s vast decks, inspect the bird's-eye maple cabinets and elegant Victorian furnishings of the captain's quarters, and try to imagine life in the cramped forecastle, where the crew slept. In the *Balclutha*'s cavernous hold are displays of various anchors, mast riggings and rudders, as well as ballast tubs and a model salmon cannery. Panels on deck give information about her history and workings.

In addition to these three ships, the steel-hulled steam tug *Hercules* (1907) and scow-schooner *Alma* (1891) are open for public viewing on a limited afternoon schedule, subject to weather. The New Jersey-built *Hercules* towed her sister ship through the Straits of Magellan on her maiden voyage, ranged north to Alaska until 1924, then towed railroad barges throughout San Francisco Bay before retiring in 1962. The *Alma* was typical of the broad, shallow, turn-of-the-century boats that carried bulk goods like hay, bricks and chicken feed along inland waterways from San Jose to Sacramento. Not open for visits, but moored for dockside viewing, is the paddle-wheel steam tug *Eppleton Hall* (1914), which operated on the River Wear near Newcastle upon Tyne, England, towing coal ships and barges.

Buena Vista Cafe

2765 Hyde St. ☎ *415-474-5044.* Best known as the first bar in the US to serve Irish coffee (a heady concoction of Irish whiskey, coffee and whipped cream), this amiable bar sold its first steaming mug of the brew in 1952. Breakfast is served all day by aproned waiters who willingly direct visitors to local attractions.

Aquatic Park Beach – This small beach fronting a grassy lawn is one of the last stretches of open shoreline along the northern waterfront. The park and the beach were created in the 1930s as part of a WPA recreational complex. While most people consider the waters of San Francisco Bay too cold for swimming, intrepid members of the century-plus-old Dolphin Club and the South End Rowing Club still take daily dips here. Look for them among the swells in their brightly colored swim caps. Asian-American line fishermen frequent the 1,850ft **Municipal Pier** (1934), along with others seeking a quiet place to stroll.

★**National Maritime Museum** – *Beach St. at Polk St. Open year-round daily 10am–5pm. Closed Jan 1, Thanksgiving Day, Dec 25. www.maritime.org/safrhome.shtml* ☎ *415-556-3002.* Resembling an ocean liner at berth on the edge of Aquatic Park, this unusual Streamline Moderne building (1939) houses a fine collection of maritime artifacts and historical displays. Its upper floors are recessed from a flat roof to create the impression of a ship's decks, a nautical effect enhanced by railings, porthole windows and cowl ventilators that look like smokestacks. It was built as the Aquatic Park Casino, centerpiece of the WPA's never-fully-realized recreational complex. Unusual slate intaglio reliefs by Sargent Johnson adorn its recessed doorway, while the interior boasts undulating undersea murals by Hilaire Hiler and a terrazzo floor designed by Richard Ayer, based on a shoal chart of the bay.

Occupying the building (which it shares with a senior center) since 1951, the museum forms part of the San Francisco Maritime National Historical Park *(p 86)*. In the entrance hall, a large anchor, the hull of a scow schooner and three fine models (including one of the Preussen, a unique, five-masted square-rigger) whet visitors' appetites for other galleries. One collection is devoted to steam-powered ocean travel from post-Civil War to the 1980s; temporary exhibits are mounted elsewhere on the first floor. A larger exhibition hall *(2nd floor)* focuses on the 1850s and '60s—the city's early years as a sea and inland port. Fisheries, whaling and shipbuilding are portrayed through unusual artifacts, including blubber-processing spoons and intricate figureheads from ships that once sailed San Francisco Bay; among them were trawlers and riverboats, ferries and yachts. Displays on the traditional arts of the sailor include knotting, modeling, whittling and scrimshaw carving. Large windows to the north, as well as an open observation deck *(3rd floor)*, offer grand views of the historic sailing ships at Hyde Street Pier.

2 Ghirardelli Chocolate Manufactory & Soda Fountain

In Ghirardelli Square. ☎ *415-771-4903.* Find out all about chocolate from the first cocoa bean to the last sweet slurp at this bustling ice cream parlor. Break into the chocolate shell of the Alcatraz Rock, Strike it Rich with butterscotch and almonds, or experience your first Earthquake: a gargantuan sundae made of eight scoops, eight toppings, bananas, nuts and cherries.

3 Earthquake Outlet

In Ghirardelli Square. ☎ *415-674-9091.* Want to be ready for the next "big one"? San Franciscans do. When things get shaky, they come here to order everything they may need, from crowbars and dust masks to water filtration units and portable commodes. You may feel more comfortable with a survival kit containing food and water rations, 12-hour lightsticks, a whistle, Mylar blanket and first-aid supplies, all stuffed into a nylon fanny pack.

★★ **Ghirardelli Square** – Kids *Block bounded by Polk, Larkin, Beach and North Point Sts.* This famed shopping and dining complex, located within a series of renovated brick factories, is an extremely popular destination for visitors and one of the finest examples of San Francisco's dedication to preserving its historic buildings.

Born and trained in Rapallo, Italy, Domingo Ghirardelli came to San Francisco in 1849, eventually opening a small chocolate factory at 415 Jackson Street. In 1865 he discovered that a bag of chocolate hung in a warm room would release its cocoa butter and that the remaining residue could be ground into a fine powder. This "broma" chocolate, as it was known, became the company's featured product. After Ghirardelli's retirement in 1892, his sons relocated the business, purchasing an entire city block including the Pioneer Woolen Mill (1859). Over the next 30 years, working with architect William Mooser, they transformed the complex into the Ghirardelli Chocolate Factory, adding a comfortable central courtyard where workers enjoyed picnic lunches. The now-famous **Clock Tower** (1916) and the enormous electric sign, lowered into place in 1915, beamed a comforting welcome to ships passing through the Golden Gate until they were darkened for defense purposes during World War II.

The manufacturing operation relocated to a new factory across the bay in San Leandro in 1962. That left the old chocolate works imperiled until visionary shipping heir William Matson Roth stepped in. Purchasing the block, he set about an ambitious plan to redevelop it as a fine shopping and dining complex. The landmark redesign (1968, Wurster, Bernardi & Emmons) is renowned as one of the city's premier examples of adaptive reuse. Several new structures were added to the open courtyard, linking the upscale galleries, boutiques and restaurants housed in the old factory buildings. Exposed brick walls and highly polished hardwood floors have been preserved throughout the interiors, and pieces of obsolete chocolate machinery harken back to Ghirardelli Square's industrial origins.

EXCURSION

★★★ **Alcatraz** – *Description p 75.*

The ✗ symbol indicates that eating facilities can be found on the premises of the sight.

11 • GOLDEN GATE BRIDGE★★★

Time: 2 hours. Muni bus 28–19th Ave. or 29–Sunset
Map p 100

Stretching across the narrow strait of the Golden Gate above the swirling union of the Pacific Ocean and San Francisco Bay, this elegant Art Deco suspension bridge remains one of San Francisco's most beloved symbols.

Historical Notes

"The Bridge That Could Not Be Built" – Imagined by a madman in 1869, proposed intermittently over the next four decades by saner visionaries, the bridge across the treacherous strait between the San Francisco Peninsula and Marin County elicited passionate emotions and aggressive resistance at every stage of its conception. Few took the idea seriously until 1916, when automotive transportation was fast becoming a way of life. The city's Board of Supervisors commissioned the first feasibility study two years later.

Initial cost estimates for the structure ran as high as $100 million, but Joseph Strauss, a tireless and innovative engineer who already had built more than 400 bridges around the world, claimed that he could span the "unspannable" passage for a mere $27 million. Excited by Strauss' plan, citizens of counties from San Francisco to the Oregon border offered their financial and political support. Two major foes, however, stood in the way: the powerful Southern Pacific Railroad (sole owner of all transbay ferry operations), which stood only to lose from Strauss' railless design; and the US War Department, which feared that the bridge would hinder navigation and provide a target for enemy bombs in the event of war. Other naysayers claimed that the deep and turbulent waters of the bay were too treacherous for such an undertaking, and still others decried Strauss' estimate as being nearly $75 million too low.

For years parties on both sides wrangled. When the War Department withdrew its opposition in 1924, the Southern Pacific filed a battery of lawsuits designed to keep the project in litigation for decades. Soon thereafter, several counties that originally had backed the plan withdrew their support, citing danger and expense as reasons to abandon the construction attempt. Since no federal or state funding was to be allocated, the remaining counties faced an even greater financial burden if they wanted to be linked to the city across the bay. By the time the last obstacles were removed—the railroad finally dropped its lawsuits under public pressure—the Great Depression had crushed the economy and citizens couldn't afford the bonds issued for public support. Then A.P. Giannini, visionary founder of the Bank of Italy, stepped

Larry Ulrich/Tony Stone Images

Golden Gate Bridge from Baker Beach

forward and announced that his bank would finance the bridge. In 1933, nearly 12 years after Joseph Strauss first submitted his proposal, that groundbreaking ceremonies finally took place.

Spanning the Gate – Unemployed laborers turned out in droves to compete for plum jobs on the bridge once construction began in January 1933. Not only did the project offer steady employment for thousands of men during the height of the Depression; it also provided the safest conditions yet found on a building site. Construction lore at the time held that one life would be lost for every million dollars spent, but Strauss and his principal assistant engineer, Clifford Paine, broke that grim law by enforcing unprecedented safety procedures that have since become standard, including safety belts, nets and filter glasses to block the blinding sun. Their stringency paid off: The first fatal accident, the toppling of a derrick onto a young steel worker, did not occur until the fourth year of construction. Only three months before the bridge opened, the workers' euphoria about the project's impending completion shattered when a scaffold suspended below the roadway tore loose and plummeted into the safety net, carrying a dozen men with it. The net held for an instant, then ripped open, dropping the victims into the deepest part of the channel. Two survived the plunge, but 10 men were lost in the vicious currents.

Despite this tragedy, the Golden Gate Bridge was hailed as a model of safety, economy and grace at its inauguration on May 27, 1937. A crowd of over 200,000 surged across the span on foot on opening day. Automobiles followed next, continuing a week-long round of festivities celebrating the conquest of the "unbridgeable" Golden Gate. The final cost was around $35 million.

Today, nearly 130,000 vehicles traverse the bridge daily, while pedestrians take to its sidewalks to admire its soaring towers, graceful cables and wondrous views.

The bridge itself can be viewed from afar at many points in San Francisco and Marin County, especially from LAND'S END, the PRESIDIO, MARIN HEADLANDS, the MARINA DISTRICT and FISHERMAN'S WHARF.

The Golden Gate Bridge

Measuring 1.22mi from end to end, the Golden Gate Bridge stood for many years as the world's longest suspension bridge until it was superseded by the Verrazano Narrows Bridge in 1964. Unlike more rigid types of bridges, a suspension bridge relies on gravity for its stability: the massive weight of the roadway, suspended from cables anchored on land, keeps the structure from falling. The cables provide enough flexibility for the midspan of the bridge to deflect transversely up to 27ft in high winds without jeopardizing the structure's integrity.

There are five main components to a suspension bridge: piers, anchorages, towers, cables and a roadway, constructed in that order. The Golden Gate Bridge's two **piers** form the bases of the towers. The Marin pier stands close to shore, but the San Francisco pier had to be poured a quarter-mile offshore in 100ft of water because the nearer bedrock was deemed unstable. An oval concrete fender, 27.5ft thick at its top and as long as a football field, surrounds this southern pier, protecting it from battering waves and collisions. The two **anchorages,** each a collection of massive concrete

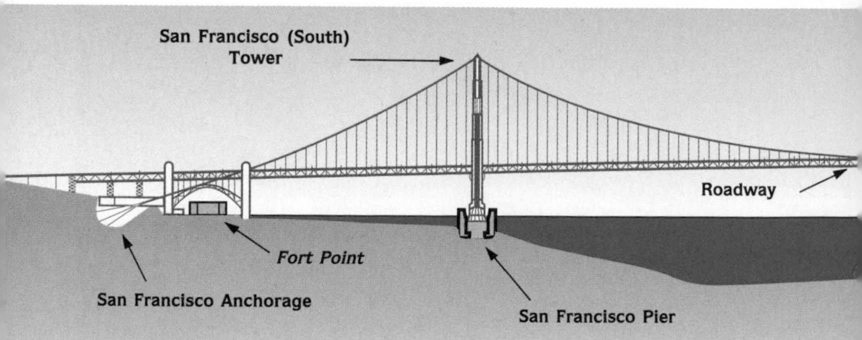

- Length of suspended bridge : 6,450ft • Length of span between towers : 4,200ft
- Height of towers : 746ft • Combined weight of towers : 88 million lbs
- Dia. of cables : 36 3/8" • Total length of wire used in cables : 80,000 miles

VISIT

Bridging the Golden Gate (1937)

Viewing Area – Kids *Access from US-101 or from Lincoln Blvd. $3 toll, southbound only. Pedestrian access to the bridge daily 5am–9pm, east sidewalk only. ☎ 415-921-5858.* A cross section of a cable, a dignified statue of Joseph Strauss and panel displays lead from the parking area to a series of viewing platforms where visitors can drink in the sight of the bridge's massive towers and cables. For closeup inspections, a stroll across the bridge on the east sidewalk is a must, but wear a jacket to ward off stiff winds. Walk to the center of the span for privileged **views**★★ of ALCATRAZ, the Marin Headlands and the Pacific Ocean. From here, visitors can get a sense of Strauss' magnificent accomplishment by gazing up the sleek, looping cables that rise in a smooth arc to the top of the towers.

Cross to the **Vista Point** on the Marin County side for lovely **views**★★ of the bridge from the north, backdropped by the forested hills of the Presidio.

blocks able to withstand 63 million pounds of pull from the cables, were sunk into pits deep enough to hold a 12-story building. The twin steel **towers** rise 746ft (65 stories) above the piers, each supporting a total load of 123 million pounds from the two main cables. The massive **cables**, spun out of 80,000mi of wire, rest in saddles at the tops of the towers and are embedded into the anchorages on land. Under normal conditions (70°F and no load on the span), the cables bend the towers toward the shore by 6in. The steel-reinforced **roadway** hangs from ropes attached to the cables at 50ft intervals.

Since the Golden Gate Bridge's inauguration, weather conditions have forced it to close only three times. The bridge is continually maintained by a team of inspectors, electricians, ironworkers and painters. Since 1937, the bridge has been repainted repeatedly to prevent rust and corrosion from salt air, fog, high winds and auto exhaust. Its trademark shade of orange vermilion, dubbed "International Orange," was selected for aesthetic reasons.

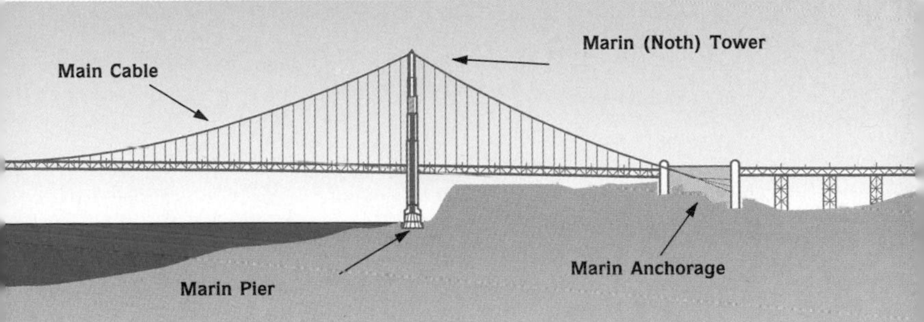

- Clearance above highest tide : 220 ft • Weight of each cable anchorage : 240 million lbs
- Weight of cables, suspenders, accessories : 490 million lbs (24,500 tons)
- Total amount of steel used : 1.66 billion lbs. (83,000 tons)

12 • MARINA DISTRICT★

Time: 1/2 day. MUNI bus 28–19th Ave., 30–Stockton or 47–Van Ness.
Map pp 96-97

Ensconced on San Francisco's northern waterfront between Van Ness Avenue, THE PRESIDIO and Lombard Street, the Marina District is one of the city's most architecturally uniform residential neighborhoods. Its many blocks of pale, stucco facades are enlivened by an abundance of Mediterranean Revival-style architectural details, including columns, tile roofs, and arched windows and doors. The most desirable homes, bordering the broad swath of Marina Green, boast views over San Francisco Bay.

Historical Notes

Formerly a muddy, marshy inlet, the area where the Marina District now lies failed to attract early Spanish settlers, though the high ground hemming it on the east and west greatly interested military commanders charged with guarding the Golden Gate. Spanish soldiers established the PRESIDIO on the rise to the west in 1776, and in 1797 emplaced a battery of five bronze cannons atop the knoll now known as Black Point, to the east. The guns were never used, but in 1850 the site caught the eye of American military strategists who established an army reservation there. To stave off Confederate attack during the Civil War, the Union Army terraced Black Point and installed a new battery of 12 cannons. Like its predecessor, this battery never saw battle; it was eventually incorporated into Fort Mason *(p 94)*.

Development came slowly to the mud flats, sand dunes and marshes between Black Point and the Presidio. At the beginning of the 19C, dairy farms covered the hills and valleys to the south (present-day COW HOLLOW) and a roadhouse stood on the site of the Palace of Fine Arts *(p 96)*, an area then called Harbor View. In 1911, city boosters seeking a favorable location for a world's fair—to promote the rebirth of the city after the 1906 earthquake and fire, and to celebrate the opening of the Panama Canal—decided upon this largely empty tract. The Army Corps of Engineers erected a seawall along the muddy waterfront and by 1913 had filled the 600 acres inside it with tons of sand and earthquake debris, creating a flat, attractive site upon which to erect the buildings of the Panama-Pacific International Exposition of 1915.

The Panama-Pacific International Exposition of 1915

As stewards of the West Coast's busiest port in the early 20C, San Francisco residents took keen interest in the construction of the Panama Canal. The resurrection of the city from the 1906 earthquake and fire, and increasing competition from the port at Los Angeles, only heightened San Franciscans' resolve to celebrate the canal's completion in a way that would unequivocally announce to the world that the city was rebuilt, rejuvenated and ready to resume its place as the economic and cultural center of the American Pacific coast.

On a 635-acre tract of reclaimed land, an esteemed group of architects, including Louis C. Mullgardt, Bernard Maybeck, Willis Polk and William B. Faville, set about designing a fabulous complex of pavilions representing 25 countries and 29 states. From its opening day in February 1915, the fair dazzled the public with its attractions and architecture. Indirect lighting, an innovation of the era, accented a fantasy city of Renaissance palazzos, Spanish missions, Classical temples and Byzantine domes. The Great Palace of Machinery was vast enough for an airplane to fly through it.

At the close of the fair, all of its structures were razed except the Palace of Fine Arts. Developers took over, laying out residential streets and building choice homes for sale. The Marina District, as it then became known, gained a reputation as a desirable middle-class address.

Ironically, the same uncompacted landfill laid down for a fair that advertised San Francisco's recovery from the 1906 earthquake proved disastrous during the Loma Prieta quake of 1989. The unstable ground beneath the Marina District liquefied during the tremor, causing several homes to collapse and heavily damaging dozens of buildings erected on the landfill.

Today the marks of Loma Prieta are largely erased and the Marina District remains an affluent residential neighborhood distinguished by its architectural harmony, its glorious views of the Golden Gate, and its tourist attractions at Fort Mason, the Palace of Fine Arts and the Exploratorium.

Visiting the Marina District – Marina Green, Chestnut Street and intervening residential streets are pleasant for strolling by day or evening. Fort Mason Center's galleries, museums and other attractions are open by day, but most theater performances are held at night; call ☎ 415-979-3010 for recorded information about weekly events and cultural offerings. Maps and information about Fort Mason and the Golden Gate National Recreation Area are available at GGNRA headquarters at Upper Fort Mason.

Street parking is usually available in the Marina District's residential areas, though time limits (usually 2hrs) are strictly enforced. Free public lots are located at Fort Mason Center *(entrance at Marina Blvd. and Buchanan St.)* and the Exploratorium *(westbound vehicles take Richardson Ave. to Lyon St. entrance; eastbound vehicles enter from Marina Blvd.)* but both fill up quickly on afternoons and weekends. Limited free parking is available at Upper Fort Mason, in the Marina Yacht Harbor and along Marina Green. Walkers may enjoy strolling all or part of the Golden Gate Promenade, a popular and scenic byway that skirts Fort Mason and Marina Green on its 3.5mi route from Aquatic Park Beach *(p 87)* to the GOLDEN GATE BRIDGE.

The Oregon State pavilion resembled the Parthenon, only using redwood trunks instead of marble pillars. Visitors were awed by a working scale model of the Panama Canal. At the center rose the Tower of Jewels, covered with more than 100,000 cut-glass jewels backed by tiny mirrors and suspended on wires, so that the tower appeared to shimmer in the breeze. Most beloved by San Franciscans was the Palace of Fine Arts *(p 96)*. The fair was acclaimed far and wide as the most ambitious event ever hosted by the city, attracting nearly 20 million visitors in its 10 months of operation and earning a substantial profit—but ultimately failing to lure back the shipping business lost to Los Angeles' growing port.

Constructed primarily of wood and plaster, the fair buildings (save the Palace of Fine Arts) were demolished at the exposition's close in December 1915. Of the original construction, only the Marina Yacht Harbor and the reconstructed Palace of Fine Arts remain today.

California Historical Society, San Francisco. James A. Heynemann Collection. FN-22832.

SIGHTS

★**Upper Fort Mason** – The military reservation that would become Fort Mason developed here, on the gentle slope and broad crown of a low hill overlooking the bay. The Army failed to occupy the attractive site for more than a decade after 1850, however, and several well-to-do civilian families had, in the interim, erected homes on Black Point before Union forces repossessed the property in 1863 during the Civil War. Named in 1881 for Colonel Richard Mason, California's first military governor (1847-49), the outpost formed the western command center for the US Army during the Indian Wars of the late 19C. Headquarters for General Frederick Funston's interim government were installed here in the anxious hours immediately following the 1906 quake, and tents were set up on the fort's broad meadow to house refugees from the devastated areas of the city.

Though operated as part of the Golden Gate National Recreation Area since 1972, Upper Fort Mason maintains the clean, orderly feel of a 19C Army command post. Military personnel continue to occupy some of its many white, wood-frame buildings.

GGNRA Headquarters – *Bldg. 201, MacArthur St. Open year-round Mon–Fri 9:30am–4:30pm.* ♿ P ☎ *415-556-0561.* Built in 1901, this three-story structure served briefly as an army hospital before its conversion to administrative offices after 1906. Inside, visitors can obtain abundant maps and information on GGNRA activities, and limited material on other national parks of the West.

Behind the headquarters building lies the charming **Fort Mason Community Garden**, a public plot where local residents may register for space to grow vegetables, flowers and root crops (more than 50 such gardens exist in the city). From the garden, a stroll along Pope Street leads past several examples of early military construction, including a wooden base chapel (1942). Originally a barracks, the American Youth Hostel at the head of the street dates from the Civil War period.

Black Point Battery – *North end of Franklin St.* In 1797, Spanish soldiers installed five-gun Batéria San José atop this serene bluff overlooking San Francisco Bay. The homes erected—without permission—by civilians in 1855 were confiscated by the army in 1863; several remain today along the east side of Franklin Street and are used as officers' quarters. The most prominent of the civilian "squatters" was the explorer and politician John C. Frémont, whose house was demolished when Black Point was terraced for gun emplacements. Though the guns have been removed, Black Point Battery still offers lovely **views** east to tall-masted ships and small boats anchored off AQUATIC PARK, with the towers of downtown San Francisco and the hills of the East Bay beyond.

The Great Meadow – *Near Bay and Laguna Sts.* Site of a tent city erected to shelter thousands of refugees from the 1906 quake, this broad, undulating lawn today draws picnickers and sunbathers, and is the site of the annual **San Francisco Blues Festival** *(p 219)*. In the meadow stand a statue of the Madonna **(1)** by Italian-American sculptor Beniamino Bufano and a bronze figure of Bay Area Congressman Phillip Burton **(2)**, whose efforts spearheaded creation of the GGNRA *(p 95)*.

★**Fort Mason Center** – *Information* ☎ *415-441-3400.* Built on landfill during the early years of the 20C, this bayside complex of barracks, warehouses and docks served as the official embarkation point for Americans serving in Pacific theaters of war from 1910 through the Korean War. More than 1.5 million GIs and 23 million tons of cargo shipped out from its three sturdy docks during World War II, making Fort Mason the second largest Army port in the US at that time.

This lower, bayside section of Fort Mason was decommissioned for civilian use in 1962 and was completely transformed as a cultural and community complex by 1977. Today its renovated military structures (dubbed "Landmark Buildings A-E") house theaters and performance spaces, galleries, philanthropic organizations, museums, cafes and other cultural venues. By day the center bustles with the comings and goings of museum visitors, performers and professionals; evenings draw theatergoers to any of several stages, including the **Cowell Theater**, built over the water on the middle pier that also houses the Herbst Pavilion; the **Magic Theatre** *(Bldg. D, 3rd floor)*, which produces innovative plays from established and emerging writers; the **Young Performers Theatre** *(Bldg. C, 3rd floor)*, specializing in dramatics for children; and the **Bayfront Theater** *(Bldg. B, 3rd floor)*, home of improvisational "theatersports." Well worth a peek are the **San Francisco Children's Art Center** Kids *(Bldg. C, 1st floor; open to children only, year-round Mon–Sat 9am–5:30pm; closed school holiday weeks; class schedules vary;* ♿ P ☎ *415-771-0292)*; and the **San Francisco**

1 Green's
Fort Mason Center, Bldg. A. ☎ *415-771-6222.* Opened in 1979 by disciples of the San Francisco Zen Center, this gourmet vegetarian restaurant (its wine list is a national award winner) gets much of its produce from the center's Green Gulch Farm in Marin County. Reserve ahead for lunch or dinner, or stop in and rest your weary feet with coffee and a home made scone while drinking in the lovely view of the bay and the Golden Gate Bridge.

Museum of Modern Art Rental Gallery *(Bldg. A; open Sept–Jul Tue–Sat 11:30am–5:30pm; closed major holidays; P www.sfmoma.org/artfinder ☎ 415-441-4777)*, where rotating exhibits of contemporary art are displayed on the ground floor and mezzanine. *General theater listings and ticket information pp 233-234; recorded Fort Mason Center event information ☎ 415-979-3010.*

★**Mexican Museum** – *Bldg. D, 1st floor. Open year-round Wed–Fri noon–5pm, weekends 11am–5pm. Closed up to 4 wks between shows. $3. ♿ P ☎ 415-441-0404.* This intriguing museum houses a large, permanent collection of pre-Hispanic, Colonial, folk and contemporary Latin American arts and artifacts, as well as Chicano arts of the US. Limited space allows display of only a small percentage of the collection at any one time. Changing exhibits can include vessels and figures from the Maya, Aztec, Olmec and other ancient cultures of Mexico; folk art costumes, toys, jewelry and masks; and contemporary fine arts. Temporary and traveling exhibitions of Latino art and historical materials supplement the museum's holdings. The museum shop, **La Tienda**, sells a colorful and fascinating array of Mexican arts, crafts, masks, baskets, pottery, toys, books, cards, clothing and more. The Mexican Museum also sponsors tours of murals around San Francisco *(inquire at reception desk). The museum is scheduled to move to a new, permanent home near Yerba Buena Gardens by 2001.*

J. Porter Shaw Library – *Bldg. E, 3rd floor. Open year-round Tue 5pm–8pm, Wed–Fri 1pm–5pm, Sat 10am–5pm. Closed major holidays. ♿ P ☎ 415-556-9874.* Operated by the San Francisco Maritime National Historical Park, whose headquarters are one floor below, this library of maritime history maintains a collection of about 32,000 books plus oral history archives, sea chanteys, recorded interviews, vessel registers, photographs and other nautical items centering on West Coast shipping and whaling.

San Francisco African American Historical & Cultural Society – *Bldg. C, 1st floor. Open year-round Wed–Sun noon–5pm. $2 contribution requested. Guided tours available. ♿ P ☎ 415-441-0640.* Changing exhibits highlight achievements, people and events related to the African-American experience, particularly in California. The museum also mounts exhibits of work by African-American artists.

Museo ItaloAmericano – *Bldg. C, 1st floor. Open year-round Wed–Sun noon–5pm. Closed major holidays. $2. ♿ P www.well.com/~museo ☎ 415-673-2200.* In addition to a permanent exhibition of modern Italian and Italian-American art and temporary displays of work by contemporary artists, this museum and cultural center sponsors community education programs, including Italian language classes.

San Francisco Craft & Folk Art Museum – *Bldg. A. Open year-round Tue–Fri & Sun 11am–5pm, Sat 10am–5pm (1st Wed 7pm). Closed major holidays. $3. Guided tours (45min) available 1st Wed & 2nd Fri 1:30pm, 1-month advance reservations required. P ☎ 415-775-0991.* Offering rotating exhibits of historical folk art and contemporary crafts from around the world, this small museum also operates a wonderful gift shop selling an international assortment of handmade toys, art and mementos.

Marina Green – Encompassing an expansive stretch of Marina District waterfront between Webster and Scott Streets, this broad, 10-acre greensward is popular with locals for its stiff breezes—ideal for kite-flying—and for its stupendous **views**★★ of San Francisco Bay, the GOLDEN GATE BRIDGE and yachts anchored offshore. A favored spot of sunbathers, in-line skaters, volleyball players and joggers, the lawn is bor-

■ Golden Gate National Recreation Area

Embracing San Francisco's northern and western boundaries as well as Angel Island, Alcatraz and a significant portion of coastal Marin County, the Golden Gate National Recreation Area (usually called the GGNRA) was established by act of Congress in 1972. The 26,000-acre system of national parks, encompassing historic landmarks, military sites, redwood forests, beaches and undeveloped coastal lands, came about largely through the efforts of US Congressman Phillip Burton, who championed the movement to preserve the area's unused military lands as parks for nature conservation and recreation. Today the GGNRA attracts more than 25 million visitors annually.

GGNRA sites described in this guide include:

- **Alcatraz** *(p. 75)*
- **Fort Mason** *(p. 94)*
- **Crissy Field** *(p. 101)*
- **The Presidio** *(p. 98)*
- **China Beach** *(p. 159)*
- **Cliff House** *(p. 152)*
- **Fort Funston** *(p. 150)*
- **Tennessee Valley** *(p. 181)*
- **Mount Tamalpais** *(p. 182)*
- **Stinson Beach** *(p. 184)*
- **San Francisco Maritime National Historical Park** *(pp. 86-87)*
- **Marina Green** *(p. 95)*
- **Fort Point National Historic Site** *(p. 102)*
- **Baker Beach** *(p. 102)*
- **Land's End** *(p. 151)*
- **Ocean Beach** *(p. 149)*
- **Marin Headlands** *(p. 179)*
- **Muir Woods National Monument** *(p. 183)*
- **Muir Beach** *(p. 184)*
- **Point Reyes National Seashore** *(p. 185)*

dered by handsome dwellings in a diverse array of architectural styles. Most were built in the 1920s and incorporate Spanish and Italian Baroque details inspired by the 1915 Panama-Pacific International Exposition.

Enclosed by a 1,500ft jetty extending parallel to Marina Green, the **Marina Yacht Harbor** encloses a flotilla of boats, many of them belonging to members of the private St. Francis Yacht Club, which occupies an attractive, tile-roofed structure (1928, Willis Polk). Visitors who brave the walk to the end of the jetty can see the "wave organ," a sculpted jumble of concrete and stone embedded with pipes, each with one end sunk beneath the surface of the harbor. One hears the gurgling "music" of the sea, theoretically, by putting an ear to an exposed pipe end.

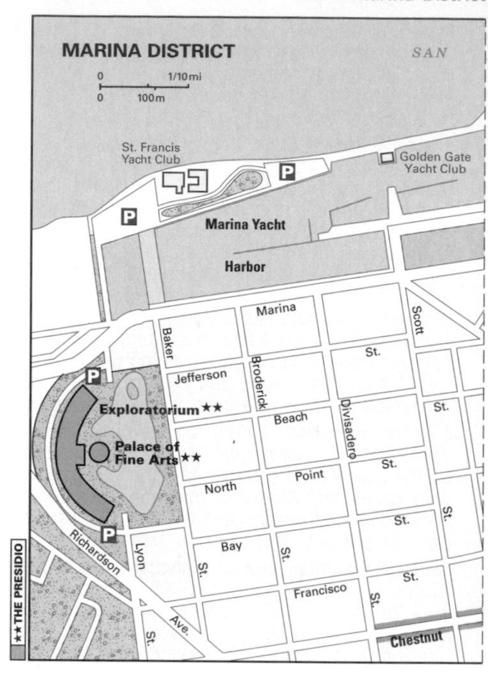

★★ Palace of Fine Arts – *Baker and Beach Sts.* Ranking among San Francisco's best-known landmarks, this grand rotunda and peristyle were replicated from structures designed by renowned architect Bernard Maybeck to house art exhibits for the 1915 Panama-Pacific International Exposition. The original building, designed to be impermanent, was framed in lath and chicken wire and covered with a plaster and burlap-fiber mixture called "staff," its surface sprayed to resemble travertine. When the buildings of the fair were torn down to make way for residential development, aesthetically-minded citizens lobbied to spare the Palace of Fine Arts. No efforts were made to strengthen the building, however, and it slowly disintegrated until 1962, when a plan was made for restoration. After funds were raised, workers made casts of the columns, statuary and artistic details, and the building was entirely reconstructed in concrete and steel between 1964 and 1967.

Maybeck's design was purely romantic in concept, inspired largely by the work of 18C engraver Giovanni Piranesi and *The Isle of the Dead*, a 19C painting depicting a royal tomb. Maybeck himself described the building as "an old Roman ruin" and stated his intent to project sadness. Reinforcing the sense of mystery and melancholy, the female figures sculpted by Ulric Ellerhusen along the top of the peristyle face inward, their faces buried in their arms.

M. Ueda/Wenger International Photography

Palace of Fine Arts

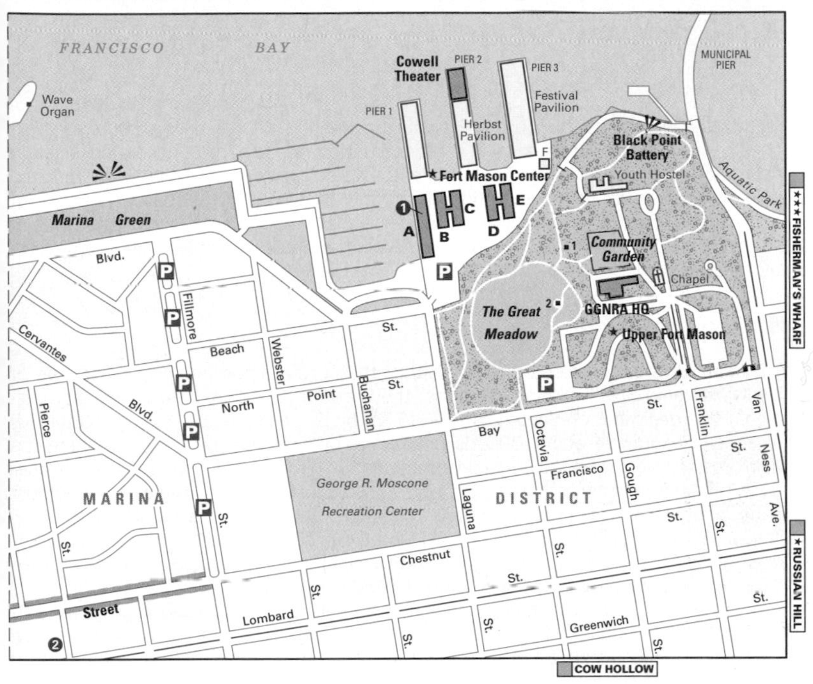

The rotunda, which measures 110ft high and 135ft across, is decorated with eight large panels carved in low relief. Angels look down from the interior of the dome: two of the original angels, which stand 14ft tall, are preserved inside the Exploratorium. On clear, calm days, the large duck pond spreading from the foot of the rotunda reflects mirror images.

★★ Exploratorium –  *1/2 day. 3601 Lyon St. Open Memorial Day–Labor Day daily 10am–6pm (Wed 9pm). Rest of the year Tue–Sun 10am–5pm (Wed 9pm). Closed Thanksgiving Day & Dec 25. $9, free 1st Wed. www.exploratorium.edu ☎ 415-397-5673. (Tactile Dome $3 additional admission; entry at 10:15am, noon, 1:45pm, 3:30pm & 5:15pm; reservations suggested; ☎ 415-561-0362.)* Located in the cavernous, semicircular structure behind the Palace of Fine Arts rotunda, this innovative museum of science, art and human perception has served as a model for similar science museums around the world since its opening in 1969. The Exploratorium's creator, Frank Oppenheimer, maintained a novel philosophy that a museum can best teach science through "hands-on" participation.

The museum boasts more than 650 exhibits in physics, electricity, life sciences, thermodynamics, weather, light, psychology, linguistics, sense perception and a host of other subjects. By pushing buttons, rotating wheels, peering through prisms, activating motors, engineering arches, arranging chimes, shouting into tubes and performing a wide variety of other actions, visitors are encouraged to set experiments in motion, observe the results and speculate on the causes. Instructions and explanations accompany each exhibit, and staff members are available to answer questions. Among the most popular exhibits are the miniature **tornado demonstration**; the photosensitive **Shadow Box**, where people's shadows are temporarily recorded on a wall; and the **distorted room**, where visitors can enter an optical illusion. New exhibits are continually being developed in the extensive workshops adjacent to the main floor, in full view of visitors.

Not to be missed is the soundproof, pitch-black **Tactile Dome**, a multilevel crawl chamber through which visitors must find their way only by sense of touch. It is not recommended for claustrophobes.

Chestnut Street – The four blocks of Chestnut Street between Divisadero and Fillmore Streets comprise the Marina District's main commercial avenue. A pleasant thoroughfare for shopping, dining and strolling, Chestnut Street projects a comfortable, friendly, middle-class atmosphere reminiscent of a small-town main street.

2 California Wine Merchant

3237 Pierce St. ☎ 415-567-0646. For more than 20 years, owners Greg and Deborah O'Flynn have tracked the astonishing growth and variety of California wines. You won't see the big names here: Their no-gimmicks shop, once the refrigerated portion of a defunct creamery, specializes in vintages from top-of-the-line, small-production wineries in California and the Pacific Northwest.

13 • THE PRESIDIO★★

Time: 3 hours. MUNI bus 28–19th Avenue, 29–Sunset, 41–Union, 43–Masonic or 45–Union-Stockton.
Map pp 100-101

For more than two centuries, the Presidio's privileged setting on 1,480 acres overlooking the Golden Gate earned it a reputation as the most beautiful military installation in North America. Residents and visitors are drawn to the lushly forested expanse to enjoy its handsome and eclectic mix of architectural styles, its traces of San Francisco's military history, and the spectacular views extending from its miles of wooded trails. Closed as an army base in 1994, the Presidio currently faces an uncertain future under the aegis of the National Park Service.

Historical Notes

A Distant Outpost – Selected as the site of the northernmost military installation of the far-reaching Spanish colonial empire, the Presidio (the word means "military garrison") was dedicated on September 17, 1776, by Lt. José Joaquin Moraga. Originally an adobe quadrangle about 300yds on each side located approximately where the Main Post now stands, the Presidio ranks as San Francisco's first European settlement, predating MISSION DOLORES by a month. The Spanish never considered the outpost to be of primary importance despite its strategic location at the mouth of the bay. Official disinterest, combined with decades of rain, earthquakes, wind and salt air, kept the lonely fortress in a perpetual state of disrepair, even after Mexico acquired it (along with independence from Spain) in 1821.

The Presidio's outlook changed in 1846 when John C. Frémont and a group of civilians staged the capture of the crumbling, largely defenseless fort from the Mexican government. The American flag was raised over the decaying garrison following cession of California to the US in 1848. San Francisco's growth as a commercial hub during the Gold Rush caused President Millard Fillmore to issue an executive order in 1850 reserving the property for military use. Over the next decade the fort was restored and enlarged, while a series of other installations was erected around the bay, including FORT POINT and ALCATRAZ.

The timing of this military construction was fortuitous. Following the outbreak of the Civil War, defense of San Francisco Bay moved to top priority from the Union's point of view. Gold and silver from California and Nevada mines were at stake. The Presidio undertook a major military buildup to guard against invasion by Confederate forces.

Following the Civil War, the Presidio housed US troops engaged in conflicts with the Modoc, Apache and other Native American tribes across the West. During this time the magnificent eucalyptus, cypress and pine forests were planted on the rolling lands of the base, both to beautify it and to protect its barren, sandy, windswept terrain from erosion, and the coastal defense batteries *(p 102)* along the bayfront were constructed. After 1898, as frontier outposts across the West were closed, the Presidio served as the launching pad for American expansion into the Pacific. During the Spanish-American War, thousands of soldiers camped on the grounds before sailing for the Philippines.

The presence of a large, standing army proved vital at the time of the 1906 earthquake and fire. Presidio troops helped maintain order as martial law was proclaimed, and more than 16,000 refugees camped on the fort's open lands. When the US entered World War I, troops trained here for combat in France. During World War II, the Presidio became headquarters for the Western Defense Command, as nearly two million troops shipped out from San Francisco. In the 1950s the base was named the command center for Nike missile defense of the bay and served as headquarters for the Sixth US Army until 1994.

Swords to Plowshares – In 1962 the site was named a National Historic Landmark. When the Golden Gate National Recreation Area (GGNRA) was created a decade later, Congress tagged the Presidio, whose military importance had waned, for future inclusion in the park. In 1989 the Presidio was designated for closure as part of a general defense reduction and consolidation, and on October 1, 1994, the Sixth Army marched off the grounds for the last time as the Presidio came under the supervision of the National Park Service. The remnants of the earliest 18C structures were discovered beneath the Main Post parking lot in 1996, shedding new light on what was believed to be the size of the original Presidio.

Today an official unit of the GGNRA, the property is managed by a presidentially appointed, nonprofit trust board charged with maintaining the Presidio's aesthetic, ecological and historic integrity while weaning it from federal dollars by 2013. Ensuring public access to the fine Spanish Colonial, Georgian, Mission Revival and Victorian buildings on the grounds, as well as to the site's hiking trails and unique natural habitats, is central to every decision.

Visiting the Presidio – Visitors can enter the Presidio by one of its three historic gates, or by **Lincoln Boulevard** from the southwest; the latter skirts the Coastal Defense Batteries, offering stunning views in the south-to-north direction. The Lombard Gate *(Lombard St. at Lyon St.)*, the most widely used entrance, is convenient to the MARINA DISTRICT and the PALACE OF FINE ARTS. The Presidio Boulevard Gate *(Presidio Blvd. at Pacific St.)* and the Arguello Boulevard Gate *(Arguello Blvd. at Pacific St.)* provide entry from the southern border of the Presidio. From all three gates, signs point the way to the Main Post. Parking lots abound on the property.

The ranger- and docent-staffed **William Penn Mott Jr. Visitor Center** *(open year-round daily 9am–5pm; closed Jan 1, Thanksgiving Day, Dec 25; ♿ P ☎ 415-561-4323)* at the Main Post, Building 102, is a good place to begin a visit, offering maps, books and other information including Main Post walking-tour brochures. Check the weather before setting out—coastal fog often lingers longer here than in other areas of the city, and a jacket or sweater may come in handy. While at the center, inquire about temporary shows mounted at the **Herbst International Exhibition Hall**, a former commissary renovated to house traveling exhibitions.

Formerly a private club reserved for Presidio officers, the **Presidio Golf Course** *(300 Finley Rd. ☎ 415-561-4653)* today welcomes all golfers to its scenic links.

SIGHTS

★★**Main Post** – Although no longer the efficient headquarters of a bustling military base, the Main Post remains the focal point of activity at the Presidio, featuring historic barracks, a comely row of officers' housing, and artillery from the Spanish colonial period.

At the southern end of the large central Parade Ground stands **Pershing Square**, former location of the home of General John "Black Jack" Pershing, later commander of the American Expeditionary Forces in Europe during World War I. Pershing's wife and daughters perished in a 1915 blaze that destroyed the house (a son survived); a flagpole marks the site. The flagpole also marks the corner of the original adobe and thatched-roof Presidio compound built by the Spanish in 1776. On either side stand two bronze **cannons**, cast in the late 17C and brought here to protect the little Spanish fort.

The Main Post reveals a broad sampling of the architectural styles represented on the grounds of the Presidio. The stately brick **barracks**★ (c.1890) stretching along Montgomery Street on the west side of the Parade Ground once housed soldiers of the Spanish-American War. The dignified row today contains the Presidio's main visitor center and offices of the GGNRA rangers administering the park. Tree-lined Funston Avenue, on the east side of the Parade Ground, was reserved for officers. The Neoclassical and Italianate cottages (1863) at the southern corner, known as **Officers' Row**★, originally faced the opposite direction but were turned towards the east in the 1870s to present a more pleasant aspect to visitors. Further along Funston Avenue, more elaborate residences representing several Victorian substyles were reserved for higher-ranking officers.

★**Presidio Museum** – Kids *Funston Ave. at Lincoln Blvd. Open year round Wed–Sun noon–4pm. Closed Jan 1, Thanksgiving Day, Dec 25. ♿ P ☎ 415-561-4331.* Originally built as the Post Hospital (1857), this handsome structure today houses a small

Barracks, Main Post

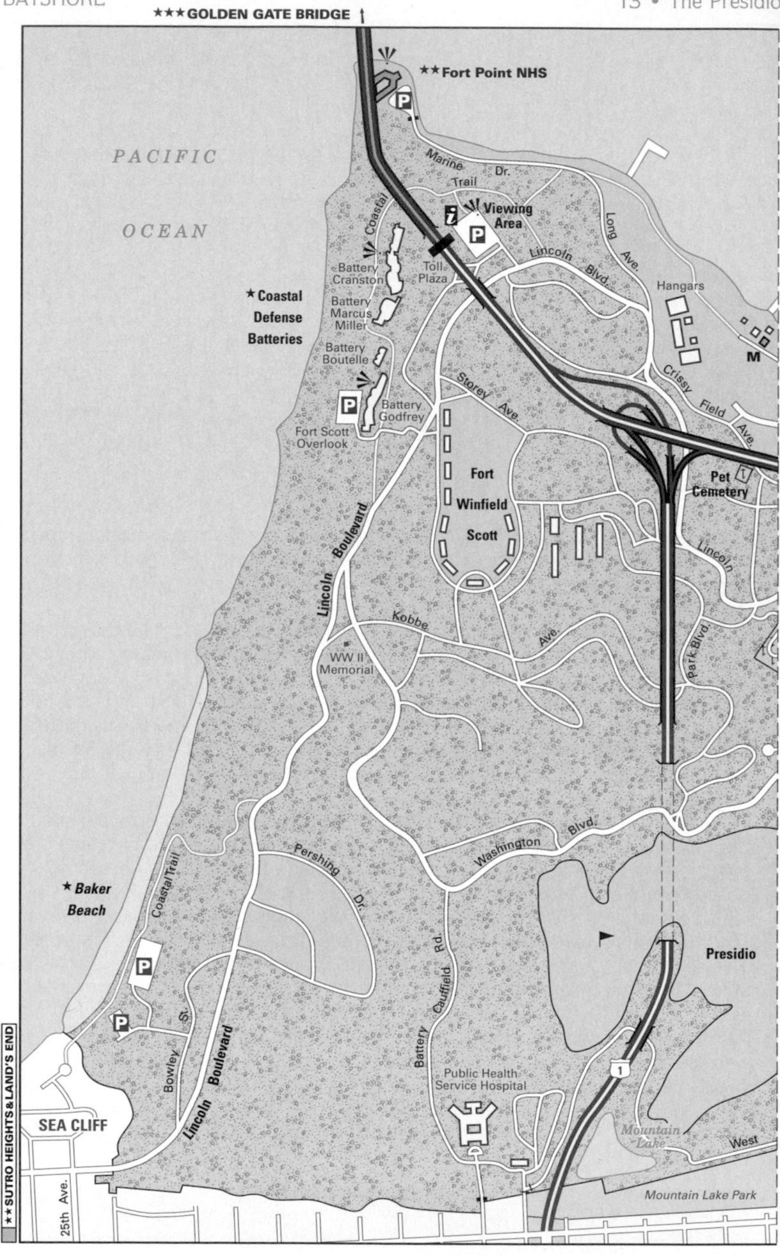

but intriguing museum with exhibits on the colonial and military history of the Presidio, an impressive array of US Army uniforms and artifacts, and historic turn-of-the-century photos. Especially interesting are **dioramas** of the Presidio under the Spanish (c.1800), the 1906 earthquake and fire, and the 1915 Panama-Pacific International Exposition, all created for the 1939 world's fair on TREASURE ISLAND. One exhibit explores the plight of Japanese-American citizens interned in detention camps during World War II, while another chronicles the little-known story of *nisei* (second-generation US citizens of Japanese descent) who served as translators during and after the war. Behind the museum, visitors may inspect two **refugee cottages** that were used to house San Franciscans left homeless by the 1906 disaster. One has been restored with period furnishings.

★**San Francisco National Military Cemetery** – *Entrance off Sheridan St. at Lincoln Blvd.* In 1884 the Presidio's 28-acre burial ground was designated a National Military Cemetery, allowing any US veteran the privilege of being buried here. Graves date from as far back as the Civil War. Well-known persons laid to rest here include General Frederick Funston, acting Presidio commander during the 1906 earthquake and fire, and US Representative Phillip Burton, sponsor and champion of the Golden Gate National Recreation Area. Eucalyptus and pine woods surround the cemetery.

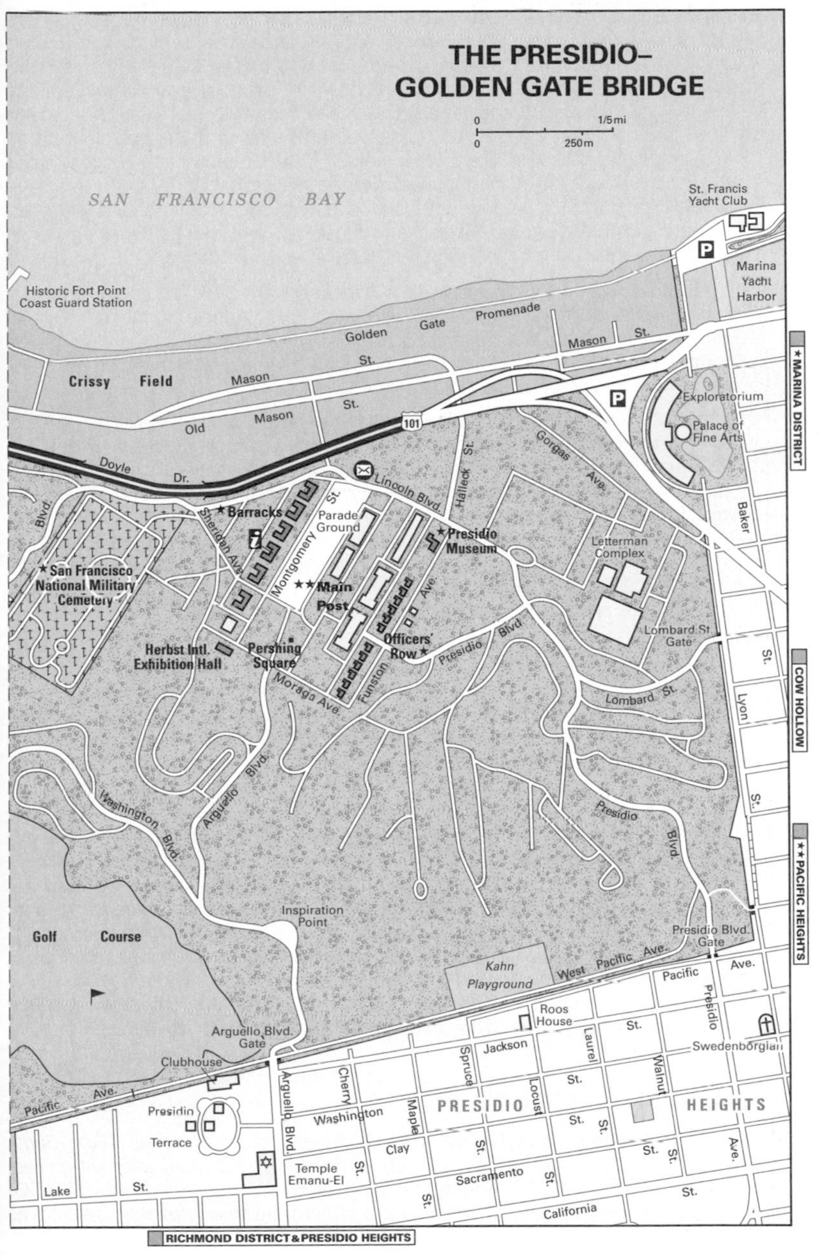

A short distance away, beneath the Crissy Field Avenue overpass leading to the GOLDEN GATE BRIDGE, lies a small **Pet Cemetery** Kids, worth a quick peek to see the whimsical headstones marking the graves of generations of Presidio household pets.

Crissy Field – *Crissy Field Ave. off Lincoln Blvd.* Once a soggy marsh drained and filled for the 1915 Panama-Pacific International Exposition, this broad, flat field served as an Army aircraft testing site from 1919 to 1936. Many of the original buildings still stand, including the old hangars that once housed cloth biplanes. The area is popular with strollers, picnickers, dog-walkers and windsurfers, who on fine days raise colorful sails here for a few brisk turns on the waves. *A two-year restoration project is scheduled for completion in late summer 2000.*

At the western end of the field is the former commander's residence, now headquarters for the State of the World Forum established by ex-Soviet Union President Mikhail Gorbachev. Adjacent, in the former Fort Point Coast Guard Station (1890), are offices of the National Oceanic and Atmospheric Administration (NOAA) and Farallones Marine Sanctuary Association.

Gulf of the Farallones National Marine Sanctuary Visitors Center (M) – Kids *Bldg. 991, Crissy Field Ave. Open year-round Wed–Sun 10am–5pm. Closed Jan 1, Thanksgiving Day, Dec 25.* *www.nos.noaa.gov/nmsp/gfnms* ☎ *415-561-6622.* Exhibits describe research and conservation efforts in the 948sq mi sanctuary, whose boundaries embrace Marin County coastlines to the mean high-tide mark and the rocky Farallon Islands (26mi west of the Golden Gate), home to the largest concentration of breeding seabirds in the continental US. The sanctuary also harbors more than two dozen species of marine mammals. In the visitor center are a live tidepool tank; interactive computer displays outlining such sanctuary activities as whalewatching, birdwatching, fishing and kayaking; and murals depicting life in the Gulf of the Farallones and adjacent Cordell Bank sanctuaries.

Fort Winfield Scott – *Entrance on Kobbe Ave. near Park Blvd.* A horseshoe-shaped group of white, Mission Revival-style barracks, Fort Winfield Scott was built in 1910 to house the Coast Artillery Corps. The only complex in the Presidio of uniform architectural style, Fort Scott provides a quiet, attractive setting from which to view the piers of the Golden Gate Bridge.

★**Coastal Defense Batteries** – Scattered along the cliffs that border Lincoln Avenue between Fort Point and Baker Beach, these crumbling concrete bunkers offer spectacular **views**★★★ of the sea, the Marin Headlands and the Golden Gate Bridge. Linked by the Coastal Trail *(p 155)*, the batteries were constructed from 1853 to 1910 to protect San Francisco Bay from invasion by sea. As with most of the fortifications around the bay, however, their guns were never fired in defense. The best way to enjoy the view is to stroll along the Coastal Trail south from the Golden Gate Bridge toll plaza through Battery Cranston (1897), Battery Marcus Miller (1891), Battery Boutelle (1900) and Battery Godfrey (1895) to the Fort Scott Overlook.

★**Baker Beach** – *Bowley St. off Lincoln Ave., southwest corner of the Presidio.* Perhaps the city's most popular beach, as much for its smooth sand as for the high dunes that protect it from all but the coldest winds, Baker Beach attracts two types of beachgoer. The southern end, near the parking lot, draws families and adolescents. The northern end, which offers a more dramatic view of the Golden Gate Bridge and the sage-covered cliffs, is popular with devotees of nude sunbathing—an activity tolerated (although not officially permitted) on federal land.

"...and the next day before the dawn we were lying to upon the Oakland side of San Francisco Bay. The day was breaking as we crossed the ferry; the fog was rising over the citied hills of San Francisco; the bay was perfect—not a ripple, scarce a stain, upon its blue expanse; everything was waiting, breathless, for the sun. A spot of cloudy gold lit first upon the head of Tamalpais, and then widened downward on its shapely shoulder; the air seemed to awaken, and began to sparkle; and suddenly 'The tall hills Titan discovered,' and the city of San Francisco, and the bay of gold and corn were lit from end to end with summer daylight."

Robert Louis Stevenson, *Arriving in San Francisco* **(1879)**

ADDITIONAL SIGHT

★**Fort Point National Historic Site** – Kids *Open year-round Wed–Sun 10am–5pm. Closed Jan 1, Thanksgiving Day, Dec 25. Guided tours (30min) and self-guided audio headset tours ($2.50; 45min) available.* *www.nps.gov/fopo* ☎ *415-556-1693.* Tucked beneath a steel arch at the southern anchorage of the GOLDEN GATE BRIDGE, this impressive, multistoried brick-and-granite fort stands as a fine example of Civil War-era masonry and military architecture. Designed as the first of three enormous fortifications to guard the entrance to San Francisco Bay (the other two were to be built on Alcatraz Island and at Lime Point, now the northern anchorage of the bridge), Fort Point was erected in 1861 atop the site of Castillo de San Joaquín (1794), an abandoned Spanish gun battery.

The original design, calling for a rectangular structure of granite blocks, was modified (after construction began) to a brick fortress with defensive towers on the east and west. Master brickmasons were hired to build the structure; their fine craftsmanship remains evident throughout. As the Civil War approached, the US military, anticipating Confederate attacks on San Francisco Bay, ordered the uncompleted and unarmed fort occupied. For months a garrison stood guard over empty gun casements.

Like other military installations around the bay, Fort Point's ordnance was never fired in defense. By 1885 its guns were considered obsolete and were removed for scrap. Long periods of minimal occupation or complete abandonment followed, with the thick walls occasionally serving as a damp, lonely barracks for unlucky companies of soldiers.

Initial plans for the Golden Gate Bridge placed Fort Point on the exact spot where Joseph Strauss, the bridge's designer, intended to sink the southern anchorage. After visiting the fort, Strauss was so impressed by the quality of its masonry that he designed a massive steel arch over the fort to preserve it.

Visit – Restored and rebuilt by the National Park Service in the 1970s, Fort Point provides visitors with an excellent glimpse into military life on the California coast in the late 19C. Information panels throughout the building detail the history of the fort and the lives of the soldiers stationed there. Just inside the "sally port," the only entrance to the structure, lies a Spanish bronze cannon (1684), saved from Castillo de San Joaquín, and a huge 1844 Rodman cannon, typical of those that once guarded the Golden Gate. To the right of the sally port, the former sutler's store (post exchange) houses a visitor center, bookstore and small theater presenting slide shows and short films about the fort and the Golden Gate Bridge. Handcut granite spiral staircases lead to the upper tiers, with their intricate masonry and arching ceilings. Officers' quarters and privates' barracks are hung with historical photographs, and there are exhibits documenting the experiences of 20C African-American soldiers and the wartime contributions of American women. From the top-level barbettes, visitors can marvel at a unique and stunning **view★★** of the southern pier and underbelly of the Golden Gate Bridge.

14 • COW HOLLOW

Time: 2 hours. Muni bus 22–Fillmore, 41–Union or 45–Union-Stockton.
Map below

Despite its homely name and prevailing residential character, Cow Hollow is best known for its charming, trendy shops and restaurants housed in attractive Victorians along bustling Union Street. Eccentric but friendly, the neighborhood reveals itself to visitors who explore on foot.

Historical Notes

Tucked between the steep slopes of present-day PACIFIC HEIGHTS and the sand dunes of a shallow inlet later reclaimed as the MARINA DISTRICT, the rolling "hollow" was known as Golden Gate Valley in the mid-19C, when herds of cattle from more than 30 dairy farms grazed upon its dales and hills. The availability of bovine carcasses also attracted tanneries, slaughterhouses and related industries. By the 1870s, the valley was dubbed "Cow Hollow" for its less endearing pastoral qualities. Wealthy residents of Pacific Heights complained about the stench rising from the valley until, in 1891, the city ordered the businesses closed and the "hollow" filled in.

Developers readily transformed Cow Hollow's pastures into a respectable neighborhood of two- and three-story wood-frame houses. Buildings along Union Street, the main thoroughfare, survived the earthquake and fire of 1906, and the area enjoyed a boom as it greeted merchants and residents fleeing the burned-out areas of San Francisco. Local businesses catered primarily to neighborhood shoppers until the 1950s, when antique shops, furniture showrooms and interior decorators began renting Union Street's Victorian storefronts, attracting clients from other parts of the city. Other fashionable shops and restaurants followed suit, converting Victorian houses and courtyards for retail use and increasing Union Street's popularity as an intriguing shopping district. Although later refurbishments have in some cases teetered toward preciousness, much of Cow Hollow's genteel, turn-of-the century architecture survives intact, along with several evocative reminders of its rural past.

COW HOLLOW
PACIFIC HEIGHTS
JAPANTOWN
0 1/10mi
0 100m
Lombard St.
Greenwich St.
Union St.
Lyon
Baker
Broderick St.
Divisadero St.
Green
Vallejo St.
PACIFIC HEIGHTS
Lyon Street Steps
Broadway
Pacific Ave.
Jackson St.
Swedenborgian Church
Washington St.
★★ THE PRESIDIO

SIGHTS

★**Octagon House** – *2645 Gough St. Open Feb–Dec 2nd & 4th Thu & 2nd Sun noon–3pm. Closed major holidays. Contribution requested. Guided tours (30min) available. ☎ 415-441-7512.* Built in 1861 by William C. McElroy, this small house was moved from a nearby lot to its present site in 1953 by the National Society of Colonial Dames of America in California, which uses it as a museum for its collection of decorative arts from the Colonial and Federal periods. The two-story structure took its curious shape from Orson Squire Fowler's popular 1848 book, *A Home for All*, which theorized that octagonal houses provided more light, space and ventilation than conventional square-cornered houses, and were consequently healthier. The interior floor plan was substantially altered when the central stairwell was moved to the west wall by its present owners. Most of the rooms on the second floor, which is naturally lit by a central octagonal cupola that protrudes above the main roof, retain their original dimensions.

The museum displays many fine pieces of early American furniture, portraits, samplers, looking glasses, pewter and silverware, as well as examples of ceramics and other decorative items from the lively import trade during the Colonial era and early Republic. One room houses a collection of signatures and handwritten documents by all but two of the signatories to the Declaration of Independence, including Thomas Jefferson, John Hancock, Benjamin Franklin and John Adams.

★**Union Street** – Lined with refurbished Victorians, Union Street's eight-block retail district between Van Ness Avenue and Steiner Street invites leisurely exploration. Pedestrians are free to wander through pleasant courtyards and patios, between and behind old houses now converted to boutiques, galleries, arts-and-crafts shops and small, urbane restaurants. Particularly attractive are the bed-and-breakfast inns of **Charlton Court** *(south side of Union St. between Laguna and Buchanan Sts.)*, a quiet lane thought to have once served as a depot for milk wagons. The house and barn (c.1870) of James W. Cudworth, Cow Hollow's first dairyman, still stand behind a palm tree at no. 2040; they now house designer boutiques. A roofed passage at no. 2164/2166 leads to an old barn and leafy carriage yard, where plants and garden ornaments are displayed for sale. Cow Hollow's most unusual building, visible to the north from the corner of Union and Webster, is the former main temple of the **Vedanta Society of Northern California** *(2963 Webster St.)*. Built by Joseph Leonard

1 La Nouvelle Patisserie
2184 Union St. ☎ *415-931-7655.* Tender brioches and flaky croissants provide the chorus line for a show-stopping lineup of glorious French pastries, including chocolate ganache sponge cake, napoleons with caramelized topping and towering croquembouche, all created by master patissier Jean-Yves Duperret.

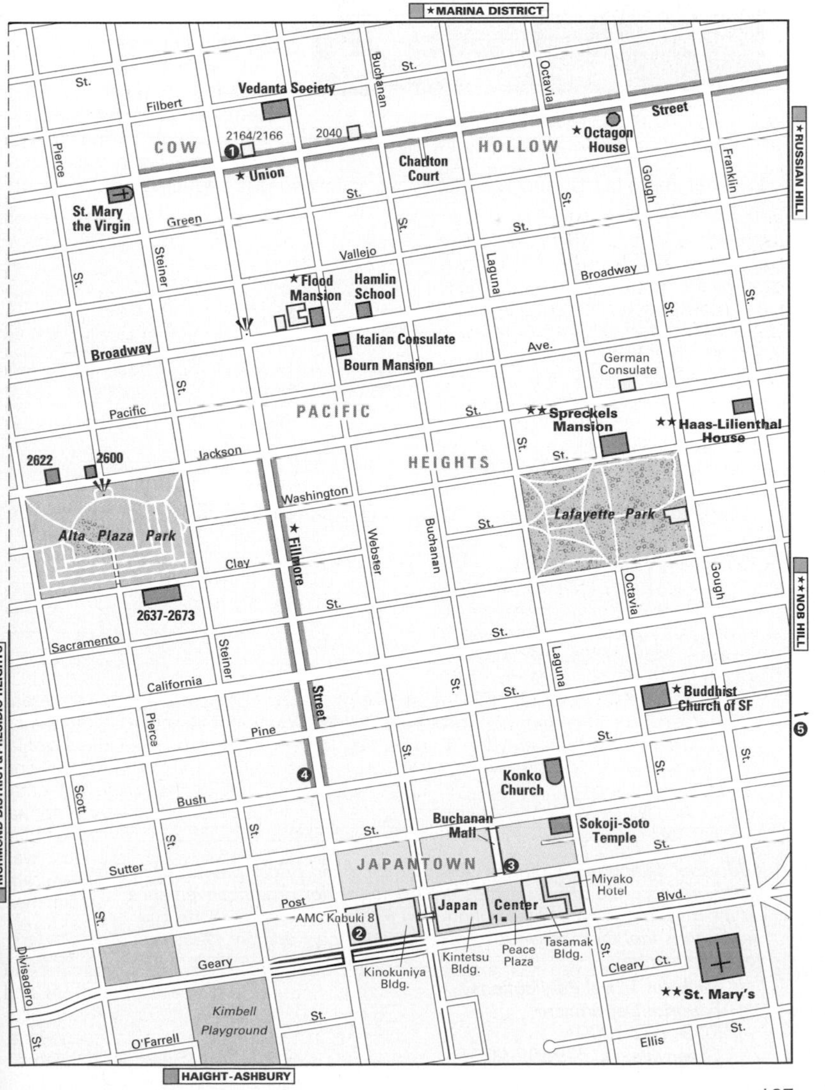

© Robert Holmes

Shopping on Union Street

in 1905 after a design by Swami Trigunatita, the three-story wooden building sports an ecumenical medley of ornamentation intended to represent religions and cultures of the world.

St. Mary the Virgin Episcopal Church – *2325 Union St. Open year-round Mon–Fri 9am–5pm, Sun during services. Closed major holidays and Christmas week.* ♿ ☎ *415-921-3665.* Partially hidden behind its fence and lych-gate, this charming church (1891) evokes the feel of an English country parsonage, though its wooden frame and redwood-shingle cladding herald the Arts and Crafts style characteristic of northern California architecture. Peace and tranquillity pervade the quiet, A-frame sanctuary and grounds. The gushing spring in the entry courtyard was used to water dairy herds, and is one of Cow Hollow's most beguiling reminders of its bucolic past.

Addresses, telephone numbers, opening hours and prices published in this guide are accurate at press time. We apologize for any inconvenience resulting from outdated information, and we welcome corrections and suggestions that may assist us in preparing the next edition. Please send us your comments:

Michelin Travel Publications
Editorial Department
P. O. Box 19001
Greenville, SC 29602-9001

15 • GOLDEN GATE PARK★★★

Time: 2 days.

Map p 109

Encompassing more than 1,017 acres of meadows, gardens and public buildings, verdant Golden Gate Park is the largest cultivated urban park in the US. Stretching 3mi inland from OCEAN BEACH to Stanyan Street, the roughly .5mi wide park accommodates 27mi of footpaths and 7.5mi of equestrian trails, all linking an enchantingly natural, yet entirely man-made, landscape of lakes, waterfalls, swales and woods.

Historical Notes

A Great Sand Waste – As San Francisco prospered in the 1860s, William Ralston and other city boosters began laying plans for a city park to rival designs for Central Park, at that time under construction in New York. They selected a roughly rectangular tract of the sandy scrublands known as the Outer Lands as an affordable, if not quite ideal, location. When Mayor H.P. Coon consulted with Frederick Law Olmsted, designer of Central Park, the famous landscape architect eyed the dunes and advised that large trees would never grow on the site. Undaunted, city planners in 1871 contracted an engineer and surveyor named William Hammond Hall to build a park on the maligned tract.

Raising a bulwark behind Ocean Beach to deflect ocean winds, Hall graded the inland dunes into gentle hills and valleys, securing them by sowing barley, lupine and ammophila grass. When this natural matting had taken root, he began to plant trees. Starting on the eastern end of the park, Hall laid out roads in a meandering fashion, partly to discourage speeding but also to imitate the leisurely ambience of a rural road. His urbane carriage entry, a narrow strip of greenery called the **Panhandle**, today harbors the park's largest and oldest trees.

By the late 1870s, the new park was a resounding public success. Corrupt city officials, however, embezzled budgeted funds, neglected maintenance and allowed private concessionaires to stake claims to park land. After being falsely accused of corruption in 1876, Hall resigned his commission as park superintendent. Golden Gate Park plunged into a decline that went unchecked until 1886, when a new civic administration asked Hall to return as an adviser.

"Uncle John" – In 1890 Hall appointed **John McLaren** (1846-1943) as the new park superintendent. Born in Stirling, Scotland, McLaren cut his horticultural teeth working as a gardener on great Scottish estates and in Edinburgh's Royal Botanical Gardens before coming to California in 1872. Prior to his park appointment, McLaren landscaped large estates for wealthy Bay Area patrons and tended his commercial plant nursery in nearby San Mateo. Fondly known as "Uncle John" by his staff and an admiring public, the cantankerous McLaren ran Golden Gate Park with a forceful, patriarchal hand. Believing that a park should provide a sylvan refuge from city life, McLaren fought hard against new buildings, concessions, statues and other urban encroachments. Continuously battling would-be developers, personally planting millions of flowers, bulbs and trees, and tirelessly driving himself and his gardeners toward perfection, McLaren devoted himself to the park for 53 years. In addition, he found time for other projects, including BUENA VISTA PARK, HUNTINGTON PARK and the 1915 Panama-Pacific International Exposition. By the time of his death at 97, McLaren had succeeded in cultivating one of the world's most varied gardens.

The Midwinter Fair of 1894 – Four years after McLaren's appointment, Michael H. de Young, inspired by the World's Columbian Exposition of 1893 in Chicago, successfully convinced city officials that San Francisco should mount its own fair at Golden Gate Park to promote the city's splendid winter climate. Five fancifully domed and spired buildings and a 266ft Electric Tower were erected around a quadrangle called the Great Court, and the California Midwinter International Exposition of 1894 (also called the Midwinter Fair) opened on January 27. All of California's counties, four other states and more than 19 foreign countries participated, drawing some 2.5 million visitors during its six months of operation. Today visitors flock to the site, now the **Music Concourse**, to hear Sunday concerts in Spreckels Bandshell (1899) and to tour the Asian Art Museum; the M.H. de Young Memorial Museum; and the aquarium, planetarium and manifold other exhibits of the California Academy of Sciences.

Besides its exalted role as a leafy retreat, Golden Gate Park has served many uses during the 20C. Refugees set up temporary homes here after the 1906 earthquake. Thousands flocked here during the "Summer of Love" in 1967, when hippies hung out and crowds gathered for mass celebrations and concerts at Speedway Meadow. For most San Franciscans, Golden Gate Park serves as a big backyard—a place for family picnics, neighborhood baseball games, outdoor sports and contemplative strolls.

SIGHTS

★**Conservatory of Flowers** – This ornate Victorian glass palace shelters more than 20,000 rare and exotic plants under an octagonal central dome and two flanking wings. Golden Gate Park's oldest structure, the lacy white wood-frame building was prefabricated in Dublin, Ireland, and shipped to the San Jose estate of James Lick for installation. Arriving after Lick's death in 1876, the disassembled structure

Practical Information ....Area Code: 415

Getting There – [Muni] from Market St. take **5-Fulton**, **21-Hayes** and walk into park from 8th & Fulton, or take **71-Haight–Noriega** or **N-Judah** and connect with **44-O'Shaughnessy** or walk from 9th Ave. From Fisherman's Wharf (Van Ness Ave. and North Point), take southbound **42-Downtown Loop**, **47-Van Ness** or **49-Van Ness/Mission** down Van Ness, transfer at McAllister to **5-Fulton**, walk into park at 8th Ave. From Union Square, take **38-Geary**, transfer to **44-O'Shaughnessy** at 6th Ave. From the east, Fell St. leads directly into the park, which is bounded by Fulton and Stanyan Sts., Lincoln Way and the Great Highway; Park Presidio Blvd. enters it from the north, 19th Ave. from the south. Call ☎ 673-6864 for more information.

Getting Around – Golden Gate Park is laced with curving drives that emerge to connect with the city's street grid at some 20 points along the park perimeter. Two principal thoroughfares traverse the park from east to west: John F. Kennedy Dr. (north) and Martin Luther King, Jr. Dr. (south). On Sundays and most holidays John F. Kennedy Dr. between Kezar Dr. and Transverse Dr. is closed to vehicular traffic. Similarly, on Saturdays, Middle Dr. W. closes between Transverse Dr. and Martin Luther King, Jr. Dr. (south of the Polo Field). **Parking** (street and lots) is available throughout the park, though spaces fill quickly on sunny Sundays. Disabled-parking spaces are located in the Music Concourse *(fee charged at Music Concourse lot on weekends and holidays)*. The principal botanical and cultural attractions are situated in the park's eastern half; recreation areas occupy the western section.

Visitor Information – Park maps and event information are available at the **Beach Chalet** visitor center *(p 122)* or at **McLaren Lodge** (Fell and Stanyan St. at park's east entrance; open year-round Mon–Fri 8am–5pm; ☎ 831-2700). The *Golden Gate Park Explorer Pass* ($12.50) allows the visitor one-time access to all four of the park's main cultural attractions (California Academy of Sciences *p 119*, Asian Art Museum *p 114*, M.H. de Young Museum *p 111* and Japanese Tea Garden *p 110)*; passes are available at the Academy of Sciences and the Visitors Information Center at Hallidie Plaza *(p 230)*. **Food** concessions are located in the Concourse area, Children's Playground and Stow Lake boathouse; restaurants at the de Young Museum, California Academy of Sciences and the Beach Chalet.

Recreation – Public sports facilities include baseball/softball diamonds at Big Rec Ball Field *(☎ 753-7024)* and tennis courts *(☎ 753-7027)* north of the Children's Playground. Guided horseback trail rides depart from Golden Gate Park stables located north of Golden Gate Park Stadium *(reservations required; ☎ 668-7360)*. Pedal, electric and row boats may be rented at Stow Lake *(year-round Mon–Fri 10am–4pm, weekends 9am–4pm; ☎ 752-0347)*. The nine-hole Golden Gate Park Golf Course is located near 47th Ave. and John F. Kennedy Dr. *(☎ 751-8987)*. Paved biking and skating trails ramble the park; Middle Dr. W. is a car-free skaters' haven on Saturdays, while a portion of John F. Kennedy Dr. is dedicated to skaters and bicyclists on Sundays & holidays *(rentals at several shops near the park along Stanyan St., and behind Stow Lake Boathouse, ☎ 668-6699)*. Extensive hiking paths wind through the park, and a variety of walking tours are conducted May–Oct *(free; ♿ for information ☎ 263-0991)*.

was purchased by a consortium of San Francisco businessmen led by Leland Stanford, and donated to Golden Gate Park. The central rotunda offers an introduction to a miniature rain forest; the east wing features smaller tropical plants and a lily pond; the west wing is devoted to economic and medicinal plants. Seasonal blooms in formal geometric designs grace the parterres in front. *Note: Conservatory closed indefinitely for repair.*

John McLaren Rhododendron Dell – At the heart of this 20-acre garden *(blooms in spring)* stands a statue of John McLaren **(1)** contemplating a pinecone. The life-size proportions and quiet, natural pose contrast pointedly with the host of heroic bronze figures that surround the nearby Music Concourse, an ironic contradiction to McLaren's lifelong campaign to keep statues from cluttering the natural scenery of the park. Stroll to the nearby bower of enormous tree ferns to experience the sensation of having entered a world of giants.

Children's Playground – [Kids] ✗ A pioneering concept when it opened in 1888, this municipal playground was centered on the sandstone Sharon Building, which provided refreshments, stored playground equipment and stabled goats for the

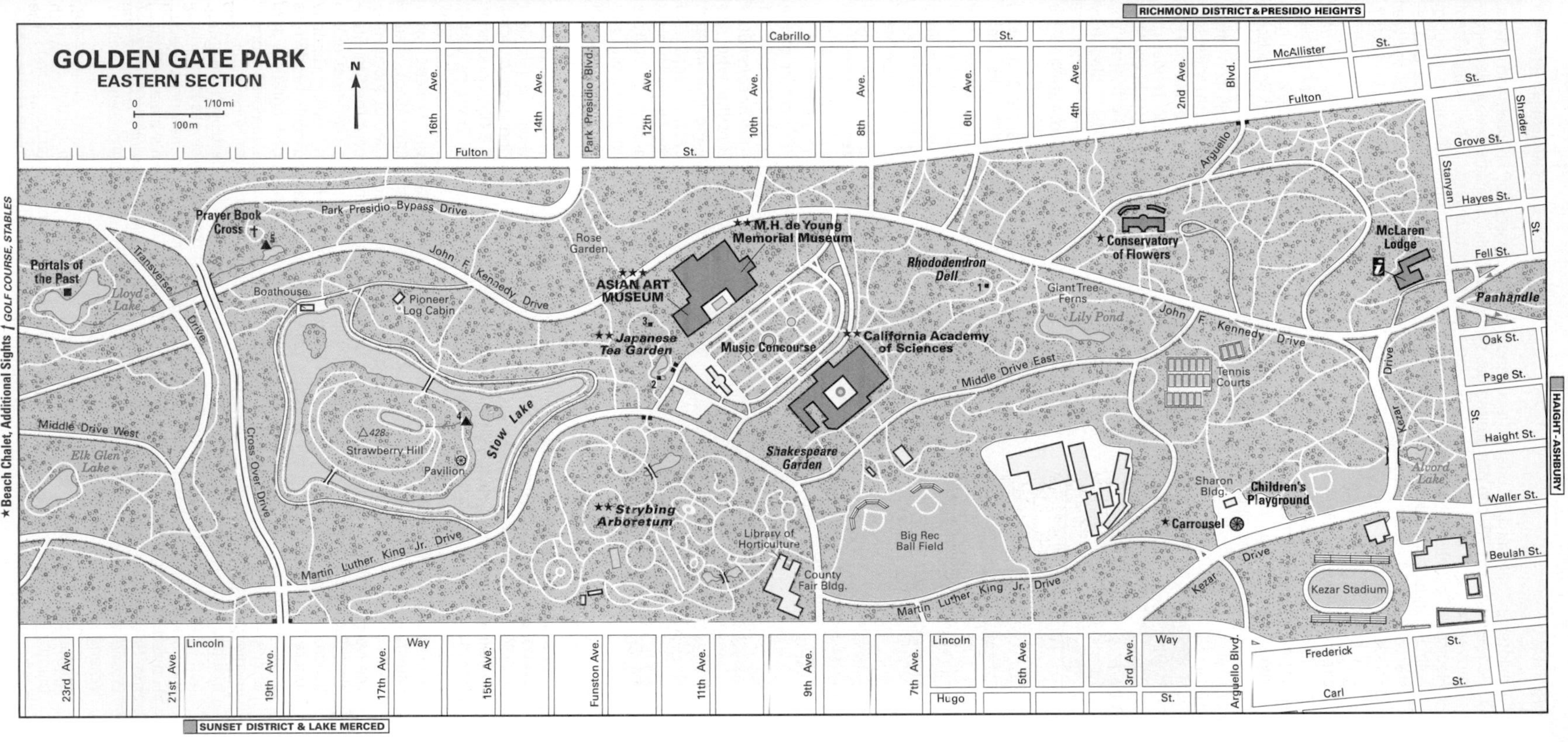

GOLDEN GATE PARK
EASTERN SECTION
0 1/10 mi
0 100 m
N
RICHMOND DISTRICT & PRESIDIO HEIGHTS
HAIGHT-ASHBURY
SUNSET DISTRICT & LAKE MERCED
★ Beach Chalet, Additional Sights / GOLF COURSE, STABLES
Cabrillo
St.
McAllister
Fulton
Shrader
Grove St.
Stanyan
Hayes St.
Fell St.
Panhandle
Oak St.
Page St.
Haight St.
Waller St.
Beulah St.
Frederick
Carl
16th Ave.
14th Ave.
Park Presidio Blvd.
12th Ave.
10th Ave.
8th Ave.
6th Ave.
4th Ave.
2nd Ave.
Blvd.
Arguello
23rd Ave.
21st Ave.
Lincoln
19th Ave.
17th Ave.
Way
15th Ave.
Funston Ave.
11th Ave.
9th Ave.
7th Ave.
Hugo
5th Ave.
3rd Ave.
Arguello Blvd.
Prayer Book Cross
Park Presidio Bypass Drive
Portals of the Past
Lloyd Lake
Transverse Drive
Boathouse
Pioneer Log Cabin
John F. Kennedy Drive
Rose Garden
★★M.H. de Young Memorial Museum
★★★ ASIAN ART MUSEUM
★★ Japanese Tea Garden
Music Concourse
★★ California Academy of Sciences
Rhododendron Dell
Giant Tree Ferns
Lily Pond
★ Conservatory of Flowers
McLaren Lodge
Middle Drive West
Elk Glen Lake
Cross Over Drive
Strawberry Hill
428
Pavilion
Stow Lake
Middle Drive East
Tennis Courts
Kezar Drive
Alvord Lake
Shakespeare Garden
★★ Strybing Arboretum
Library of Horticulture
County Fair Bldg.
Big Rec Ball Field
Sharon Bldg.
Children's Playground
★ Carrousel
Kezar Stadium
Martin Luther King Jr. Drive

children's "barnyard." Today it is a venue for art classes for children and adults. Redesigned in 1978, the playground has swings and slides, a sandbox, a play structure and a new, goat-free version of the barnyard. The magnificent Herschell-Spillman **Carrousel★**, housed with its princely stable of carved wooden animals under a dome supported by 16 fluted columns, was built in 1912 and restored in 1984 *(open Memorial Day–Labor Day daily 10am–6pm; rest of the year Fri–Sun 10am–4:30pm; closed Jan 1, Thanksgiving Day, Dec 25; $1/adult, 25¢/child; ☎ 415-759-5884)*.

★★ **Japanese Tea Garden** – Kids *Open Apr–Oct daily 9am–5:30pm. Rest of the year daily 8:30am–5pm. $3.50.* ✗ P ☎ *415-831-2700.* Harboring a delightful maze of winding paths, stone lanterns, ornamental ponds, bonsai, a wooden pagoda, a Zen garden and a teahouse, this tranquil, five-acre garden has been one of San Francisco's premier attractions since it was built for the Midwinter Fair of 1894. After the fair closed, the garden continued operating under the direction of master gardener Makoto Hagiwara, who also tended the tea concession and is credited with inventing the fortune cookie here in 1909. A plaque by the front entrance honors the memory of Hagiwara and his family.

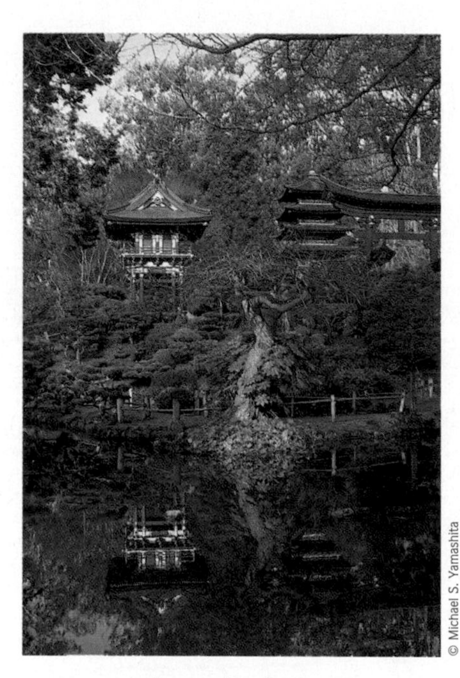

© Michael S. Yamashita

Japanese Tea Garden

The garden is most colorful around April, when its cherry trees burst into bloom. The exquisitely crafted ceremonial gateway at the front entrance is a traditional feature of Japanese shrines. Inside, the steeply arching wooden **Moon Bridge (2)** takes its name from the orb formed by the bridge and its reflection in the pond below. Near the center of the garden sits a 10.5ft statue of *Amazarashi-no-hotoke-Buddha* ("the Buddha who sits through sun and rain without shelter"); cast in Japan in 1790, it is the largest bronze Buddha outside Asia. Visitors enjoy sipping green tea and nibbling delicate cookies in the open-air **teahouse (3)**.

★★ **Strybing Arboretum** – *Open year-round Mon–Fri 8am–4:30pm, weekends & holidays 10am–5pm. Guided tours (1hr) available Mon–Fri 1:30pm, weekends 10:30am & 1:30pm. Contribution requested.* ✗ P ☎ *415-661-1316.* Covering some 70 acres of rolling terrain, this outstanding botanical collection comprises 6,000 species of plants from all over the world. Arranged around a large, central lawn, its varied gardens shelter secluded benches and gentle pathways that invite leisurely contemplation. The arboretum emphasizes regions of Mediterranean climate, with significant collections from California, the Cape Province of South Africa, southwestern Australia and Chile. Other attractions include a hillside garden of succulents; the New World Cloud Forest, where special mist emitters supplement the San Francisco fog; the verdant Redwood Nature Trail; the Primitive Plant Garden of moss, lichen, cycads, horsetails, tree ferns and conifers; and the Moon-Viewing Garden, where East Asian plants grow around a reflecting pond in a landscape inspired by classical Chinese and Japanese principles. The adjacent Garden of Fragrances and Biblical Garden share a handsome retaining wall built of stones removed from a medieval Spanish monastery purchased by William Randolph Hearst, who had it dismantled and shipped to Golden Gate Park for reassembly. A fire destroyed the crates and identifying markings, leaving a great pile of indistinguishable stones from which the Park Department has drawn over the decades for a variety of masonry projects. Housed in the County Fair Building to the left of the Arboretum's main entrance, the **Helen Crocker Russell Library of Horticulture** *(open daily year-round 10am–4pm; closed major holidays)* maintains more than 12,000 volumes and presents exhibits *(changing quarterly)* of botanical prints and other art.

Shakespeare Garden – Established in 1928, this small English garden nurtures plants mentioned in the works of William Shakespeare. The locked box in the back wall contains a bust of the Bard, a copy cast from the sculpted image at the poet's tomb. That image was carved by Gerard Johnson after Shakespeare's death in 1616. *Visitors who wish to see the bust must make prior arrangements at the McLaren Lodge (p 108).*

Stow Lake – Kids Serving as the park's main irrigation reservoir, this moat surrounding Strawberry Hill is the largest of the 15 man-made lakes and ponds that dot Golden Gate Park. Swarms of waterfowl share the water with a flotilla of small boats, which may be rented from the boathouse on the northwest shore *(p 108)*. The 428ft summit of Strawberry Hill, reached by footpath, is the highest point in the park and was famed for its panoramas of the city before trees grew to block the view. Constructed in 1894, a **waterfall (4)** named for industrialist Collis P. Huntington *(p 14)* cascades 125ft from the summit to the surface of the lake. A decorative Chinese moon-viewing pavilion stands on the island's eastern shore. Immediately north of Stow Lake, **Prayer Book Cross**, a 57ft Celtic cross carved of sandstone, dominates the hill above **Rainbow Falls (5)**.

★★M. H. DE YOUNG MEMORIAL MUSEUM *3hrs*

Open year-round Tue–Sun 9:30am–5pm (1st Wed 8:45pm). Closed major holidays. $7 (includes admission to Asian Art Museum; free 1st Wed). Guided tours available. X ♿ P *www.thinker.org* ☎ *415-863-3330.*

From an initial hodgepodge collection begun in the late 19C, the M.H. de Young Memorial Museum has developed into a mature art museum specializing in American fine and decorative arts from the pre-Columbian era to the present. Though architecturally undistinguished, it is a proud presence in Golden Gate Park and serves as a major West Coast venue for important traveling exhibitions.

Building a Museum, Building a City – The museum was established by local newspaperman **Michael H. de Young**, co-founder of *the San Francisco Chronicle*. Inspired by the World's Columbian Exposition in Chicago in 1893, de Young pulled together a similar spectacle, the California Midwinter International Exposition *(p 107)*, the following year. When the fair closed, de Young persuaded the city's Park Commission to preserve the Egyptian Revival-style Fine Arts Building as a museum dedicated to the memory of the great fair.
Soon after the museum opened in March 1895, de Young, collecting with more enthusiasm than connoisseurship, began to amass a great miscellany of artwork, historic artifacts and natural history exhibits. Many of these objects have since been removed from display, but one of the early purchases, *Caius Marius Amid the Ruins of Carthage* (1807) by American painter John Vanderlyn, proved very astute. As a bold if unsuccessful attempt to establish an American school of monumental history painting, the Vanderlyn work was significant enough to attract the interest of benefactors—among them John D. Rockefeller III—seeking to endow an institution committed to building a fine American painting collection.
In 1919 Louis C. Mullgardt, architectural coordinator of the Panama-Pacific International Exposition of 1915 *(p 92)*, completed an east wing addition to accommodate the museum's growing collections. The central section and tower were added in 1921 and the original Fine Arts building was demolished as unsafe in 1929. Galleries for temporary exhibitions were constructed in the early 1930s and the west wing (present home of the Asian Art Museum) was completed in 1965.
Throughout the de Young's century-plus life, several benefactors have elevated specific collections in ways that have redefined its character. Local arts patron Phyllis Wattis for decades fostered acquisition of indigenous art, from Africa and Oceania in particular. The promised bequest of the San Francisco-based Land Collection brings greater refinement to the pre-Columbian holdings. The Carolyn and H. McCoy Jones gift of village and tribal weavings from the Near East and Central Asia inspired the creation of a separate exhibition space for ethnographic textiles. But the museum's primary focus was established in 1978 when Blanchette and John D. Rockefeller III bequeathed to the museum their extraordinary personal collection of American painting and works on paper. This immensely important gift of some 137 works propelled the de Young to first-class status among American art museums. In 1996 Harry W. and Mary Margaret Anderson presented 655 works of American printmaking from 1962 to 1991, a collection rich in the work of postwar artists such as Jasper Johns, Robert Motherwell, Roy Lichtenstein, Frank Stella and Claes Oldenburg.

A Complementary Union – In 1970 the de Young was united with the California Palace of the Legion of Honor under a single administration called the **Fine Arts Museums of San Francisco**. As a result, the identities of the two institutions have been more clearly defined and their holdings redistributed accordingly. The Legion is now solely devoted to European art, from antiquity to modern, whereas the de Young specializes in historical American art with significant holdings in textiles, African art, Oceanic art and the pre-Columbian arts of the Americas. The arrangement enables the two museums to share conservation and education resources, while the division of functions promotes acquisition without competition or duplication. Today both museums curate and host important large-scale temporary and traveling exhibitions while seeking constantly to expand and upgrade their permanent collections. Current plans aim at strengthening the de Young's profile in early-20C American and late-20C Bay Area art, with a view to presenting contemporary art in the context of earlier traditions.

The Asian Art Museum *(p 114)*, which presently occupies the west wing of the de Young building, is slated to move to new quarters in the city's former Main Library at CIVIC CENTER soon after the turn of the century.

Visiting the de Young – A notice board just past the entrance posts scheduled docent tours, and the nearby information desk provides updated maps of the galleries. American art, for the most part, is displayed in chronological order, beginning in the galleries leading left past the bookstore and continuing clockwise around the central, skylit **Hearst Court**. Silver and glass are displayed in wall cases in the corridors linking the central core of galleries. The African, Oceanic, Art of the Americas and Textiles collections are exhibited to the east (right) of the entry hallway. Temporary exhibitions are normally mounted in galleries to the south and east of Hearst Court.

Gallery One Kids is dedicated to orienting children to art and aspects of museum work. Stop here for an entertaining introduction to why and how art objects are made, what labels mean, and other topics. Tables accommodate reading and art-making by children, and a computer station accesses the database of more than 80,000 works in the Fine Arts Museums' Achenbach Foundation for Graphic Arts *(p 156)*.

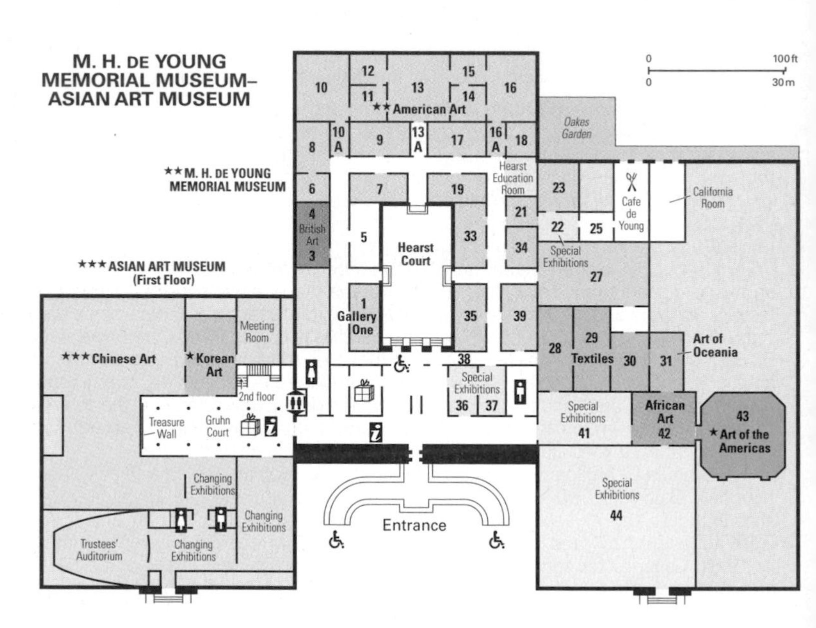

★★American Art

The American collection reveals great depth in portrait, landscape and genre painting, with special emphasis in *trompe l'œil* still life. Contemporaneous decorative arts pieces—furniture, silver, glass and porcelain—are displayed with the fine art of a given period.

Portraiture – Only 30 works painted in 17C Boston are known to exist, 26 of these without specific attribution. One of them, *The Mason Children* (1670), forms part of a group of eight portraits of the children of the Freake, Gibbs and Mason families painted by an unknown artist (or several artists) known only as the **Freake-Gibbs Painter**. The work, which presents the subjects in strict frontal arrangement, is the oldest known painting in the country to depict more than two people. *Mrs. Daniel Sargent (Mary Turner Sargent)* (1763), by the self-taught master **John Singleton Copley**, shows release from the rigidity of early Colonial painting: The subject is turned obliquely from the perspective of the artist, who painstakingly reproduced the elegant costume. Two portraits (c.1806) by **Gilbert Stuart**, a favorite painter of the wealthy and powerful in the new Republic, reveal the elegance that characterizes Stuart's celebrated portraits, such as the one of George Washington that appears on the one-dollar bill.

Works by **John Singer Sargent**, America's foremost portraitist of the leisure class, and Impressionist **Mary Cassatt** (*Mrs. Robert S. Cassatt, the Artist's Mother*, c.1889) testify to the international success these painters gained during their lifetimes.

Landscape – Works by **Albert Bierstadt** and **Thomas Moran**, best known for their grandiose landscapes of the West, and by the Hudson River school painters **Thomas Cole** and **Frederic Church**, highlight the museum's collection of American landscape painting. **William Stanley Haseltine**'s handling of light in *Ruins of the Roman Theatre at Taormina, Sicily* (1889) suggests the advent of Impressionism, though the subject matter clings to the romantic architectural ruin dear to the 19C sensibility. The work of California painters **Thomas Hill**, **William Keith** and **Virgil Williams** celebrates nature in the West.

Fine Arts Museums of San Francisco

Caroline de Bassano, Marquise d'Espeuilles (1884) by John Singer Sargent

Still Life and Trompe-l'Œil – The de Young holds a number of *trompe l'œil* works (the term derives from the French expression "deceives the eye") that became especially popular in America following the showing of *After the Hunt* by **William Harnett** at the Paris Salon of 1885. Harnett and **John Frederick Peto** (*Job Lot Cheap* and *The Cup We All Race 4*, both c.1900) go beyond illusionism, leading viewers to question the nature of reality itself as well as that of the picture plane.

Genre and Regionalist Painting – Well endowed with works by painters who preferred to depict everyday life to grandiose subjects, the museum contains outstanding pieces by **George Caleb Bingham** (*Boatmen on the Missouri*, 1846), **Winslow Homer** (*The Bright Side*, 1865), **George Catlin** (*Fire in a Missouri Meadow and a Party of Sioux Indians Escaping From It*, 1871), **Thomas Anshutz** (*The Ironworkers' Noontime*, 1880) and **Thomas Hovenden** (*The Last Moments of John Brown*, 1884). Regionalists **Grant Wood** (*Dinner for Threshers*, 1934) and **Thomas Hart Benton** (*Susanna and the Elders*, 1938) bring dignity to scenes of rural life near their Midwestern homes.

Period Rooms and Decorative Arts – A George III (1760-1820) dining room *(Gallery 4)* in the style of **Robert Adam** reveals the influence on English and early American neoclassicism of the then newly rediscovered Roman cities of Pompeii and Herculaneum. A Federal parlor *(Gallery 6)* from 1805 relies on lighter, straighter lines and touches of exoticism. Silver and glassware are featured in corridor display windows.
Especially worth noting is a passageway *(Gallery 10A)* lined with **Joseph Dufour** wallpaper entitled *Savages of the Pacific Ocean* (1806); the elaborately designed and colored paper depicts scenic idealizations of narrative incidents described and illustrated in Captain James Cook's journals of his Pacific explorations in the 1770s. Beneath stands a set of oak and beech "elastic" side chairs made in Boston by **Samuel Gragg** around 1808; the steam-formed chairs were a precursor to the bentwood styles later popularized in the US.

Sculpture – 19C American sculpture is primarily exhibited in two rooms. Marble works in Gallery 11 include **William Wetmore Story**'s *King Saul* (1882). Featured among bronzes in Gallery 14 are **Frederic Remington**'s *The Bronco Buster* (1895) and 11 works by **Arthur Putnam**. Other sculptures—presented singly or in small groups in other galleries—include **Robert Boardman Howard**'s *Scavenger* (1948) and **Alexander Calder**'s *Stabile* (1967), both in Gallery 35.

Textiles

Although the museum regularly rotates objects from its holdings of world textiles, visitors to low-lit Galleries 28–30 are certain to see fine traditional weavings from the Near East and Central Asia. These include the finest collection of high-quality Anatolian *kilims* (flat-woven pileless tapestries) outside Turkey. Textiles produced by nomadic Turks as tent and yurt furnishings adhere to a traditional vocabulary of tribal designs, and often employ a deep-red pigment made from the native madder plant. Doorway embroideries, prayer rugs and bed coverings made by artisans in settled Uzbek and Turkmen tribes reflect a more varied exposure to materials and design through commercial relations.

African Art

The exhibit contains pieces from a cross section of agricultural sub-Saharan cultures, mostly West African. Pieces like the stylized Luba figures from Zaire were among the first African sculptures to influence Western artists. Because most of the materials of African art—wood, fiber, hide, hair, bark and shell—are organic and highly perishable in tropical conditions, the museum's pieces are relatively young, dating mainly from the late 19C and 20C.

Slender, attenuated wooden sculptures of Zaire's Lengola culture, beaded cloth sculptures of the Bamileke from Cameroon, and carved granary doors made by the Dogon of Mali are commanding presences. In spite of their visual appeal, the objects shown here—shrine and ancestor figures, masks, headdresses, containers and items of regalia—were not created simply for beauty. These objects are purposeful, ceremonial conduits to powers in the spirit and animal worlds. The tribal community assures its own vitality by keeping this religious and cultural circuitry intact.

Art of Oceania

This small but beautiful collection concentrates on the pre-World War II arts of Polynesia, Melanesia and Micronesia. In these highly stratified island societies, artists were often esteemed as mediators between the realms of the human and the divine; remarkable masks such as those displayed from New Ireland helped to bridge the gap. In some communities, the artistic process was a communal one; an example is a handsome Maori canoe prow from New Zealand, carved with a stone adze.

★Arts of the Americas

Arrayed in one large room, ceremonial and funerary objects from Mesoamerica and Central and South America reflect the span from 1200 BC to AD 1520, after which time European intervention began to change the nature of the indigenous cultures. Especially worth noting are **wall murals** (painted with natural pigments on a backing of volcanic ash and mud) from the ancient city of Teotihuacán and artworks from the Olmec culture, including two hollow earthenware sculptures of crawling babies. One of the figures (c.1200-900 BC) holds aloft a ball, which prefigures the ritual ball court games played throughout Mesoamerica until the Spanish conquest. Delightfully lively, refined Colima ceramic animals and figures intended to accompany the dead to the next world were excavated from shaft tombs along Mexico's west coast.

Other displays present objects, many of gold or jade, from Maya, Mixtec, Aztec and Intermediate Andean cultures. Iconographies of surface decoration relate to shamanic rituals, sacred warfare and the afterlife.

Examples of indigenous art from the west coast of North America include fine Native American **baskets** (note the brilliantly colored Pomo feathered baskets) that reveal how precisely their makers understood seasonal variations in native vegetation. Offerings and storage containers for intertribal "potlatch" gatherings of Northwest Coast natives are arrayed at the base of a darkly pigmented 20ft Tsimshian **totem pole**, a rare 19C relic in which ancestral animal spirits rise one from another.

★★★ASIAN ART MUSEUM *1/2 day*

Open year-round Tue–Sun 9:30am–5pm (1st Wed 8:45pm). Closed major holidays. $7 (includes admission to M.H. de Young Memorial Museum; free 1st Wed). Guided tours (1hr) available. ✗ ♿ 🅿 *www.asianart.org* ☎ *415-379-8880.*

Possessing what is today considered the finest collection of Asian art in the nation, this museum was born of the efforts of collector and Olympic advocate Avery Brundage. With particular strengths in Chinese art, including jades, ceramics, ritual bronzes and paintings from the Ming and Qing dynasties, the collection of some 12,000 works also boasts the nation's most comprehensive assemblage of Japanese art; significant holdings of Indian and Southeast Asian religious statuary; and Korean, Himalayan and Near Eastern artwork.

Collector and Olympian – The museum's founder, **Avery Brundage** (1887-1975), represented the US in the decathlon during the 1912 Olympics in Stockholm, Sweden, and enjoyed an extremely prosperous career as an engineering executive before being appointed to the International Olympic Committee in the 1920s. During his extensive travels around the world in this capacity, he became fascinated by East Asian cultures, adopted a Taoist philosophy, and launched a collection of Japanese woodblock prints and *netsuke*—carved bone toggles used to fasten men's kimono sashes. His passion for collecting broadened in the 1930s to embrace 3,000-year-old Chinese bronzes, Chinese ceramics and objects from Korea, Southeast Asia, India and its neighbors, and the Middle East.

By the 1950s, Brundage began to search for a permanent museum that could conserve and display his then-uncatalogued collection of some 5,000 pieces of art. Anticipating a growing awareness of the need for closer relations with Pacific Rim nations, and believing his museum would be a "bridge of international knowledge and respect" between the East and the West, he selected San Francisco—with its growing reputation as a "gateway to the Pacific Rim"—as an ideal location for the new museum. After protracted negotiations, Brundage presented a portion of his collection to the city in 1959. The city-owned Asian Art Museum opened in 1966. Following Brundage's death in 1975, the museum continued to acquire and catalog Asian artwork. Other benefactors stepped forward to donate works, including important collections of Indian miniature paintings, Thai ceramics, and other Chinese and Japanese works. With space to display only 12 to 15 percent of the collection at any given time, the museum has long outgrown its present home. In the early 1990s, the city decided to relocate the Asian Art Museum to the former Main Library building at CIVIC CENTER, a venue that will offer more than three times the display space after renovation. The move is expected to occur early in the 21C.

Visiting the Asian Art Museum – Enter through the Gruhn Court from the west side of the M.H. de Young Museum (admission fee permits entry to both museums). Three galleries to the left of the court host high-quality temporary exhibitions. Against the court's west side, the brilliant Treasure Wall, designed after Qing dynasty Empress Dowager Cixi's treasure case in Beijing's Forbidden City, contains colorful ceramics, sculptures and carvings from throughout Asia and serves as an overview of the museum's collections.

The Chinese and Korean galleries occupy the museum's first floor; the second floor houses the Japanese, Himalayan, Southeast Asian and Indian galleries; Near Eastern artifacts are displayed along the second-floor loggia. To accommodate its limited display space, the museum regularly rotates exhibits so that even objects of primary importance are not always on view.

★★★Chinese Art *1st floor*

Comprising over half the museum's holdings, the Chinese collection numbers some 6,000 bronzes, sculptures, paintings and decorative arts. The works exemplify the beauty and diversity of Chinese art from Neolithic times to the present, while the comprehensive collection of pottery, vases, tableware and figurines thoroughly illustrates the momentous history of ceramics in China.

The Neolithic Age in China yielded a wealth of earthenware pottery, stone crafts and jade. The museum's oldest pot, a small earthenware **bottle** from the Yangshou culture, dates from 4800-3600 BC. **Oracle bones**, created by priests to divine the future, represent the first evidence of written language in China. Neolithic artisans were already producing **jades** in the characteristic doughnut shape, called *bi*, which has remained a popular finished shape for jade throughout Chinese history. Harder than steel, jade was revered for its durability, and was believed to possess a life-preserving property. The museum's collection of Shang dynasty ritual bronzes, made to contain tomb offerings, is dominated by three-legged pots called *ding*, decorated on the outer surfaces with intricate spirals and monster heads. An especial highlight is a **ritual vessel** (12C BC)

Asian Art Museum of San Francisco, Avery Brundage Collection

Horse with Bridle, Tang Dynasty

shaped like a rhinoceros. Composite animals and decorative surface carvings characterize later Zhou dynasty bronzes; jade carving also showed increasing sophistication. Animal motifs—including fish, birds and tigers—were very popular.

Depleting resources of bronze caused the Han dynasty government to ban the placement of ritual bronzes in tombs except among aristocrats, resulting in alternative use of pottery tomb offerings. Stoneware and lacquerware also developed during this era; the museum owns China's oldest-known **lacquer vessel** (1 AD) with a maker's mark.

Indian (and, by association, Hellenistic) influences permeate early works of Chinese Buddhist art. Among them is the earliest known Chinese **Buddha image** (AD 338), a gilt bronze representation of the Indian prince who became the Buddha—recognizable by its extended earlobes and a cranial protuberance signifying wisdom. The statue makes an interesting contrast with later figures, which adopt distinctly Chinese characteristics.

The worldly confidence of the Tang dynasty encouraged an appreciation of simplicity, exemplified by the draperies on Buddhist images. Their cultural dynamism also shows in secular works, particularly in the **sancai tomb figures**—three-color ceramic statues that vigorously depict horses, Bactrian camels and foreign traders. The Tang dynasty also developed cobalt-blue glazes and true porcelain, a hard, white ceramic of kaolin clay that rings when struck.

Ceramics reached a peak during the Song dynasty with the development of green celadon glazes, light-blue Jun ware and the opaque, glassy, blue-green glaze of Longquan ware. Although the Chinese court settled for nothing less than perfection in ceramics, a rougher form of pottery was introduced to Japan during this dynasty, ironically carried home from southern Chinese monasteries by Japanese monks. Particularly interesting are the bronze wire burial suit and bronze mask from the short-lived Liao dynasty.

Highlights of the Chinese Dynasties

Neolithic Period (c.5000-16C BC): Regional cultures emerge, with distinct craft traditions in clay, stone, bone, basketry and textiles.

Shang Dynasty (1122-1028 BC): Transition to Bronze Age is marked by the rise of cities and rival clans. Remarkable piece-mold technique is invented for casting shapely bronze vessels.

Zhou Dynasty (1122-256 BC): During unsettled period of state-making, increasing prosperity creates a market for objects of extreme technical refinement and splendor.

Qin Dynasty (221-206 BC): Short-lived dynasty, established by the first emperor, marks beginnings of imperial China; Great Wall is unified from existing walls and a common script is established.

Han Dynasty (206 BC-AD 220): Major dynasty forges a single Chinese nation and imposes a long period of peace marked by expansion and the coming of Buddhism. Prosperity encourages trade along the Silk Road, bringing in foreign influences. The decorative dragon becomes prominent, along with layered and inlaid bronzework.

Six Dynasties (AD 317-589): Empire splits into rival states.

Sui Dynasty (AD 581-618): Empire is reunited; Grand Canal is built. Potters improve glazing techniques.

Tang Dynasty (AD 618-907): Expansive dynasty blossoms into a splendid and powerful nation, open to international trade and spreading Chinese influence abroad, most spectacularly to Japan. Aristocratic burial rites become increasingly elaborate and tomb furnishings proliferate in quality and quantity. Buddhism flourishes. AD 907-1125: Empire breaks down into individual states, including the **Liao dynasty** (937-1125), a northern kingdom established by nomadic Khitan people.

Song Dynasty (AD 960-1279): Humanistic age of extreme aesthetic richness is renowned for fine and varied ceramics and painting. Nomads invade the north to establish the **Jin dynasty** (1115-1234), but the court moves south to Hangzhou and continues to govern as a sub-dynasty known as the **Southern Song** (1217-1279).

Yuan Dynasty (AD 1279-1368): Mongol dynasty favors blue-and-white porcelains to trade with Islamic nations.

Ming Dynasty (AD 1368-1644): Return to native rule is a classic age of blue-and-white wares.

Qing Dynasty (AD 1644-1911): Period of foreign rule under Manchus features delicate ceramics of brilliant color and eggshell translucency. Contact with Western nations increases

During the Yuan dynasty, potters added kaolin clay, making glazes thicker and more opaque. The Ming dynasty is noted for the proliferation of glazing and decorating techniques, including the development of five-color ware. Western tastes were profoundly influenced by the blue-and-white ware exported from the late Ming dynasty onward.

Unlike post-Renaissance art from the West, which relies on a fixed perspective, Chinese (and Japanese) **landscape painting** traditionally employs a "floating" perspective that invites the eye to enter the painting and to move from feature to feature, promoting a meditation on nature. The museum's broad collection focuses on Ming and Qing masters and includes monumental landscapes and still-life scrolls from the 13C to the present. The museum also holds many examples of **calligraphy**, emphasizing the different script styles of the Ming dynasty.

★Korean Art *1st floor*

Comprising some 500 objects, the Korean collection features hanging scrolls, stoneware ceramics from the Three Kingdoms and United Silla periods (57 BC-AD 935), gold jewelry, ash-glazed funerary pottery (cinerary ware) and a wide-ranging exhibit of celadon-glazed vessels from the Koryo period (AD 918-1392). Though less prolific than their Chinese counterparts, Korean potters produced many unique ceramic forms, including gourd-shaped bottles with red-pigment celadon glaze. Two slate **daggers** (c.500-600 BC) are the museum's oldest Korean artifacts. The important collection of Buddhist objects includes sculptures, bronze vessels and implements, paintings, lacquerware and furniture. Of particular note is a gilt bronze sculpture of *Amitabha Buddha* (8C), the largest specimen of such quality in a Western collection; and exceptional portraits, including *Buddha Amithaba and Eight Great Bodhisattvas* (14C) and the later *A King of Hell* (16C).

★★Japanese Art *2nd floor*

With more than 4,200 objects, the museum's Japanese holdings offer the most comprehensive overview of Japanese art in the US. Gallery highlights feature screens and scroll paintings, ceramics, archaeological bronzes, religious sculptures, swords and decorative arts. The museum also has splendid collections of *netsuke* miniatures in horn and ivory, and Japanese calligraphy representing different styles and formats from the 12C-20C.

■ History of Japan

Prehistoric Age (c.12,000 BC-AD 552): Contact with China and Korea after c.300 BC brings new technologies to existing pottery culture; metal tools and bronze bells *(dotaku)* develop. During **Kofun Period** (AD 250-552), imperial Japan takes form.

Asuka to Nara Periods (552-710): Buddhism enters Japan from China via Korea. Along with religious influences, Japan imports Chinese writing, tea and styles of architecture, sculpture and painting.

Heian Period (794-1185): Capital moves from Nara to Heian-kyo (present-day Kyoto).

Kamakura Period (1185-1333): Rise of the warrior class of samurai. Zen (a sect of Buddhism encouraging intellectual spiritualism based on meditation) arrives from southern China. The arts and the tea ceremony become secularized.

Muromachi Period (1333-1573): Under strong shogunate rule, a flourishing of Zen Buddhism—and reaction against it—infuses the arts, particularly painting and the tea ceremony.

Momoyama Period (1573-1615): Warlords battle for control of Japan while Western traders and missionaries make their first landings on the Japanese coast.

Edo Period (1615-1868): The shogun Tokugawa Ieyasu moves the capital to Tokyo and seals the country from foreign arrivals; a strict class structure (samurai, farmers, craftsmen and merchants) is established. Ensuing prosperity allows the diffusion of art through a broad swath of society.

Meiji Period (1868-1912): Following the 1853-54 visit of US Commodore Matthew Perry, Japan is compelled to abandon isolationist policies and open trade with the US and Europe. Modernization becomes paramount after a new imperial government overthrows the weakening Tokugawa shogunate.

Among the museum's treasures from Japan's Prehistoric Age are earthenware pottery, bronze *dotaku* (bells), mirrors and weapons, and a wealth of *haniwa* (retaining posts for burial mounds) fashioned in the shapes of animals, houses, boats and people. Japanese sculptures of the Nara to Meiji periods were made of wood, bronze and dry-lacquer, a technique that involves applying lacquer-soaked cloths to a clay core that is later removed.

Buddhist temples of various sects were built during the entire history of Japan, many with powerful statues of ferocious temple guardians standing on misshapen demons known as the "dwarves of ignorance." Buddhist sculpture and painting reached their zenith during the Kamakura period. The arrival of Zen inspired extensive artistic expression, characterized in painting by monotone landscapes that fade to blankness. The demand for **samurai swords** pushed the manufacture of Japanese steel to a high art, involving ritual instructions that required repeated pounding, folding and immersions in water.

Nearly 200 screens (only a handful of them on display at any one time) represent the major schools and styles of Japanese painting. Among them are the colorful Yamato-e style; the monochrome Kanga landscapes, which harkened back to classical Chinese ink paintings and literary themes; and the abstract, minimalist Haboku (splashed ink) style, a technique expressive of Zen spontaneity. By the middle of the Muromachi period, non-religious painters of the Kano school—which rejected the rich narrative traditions of painting to emphasize poetic simplicity of image and line—plied their arts on large screens that were used for blocking drafts and brightening dark castles.

Worth noting is a traditional **Japanese tea ceremony exhibit**, displaying a whisk for frothing the tea and roughly formed Temmoku teaware—a reflection of the secular Japanese appreciation for *wabi* (poverty) and *sabi* (rusticity).

The arrival of Western missionaries during the turbulent Momoyama period served as a favorite subject of secular painters. Many painting schools flourished during the Edo period, as did the arts of lacquerware, ceramics and stage drama. The collection numbers many highly decorated items from this era, including *inro* (small cases for personal effects), a fine *koto* (13-stringed zither), an exquisitely lacquered palanquin, and popular woodblock prints. The Meiji period enriched contact between Japanese artists and the outside world, both reaffirming the value of traditional arts and introducing new themes, styles and techniques.

★Tibetan and Himalayan Art *2nd floor*

This fascinating gallery contains about 300 items from Nepal, Tibet and Bhutan. The overwhelming emphasis is on religious art, including scriptures, gilt bronze sculptures of Hindu and Buddhist gods, and Nepalese and Tibetan scroll paintings known as *thangkas.*

Bhutan is renowned for its textiles woven on backstrap and floor looms, in cotton, wool and silk. Patterns, usually with stripes—vertical for men and horizontal for women—differ between households.

Brilliantly colored Nepalese painting is invariably religious. Both Hindu and Buddhist subjects are popular and coexist peacefully. Exhibits embrace some spectacular shrines produced by Newar artisans from the 8C-19C, mostly metalwork inlaid with semiprecious stones.

The arts of Tibet are heavily influenced by Nepal, India and China. Buddhism in Tibet dates from the 7C, introduced by the Chinese and Nepalese queens of King Srongtsen Gampo. The dominant Buddhist school, Tantrism, is based on the belief that enlightenment can be achieved through esoteric practices. Tibetan artworks, with their fantastic, terrifying and beautiful imagery, are unique expressions of Buddhist practice and wisdom.

The museum's *thangka* collection is one of the largest in a public American institution. Numbering 120 examples from the 12C-20C, these scrolls are made of sized cotton and brilliantly painted. Only a small number are exhibited at any given time. Tibetan ritual implements are made of precious metal and gems, and even human bone. The most common Buddhist ritual implements in Tibet are the bell *(drilbu)* and thunderbolt *(dorje)*, respectively representing the feminine attribute of wisdom and the male property of skillful means, both necessary for enlightenment.

★★Indian Art *2nd floor*

A wealth of religious statues in stone, bronze, terra-cotta and wood represent sculptural styles from every regional school and span all major periods of Indian art from the 3C BC to AD 19C. The collection also boasts carved ivories, jades and fine miniature paintings, as well as artists' prints of British India (c.1780-1910).

The distinctive Gandhara style of sculpture developed northwest of India in what is now southern Afghanistan and northern Pakistan. Situated at a crossroads on the Silk Road between East and West, hence in a unique position to receive and transmit artistic influences, Gandhara was culturally influenced by the Greek armies under Alexander, and later by Hellenistic and Roman travelers. Eventually it became a center of Buddhist art. Gandhara sculpture reflects a Greek and Roman style of carving, as illustrated by the splendid rendition of a 2C-3C Bodhisattva adorned with earrings, mustache, flowing robes, elaborate hairstyle and copious jewelry. Outstanding are eight fragments of **friezes** depicting the life of Shakyamuni, the Indian prince who became the Buddha, from birth (emerging from the right side of his mother, Maya) to his death on a couch while teaching his grieving disciples. More typically "Indian" in flavor is the Hindu and Jain sculpture of Mathura, capital of the Kushan empire. South Indian sculpture employed mostly hard granitic rock, though bronze statues were also created. The region around the city of Mysore produced delicate carving from schist: an example is a seated Ganesha (13C)—one of 14 museum statues of the elephant-headed god—which regularly receives "offerings" from museum patrons.

Sandstone dominated the sculpture of central and western India. Many works decorated the outsides of temples. A prominent example from central India is a 5C **lingam**, a phallic symbol and cult image of the Hindu god Shiva. Pala sculptures from east India are carved in a fine-grained schist that permitted intricate details, smooth surfaces and technical sophistication. The style directly influenced the art of Burma, Malaysia, Java, Nepal and Tibet.

■ Selected Hindu Deities

Brahma: The Creator, one of the Hindu triad of supreme gods.

Devi: A Hindu goddess who takes many forms, including Uma, the consort of Shiva; Parvati, the mother of Ganesha; and the ferocious Durga, slayer of the Buffalo Demon.

Ganesha: The elephant-headed son of Shiva and Parvati, beloved as the god of wisdom and wealth.

Krishna: An incarnation of Vishnu and among the most beloved of Hindu gods. Krishna is often depicted as a handsome young man with blue skin.

Shiva: The Destroyer, one of the Hindu triad of supreme gods and the most widely worshipped. Shiva wears his hair matted, carries a cobra and trident, and appears as a teacher, an itinerant wanderer or a terrible force of destruction. By virtue of clearing chaff for new growth, he is also a creator.

Vishnu: The Preserver, one of the Hindu triad of supreme gods. Vishnu wears a crown and carries a conch, lotus, discus and club, and can take many forms.

★Southeast Asian Art *2nd floor*

The collection comprises more than 500 pieces from mainland and insular Southeast Asia (Thailand, Burma, Laos, Cambodia, Vietnam, Malaysia, Indonesia and the Philippines). Sculptures constitute much of the collection, which has grown to include textiles (especially Thai and Lao silks), weaponry (highlighted by examples of the sinuous gilt *kris*, a Malay-Indonesian dagger), jewelry and manuscripts. Hindu and Buddhist sculptural motifs influenced by Indian art have been vigorously and monumentally reinterpreted; indigenous media and styles are also represented. A spectacular example is a 12C Cambodian carved-stone lintel depicting an army of monkeys attacking the demon Kumbhakarna, from the Indian epic *The Ramayana*. The holdings also include an important collection of Thai ceramics.

Islamic and Ancient Persian Art *2nd floor loggia*

The museum owns about 450 Near Eastern objects spanning 6,000 years from prehistoric through Islamic medieval periods, including painted earthenware, glazed ceramics and metal objects. Particularly fine are the Luristani bronzes (c.1000-650 BC) and ceramics from the 15C Timurid dynasty of Tamerlane, who ruled from Samarkand.

★★CALIFORNIA ACADEMY OF SCIENCES *1/2 day*

Kids *Open Memorial Day–Labor Day daily 9am–6pm. Rest of the year daily 10am–5pm. 1st Wed each month 10am–8:45pm. $8.50 (free 1st Wed). Guided tours (2hrs 30min) available.* ✗ ♿ P *www.calacademy.org ☎ 415-750-7145.*

The oldest scientific institution in the West, the California Academy of Sciences has maintained its sense of mission—to explore and interpret the natural world—while celebrating nature's biodiversity and the endlessly varied survival strategies among its species. Three separate divisions compose this multifaceted institution: the Natural History Museum, one of the 10 largest in the world, harboring more than

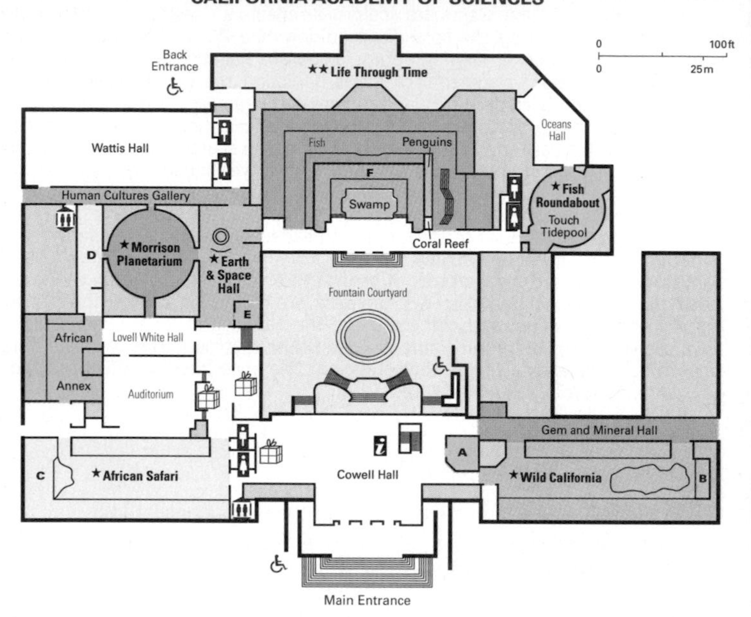

14 million specimens; the Steinhart Aquarium, oldest in the US, presenting more than 185 exhibits; and the Morrison Planetarium, taking the theme of development over time beyond the limits of Earth and into the far reaches of space.

A Center for Science – Founded in 1853 in a surge of post-Gold Rush enthusiasm for knowledge about California's physical environment, the Academy of Sciences began as a clubby group of naturalists who collected specimens and presented scholarly papers in an office on Clay Street. As public interest in its educational and information-gathering efforts increased, the Academy began to function as a natural-history museum. In 1891 the organization took up residence at 833 Market Street, in a building bequeathed by local philanthropist James Lick. Charles Crocker and Leland Stanford were among those who donated funds for an exhibit to display birds, mammals, plants and other specimens from the collections.

The Market Street building and most of its contents were destroyed by the earthquake and fire of 1906, but the institution had become so popular that San Francisco's citizenry voted to re-establish it in Golden Gate Park. The first unit of the present facility, the North American Hall of Birds and Mammals, opened in 1916. Subsequent developments through the 20C expanded the natural-history museum and added the Steinhart Aquarium in 1923 and the Morrison Planetarium in 1952. Today, through interpretive displays and study collections, the Academy functions as a respected center for scientific study. Its eight departments—Anthropology, Aquatic Biology, Botany, Entomology, Herpetology, Ichthyology, Invertebrate Zoology and Geology, and Ornithology and Mammalogy—maintain impressive holdings and pursue active research. The **Biodiversity Resource Center (A)** provides access (through videotapes, optical laser disks and CD-ROM databases) to information on efforts to preserve biodiversity worldwide. The **Academy Library** holds 170,000 books and 2,100 current journals.

Visiting the Academy of Sciences – From the ticket booth, visitors enter **Cowell Hall**, where the skeleton of a Canadian tyrannosaur extends a greeting from an era that ended 65 million years ago. The hall hosts temporary and traveling exhibits; a small shop selling children's books and toys; and the Academy Store, with books, gift items and contemporary ethnic artworks for sale. From Cowell Hall, steps lead down to a full-service cafeteria opening onto a cheerful patio. Natural-history exhibit halls extend to the sides, while the Steinhart Aquarium lies directly opposite, across the Fountain Courtyard.

★★Natural History Museum

In this section of the tripartite Academy, interpretive exhibits invite visitor participation. In addition to the permanent displays, two major special exhibitions are mounted each year in **Wattis Hall**.

★**Wild California** – This long, cavernous hall originally housed the North American Hall of Birds and Mammals. Current dioramas present habitat groups in California's widely varied multitude of ecosystems, including bobcats prowling the glades of the Oak Woodland, pronghorn antelopes grazing the plains of the Great Basin, and grizzly bears clawing for roots on the Montane Slope. Wall-mounted speaker phones give detailed information related to video sequences shown on monitors at each habitat. At the far end of the hall, behind a replicated battleground for life-size elephant seals, a saltwater **surge tank (B)** recreates the surf zone on the rugged Farallon Islands off San Francisco's Pacific Coast.

In the **Gem and Mineral Hall** *(adjacent to Wild California)*, displays drawn from the Academy's permanent collection distinguish gems from minerals and minerals from rock. Specimens are organized from simplest to most complex chemical composition according to the Dana System of Mineralogy, and are grouped according to type and structure.

★**African Safari** – Denizens of Africa's tropical heart inhabit the masterfully painted dioramas of this enormous, barrel-vaulted hall. Created in 1934, the room exhibits giraffes, antelopes, gazelles and other large herbivores sustained by savanna grasses over most of the African continent. Their carnivorous predators, including lions, cheetahs, jackals and leopards, illustrate the interdependence of the region's life forms. The most dramatic exhibit is the **Watering Hole (C)**, showcasing a populous and interdependent community of animals gathered to drink while lighting effects and sounds—recorded on location in Africa—mimic a shortened version of the diurnal cycle.
Around the corner in the **African Annex**, nine more dioramas begin with a pair of delicate gerenuk browsing on thornbush and lead up to a life-size hippopotamus and rhinoceros.

In the **Far Side of Science (D)** gallery, original cartoons by Gary Larson embody the artist's zany take on the scientific method. The **Human Cultures Gallery** showcases changing anthropological and photographic displays.

★**Earth and Space Hall** – Visitors can discover earthquakes, volcanoes and space exploration through exhibits designed to promote understanding of the Earth's position in the solar system and the dynamic forces within it. Sundials, pendulums, chronometers and navigational devices illustrate the ways time and distance have been measured throughout history, while other displays present space voyaging and the Hubble space telescope. Step on a scale to find out how much you'd weigh on various planets, view a moon rock collected by astronauts on the Apollo 17 mission, or watch an immense Foucault pendulum knock down a peg every 22 minutes to confirm the Earth's rotation beneath its swing. Perhaps most memorable are the images screened in the **EarthQuake Theater (E)**, simulating tremors as strong as 8.3 on the Richter Scale—equal in magnitude to the great San Francisco quake of 1906.

★★**Life Through Time** – *Self-guided audio tours ($1) available for rental at main ticket booth.* This challenging, yet enormously informative, permanent exhibit traces evolutionary adaptations of body structures over 3.5 billion years. An interactive computer program called "LIFEmap" allows users to select a life form and explore its sequence of development, learning through the use of branching diagrams how all living things are interconnected and why certain forms are more closely related than others. An entire wall composed of striated layers of fossil-bearing rock shows relative geological age, and the highlight exhibit, **Age of Dinosaurs**, traces changes in morphology as the immense creatures adapted to life on land—and then failed to adapt to abrupt geological change.

★Morrison Planetarium

Enter through Earth and Space Hall. Shows Jul–Aug Mon–Fri 11am, 12:30pm, 2pm & 3:30pm, weekends 11am–4pm each hour. Rest of the year Mon–Fri 2pm, weekends 11am–4pm each hour. Closed Thanksgiving Day and Dec 25. $2.50. ♿ www.calacademy.org/planetarium ☎ 415-750-7141.

The Academy's planetarium was the first to be constructed entirely in the US. Its star projector, the instrument that casts images upon the central dome, was successfully improvised in 1948 by Academy technicians who had gained expertise making and repairing optical instruments for the US Navy during World War II. The planetarium staff produces some six shows a year on such topics as recent discoveries, celestial navigation and upcoming astronomical events: comets, meteor showers and eclipses.

★Steinhart Aquarium

Open same hours as California Academy of Sciences. Guided tours (1hr) available. www.calacademy.org/aquarium ☎ 415-750-7145.

Founded in 1923 and still the oldest operating aquarium in the US, the Steinhart boasts an unusually diverse collection of fish from around the globe. Strolling past the various aquariums, visitors learn why fish school, see how environmental degradation affects undersea life, explore the effects of wave action, witness camouflage techniques enabling ocean and freshwater fish to blend into their various habitats, and observe symbiotic partnerships (such as that between the grouper and wrasse). *The aquarium will remain open through a seismic retrofitting program slated to begin in 1999.*

Visit – In the steamy **Swamp** near the aquarium's entry, dim-eyed crocodilians laze about in foliage-filtered light. Proceed clockwise around the **Reptiles and Amphibians (F)** to the darkened hall where freshwater and saltwater fish glide and glimmer in lighted tanks. Don't miss the display of fish that use electricity for communication and defense (the electric eel may be hard to spot when inactive). Past the **Penguin Environment**, with its breeding colony of South African black-footed penguins (sometimes called "jackass penguins" for their characteristic braying noise), lies the **Coral Reef**, an entire symbiotic community of coral plants and invertebrate animals. The reef is among the first ever to be maintained in an aquarium. One of the most intriguing exhibits, the **Fish Roundabout★**, places visitors in the center of a doughnut-shaped, 100,000-gallon tank to observe the schooling behavior of fast-swimming ocean fish. At its base, the **Touch Tidepool** draws children, especially, to extend their fingers toward a sea anemone's tentacles or study the underside of a starfish. *(Visitors can watch fish being fed at 2pm daily, penguins at 11:30am and 4pm daily.)*

ADDITIONAL SIGHTS IN THE PARK

The western section of Golden Gate Park, from Stow Lake to the ocean, abounds with great stretches of meadows, woods, sports facilities and minor attractions. Reflected in Lloyd Lake, the portico known as **Portals of the Past** is all that remains of a Nob Hill mansion destroyed in the earthquake and fire of 1906; it was moved here in 1909 to commemorate the disaster. Halfway to the ocean from Stow Lake lies the immense **Polo Field**; although it no longer hosts polo matches, simultaneous football, rugby, soccer and lacrosse games are often held here, and runners, bicyclists and equestrians avail themselves of its concentric tracks.

At **Spreckels Lake**, model-boat enthusiasts launch their own radio-controlled vessels. A bit farther west along John F. Kennedy Drive, at the **Bison Paddock** Kids, a small herd of the shaggy beasts grazes under eucalyptus trees.

In the northwest corner of the park, the small but beautifully cultivated **Queen Wilhelmina Garden** *(blooms early spring)* provides a setting for the **Dutch Windmill★** Kids (1902), one of the world's largest, which pumped water for park irrigation until 1929. The windmill was restored for decorative purposes in 1981. Its companion, the **Murphy Windmill** (1905) in the park's southwest corner, still awaits restoration.

★**Beach Chalet** – *Open year-round daily 9am–6pm. Closed Dec 25. Guided tours (30min) available.* ✗ ♿ P ☎ *415-751-2766.* The last structure ever designed by architect Willis Polk, this Spanish Colonial-style pavilion (1921)—bordering the Great Highway on the park's western edge—operated for years as a workingman's bar. The structure is graced with some of San Francisco's finest WPA-funded **murals★**, a series of frescoes executed in 1937 by Lucien Labaudt. Contrary to the serious toil honored in the contemporaneous murals at COIT TOWER, the Beach Chalet scenes depict recreation and diversion in the city. The frescoes today have been carefully restored, and the building's main floor has been modified to serve as a park **visitor center**. Check here to review the park's history, receive a map locating its attractions and learn of current programs or events. An elegantly sinuous banister, designed by Labaudt in the form of a serpent and carved of honey-hued magnolia wood, leads to a second-floor brew pub and restaurant.

16 • HAIGHT-ASHBURY

Time: 2 hours. MUNI bus 6–Parnassus, 7–Haight, 33–Stanyan, 37–Corbett, 43–Masonic, 66–Quintara or 71–Haight-Noriega; streetcar N–Judah.

Map p 123

Although three decades have passed since the Human Be-In and the Summer of Love, a countercultural ethos still clings to Haight-Ashbury, usually called "the Haight." Named for the two streets intersecting at its heart, this neighborhood draws hordes of young people to its parks and sidewalks, thrift stores and coffeehouses. With 90 percent of its housing stock predating 1922, the Haight boasts some of the city's loveliest Victorian homes, which have attracted a steady influx of ambitious remodelers since the mid-1970s. Today this area, nestled between GOLDEN GATE PARK and its Panhandle, Buena Vista Park and Frederick Street, manages to nurture both its turn-of-the-century roots and its anarchic ones to create a colorful, eclectic community.

Historical Notes

Culture... – Prior to its development in the early 1870s, the neighborhood was a sandy scrubland sparsely populated by farmers. As San Francisco's population skyrocketed, a committee of city officials—Supervisors Clayton, Ashbury, Cole, Shrader and Stanyan among them—determined the city's westward expansion. In addition to establishing a street grid (imposing their own names on several streets), the supervisors reserved large spaces for public use, including Golden Gate Park and its Panhandle *(p 107)*.

As these parks developed, a resort area took shape in the neighborhood surrounding Stanyan Street. The Haight Street Cable Railroad began regular runs from Market Street in 1883; hotels, restaurants, saloons and shops appeared; and a California League baseball field was built in 1887 north of Waller Street. Beginning in 1895 **The Chutes**, an amusement park on the south side of Haight Street between Cole and Clayton streets, drew large crowds with its vaudeville theater, zoo, carnival rides and 300ft water slide. Property values quintupled and new homes proliferated so rapidly that the architectural style of the day, Queen Anne, continues to characterize the Haight a century later.

By the early 1900s the area was predominantly residential. As the baseball field and amusement park were dismantled, new shops and restaurants opened along Haight Street between Stanyan Street and Masonic Avenue. For two decades, the neighborhood remained solidly middle-class. In the 1920s the advent of the automobile opened relatively far-flung Twin Peaks and the Sunset District to development, diminishing the Haight's appeal as a "streetcar suburb." During the Great Depression, many Haight-Ashbury homes were sold or divided into apartments; rents plunged and buildings deteriorated as absentee ownership rose.

... And Counterculture – By the 1950s the neighborhood hosted an eclectic mix of students, gays, blacks and beatniks fleeing tourist-ridden NORTH BEACH. A decade later, the Haight blossomed into a countercultural haven, celebrating rock music, mind-altering drugs and free love. An estimated 20,000 people crammed into Golden Gate Park in January 1967 for Timothy Leary and Allen Ginsberg's **Human Be-In**, an anti-establishment celebration featuring poetry readings and rock concerts. Jerry Garcia's Grateful Dead held court at 710 Ashbury Street; neighbors included Janis Joplin and members of Jefferson Airplane. Together these musicians invented the wandering, melodic San Francisco Sound that would catapult them to international fame. The Haight-Ashbury craze reached its peak later that year during what became known as the **Summer of Love**, when an estimated 75,000 participants flocked to the neighborhood, sleeping in Golden Gate Park and attending free rock concerts and parties.

In 1968, many hippies left the Haight for rural communes, and heroin replaced LSD and marijuana as the drug of choice. By 1971, more than a third of the shops on Haight Street were boarded up, and violent crime soared. Yet the neighborhood sur-

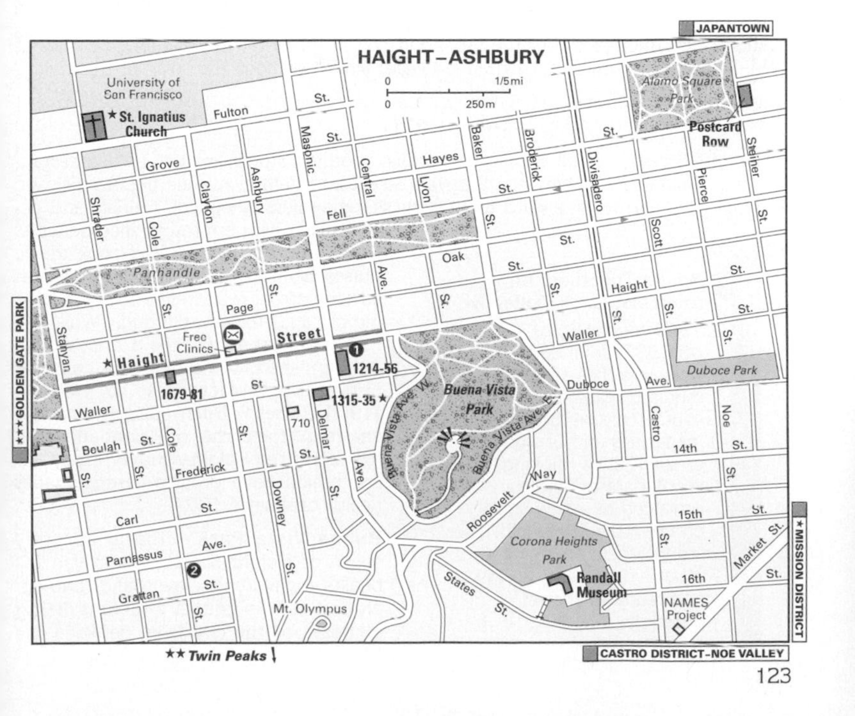

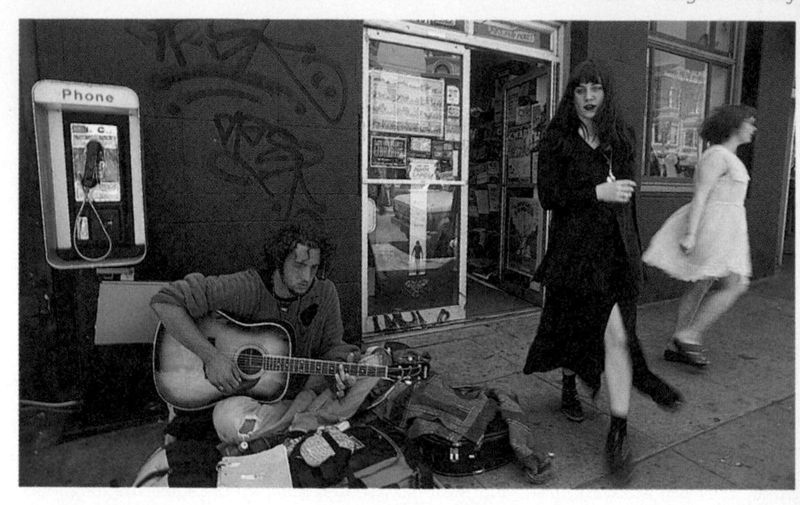

Hanging in the Haight

vived to experience a gentrification movement later that decade. Crime dropped as incomes and property values rose. By the 1980s the Haight had re-emerged as the middle-class enclave it had been a century before.

Today the Haight is more mainstream than it was during its 1960s heyday. Despite citizen protest, several chain stores have appeared in the neighborhood, and a new wave of upscale designer-clothing shops and restaurants have opened to serve a burgeoning professional class. Nonetheless, the countercultural heart of the Haight still beats. Disaffected youths congregate on street corners and in Golden Gate Park, along with middle-aged denizens whose appearance seems only to have grayed since 1967. Quirky collectors flock to the area's comic shops and vintage magazine stores, and hipsters hang out in Haight Street cafes. Here, even as the Queen Annes are restored to their turn-of-the-century beauty, vestiges of the 1960s live on.

Residential Architecture – Hundreds of unique, eye-catching Victorian period houses, most in the substyle known as Queen Anne, ornament Haight-Ashbury. Characterized by asymmetrical massing, a panoply of external surfaces and designs, bay windows and sometimes turrets, the homes date primarily from the building boom of the 1880s and 1890s. Because houses in the Haight were so much in demand, Queen Annes were frequently built in rows of four or five similar structures, but a variety of color and detailing options provided ample opportunity for homeowners to distinguish their abodes from their neighbors'. A stroll along Central Avenue or Page, Masonic or Waller streets reveals fanciful examples of Queen Annes, many restored during the gentrification trend that has swept the neighborhood in the last two decades. The rows at **1214–1256 Masonic Avenue** and **1315–1335 Waller Street★** embody the spirit of the style.

SIGHTS

★**Haight Street** – Lined with coffee shops, clothing stores, nightclubs and restaurants, Haight Street between Stanyan Street and Central Avenue bustles day and night. The narrow sidewalks teem with skateboarders, shoppers, tourists and occasional street performers; incense wafts from New Age shops; and rock music pulses from large, frenetic thrift stores where patrons wait in line to trade their old old duds for new old duds. While the buildings here are not the district's most distinguished, some, like the colorful, curvaceous structure at **no. 1679–81** (1904, James F. Dunn), display a certain charm. At the corner of Haight and Clayton stand the Haight-Ashbury Free Clinics, which have provided free, quality health care since 1967.

Bound Together: An Anarchist Book Collective

1369 Haight St. ☎ 415-431-8355. For 20 years this outlet has served up required reading for the counterculture: books, magazines and pamphlets on alternative thinking, vegetarianism, and the remaking of a new society on the ruins of the old. The storekeepers are volunteers, often writers, easy to talk to and ready to answer questions.

Buena Vista Park – Rising abruptly south of Haight Street, this sylvan hill boasts a children's playground, two secluded tennis courts and tantalizing glimpses of the city from between the trees that crowd its steep slopes. The 36.5-acre park was reserved for public use in 1867, and John McLaren *(p 000)* supervised the planting of cypress, live oak, pine and eucalyptus trees during the early 1900s. In recent years, non-native plants have been removed and underbrush cleared from the hillside. Visitors who make the bracing climb along footpaths to the summit are rewarded with sweeping **views** of San Francisco's residential areas stretching away toward bay and ocean.

★**St. Ignatius Church** – *650 Parker Ave. at Fulton St. Open year-round Sun–Fri 8am–5pm, Sat 8am–6pm. ☎ 415-422-2188.* This imposing domed Renaissance Revival church (1914, Charles J. Devlin), on the campus of the Jesuit-affiliated University of San Francisco, features two 213ft towers on either side of a facade dominated by Corinthian columns atop Ionic columns, separated by a portico. A campanile at the northeast corner houses a three-ton bell cast in England in 1859. The interior design is based upon early Christian basilicas. A deeply coffered ceiling, freestanding columns and arches provide a dramatic framework for the sanctuary, whose paintings, iconography and ornate stained-glass windows were added between 1938 and 1962. The centerpiece is a polychrome white-oak baldachin that stands over an altar of Italian marble with Moroccan onyx inlays, containing relics of St. Ignatius.

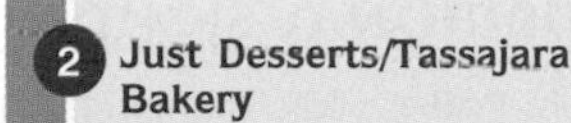

2 Just Desserts/Tassajara Bakery

1000 Cole St. ☎ 415-664-8947. Founded by the San Francisco Zen Center, this natural-foods eatery draws students and staff from the nearby UCSF medical school, who stoke up with vegetarian sandwiches and bowls of hearty homemade soup. The potato-and-cottage-cheese bread regularly sells out, as do the thick-crust hearth loaves baked directly on the oven shelf.

Postcard Row: Alamo Square Victorians

The row of Victorians located at 710-720 Steiner Street, between Hayes and Grove Streets, strikes a familiar chord with most San Francisco visitors. One of the most photographed vantages in the city, "Postcard Row" stands before a remarkable, snapshot-ready backdrop featuring many San Francisco landmarks, including the Bank of America Center and the Transamerica Pyramid. Lush, grassy Alamo Square Park across the street conveniently allows photographers ample time to focus.
Distinguished externally by color and by window and door treatments, the three-story, wooden, gable-roofed houses were completed in 1895 and sold for $3,500 apiece by Irish-born carpenter and real-estate developer Matthew Kavanagh, who lived at no. 722 from 1892-1900. All seven homes are private, one- or two-family dwellings, although no. 716 was divided into seven apartments from the 1920s until the 1950s. The J. Frank Moroney house at no. 710, distinguished by its jewel-encrusted stained-glass windows and ornate gable, originally belonged to a socialite couple from New York, then changed hands nearly seven times throughout the century. The house was extensively renovated in 1967, and was sold for $87,500 in 1974.

ADDITIONAL SIGHTS

★★**Twin Peaks** – Kids *From Haight St. drive south on Clayton St. to Carmel St.; cross and continue up Twin Peaks Blvd. to Christmas Tree Point on the left.*

These two high points dominate the western skyline as seen from downtown and are generally more visible from most areas of the city than Mt. Davidson, highest point in San Francisco at 929ft. The two distinct but closely adjacent peaks reach 904ft (north peak) and 922ft (south peak). Most visitors content themselves with the grand **panorama**★★★ of the northern and eastern sides of the city from the parking lot at Christmas Tree Point, although it is possible to climb up the grassy slopes of either peak for the view to the west as well. On clear days, MOUNT DIABLO to the east, in Contra Costa County, and MOUNT TAMALPAIS to the north, in Marin County, come into view.

Renowned architect Bernard Maybeck, who designed the PALACE OF FINE ARTS for the 1915 Panama-Pacific International Exhibition, developed grandiose plans for Twin Peaks, including a great monument at the summit with waterfalls cascading to the valley below. The plans never materialized. Today visitors and locals throng the viewpoint, particularly on weekend afternoons.

Josephine D. Randall Jr. Museum – Kids *199 Museum Way, Corona Heights. From Haight St., take Masonic Ave. south to Roosevelt Way; turn left here, and right after three blocks on Museum Way. Open year–round Tue–Sat 10am–5pm. Closed major holidays. ☎ 415-554-9600.* This family-oriented science museum sits at the end of a dead-end street with a view over the Mission District. Interactive exhibits include a lapidary studio, a greenhouse, a seismology laboratory and a live-animal nursery. School science fairs are staged throughout the year. Public classes include such subjects as mushrooms, spiders, carnivorous plants and "Zen and sawdust."

■ San Francisco Viewpoints

A city famed for its views, San Francisco offers vistas at nearly every turn, from urban cityscapes to natural landscapes. Viewpoints on the following list are guaranteed to delight (weather permitting); views from each rate★★★. See individual sight descriptions for further information.

Alamo Square *(p 125)* – The quintessential postcard view of the downtown skyline looming behind a row of picture-perfect Victorians.

Angel Island *(p 192)* – An oasis of tranquillity in the middle of the bay, the summit of Mt. Livermore offers an unobstructed 360° view of the entire Bay Area.

Coit Tower *(p 65)* – A sweeping yet intimate overview encompasses the northern waterfront, Marin County and East Bay as well as the quieter corners of North Beach and Russian Hill.

Land's End *(p 155)* – An enchanting and dramatic overview of sea, rocky coastline, sweeping tide and Golden Gate Bridge.

Marin Headlands *(p 180)* – Turnouts along Conzelman Road provide ample opportunity to soak in an ever-broadening panorama of bay, bridge and city.

Mount Diablo *(p 175)* – One of the region's most extensive panoramas encompasses not just the Bay Area but a good bit of the rest of California.

Mount Tamalpais *(p 183)* – A virtual map of the Bay Area spreads out from this majestic peak. Low-lying fog can make the view especially interesting, because the summit remains in the clear while building tops and bridge piers can be seen poking up through the puffy white layer.

Treasure Island *(p 80)* – An outstanding scape of the famed towers of the Financial District, with the Ferry Building and Bay Bridge in the foreground.

Twin Peaks *(above)* – One of the city's best-known and most-frequented tourist stops, a good place to get an overall impression of the city's layout.

17 • JAPANTOWN

Time: 3 hours. MUNI bus 38–Geary, 2–Clement, 3–Jackson or 4–Sutter.
Map p 105

Known as Nihonmachi by local residents, Japantown is a locus of Japanese-American cultural life in the Bay Area. Its tidy, six-block core, bounded by Fillmore, Sutter and Laguna Streets and Geary Boulevard, displays some of the city's finer groupings of well-maintained Victorian houses alongside neat but simple modern buildings, many with stucco and half-timbered exteriors that evoke the traditional countryside architecture of Japan. By comparison with teeming CHINATOWN, Japantown is a much more subdued, orderly and open neighborhood, both architecturally and socially. Its well-organized identity is perhaps best epitomized by the Japan Center shopping, dining and entertainment complex at the heart of the community.

Historical Notes

A few Japanese came to San Francisco after the Meiji revolution of 1868 but arrivals did not peak until the first decade of the 20C. Anti-Asian sentiment slowed Japanese immigration considerably by the 1920s. Most new arrivals settled in the area today known as SOUTH OF MARKET, but when that neighborhood was devastated by the earthquake and fire of 1906, residents took refuge in the Western Addition. The new community, popularly known as "Little Osaka," harbored about 7,000 Japanese-American residents within a 20-block rectangle formed by Fillmore, Pine, Octavia and O'Farrell Streets.

Little Osaka was abandoned during World War II when anti-Japanese hysteria following the Pearl Harbor attack culminated in Executive Order 9066, forcing the evacuation of 112,000 Japanese-Americans to internment camps. Empty residences soon were inhabited by an influx of civilian workers, many of them black, who came to fill wartime shipyard jobs. After the war's end, many Japanese Americans returned to San Francisco, though few resettled in the old neighborhood. Diminished from its prewar size, Japantown took on its present appearance in the late 1960s and '70s after massive urban renewal projects cleared blocks of Victorian housing and widened Geary Boulevard. Since then, new construction has generally echoed Japanese architectural themes.

Visiting Japantown – Japantown comes alive in the evening when diners and moviegoers flock to its many restaurants and its celebrated AMC Kabuki 8 Theatre complex. The greatest crowds gather on festival days. During the spectacular **Cherry Blossom Festival** in mid- to late April *(p 218)*, thousands congregate to enjoy Japanese arts and crafts, foods and music, *taiko* drumming, dancing and a colorful parade.

SIGHTS

Japan Center – *Bounded by Geary Blvd. and Fillmore, Post and Laguna Sts. Open daily year-round. Most shops open daily 10am–5:30pm, restaurants 9pm & lounges until midnight. Closed Jan 1, Thanksgiving Day, Dec 25.* ✗ ♿ P ☎ *415-922-6776.* Reminiscent of contemporary Japanese architecture—and therefore more blandly international than traditional in style—this five-building complex (1968, Minoru Yamasaki) of galleries, shops, restaurants, cinemas and the deluxe Miyako Hotel serves as a focal point for community celebrations. Its most striking Japanese touch is the **Peace Pagoda (1)**, inspired by the miniature round pagodas dedicated to eternal peace by Empress Koken more than 1,200 years ago in Nara, Japan. Rising 110ft above the plaza in five copper-roofed concrete tiers, the pagoda is capped by a golden ball atop a copper spire, symbolizing virtue.

From the Peace Plaza, stroll west through the Kintetsu and Kinokuniya buildings, linked by an arching bridge over Webster Street. They are home to a colorful row of Japanese restaurants, galleries, music and video stores, electronics stores, antiques shops, a Japanese bookstore and the Ikenobo Ikebana (flower-arranging) Society. The complex's westernmost building houses the AMC Kabuki 8 Theatres, a popular venue for first-run films and for the annual **San Francisco International Film Festival** in April and May *(p 218)*.

Buchanan (Nihonmachi) Mall – *Buchanan St., between Sutter and Post Sts.* Completed in 1976, this quiet, attractive outdoor pedestrian street evokes the atmosphere of a Japanese village, with cobbled paving and "half-timbered" buildings. A small police *koban* (kiosk) stands

Kabuki Hot Spring
1750 Geary Blvd. in Japan Center. ☎ *415-922-6000.*
A sojourn in this traditional bathhouse will revive even the most bone-weary traveler. In keeping with Japanese bathing ritual, one must first shower to get clean *before* bathing. Sign up for one of several plans including steams, hot soaks and *shiatsu* massage, and emerge relaxed, refreshed and squeaky clean.

 **Soko Hardware**
1698 Post St. ☎ 415-931-5510. Nestling up to hammers and screwdrivers, a glorious array of housewares such as tatami mats, mulberry wrapping paper, rice cookers and flower-arranging supplies brings Japan to San Francisco. Downstairs you'll find Japanese tools and plastic-shrimp sushi displayed next to sink faucets and extension cords.

at the Post Street end of the mall near a Japanese hardware store, while traditional restaurants and shops selling Japanese furniture, stationery, chinaware, gifts, kimonos and publications line its sides.

Konko Church of San Francisco – *1909 Bush St. Open year-round Mon–Sat 6:30am–6pm, Sun 8am–3pm. Guided tours (1hr) available, reservations recommended. ☎ 415-931-0453.* With a handsome "half-timbered" exterior surface and timbers jutting from the roof, this steel-frame building (1973, Van Bourg, Nakamura and Associates) blends traditional Japanese aesthetics with modern engineering. The interior incorporates a traditionally austere, natural-wood Shinto altar with Christian influences such as pews. English-language services are held Sundays. Inspired by a Japanese farmer's revelation in 1859, the Konko (Eternal Golden Light) religion advocates earthly happiness and respect for all life by encouraging reverence for the Principal Parent of the Universe *(Tenchi Kane no Kami)* and by practicing personal meditation and study.

Sokoji-Soto Zen Buddhist Temple – *1691 Laguna St. ☎ 415-346-7540.* Dedicated in 1984, this overseas-mission temple building is handsomely clad with half-timbered stucco facing. Images of Koso-Dogen Zenji and Taiso-Keizan Zenji, celebrated as the founders of the Soto sect of Zen, flank the golden image of Shakyamuni Buddha at the center of the elaborate altar. The temple is attended by monks in traditional robes.

★**Buddhist Church of San Francisco** – *1881 Pine St. Open year-round Mon–Fri 10am–5pm, Sat 9am–noon, Sun 9am–4pm. Closed major holidays. Guided tours (1hr) available, reservations suggested. Contribution requested. ☎ 415-776-3158.* This most exquisite of Japantown temple interiors occupies the second floor of an otherwise unprepossessing building (1938, Gentoko Shimamato) capped by a stupa containing a relic of the Buddha. The Jodo Shinshu (True Pure Land) sect of Buddhism has long adopted such American cultural influences as pews, pulpit, homily books and an organ, but the golden altar embodies Japanese tradition. A small standing image of Amida Buddha occupies the central position, raising his right hand in reassurance and lowering his left in a blessing. He is flanked on the right by an image of Shinran Shonin (1173-1262), founder of the Jodo Shinshu sect. Worshipers leave offerings of flowers, candies and other goods, though not in ritual worship of the images, which are revered only as symbols of the Buddha's compassion and wisdom. Jodo Shinshu's **Buddhist Church of America** headquarters share this building with a separate entrance *(1710 Octavia St.)*.

ADDITIONAL SIGHT

★★**St. Mary's Cathedral** – *1111 Gough St, at Geary Blvd. Open year-round daily 6:45am–4:30pm. Guided tours available Apr–Oct Mon–Fri 9am–noon. Organ recitals Sun 3:30pm.* ♿ 🅿 *☎ 415-567-2020.* Sheathed in white travertine marble and visible from miles around the city, San Francisco's third Catholic cathedral crowns a shallow rise known as Cathedral Hill. Commissioned after a fire burned down its Van Ness Avenue predecessor in 1962, the striking, contemporary cathedral (McSweeney, Ryan & Lee; Belluschi; Nervi) was dedicated in 1971.

Enter through the main doors facing Geary Boulevard to see the bronze overpanel, an image of Christ rising above human figures to represent the ecumenical search for God throughout civilization. Backed by stained glass, the overpanel is also impressive when viewed from the interior.

The building's most daring design attribute is its reinforced concrete **cupola**, formed of hyperbolic paraboloids that join to enclose a soaring atrium. At the level of the congregation, clear glass panels afford fine views of the city. Unobstructed views of the massive marble altar can be had from all 2,400 seats. Narrow stained-glass windows rise steeply from the four compass points to meet at the cupola's apex, forming a brilliant cross 190ft above the sanctuary floor. Suspended on wires 75ft above the altar is a contemporary **baldachin**, a shimmering canopy of anodized aluminum rods designed by Richard Lippold to sparkle in the slightest breeze. A magnificent, 4,842-pipe Ruffatti organ perches on a concrete pedestal. Cast-bronze shrines by Enrico Manfrini and Mario Rudelli depict events in the lives of Mary and Jesus.

18 • PACIFIC HEIGHTS★★

Time: 3 hours. MUNI bus 3–Jackson, 22–Fillmore, 24–Divisadero, 41–Union, 45–Union-Stockton or 83–Pacific.
Map pp 104-105

Stretching along a high east-west ridge between Van Ness Avenue and THE PRESIDIO, this elegant residential neighborhood holds some of the city's finest houses and loveliest views. The name Pacific Heights connotes San Francisco wealth, and its reputation is fully deserved: no other neighborhood gives a grander vision of the life of affluent San Franciscans.

Historical Notes

Ridgetop for the Elite – The area today known as Pacific Heights occupies a favored location equidistant from San Francisco's three main historic centers: the MISSION DOLORES, the Presidio and the commercial area around Yerba Buena Cove (today the FINANCIAL DISTRICT). Trails linking these three centers converged near the highest point of the ridge, called the *divisadero*, but the neighborhood's precipitous streets were not developed until late in the 19C, after other areas of the city had already been established. In the mid-1850s the street grid was extended west from Van Ness Avenue, but as late as 1880 only a few houses had been built here.
Improvements in public transportation, most notably the invention of the cable car *(p 59)*, brought the area within easy reach of downtown, and at the end of the 1870s Pacific Heights experienced a sudden surge of growth. This first of many real-estate booms was focused upon the easternmost edges of the district, where huge mansions were constructed along Van Ness Avenue by the city's most successful merchants. Almost all of these early residences were destroyed in the great earthquake and fire of 1906, many of them having been dynamited by the US Army to create a firebreak.
Throughout the last decades of the 19C, on smaller parcels all over Pacific Heights, speculative developers built more modest but still impressive homes. Often erecting between five and ten houses at a time, side-by-side on the narrow lots, contractors followed formulaic plans but decorated the exteriors in a variety of ornamental motifs, from Gothic to Italianate to many combinations thereof. The prefabricated decorative elements commonly applied earned these houses the nickname "Gingerbread," and the many surviving examples are among San Francisco's most cherished architectural treasures.
In the decade following the 1906 catastrophe, many wealthy San Franciscans who had lost homes on NOB HILL and elsewhere resettled in Pacific Heights, attracted by the neighborhood's bay views and peaceful, noncommercial ambience. Most of the largest homes here date from this decade-long period, a time of great energy in every aspect of San Francisco's civic life. Along Broadway, for example, Comstock mining magnate James Leary Flood built a pair of mansions, each of which would cost $25 to $50 million today, while many bankers, industrialists and other civic leaders built stately homes.
Only the very rich could afford to maintain such massive and money-consuming establishments, and beginning in the 1920s, apartment towers were built to lodge the city's elite on a more modest scale. Some of these buildings today rank among San Francisco's most desirable residences, their full-floor units rising 10 or more stories and offering splendid views. Smaller, more conventional apartments aimed at young professionals working in downtown offices arose in the eastern half of Pacific Heights during this period.
Today many Pacific Heights mansions house schools or consulates, such as those of Italy *(2151 Broadway)* and Germany *(1960 Jackson St.)*, but the vast majority remain private homes. One of the few earthquake survivors, the Haas-Lilienthal House *(p 131)*, today serves as the city's finest house museum. Although choice residential areas have appeared in other parts of the city, the neighborhood retains its reputation as a preferred address of moneyed San Francisco.

An Architectural Smorgasbord – Pacific Heights' wealthy denizens spent fortunes ensuring that their residences reflected their financial and social status. As a result, the neighborhood constitutes a showcase of design. A slow meander along its quiet streets reveals examples of almost every architectural style and period that exist in San Francisco. Elite taste leaned toward refined, Classical motifs. Many architects looked to the Italian Renaissance palazzo for inspiration, and most followed the rules and precepts established by the École des Beaux Arts in Paris, which many of them had attended. Stone or brick was a popular building material, and designs tended to follow one consistent historical style rather than mix aspects from different periods.
Apart from the palaces and mansions of San Francisco's wealthiest elite, the great majority of homes here were built in the 1880s and '90s for well-to-do families by speculative developers, usually without the services of an architect. Almost all of these "Gingerbread Victorians" were built of wood, with molding, trim and other decorative elements ordered from pattern books and catalogs then widely available to the mass market. Fish-scale shingles, ogive-arched window frames and finely carved verge boards could be bought directly from lumber mills and added to the design at the whim of the builder or homeowner.

Visiting Pacific Heights – Bear the terrain in mind when planning a visit to the "Heights." Streets ascend and descend abruptly, sometimes as much as 100ft in one block, to accommodate the willy-nilly fluctuations of the landscape. Public transportation is handy, and street parking is generally easier to find on the west side of the neighborhood than elsewhere in the city.
To get a sense of life in Pacific Heights, visit during early evening when the people who live here jog the streets or walk their dogs. The area also enjoys breathtaking sunset vistas from its many viewpoints.

SIGHTS

Lyon Street Steps – *Between Broadway and Green St.* Too steep for vehicular traffic, this part of Lyon Street was landscaped around 1915 and today forms one of the city's most attractive public spaces. Dropping toward the bay from the west end of Broadway along the eastern wall of the Presidio, the steps offer a memorable **view★★** out over the great reddish dome of the palace of fine arts across the bay to ANGEL ISLAND and MOUNT TAMALPAIS. Flower beds and other plantings soften the carefully choreographed Beaux Arts stairs, landings and balustrades, and benches offer a place to rest while taking in the view. The corner of Broadway and Lyon offers pedestrian access to the forests of the Presidio; two blocks south stands one of the city's architectural treasures, the SWEDENBORGIAN CHURCH.

Alta Plaza Park –  *Bounded by Jackson, Scott, Clay and Steiner Sts.* Set aside as a public park when the city annexed the Western Addition in the mid-1850s, the lush green oasis of Alta Plaza lies at the heart of Pacific Heights. Basketball and tennis courts and a children's playground occupy the center of the park, and the green lawns are a favorite picnic spot. Terraces drop down on Alta Plaza's south side, forming a distinctive ziggurat of concrete and shrubbery.
The houses facing the terraces are among the oldest in Pacific Heights: a series of elaborate Italianate Victorian houses at **2637–2673 Clay Street**, all designed and built by the same contractor in 1875.
On the north side of the park, Jackson Street features a pair of houses created by two influential turn-of-the-century architects whose use of Classical Beaux-Arts models contrasts with the lighthearted playfulness of other Victorian-era designs. The former Music and Arts Institute at **2622 Jackson Street** was the first of architect Willis Polk's many commissions in the city. Built of stone in 1894 and styled like a Renaissance-era Tuscan villa, the house was acclaimed by the *San Francisco Examiner* as "the first Classical residence in San Francisco." Nearby, the angular brick facade of **2600 Jackson Street** was designed by Ernest Coxhead and built in 1895 by industrialist Irving Scott as a wedding present for his daughter.

4 Leon's Bar-B-Q
1911 Fillmore St. ☎ *415-922-2436.* Escape tony Pacific Heights and come here to eat ribs with your fingers and drink beer from a bottle. Leon's is what Fillmore south of California Street was all about before Japantown became Japantown and the neighborhood went high-style. Take one of the red Naugahyde booths for two, or step to the back for a larger table.

★ Fillmore Street – Lively, inviting and unpretentious, Pacific Heights' only commercial district lies along Fillmore Street between Jackson and Bush streets. Its art cinema, boutiques, restaurants and cafes are good places to take a break while walking around the neighborhood.
Four blocks south of California Street, Fillmore runs past the JAPAN CENTER and through the heart of the Western Addition. To the north, it reaches the edge of Pacific Heights at Broadway, where it offers one of the city's finest bay **views★** before dropping swiftly down into COW HOLLOW and the MARINA DISTRICT.

★ Broadway Mansions – *Broadway between Fillmore and Buchanan Sts.* These two elegant blocks of Broadway bear witness to the emergence of Pacific Heights as home to the city's elite after the 1906 earthquake. One of the finest buildings in the city is the former **Flood Mansion★** *(no. 2222)*, designed by local architects Bliss and Faville in 1912 for James Leary Flood. The house is a refined and beautifully crafted version of an Italian Renaissance palazzo, its Tennessee marble hung on an earthquake-resistant steel frame. A pair of brick mansions, both dating from the same period, stand alongside the Flood Mansion; all three now house private schools.
Just south of Broadway, the **Bourn Mansion** *(2550 Webster St.)* was designed by Willis Polk in 1896 for William Bourn, the mining magnate for whom Polk also created the magnificent FILOLI estate south of San Francisco. Designed as a pied-à-terre, the stately home contains only two bedrooms; rough clinker brick softens the Classical formality of the facade. Most unusually, the design plays down the importance of the entrance, which is set back in a deep vestibule beneath the upper-floor balcony.

Farther east along Broadway lie two other remarkable mansions, the stately **Italian Consulate** *(no. 2151)*, and the blue-and-gray, Baroque Revival-style **Hamlin School** *(no. 2120)*. James Flood had the latter (1901) constructed on land owned by his sister, then moved to the Flood Mansion after its completion. It too is now a private school.

★★ **Spreckels Mansion** – *2080 Washington St.* Of all the many grand mansions in Pacific Heights, none is more ostentatious than the elaborate French Baroque-style palace built in 1913 for sugar magnate Adolph Spreckels and his wife, Alma de Bretteville Spreckels *(p 155)*. The main facade consists of a series of five arched windows separated by pairs of ornate Ionic columns. The house faces onto lushly landscaped **Lafayette Park.** The rear gardens, which drop steeply down to Jackson Street, boast a covered swimming pool.

5 Dawydiak Cars
Bush St. at Franklin St. ☎ *415-928-2277.* The Bay Area—not too hot, not too cold, steep hills, two-lane highways—is sports-car territory. This longstanding dealer (pronounced "da-WID-ee-yak") specializes in European sports models from 1955 to the early 1990s, with an emphasis on Porsches. Daydream among the 25–30 cars in the 8,000sq ft showroom; the knowledgeable sales staff is happy to answer questions.

★★ **Haas-Lilienthal House** – *2007 Franklin St. Visit by guided tour (1hr) only, year-round Wed noon–3:15pm & Sun 11am–4pm. Closed major holidays. $5. www.sfheritage.org* ☎ *415-441-3000.* One of San Francisco's few Victorian-era residences open to the public, this imposing gray edifice (1886, Peter R. Schmidt) is among the last survivors of the many ornate single-family houses that once filled this eastern Pacific Heights neighborhood. Unlike the grandiose mansions constructed atop Nob Hill, this elegant residence typifies the architectural aspirations of the city's upper-middle class at the end of the 19C. Constructed for William Haas, a prominent wholesaler, the house was donated by his descendants to the Foundation for San Francisco's Architectural Heritage, which currently maintains the property as a house museum and headquarters.

The exterior embellishments are typical of the Queen Anne style and include a variety of patterned siding, ornately bracketed gables and a deceptive corner tower with windows 10ft above the floor. The basement, which at times was used as a ballroom, now holds a display of photographs showing the house in its pre-1906 neighborhood context. Upper-floor rooms, including two parlors, a dining room and one of the original six bedrooms, are furnished in a range of decorative styles dating from the 1880s to the 1920s.

Spreckels Mansion

Cross-references to sights described in this guide are indicated by SMALL CAPITALS. Consult the index for the appropriate page number.

19 • RICHMOND DISTRICT and PRESIDIO HEIGHTS

Time: 3 hours. Richmond District: MUNI bus 38–Geary, 1–California, 2–Clement or 4–Sutter. Presidio Heights: MUNI bus 3–Jackson or 43–Masonic.
Map p 133

One of San Francisco's most ethnically diverse neighborhoods and a haven of the middle class, the Richmond District is a relatively flat expanse of undistinguished row houses sandwiched between Masonic Avenue to the east, California Street to the north, GOLDEN GATE PARK to the south and the Pacific Ocean to the west. Just to the north, between California Street and THE PRESIDIO, lies Presidio Heights, a wealthier residential enclave comprised largely of spacious, single-family homes.

Historical Notes

Though today socially and economically distinct, the Richmond District and Presidio Heights were both once part of the Outer Lands, a vast expanse of scrub plants and dunes extending west from the developed areas of the city to the Pacific Ocean. Recluses and outlaws took refuge in the "Great Sand Waste," as it was called, and cemeteries occupied its eastern edge. During the final two decades of the 19C, Adolph Sutro *(p 151)* purchased vast amounts of the sandy acreage quite cheaply, opening the land for development and building a steam railway along the present course of California Street to his Cliff House and monumental bathhouse at LAND'S END, on the western edge of the city.

Construction in the Richmond District proceeded quickly after the 1906 earthquake and accelerated after a municipal railway line began operating along Geary Boulevard in 1912. Two years later, Mayor Jim Rolph ordered all San Francisco's cemeteries closed and removed south of the city limits to the town of Colma, spurring construction of yet more single-family row houses until the Great Depression struck in 1929. These new tracts drew residents of broad ethnic diversity, including White Russians fleeing the 1917 Russian Revolution, Jews from Eastern Europe and, after World War II, Japanese-Americans returning from internment camps. Chinese-Americans have formed the largest ethnic group since the 1970s, but the 1990s have witnessed a resurgence of Russian immigration.

Presidio Heights developed more slowly, lot by lot, as wealthy families hired architects to build unique, often palatial homes. A casual stroll through the neighborhood, especially along Pacific Avenue, Jackson Street and Washington Street, reveals a broad variety of architectural styles including Norman, Tudor, Italianate, Queen Anne and Romanesque. Specially designed door knockers, mailboxes, gates, gardens and a host of other intriguing ornamental details add to the visual appeal. Particularly worth noting is **Roos House** *(3500 Jackson St.)*, a massive, half-timbered residence designed in 1909 by renowned Arts and Crafts practitioner Bernard Maybeck.

SIGHTS

San Francisco Columbarium – *1 Loraine Court. Open year-round Mon–Fri 10am–5pm, weekends 10am–2pm. Guided tours (1hr 30min) available, 1-week advance reservations required.* ♿ P ☎ *415-221-1838.* Owned and operated by the Neptune Society of California, a cremation organization, this copper-roofed, Neoclassical rotunda recalls the days when cemeteries covered the Richmond's shallow dunes. Originally erected as part of the Oddfellows Cemetery, the columbarium was spared when the graves were removed in 1914. Today it contains more than 4,400 niches for cremated remains, including those of several prominent San Francisco families. The flamboyant interior is adorned with stained glass and brightly painted plaster filigree; individually decorated niches are arranged around four circular levels.

Clement Street – The more charming of the Richmond's main shopping thoroughfares (the other being Geary Boulevard), Clement Street is popular among neighborhood residents for its grocery markets, bookshops and household-goods stores. Locals and visitors alike, however, flock here for the many excellent yet understated restaurants that line the street west of Arguello Boulevard. The 12-block stretch between Arguello and Park Presidio boulevards is sometimes known as "New Chinatown" because so many of its residents have relocated from downtown's CHINATOWN since the 1970s. Although Asian restaurants predominate, a culturally diverse community thrives on Clement Street with its Continental bistros, Russian and Italian restaurants, Irish pub, dessert parlor, Western saloon and other diversions.

★**Temple Emanu-El** – *2 Lake St. Visit by guided tour only, year-round Mon–Fri 1pm–3pm. Closed Jewish holidays.* ♿ ☎ *415-751-2535.* Rising 150ft from the ground and visible for miles, this synagogue's spectacular, orange-tiled, Byzantine-style dome crowns a massive, architecturally unified complex of offices and meeting halls. Designed by Sylvain Schnaittacher, John Bakewell and Arthur Brown, Jr., the building was dedicated in 1926 as the third synagogue for the venerable Emanu-El congregation, founded in San Francisco in 1850. Outside the sanctuary's front doors, the cloistered courtyard is dotted with plants named in the Bible as well as a lion-headed fountain. Visitors enter through the vestibule, its ceiling decorated with a brilliant blue and yellow fresco of a star-studded sky. The temple, which seats 1,700 people, is lit by two stained-glass windows representing fire (west) and water (east). Four massive bronze chandeliers symbolize the tears of the Jews. At the altar, the Ark of the Covenant stands under a marble canopy, housed in a gilded bronze tabernacle box inlaid with cloisonné; the box was built in London by Californians Frank Igerson and George Dennison.

1 V. Breier Contemporary and Traditional Craft
3091 Sacramento St. ☎ *415-929-7173.* This charming shop displays an eclectic mix of folk art, furniture and contemporary crafts, much of it produced by Bay Area artists. Ceramics and glass occupy the front room, while sculpture ornaments the garden out back.

Immediately north of the synagogue lies **Presidio Terrace**, an exclusive residential enclave since 1905. Pass through the gate to admire elegant homes, many by noteworthy architects, including no. 15 (1905, Bakewell & Brown), no. 34 (c.1910, George Applegarth) and no. 36 (1911, Julia Morgan).

Sacramento Street – The discreet but charming stretch of Sacramento Street between Lyon and Spruce Streets forms the elite shopping district of Presidio Heights. More subdued than popular UNION STREET or FILLMORE STREET, Sacramento Street's upscale boutiques, intimate restaurants and small cinema cater to a mostly local clientele.

★★Swedenborgian Church – *2107 Lyon St. Open year-round Mon–Fri 8:30am–4:30pm, Sun service 11am.* ☎ *415-346-6466.* This diminutive, lovingly crafted wood-and-brick chapel, officially named the Church of the New Jerusalem, is better known as the Swedenborgian Church after Swedish scientist, philosopher and religious writer Emanuel Swedenborg, whose doctrines inspire the congregation. A fine example of Arts and Crafts design and construction, the church was

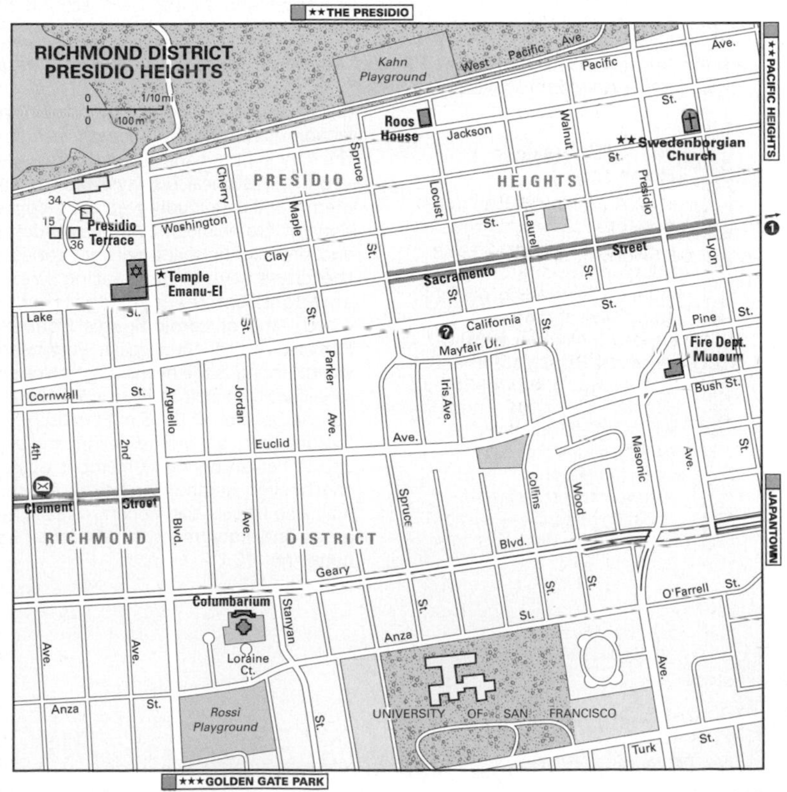

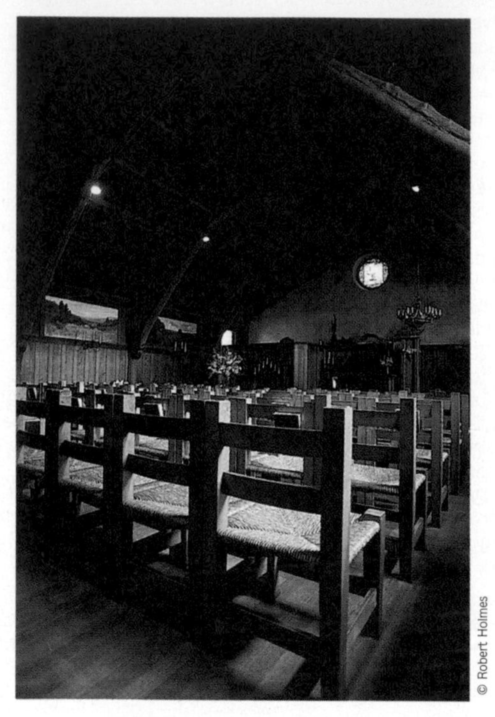

© Robert Holmes

Swedenborgian Church, interior

conceived in 1895 by the congregation's founder, the Reverend Joseph Worcester, himself an architect who enlisted the help of many talented friends. Bruce Porter sketched the design from an Italian original, while A. Page Brown served as chief architect and Bernard Maybeck as draftsman. Willis Polk designed the adjacent Parish House.

The church interior replicates the natural beauty of a California woodland. A massive fireplace along the west wall warms the entrance on chilly mornings. The ceiling is supported by bark-covered branches of native California madrone. Landscape painter William Keith contributed the pastoral scenes of the California countryside along the north wall, while Porter designed the windows along the south wall to admit a view of garden trees. The solid chairs were built by hand, without nails, of maple wood and woven tule rushes from the Sacramento River delta. A giant clam shell near the altar is the baptismal font in which poet Robert Frost, among many others, was submerged and sanctified as an infant. Outside, herringbone-patterned brick walkways frame lush gardens planted with trees and shrubs from around the world, symbolizing universality.

San Francisco Fire Department Pioneer Memorial Museum – Kids *655 Presidio Ave. Open year-round Thu–Sun 1pm–4pm.* ♿ ☎ *415-558-3546*. This converted firehouse garage houses a wonderful collection of historic fire engines, including the city's first hand-drawn pump cart (1849). Historical displays, photos and memorabilia, including eclectic collections of fire helmets, hydrants, uniforms and fire extinguishers, tell the stories of the city's several devastating fires—among them the conflagration of 1906—and of heroic figures from San Francisco's firefighting past. Particularly worth noting is the helmet that belonged to Lillie Hitchcock Coit *(p 65)*, the eccentric booster of the San Francisco Fire Department; an ornate certificate proclaims her an honorary member of Knickerbocker Engine Co. No. 5. Visitors may also inspect the modern-day fire engines and equipment in adjacent Firehouse no. 10.

Judith Ets-Hokin's Homechef

3527 California St. ☎ *415-668-3191*. Stop into this elegantly stocked store for gourmet cooks to browse among specialty ingredients, equipment and other supplies. Just down the street, at 3501 California St. (upstairs), sign up for the Homechef cooking school, which offers onetime and series classes covering everything from Mediterranean meals to Thai treats.

The Kids symbol indicates areas of special interest to children.

20 • CASTRO DISTRICT and NOE VALLEY

Time: 1 hour. MUNI bus 24–Divisadero; streetcars F–Market, K–Ingleside, L–Taraval or M–Oceanview to Castro St. station; Map p 138

Bounded roughly by 16th, 22nd, Douglass and Dolores Streets, this lively neighborhood forms the heart of San Francisco's vibrant gay community. Bars, restaurants, trendy clothing stores and boutiques crowd together along Castro, Market and 18th Streets, while residential side streets lined with beautifully refurbished Victorians invite leisurely exploration.

Historical Notes

Pastoral Beginnings – Part of a 4,000-acre land grant given to San Francisco's last Mexican mayor, José de Jesus Noe, the present-day Castro District and neighboring Noe Valley were used primarily for cattle-ranching and sheep-grazing until shortly after the Gold Rush. In 1854, during a citywide wave of land speculation, a wealthy produce merchant named John Meirs Horner bought much of Noe's ranch, platted a street grid, and began peddling land tracts to working-class Irish and German immigrants. By 1887 the Market Street Cable Railway extended down Castro Street, linking Eureka and Noe Valleys and opening the 21st Street summit to development.

As the district sustained only minor damage in the 1906 earthquake and fire, campgrounds for refugees were quickly erected. Many of the temporary residents opted to stay, and a tight-knit working-class community thrived well into the 1920s, when a commercial building boom graced Castro Street with the majestic Castro Theatre and several other fine structures. The district's social fabric changed after the Twin Peaks Tunnel opened in 1917, leading some residents to relocate to newly developing areas to the west. The Great Depression forced many landowners to divide and rent out single-family homes; federal housing subsidies in the 1950s further encouraged the working-class families' slow march out of the city.

A New Alternative – The area experienced a marked change during the 1960s and '70s when members of San Francisco's gay community began purchasing the homes vacated by the working class. Gay bars appeared along Castro Street in the early'70s and the Castro District became a gay enclave, overt about its new identity thanks to the social liberalization of the period and significant gains in gay civil rights. In 1977 residents of the Castro were instrumental in electing **Harvey Milk**, one of their own, to the city's Board of Supervisors, making him the first openly-gay elected official in US history. Milk's life and career were cut short the following year when he and Mayor George Moscone were gunned down at City Hall by City Supervisor Dan White. In 1978, largely due to the presence of gay men in city and state political arenas, San Francisco passed the Gay Bill of Civil Rights, forbidding discrimination in housing and employment on the basis of sexual orientation.

Crisis struck the neighborhood in the 1980s with the onset of the AIDS epidemic. In response, public-education organizations, support groups and health-news clearinghouses have taken root all over the Castro. Today an upbeat, neighborly attitude pervades the district. On thronged commercial thoroughfares, dance music pulses in many shops, whose creative, sometimes outrageous window displays are among the most eye-catching in the city. Along the quiet residential streets, rainbow flags symbolizing gay liberation brighten the windows of many Victorian homes.

Visiting the Castro District During the day, the Castro hums with the comings and goings of residents and visitors. Shoppers flood Castro Street and its cross streets, where neighbors stop and chat on crowded sidewalks. At night, neon signs of bars and the spectacular Castro Theatre *(p 136)* light up, dance music is ratcheted up a few notches, denizens and visitors alike put on their finery and the air buzzes with palpable energy. Street parking in the area can be exceedingly difficult to find. Many public transportation lines serve the area, most stopping at Harvey Milk Plaza (Castro Street station) at the intersection of Market, 17th and Castro Streets.

In October, the **Castro Street Fair** draws large crowds to hear local rock bands perform and to see the work of local artists and entrepreneurs.

CASTRO DISTRICT

Castro Street – Flanked with bookstores and bars, salons and cafes, the bustling shopping strip between Market and 19th Streets has served the neighborhood since the 1850s. Named for Vincent Castro, an early Mexican rancher, the busy thoroughfare overflows day and night with foot and car traffic.

In recent years, **Market Street** between Castro and Church has also become a vibrant shopping strip. Full-grown Canary Island palm trees were planted along the median in 1994, adding a welcome touch of green. In 1995, the refurbished streetcars of the historic F-Market line began clanging through, balancing the trend-setting designer clothing boutiques, funky gift shops and tony new restaurants with a charming touch of the past. The San Francisco chapter of the **NAMES Project** *(2362-A Market St.; open year-round Mon–Fri 9am–5pm; quilting bee every Wed 7pm–10pm; 1hr guided tour available, reservations requested; closed major holidays; ♿ www.aidsquilt.org ☎ 415-882-5500)* occupies a small storefront near the Castro Street intersection. Called the "largest community art project in the world," the Project sponsors the AIDS Memorial Quilt *(below)*. Visitors are welcome to step inside to view the panel storage areas and the small sewing workshop.

★**Castro Theatre** – *429 Castro St. Open year-round daily, at showtimes. Theater interior accessible on Cruisin' the Castro tour (p 231). ♿ ☎ 415-621-6120.* Declared a San Francisco Historic Landmark in 1977, this splendid Spanish Renaissance Revival theater (1922, Timothy Pflueger) represents the city's finest example of early-20C movie-palace architecture. The front exterior facade features Spanish Colonial-style ornamentation above the low-hanging marquee and a huge, pink-neon sign,

The AIDS Memorial Quilt

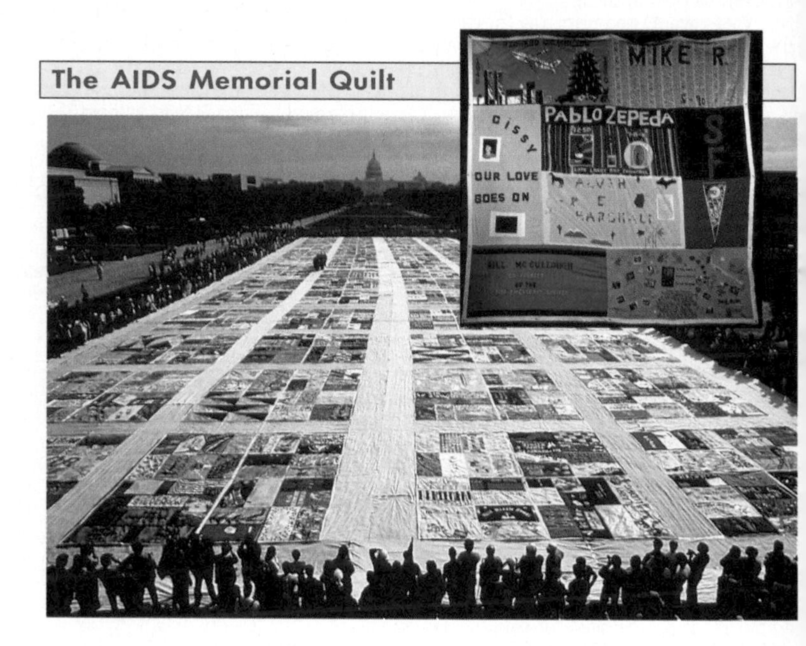

Invoking both an American tradition of quilting and a historic practice of honoring the dead with national monuments, the AIDS Memorial Quilt, sponsored by the NAMES Project Foundation *(above)*, represents a unique, moving response to the epidemic of Acquired Immune Deficiency Syndrome that has asserted itself throughout the world since the early 1980s. Composed of coffin-sized 3ft-by-6ft panels, each handmade in memory of someone who died of the virus, the quilt tours the world in sections to increase AIDS awareness and raise funds for North American AIDS-service organizations.

The idea for the quilt originated with Cleve Jones, a San Francisco gay-rights activist. In 1985, after learning that more than 1,000 city residents had died of AIDS-related illnesses, Jones asked participants in the 1985 memorial march for Harvey Milk to carry signs bearing the names of friends and acquaintances who had succumbed to the virus. At the end of the march, the posters were affixed to the facade of the San Francisco Federal Building, and the resulting patchwork resembled a quilt.

In 1986, Jones founded the NAMES Project, and in spring 1987 he made the first cloth panel in memory of his best friend. Soon, handmade panels adorned with such diverse materials as spray paint, leather, sequins and photographs began arriving at the NAMES Project headquarters in San Francisco from all over the country.

In October 1987, when the quilt was displayed for the first time in Washington DC, it comprised 1,920 panels and covered a space larger than a football field. The 1996 display in the capital was made up of an estimated 41,000 panels, covering roughly 29 football fields. But while the rapid expansion of the quilt constitutes a serious and moving reminder of the growing proportions of the epidemic, its panels remain very personal. Colorful, quizzical, kitschy, campy, each individual square celebrates the uniqueness, spirit and *joie de vivre* of one who has died.

both added in 1937. The grand, 1,450-seat interior's gently curved green and gold-leaf ceiling, two-story proscenium framed by columns and an ornate lintel, and sumptuous murals combine to create a magical ambience. Attend one of the two nightly screenings to hear resident musicians playing the Mighty Wurlitzer organ, which slowly rises from the orchestra pit for the performance, then sinks back down as the lights dim. Screening kitsch classics, foreign movies, silent-era gems and low-budget experimental films most of the year, the Castro Theatre also hosts several annual film festivals, including the San Francisco International Film Festival.

NOE VALLEY

Cradled in the lowlands south of the Castro District, Noe Valley features wide, Victorian cottage-lined streets intersecting a quaint, bustling shopping strip. Like the Castro, the neighborhood was part of José de Jesus Noe's huge ranch until well into the 1850s, and harbored a thriving community of working-class immigrants through the mid-20C. In the 1970s the area gained popularity with hippies and artists, and the enclave was nicknamed "Nowhere Valley" and "Granola Valley" due to its relative isolation and liberal-thinking population.

Today residents can only wish for such anonymity—in recent years Noe Valley has become a desirable neighborhood for young professionals starting families. Its colorful commercial thoroughfare, **24th Street** *(between Dolores and Diamond Sts.)*, retains its modest appeal. During the day, the awning-covered sidewalks fill with denizens walking dogs and pushing strollers; cafes overflow with latte-sipping, newspaper-reading customers; and designer clothing shops, bookstores, flower stands and wine merchants beckon shoppers with creative window displays.

1 Joseph Schmidt Confections

3489 16th St. ☎ 415-861-8682. Think of this place as an art gallery where chocolate is the medium. The *objets d'art* range from truffles to chocolate fish, mushrooms, tulips, even graduation mortar boards. Flavors and shapes change with the seasons, but the city's year-round cool temperatures keep the art from melting.

2 Isak Lindenauer Antiques

4143 19th St. ☎ 415-552-6436. This small antiques dealer began specializing in Arts and Crafts and Mission-style furniture and fixtures long before the styles were widely collected. It's well worth a stop—Lindenauer might have just taken delivery of a new shipment of Gustav Stickley pieces.

3 Global Exchange

3900 24th St. ☎ 415-648-8068. A fair return to the craftsperson is the idea behind this nonprofit shop. Handicrafts from 40 countries (many of them developing nations) show up in this small space. Children's overalls from Guatemala, soapstone carvings from Kenya and Indonesian slide whistles are typical of the variety of attractively priced items for sale. Other Global Exchange stores are at 2017 Mission Street and in Berkeley at 2840 College Avenue.

21 • MISSION DISTRICT★

Time: 3 hours. MUNI bus 14-Mission, 22–Fillmore, 33–Stanyan or 48–Quintara/24th St.
BART 16th St. or 24th St. station.
Map pp 138-139

Embracing numerous peoples and cultures while maintaining a festive Latino flavor, San Francisco's oldest neighborhood occupies a vast area roughly bounded by Potrero Avenue and Dolores, 14th and Cesar Chavez streets. A series of hills ripples along the scenic western edge of the district, offering some protection against chill fogs and ocean winds; as a result, "the Mission" boasts one of the city's warmer microclimates. The vibrant, gritty, colorful heart of the Mission District thrives along 24th Street, a narrow, tree-lined thoroughfare jammed with small shops, groceries, *taquerías* and restaurants.

Historical Notes

A City is Born – San Francisco was founded in the Mission District. In 1776, Spanish explorer Juan Bautista de Anza staked out the location for a Catholic mission in this warm valley near an Ohlone settlement, and on June 29 of that year, Franciscan priests Pedro Cambón and Francisco Palou celebrated Mass to establish the new mission, dedicating it to St. Francis of Assisi.

A primitive village grew up in the vicinity of the mission compound, but the surrounding lands remained largely uncultivated because the soil was poor. After secularization of the mission in 1834, wealthy Californio ranchers used the property for cattle grazing, although Yankee squatters' rights prevailed after the US won the Mexican-American War in 1848.

Like the rest of San Francisco, the Mission District boomed with the onset of the Gold Rush. In 1851, a 40ft-wide plank road was laid through the marshy SOUTH OF MARKET area, providing a connection to the flourishing downtown waterfront and opening the neighborhood to development. A street grid was platted, with 16th Street serving as the main commercial thoroughfare. Although several wealthy San Francisco families, including the Spreckelses and the Phelans, built lavish weekend homes in the area, the Mission District mostly attracted working-class people, many of them immigrants from Germany and Scandinavia (and later, Italy and Ireland), who had arrived on trade vessels and stayed to work in the shipyards and factories of the burgeoning city.

Latino Enclave – Much of the district survived the earthquake and fire of 1906, and many of those left homeless by the conflagration resettled here. Working-class families moved in, drawn to jobs available in the factories, breweries and warehouses burgeoning in the Mission District's northeast corner. Throughout the 1920s, Mexicans fleeing the revolution in their homeland swelled the ranks of Latinos in the core of the Mission; in subsequent decades, new waves of first- and second-generation Latinos replaced many European-descended families. Social and political unrest in Central and South America since the 1970s has fueled a steady influx of new immigrants from these regions.

The area east of Valencia and south of 16th Street today remains predominantly Latino and largely working-class. In the industrial northeast corner of the district, artists have begun to transform empty warehouses into sleek living and working spaces, studios and theaters, giving rise to a small but trendy cafe and bar scene. On the western edge of the district, chic new restaurants and watering holes have begun to crop up beside secondhand bookstores and thrift shops, drawing a wealthier crowd into what formerly had been an inexpensive enclave for avant-garde artists, students and political activists.

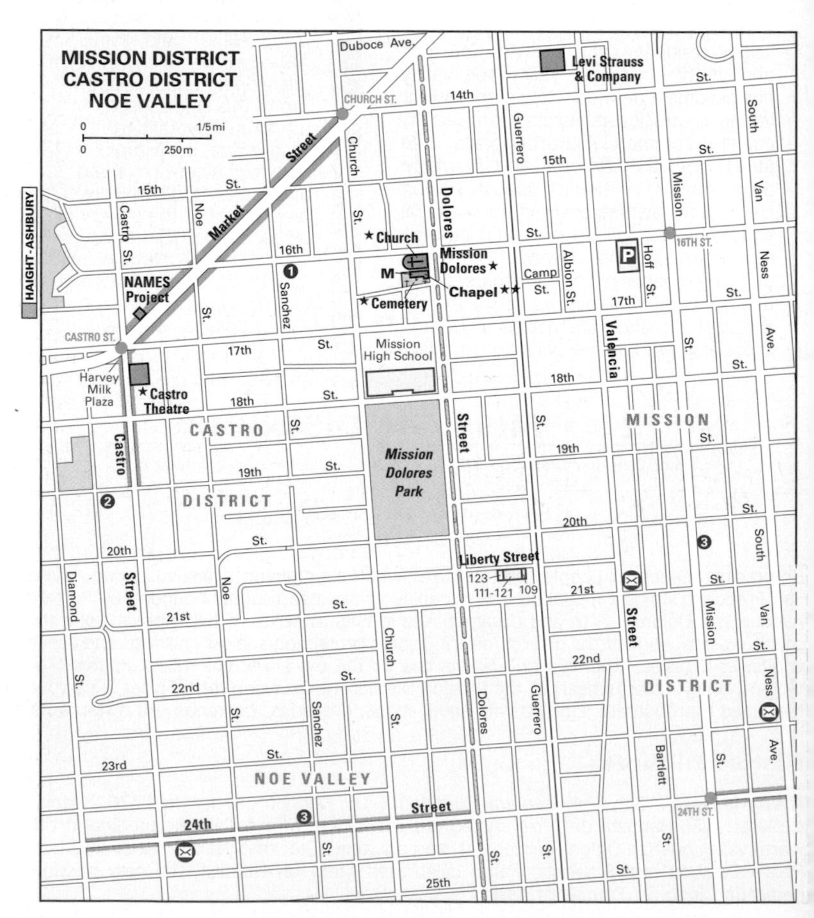

Visiting the Mission District – During the day, and especially on weekends, the Mission District's commercial thoroughfares hum with activity. Shops and sidewalks teem with people, lines lead out the doors of the most popular *taquerías*, and strains of salsa music fill the air. At night, restaurants and bars on Valencia Street, and on 16th and 22nd between Valencia and Guerrero streets, often fill to capacity and remain so until last call.

While many parts of the Mission are safe, the neighborhood's rough-and-tumble character can be intimidating. At night, keep to Valencia and 16th Streets and the areas south and west of them, except to access the BART stations on Mission Street. Street parking is relatively easy to find, though meters and time limits are strictly enforced day and night.

Exuberant celebrations occur regularly, including *Cinco de Mayo (1st Sun in May)*, *Carnaval San Francisco (Memorial Day Sun)*, and the *Latino Summer Fiesta (second Saturday in September)*. For information, contact the Mission Economic Cultural Association ☏ 415-826-1401.

SIGHTS

★**Mission Dolores (Mission San Francisco de Asís)** – *16th and Dolores Sts. Open May–Oct daily 9am–4:30pm. Rest of the year daily 10am–4pm. Closed Jan 1, Easter Sunday, Thanksgiving Day, Dec 25. $2 contribution requested. ♿ ☏ 415-621-8203.* Flanked by a historic cemetery and a lavishly ornamented 20C basilica, San Francisco's oldest extant structure serves as a distinct reminder of the city's Spanish heritage and as a repository of some of the area's early European history. The sixth mission in the Alta California chain was first established in 1776 near the present-day corner of Camp and Albion streets, two blocks east of its present site. A nearby lake named for Our Lady of Sorrows (Nuestra Senora de los Dolores) gave the mission its centuries-old nickname, Mission Dolores. The present chapel was completed in 1791, though poor soil and illness among the neophytes impeded the mission's growth. By the time it was secularized in 1834, the neophytes had largely abandoned it, and the property was occupied by squatters during the raucous days of the Gold Rush *(illustration p 13)*. The Catholic Church reacquired the property in 1860, erecting a series of larger churches alongside the old chapel to accommodate a growing congregation. The present **church**★ (1918), with its gloriously ornate Churrigueresque facade, was designated a basilica in 1952.

Visit – A remarkably sturdy structure, the **chapel**★★ has survived major earthquakes in 1868, 1906 and 1989 as well as abandonment and neglect. Today it appears much as it did in 1791, thanks to a conscientious restoration program completed in 1995. Cement stucco covers 4ft-thick adobe walls, while amber-colored windows bathe the interior in warm light. The ornate, hand-carved reredos and side altars were imported from Mexico in 1780, and bronze bells occupying niches high in the chapel's front exterior facade were brought as gifts in 1792, 1795 and 1797. The remarkable, multicolored motifs painted on the high, beamed ceiling are patterned after Ohlone basket designs.

A small passage north of the chapel contains a splendid **diorama** of the mission as it appeared in 1799; the model was created for the Golden Gate International Exposition of 1939-40 *(p 80)*. The mission's small **museum (M)** houses shards and shreds of artifacts discovered during restorations, as well as baptismal records and vestments dating from the colonial period. A section of the wall plaster is cut away and covered with glass to show the thick adobe bricks within. On the south side extends a tranquil **cemetery**★; here, amid verdant, varied plantings, are buried many of San Francisco's early leaders, including Luis Antonio Arguello (1784-1830), first governor of California under Mexican rule; Francisco De Haro (1803-1848), first mayor of San Francisco; and many others whose names grace nearby streets.

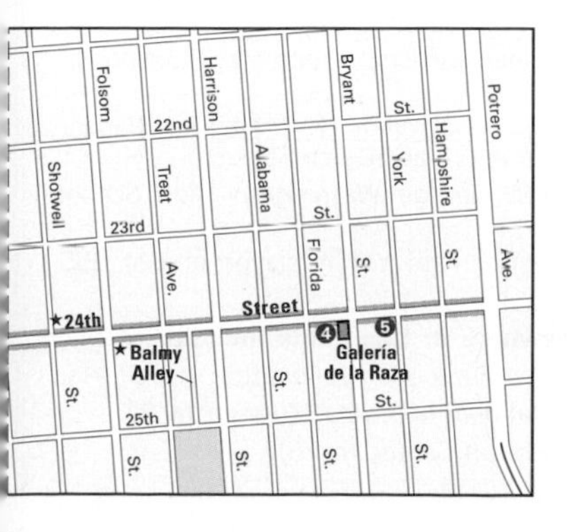

Dolores Street – *Between 16th and 21st Sts.* Rolling hills, lofty palm trees and an eye-catching assemblage of architectural styles characterize this attractive stretch of Dolores Street. At 18th Street, Mission Dolores' architecture is echoed in the huge, red-tile-roofed Mission High School (1926, John Reid, Jr.); exemplifying the city's diversity, its student body hails from more than 30 countries. Lush, hilly **Mission Dolores Park**, stretching from 18th to 20th Street on the west side of the street, was laid out in 1905 and served as a cemetery for two Jewish temples.

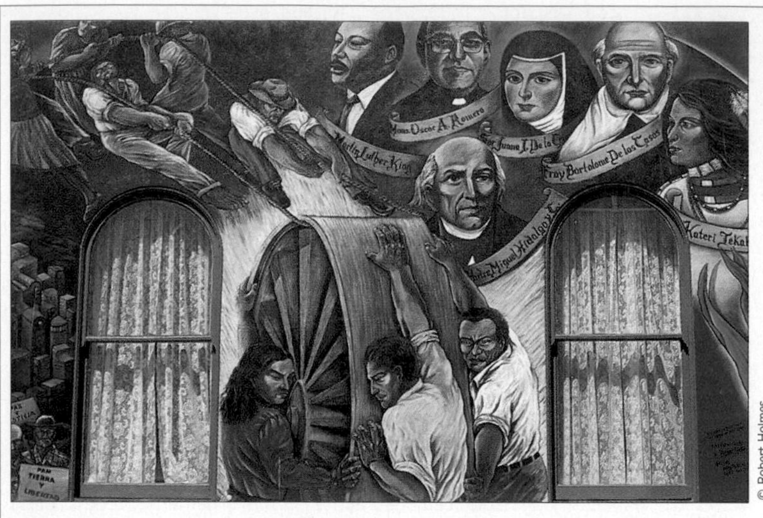

© Robert Holmes

Five Hundred Years of Resistance, detail (1993) © by Isaías Mata

■ Speaking Walls: The Murals of San Francisco

San Francisco tallies more than 500 wall paintings within its 49 square miles. Some record traditional history, while others serve as vibrant pictorial voices for communities without expression in mainstream art institutions—groups united by race, ethnicity, class, gender or politics. The great Mexican muralist **Diego Rivera** visited the city during the early 1930s, executing important works at the San Francisco Art Institute and the Pacific Exchange. Fresco murals at Coit Tower and the Beach Chalet reflect Rivera's influence during this period. During the late 1960s, **David Alfaro Siqueiros** improved techniques for outdoor painting, and the Mission District witnessed an explosion of outdoor art the following decade.

The fences, walls and garage doors of Balmy Alley, off 24th Street, were originally decorated by schoolchildren. Many Mission District artists painted their first murals in the alley, including Patricia Rodríguez, Graciela Carillo and Irene Pérez, who later founded Mujeres Muralistas, a group of women artists who pictured the beauty of their cultures. Many of those early murals were subsequently replaced in the 1980s by the **PLACA** group—this time with themes of the struggle for peace in Central America.

Following is a brief list of exceptionally interesting murals. For more information, call the Precita Eyes Mural Arts Center, which offers lectures and walking tours of Mission District murals (*☎ 415-285-2287*).

Las Lechugueras (1983) by Juana Alicia; Taquería San Francisco at 24th and York Streets.

New World Tree (1987) by Juana Alicia, Susan Cervantes, Raúl Martínez; Mission Pool on 19th Street near Valencia Street.

Silent Language of the Soul (1990) by Juana Alicia and Susan Cervantes; Cesar Chavez Elementary School at Shotwell and 22nd Streets.

The Dream Theater Murals (1991) by Neil Levine; Little Hollywood Launderette (interior) on Market Street at Laguna Street.

Five Hundred Years of Resistance (1993) by Isaías Mata; St. Peter's Church on 24th Street at Florida Street.

Maestrapeace (1995) by various women artists; Women's Building at 3543 18th Street.

Prime Time/No Time and *Just Us* (1980), *Venceremos* (1981) by Ray Patlan; New College of California Law School (interior) at 50 Fell Street.

Life of Washington by Victor Arnautoff; George Washington High School (interior) at 32nd and Anza Streets.

Chinese American History (1988) by Victor Fan; YMCA playground at 855 Sacramento Street.

Other mural locations described elsewhere in this guide include:

Balmy Alley (p 141)
Beach Chalet (p 122)
Coit Tower (p 65)
San Francisco Art Institute (p 70)
National Maritime Museum (p 87)
Rincon Center (p 78)

South of the park lies **Liberty Street** *(between 20th and 21st Sts.)*, lined with Victorians dating from the 1860s. All major styles are represented, including Italianate *(no. 109)*, Stick *(nos. 111–121)*, and Queen Anne *(no. 123)*.

★**24th Street** – *Between Mission and Potrero Sts.* This lively, tree-lined shopping strip exudes the gritty, exuberant aura of the Mission District. Community residents flock here daily to pick up produce, meats, cheeses and baked goods from the many tiny shops and markets. Bright awnings shadow fruit stands overflowing with exotic picks; salsa music pours from music stores and slow-moving cars; Spanish rolls off the tongues of shopkeepers and shoppers alike; and a host of modest eateries serve up a plethora of Latin American cuisines.

Stroll down **Balmy Alley**★ *(between Treat and Harrison Sts.)* to admire the colorful murals adorning nearly every garage door and wall surface. Occupying an unassuming corner storefront, **Galería de la Raza** *(corner of 24th and Bryant Sts.)* has sustained and nurtured the Chicano art movement for more than 25 years through exhibitions, events, and performances. The gallery showcases new artists along with established ones, and exhibits, which change every four to six weeks, reflect Chicano and Latino social and cultural issues.

4 Studio 24

2857 24th St. ☎ *415-826-8009.* Adjacent to Galería de la Raza, this colorful retail shop stocks handcrafts and contemporary and traditional folk art from Mexico and Central and South America.

5 St. Francis Fountain

2801 24th St. ☎ *415-826-4200.* The city's only surviving soda fountain was last remodeled (pink on pink) the year Harry S Truman was elected president. Take a booth or a stool at the counter and sip a soda or belly-up to the house gut-buster challenge: five scoops of different flavors of ice cream, two toppings, whipped cream and a banana.

Valencia Street – *Between 16th and 23rd Sts.* In recent years a profusion of coffeehouses, restaurants, thrift stores and bars has sprung up along this section of Valencia Street and the cross streets linking it to Guerrero Street, transforming the former working-class neighborhood into a trendy "new Bohemia." While still a bit down at the heel, the area has become a magnet for the young and the hip, and for immigrants from the Middle East and North Africa as well as Latin America. Regulars drift through its coffeehouses, used bookstores and thrift shops by day; at night, strolling mariachi bands enliven its already-teeming restaurants, bars and clubs.

Levi Strauss & Company – Kids *250 Valencia St. Visit by guided tour (1hr 30min) only, year-round Tue–Wed 9am, 11am & 1:30pm. Reservations required. Closed 1st 2 weeks in Jul & late Dec–early Jan.* ♿ ☎ *415-565-9159.* Located in an attractive, canary-yellow building (1906), this factory represents a tiny link in the enormous, international Levi's chain. In 1873, German-born Levi Strauss and his partners patented the design he had developed while in San Francisco making "waist-high" overalls for miners during the Gold Rush. The design included the now-famous back-pocket design and reinforced copper rivets. The guided tour includes a video *(10min)*, a tour of the Levi's museum and a stroll through the loud factory floor where jeans are designed and sewn.

22 • SOUTH OF MARKET★★

Time: 6 hours. Muni bus 9–San Bruno, 14–Mission, 15–Third, 19–Polk, 30–Stockton or 45–Union-Stockton.

BART Montgomery St. or Powell St. stations.

Map p 147

San Francisco's hardscrabble history meets its high-tech future in the area known as South of Market, a heterogeneous industrial zone bounded by Market, Townsend and 13th streets and the EMBARCADERO. Like New York City's SoHo (which inspired South of Market's sobriquet, "SoMa"), the area is largely dominated by warehouse and factory structures. Yet this visually desolate quarter pulses with some of the city's most vibrant cultural activity. Several renowned art museums and galleries have recently made their homes on and around Third and Fourth Streets, along with an enormous convention center and the city's burgeoning multimedia industry. Constraints on development in the neighboring FINANCIAL DISTRICT have brought new office towers to SoMa's northeastern corner. Elsewhere, erstwhile industrial buildings are reborn as sleek, spacious restaurants, ultrahip clubs, theaters, lofts and cafes.

Historical Notes

"South of the Slot" – In 1847, Irish engineer and surveyor Jasper O'Farrell platted the area with streets parallel and perpendicular to Market Street, a 120ft-wide thoroughfare laid diagonally through the city from the Embarcadero to TWIN PEAKS. Anticipating industrial development on this flat terrain fronting the bay, O'Farrell planned SoMa's blocks four times larger than those north of Market, and made the streets twice as wide. Gasworks, shipyards, refineries, foundries and breweries took root along the waterfront, and workers settled in boardinghouses near the Embarcadero and in a large tent community euphemistically called "Happy Valley." Wealthy business owners built elegant Victorian mansions atop nearby **Rincon Hill**, a high sand ridge separating Yerba Buena Cove and Mission Bay. At the foot of the hill lay South Park *(p 147)*, an attractive enclave of Georgian townhouses encircling a private oval common.

Wharves, factories and shanties quickly occupied the landfilled waterfronts of Yerba Buena Cove and Mission Bay, and in 1869 Rincon Hill was bisected to facilitate industrial traffic. As unattractive development on the flats continued to encroach on their elite enclave, the well-to-do deserted South of Market, particularly after the 1873 invention of the cable car made it possible to build on NOB HILL and other slopes west of downtown. The neighborhood gained the nickname "South of the Slot" after the Market Street cable car line was established in 1876.

Neighborhood in Transition – After the earthquake and fire of 1906 razed the sector, the neighborhood's population remained largely male and working-class until the 1950s, when real-estate developers recognized South of Market's potential as an adjunct to the downtown Financial District. Decades of conflict among residents, city planners and developers culminated in 1981 with the completion of **Moscone Convention Center** (Hellmuth, Obata and Kassabaum); later additions came in 1988 and 1991. Occupying the blocks bounded by Howard, Folsom, Third and Fourth streets, the modern center encloses 442,000sq ft of exhibition space.

Today architects, graphic designers, performing artists, filmmakers and cyber-artists make South of Market their home. New apartments and condominiums, particularly along the Embarcadero and around South Beach, have encouraged an influx of downtown workers to take up residence here. A proliferation of clothing manufacturers' outlets *(p 241)* draws bargain-hunters by the busload. The lively after-dark scene between Eighth and Tenth Streets and along Eleventh Street between Folsom and Harrison offers jazz clubs and rock discos, microbreweries and bistros, theaters, galleries and experimental performance spaces housed in converted industrial buildings. The recent completion of Yerba Buena Gardens *(p 145)* and the San Francisco Museum of Modern Art *(below)*, and the ongoing construction of new museums and cultural complexes, presages the continuation of South of Market's seemingly perpetual state of transition.

Visiting South of Market – Most attractions in the South of Market district are within easy walking distance of Yerba Buena Gardens, and it makes sense to center your sightseeing there. At midday, office workers gather on the Esplanade for lunch and enjoy free concerts held regularly in the outdoor bandshell *(for performance schedule ☎ 415-978-2787)* Most museums and galleries, including the San Francisco Museum of Modern Art, open at 11am; most are closed certain days of the week, but may (as in the case of SFMOMA) stay open late one evening.

After dark it's best to travel by car or taxi. Surface lots dot the areas around Yerba Buena Gardens, and street parking is usually easy to find after rush hour ends around 7pm. The large garage at Fifth and Mission Streets offers abundant parking in a location convenient to many sights. Some restaurants and many clubs stay open well past midnight.

★★SAN FRANCISCO MUSEUM OF MODERN ART

151 3rd St. Open Memorial Day–Labor Day Thu–Tue 10am–6pm (Thu 9pm). Rest of the year Thu–Tue 11am–6pm (Thu 9pm). Closed major holidays. $8 (free 1st Tue, 1/2 price Thu 6pm–9pm). Guided tours (1hr) available. ✗ ♿ www.sfmoma.org ☎ 415-357-4000.

San Francisco's premier showcase for modern art occupies an innovative contemporary building that makes a striking new addition to the city's skyline. After an extended and awkward tenancy in its longtime quarters at CIVIC CENTER, the museum (popularly known as "SF-MOMA") is coming of age in its new home facing South of Market's thriving arts center at YERBA BUENA GARDENS.

Growing Pains – The present-day museum began in 1871 as the San Francisco Art Association, a group of artists and art lovers determined to promote artistic expression and appreciation in the Bay Area. Housed at the Palace of Fine Arts after the Panama-Pacific International Exposition of 1915 *(p 92)*, the organization, renamed the San Francisco Museum of Art, moved in 1935 to new quarters in the War Memorial Veterans Building at Civic Center. Founding director Grace

McCann Morley conceived an ambitious program of more than 70 shows a year highlighting pivotal movements and seminal works of contemporary art, and the museum quickly gained a reputation for bringing new and challenging works before the public eye. It organized the first solo exhibitions of works by then-unknown artists Arshile Gorky, Clyfford Still, Jackson Pollock, Robert Motherwell and Mark Rothko.

As early as 1970, despite several expansions and renovations, problems inherent in the Veterans Building space—lack of climate control, no ground-floor presence, insufficient gallery space and inadequate storage—inhibited the flow of donations and caused certain important traveling shows to bypass the Museum of Art. In 1988, the board of trustees initiated massive fundraising efforts to begin construction of a new home for the museum on land situated across from Yerba Buena Gardens. Swiss architect Mario Botta, reputed for humanistic modernism and skillful use of natural light, was selected to design the new space, with Hellmuth, Obata & Kassabaum, Inc. as the architect of record. The commission represented Botta's first building in the US and his first major museum.

Modern Home for Modern Art – Botta's design is a striking composition of symmetrically arranged, stepped-back, brick-clad masses. Though at first glance the building appears simple and blocky, fine brickwork creates a rhythmic play of light and shadow across its exterior, and such details as exposed expansion joints are worth a careful look. Piercing the center of the building is a massive shaft, set off from the red-brown brick by stripes of alternating black and white stone. Botta created a huge skylight by slanting the top of the cylinder toward Third Street and facing the slanted surface with glass. This great central oculus serves as both beacon and receptor: It announces the museum's presence in the cityscape while suffusing the building's upper galleries and atrium with natural light.

Botta, who studied and worked extensively in Italy and was much influenced by that country's public architecture, envisioned the museum's interior street level as a piazza-like urban space. Paved in alternating bands of polished and unpolished black marble, the stunning central **atrium★★** leads to a stylish cafe, a bookstore, a 299-seat theater, classrooms and special-events spaces. Its open design reveals the building's spatial arrangement at a glance, giving a clear sense of five levels arrayed around the great, catwalk-crossed tower shaft and accessed by a majestic stairway.

In the galleries, the colors of structural and finish materials provide a neutral backdrop for artworks. The blacks and grays of stone and the slickness of glass and steel play against the somber warmth of wood tones. Nordic birch sheathes the wainscoting, and the maple floors are sprung to reduce foot fatigue.

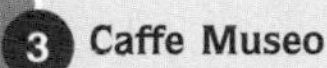

3 Caffe Museo

In the SFMOMA. ☎ 415-357-4500. Glowing woods and fixtures match the museum's decor at this elegant cafe, the perfect place to refresh with an espresso, a vegetarian pasta, a focaccia sandwich or other light, Italian fare. Eat in, or take a table on the sidewalk to view the comings and goings at Yerba Buena Gardens across the street.

The Collections – Now numbering more than 17,000 works of art, the permanent collection was initiated in 1935, just six years after the Museum of Modern Art was founded in New York City. The initial gift of 36 works—including Diego Rivera's *The Flower Carrier*—was presented by local insurance magnate Albert M. Bender, one of the institution's founding trustees. Through the 20C the holdings grew steadily in size and scope while staying true to the museum's contemporary bent. Acquisition of painting and sculpture remained a focus, with major donations bestowed by influential San Franciscans such as architect Timothy Pflueger (whose landmark PACIFIC TELEPHONE BUILDING backdrops the museum building to the east), Elise Stern Haas and Harriet Lane Levy. American abstract artist Clyfford Still's gift of 28 paintings is one of the treasures of the museum's holdings. Today the painting and sculpture collections represent all major movements of modern art, with significant strengths in early Modernism and works by California and Bay Area artists.

As early as 1936, the museum began to present photography as a fine-art medium, and gifts of works by Alfred Stieglitz, Ansel Adams, Imogen Cunningham and other members of the Group f.64 *(p 26)* augmented the photography collection. An initial architectural show in 1940 gave rise to the museum's Department of Architecture and Design; further exhibitions of the work of such noted architects as Le Corbusier and American designers Charles and Ray Eames have helped to secure the museum's reputation in this field. The Department of Media Arts, established in 1988 and one of only five such curatorial chairs in the US, celebrates the Bay Area's position as a hub of activity in video, film and computer-processed imagery.

Visit *3hrs.*

First-time visitors to the museum are advised to take the interactive CD-ROM-based audio tour *($3; rental table on 1st floor)* recorded by museum curators and directors; the tour provides excellent insights into the collection and its highlights. Be sure to stop by the computer-equipped study alcove *(2nd floor)* where users can sample various programs, among them a survey of key ideas and issues in 20C art with reference to the permanent collection, and a multimedia archive of California artists. The museum's library and graphic arts research center *(lower level)* are open to the public by appointment only.

In addition to hosting important traveling shows, the museum maintains an active program of changing thematic exhibitions from the permanent collection. Much gallery space is reserved for this purpose. Bear in mind that only part of the permanent collection is on view at any given time.

Second floor – Paintings, sculpture and works of architecture and design drawn from the permanent collection occupy galleries here. Though artworks are frequently rotated, visitors are likely to see mainstays of the painting collection. Henri Matisse's landmark *Femme au Chapeau* (1905) created outrage when it was exhibited at the Paris Salon d'Automne of 1905; critical response to the painting, and to similar works exhibited with it, gave rise to the term "Fauvism" to describe the use of vivid, non-naturalistic colors. Georges Braque's *Violin and Candlestick* (1910), created during the height of Cubism, represents objects simultaneously from multiple points of view. A small gallery rotates works by Paul Klee, who participated briefly in the *Blaue Reiter* movement; the 100 Klee works promised the museum by benefactor Dr. Carl Djerassi span the length of the Swiss artist's career. Visitors should not miss Mexican muralist Diego Rivera's sympathetically idealized paean to peons, *The Flower Carrier* (1935), nor self-taught artist Frida Kahlo's insightfully detailed portrait of herself and her husband, *Frieda and Diego Rivera* (1931), which she painted especially for museum trustee Albert Bender, her friend and patron.

Jackson Pollock's immensely influential *Guardians of the Secret* (1943), one of the museum's most important pieces, opened the gateway to American Abstract Expressionism as well as to Pollock's own "drip" period. One gallery is dedicated to displaying selections from the museum's 30 huge, abstract canvases by Clyfford Still.

Berkeley painter Joan Brown's *Noel in the Kitchen* (c.1964), embodies the Bay Area Figurative movement's return to recognizable subject matter in the aftermath of Abstract Expressionism. Other California artists whose work may be on view include Richard Diebenkorn, Elmer Bischoff, David Park, Robert Arneson, Edward Keinholz, Wayne Thiebaud and Bruce Connor. Works by Jasper Johns, Robert Rauschenberg and Pop artists James Rosenquist and Andy Warhol reflect the styles

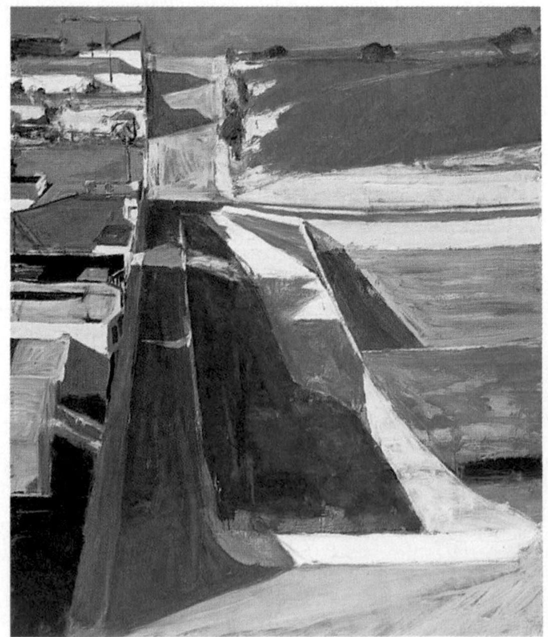

Don Myer Photography/San Francisco Museum of Modern Art

Cityscape I (1963) by Richard Diebenkorn

that evolved in the postwar period in reaction to Abstract Expressionism. Other noteworthy works include paintings by Pablo Picasso, Joan Míro, Salvador Dalí, Georgia O'Keeffe, Roy Lichtenstein and Mark Rothko.
The Department of Architecture and Design taps its permanent collection to present frequently changing shows on furniture, graphic arts, building design and even urban design.

Third Floor – Lower ceilings here keep scale appropriate to exhibitions of photography and works on paper. The museum's 9,000-piece photography collection is international in scope and rich in both historic and contemporary holdings. Strengths Include works by mid-20C American masters Edward Weston, Imogen Cunningham, Ansel Adams, Edward Steichen, Diane Arbus, Margaret Bourke-White, Robert Mapplethorpe and Alfred Steiglitz (including one portrait of his wife, painter Georgia O'Keeffe).

Fourth and Fifth Floors – These two levels are devoted to the exhibition of large-scale, contemporary pieces and installations, sometimes including works from the permanent collection. The entire floor is engineered to handle the technical requirements of experimental work, and movable nonbearing walls allow the spaces to be reconfigured as necessary. Natural light washes the white surfaces of these high-ceilinged upper galleries, though subtle screens and filters can adjust its quality. Be sure to venture across the fifth floor's dramatic steel bowstring-truss **catwalk**★ soaring 125ft over the lobby floor for a superb (if decidedly vertiginous) overview of the central shaft.

★★YERBA BUENA GARDENS

Uniting two theaters, three galleries, an outdoor cafe and a beautifully manicured esplanade, Yerba Buena Gardens (bounded by Third, Fourth, Mission and Howard Streets) is fast becoming an important cultural and artistic hub. Specializing in exhibitions and performances that reflect northern California's diverse populations, its Center for the Arts mixes the work of internationally renowned artists with that of local emerging ones, providing a unique, democratic forum that challenges the artistic establishment even as it celebrates artistic expression.

★**Yerba Buena Center for the Arts (A)** – *Open year-round Tue–Sun 11am–6pm. Closed major holidays. $5. ♿ ☎ 415-978-2787.* Exploring such issues as race, class, gender, history, technology and art itself, the changing exhibitions in this low-slung, modernistic building (1993, Fumihiko Maki) reflect the cultural diversity and experimental élan of the Bay Area. Designed to resemble an ocean liner—its tall flagpole suggesting a mast and the angled Mission Street facade recalling a stern—the structure contains a 755-seat performance space, two cavernous first-floor galleries and a sculpture plaza. Upstairs, a high-tech gallery accommodates film, video and multimedia installations, while an open terrace overlooks the large downstairs gallery and spacious lobby. Temporary exhibitions of work by new artists change quarterly.
Adjacent to the galleries stands the 750-seat **Yerba Buena Center for the Arts Theater (B)** (1993, James Stewart Polshek and Partners). Exposed steel cross beams emphasize its boxy, geometrical design, accented by red and yellow flourishes around the lobby and entranceway. The theater hosts presentations by local and touring performance groups that share the center's goal of promoting multiculturalism.

Esplanade (C) – Incorporating gently rolling hills, trees, gardens, eclectic sculptures and an outdoor performance area, the handsome, 5.5-acre Esplanade is a quiet haven. Paths meander about the ground level, which lies atop an underground extension of Moscone Center. The south side is dominated by *Revelations*, a site-specific memorial to Dr. Martin Luther King, Jr., curtained by an exhilarating waterfall. On the second-story terrace lies the Sister City Garden, featuring plants and shrubs from the 14 international cities that nurture cultural and political relations with San Francisco. Note especially the fine sculptures that stud the Esplanade, including wild-eyed *Shaking Man* by Terry Allen *(terrace level)* and *Deep Gradient/Suspect Terrain*, a 20ft steel-and-glass sinking "ship" by John Roloff in the east garden.

Rooftop at Yerba Buena Gardens (D) – Kids *750 Folsom St. Open year-round daily 10:30am–11pm. ☎ 415-777-3727.* This long-awaited $56 million children's complex opened in autumn 1998 atop the west wing of Moscone Convention Center's South Hall. Highlighted by an illuminated, glass-enclosed Charles Looff carousel (constructed c.1906 and subsequently a fixture at the Playland-at-the-Beach amusement park, *p 152*), it includes a year-round ice-skating rink, a 12-lane bowling center, an interactive playground and learning garden, a labyrinth of hedges, and an outdoor amphitheater. Rooftop's cornerstone is **Zeum** *(221 4th St.; open year-round Mon–Fri noon–6pm, weekends 11am–5pm; $7; ♿ ☎ 415-777-2800)*, a 34,000sq ft high-tech studio and theater for the visual and performing arts, designed by architect Adele Naude Santos.

On the opposite corner of Howard Street, at Fourth and Mission, Sony Entertainment's four-story, 350,000sq ft **Metréon** entertainment complex is scheduled for completion in summer 1999. In 2001, the Mexican Museum *(p 95)* and **The Jewish Museum San Francisco** *(☎ 415-788-9990)* intend to move into new facilities in the Mission Street area between Third and Fourth.

ADDITIONAL SIGHTS

★**Pacific Telephone Building** – *140 New Montgomery St.* "We wanted to get a solid mass with a textural surface treatment and a silhouette that set firmly on the ground," wrote architect Timothy Pflueger of the Pacific Telephone Building, which he designed in the early 1920s. Completed in 1925, the 30-story structure stood as the only skyscraper south of Market Street for decades. Today the restored building still boasts an elegant terra-cotta facade and brass doorways topped by ogee arches. The elegant **lobby★** is well worth a visit for its black marble walls and columns, intricate plaster ceiling designed with Asian motifs, and its display cases with memorabilia illustrating the building's history. The modest **Pacific Bell Museum** *(enter from lobby; open Tue–Thu 10am–2pm; ☎ 415-394-2574)* has a variety of offbeat exhibits on telephone history.

California Historical Society – *678 Mission St. Open year-round Tue–Sat 11am–5pm. $2 (free 1st Tue). ♿ www.calhist.org ☎ 415-357-1848.* The state's official historical society, this century-plus-old organization carries out an active program of research, collection and exhibition on California's colorful, rambunctious past. In its attractive building (1922) near Yerba Buena Gardens, the society maintains holdings *(available for study by appointment)* of books, manuscripts, original documents, journals, maps, photographs and fine and decorative arts covering the great sweep of California's history, with some publications dating from the 17C. A spacious public gallery on the first level houses changing thematic exhibits curated by society staff, as well as traveling exhibits organized by other historical institutions. There also is an excellent specialty bookshop off the lobby.

Marriott San Francisco Hotel – *55 4th St.* Although adjacent buildings tend to obscure its futuristic 39-story profile, this Postmodern building (1989, Anthony Lumsden) is a landmark in the South of Market district. The Marriott's neo-Deco silhouette and fan-shaped windows once led to its being labeled "the Jukebox" by a local columnist. It is best viewed looking south down Grant Avenue from Chinatown.

Cartoon Art Museum (M²) – *814 Mission St., 2nd floor. Open year-round Wed–Fri 11am–5pm, Sat 10am–5pm, Sun 1pm–5pm. Closed major holidays. $5. ♿ ☎ 415-227-8666.* Housed in the former *Call-Bulletin* newspaper building, this museum displays comics that wed drawing and text to sometimes humorous, sometimes shocking effect. Founded in 1984 to foster appreciation of cartoon art, the museum has since amassed an 11,000-piece permanent collection, including work dating from the late 18C. Samples of these works are displayed alongside temporary exhibits of international and local cartoonists, many of whom use the medium to critique the status quo.

© Charles Schulz/Cartoon Art Museum

Self-portrait, *Peanuts* Cartoonist

Old Mint – *88 5th St. Not open to the public.* With its six great Doric columns and pyramidal granite staircase, the Old Mint (1874, Alfred B. Mullet) remains one of San Francisco's finest Neoclassical buildings. Made of brick with stone facing, the structure served as a US Mint from 1874 to 1937, narrowly surviving the fire of 1906 when employees, with the help of soldiers and a tiny firehose, fought the flames to save $200 million in silver and gold. The building's grand entrance, elevated 12ft above the sidewalk, suggests power and indomitability. The structure was designated a National Historic Landmark in 1966. Damaged in the 1989 earthquake, the Old Mint closed its doors in 1995.

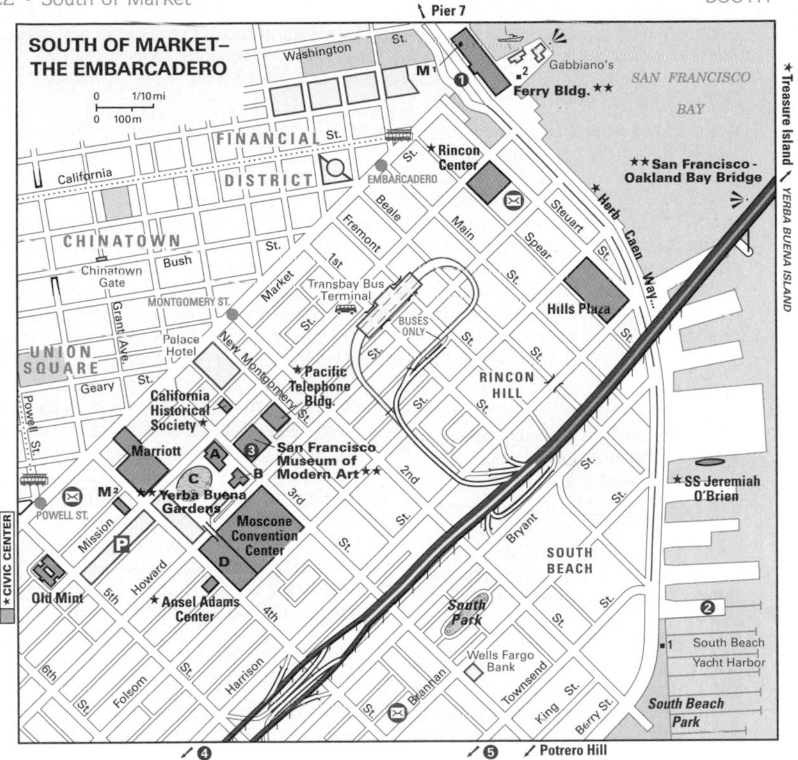

★Ansel Adams Center/Friends of Photography – *250 4th St. Open year-round daily 11am–5pm (8pm 1st Thu). Closed Jan 1, Thanksgiving Day, Dec 25. $5.* ♿ ☎ *415-495-7000.* Tucked in a converted industrial building, this award-winning museum exhibits fine historic and contemporary photographs and works in other visual media. Established in 1989, the center was named for San Francisco-born artist **Ansel Adams** (1902-1984), whose dramatic photographs of the American Southwest brought photography newfound respect as an art form in the 1930s. In these early works, as well as in his later Sierra Club books and photographs of Japanese-Americans interned during World War II, Adams sought to fuse his passions for social justice and environmental preservation with his desire to bring photography recognition in the larger artistic community. The Friends of Photography, founded in 1967 by Adams and a group of renowned artists and historians, continues to promote the photographer's goals. At the museum, five spacious, well-lit rooms feature exhibits. One gallery is primarily dedicated to Adams' life and work; others present temporary and/or traveling exhibits.

South Park – *Bounded by 2nd, 3rd, Brannan and Bryant Sts.* Modest apartment houses, unique shops, restaurants and a charming cafe flank this sedate, tree-filled, oval-shaped park, bringing a touch of gentility to a warehouse-dominated neighborhood. Designed in the early 1850s to resemble London's Berkeley Square, South Park, like nearby Rincon Hill, was home to San Francisco's high society until the early 1870s. In 1876, writer Jack London was born nearby at Third and Brannan Streets. (A plaque on the Wells Fargo bank at 601 Third Street marks his birthplace.) Today the eclectic surface treatments of South Park's homes and storefronts bear witness to the growing presence of design firms in the neighborhood.

4 Slim's

333 11th St. ☎ *415-621-3330.* Reggae, jazz, country and alternative acoustic all have a home at this longstanding nightclub, but mosh-diving and head-slamming do not, as a sign on the wall warns. Bonnie Raitt, Melissa Etheridge and Pearl Jam all have appeared at the popular venue, owned by veteran rocker Boz Skaggs. Clubbers can dine on the balcony or dance on the huge floor.

Potrero Hill

This eclectic residential neighborhood in the heights below South of Market features windswept streets, lovely views, comfortable commercial strips and several historic factories that recall the area's industrial origins. In recent years, much of San Francisco's design-industry activity has relocated along De Haro Street between 16th and Mariposa streets; trendy cafes and restaurants do an active business here. **Eighteenth Street** between Arkansas and Mississippi streets harbors a cozy commercial strip of shops and restaurants, boasting scenic **views★** of downtown from its north-south cross streets.

Anchor Brewing Company – *1705 Mariposa St. Tap room and gift shop open year-round Mon–Fri 9am–5pm. Brewery visit by guided tour (1hr 30min) only, year-round Mon–Fri 2pm. Reservations required 4–8 weeks in advance. Closed major holidays. ♿ ☎ 415-863-8350.* Housed in an attractive, Art Deco factory (1937), Anchor Brewing Company has earned a national reputation for brewing **Anchor Steam Beer**, a tart, amber lager that has gained fame as a local specialty. The company sparked a 1990s trend in the US toward beers produced by small manufacturers, called "microbreweries."

Founded in 1896, Anchor began as one of many local breweries that aimed at quenching San Franciscans' thirsts. By 1965, the brewery, then located at Eighth and Bryant streets, was ready to close its doors when Fritz Maytag, heir to the Maytag appliance fortune, bought the company. After more than a decade of struggling to perfect his brew, Maytag moved the operation to this location in 1979.

Inside, the second-floor tasting room is arranged like an old-fashioned pub, with a long oak bar and brewery memorabilia decorating the walls; on tap is every Anchor brew made. Guided tours include a visit to the factory's main room, where barley, hops and malt begin the long transformation into beer, and to the high-speed bottling room.

★ Basic Brown Bear Factory – Kids *444 De Haro St. Open year-round Mon–Sat 10am–5pm, Sun noon–5pm. Closed major holidays. Guided tours (30min) available Sun–Fri 1pm, Sat 11am & 1pm. ♿ www.basicbrownbear.com ☎ 415-626-0781 or 800-554-1910.* Within this diminutive gray warehouse resides a veritable Santa's workshop. A small crew of workers cuts, sews and stuffs virtually every size and shape of teddy bear imaginable—from the long-legged "Natalie" bear, reminiscent of early toy bears, to the mammoth "California" bear, hunched over on all fours. The two front rooms of the factory are stacked floor-to-ceiling with stuffed and unstuffed bears; visitors may select and stuff their own. An entertaining guided tour leads from the showroom to the cutting room, where bears are cut en masse from patterns; then to the sewing room, where the pieces are stitched together and eyes attached; then to the stuffing room, where polyester fill is blown into the bears by a machine invented to stuff life jackets during World War II. Along the way, guides relate the nuts and bolts of bearmaking and recount the history of teddy bears, from the story of how they were named (in 1903, for US President Theodore Roosevelt) to how they were made to be safe and durable for kids. The Bear Factory has a smaller outlet at The Cannery *(p 85)* on Fisherman's Wharf.

5 Butterfield & Butterfield Auctioneers and Appraisers

220 San Bruno Ave. ☎ 415-861-7500. Previews occur two or three weekends a month at the largest US auction house outside New York City. Specialties include California paintings, fine and rare wines, American and European arms and armor, Asian art, memorabilia and prints. Around the corner at Butterfield West, less pricey items go on the block two weekends a month, luring those who like the idea of finding a treasure and landing it for a pittance.

Consult the practical information section at the end of the guide for details on annual events, sports, recreation, restaurants, shopping and entertainment.

23 • SUNSET DISTRICT and LAKE MERCED

Time: 1/2 day
Map p 2

Bounded on the east by Stanyan Street, on the west by the Pacific Ocean and on the north by GOLDEN GATE PARK, the Sunset District encompasses a broad, flat grid of regularly spaced residential streets with row after orderly row of tract houses. Most attractions lie along the coast or scattered around natural Lake Merced in San Francisco's southwesternmost corner.

Historical Notes

Part of the wind-scoured expanse of sand dunes known as the Outer Lands during the city's early decades, the Sunset is today a wind-scoured expanse of stucco row houses that were erected after construction of a streetcar tunnel under Twin Peaks opened the area to residential development in the 1930s. During the ensuing building frenzy, contractors literally raced each other up and down the newly platted streets, throwing up affordable, mass-produced row houses. Although derided by architectural critics for their "cookie-cutter" sameness, the bungalows nonetheless offered the possibility of home ownership to people of less-than-substantial means. The Sunset's two most interesting neighborhoods, **Forest Hill** *(east end of Taraval St.)* and **St. Francis Wood** *(east end of Sloat Blvd.)*, predate the Twin Peaks tunnel.

The Sunset District harbors the main campus of San Francisco State University and the medical center of the University of California at San Francisco. Extending across the district's southern border is Lake Merced, a pleasant body of water that is a popular recreation destination for the golf course and biking and running trails that line its shores. The area's most visible landmark is the distinctive **Sutro Tower**, a pronged, red-and-white-striped television transmitter perched atop Mt. Sutro, which rises above the district on the northeast. The tower is the city's tallest structure.

SIGHTS

★**Ocean Beach** – Kids MUNI *streetcars L–Taraval or N–Judah.* This expansive beach creates a broad, sandy seam between San Francisco and the Pacific Ocean. Pounding surf and a dangerous undertow make swimming here unwise, although schools of surfers in gleaming wetsuits often float out from the beach at the foot of Taraval Street to await the perfect wave. A paved **promenade**, landscaped with dune-stabilizing grasses and shrubs, extends 3mi from Sloat Boulevard to just south of CLIFF HOUSE, making the beach extremely popular with bikers, walkers and runners.

Sigmund Stern Grove – *Entrances off Crestlake and Vale Sts., a block north of Sloat Blvd. seven blocks west of 19th Ave.* MUNI *bus 23–Monterey or 28–19th Ave. Open year-round daily 10am–6pm. Concerts: mid-Jun–mid-Aug Sun 2pm.* P *www.sterngrove.org ☎ 415-831-5500.* Presented to the city as a park in 1931 by Mrs. Sigmund Stern in memory of her husband, this 63-acre sylvan "grove" lies at the bottom of an east-west-running ravine. Redwoods and fragrant eucalyptus trees hem the sides of the narrow valley surrounding Stage Meadow, which forms a natural amphitheater. Free musical performances are staged as part of a popular, long-running concert series also endowed by Mrs. Stern. Music lovers of every stripe bring blankets and picnic fare to enjoy concerts in a range of musical styles from jazz to opera. Pre-performance lectures and demonstrations are held just east of Stage Meadow in the dignified, Victorian **Trocadero** (1892), built by George M. Greene and popular as a saloon until Prohibition.

★**San Francisco Zoo** – Kids *Sloat Blvd. at 45th Ave.* MUNI *bus 18–46th Ave. or 23–Monterey; streetcar L–Taraval. Open year-round daily 10am–5pm. $9. Guided*

2 PJ's Oyster Bed
737 Irving St. ☎ 415-566-7775. This informal, popular "Bayou by the Bay" serves hearty, delicious seafood and oysters. Come in good voice or be muted by the roar of music, patrons and steam-inhaling fans. Portions are hearty—for each meal you eat, you'll have a second to take home.

3 Casa Aguila
1240 Noriega St. ☎ 415-661-5593. The owners circulate sangria, chips and salsa to sustain the inevitable crowd of patrons-in-waiting outside this small, imaginatively decorated Mexican restaurant. Helpings are huge, especially the signature dish, *la parillada*, a mound of seafood, pork, chicken or some of each, served on a flame-heated stand.

tours (1hr) available Sat 11am. ✗ 🅿 *www.sfzoo.org* ☎ *415-753-7080.* Set on 125 undulating acres on the southern fringe of the Sunset District, San Francisco's zoo has overcome its fog-draped site and dispiriting institutional history to welcome some 900,000 visitors a year.

The zoo's original plan took shape in the 1930s, a legacy of the WPA-assisted public construction common among zoos of that era. By the 1980s, its diminutive concrete enclosures had been eclipsed by the cageless, "natural habitat" displays adopted by other zoos in the country. In 1993, with the zoo facing loss of its accreditation, a partnership was formed between the city and the nonprofit San Francisco Zoological Society to manage it and raise funds for physical renovation, species conservation and breeding programs.

In 1997, San Franciscans approved a $48 million bond to rebuild two-thirds of the zoo by 2004, focusing on more naturalistic habitats for its 1,000 denizens—including an African savanna, a South American jungle, and new quarters for lions, elephants, rhinos, chimpanzees, orangutans and the fauna of Madagascar. Improved visitor amenities, including shops and food outlets, will cluster near a new main entrance. An Education Center and Animal Resource Center are slated to open in 1999.

Visit – For now, begin your visit with a ride on the **Safari Train** *(30min)*, then return to linger at spots of particular interest. Just past the entrance, the **Children's Zoo** features an insect zoo, terrariums at kids' eye level, and a petting barnyard where human youngsters can make friends with domestic animals. Admire the graceful inhabitants of **Flamingo Lake**, then continue to the superb **Primate Discovery Center★**, where 15 species of rare and endangered monkeys and prosimians cavort and swing in open atriums. The adjacent **Aye-Aye Forest** houses endangered aye-ayes, the first breeding pair of these rare nocturnal primates to be exhibited in public. A spur trail leads to **Gorilla World**, a lushly landscaped, one-acre domain where a six-member society of lowland gorillas acts out the rules of its own hierarchy.

For a glimpse of animal life below the Equator, stroll left from the main entrance to the **Australian Walkabout**, an outdoor habitat for kangaroos (one of them albino), wallabies and emus. Nearby are the **Billabong**, home to waterfowl from Down Under; **Koala Crossing**, patterned after an Outback station; and **Rainbow Landing**, an aviary aflutter with colorful lorikeets. The **Feline Conservation Center**, near the zoo's South Gate, harbors small and medium-sized cats—including snow leopards, jaguars and panthers—for breeding and study. Visitors to Penguin Island can view the world's most successful breeding colony of Magellanic penguins. Other animals on view may include tigers (Siberian and Sumatran) and bears (spectacled, polar and Kodiak). Before departing, take a spin around the track on **Little Puffer**, a miniature turn-of-the-20C steam train gleamingly restored and brought back from premature retirement in July 1998.

Fort Funston – *Enter from Rte. 35 (Skyline Blvd.) just south of John Muir Dr.* MUNI *bus 18–46th Ave.* This expansive former military post overlooking the Pacific Ocean was established in 1898 during the Spanish-American War. As with all of San Francisco's coastal fortifications, it was never tested in combat. Originally called the Laguna Merced Military Reservation, the fort was renamed in 1917 in honor of General Frederick Funston, the Presidio co-commandant who organized military forces to maintain order in San Francisco in the aftermath of the 1906 earthquake and fire. With the approach of World War II, heavy cannonry was installed; Battery Richmond Davis, built in 1938, held two 16in guns. In a strategy worthy of Lewis Carroll, destinationless "roads" were created within Funston's grounds at this time to confound any invaders arriving by sea.

Today the former military lands (decommissioned in 1963) are managed by the Golden Gate National Recreation Area as a 250-acre park. Ice plants cloak the dunes atop bluffs that rise 200ft above a clean sand beach; these dunes are considered among the finest hang-gliding spots in the US. Visitors gather on a wooden viewing deck for expansive shoreline vistas and to watch the aerialists in flight with their colorful craft. The grounds are also a popular place for urbanites to run their dogs. The north end of the park is a stopover for migratory Central and South American bank swallows, which burrow into the bluffs and nest there from April through July.

Visit – Stop at the small **visitor center** *(open year-round weekends noon–4pm;* ♿ 🅿 ☎ *415-239-2366)* at the edge of the parking lot (once a Nike missile site) to take in displays on Fort Funston's history, and to acquire park maps and other information. Knock on the adjacent park rangers' door for information when the visitor center is closed. The nearby Environmental Science Center maintains a native plant nursery behind the structures. Scenic **Sunset Trail** *(.75mi)* meanders atop the wind-swept dunes and past Battery Davis before looping back to the parking lot. Long-distance hikers may link this trail to other sections of the Coastal Trail for a 4.7mi walk to CLIFF HOUSE or a 9.1mi ramble to FORT POINT.

San Francisco State University – *1600 Holloway Ave. at 19th Ave.* MUNI *bus Mline 19th Ave.* ♿ ☎ *415-338-1111.* Founded in 1899 as a two-year teacher-training college, this was the first normal school in the nation to require a high-school diploma for admission. The college had a high national profile during the late 1960s, as student protests against racial discrimination, the Vietnam War, the military draft and "irrelevant" college classes culminated in November 1968 in the longest campus strike in US history. Acting university president S.I. Hayakawa refused to give in to the students, and strife finally ended in March 1969 with both sides claiming victory. A lasting legacy was the establishment of the nation's first School of Ethnic Studies and an expanded Black Studies Department. Today the 93-acre campus is academic home to nearly 27,000 students.

An emphasis on multiculturalism is evident at the fine **Art Department Gallery** *(upper level of Fine Arts Bldg.; open Sept–May noon–4pm; closed major holidays; ☎ 415-338-6535)*, whose changing exhibits focus on notable artists of African, Asian and Hispanic ancestry. Two Ruth Asawa sculptures stand on either side of the lobby *(inquire in the gallery for a self-guided map to large-scale campus sculptures)*. Other notable SFSU sites include the **American Poetry Archives** *(Humanities Bldg., ☎ 415-338-1056)*, the world's largest videotaped collection of poets reading their own works; and the **Sutro Library** *(480 Winston Dr., ☎ 415-731-4477)*, one of the West's earliest and largest collections of books, inherited from the estate of Adolph Sutro *(below)*.

24 • SUTRO HEIGHTS and LAND'S END★★

Time: 6 hours. MUNI bus 18–46th Ave. or 38–Geary
Map pp 152-153

The rugged northwestern corner of the San Francisco Peninsula between Ocean Beach and Lincoln Park has drawn visitors to its rocky cliffs and sheltered coves since the days when Ohlone Indians camped here. Comprising ghostly ruins, a historical roadhouse, brush-lined trails and breathtaking views, this stretch of the Golden Gate National Recreation Area (GGNRA) provides an impressive natural refuge at the edge of bustling San Francisco.

Its highlight is the California Palace of the Legion of Honor, San Francisco's preeminent repository for European art. Extending its pristine colonnaded wings toward the rugged shores of the Golden Gate, the museum enjoys a spectacular setting amid the Monterey pines and cypresses of Lincoln Park.

Historical Notes

Oceanfront Outings – Settlement came slowly to San Francisco's coastline. In the early days of the Gold Rush, a few intrepid Europeans tried to homestead here, but it wasn't until the mid-1850s that Seal Rock House, an early precursor to today's Cliff House *(p 152)*, was constructed near the shore, drawing city dwellers on Sunday beach outings. In the mid-1860s, prominent San Francisco families—including the Crockers, Stanfords and Hearsts—adopted the area as their summer playground. In the last two decades of the 19C, however, the area lost its upper-class cachet, largely thanks to a populist-minded entrepreneur named Adolph Sutro.

The Comstock King – In 1851 at the age of 21, Prussian-born **Adolph Sutro** (1830-1898) arrived in San Francisco in search of Gold Rush riches. After establishing himself as a tobacconist, the self-educated engineer relocated in 1860 to Virginia City, Nevada, where fortunes were being made from the Comstock Lode. Silver, not gold, lay in the lode's blue clay, but mining proved treacherous due to poor ventilation and water in the shafts. Sutro designed a 4mi-long passage beneath the silver vein, wrangling for nearly 15 years with banks, mine owners and investors over funds to build it. When

Marilyn Blaisdell Collection

Adolph Sutro in his Library (c.1885)

the Sutro Tunnel finally opened, its brilliant engineer was dubbed the Comstock King. A shrewd businessman, Sutro sold his shares in the tunnel just prior to the crash of the mine stock in 1880. Returning to San Francisco, he quickly invested his fortune in land, eventually coming to own one-twelfth of all the property in the city, including hundreds of acres of wind-swept sand dunes between downtown and the ocean. His enormously popular Sutro Baths (p 154), his lush estate atop Sutro Heights, his five-cent railway and his rebuilt Cliff House ballooned the oceanfront's reputation as a favorite leisure destination for pleasure-seeking San Franciscans of every economic stripe.

A Popular Playland – By 1921 a beachside entertainment zone of dance halls, rides and other amusements had sprung up between Sutro Heights and Golden Gate Park. Renamed **Playland-at-the-Beach** in 1928, the strip resounded with shrieks of pleasure from the "Big Dipper" roller coaster and sprightly music from a Looff carousel (since restored and relocated to the new Rooftop children's center at Yerba Buena Gardens, *p 145*). Streetcars brought revelers from downtown to practice their marksmanship in the shooting galleries, whoosh down the Fun House slide and munch on waffles, hot dogs and chocolate-covered ice-cream cookie sandwiches.

By the mid-20C Playland had fallen into seediness; it succumbed to the wrecking ball in 1972. In the mid-1970s much of San Francisco's west coast, including Ocean Beach, Sutro Heights and Land's End, were acquired by the National Park Service as part of the GGNRA. Today this region's dramatic natural beauty, its most enduring resource, has again become its central attraction.

Visiting Sutro Heights and Land's End – This area is very popular with visitors, especially in summer. Parking spaces just in front of Cliff House tend to fill quickly, but lots may be found above Sutro Baths on Merrie Way; across Point Lobos Avenue from Merrie Way; and at Fort Miley beside the *USS San Francisco* memorial.

Note that the cliffs are unstable: When hiking, keep to designated paths. When exploring near the water, never turn your back on the ocean as waves can be extremely unpredictable. High tides tend to arrive suddenly, and sneaker waves—large waves that rise without warning—pose a threat to the careless.

SIGHTS

★**Cliff House** – *1090 Point Lobos Ave. Open year-round daily 9am–10:30pm (Fri–Sat 8:30am–11pm).* ✂ ♿ P *www.cliffhouse.com* ☎ *415-386-3330.* Best known for its spectacular setting, Cliff House perches atop a high bluff overlooking the Pacific Ocean. Although today's modern structure lacks the awe-inspiring grandeur of Adolph Sutro's version, it recalls the area's turn-of-the-century heyday as San Francisco's preeminent leisure destination.

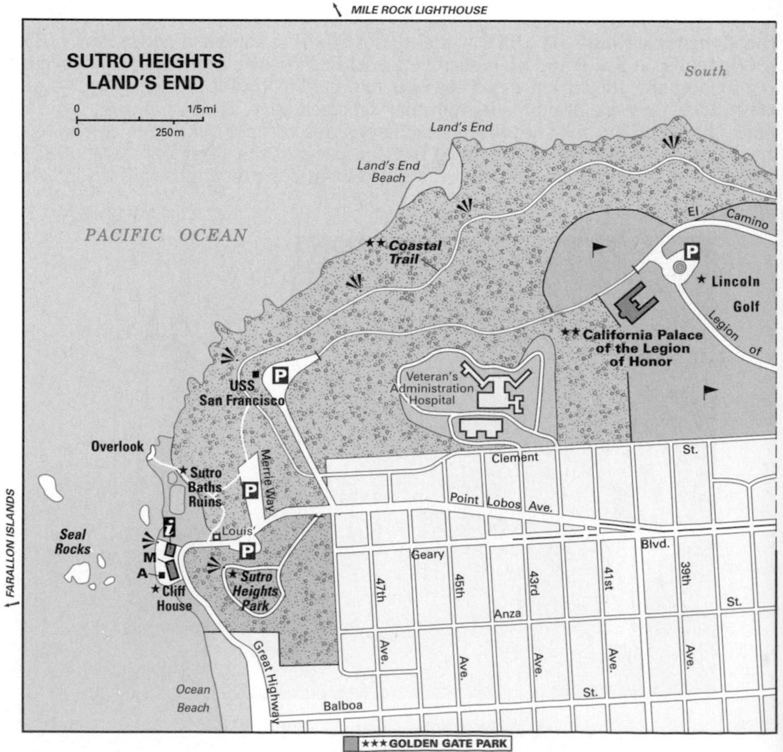

California Historical Society, San Francisco. FN-27271

Cliff House (1896-1907)

The present building is the third incarnation of a white clapboard roadhouse erected in 1863 by real-estate tycoon Charles Butler, who hoped to spark Coney Island-style development of the adjacent coastal area. By the 1880s it had acquired a somewhat unsavory reputation as a gambling hall to which "gentlemen" repaired for afternoon trysts. Adolph Sutro, who bought the property in 1881, cleaned up its tawdry image and remade it as a family resort, building the Sutro Railroad to transport the general public to and from the city.

This first Cliff House burned to the ground on Christmas Day 1894, but Sutro lost no time in hiring architects Emile Lemme and C.J. Colley to design its replacement: a flamboyant, eight-story, many-spired confection resembling a French chateau. Critics decried Sutro's extravagance, but the public loved the ornate castle and its restaurants, art galleries, luxurious parlors with panoramic ocean views, private lunch rooms and observation tower 200ft above the sea. Its glory was short-lived, however—the building survived the 1906 earthquake only to succumb to fire the following year.

In 1909 the Reid Brothers, architects of the Fairmont Hotel, designed the third and present Cliff House. The resort remained popular through Prohibition, but was abandoned for extended periods in the mid-20C. Many times renovated and modernized, Cliff House was acquired by the National Park Service in 1977.

Today visitors flock here to enjoy stiff breezes, stunning **views**★★ of Ocean Beach, and glimpses of brown pelicans, cormorants and—at certain times of the year—sea lions roosting on **Seal Rocks**, just offshore. A well-stocked **visitor center**★ *(open year-round daily 10am–5pm; closed Jan 1, Thanksgiving Day, Dec 25; 1hr guided tours available, reservations required; www.nps.gov/goga* ♿ P ☎ *415-556-8642)* on the lower deck offers maps and information about the entire GGNRA, as well as photos of Cliff House, Ocean Beach and Sutro Baths as they appeared at the turn of the century.

Musée Mécanique (M) – Kids *Open Jun–Aug daily 10am–8pm. Rest of the year Mon–Fri 11am–7pm, weekends & holidays 10am–8pm.* ♿ P ☎ *415-386-1170.* Situated opposite the visitor center on Cliff House's lower terrace, this small gallery contains a curious collection of antique mechanical amusements, including coin-operated player pianos and orchestrions, mobile dioramas made entirely of toothpicks, and penny-arcade picture machines. Many of the mechanisms were collected from Playland *(p 52)*, most notably "Laughing Sal," whose rambunctious guffaws—audible from a considerable distance—recall the days when small change could still buy a laugh. Historic photographs of Playland line several walls, and a room at the rear houses modern arcade games.

Camera Obscura (A) – Kids *Open year-round daily 11am–sunset. Closed rainy & foggy days. $1.* ♿ P ☎ *415-750-0415.* Housed in a small building near the Musée Mécanique, this curious instrument employs a mirror and two opposing lenses to magnify and project views of the surrounding area onto a 6ft parabolic screen. The motorized contraption completes a 360° rotation every 6min, giving visitors close-up views of Ocean Beach, Seal Rocks and the rugged coastline stretching away to the north.

★**Sutro Baths Ruins** – *Access by footpath from Louis' Restaurant or steps from the end of the Merrie Way parking lot.* The haunting vestiges of the once-grand Sutro Baths *(below)* lie in a cove just north of Cliff House. Lupine and ice plants cover the hills surrounding the concrete foundations that hardly evoke the grandeur of the disappeared structure they once supported. Sea birds bathe in the brackish pools. A tunnel, originally used to dump dirt dredged from the baths, pierces the bluff to the north, leading to a stretch of craggy coastline. The tunnel crosses a sea cave where the sound of rushing waves reverberates on rocky walls. Above the tunnel, an upper path leads to an **overlook** from which the remains of long-grounded ships can be spotted at low tide.

Sutro Baths

Adolph Sutro's most beloved contribution to the city was perhaps the fabulous Sutro Baths, an elaborate and luxurious public swimming facility the millionaire erected among the rocks below his Sutro Heights estate. In 1891, construction began on the three-story, glass-domed structure, designed by Sutro to utilize tidal ebb and flow to fill and empty its pools. After its completion in 1894, city dwellers paid five cents to travel out to the baths on Sutro's own railroad. From the Greek-inspired entrance portal, they descended a magnificent stairway bounded by palm trees to a cavernous main hall with seven saltwater swimming pools, ranging in temperature from bathwater-warm to ocean-cold. Patrons could change into rented woolen swimming suits in one of 500 private dressing rooms, lounge on bleachers seating 5,300 people, dine in any of three restaurants, or simply wonder at an astounding display of artifacts and curiosities collected by the Comstock King for the glorious structure. There were seven slides, one for each pool, and 30 swinging rings strung above the 1.8 million gallons of water.

Despite their enormous popularity, the baths operated at a financial loss, and in 1934 Sutro's heirs covered part of the swimming pools with a skating rink and basketball courts. After World War II, the deteriorated pools were closed. The skating rink continued to operate until 1966, when plans were made to demolish the structure and build apartments on the site. A fire of unexplained origin hastened the building's demise but the apartments were never built and the National Park Service acquired the property in 1980.

★★**Coastal Trail** – *3.4mi loop. From the Merrie Way parking lot, follow the sandy path to the wide main trail.* This well-maintained loop trail provides an invigorating walk along San Francisco's northwesternmost headland, a wild, heavily wooded shoreline boasting spectacular **views**★★★ of the ocean, the GOLDEN GATE BRIDGE and the MARIN HEADLANDS. For part of its length, the lower trail follows an old railroad bed atop sheer bluffs that plunge abruptly to swirling waters. Eucalyptus trees scent the hills rising to the south, while Monterey pines and firs hold the crumbling cliffs in place with their gnarled, winding roots. Stairs scale the steeper inclines, and several smaller trails lead off the main path, one of them to the secluded Land's End Beach often frequented by members of the city's gay community. The main trail, narrow and winding in places, leads to a viewing platform overlooking the posh Sea Cliff neighborhood *(p 159)*. Walk down the steps to the end of the overlook for a lovely view of rocky Eagle's Point.

The return route leads up from the overlook to follow a wide, paved berm along El Camino del Mar through the **Lincoln Park Golf Course**★ *(p 243)*. These city-owned public links, landscaped by John McLaren *(p 107)* in 1909, boast spectacular views from the fairways. Pass to the right of the CALIFORNIA PALACE OF THE LEGION OF HONOR through a parking lot above the golf course to rejoin the footpath, which leads to the trail's end at the Fort Miley parking lot. Across from here, part of the bullet-torn bridge of the **USS San Francisco** commemorates the commander and crew of this vessel, which was heavily damaged in the naval Battle of Guadalcanal (1942).

★**Sutro Heights Park** – *Point Lobos Ave. at 48th Ave.* The grounds of Adolph Sutro's former estate occupy a striking promontory overlooking Cliff House and Ocean Beach. Although Sutro's residence was demolished in 1939, the property remains a lush paradise of well-tended lawns and stately groves of distinctive trees. Sutro chanced upon the commanding site in 1881 while enjoying a leisurely buggy ride, and purchased it forthwith. The small cottage that stood on the property was enlarged to a comfortable, though not opulent, country home. Sutro lavished most of his attention on the grounds, importing drought-resistant flowers and trees from all over the world, including Norfolk Island pines, Canary Island date palms and Monterey cypresses. He designed a wind-powered watering system, constructed a large glass conservatory for delicate plants, and installed more than 200 statues of mythical and historical figures, many of questionable artistic merit. Ever the populist, Sutro placed a sign at the entrance inviting the public "to walk, ride, and drive therein." After his death in 1898, Sutro's daughter Emma continued this open-door policy, bequeathing the estate to the city as a public park in 1938. In 1976, the National Park Service acquired Sutro Heights, now maintained as part of the GGNRA.

Visit – Two stone lions, copies of originals now housed in Park Service archives, flank the park's entrance. To the left of the broad driveway, figures of a stag and the goddess Diana rise among the foliage. Sutro's glass conservatory (now demolished) stood to the east of the circular drive that served as a carriage turnaround. A white Victorian gazebo—originally the property's wellhouse—lies to the west on a grassy lawn where intricate carpets of brightly colored flowers once flourished. Follow the wide dirt path past the gazebo, veering left off the main driveway to Sutro's now-overgrown viewing parapet to enjoy some of the area's finest ocean **views**★★; on the clearest days, the Farallon Islands, a protected wildlife refuge 26mi offshore, can be spied on the horizon. Descend the stone stairs to see the lovely terraced gardens on its sheltered south side, replanted by the WPA after Sutro Heights became a public park.

★★CALIFORNIA PALACE OF THE LEGION OF HONOR

map p 154

Legion of Honor Dr. and El Camino del Mar, Lincoln Park. Open year-round Tue–Sun 9:30am–5pm. Closed major holidays. $7 (free 2nd Wed). Guided tours available. X ♿ P *www.thinker.org* ☎ *415-863-3330.*

A gift to San Francisco from **Alma de Bretteville Spreckels**, this museum houses her personal collection of great sculptures by Auguste Rodin, plus a treasury of European, particularly French, art.

Historical Notes – Born in San Francisco to impoverished European immigrants, Alma de Bretteville (1881-1968) inherited the energy of her hard-working mother and the imagination of her father, whose pride in the faded nobility of the French de Bretteville lineage instilled in his daughter a sense not only of personal destiny, but even of *noblesse oblige*. Alma developed into a statuesque, willful, mostly self-educated woman who defied convention in many ways. After several years of a socially unacknowledged liaison, she married sugar magnate **Adolph Spreckels** in 1908. In 1914 she met and fell under the influence of American-born dancer Löie Fuller, the toast of Belle Epoque Paris, who convinced her that her destiny was to become a great patron of the arts with Löie as her agent and chief advisor.

The Thinker by Auguste Rodin

Today the Legion of Honor still expresses the determined grandeur of Alma, who would have liked to have grown up in an art-filled palace and perhaps sought vindication of her social status in the construction of this one. At her request, the building (1924, George Applegarth) was modeled after the 1915 Panama-Pacific International Exposition's French Pavilion. The pavilion was itself a version of the Hôtel de Salm, an 18C Parisian residence designated by Napoleon in 1804 as the Palais de la Légion d'Honneur. (That building's semicircular rotunda so impressed Thomas Jefferson that he incorporated it into his design for Monticello.) On Armistice Day 1924, the new museum was dedicated to the 3,600 Californians who had perished in World War I, declaring the wish of the founders to "honor the dead while serving the living."

The Collection – Dance-related art and European decorative arts formed the initial core of the museum's holdings, along with one of the finest collections of works by French sculptor Auguste Rodin (1840-1917) outside the Musée Rodin in Paris. Alma, who had been introduced to Rodin in 1914, acquired many of the pieces during the artist's lifetime, when his sculptures were cast by his favorite *fondeur*, Alexis Rudier. The museum now owns 106 sculptures by Rodin, of which perhaps the most famous, *The Thinker* (1880), greets visitors in the museum's Court of Honor.

In 1950, the Legion received the city-owned **Achenbach Foundation for Graphic Arts**. This immensely important body of works on paper today numbers 80,000 prints, drawings, photographs, and illustrated books, including the 3,000-work archive of Crown Point Press and special collections of theater and dance designs, Asian miniatures and prints, and early photography.

Along with the M.H. DE YOUNG MEMORIAL MUSEUM, the Legion of Honor forms part of the Fine Arts Museums of San Francisco *(p 111)*, whose European collections it houses. The museum reopened in 1995 after a three-year overhaul to seismically strengthen the building while expanding and improving the interior. Although the structure had to be gutted in the process, its shell remained intact. A square-based glass pyramid was added to the outdoor Court of Honor, offering homage to I.M. Pei's famed glass structure at the Louvre; like Pei's pyramid, this one serves as a skylight for spaces on the lower level.

Visit *1/2 day.*

Arrayed with neoclassical symmetry around the central rotunda, the 19 main-floor galleries present a selective, chronologically organized survey of medieval to modern European art. *(The Medieval and Renaissance period collections normally displayed in galleries 1 through 5 have been replaced by temporary exhibitions moved from the de Young Museum pending completion of seismic refitting there.)* Throughout the main floor, paintings are exhibited with sculptures, textiles and decorative arts of the same period. Large galleries on the lower level host temporary exhibitions, along with rotating displays of works from the Achenbach Foundation for Graphic Arts. The Achenbach Study Center permits computer access to digitized images by subject as well as by artist and title. Greek, Etruscan, Roman and Egyptian antiquities and porcelain collections are shown here, and the museum's bookstore, cafe, theater and restrooms are also located on the lower level.

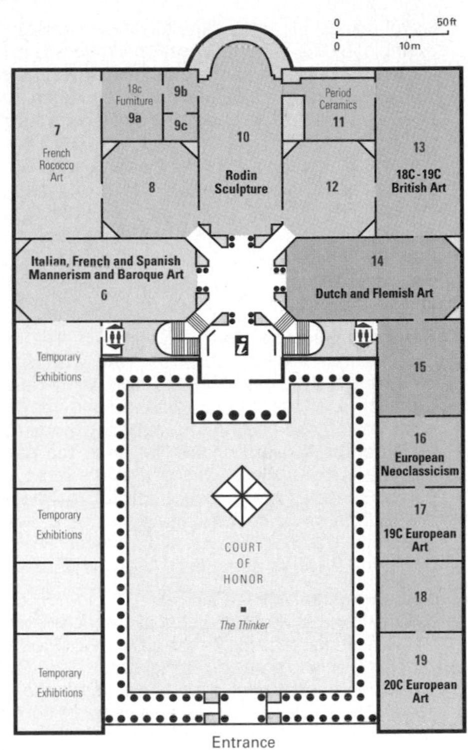

Mannerism and Baroque Art – *Galleries 6 and 7.* The progressively idealized human form and increasingly secular subject matter of High Renaissance art yielded around 1520 to the figural elongation and harsh coloring associated with Mannerism. El Greco was a master of this style: In his *St. John the Baptist* (c.1600), a strange play of light, like that of an electrical storm, charges the picture and the elongated central figure.
The Baroque style, which emerged in Rome around 1600 as a conscious reaction to the artificiality of the Mannerist style, reflects the scientific discoveries of the period, including the inventions of the telescope and microscope. Revolutionary ideas were interpreted with great variety by each national school. Representation of movement in space and time, and a fascination with light effects and the emotional state, contribute to the style's unmistakable vigor and theatricality. Especially worth note are the Georges de la Tour companion portraits, *Old Man* and *Old Woman* (c.1618); and *Samson and the Honeycomb* by Il Guercino (c.1657), which exemplifies the Baroque style with rounded forms, individualized faces, blowing trees, flying hair and a sumptuous play of light.
The rococo style flourished in mid-18C France. Jean-Antoine Watteau, François Boucher, Jean-Honoré Fragonard and Venetian painter Giovanni Battista Tiepolo all employed a rich profusion of ornament, asymmetrical motifs, pastel colors and exquisite craftsmanship to create an ambience of pleasure. A **marquetry table** (1680-90), a marvel of inlaid oak, fruitwood, metal, horn and tortoise shell, merits careful inspection; the work is attributed to André-Charles Boulle, a renowned French cabinetmaker who was retained by Louis XIV to create pieces to ornament Versailles.

Rodin Sculpture – *Galleries 8, 10 and 12.* Skylights and high, arched windows bring a changing play of natural light over the surfaces of great works by Auguste Rodin, widely acknowledged as the "father of modern sculpture." Gallery 10 displays large casts, including the justly famous *Burghers of Calais* (cast c.1889), *The Kiss* (cast c.1887) and *The Three Shades* (cast c.1880). (*Burghers* and *The Kiss* are sometimes displayed in smaller versions to make room for other, less-well-known Rodin sculptures.) Rodin's raw, unfinished bases proclaim his struggle to wrest form and meaning from mass—a stylistic trait shared by the sculptor's inspiration, Michelangelo. Sculptures by Rodin contemporaries share gallery 12.

Galleries 9 and 11 are period spaces containing examples of the museum's fine collection of 18C furniture and ormolu-mounted ceramics.

18C-19C British Art – *Gallery 13.* Founded in 1768, the Royal Academy of the Arts moved to elevate British painting to a significant current within the mainstream of European art. Guided by its president, Sir Joshua Reynolds, the academy championed history painting but also encouraged portraiture and landscape. Reynolds' *Anne, Viscountess Townshend* (1779) places the subject against a carved relief suggesting ancient Greece. By the early 19C, landscape painting, thanks in particular to Thomas Gainsborough (*Landscape with Country Carts*, c.1784) and John Constable, emerged as the primary genre. Later artists such as John Martin interpreted the elements in a more dramatic manner. Examples of *chinoiserie* decoration include a scarlet-lacquered bureau-cabinet and a commode by Pierre Langlois.

Dutch and Flemish Art – *Galleries 14 and 15.* Protestant Holland and Catholic Flanders split politically in the early 17C, forging divergent artistic styles. In the Netherlands, Rembrandt and his school documented the citizenry and their surroundings in portraits, still lifes, landscapes and genre paintings. One fine example, by the master himself, portrays sea captain *Joris de Culerii* (1632). Artists centered around Flanders continued under the patronage of monarchy and Church, employing richer colors and concentrating on religious subjects. Anthony van Dyck's *Portrait of a Lady* (c.1620) communicates the aristocratic status of its subject, while *The Tribute Money* (c.1612) by Flemish master Peter Paul Rubens employs sumptuous color and drama, expressing a Counter-Reformation mission to attract the faithful. Smaller Dutch pictures, such as Willem van Aelst's remarkable still life, *Flowers in a Silver Vase* (1663), detail everyday life in a great center of commerce, while Flemish works express their connection to aristocracy. Frans Pourbus the Younger's *Portrait of a Lady* (1591), though formal and restrained, depicts clothing materials of great richness—all in black, the color most fashionable at the turn of the 16C.

European Neoclassicism – *Gallery 16.* The excavations of Pompeii and Herculaneum in the mid-18C inspired new enthusiasm for antiquity, expressed in art through the sober elevation of civic virtue and public morality in reaction to the exuberance of the rococo. First among the revolutionary painters was Jacques-Louis David, who became a foremost exponent of the new classicism following the exhibition of his *Oath of the Horatii* at the Paris Salon of 1785; two of his paintings are in this gallery. One of David's most successful pupils was the portraitist Baron François Gerard, court painter to Napoleon. Pierre-Henri de Valenciennes' *A Capriccio of Rome with the Finish of a Marathon* (1788) reflects the classical landscape tradition of the 17C master Poussin. Fine French silver by Martin-Guillaume Biennais and Henri Auguste is on view in this gallery.

19C European Art – *Galleries 17 and 18.* Europe in the 19C, with Paris as its nominal capital, witnessed one of the richest and most complex periods in Western art. Reflecting the radical changes in social, political and intellectual spheres, a wide variety of artistic styles rapidly evolved. Jean-Baptiste Camille Corot (*View of Rome: The Bridge and Castel Sant'Angelo with the Cupola of St. Peter's*, c.1827) pioneered landscapes based on sensations of light and color, influencing the Barbizon School and later the Impressionists. *Equestrian Portrait of Charles V* (c.1814) by Théodore Géricault displays the restless searching and dash of Romanticism, and Jean-Léon Gérôme's *The Bath* (c.1880-85) reveals a new exoticism, with the white-fleshed bather passive amid the vivid Islamic tiles of the oriental setting. Another remarkable work is Konstantin Makovsky's *The Russian Bride's Attire* (1889), which depicts costumes from various periods of Russian history in attendants' dresses.

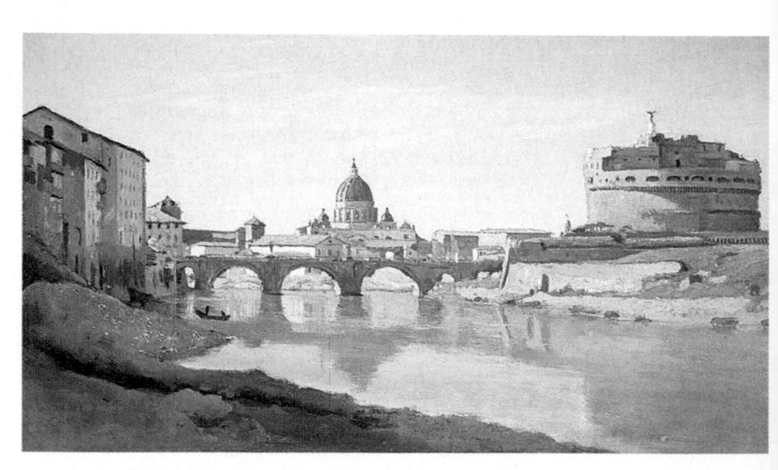

View of Rome: The Bridge and Castel Sant'Angelo with the Cupola of St. Peter's (1827) by Jean-Baptiste Camille Corot

In the late 19C, painters began to develop a new visual vocabulary to record their close scrutiny of nature and contemporary life. Depicting the transient moment with spontaneous brushwork, blurred outlines and colors in vibrant interrelation, the Impressionists were rejected by the Paris Salon of 1873; in response, they mounted their own, immensely influential exhibition. Realism and themes of modern urban life absorbed artists such as Edgar Degas *(Musicians in the Orchestra*, 1870) and Edouard Manet (*At the Milliner's*, 1881). Works by Pierre-August Renoir, such as *Landscape at Beaulieu* (1893), show the dissolution of outline into warm color. *Eiffel Tower* (1889) reveals Georges Seurat's experimentation with pointillism, a technique in which adjacent dots of color are "read" by the viewer's eye to produce a coherent image. Paul Cézanne's *Forest Interior* (c.1898) anticipates Cubism in its rendering of a constructed scene from more than one viewpoint.

20C European Art – *Gallery 19.* A great wave of artistic experimentation broke over Europe soon after the beginning of the 20C, inaugurating movements such as Cubism, Futurism, German Expressionism and Surrealism. Anchored by a late Claude Monet *Water Lilies* (c.1914-17), the gallery showcases two of Pablo Picasso's stylistic transformations; two paintings demonstrating Henri Matisse's mastery of abstract design and color; and works by other innovative 20C artists such as Georges Braque and Salvador Dalí. A black lacquer and straw table and chairs by creative designer Armand-Albert Rateau are also on view here.

ADDITIONAL SIGHTS

★**Sea Cliff** – *Entrance from El Camino del Mar at 27th Ave.* This secluded residential enclave forms a strikingly civilized corner amid San Francisco's wild coastal landscape. Curving, gently sloping streets accommodate the neighborhood's rolling terrain, winding among luxurious Mediterranean-style homes sheathed in brick or pale stucco. Most buildings here date from the 1920s. An early local example of planned residential development, the quiet, elegant neighborhood is considered one of the city's most desirable addresses.

China Beach – Kids *End of Seacliff Ave. off El Camino del Mar at 27th Ave. Parking available at beach entrance or on El Camino del Mar.* Fringing a gentle cove, this pleasant strip of sand is one of the few places in the city where swimming is safe, though its cold ocean waters tempt few. Sheltered from the Golden Gate's incessant winds by a jutting headland, the beach was nicknamed for Chinese fishermen who camped here in the 19C. Large shower rooms, a broad deck and a small grassy area with tables and barbecue grills make China Beach a favored place for sunning and recreation.

Consult the practical information section at the end of the guide for travel tips, useful addresses and phone numbers, and a wealth of details on shopping, recreation, entertainment and annual events.

Excursions

25 • BERKELEY★★

Population: 103,343.
Time: 1 day. bart Berkeley station.
Maps pp 165 and 167

Intellectual and cultural vitality characterize this university city, remarkable for its academic invention, political turmoil, social experimentation and vibrant artistic, architectural and culinary expression. Although the University of California campus has always been the powerhouse behind Berkeley's sometimes-celebrated, sometimes-reviled dynamism, the majority of the city's inhabitants live and work at some remove from academia, in urban communities that stretch from the largely industrial "flatlands" of Ocean View, through the downtown business precinct along Shattuck Avenue, to the beautiful, tree-filled neighborhoods of Claremont, Elmwood and the North Berkeley hills.

Historical Notes

From Cows to "Cal" – Like OAKLAND, the lands of present-day Berkeley pastured cattle before becoming part of Luis María Peralta's Rancho San Antonio in 1820. The land was eventually overtaken by squatters. In 1852, Francis Kittredge Shattuck subdivided lands along the middle course of Strawberry Creek into farms; the nearest town, Ocean View, sprang up more than a mile away along the bay shore. Not until the 1860s, when a site on the upper forks of Strawberry Creek was selected for an institution of higher learning, did shops and hotels begin to sprout along Shattuck's farm road, today's **Shattuck Avenue**.

In 1866 the fledgling community at the edge of the undeveloped campus was named after the Irish bishop and philosopher George Berkeley (1685-1753), author of the oft-quoted line, "Westward the course of empire takes its way." For the next four decades, after it merged with Ocean View, the town grew up steadily around "Cal," as the university is called. In the aftermath of San Francisco's great earthquake and fire of 1906, a tidal wave of new settlers flooded Berkeley and housing tracts filled the farm and grazing lands. By 1916, wooden buildings along Shattuck Avenue had been replaced with substantial masonry structures, many of which still stand today.

Cultural Ferment – Berkeley has long enjoyed a reputation for attracting intellectuals, idealists and eccentrics whose diverse and often highly cultivated tastes have left their mark on the city's history, architecture and ambience. While Beaux Arts aesthetics and pockets of greenery became the hallmark of campus architecture in the early 20C, builders beyond the university property integrated leafy yards and landscaped footpaths with neighborhoods of highly original and imaginative architecture. A gastronomic version of this passion for art and nature swept Berkeley in 1971 when Alice Waters opened her famed Chez Panisse restaurant, giving rise to California Cuisine *(p 32)* and lending the moniker **Gourmet Ghetto** to upper Shattuck Avenue *(between Rose and Virginia Sts.)*. Today Berkeley revels in its numerous fine restaurants—including a rich array of ethnic eateries—located particularly in the neighborhoods along **Solano Avenue**★ in north Berkeley, the erstwhile industrial sector along **4th Street** *(north of University Ave.)*, and behind the early-20C storefronts of the **Elmwood** shopping district *(along College Ave. at the intersection of Ashby Ave.)*. Bookstores, cinemas, coffeehouses and craft shops also thrive in these areas.

Berkeley's penchant for idealism fueled the student protest movements of the 1960s, spreading its reputation as a hotbed of radicalism. Among the events that catapulted the city into the forefront of national attention were the **Free Speech Movement** and the Vietnam War protests of the 1960s. Though now considerably mellowed from the late 1970s and early 1980s—when Berkeley's government cultivated its own foreign policy, promoted itself as a model for socialism, and was widely referred to as "the People's Republic of Berkeley"—the city retains many reminders of its radical heyday

Visiting Berkeley – Stop at the Berkeley Convention & Visitors Bureau **Visitor Inform tion Center** *(2015 Center St. 1st floor; open year-round Mon–Fri 9am–5pm; clos major holidays; ♿ ☎ 510-549-7040 or 800-847-4823)* for maps and informat

Guided tours of the UC Berkeley campus depart from the **Campus Visitor Center** *(101 versity Hall, 2200 University Ave.; open year-round Mon–Fri 8:30am–4:30pm; Dec 25–Jan 1; 1hr 30min guided tours available Mon–Sat 10am and Sun 1 ☎ 510-642-5215)*.

Although the student population diminishes during spring, summer and C vacations, Berkeley bustles day and night throughout the year. Restaurants feehouses near campus hum from morning to late evening, and theaters, and cinemas offer a wide variety of entertainment.

Street parking near the campus is difficult to find, and posted restrictions Berkeley are strictly enforced. Try the city pay lots on Allston Way or C located three blocks from the Campus Visitor Center. University par usually fill by afternoon during term; small pay lots are found farther away at t Botanical Garden, and the Lawrence Hall of Science, both connected to the mai campus by shuttle *(50¢)*. Neighborhoods away from the campus offer easier street parking. From San Francisco, it's best to take BART to the Berkeley station and either walk one block east (uphill) to the campus or ride a campus perimeter shuttle bus from Shattuck Avenue to Mining Circle *(operates year-round Mon–Fri 7am–6pm; 25¢; ☎ 510-642-5149)*.

**UNIVERSITY OF CALIFORNIA, BERKELEY *Map p 165*

The first and most prestigious campus of the acclaimed University of California system, UC Berkeley is noteworthy for its varied architecture and profuse landscaping, its outstanding museums and research collections, its notoriety in the 1960s and '70s as a hotbed of student activism, and its myriad contributions to human knowledge, especially in the field of nuclear physics.

The university owes its creation to clergymen scholars from the eastern US, led by the Rev. Samuel Hopkins Willey and the Rev. Henry Durant, who chartered the College of California in OAKLAND in 1854. Seeking to expand two years later, the trustees acquired lands on the twin forks of Strawberry Creek, officially dedicating their enterprise in 1861 at **Founders' Rock (1)**, still visible on campus today *(corner of Hearst Ave. and Gayley Rd.)*.

In 1864, landscape architect Frederick Law Olmsted was commissioned to plan the college grounds and an adjacent residential neighborhood. Olmsted aligned the campus on an east-west axis, but a shortage of funds curtailed construction of this initial plan. In 1867, the college merged with the state-sponsored Agricultural, Mining and Mechanical Arts College, and the new institution was dedicated the following year as the University of California.

Athens of the West – At the turn of the century, noted philanthropist and university regent **Phoebe Apperson Hearst** financed a competition to expand construction of the main campus "with landscape gardening and architecture forming one composition." Supported by Hearst moneys and state funds, architect John Galen Howard set out to make Berkeley the "Athens of the West," establishing Beaux Arts as the hallmark architectural style with a phalanx of white granite buildings sporting red-tile roofs and Neoclassical ornamentation. In the course of expansions during the first half of the 20C, campus architecture diversified with the addition of buildings by such noteworthy architects as Bernard Maybeck, Julia Morgan, George Kelham and Arthur Brown, Jr.

In addition to its 178-acre main campus, the university embraces 1,054 acres in the steep Berkeley Hills, including lands occupied by the Lawrence Berkeley Lab *(not open to the public)*. Founded by Ernest O. Lawrence (1901-1958) as the Radiation Laboratory in 1936, the laboratory housed several progressively more powerful cyclotrons that fueled profound breakthroughs in 20C physics, including Glenn Seaborg's 1941 discovery of plutonium, an event that heralded the Atomic Age.

Today, with 14 separate colleges and schools, 1,460 faculty members and an ethnically diverse student body that numbers some 30,000, UC Berkeley ranks among the nation's leading universities. Many of its graduate programs are annually rated

© Robert Holmes

Sather Gate, UC Berkeley

at or near the top of national standings, and Berkeley graduates earn more PhDs than those of any other American university. Eight Nobel laureates are among the current faculty: three physicists, two chemists, two economists and a poet. An active center of culture and sports, the campus hosts frequent concerts, film screenings, club meetings, lectures and sporting contests. The year's biggest sporting event is the November football game against cross-bay archrival Stanford University—called, simply, The Big Game.

Walking Tour *1/2 day*

Begin at West Gate (Oxford St. between University Ave. and Center St.).

Planted in 1877, the **Eucalyptus Grove** on the south side of University Drive contains the tallest hardwood trees in North America. Some measure nearly 200ft in height.

★**Valley Life Sciences Building** – The largest academic building in the nation when it was completed (1930, George Kelham), this massive pseudo-Egyptian "temple" to science supports dense rows of immense pilasters; it is intriguingly decorated with bas-relief tableaux, American bison skulls, saber-tooth tiger heads, griffins and other designs. The interior, renovated in 1994, houses laboratories and world-class natural-history specimen collections, including the **Museum of Paleontology**★ **(M¹)** Kids *(open year-round daily 8am–5pm; ♿ www.ucmp.berkeley.edu ☎ 510-642-1821).* One of the oldest (1921), largest and most important collections in the country, it contains more than five million invertebrates and 135,000 catalogued vertebrate specimens, including the largest triceratops skull ever found, giant clams, a frozen mammoth *(not on display)*, an ichthyosaur skeleton and the assembled skeleton of a *Tyrannosaurus rex*. Only a small portion of the collection is displayed at any given time, in cases spread over three floors surrounding a spiral staircase.

Walk east of the building on the pedestrian walkway, past the flagpole. Beyond California Hall, turn uphill toward the Campanile.

Campanile Way passes among a quartet of monumental Neoclassical structures, all designed by John Galen Howard, including **California Hall (A)** (1905), **Durant Hall (B)** (1912) and **Wheeler Hall (C)** (1918), headquarters of the English department. The grandest of the four structures, **Doe Library**★ (1911; additions in 1917 and 1995) recalls a Roman temple with a Corinthian colonnade on its northern facade. As the university's central book repository, the library manages holdings of more than eight million bound volumes and 90,000 periodicals, housed throughout the campus and in its extensive underground "stacks." On the ground floor, the wood-paneled **Morrison Library** provides a cozy haven for casual readers. Upstairs, note the barrel-vaulted Reference Room and the old circulation hall with its magnificent coffered bronze ceiling and suspended lamps.

Bancroft Library (D) – *Open year-round Mon–Fri 9am–5pm, Sat 1pm–5pm. Hours vary university holidays. ♿ ☎ 510-642-3781.* This annex (1948, Arthur Brown, Jr.) on the east side of the Doe Library stores rare books, manuscripts, archival materials and special collections, including the country's largest assemblage of manuscripts, notebooks and papers belonging to author Mark Twain. The Bancroft is famed for its extensive holdings of Western Americana amassed by 19C San Francisco bookseller Hubert Howe Bancroft (1832-1918). Treasures periodically rotated through the library anteroom include paintings of the old West, first editions and printed posters. The **Plate of Brass** displayed was long believed to have been left by Sir Francis Drake when he landed on the northern California coast in 1579 *(p 12)*. Metallurgists have since demonstrated that the plate, discovered in Marin County in 1936, is a clever hoax.

South of the Bancroft Library stands the oldest building on campus, the red-brick **South Hall (E)** (1873, David Farquharson), built in the French Second Empire style. Once the university president's office, the building now houses the School of Information Management and Systems.

Ascend the stairs to the Campanile.

★★**The Campanile (Sather Tower)** – Kids *Open year-round Mon–Fri 10am–4pm, S 10am–2pm & 3pm–5pm. Closed Dec 25–Jan 1. $1. ☎ 510-642-5215.* Modele the bell tower in Venice's St. Marks Square, this 307ft, steel-framed, granite shaft (1914, John Galen Howard) is crowned by a quartet of obelisks surmo with bronze urns, and a soaring central spire capped by a bronze lantern. A rial to university benefactor Jane K. Sather, the Campanile houses a carill bells. From its open-air observation platform, arched windows frame **views**★★ of the Berkeley hills, downtown Oakland, San Francisco Bay and ing geometry of the campus, with Campanile Way delineating the ea drafted in Olmsted's campus plan of 1864. When school is in session at a keyboard play the bells from an enclosure at the platform's ce nating, if deafening, performance *(Mon–Sat 7:50am, noon & 6pm*

Walk north from the Campanile, turning right at the first corner

Hearst Memorial Mining Building – Clad in granite and roofed in red tiles, this Beaux Arts building (1907, John Galen Howard and Julia Morgan) was named for Senator George Hearst, who made his fortune in mining. The facade bears three archways and a row of corbels carved to resemble men and women straining to support the massive wooden cornices. Inside, exposed metal columns and girders frame a lobby that soars three floors up to three domes in a vaulted ceiling. Normally housing offices, laboratories and classrooms, the building was emptied for seismic upgrading in 1998, a project expected to require several years.

Walk south across Mining Circle and cross University Dr.

The route passes **LeConte Hall (F)**, the physics building where J. Robert Oppenheimer (1904-1967), Edward Teller and other physicists drafted a blueprint of the first atomic bomb in the summer of 1942.

Turn right, then left, crossing Strawberry Creek under an arch with a Latin inscription, and over a concrete footbridge.

At the lush green known as Faculty Glade, a path beside Strawberry Creek leads east behind the partially wood-shingled **Faculty Club (G)** (1902, Bernard Maybeck), which blends beautifully with the surrounding oaks, laurels and redwoods. After crossing and recrossing the creek on adjacent bridges, pass behind the redwood log **Senior Hall (H)** (1906, John Galen Howard) and turn left onto a flagstone path that leads past the cabin to the brown-shingled **Women's Faculty Club (J)** (1923, John Galen Howard), ensconced in a pretty English garden.

Pass along the front of the club, climb steps and cross to ascend a broad stairway on the north side of Cheit Hall.

The assemblage of buildings constituting the **Haas School of Business★** (1995, Moore/Ruble/Yudell/VBN) projects the atmosphere of a prosperous quarter in a north German city, complete with street lamps, gabled roofline, multi-paned windows and an enclosed parapet walk above its arching western gateway. Pass under the eastern portal arch to Piedmont Avenue, and look left to the concrete, Tudor Revival "castle" of **Bowles Hall (K)** (1929, George Kelham), rising magnificently on a hillside and surmounted by chimneys, gables and steep, red-tiled roofs. Hidden by trees a little farther to the north, the outdoor **Hearst Greek Theater** (1903, John Galen Howard and Julia Morgan) was modeled after the ancient amphitheater at Epidarus. Directly across the street stands **California Memorial Stadium** (1923, John Galen Howard), home field for the Cal Bears football team.

Turn right and walk to Bancroft Ave.

International House (L) – *2299 Piedmont Ave.* Iberian flourishes highlight this residential and cultural center (1930, George Kelham), the Berkeley branch of a movement to encourage cultural exchange between Americans and foreigners. A Moorish domed tower and balconies dominate the exterior. Many of the large public rooms and hallways inside, including the Great Hall and the International Cafe, reveal traditional Spanish decorative elements such as red-tile floors, carved-wood doors and iron chandeliers.

Walk down the south side of Bancroft Ave.

★**UC Berkeley Art Museum** – *2626 Bancroft Way. Open year-round Wed–Sun 11am–5pm (Thu 9pm). Closed university holidays. $6. www.bampfa.berkeley.edu ☎ 510-642-0808.* Housing one of the largest university art collec-

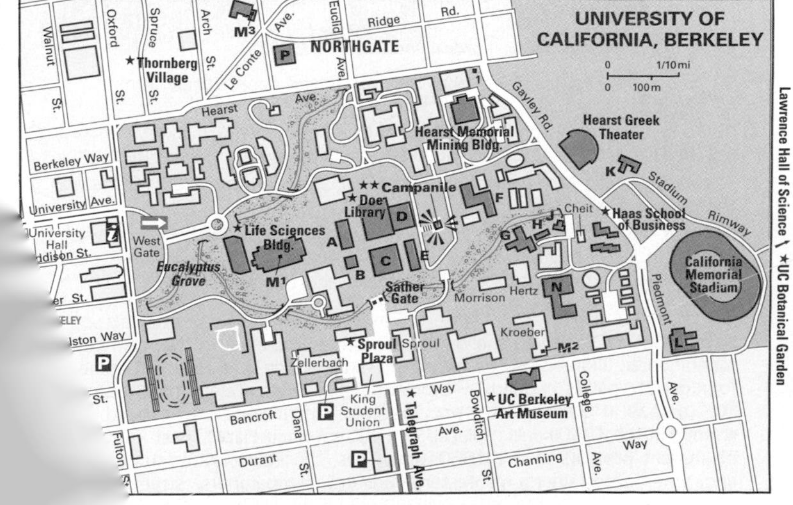

tions in the US, the museum was born in 1963 when Abstract Expressionist painter Hans Hofmann (1880-1966), having left Nazi Germany with the aid of two UC professors, donated 45 paintings and $250,000 to the university. The distinctive building (1970, Mario Ciampi, Richard Jorasch and Ronald Wagner) unfolds like a paper fan. Its stark, spacious interior features 10 cantilevered exhibition terraces linked by ramps and stairs. In addition to Hofmann's work (displayed in Gallery A on a rotating basis), the 9,000-piece permanent collection is strong in 20C art, pre-20C European painting, Asian ceramics and painting, and contemporary art. Sculpture is displayed in an outdoor garden that wraps around the north and west sides of the building. The museum also mounts changing exhibitions from university and traveling collections.

The lower level houses the renowned **Pacific Film Archive★** with some 8,000 films, videos and rare prints of classic films emphasizing Japanese, Soviet and American art cinema *(2621 Durant Ave.; shows year-round nightly, hours vary; closed university holidays; $6;* ✗ ♿ 🅿 ☎ *510-642-1412).*

Backtrack up Bancroft Ave. to College Ave. and cross the street to Kroeber Hall.

Phoebe Hearst Museum of Anthropology (M²) – *103 Kroeber Hall. Open year-round Wed–Sun 10am–4:30pm (Sept–May Thu 9pm). Closed university holidays. $2.* ♿ 🅿 *www.qal.berkeley.edu/~hearst* ☎ *510-643-7648.* Among the country's most significant anthropological research museums, the Hearst was established around a core collection obtained in a series of expeditions funded by Phoebe Apperson Hearst, starting in 1899. Today the **collections★** have grown to contain some four million artifacts from around the world, with emphasis on California archaeology, ancient Peru, Classical Greece and Italy, ancient Egypt, Central American textiles and ethnological artifacts from West Africa, Oceania and the Arctic and sub-Arctic regions. Varied temporary exhibitions are drawn from this vast collection. A single permanent exhibit displays the handicrafts of Ishi, who in 1911 appeared in Oroville, California, on the verge of starvation. Believing him to be the last surviving member of the Yahi tribe, Berkeley anthropologist Alfred Louis Kroeber invited Ishi to live at the museum (then located in San Francisco), where he was encouraged to demonstrate the techniques of his native culture by making tools and crafts until his death in 1916.

Eugene Prince/Phoebe Hearst Museum of Anthropology

Painted Cloth (1000-1450 AD), Chimú Capac Culture, Peru

Rising across the courtyard northeast of Kroeber Hall, the 10-story concrete **Wurster Hall (N)** (1964, DeMars, Escherick, Olsen) is a striking example of the Brutalist style

Passing between Morrison and Hertz Halls, turn left at Faculty Glade and follo the creek downstream.

Pause at the wall of the old brick powerhouse to admire Byzantine-inspired mos created in 1936 by WPA-sponsored artists Helen Bruton and Florence Swift scenes depict a group of artists, musicians and dancers.

Continue west to Sproul Plaza.

Sather Gate – Spanning the broad pedestrian entrance to the main cam monumental, filigreed bronze gateway (1910, John Galen Howard) arche four granite pillars capped by banded glass globes. Telegraph Avenue the campus at Sather Gate, but the commercial zone was cleared Avenue in the 1950s and replaced in 1960 by **Sproul Plaza★**. Best know of student protests in the 1960s and '70s, the Plaza draws studer and other entertainers, protesters, political campaigners, street eccentrics of every stripe. Commemorating its revolutionary birthright, a 6in circle at the center of the plaza is ceremonially declared an extraterritorial zone "not subject to any entity's jurisdiction."

On the plaza's east side stands Sproul Hall, which houses university administrative offices. The King Student Union complex on the west side contains food services, bookstores, sundry shops and Zellerbach Auditorium, the university's largest enclosed performance venue.

Additional Sights on Campus

★**UC Botanical Garden** – *Centennial Dr. Open Memorial Day–Labor Day daily 9am–7pm. Rest of the year daily 9am–4:45pm. Closed Dec 25. $3 (free Thu). Guided tours (1hr) available Thu, Sat–Sun 1:30pm.* ♿ P ☎ *510-643-2755.* Some 13,000 species of plants grace the slopes of Strawberry Canyon in a sylvan setting above the main campus, overlooking the bay. University scientists have nurtured exotic plants collected from the wild since 1890, though this 34-acre site was established in the 1920s. Most of the garden is organized geographically, in sections representing the flora of Asia, Africa, the Mediterranean and Europe, New Zealand, Australia, Meso-America, North America and California. Other thematic gardens nurture palms and cycads, old roses and Chinese medicinal herbs. A sequoia forest and redwood grove are located across Centennial Drive.

Lawrence Hall of Science – Kids *Centennial Dr. Open year-round daily 10am–5pm. Closed Labor Day, Thanksgiving Day & Dec 24–25. $6.* ✕ P *www.lhs.berkeley.edu* ☎ *510-642-5132.* Dramatically situated high in the Berkeley hills, this futuristic museum (1968, Anshen and Allen) is dedicated to teaching children about physics, biology, chemistry, navigation, mathematics, computers and lasers through interactive exhibits, laboratories and a comprehensive program of classes. The planetarium complements an active Saturday-night astronomy program. Frequently changing temporary exhibits feature mechanical creatures, the mysteries of chemistry, and a variety of science topics ranging from prehistoric life to space travel. The **view**★ from the front patio overlooks much of the northern Bay Area.

SIGHTS IN BERKELEY

★**Telegraph Avenue** – *Between Bancroft and Dwight Ways.* From morning through late evening this impelling thoroughfare flows with students, bibliophiles, crafts sellers, street people and tourists, all of whom frequent its many coffeehouses, bookstores, eateries and shops. East of the avenue, sandwiched between Dwight Way and Haste Street, **People's Park** remains a potent symbol of Berkeley radicalism. Seized from the university by students and political activists in 1969, the park sparked a series of riots and running battles between police and protesters before a sort of truce was reached, in which the city of Berkeley manages the property in partnership with the university.

★★**First Church of Christ, Scientist** – *2619 Dwight Way. Visit by guided tour (45min) only, year-round 1st Sun of each month 12:15pm, or by reservation (☎ 510-845-7714).* P ☎ *510-845-7199.* Bernard Maybeck harmonized a wealth of different styles to create a unique, Arts and Crafts-style structure of surpassing beauty and serenity. Dedicated in 1916, the church fuses multiple rooflines—typical of a Japanese temple—with Spanish tiles and rectangular, fluted columns supporting trellises hung with wisteria. In the [illegible]hape of a Greek cross, the sunken audi[illegible]rium is naturally lit by side windows and [illegible]gonally spanned with arching beams, [illegible]parting a feeling of great spaciousness. [illegible] the exquisite craftsmanship of the [illegible]d woodwork in the ceiling beams.

[illegible] **L. Magnes Museum** – *2911 Rus[illegible] Open year-round Mon–Thu & Sun [illegible]pm. Closed major & Jewish holi[illegible]ided tours (1hr) available Wed & [illegible]w.jfed.org/magnes/magnes.htm*

1 Bookstores on Telegraph

The stretch of Telegraph Avenue between Haste St. and Dwight Way has satisfied many a Berkeleyite's literary longings. **Cody's** *(no. 2454 ☎ 510-845-7852)*, one of the largest independent bookstores in the Bay Area, stocks general interest books, with specialties in computers, psychiatry, fiction and children's books. **Moe's** *(no. 2476 ☎ 510-849-2087)* sells good used books on four floors; an antiquarian section occupies the top floor. Metaphysics and religion are the specialties at **Shambhala**, *(no. 2482 ☎ 510-848-8443)* along with witchcraft, meditation and acupuncture. At the end of the block, **Shakespeare & Co.** *(no. 2499 ☎ 510-841-8916)* stocks its tall shelves and narrow aisles with used books, including a number of discounted review copies.

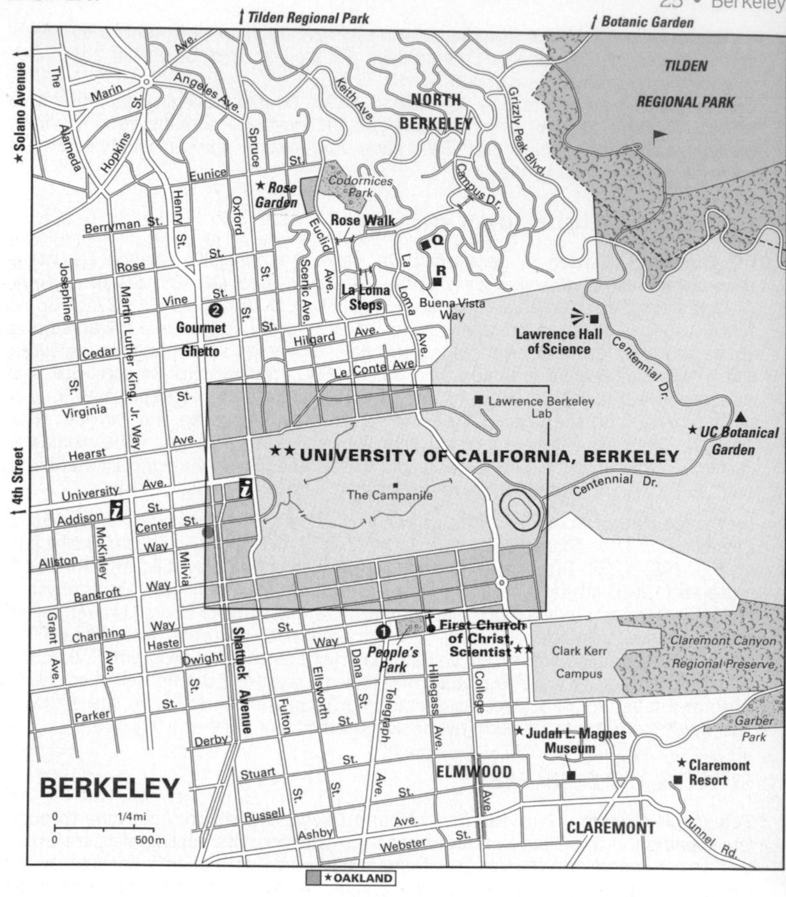

☎ *510-549-6950.* Set amid shaded grounds landscaped by John McLaren *(p 107)*, an imposing mansion (1908) houses the nation's third-largest museum of Jewish history and art. Named for a prominent San Francisco rabbi, the museum sponsors changing exhibits *(main level)* highlighting Jewish history and the works of 19C and 20C Jewish artists and photographers. Galleries on the upper level are reserved for rotating exhibits of ceremonial and cultural items from the museum collections, including Hanukkah lamps, amulets, Bibles, Torah pointers, wedding robes, Torah cases and arks, and Sephardic artifacts from around the world.

★**Claremont Resort** – *41 Tunnel Rd. Open daily year-round.* *www.claremontresort.com* ☎ *510-843-3000.* Looming like a white castle in the hills between Berkeley and Oakland, this stately old hotel (1915, Charles Dickey) forms the centerpiece of an upscale resort. The proposal to build it originally was floated in the first decade of the 20C by three East Bay businessmen, one of whom subsequently won the entire property from his partners in a game of checkers. A reputation for dullness dogged the hotel for many years, largely because laws forbade the sale of liquor within a mile of the UC Berkeley campus. An enterprising student actually measured the distance in 1936, however, and discovered that the southern end o the hotel lay beyond the mile radius; th following year, the Terrace Lounge o ned on the "wet" side of the invisible l where it remains to this day.

> **2 Peet's Coffee & Tea**
> *2124 Vine St.* ☎ *510-841-0564.* Berkeley-born Peet's places nearly as much value upon educating customers about coffee as it does to making a sale. The 30-year-old anchor store of the popular Peet's chain doesn't have a sign out front—regulars know where to go. Bean up while perusing the wide variety of coffee fixings and paraphernalia for sale.

Tilden Regional Park – Kids *From B ley take Spruce St. to Grizzly Peak cross and make a sharp left on Ca Follow signs to the Nature Are daily year-round dawn–dusk.* ☎ *510-635-0135.* Sprawling o acres on the eastern side of above Berkeley, this pre undeveloped preserve offers v

tions to people of all ages, including swimming and fishing in Lake Anza, golf, pony rides, picnicking, group camping, hiking trails, a petting zoo and miniature train rides. Also here is the **Tilden Nature Study Area** *(open year-round Tue–Sun 10am–5pm; closed Jan 1, Thanksgiving Day, Dec 25; guided tours available weekends; ♿ 🅿 www.ebparks.org ☎ 510-525-2233)*. Within the park, the 10-acre **Botanic Garden** cultivates the world's largest collection of California native plants. Landscaped on picturesque terraces along the banks of Wildcat Creek, the garden's more-than-1,500 species are divided into 10 separate sections that correspond with geographical regions of the state.

Northgate – This neighborhood was named for its location immediately outside the north entrance to the University of California campus. Above the first block of Euclid Avenue, lined with pleasant shops and restaurants, the rise where Ridge Road intersects with LeConte Avenue has been dubbed "Holy Hill" for its uncanny concentration of theological schools.

Paramount among the venerable institutions is the **Graduate Theological Union (P)** *(2465 LeConte Ave.)*, a Georgian Revival mansion built of red clinker-brick in the 1920s. Administering a union of nine schools and 1,400 students, the Union also runs the Flora Lamson Hewlett Library *(2400 Ridge Rd.)*, one of the country's largest theological collections. Walter J. Ratcliff's Holbrook Building *(1798 Scenic Ave.)*, an impressive Tudor Revival structure, is part of the Pacific School of Religion, oldest seminary in the western US. Its **Badé Museum (M³)** contains a gallery of contemporary art, a table that once belonged to John Muir and an extensive collection of antiquities excavated in the early 20C by Dr. William Badé at the archaeological site of Mizpah of Benjamin in Israel *(open year-round Mon–Fri 11am–1pm, closed major holidays & last week in Dec; guided tours available by reservation only; ♿ ☎ 510-849-8272)*.

Thornberg Village★, better known locally as Normandy Village *(1817–1839 and 1781–1783 Spruce St.)*, lies one block west of Holy Hill. Erected in 1927–28 in "Hansel and Gretel" style by William R. Yelland, the residential complex is a storybook fantasy of Gothic arches and towers, playful brickwork, eccentrically peaked rooflines, faux-leaded windows, carved-wood gargoyles, handcrafted lanterns, cobbled drives and meandering stairways.

North Berkeley Hills – Long a magnet for well-educated residents with cultivated tastes, the steep hills north of the UC Berkeley campus began to earn their reputation for high aestheticism after the turn of the century, when streets were laid out along hill contours instead of the more typical grid pattern. Encouraged by the Hillside Club, a social organization with strong interests in preserving the natural beauty of the hills, developers introduced landscaped footpaths and stairways to complement the Arts and Crafts and brown-shingled houses that dominated the neighborhood, and that are still recognized as the hallmark of residential architecture in Berkeley. When a wildfire destroyed between 500 and 600 neighborhood homes in 1923, many residents rebuilt in an eclectic array of period revival styles inspired by Norman castles, Swiss chalets, Spanish missions, Tudor mansions, Italian villas, and Japanese and classic Greek temples.

Today the area offers pleasant if strenuous strolls along its streets and paths, including **Rose Walk** *(linking Euclid and LeRoy Aves.)* and **La Loma Steps** *(between LeRoy Ave. and Buena Vista Way)*. At the heart of the neighborhood, the four-acre Berkeley Municipal **Rose Garden★** *(Euclid Ave. north of Bayview Pl.)* flourishes on terraces that descend down the canyon of Codornices Creek. Funded by WPA grants, the garden was completed in 1937, and today contains more than 3,000 rose bushes of 250 species. One spectacularly eccentric house, the **Hume Cloister (Q)** *(2900 Buena Vista Way)*, replicates a 13C French monastery. An even more unusual structure, the **Temple of the Wings (R)** *(2800 Buena Vista Way)* with a pair of Corinthian colonnades joined to a central dance stage, was designed by Bernard Maybeck and completed in 1914.

26 • OAKLAND★

Population 367,230

Time: 1 day. BART 12th Street/City Center or Lake Merritt station.

Alameda/Oakland ferry to Jack London Square.

Map p 171

…g directly across the bay from San Francisco and linked to it by the SAN FRANCISCO-…ND BAY BRIDGE, bustling Oakland boasts a large and busy port, gleaming waterfront …vic-center districts, an exceptional museum and a profusion of ambitiously re-…mid-19C to 20C residential and commercial buildings.

…ical Notes

…' Rights – After the founding of MISSION DOLORES in San Francisco, the Ohlone …s of the East Bay provided pasture for mission cattle. In 1820, when Luis …a retired from military duties in nearby San Jose, the king of Spain granted …cres of East Bay rangeland. Embracing the future sites of Oakland, Piedmont, Emeryville and BERKELEY. Peralta's Rancho San Antonio prospered by shipping tanned cowhides to eastern US markets from the family's bayside boat landing, the Embarcadero de Temescal.

The Gold Rush of 1849 signaled the end of the pastoral life on Rancho San Antonio as large numbers of prospectors traveling from San Francisco passed through the *contra costa*, the "opposite coast," en route to the Sierra Nevada goldfields. Interlopers soon began to log and mill East Bay redwood forests, and squatters carved out farms on the fringes of the ranch. The Peraltas eventually lost most of their lands as a town began to take shape near the former site of the Embarcadero de Temescal.

Boom and Decline – Incorporated on May 4, 1852, and named for its expansive groves of oak trees, the young settlement of Oakland soon acquired a wholesome reputation as a quiet community of houses, shops, churches, farms and schools, with regular ferry service to the woollier city across the bay. The arrival of the transcontinental railroad in 1869 established Oakland as a regional transportation hub, and shops, hotels and restaurants sprang up along Eighth, Ninth and Washington Streets—the area today known as Old Oakland *(p 172)*. When the 1906 earthquake and fire devastated San Francisco, Oakland sheltered more than 150,000 refugees, many of whom elected to remain.

Skyscrapers grew up along Broadway through the early 20C, and the city was joined to San Francisco by the largest civil engineering project of the time, the SAN FRANCISCO-OAKLAND BAY BRIDGE. Oakland's population grew by a third during the years of World War II when the Kaiser Shipyards attracted thousands of workers. The end of the war, however, brought economic decline and social unrest. In the 1960s Oakland suffered through race riots and rising rates of urban poverty and violent crime. Natural disasters have also taken their toll—the Loma Prieta earthquake of 1989 collapsed the "Cypress Structure" section of the double-deck I-880 freeway through West Oakland, while a devastating hill fire in 1991 razed substantial residential areas.

A Gradual Rebuilding – Although vacant storefronts continue to haunt Broadway, major civil-engineering programs have brought a measure of recovery to downtown. The expanded, modernized **Port of Oakland** now ranks among the top 20 in the world. In addition, the opening of eight BART stations in Oakland in 1974, the re-establishment of passenger ferry service to San Francisco in 1989, and the completion of a new Amtrak passenger station in 1995 have renewed Oakland's traditional role as a Bay Area transportation center. The City Center and Jack London Square areas underwent massive redevelopment in the 1980s, and the city has aggressively preserved its rich architectural heritage, buying and refurbishing scores of Victorian and 20C houses and commercial buildings in Old Oakland and Preservation Park. Gentrified neighborhood shopping precincts, including **Piedmont Avenue** *(between MacArthur Blvd. and Pleasant Valley Ave.)* and **College Avenue** in the Rockridge district, attract shoppers and diners by day and evening.

Visiting Oakland – Downtown Oakland bustles only during weekday business hours, by far the best time to visit the area. Parking is available in downtown garages, but it's best to take BART to the 12th Street/City Center station. That station is also convenient to Chinatown and Old Oakland.

The Lake Merritt BART station accesses the Oakland Museum of California and the south side of Lake Merritt. Parking is available in the museum's basement garage and on the north and west sides of the lake.

Jack London Square offers abundant garage parking, with discounts offered to patrons of the square's shops and restaurants. The immediate waterfront area is a pleasure to explore on foot throughout the day and evening, though the Oakland Produce Market is best seen in the early morning. The **Alameda-Oakland Ferry** *(p 232)* from San Francisco docks near Jack London Square after its scenic trip across the bay.

For maps and visitor information, stop at the **Oakland City Store** *(Plaza Level, 12th St. BART station, 1333 Broadway; open year-round Mon–Fri 10am–4pm; ♿ ☎ 510-286-8727)* or the **Visitor Information Center** *(Jack London Square, Broadway & Water Sts.; open year-round daily 11am–5pm ☎ 510-208-4646)*.

SIGHTS

Downtown *12th St./City Center station.*

City Hall – *1 Frank Ogawa Plaza. Open year-round Mon–Fri 9am–5pm. C[losed] major holidays. ♿ ☎ 510-444-2489.* The present-day center of dow[ntown] Oakland was ordained by city planners to be the dynamic intersection [where] Broadway, San Pablo Avenue and 14th Street converged. Since the openin[g of City] Center in the 1980s, the focus of business has shifted one block south, [but City] Hall still dominates that prominent (if now eclipsed) intersection. A vaulti[ng symbol] of the city's progressive spirit, when it was completed in 1914 (Palmer, [Hornbostel] & Jones), the 18-story shaft rises from a three-story Beaux Arts podi[um topped] by a Baroque-style clock tower. Inside, an elegant staircase leads fro[m ...] to a third-floor Council Chamber.

★**City Center** – The pleasantly landscaped John B. Williams Plaza conducts pedestrians via escalators upward from the sunken BART station to this open-air mall. At its center stands a brightly painted metal **sculpture (1)** by Roslyn Magzilli entitled *There* (1981). The title is a jocular allusion to Gertrude Stein's famous (and usually misinterpreted as spiteful) observation—"There is no there there"—following a visit to her childhood hometown after an absence of many years. To the west, three-story rows of modern commercial buildings, designed by Horace Gilford, frame a striking view of the Federal Building's twin towers. East from the plaza, sight lines converge on the 21-story **Oakland Tribune Building** *(13th and Franklin Sts.)*. The jaunty landmark (1923, Edward Foulkes), designed to recall an Italian campanile but capped with a copper-clad, French chateau-style roof, housed the offices of *The Oakland Tribune* until the newspaper moved to Jack London Square in 1992.

★**Federal Building** – Some 5,000 employees occupy the offices of this monumental, twin-towered structure, the largest building in Alameda County. Completed in 1993, the limestone-clad towers contain federal courts, offices and a public auditorium, and are linked by a 75ft glass rotunda that serves as a lobby. A marble map of the Bay Area spreads across the rotunda floor.

Preservation Park – *Bounded by Martin Luther King, Jr. Dr. and 12th, 14th and Castro Sts.* These splendidly landscaped Victorian homes were relocated from their original sites and restored as a charming office park. Labels recount the history of each of the houses, which span the decades from about 1870 to 1910. Worth a special visit is the Italianate **Pardee Home Museum**★ *(672 11th St.; visit by 1hr 30min guided tour only, year-round Fri–Sat noon; closed major holidays; $5; ☎ 510-444-2187)*, family mansion of two Oakland mayors: Enoch Pardee and, later, his son George. The latter also held the office of California governor from 1903-07. Built in 1868, the mansion is maintained as it was in 1981 at the death of George Pardee's daughter. Tours reveal a hodgepodge of furnishings and thousands of *objets d'art* collected and displayed by George's wife.

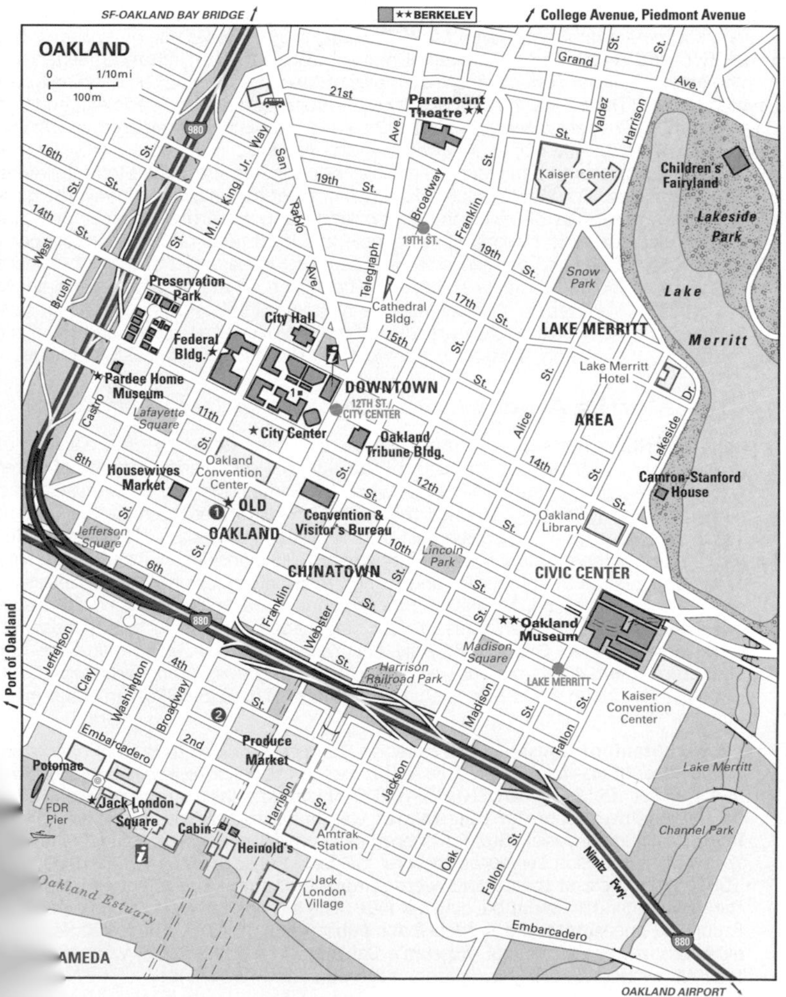

★**Old Oakland** – *Bounded by Broadway, Washington, 8th and 10th Sts.* This restored historic district formed the heart of downtown Oakland during the 1870s. Today it remains an extraordinary grouping of 19C commercial buildings. The shops, hotels and restaurants were built between 1868 and 1880 for the throngs of travelers passing through the Central Pacific passenger depot at Seventh and Broadway (terminus of the first transcontinental railroad); the sturdy, two- and three-story structures were restored in the 1980s. Splendid showcases of Victorian craftsmanship, they display a medley of brick and granite masonry, elegant cornices and elaborate ornamentation.

Exotic culinary items abound at the commodious **Housewives Market** *(Clay and 9th Sts.)*, which shelters an ethnically diverse emporium of food counters, produce and fish markets, butcher shops and other stalls.

G.B. Ratto & Co.
821 E. Washington St. at 9th St. 510-832-6503. An Oakland institution, this venerable specialty-food emporium has catered to the particularities of East Bay tastes for 100 years. Linger over the lengthy cheese counter beneath hanging salamis, check out the myriad flours, beans and spices stored in burlap sacks, and wend your way to the back, where vinegar ages in barrels.

Oakland Chinatown – *Bounded by Broadway, 7th, 10th and Harrison Sts.* Although the first Chinese immigrants arrived in Oakland in the early 1850s, they gathered in the present nine-square-block quarter during the 1870s. Unlike its San Francisco counterpart, Oakland's Chinatown does not court tourists, although many visitors enjoy exploring the bustling array of shops and markets, and tasting Asian foods.

★★**Paramount Theatre** – *2025 Broadway. 19th St. Visit by guided tour (1hr 30min) only, year-round 1st & 3rd Sat 10am. Closed major holidays. $1. 510-465-6400.* This monumental movie palace (1931, Timothy Pflueger) represents one of the nation's finest examples of Moderne design. The building's resplendent Art Deco detailing describes flowers, foliage, birds and people in addition to the more abstract designs typical of the style. Authentically restored in 1973, it is now owned by the city as a performing-arts facility.

The exterior boasts two majestic tile mosaics of puppeteers, divided by the towering Paramount sign. The amber-colored *Fountain of Light* dominates the lobby; the glass sculpture appears to be rising in spectacular billows toward a green-lit grillwork ceiling. With seating for nearly 3,000 people, the lavish auditorium features a gold-lit filigreed ceiling, and paneled side walls sculpted in bas-relief scenes of maidens and warriors. Ralph Stackpole sculpted the horsemen on the orchestral panel above the stage. A Wurlitzer organ mounted on a hydraulic lift rises to stage level for performances. Also worth a gaze are the splendidly decorated men's and women's restrooms, the curving foyers, and the women's Black Lacquer Smoking Lounge.

Lake Merritt Area *Northeast of downtown. Lake Merritt station.*

Lake Merritt – The shores of this 155-acre saltwater tidal lake offer a haven of green serenity near the bustling heart of the city. The shimmering expanse of water was a marshy tidal slough until 1869, when Dr. Samuel Merritt, an ex-mayor who owned land on its shores, dammed the outlet at 12th Street to create the lake. In 1870, he successfully lobbied the California legislature to declare it an official wildlife refuge. Although many private landowners built mansions at its edge, the city eventually secured the properties and turned them into public parkland. A pleasant esplanade winds around the lake's 3.5mi shoreline, broadening on the northern side into **Lakeside Park**. This lush oasis of 122 oak-shaded acres includes a bandstand, show gardens, and **Children's Fairyland** Kids *(open Apr–mid-Jun & mid-Sept–Nov Wed–Sun 10am–4pm; mid-Jun–early Sept daily 10am–4:30pm, weekends 5pm; Dec–Mar Fri–Sun 10am–4:30pm; $3.25; 510-238-6876)*, an amusement park for the very young.

Camron-Stanford House – *1418 Lakeside Dr. Visit by guided tour (1hr) only, year round Wed 11am–4pm & Sun 1pm–5pm, rest of the week by appointment. Close Jan 1 & Dec 25. $4. 510-836-1976.* This sedate Italianate residence (187 on the southwest shore of Lake Merritt was home to a succession of promin figures, including Josiah Stanford, brother of railroad magnate Leland Stanf *(p 14)*. The mansion served as the first Oakland Public Museum from 1910 1967, when most of the exhibits were removed for storage pending completic the new Oakland Museum building *(p 173)*. The interior was painstakingly res to its 19C appearance and reopened for public tours in 1978. The lower flo exhibits some of the original museum's Oakland history collections, while th floor showcases Victorian-era interior decoration and furnishings.

Lake Merritt

★★**Oakland Museum of California** – Kids *1000 Oak St. Open year-round Wed–Sat 10am–5pm (Fri 9pm), Sun noon–5pm. Closed Jan 1, Jul 4, Thanksgiving Day, Dec 25. $6 (free Fri 5pm–9pm). Guided tours available Wed–Fri noon–5pm, weekends 1:30pm.* ✗ ♿ P *www.museumca.org* ☎ *510-238-2200 or 888-625-6873.* A city showpiece, this 7.7-acre cultural complex celebrates California's natural and human history and its art. A setting for public art and celebration, the museum's innovative gardens—a geometric weave of landscaped passages, courtyards, terraces and stairways—encourage visitors to explore the building from its sunken central lawn court to its scenic rooftops.

In the early 1960s, city officials and private individuals launched a massive public campaign to build a grand new museum complex that would help revive decaying inner-city Oakland. The facility consolidated three existing collections—the Snow Museum, which focused on natural history; the Oakland Public Museum, devoted to Native Californian ethnology and the state's pioneer history; and the Oakland Art Museum.

Internationally acclaimed architect Eero Saarinen was the leading candidate to design the museum when he died unexpectedly in 1961. His colleague, Kevin Roche, was then chosen to undertake the project. With assistance from architectural technologist John Dinkeloo, Roche created a series of tiered horizontal galleries around a central courtyard, overhung with terraced roof gardens. Composed solely of reinforced concrete, plate glass and wood, the building's strongly angular lines are graced by statuary and softened with flowers, shrubs and trees—including orchard varieties like olive and pear that recall the state's important agricultural roots. The museum opened in 1969 to rave reviews, with *New York Times* critic Ada Louise Huxtable calling it "one of the most thoughtful revolutionary structures in the world."

The three main departments—natural history, history and art—occupy the principal halls on three separate levels of the building. The **Great Hall** features major traveling exhibitions, art shows and temporary presentations drawn from the museum's own collections.

Hall of California Ecology – *1st level.* Inspired by Elna Bakker's book *An Island Called California*, this hall (also known as the Natural Sciences Gallery) is ingeniously arranged to guide visitors on a walk eastward through central California to experience the astounding breadth and richness of the state's geography and biodiversity. Detailed dioramas of native flora and fauna re-create eight distinct biotic zones that stretch across the middle of the state: the Coastline, the foggy Coastal Mountains, the dry Inner Coast Ranges, the Central Valley, the Sierra Slope, the High Sierra, the sagebrush deserts of the Great Basin, and the rocky Mojave Desert. Located off the main hall is the Aquatic California Gallery, where brilliantly realistic displays in resin illustrate life in the state's coastal and delta waters, salt marshes and freshwater streams.

vell Hall of California History – *2nd level.* The hall's permanent exhibition— *Cali- nia: A Place, A People, A Dream*—traces the state's human history through rical tableaux and displays of 6,000 artifacts. Beginning with **First People**, the ition reveals the diversity of California's native cultures through their rituals, try, fetishes, stone tools and clothing. In **Explorers, Priests and Colonists**, the hard- and successes of the Spanish-Mexican period are explored through church s, navigational equipment, a sample of an adobe wall and the tools of the early colonists. **Immigrants and Settlers** are recalled in a model pioneer's cabin with its rustic kitchen. **Adventurers and Goldseekers** re-creates the raucous boom times of the mid-19C, complete with an archetypal assay office and 5oz of gold nuggets. **Founders, Organizers and Developers** chronicles the lives of Victorian-era citizens through displays of day-to-day paraphernalia from home, city and farm, including a rural "mud wagon," a millionaire's black carriage and a gleaming fire truck. Finally, **Seekers, Innovators and Achievers** celebrates the 20C "California Dream" of a better life for all who come here, whether surfers, Hollywood stars, backpackers, beatniks, hippies, immigrants or Silicon Valley inventors. At the rear of the hall sits Ivan and Elliot Schwartz's striking sculpture, *Dreamers*, created by fusing masks, cast from the faces of real Californians, to clothed figures and spraying all with white plaster. A special gallery features changing exhibits on historical subjects, and three computer stations provide in-depth information.

Gallery of California Art – *3rd level.* Devoted to works by artists who have lived, worked or studied in California, the collection contains paintings, sculptures, drawings, prints, photographs and mixed-media works from the early 19C to the present. Of special note are the 19C California landscapes, including paintings of the Sierra Nevada by Thomas Moran, Albert Bierstadt, Thomas Hill and William Keith. The museum holds the largest collection of work from California Arts and Crafts practitioners Arthur and Lucia Kleinhans Mathews, including murals, frames and furniture. California Impressionist works are represented by Guy Rose, Joseph Raphael and E. Charlton Fortune, and by the Oakland-based "Society of Six" landscapists: William Clapp, August Gay, Selden Gile, Maurice Logan, Louis Siegriest and Bernard von Eichman. Works by Richard Diebenkorn, Elmer Bischoff and other Abstract Expressionists, as well as adherents of the Bay Area Figurative movement, are in the collection. The museum owns the world's largest collection of Dorothea Lange's photographs and negatives, and photography by such group f.64 members as Edward Weston, Ansel Adams and Imogen Cunningham.

ADDITIONAL SIGHTS

★**Jack London Square** – Kids *Along the Embarcadero from Clay to Alice St. Farmers' market year-round Sun 10am–2pm.* ✂ ♿ ☎ *925-426-5420.* Stretching along the busy Inner Harbor of the Oakland Estuary southeast of Broadway, this once-gritty dock area has been developed as an attractive complex of shops, restaurants, hotels, cinemas, a farmers' market and yacht harbor. Oakland's Amtrak passenger lines, Oakland Estuary water-taxi service, and ferries from San Francisco converge near the marina.

The square was named for writer Jack London *(p 29)*, who lived in Oakland as a boy and young man. His adventurous spirit is recalled in the historic **Jack London Cabin**, a reconstruction from original timbers of the rustic, single-room log cabin that London occupied during the winter of 1897-98 while prospecting for gold in the Yukon Territory. Near the cabin stands one of London's favorite watering holes, **Heinold's First and Last Chance Saloon** (1883), built of the timbers of a whaling ship. Still operating as a bar, Heinold's was also patronized by such authors as Ambrose Bierce, Joaquin Miller and, for a short time, Robert Louis Stevenson. It was declared a National Literary Monument in 1997.

The Potomac – *FDR Pier, end of Clay St. Open year-round Wed & Fri 10am–2pm, Sun 11am–3pm, weather permitting. $3. Guided tours available Wed & Fri 10am–1:15pm, Sun 11am–2:15pm.* P ☎ *510-839-8256.* Franklin Delano Roosevelt's presidential yacht lies berthed at FDR Pier off Jack London Square. Now owned by a nonprofit association, the 165ft former Coast Guard cutter was built in 1934 and officially recommissioned as a US Navy vessel for the use of the Commander in Chief two years later. Today the *Potomac* has been renovated to match its appearance when it served as a presidential retreat on the Potomac River and along the Atlantic seaboard. Points of interest on the tour include the Presidential Cabin, the engine room, and a radio room from which Roosevelt made a national broadcast on March 29, 1941.

Corrugated metal awnings roof the si[illegible] walks of the **Oakland Produce Ma[illegible]** *(2 blocks east of Jack London Squ[illegible]* From early morning to early after[illegible] workers on forklifts shuttle crates o[illegible] fruits and vegetables between [illegible] trucks and warehouse buildings, [illegible] which have been brokering whole[illegible] duce since 1917. Some wareho[illegible] have been converted to restaur[illegible]

> **2 Oakland Grill**
> *301 Franklin St. at 3rd St.* ☎ *510-835-1176.* Get to this produce district eatery around 8am to down a hearty breakfast against a backdrop of fruits and vegetables being unloaded and readied for sale. All four buildings on this nostalgic corner sport corrugated metal awnings. Just to say you did it, try the scrambled egg whites, listed on the menu as "Ono Yoko."

27 • AROUND THE EAST BAY

Map of Principal Sights p 4

East of the ridgeline backdropping the cities of BERKELEY and OAKLAND, pleasant suburban towns dot a series of hills and valleys overshadowed by Mt. Diablo. Visible from many of San Francisco's loftier viewpoints, this regal peak looms over the San Ramon and Diablo Valleys, which drain north to the narrow Carquinez Straits in the northeast part of San Francisco Bay. Martinez, Concord, Walnut Creek, Alamo, Danville and other residential communities spread over the valley floors, while exclusive developments extend higher into the grassy hills. The historic Solano County towns of Vallejo and Benicia guard either end of Carquinez Straits.

SIGHTS

★**Mount Diablo State Park** – Kids *2hrs. 35mi from San Francisco. Take I-80 east across the Bay Bridge, then I-580 to Rte. 24 north and east through the Caldecott Tunnel, exiting in downtown Walnut Creek on Ygnacio Valley Rd. Continue east about 3mi to Oak Grove Rd. Turn right, then immediately left and continue to North Gate Rd., which leads past the state park office en route to the summit. Park open year-round daily 8am–dusk. Closed during very high fire-risk days. $5/car.* ⚠ P *Summit Museum open Memorial Day–Labor Day Wed–Sun 11am–5pm. Rest of the year Wed–Sun 10am–4pm.* ♿ P *www.mdia.org ☎ 925-837-2525.* The sweeping, panoramic **view**★★★ from the 3,849ft summit of Mt. Diablo is said to encompass more than 40,000sq mi. That would make it the second most extensive view over land from any point on earth, after Africa's Mt. Kilimanjaro. On clear days, the naked eye can easily pick out such far-flung landmarks as San Francisco (27mi west), the Farallon Islands (62mi west), Mt. Lassen (165mi northeast), the Sacramento River Delta to the north, and the long wall of the Sierra Nevada range to the east. A good pair of binoculars can bring Yosemite National Park's El Capitan (130mi east) into focus. From this remarkable vantage point, Colonel Leander Ransom in 1851 established the Mt. Diablo Base and Meridian, used to make the first surveyed maps of Northern California and Nevada. A year later, R.D. Cutts mapped the state's northern waterways for the Coast Survey from here.

Both survey marks still can be seen upon the rock now enclosed by the small **Summit Museum,** built of locally quarried sandstone by the Civilian Conservation Corps in 1940. Exhibits within the museum focus on Mt. Diablo's geology and its natural and human history; telescopes mounted on an observation deck assist viewing of distant sites. *Note: summer fogs often obscure views.*

On the mountain's flanks are extensive outcrops of fossilized seashells and prehistoric mammal bones. The park also is home to some 400 plant species, as well as deer, cougar, coyote, bobcat and about 200 species of birds, including bald eagles. Mt. Diablo offers camping, picnicking, hiking on more than 150mi of trails, and climbing in the weird sandstone formations known as **Rock City**. A new visitor center is under construction in the Mitchell Canyon section of the park.

Lindsay Wildlife Museum – Kids *1hr. 45mi from San Francisco in Walnut Creek. Take I-80 east across the Bay Bridge, then Rte. 24 north to I-680 north to Walnut Creek. Exit at Geary Rd./Treat Blvd.; turn left on Geary Rd., left on Buena Vista Ave., then right on 1st Ave. to the museum. Open mid-Jun–Labor Day Tue–Sun 10am–5pm. Rest of the year Tue–Fri noon–5pm, weekends 10am–5pm. Closed Labor Day week. $4.50.* ♿ P *www.wildlife-museum.org ☎ 925-935-1978.* This community-oriented natural-history museum performs the work of a wildlife-rehabilitation hospital, the largest such facility in the country. Injured animals that cannot be returned to the wild live out their days here, under conditions carefully designed to satisfy both their physical and psychological needs. Eagles, hawks and other raptors roost on perches, while rabbits, lynx, coyote and other mammals cavort below eye level. Live reptiles and amphibians, as well as mounted insect collections, introduce yet more local fauna.

★★**Eugene O'Neill National Historic Site** – *3hrs. 28mi from San Francisco, in Danville. Take I-80 east across the Bay Bridge, then Rte. 24 east to I-680 south. Exit on Diablo Rd. and head west, turning left on Hartz Ave. and right on Church St. National Park Service van picks up visitors in parking lot at corner of Railroad Ave. and Church St. for ride to Tao House. Visit by guided tour (2hrs 30min) only, year-round Wed–Sun 10am & 12:30pm. Reservations required. www.nps.gov/euon ☎ 925-838-0249.* Situated on a scenic knoll in the shadow of Las Trampas Ridge, this modest yet comfortable dwelling was home for more than six years to playwright **Eugene O'Neill**. Author of nearly 60 plays, winner of four Pulitzer Prizes for drama, and the only American playwright to win the Nobel Prize for Literature, O'Neill is one of the nation's best known and most influential dramatists.

Tragedy and Triumph – The son of a successful traveling actor, Eugene O'Neill was born in 1888 in a New York City hotel and raised largely "on the road" by a loving but troubled family. O'Neill's personal life was filled with difficulties. His mother was addicted to morphine and his brother to alcohol. His son committed suicide and he was bitterly estranged from his daughter, Oona, following her marriage to comic actor Charlie Chaplin. Suffering from tuberculosis, alcoholism and severe depression himself, O'Neill overcame his afflictions to find fulfillment first as a seaman and ultimately as a playwright. His heavily autobiographical tragedies helped transform American theater from an arena of pure entertainment into a high art form. O'Neill's six years at Tao House, a then-remote California home he built with his third wife, Carlotta, were among the happiest and most productive of his life.

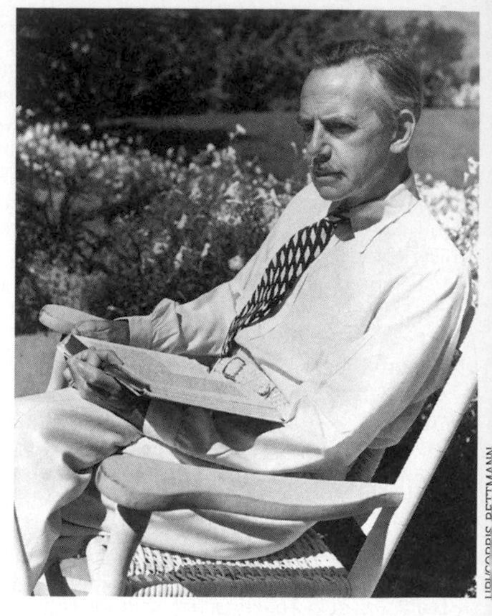

Eugene O'Neill (1937)

In 1937, the intensely private O'Neills bought 158 acres of almond and walnut orchards on the flank of Las Trampas Ridge, attracted by the site's remoteness and its handsome views of Mt. Diablo and the San Ramon Valley. Designed by architect Frederick Confer, their white, two-story Monterey-style house was built of reinforced concrete blocks (baselite) intended to resemble adobe brick, with a black-tile roof and verandas on the second floor. The couple christened their home **Tao House** after Carlotta's taste for chinoiserie and Eugene's interest in the Taoist philosophy. Here O'Neill wrote six plays, including four of his greatest: *The Iceman Cometh, Hughie, A Moon for the Misbegotten* (whose intended setting is thought to be the old barn on this property) and his masterpiece, *A Long Day's Journey into Night.*

O'Neill's degenerative illness and an inability to hire local assistance during World War II forced the couple to sell the house in February 1944 and return to the East Coast, where the playwright died in 1953. After the property became a National Historic Site in 1980, the National Park Service began efforts to restore the home and furnishings to their original appearance.

Visit – On the downstairs floor, guided tours lead through the kitchen, living room, guest room (which hosted Bennett Cerf, Somerset Maugham and John Ford), and "Rosie's Room," named for O'Neill's cherished player piano. Upstairs are O'Neill's writing den, which he furnished in a style fitting for a shipboard cabin, and the couple's bedrooms—the writer's still containing his original bed, an antique Chinese opium couch from Gump's. The 13-acre site also preserves the pool built for the playwright, an avid swimmer, and the grave of the O'Neills' beloved dog, Blemie.

Blackhawk Automotive Museum – Kids *2hrs. 33mi from San Francisco, in Danville. Take I-80 east across the Bay Bridge, then I-580 to Rte. 24 to I-680 to Danville. Exit at Sycamore Valley Blvd. (which becomes Camino Tassajara), and continue 5mi to Blackhawk Plaza. Open year-round Wed–Sun 10am–5pm. Closed Jan 1, Thanksgiving Day, Dec 25. $8. Guided tours (1hr) available weekends 2pm.* ♿ P *www.blackhawkauto.org* ☎ *925-736-2277.* At the eastern end of Blackhawk Plaza—a beautiful, Mediterranean-style luxury shopping complex landscaped with a cascading artificial creek—rises the red-granite and glass facade of this museum. It houses Kenneth Behring's stunning **collection**★★ of some 120 beautifully restored vintage automobiles spanning the decades from the 1890s to the 1980s. Informatively labeled and attractively arranged through two levels, the rare and historic vehicles are presented as works of art. From the ground floor, an interior hall leads to the Behring Automotive Art Galleries, comprising nearly 4,000 pieces of automotive art and memorabilia.

★**John Muir National Historic Site** – *2hrs. 30mi from San Francisco, in Martin... Take I-80 east across the Bay Bridge and continue north to Rte. 4 East. Exit Alhambra Blvd. in Martinez. Open year-round Wed–Sun 10am–4:30pm. Clo...*

major holidays. $2. ✗ ♿ P *www.nps.gov/jomu* ☎ *925-228-8860.* This comfortable home surrounded by orchards formed part of the 2,600-acre fruit ranch owned by **John Muir** (1838-1914). The legendary conservationist resided here during the final decades of his life, tending his orchards and writing many of the works that have since become landmarks of the environmental movement.

Born near Dunbar, Scotland, Muir arrived in Wisconsin with his family at the age of 10. Detesting the drudgery of farm work, he eventually departed to pursue the life of a wandering botanist, walking first to the Gulf of Mexico in 1867, where he took ship passage for San Francisco. His many visits to the Sierra Nevada invoked a lifelong love for rugged wilderness. A fine scientist and gifted writer, Muir published observations of nature that attracted a following among East Coast readers and opened minds to the then-novel idea of conserving wilderness lands. Muir helped found and served as the first president of the Sierra Club, and eventually prevailed upon the US Congress to bolster the young National Parks movement with new or expanded parklands in the Sierra Nevada and elsewhere.

Visit – Built in 1882 by Muir's father-in-law, Dr. John Strenzel, this two-story, Italianate frame residence was John Muir's home from 1890 until his death. The house today reflects the Victorian proclivities of the Strenzel family more than Muir's own simple tastes. The conservationist wrote many of his influential books in the second-floor "scribble den," which retains his original chair and desk.

Muir himself planted the large *Sequoia giganteum* (giant sequoia) that grows sturdily near the northwest corner of the house. Beyond, the park preserves 326 acres of land on Mt. Wanda and a small number of pear, peach, cherry, fig, orange, pomegranate, apricot and plum trees, as well as some grape vines. Beyond the orchard stands the **Martinez Adobe** (1849), the home of Vicente Martínez, who received it as part of an early 19C land grant of 17,750 acres.

A film on Muir's life is shown in the visitor center. Muir and his family are interred in a privately owned graveyard nearby.

Benicia – *2hrs. 34mi from San Francisco. Take I-80 east across the Bay Bridge and continue north, crossing the Carquinez Bridge. Turn east on Rte. 780 to 2nd St. exit in Benicia.* Established on part of General Mariano Vallejo's *(p 206)* vast land holdings, this small, friendly community on the north shore of the Carquinez Straits was named for Vallejo's wife. The town—the second to be incorporated in the state—grew up along the 10-block stretch of First Street north of the waterfront, today a pleasant boulevard of cafes and shops. From February 11, 1853 to February 25, 1854, Benicia served as the California state capital. **Benicia Capitol State Historic Park** *(115 West G St.; open year-round daily 10am–5pm; closed Jan 1, Thanksgiving Day, Dec 25; $2;* P ☎ *707-745-3385)* preserves the old brick statehouse, furnished as it might have appeared during its 54-week tenure.

Benicia Arsenal – *From 1st St. drive east on Military East, pass through the old army gate and follow signs to the Camel Barn and the Clocktower.* The US Army founded a military reservation in Benicia in 1849, establishing the Benicia Arsenal the following year. One of four US arsenals at the time, it served until it was deactivated in 1964, after which it was converted to the Benicia Industrial Park. Many of the old military buildings today house offices and artists' studios, some of which are open to the public. Among historic reminders of the army's presence are the oldest military cemetery in the Pacific states (1849), the turreted arsenal storehouse known as the Clocktower (1859), the commandant's house, and the **Camel Barn Museum** *(2060 Camel Rd.; open year-round Wed–Sun 1pm–4pm; $2;* ♿ P ☎ *707-745-5435)*, where the army auctioned camels in 1864 after experimenting with them as pack animals in the North American deserts.

★**Marine World** – Kids *1 day. 30mi from San Francisco. Take I-80 east across the Bay Bridge and continue north; cross Carquinez Bridge and exit at Marine World Parkway (Rte. 37). Blue & Gold Fleet ferry departs from Pier 39 in San Francisco to Vallejo daily 8:45am–7:40pm. One-way 1hr; $7.50. Shuttles depart from the Vallejo dock for the park. Package including park admission $40; call for information.* ✗ ♿ P *Blue & Gold Fleet* ☎ *415-705-5555. Park open Memorial Day–Labor Day daily 10am–10pm. Late Mar–Memorial Day & Labor Day–Oct Fri–Sun 10am–8pm. $29.99, children (4-12) $20.99.* ✗ ♿ P*($6).* ☎ *707-643-6722.* This 160-acre, landscaped park combines three distinct elements—it's a zoo, an oceanarium and an amusement park rolled into one—while entertaining and educating visitors about conservation issues with various shows and exhibits. Beginning as a modest theme park in 1968 in Redwood City, 25mi south of San Francisco, it was renamed Marine World Africa USA in 1972 after a merger with a Southern California wildlife park, and relocated in 1986 to its present site in Vallejo.

Visit – A visit to the park is best structured around seven live animal performances presented up to four times daily in various outdoor amphitheaters *(shows last 20-30min; map and daily schedule available at entrance).* Prominent among these are the bottle-nosed acrobats of **Dolphin Harbor**; the **Killer Whale Show**, in which an orca dives, cavorts and splashes the audience; and the **Wildlife Theater**, where the presentation of exotic animals from around the world furthers appreciation for endangered species. Visitors can pass through a transparent viewing tunnel as sharks swim overhead in **Shark Experience★**; hand-feed giraffes at the **Giraffe Feeding Dock**; team up in a game of tug-of-war with pachyderms at **Elephant Encounter**; watch frisky walruses through a glass-walled tank at the **Walrus Experience★**; and explore the steamy jungle setting of the **Butterfly World★** in search of brilliant tropical specimens. Also worth visiting are a saltwater aquarium and **Camp Looney Tunes**, a children's ride and amusement area. From April to October, the **Water Ski and Boat Show** showcases the park's ski team in myriad waterborne stunts.

Among the most popular rides are the **DinoSphere**, which scoots visitors past a life-sized, mechanical Tyrannosaurus and through an erupting volcano; **Kong**, a suspended roller-coaster that corkscrews and drops more than 10 stories at speeds above 50mph; and the splashing plunge of **Monsoon Falls**.

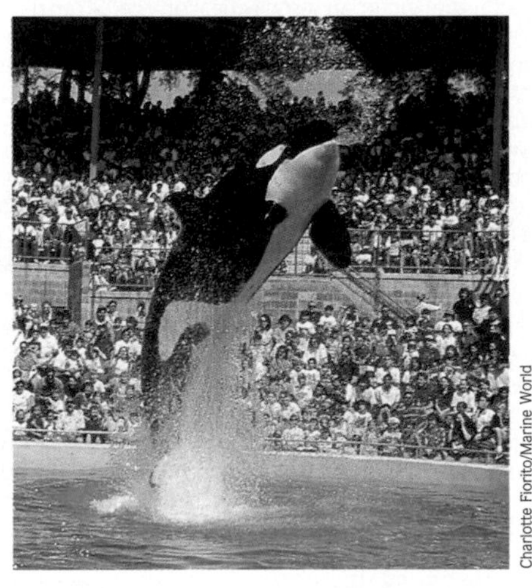

Charlotte Fiorito/Marine World

Killer Whale Show, Marine World

28 • MARIN HEADLANDS★★

Time: 3 hours. MUNI bus 76–Headlands (Sundays and holidays only)
Map p 181

Rising to the north of the Golden Gate, these 15sq mi of pristine coastal lands encompass a remarkable preserve of windswept ridges, sheltered valleys, sandy coves and scattered vestiges of the area's military history. Protected since 1972 as part of the Golden Gate National Recreation Area (and by the US Army before that), the Marin Headlands offer unequaled views of the city-fringed bay, the GOLDEN GATE BRIDGE elegantly overlapping San Francisco's skyline, and the vast Pacific Ocean stretching away to the western horizon.

Historical Notes

The headlands' strategic importance became evident to American forces soon after the US takeover of California in 1846. A fort was planned at Lime Point (today the north pier of the Golden Gate Bridge) to complement FORT POINT and ALCATRAZ in guarding the mouth of the Golden Gate. Although the Lime Point fort was never built, other defenses eventually appeared along the bluffs in the form of batteries, bunkers and gun emplacements. Many of the weapons installed on the headlands rapidly grew obsolete, to be replaced by newer armaments at Fort Baker, Fort Barry and Fort Cronkhite. None of the guns were ever fired in defense, and today the grounds of the three forts harbor a multitude of abandoned coastal defense installations ranging from post-Civil War earthen bunkers to Cold War-era Nike missile sites.
Thickly covered with coastal grasses, sagebrush, coyote brush and oak woodlands, the headlands provide habitat for lizards and snakes, elusive bobcats and foxes, and blacktailed deer. In spring, lupine, Indian paintbrush and other colorful wildflowers decorate the hillsides. Lagoons and coves attract stately egrets and herons, while fleets of brown pelicans patrol the coastal waters, and offshore rocks provide haven for seals, sea lions and nesting shorebirds.

Visiting the Marin Headlands – By car, follow US-101 north across the Golden Gate Bridge and exit at Alexander Ave. (2mi); follow Marin Headlands signs. For visitors without cars, MUNI bus 76-Headlands offers hourly transit between San Francisco and Fort Cronkhite on Sundays and holidays.
In summer, ocean-born fogs pour over these hills, freshening the air but often obscuring the stunning views of the bridge, bay and city. In fall and spring—the best seasons to visit the headlands—the hills bask in sunshine. Sundays are an especially popular time to visit; if possible, avoid the crowds by going on weekdays.
There are four campgrounds (primitive and modern) in the headlands, and hiking, biking and fishing opportunities abound. For information and reservations, contact the Marin Headlands Visitor Center *(p 180)*.

Cove Beach, Marin Headlands

SIGHTS

Fort Baker – *From San Francisco, follow US-101 north across the Golden Gate Bridge to the Alexander Ave. exit, just past Vista Pt. At Bunker Rd., turn left and follow signs to the Bay Area Discovery Museum.* Named in honor of Colonel Edward Dickinson Baker, a Civil War hero and friend of Abraham Lincoln, this attractive group of buildings and batteries was the first military post on the north side of the Golden Gate. Eight small batteries were constructed between 1873 and 1943, including the still-visible Battery Yates (1905) near Cavallo Point—the easternmost tip of Horseshoe Cove.

Today, the section east of the bridge, called **East Fort Baker**, is home to the Army's 91st Division Reserve, a US Coast Guard station, the Presidio Yacht Club and a children's museum *(below)*. Stroll the bluffs overlooking Horseshoe Cove for dramatic **views**★★ of the Golden Gate Bridge. The **Bay Trail** *(.25mi)* along the shore east of Cavallo Point offers views of the East Bay, Angel Island and Alcatraz while skirting the habitat of the endangered Mission Blue butterfly.

★**Bay Area Discovery Museum (M)** – Kids *Open mid-June–mid-Sept Tue–Sun 10am–5pm. Rest of the year Tue–Thu 9am–4pm, Fri–Sun 10am–5pm. Closed major holidays. $7.* *www.badm.org* *415-487-4398.* One of the Bay Area's excellent children's museums, this complex of six learning-oriented halls delights children ages one to ten. In the **Entrance Pavilion**, young computer whizzes head for the multimedia computer center to check out the latest educational CD-ROM programs before heading off to the science room or maze of illusions. The **San Francisco Bay**★ building highlights some of the activities and animals of the bay. Kids pretend to go crabbing off a pier, explore an undersea tunnel, or fish for salmon on the Discovery Boat. The **Architecture and Design** building helps young visitors learn how to build bridges and other structures, design interiors, or be pretend-engineers on a high-rise construction project. The **Tot Spot**'s whimsical, multicolored rooms safely occupy kiddies ages three and under, and the **Art Room** offers a variety of drop-in art activities.

★★★**Conzelman Road** – Kids *From Fort Baker, return to Alexander Ave., turn right toward US-101, pass under the freeway and continue to Conzelman Rd., following signs for Marin Headlands.* This gloriously scenic route snakes along the Marin Headlands' curvaceous bluffs past numerous abandoned military batteries. Turnouts along the way provide ample opportunity to pull over and drink in the outstanding **views**★★★ of San Francisco Bay, the Golden Gate Bridge and the Pacific Ocean. Stop at **Battery Spencer** *(.25mi)*, a massive concrete casement built in 1896 to house three cannons, for a formidable view of the city framed by the looming north pier of the bridge. The curious can crawl inside the command station overlooking a gun mount. **Battery Construction 129** *(1.75mi)*, considered the highest gun battery in the US, was begun in 1942 to house a 16in gun capable of firing shells over 20mi; construction was suspended in 1944 and the battery was never armed. From mid-August to mid-December, **Hawk Hill**★, just above Battery 129, draws legions of birders to witness the southward migration of raptors—eagles, hawks and falcons—plying the only such flyway on the West Coast.

Beyond Battery 129 the road crests and becomes a winding one-way passage that curves down along the precipitous edge of a high sea cliff. Entering decommissioned Fort Barry, it heads past Battery Rathbone-McIndoe (1905) to Batteries Alexander (1905), Wallace (1918) and Mendell (c.1905). From the latter, views extend west and north over the coastal headlands, guano-covered Bird Rock, Rodeo Valley and the stark barracks and buildings of Fort Cronkhite *(p 181)*. Point Bonita can be seen due south of Battery Mendell.

★**Point Bonita Lighthouse** – Kids *From the end of Conzelman Rd. follow Pt. Bonita Lighthouse signs to trailhead for hike (.5mi) to the lighthouse (sturdy shoes advised). Open year-round Sat–Mon 12:30pm–3:30pm. Guided tours (1hr) available weekends 12:30pm.* *www.nps.gov/goga* *415-331-1540.* Perched on the rocky tip of Point Bonita, this small lighthouse has helped guide mariners through the Golden Gate since 1855. Though automated in 1981, the sentinel still employs its original Fresnel lens, through which beacons of light were beamed to 19C passenger ships, lumber schooners and naval fleets of both world wars. Extensive restorations to the lighthouse were completed in 1996.

★**Marin Headlands Visitor Center** – Kids *From Conzelman Rd. take Field Rd. to the corner of Bunker Rd. Open year-round daily 9:30am–4:30pm. Closed Dec 25. Guided tours (1-2hrs) available. Call ahead for schedule.* *www.nps.gov/goga* *415-331-1540.* Located in Fort Barry's former post chapel (1941), this ranger station/visitor center mounts excellent, hands-on natural history displays and exhibits on the human inhabitants of the headlands—Coast Miwok, 19C *vaqueros* (Mexican and Native American cattle ranchers), Portuguese dairy ranchers, lighthouse keepers, and soldiers. Browse the well-stocked bookstore for books, field guides and maps.

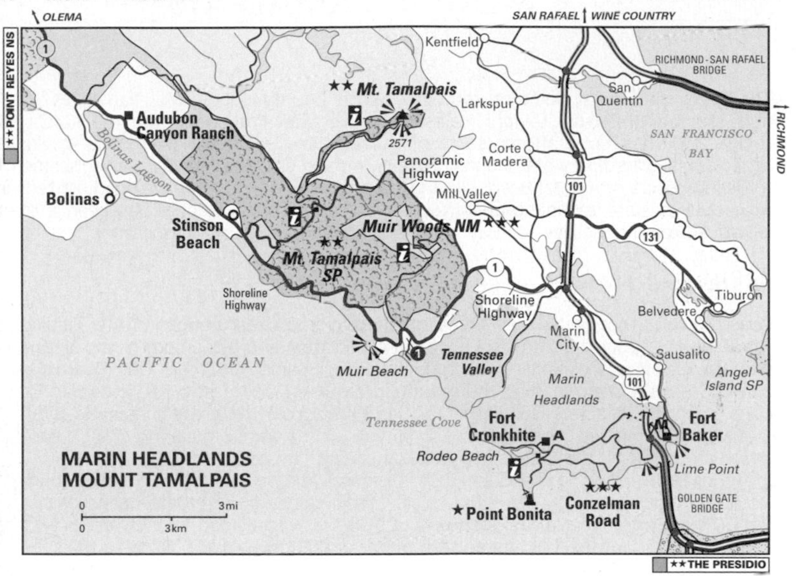

Near the visitor center lies Missile Site SF 88L, a former **Nike missile site**, one of several around the bay. Its original but unarmed Nike missiles are open to the public for viewing *(open year-round Mon–Fri & first Sun of each month 12:30pm–3:30pm; guided tours available; call in advance; ♿ P ☎ 415-331-1540).*

Fort Cronkhite – *Follow Bunker Rd. to Mitchell Rd. and continue along Rodeo Lagoon to beach parking lot.* Named for World War II commander Major Adelbert Cronkhite, the fort housed gun batteries and a Nike missile. A set of well-preserved former barracks still stands sentinel on the fort's grounds.
The waters off Fort Cronkhite's **Rodeo Beach** draw surfers, although dangerous currents and cold temperatures make it unsafe to swim here. From the beach parking area, the Coastal Trail leads to Battery Townsley *(.5 mi).*

Marine Mammal Center (A) – Kids *Follow signs from Bunker Rd. Open year-round daily 10am–4pm. Closed Jan 1, Thanksgiving Day, Dec 25. Guided tours (30min) available, reservations required. ♿ P ☎ 415-289-7325.* Since opening in 1975, this animal hospital for wild creatures has rescued, rehabilitated and released hundreds of injured and sick marine mammals found on the California coast. Visitors can see adult and juvenile sea lions, seals and otters in various stages of recuperation. The center also conducts marine-mammal research and runs educational marine environmental programs.

ADDITIONAL SIGHT

Tennessee Valley – *From the Golden Gate Bridge, take US-101 north to the Mill Valley/Stinson Beach (Hwy. 1) exit. Continue .5mi to Tennessee Valley Rd. Turn left and continue 1.5mi to trailhead parking lot.* This peaceful valley was named for the *SS Tennessee*, a 210ft steamer that ran aground on the beach here in dense fog on March 5, 1853. The ship was carrying 600 passengers from Panama to San Francisco. All survived, but the ship was destroyed.
The valley, once part of the Rancho Saucelito *(p 189)*, was later home to several Portuguese dairy ranches. Today the ranches are gone and the valley forms part of the GGNRA. A pleasant, easygoing hiking road *(2mi)* wanders down the inland valley to Tennessee Cove and the ocean. Herds of black-tailed deer have replaced the dairy cattle, hawks soar overhead and great horned owls hoot from eucalyptus trees along the way.

Consult the practical information section at the end of the guide for travel tips, useful addresses and phone numbers, and a wealth of details on shopping, recreation, entertainment and annual events.

29 • MOUNT TAMALPAIS★★

Time: 1 day

Map p 181

The geographic focal point of southern Marin County, kingly Mt. Tamalpais (pronounced tam-ul-PIE-us) towers majestically over San Francisco from the north. Its rocky, 2,571ft summit affords some of the Bay Area's finest views, while its flanks harbor an extraordinary abundance of trails, meadows, forests and other enticements to delight lovers of natural beauty and outdoor sports. Largely undeveloped, its terrain protected as state and national parklands or county watershed, it has been a treasured recreation resource for Bay Area urbanites for more than a century.

Historical Notes

Coast Miwok tribes made their home on the bay and ocean fringes of Mt. Tamalpais for at least 3,000 years prior to European exploration and settlement of the area. The mountain itself was considered sacred. In 1772, Spanish explorers Don Pedro Fages and Padre Juan Crespí named the mountain La Sierra de Nuestro Padre de San Francisco ("The Mountain of Our Father of San Francisco"). Its present name is thought to have been derived from the Coast Miwok words *tamal*, meaning "bay," and *pa* (later corrupted by the Spanish to *pais*), meaning "mountain."

In the decades following the Gold Rush, residents and visitors looked to the mountain for leisure and recreation, traveling to its scenic slopes by ferryboat, stagecoach and train. Hiking trails were established and in 1884, a wagon road to the west peak was built. By 1896 tourists could ascend from the foothill town of Mill Valley to the summit aboard the steam-powered Mill Valley and Mt. Tamalpais Scenic Railway (later known as the Mt. Tamalpais and Muir Woods Railway). Dubbed the "Crookedest Railroad in the World," the train chugged along a steep 8.2mi route, negotiating 281 curves along the way. In 1907, a "gravity car" line to Muir Woods was installed, wherein passengers glided silently down from the summit to the Muir Woods Inn before hiking or riding horse-drawn carriages to the redwood forest. The railway ceased operation in 1930.

The work of preserving Mt. Tamalpais' unspoiled beauty was set in motion by **William Kent**, an ardent and wealthy Marin County conservationist and state representative. Between 1905 and 1928, Kent made numerous gifts of land to the state and federal governments; his donations and political lobbying helped create Muir Woods National Monument and Mount Tamalpais State Park, and resulted in the mountain's present status of public ownership.

A nature lover's paradise, Mt. Tamalpais is blessed with abundant wildlife and a tremendous variety of vegetation. Some 300 species of birds have been seen soaring above the peaks or flitting in the treetops, including red-tailed hawks, turkey vultures, black ravens, Stellar's jays, quail, wrens and pileated woodpeckers. Black-tailed deer, Western gray squirrels, Sonoma chipmunks and brush rabbits all make their homes here. Nocturnal bobcats are present but rarely seen, and sightings of mountain lions and coyotes have been reported in recent years, though most large mammals were hunted out in the early 1800s.

Visiting Mt. Tamalpais – Roads through the park offer spectacular vistas of ocean, bay and rugged hills. **Shoreline Highway** (Rte. 1) takes a cliff-hugging route along the coast: From San Francisco, take US-101 north over the Golden Gate Bridge to the Mill Valley/Stinson Beach exit and turn left onto Rte. 1. The most direct route winds up the mountain's southern ridges on the **Panoramic Highway, Pantoll Road** and **Ridgecrest Road** to a vista point near the summit: from Shoreline Highway, turn right on Panoramic Highway and follow the signs to Mt. Tamalpais. The **Muir Woods Road** branches off the Panoramic Highway.

The mountain is a favored recreation destination at all times of the year. Trails and unpaved fire roads offer more than 210mi of hiking, biking and equestrian paths; contact the GGNRA headquarters at FORT MASON or the Mount Tamalpais State Park Pantoll **ranger station** *(intersection of Panoramic Hwy. and Stinson Beach Hwy.; open year-round daily 8am–1hr past dusk;* 🅿 ☎ *415-388-2070)* for maps and information on weather and trail conditions.

Spring is an especially lovely time to visit, when myriad small creeks run full, grassy ridges wear a lush green coat, and wildflowers festoon the slopes. In summer, thick fogs can blanket the mountain's lower slopes; yet the summit is often sunny and can afford extraordinary views of fog-wrapped San Francisco Bay.

While it is possible to visit all sights described on Mt. Tamalpais in one day, visitors may wish to plan more leisurely visits to individual sights. Directions to each are provided from San Francisco.

SIGHTS

★★**Mount Tamalpais State Park** – *18mi. Take US-101 north to Rte. 1 (Shoreline Hwy.). Continue to Panoramic Hwy. and turn right, following signs to the park. Open year-round daily 8am–1hr past dusk. Closed during high fire-risk days. $5/car.* ⚠ *(reservations ☎ 800-444-7275)* 🅿 ☎ *415-388-2070.* The park began as a 200-acre gift from William Kent and was later enlarged through the efforts of local hiking clubs, which helped acquire an additional 520 acres. Today it completely surrounds Muir Woods National Monument *(below)*. Nature lovers flock to Mt. Tam's spectacular trails year-round, and summer brings theatergoers to the Mountain Theatre, a woodsy natural amphitheater with terraced stone seats, that mounts popular musicals and theatrical performances on weekends during May and June *(East Ridgecrest Blvd., just east of intersection with Pantoll Rd. ☎ 415-383-1100)*.

East Peak – *From the Pantoll ranger station, take Pantoll Rd. to Ridgecrest Blvd. and continue toward the summit.* Numerous turnouts, picnic spots, trailheads and scenic overlooks mark the long ascent to a parking area a quarter-mile below the top of Mt. Tamalpais. From here, cities, towns and majestic bay appear as if on a giant raised relief map, backdropped to the east by MOUNT DIABLO, 35mi away. The 360-degree panorama is one of the finest **views★★★** in the Bay Area. On exceptionally clear winter days, the snow-capped Sierra Nevada mountains are visible 140mi to the east, as are Mt. St. Helena to the north and the Farallon Islands to the west.

Vegetation at this elevation consists mostly of the brushy mix of scrub oak and red-barked manzanita known as chaparral. From the East Peak parking lot, a short but rocky and strenuous path *(.3mi)* leads to the summit fire lookout, rebuilt in 1937 by the Civilian Conservation Corps *(closed to the public)*. The **Verna Dunshee Trail** *(.7mi)* makes a level, paved loop around the summit.

■ A Cradle for Mountain Biking

In the early 1970s, a group of local bicycle enthusiasts began modifying and equipping their traditional balloon-tired "cruiser" bikes to withstand travel across Mt. Tamalpais' rugged trails and fire roads. Riding and racing such bikes quickly became a local passion, and the ensuing years brought increasing technological innovations that resulted in today's sophisticated "mountain bikes." Mt. Tamalpais continues to attract a steady stream of bicycling enthusiasts, many of whom make the strenuous ascent to the summit on the unpaved Old Railroad and Eldridge grades.

Many trails guide hikers and bicyclists to East Peak and other points around the park. One of the more popular mountain-bike routes starts from a trailhead at **Mountain Home Inn**, a bed and breakfast lodge built on the site of a historic railroad inn *(810 Panoramic Hwy.; park in public lot across from the inn)*. The path ascends on unpaved fire roads that follow, in part, the old railway grade. Hikers may prefer to start higher on the mountain, at Pantoll, where several possible routes lead to the summit. Another popular destination is the **West Point Inn** (1904), a rustic wooden structure situated on a ridge just below the summit. Hikers, equestrians and bicyclists congregate here to refill water bottles, relax on the shady veranda and take in panoramic **views**. From the inn, the Old Railroad Grade continues to East Peak.

★★★ **Muir Woods National Monument** – Kids *17mi. Take US-101 north to Rte. 1 (Shoreline Hwy.). Continue to Panoramic Hwy. and turn right, then left on Muir Woods Rd. Open year-round daily 8am–dusk. Guided tours (1hr) available Fri–Sun 1pm. $2. www.nps.gov/muwo ☎ 415-388-2595.* Situated on the slope of Mt. Tamalpais along Redwood Creek, Muir Woods harbors one of the largest stands of ancient coast redwoods in the Bay Area. The tranquil grove of majestic red-barked trees, some 1,100 years in age, attracts more than two million visitors annually.

A Tree-Lover's Monument – The world's tallest trees, coast redwoods *(sequoia sempervirens)* can attain heights equal to that of a 36-story building. They are among the few conifers that can sprout from knotty outgrowths, called burls, as well as reproduce by seeds. The absence of resin in the trees' 6in- to 12in-thick bark, coupled with the high tannin content of the wood, renders them resistant to fire, insect damage and disease, enabling them to live for hundreds of years. Muir Woods is a relatively young grove; its oldest trees are more than a millennium old. California's tallest, oldest redwoods thrive well to the north of here in the Redwood Empire *(consult the Michelin Green Guide to California)*.

Prior to the arrival of Europeans on the west coast, millions of acres of primeval redwood forest blanketed the coastal reaches of California and southern Oregon; aggressive logging has since wiped out all but 150,000 acres. Much of Mt. Tamalpais' virgin redwood forest was logged in the years following the Gold Rush, but the trees in present-day Muir Woods escaped the lumbermen's saws and axes, owing to their relative inaccessibility. The forest became a national monument in 1908 after William Kent

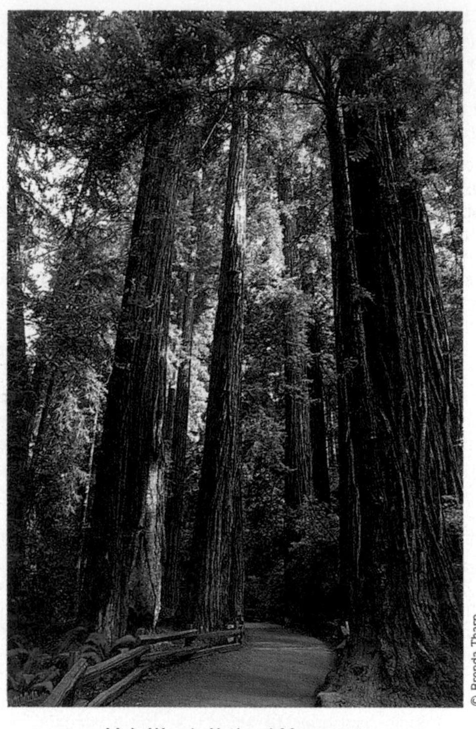
© Brenda Tharp
Muir Woods National Monument

(p 182) donated 295 acres of land in Redwood Canyon to the federal government in 1907, insisting that the park be named for conservationist John Muir *(p 177)*. In a letter of thanks to Kent, Muir wrote, "This is the best tree-lover's monument that could possibly be found in all the forests of the world."

Visit – Begin at the visitor center and adjacent bookstore, which stock trail maps and information about local natural history. From the visitor center, six miles of trails (some paved) wind about the forest floor, following the paths of Redwood Creek and Fern Creek. The **Main Trail** *(1mi)* crosses over a series of wooden bridges, looping under a dense canopy of mature redwoods that rise like spires toward the heavens. Amid groves of living trees, trunks of fallen giants lie in various states of decay in a lush undergrowth of sword ferns, azaleas and horsetail, a primitive plant whose ancestry dates back 300 million years. Muir Woods' most impressive trees stand in **Cathedral Grove** and **Bohemian Grove**, site of the park's tallest tree, measuring 253ft *(tree is unmarked)*.
The Main Trail connects to the Hillside Trail *(1.9mi loop)* or to the Ocean View, Lost and Fern Creek trails *(3.1mi loop)*. Trails in the monument also connect with unpaved hiking trails in Mount Tamalpais State Park.

ADDITIONAL SIGHTS

Muir Beach Overlook – *17mi from San Francisco; take US-101 to Rte. 1 (Shoreline Hwy.); continue to "Muir Beach" sign. From Muir Woods, take Frank Valley Rd. 2.5mi and turn right on Rte. 1 (Shoreline Hwy.).* Steps lead down to a railed promontory that affords sweeping **views★★** of the coast to the north and south. The hooded concrete burrows on the bluff behind the promontory were installed during World War II; signs illustrate how the stations were designed to target enemy vessels.
South of the overlook, Shoreline Highway passes **Muir Beach**, a small, scenic stretch of sand situated at the mouth of Redwood Creek. Tables and grills make this an excellent spot to relax, though dangerous tides and currents make swimming inadvisable.

> **1 The Pelican Inn**
> *Junction of Rte. 1 and Pacific Way (Muir Beach Rd.). ☎ 415-383-6000.*
> This thoroughly British country inn and pub was created by a fourth-generation pub owner from Surrey, England. Pub fare and pints of British and Irish brews are served up in a low-beamed dining room and at a candlelit Tudor-style bar.

Stinson Beach – *Rte. 1, 5mi north of Muir Beach Overlook.* Called Willow Camp in the late 19C, this charming beach town is a popular stop for coastal travelers. Its small but inviting assortment of restaurants and art galleries, bookstore, surf shop and outdoor Shakespeare theater draws visitors and residents from throughout San Francisco and Marin County. The excellent **beach★★**, one of the few in the area safe for swimming (when it's not being patrolled by sharks), is the town's principal attraction. In addition to swimmers, the 3.5mi sandy crescent draws surfers, sunbathers and kayakers. Stinson Beach is the finishing point for the annual Dipsea Race in which runners traverse Mt. Tamalpais from Mill Valley.

Audubon Canyon Ranch – Kids *4900 Shoreline Hwy. (Rte. 1), 8mi north of Muir Beach Overlook. Open mid-Mar–mid-Jul weekends & holidays 10am–4pm. $10 contribution requested.* P *www.egret.org* ☎ *415-868-9244.* This 1,000-acre bird sanctuary is located in a woodsy canyon adjacent to Bolinas Lagoon. In spring, the center's grounds and trails are open for observing great blue herons and white egrets nesting in the trees. A small museum mounts interesting exhibits on local geology and natural history.

Bolinas – *10mi north of Muir Beach Overlook. Take first left turn off Rte. 1 north of Bolinas Lagoon.* In a captivating setting on an off-the-beaten-path peninsula between the Pacific Ocean and Bolinas Lagoon, this picturesque community has in recent decades developed a reputation as an insular outpost of counterculture. First settled in 1835 as part of the Baulenes Rancho land grant, the town boomed during the Gold Rush when schooners came here to load timber destined for building sites in San Francisco. Today, the quaint downtown features a charming bar, a health-food store, several cafes and a small local history **museum and art gallery** *(48–50 Wharf Rd.; open Fri–Sun 1pm–5pm; closed Dec 25.* ♿ P ☎ *415-868-2006).* The pleasant beach near downtown attracts swimmers, surfers and sunbathers.

30 • POINT REYES NATIONAL SEASHORE**

Time: 1 or 2 days

Map p 186

Windy, wave-swept and often cloaked in fog, the Point Reyes Peninsula is an enchantingly varied expanse of wilderness 40mi north of San Francisco. Jutting from the west Marin County pasturelands into the Pacific Ocean, this 30mi coastal wedge harbors long sandy beaches, lush forests, rugged sea cliffs and vast wetlands, all populated by diverse animal, bird and marine life. Laced by 140mi of trails, the 102sq mi peninsula was designated a national seashore in 1962.

Historical Notes

Formed by the San Andreas Fault, the Point Reyes Peninsula rides on the eastern edge of the Pacific tectonic plate, creeping northwesterly at about 2in per year while the adjacent North American plate travels westward at a slower rate. The two plates meet in a rift zone that runs south through the Olema Valley and northwest beneath narrow Tomales Bay, which separates the peninsula from the rest of Marin County. The jut of land was thrust more than 16ft northwest of the mainland by the great earthquake of 1906. A legacy of the peninsula's ancient journey along the San Andreas Fault is

Practical Information .... Area Code: 415

Getting There – From San Francisco take US-101 north to Mill Valley/Stinson Beach exit (Rte. 1) and continue on Shoreline Hwy. to Bear Valley Rd. (27mi). For a quicker if less dramatic route, continue north on US-101 to the Greenbrae exit (10mi) to Sir Francis Drake Blvd. west, turn right on Rte. 1 and take the first left onto Bear Valley Rd.

When to Go – Weather conditions can change dramatically from one area to the next on the peninsula; visitors should always be prepared for cool winds and damp conditions. The autumn months are usually mildest. Winter, the rainiest season, is the best time to see migrating gray whales *(p 232)*.

Visitor Information – Stop by the Bear Valley Visitor Center *(below)* for maps and information on recreation, lodging and seasonal events on the peninsula. Other information centers are located at Drakes Beach and Point Reyes Lighthouse. Point Reyes National Seashore information may be accessed on the Internet at www.nps.gov/pore.

Accommodations – **Bed-and-breakfast** inns and **cabins** are available in Inverness, Olema and Point Reyes Station. A hostel is located at Point Reyes *(☎ 663-8811)*. The six camping areas on the peninsula range from primitive to modern; for reservations call Bear Valley Visitor Center (four campgrounds, all for hikers and bikers; ☎ 663-1092); Tomales Bay State Park (one campground for hikers and bikers; *no reservations necessary*); or the private Olema Ranch (one campground, cars welcomed; ☎ 663-8001).

Recreation – **Hiking**: easy and strenuous trails; stop at Bear Valley Visitor Center for maps and information. Biking: on roads and designated trails; rentals in Olema and Point Reyes Station. Guided **horseback** trail rides: Five Brooks Stables *(☎ 663-1570)*. **Birdwatching**: Point Reyes Bird Observatory (west of Bolinas); Estero de Limantour (east of Drakes Estero). **Whale Watching**: Point Reyes Lighthouse.

its granite backbone, **Inverness Ridge**, which has geologic origins in the Tehachapi Mountains 300mi to the south. Five million years ago, the peninsula occupied the site of present-day Monterey Bay; someday it will be an island sliding toward the Gulf of Alaska.

For thousands of years, Point Reyes was home to Coast Miwok Indians. The peaceable Miwoks harvested acorns and berries, fished for shellfish and salmon, and hunted deer and elk. In summer 1579, Francis Drake, an English explorer sponsored by Queen Elizabeth I, turned south from his search for a Northwest Passage and anchored his ship, the *Golden Hind*, for repairs in the vicinity of Point Reyes. The "faire and good baye" he described is thought to be the protected bay now known as Drakes Bay. Drake claimed his landfall for England, calling it "Nova Albion" after "the white bancks and cliffes" (resembling the blanched palisades of England's Dover coast) that rise over Drakes Beach.

In the next decades the area was visited by Spanish explorers, including Sebastián Vizcaíno, who in 1603 named it La Punta de Los Reyes or "Point of the Kings." In 1792, British Captain George Vancouver gave Drakes Bay its name. But Francis Drake's claim to Nova Albion was never upheld by Vancouver nor other English visitors. The area became a distant colony of Spain. After Mexican independence in 1821, Point Reyes became a center for cattle ranching, remaining so after the US takeover of California. In the 1950s, development threatened to change the peninsula forever, but fierce preservation efforts led to the creation of the Point Reyes National Seashore in 1962.

SIGHTS

Bear Valley Area

★**Bear Valley Visitor Center** – Kids *Open year-round Mon–Fri 9am–5pm, weekends & holidays 8am–5pm. Closed Dec 25.* ♿ P ☎ *415-663-1092.* Rangers on duty at this attractive, barn-like park headquarters provide information, answer questions, take campsite reservations, and post times and meeting places for guided hikes and other interpretive programs. The bookstore stocks a wide variety of posters, postcards and natural-history publications, including books about Point Reyes. Spend time in the center's fine **exhibit hall**, where displays on coastal wetlands, birdwatching hot spots, marine mammals and cultural history provide an introduction to the peninsula.

From the Visitor Center parking lot, the pleasant, easy **Earthquake Trail**★ Kids *(.6mi)* invites strollers to see the dramatic effects of ground-shifting that took place during the 1906 quake, whose epicenter was in this rift zone. One spot on the trail shows how a wooden fence split and separated as it rode with the moving ground. Also leading from the parking lot, the **Woodpecker Nature Trail** Kids *(.7mi)* offers a quick introduction to the natural wonders of Point Reyes.

Morgan Horse Ranch – Kids *Open year-round daily 10am–4:30pm.* P ☎ *415-663-1763.* Situated just behind the Visitor Center, this 100-acre ranch maintains a herd of more than a dozen compact, muscular Morgans used by park rangers for back-country patrol. A self-guided tour of the ranch (which includes a blacksmith's shop, pole barn and stables) trots visitors through two centuries of history about the Morgan, the first American breed of horse.

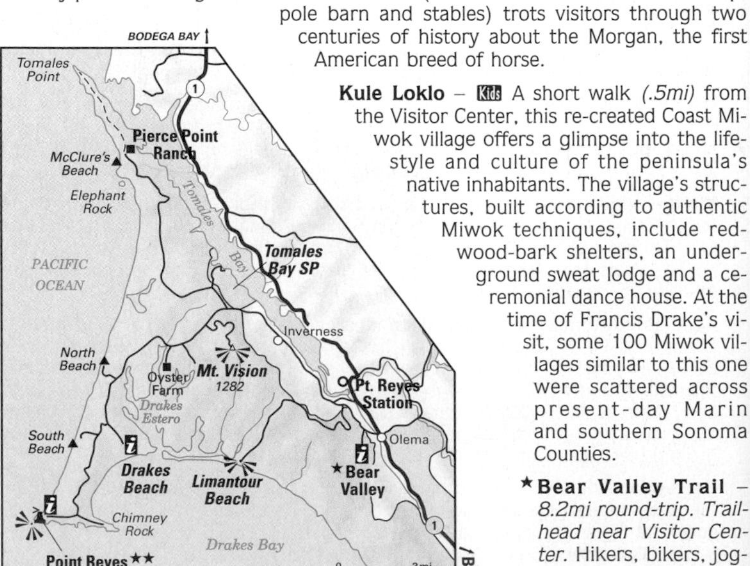

Kule Loklo – Kids A short walk *(.5mi)* from the Visitor Center, this re-created Coast Miwok village offers a glimpse into the lifestyle and culture of the peninsula's native inhabitants. The village's structures, built according to authentic Miwok techniques, include redwood-bark shelters, an underground sweat lodge and a ceremonial dance house. At the time of Francis Drake's visit, some 100 Miwok villages similar to this one were scattered across present-day Marin and southern Sonoma Counties.

★**Bear Valley Trail** – *8.2mi round-trip. Trailhead near Visitor Center.* Hikers, bikers, joggers and equestrians range this wide, easygoing path along Coast Creek. Traversing redwood forests and picnic-perfect Divide Meadow, the trail ends at the **Arch Rock viewpoint** overlooking the ocean. Several more-strenuous trails branch off the Bear Valley Trail, including the Sky, Glen and Old Pine trails; the Coast Trail intersects it near Arch Rock.

Limantour Beach – *From the visitor center, drive 1.5mi north on Bear Valley Rd. Turn left on Limantour Rd. and continue 6mi.* This splendid curve of land along Drakes Bay is famous for its fine **views** of the white cliffs of Point Reyes. At the northern end, the shoreline narrows to form Limantour Spit, which separates the wildlife-rich waters of Limantour Estero (*estero* is Spanish for "estuary") from the deeper waters of Drakes Bay. From September through May, Limantour Estero and nearby Drakes Estero are major wintering and migratory grounds for shorebirds and seabirds. Come at low tide to explore numerous tidepools.

Point Reyes Peninsula Area

The tip of Point Reyes, protruding some 15mi into the Pacific Ocean, has for centuries constituted a severe hazard for mariners making their ways along the California coast. Numerous ships have met their demise here, lost in the dense fogs and stormy weather that frequently drape the exposed jut of land. High winds and heavy surf rake the northwest-facing bluffs and pound the sands, while the beaches and estuaries on the point's southeast side enjoy sheltered, peaceful conditions.

Mount Vision – *From Bear Valley Visitor Center, turn left on Bear Valley Rd. Veer left onto Sir Francis Drake Blvd. and turn left on Mt. Vision Rd.* From the overlook en route to Mt. Vision's 1,282-ft summit, sweeping **views★★** extend over Point Reyes, Drakes Estero and the rolling Pacific Ocean. The narrow, winding road continues to the peak, where hikers can connect to several different trails scaling the flanks of Inverness Ridge.

West of Mt. Vision Road, take Drakes Estero exit off Sir Francis Drake Boulevard to **Johnson's Oyster Farm** *(open year-round Tue–Sun 8am–4:30pm; ♿ 🅿 ☎ 415-669-1149)*, a family-owned purveyor of freshly harvested oysters and other shellfish.

Drakes Beach – *Follow signs from Sir Francis Drake Blvd.* Here, visitors enjoy one of the peninsula's most serene stretches of sand, sheltered from pounding surf and stiff ocean winds. Gentle waves lap the shore, and the adjacent estuary attracts birds (and birdwatchers) year-round. The small **Kenneth C. Patrick Visitor Center** here provides information and exhibits on the marine ecosystem of Drakes Bay *(open Memorial Day–Labor Day Fri–Tue 10am–5pm; rest of the year weekends & holidays only 10am–5pm; closed Dec 25; ✗ ♿ 🅿 ☎ 415-669-1250)*.

Point Reyes Beach – *From Mt. Vision Rd., follow Sir Francis Drake Blvd. southwest for 4.7mi and turn right at sign to North Beach.* The wide, splendid, 12mi strip comprising **North Beach** and **South Beach** faces northwest—directly into the strongest winds and roughest surf of the open ocean. The beaches offer glorious walks, although strong currents make them unsafe for swimming, surfing or wading.

★★**Point Reyes Lighthouse** – Kids *From North and South Beaches, continue south on Sir Francis Drake Blvd. Lighthouse Visitor Center parking area is 22mi from Bear Valley Visitor Center. Lighthouse open year-round Thu–Mon 10am–4:30pm, weather permitting. www.nps.gov/pore ☎ 415-669-1534.* Perched halfway down the sheer south face of precipitous Point Reyes headland, this beacon guided countless mariners along the rocky Pacific shore for a century after it began operating in 1870. A steep staircase of 308 steps *(closed when winds exceed*

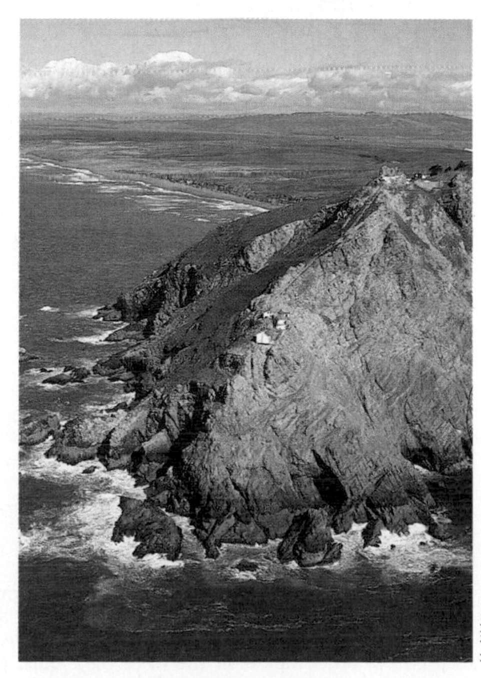

V. Atkinson

Point Reyes Lighthouse

40mph) descends to the station, where visitors can admire the three-ton Fresnel lens cast in 1867. The brass-mounted light is visible for more than 24 nautical miles and is still fully operational.

On clear days, the headlands offer excellent **views**★★★ of the coast, the Farallon Islands to the southwest and distant San Francisco. The spot is popular with birders (more than 360 species have been recorded in the area) and with whale-watchers, who congregate here to spy gray whales as they pass close to shore during their annual migration season *(December to April)*. Sea lions and seals perch on rocky abodes just east of the point. Chimney Rock is one of the best places to spot elephant seals in the Bay Area.

Tomales Point Area

Dairy and cattle ranches blanket the peninsula's northern point, set between the Pacific Ocean to the west and Tomales Bay to the east.

Pierce Point Ranch – Kids *From Bear Valley Visitor Center, take Sir Francis Drake Blvd. north 7.5mi. Turn right on Pierce Point Rd. and continue to its end. Open year-round dawn to dusk.* ♿ P ☎ *415-663-1092 (Bear Valley Visitor Center).* Established in 1858 by Vermont dairy farmer Solomon Pierce, this pastoral spread of farm buildings remains the only one of the park's 26 historic dairy and cattle ranches open to the public. A self-guided tour leads among the ranch buildings, while exhibits describe such farm activities as butter churning and hay collecting. The wide, mile-long stretch of **McClures Beach** *(turn left at the end of Pierce Point Rd.; beach accessible by a steep .5mi dirt path)* is bounded on each end by granite outcrops. At the south end, a narrow passageway through the rocks *(accessible only at low tide)* opens onto a pocket beach where cormorants nest on Elephant Rock.

The lands surrounding the beach and the ranch today form a 2,600-acre reserve for a flourishing herd of **tule elk**, reintroduced in 1978; these animals once roamed the entire peninsula before being hunted out in the late 19C. More than 150 white-spotted **axis deer** graze on the moors between Marshall Beach Trail and Estero Trail, and a similar number of **fallow deer** range over the peninsula; one-fifth of them sport pure white coats.

Tomales Bay State Park – *5mi north of Inverness. Open year-round daily 8am–sunset. $5/car.* ⛺ *(hiker/biker sites only, no cars allowed after hours)* ♿ P ☎ *415-669-1140.* Tiny **Heart's Desire Beach** and Shell Beach offer excellent opportunities for swimming and wading in sheltered Tomales Bay. Follow interpretive signs along the **Nature Trail** *(0.5mi)* to Indian Beach, where a traditional native shelter can be visited.

ADDITIONAL SIGHTS

Point Reyes Station – *2mi north of Olema by Rte. 1.* This small town grew up as a dairy center and stop along the North Pacific Coast Railroad. Although bakeries, restaurants, art galleries and antique shops now occupy some of its late-19C structures, dairy ranchers still swap stories at the local diner and load up supplies at the feed barn, preserving the community's bucolic atmosphere.

Bolinas – *Description p 185.*

31 • SAUSALITO★

Population: 7,036
Time: 1 day
Map p 190

Nestled into the bay side of the MARIN HEADLANDS just a few miles north of the GOLDEN GATE BRIDGE, this upscale residential community draws throngs of visitors on sunny days and weekends. Sausalito's winding streets, sophisticated boutiques and lush hillsides dotted with attractive homes and gardens create a relaxed yet cultured ambience, and its privileged setting affords some of the finest views of San Francisco and the bay islands.

Historical Notes

On the afternoon of August 5, 1775, the Spanish supply ship *San Carlos*, under the command of Lieutenant Juan Manuel de Ayala, dropped anchor just outside the Golden Gate. Ayala's first mate and six crew members, sent ashore to explore potential anchorage sites, became the first Europeans to enter the bay from the sea. Ayala named their chosen anchorage after the trees they found growing along freshwater streams (the Spanish word *sauces* means "willows").

Sausalito's first Anglo settler, **William Richardson**, arrived in San Francisco Bay in 1822 at age 27, while serving as first mate on a British whaler. Fluent in Spanish and conversant in several other languages, he became the first to build a habitation in San Francisco, then called Yerba Buena. In 1825, having acquired Mexican citizenship, Richardson married the daughter of the *comandante* of THE PRESIDIO. Through family connections, he eventually acquired title to the 19,572-acre Rancho del Saucelito, which stretched on the west side of the peninsula from the Marin Headlands to STINSON BEACH. In 1849, following the US takeover of California, his ownership of the property came under dispute and he was forced to sell the southern portion of the land.

Early attempts to develop the area failed and in 1868, 1,164 acres were acquired by a group of San Francisco businessmen intent on developing a resort and residential community. In 1875, the North Pacific Coast Railroad extended its tracks from San Rafael to Sausalito. Trains carrying lumber from the northern redwood forests halted here to unload their cargoes onto a fleet of ferryboats that carried travelers and commerce between rural Marin County and booming San Francisco.

In 1942, three months after the US entered World War II, the US Maritime Commission hired the W.A. Bechtel Company to construct a new West Coast shipyard capable of quickly building standard **Liberty Ships** and oil tankers. Bechtel selected 210 acres of undeveloped Sausalito waterfront as the site of the new facility, known as Marinship *(p 190)*; in 1942-43, 75,000 men and women poured into the town to build vessels for the American war effort.

Beginning just previous to the war—in the years following the 1937 completion of the Golden Gate Bridge—Sausalito also experienced an influx of writers, artists, poets and other free-spirited souls who found inexpensive refuge in the hulks of retired ferryboats and in houseboats made from the hulls of old military landing craft. The close-knit community of "floating home" dwellers persists today, continuing the 1890s tradition of houseboating on Richardson Bay *(p 192)*.

Visiting Sausalito – From San Francisco, take US-101 over the Golden Gate Bridge to the Alexander Avenue exit, just past Vista Point; continue 2mi to Bridgeway Boulevard. Street parking and public lots in Sausalito fill to capacity on weekends, leaving drivers with no option but to park on residential streets high on the hillsides. A better alternative is to take a ferry; they depart regularly from Pier 41 at FISHERMAN'S WHARF *(year-round daily 11am–4:50pm; no service Jan 1, Thanksgiving Day, Dec 25; 30min; $5.50/one way;* ✗♿ 🅿 *Blue & Gold Fleet* ☎ *415-705-5555)* or the ferry building (year-round Mon–Fri 7:40am–8pm, weekends & holidays *11:30am–6:55pm, May–Sept 8pm; no service Jan 1, Thanksgiving Day, Dec 25; 30min; $4.70/one-way;* ✗♿ 🅿 *Golden Gate Ferry* ☎ *415-923-2000)*. A visitor information kiosk at the ferry landing provides free brochures and other information.

SIGHTS

★ **Bridgeway Boulevard** – This attractive thoroughfare skirting Sausalito's waterfront was originally called Water Street. The name was changed to Bridgeway in 1937, as highway engineers had planned to route Golden Gate Bridge automobile traffic directly through Sausalito. An alternate route above the village was ultimately selected and Bridgeway instead became the anchor of a charming commercial district of restaurants, cafes, galleries and retail shops. Near the ferry landing, across from the Mission-style Sausalito Hotel, tiny **Plaza Viña del Mar** honors the city of Viña del Mar, Chile, one of Sausalito's two sister cities (the other is Sakaide, Japan). Created by resident Sausalito architect William Faville, designer of much of San Francisco's 1915 Panama-Pacific International Exposition, the park features an Italianate fountain and two whimsical, elephant-shaped light standards originally created for the fair. South of the ferry landing, Bridgeway's wide sidewalks offer delightful views★★ of San Francisco, the bay, ALCATRAZ and ANGEL ISLAND.

Sausalito Visitor Center – *777 Bridgeway, 4th level. Open year-round Tue–Sun 11:30am–4pm. Closed major holidays.* ♿ 🅿 *www.sausalito.org* ☎ *415-332-0505.* Located within the **Village Fair**, a complex of boutiques, shops and cafes, this small museum's displays trace the history of Sausalito from the days of the Coast Miwok to the present. Particularly interesting are photographs of the Golden Gate Bridge under construction, and portraits of such famous residents as actor Sterling Hayden; Sally Stanford, a San Francisco madam who became mayor of Sausalito; and infamous rum-runner and bank robber "Baby Face" Nelson.

Sausalito Yacht Harbor – Just north of the Village Fair, a forest of masts rises above Sausalito's vast flotilla of sail and motor yachts. Visitors can walk along the boardwalk fronting the harbor and on individual piers for close-up views of luxury watercraft. Several houseboats can be seen from the public walkway at the north end of the harbor.

Bulkley Avenue – *From Bridgeway, follow Princess St. (first street south of Plaza Viña del Mar) to Bulkley Ave. and turn right.* A walk up shady Bulkley Avenue, through the hills that backdrop Sausalito's waterfront, brings visitors to elegant

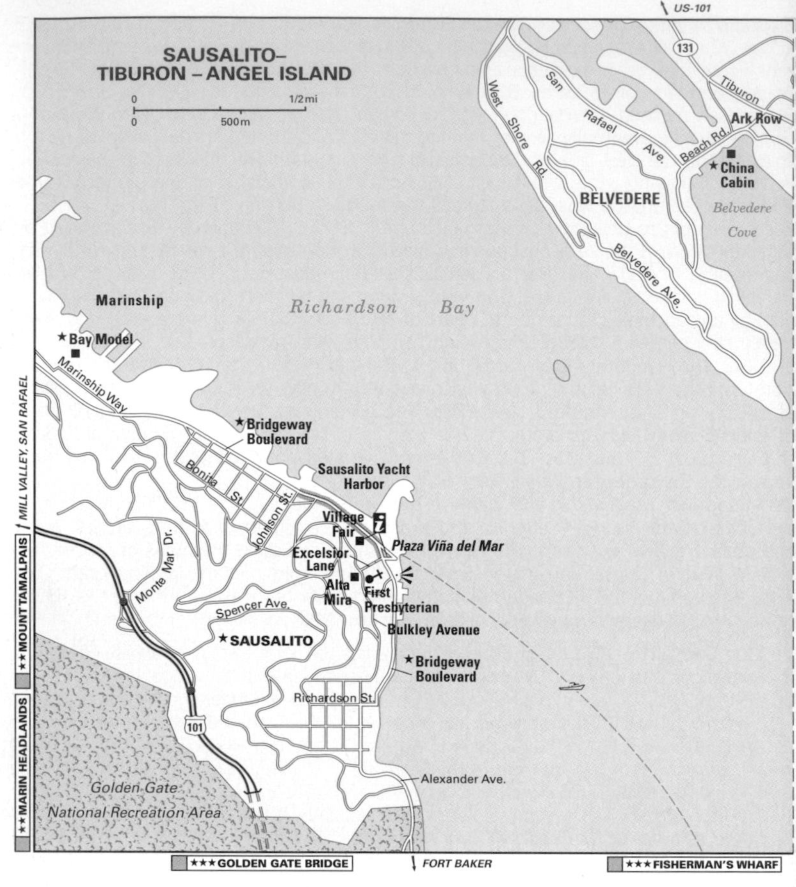

homes and contemporary compounds embellished by elaborate gardens and forests of pine, oak, acacia and eucalyptus trees. The **Alta Mira** *(no. 125)*, a sprawling, Spanish-style inn built in 1927, commands spectacular bay **views**★★ from its terrace. Opposite, the **First Presbyterian Church** (1909, Ernest Coxhead) is a striking example of the Shingle style; note its intricate wooden exterior. Just past the church, tiny **Excelsior Lane** descends the precipitous slope to the upscale shops and trendy restaurants of Bridgeway.

Marinship – *From downtown, follow Bridgeway north 1mi to Marinship Way and turn right.* This complex of warehouses and docks is all that remains of the huge shipbuilding facility that transformed Sausalito during World War II. In 1942 and 1943, more than 90 vessels were constructed here, including 15 Liberty Ships, 62 T-2 oil tankers and 16 Navy oilers, all in record time. Working three shifts around the clock, seven days a week, workers built the ships with amazing speed: one 10,000-ton tanker, the SS *Huntington Hills*, was built and delivered to America's forces in the Pacific in just 33 days. When the American fleet gathered in Tokyo Bay on August 14, 1945, to accept Japanese surrender, eight Marinship-built tankers were present, including the flagship of the Sausalito yard, the USS *Tamalpais*.

★ **Bay Model Visitor Center of the US Army Corps of Engineers** – Kids *2100 Bridgeway. Open Memorial Day–Labor Day Tue–Fri 9am–4pm, Sat 10am–6pm. Rest of the year Tue–Sat 9am–4pm. Call to confirm Sun & holiday hours.* ♿ P *www.spn.usace.army.mil/bmvc* ☎ *415-332-3870.* Located in a former Marinship warehouse, this two-acre scale model of the San Francisco Bay and Delta was originally conceived to test the effect of proposed dams on the bay. The dams were never built; today the model serves researchers measuring the effects of drought, floods, dredging, shoreline development and freshwater diversions on this vast estuary system. The self-guided tour of the model includes an introductory video, interactive displays and a walk above and beside the sprawling miniature representation of 343sq mi of bay, river, ocean and upland. Near the lobby is a fascinating display on Sausalito's remarkable World War II shipbuilding years.

Outside the Bay Model, stroll to the waterfront to see the massive 1915 steam schooner *Wapama*, which once hauled lumber up and down the Pacific coast. The wooden ship, drydocked on a barge alongside the pier, is under extensive resto-

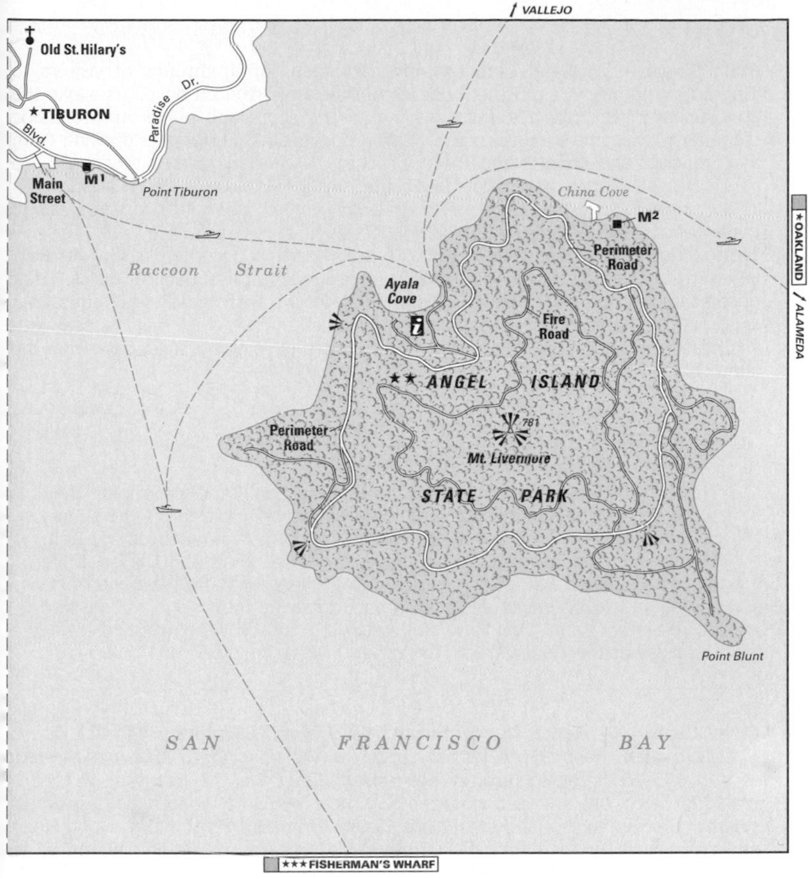

ration by a team of volunteers *(ranger talks available, for information ☎ 415-556-3002)*. It forms part of the collection of the San Francisco Maritime National Historical Park *(p 86)*.

32 • TIBURON and ANGEL ISLAND★

Map pp above

A breezy maritime ambience, a historic Main Street, a bustling waterfront promenade and popular restaurants lure visitors to this charming bayside village at the southern tip of the Tiburon peninsula.

Historical Notes

Lieutenant Juan Manuel de Ayala, the first European to visit the area, named Punta de Tiburon (Shark Point) during his 1775 voyage to explore and chart San Francisco Bay. Tiburon formed part of an 1834 Mexican land grant, the Rancho Corte Madera del Presidio, deeded to Irish immigrant John Reed. In 1884, it became a busy railroad town when a branch line of the San Francisco and North Pacific Railroad (later the Northwestern Pacific Railroad) was built along the peninsula, making it possible to travel from San Rafael and the Redwood Empire to San Francisco via train and ferry. Today, roads and a bike path along Richardson Bay mark the route of the long-defunct railroad, but traces of turn-of-the-century Tiburon still shape the character of the downtown area.

Visiting Tiburon – Ferries from San Francisco's FISHERMAN'S WHARF offer the easiest and most scenic transportation to Tiburon, especially on crowded summer weekends *(ferries depart Pier 41 May–Sept Mon–Fri 11am–4:50pm, weekends & holidays 9:30am–6:30pm; rest of the year 10:40am–5:50pm; early-morning commuter service via San Francisco Ferry Building; additional Fri & Sat evening departures in summer; no service Jan 1, Thanksgiving Day, Dec 25; 30min; $5.50; ✗♿ 🅿 Blue & Gold Fleet ☎ 415-705-5555)*. Driving from San Francisco, take US-101 north 6mi to the Tiburon Boulevard (Rte. 131) exit; continue 4mi to the town center. Parking lots are located on Tiburon Boulevard next to the Boardwalk Market, on Main Street next to the Tiburon Playhouse movie theater, and at Point Tiburon (enter from the traffic circle at the end of Tiburon Boulevard).

SIGHTS *1/2 day*

Main Street – Weekends and pleasant afternoons bring throngs of visitors to Tiburon's charming Main Street, where colorful, false-fronted buildings evoke the atmosphere of the late 19C. Walkways skirt the shore and numerous waterside restaurants welcome visitors to relax on outdoor decks. Ferryboats docking from San Francisco and Angel Island *(below)* add to the cheerful hubbub. For a glimpse of Tiburon's colorful past, stop in at the small railroad and ferry **museum (M')** *(Tiburon Blvd., 3 blocks east of ferry landing; restoration in progress; call to confirm hours ☎ 415-435-1853).*

West of downtown, Main Street turns sharply north to become pleasant **Ark Row**, where trees shade a charming collection of grounded houseboats, or "arks," that once floated on the bay as summer residences. Now transformed as boutiques and small shops, these unusual structures retain much of their yesteryear appeal with such decorative adornments as arched roofs and tiny columns. Most date from the late 19C.

■ Arks around the Bay

Through the late 19C and early 20C, numerous San Franciscans spent their summers aboard floating homes known as "arks," moored off the shores of Sausalito and other southern Marin County towns such as Tiburon. Popular summer retreats, these quaint structures enhanced the good life on San Francisco Bay and Richardson Bay. Some of them have been preserved on land as shops and homes on Bridgeway (north end of Sausalito Yacht Harbor) and "Ark Row" (downtown Tiburon). A refurbished ark is displayed at the Hyde Street Pier in San Francisco *(p 85)*.

★**China Cabin** – *52 Beach Rd.; turn west from Tiburon Blvd. Open Apr–Oct Wed & Sun 1pm–4pm. Rest of the year by appointment only. Contribution requested. ☎ 415-435-1853.* Resting atop pilings in Belvedere Cove, this beautiful, Victorian-era social salon was salvaged from the *SS China* (1866), a wood-hulled sidewheel steamer that once traversed the Pacific Ocean, from San Francisco to Hong Kong and Yokohama, for the Pacific Mail Steamship Company. The interior, restored to its full, gilded grandeur, offers a tantalizing glimpse of the elegance and luxury of 19C social salons.

Old St. Hilary's – *Esperanza via Mar West. From Tiburon Blvd. turn east on Beach Rd. and follow signs. Open Apr–Oct Wed & Sun 1pm–4pm. Rest of the year by appointment only. Contribution requested. ♿ P ☎ 415-435-1853.* Perched on a hillside above town, this former Roman Catholic church (1888) represents an excellent example of the Carpenter Gothic style. The historic landmark is surrounded by **St. Hilary's Preserve**, which protects 217 species of wildflowers, two-thirds of them native to the Tiburon Peninsula. Scenic paths lead through the preserve, where the wildflowers bloom spectacularly in spring.

★★ANGEL ISLAND STATE PARK

This hilly, forested island, separated from Tiburon by tide-swept Raccoon Strait, is a peaceful oasis amid busy San Francisco Bay. Over its long history of human habitation, the 750-acre island—largest in the bay—has served as a Coast Miwok haven, a Spanish land-grant cattle ranch, a US military base, a quarantine station and an immigration facility.

The island was christened Isla de Los Angeles (Angels Island) by Lieutenant Juan Manuel de Ayala in 1775. After years of military use and a period (1910-40) when it served as an immigration station, the island was declared surplus property by the federal government in 1948. In 1954, citizen groups led by Marin County conservationist Caroline Livermore persuaded the California State Park Commission to acquire 37 acres surrounding Ayala Cove. In 1963 the entire island (with the exception of a Coast Guard installation at Point Blunt) became part of California's state park system. Today it draws runners, hikers, bikers and campers to its myriad trails, lofty campsites and tranquil picnic spots.

Visiting Angel Island – Angel Island is pleasant throughout the year, though summer fogs can obscure its stunning views of San Francisco and the bay. On weekends, especially during the summer, recreation enthusiasts flock to its trails and campsites. *Park open year-round daily 8am–sunset. Visitor Services open Apr Wed–Sun, May–Oct daily, Nov & Mar weekends only. ⛺ ✂ ♿ www.angelisland.com ☎ 415-435-1915.*

The Cove Cafe offers light lunch fare and outdoor dining. Open-air motorized tours *(1 hr; audio commentary; $10)* and mountain **bike** rentals *($10/hr or $25/day)* are available through Angel Island Tram Tours (☎ 415-897-0715). Sea Trek offers **sea kayak** tours *(all-day guided tour $100, reservations required, ☎ 415-488-1000)*. Limited overnight **camping** is available by advance reservation only *(www.cal-parks.ca.gov* or *☎ 800-444-7275)*.

Ferries depart from **Tiburon** *(Apr–Sept Mon–Fri 10am, 11am, 1pm & 3pm, weekends 10am–5pm each hour; rest of the year Wed–Fri call for schedule, weekends 10am–5pm each hour; one-way 10min; $6 round-trip & park admission; Angel Island-Tiburon Ferry ☎ 415-435-2131)*; from Pier 41 in **San Francisco** *(Apr Wed–Sun 10am–12:15pm, May–Oct Mon–Fri 10am–12:15pm, rest of the year weekends & holidays 9:30am–11:45am & 2pm; one-way 20min; $10 round-trip, includes park admission; ✕♿ Blue & Gold Fleet ☎ 415-773-1188)*; from **Oakland** and **Alameda** *(May–Oct weekends 10:50am & 11am, respectively; round trip 1hr; $13; P Alameda/Oakland Ferry ☎ 510-522-3300)*; and from **Vallejo** *(year-round weekends 9am; call for weekday schedule; 55min; $13; ☎ 707-643-3779)*.

Visit *1 day*

Ayala Cove – Ferries dock at this cozy little cove named for Lieutenant Juan Manuel de Ayala, who anchored his ship here for a month in 1775. The cove's broad sweep of lawn is a popular picnic spot. Stop at the state park **visitor center** *(open year-round daily 8am–sunset; guided tour & tram depart here; ☎ 415-435-1915)* for maps and brochures, and to take in exhibits on the island's history.

Perimeter Road – *5mi loop. Trailhead to left of Ayala Cove.* This mostly paved road rings the island's forested flanks and offers an easy, scenic stroll past military installations and garrisons recalling the island's human history. From various points along the road, **views★★★** take in the jagged San Francisco skyline, shiplike ALCATRAZ and the GOLDEN GATE BRIDGE spanning the mouth of San Francisco Bay. From the main path, spur roads and trails lead to several fine beaches and enclaves of historic buildings. At China Cove (North Garrison), a barracks that formerly housed Chinese, Russian, Japanese and South American immigrants today contains a small **museum★ (M²)** *(visit by 45min guided tour only, May–Oct weekends & holidays 11am–3:30pm)* commemorating the island's days as an immigration station.

The **Fire Road** *(3mi loop)* circumscribes the island at a higher elevation, providing bikers and hikers with a more challenging route.

Mt. Livermore – The 781ft summit of the island's central peak, accessible from Ayala Cove by the moderately strenuous Northridge *(2mi)* and Sunset *(2.5mi)* trails, offers an unobstructed **panorama★★★** sweeping over San Francisco, the bay and the communities surrounding it. The mountain was named for Caroline Livermore, leader of the movement to preserve Angel Island.

ADDITIONAL SIGHT

San Rafael Arcángel Mission – *10mi north of Tiburon at 5th Ave. and A St. in San Rafael. Take Rte. 131 to US-101 north and continue to Central San Rafael exit. Chapel open year-round daily 6am–4:30pm. Gift shop open year-round Mon–Sat 11am–4pm. Closed major holidays. ☎ 415-456-3016.* The 20th and penultimate mission of the California chain was founded in 1817 as an *asistencia* to MISSION DOLORES in San Francisco. The branch mission was used as a sanitarium for San Francisco parishioners in failing health, and was named for the patron saint of bodily healing.

The buildings were razed in 1870; the current replica on the site dates from 1949. Fragments from the original church are on display in the mission's gift shop.

Consult the legend on the inside front cover for an explanation of symbols and colors appearing on maps throughout this guide.

The Wine Country

Lying inland within a two-hour drive of San Francisco, the Napa Valley and Sonoma County thrive on the abundant sunshine and fertile soil that produce grapes for some of North America's finest wines. Though vineyards flourish along many of California's inland coastal areas from Eureka to San Diego County, and even as far east as the foothills of the Sierra Nevada, these areas just north of San Francisco have garnered a reputation as the state's preeminent winemaking regions. Visitors and locals flock here, drawn by the temperate climate, varied natural beauty and acclaimed wineries that make the Wine Country one of California's foremost tourist destinations.

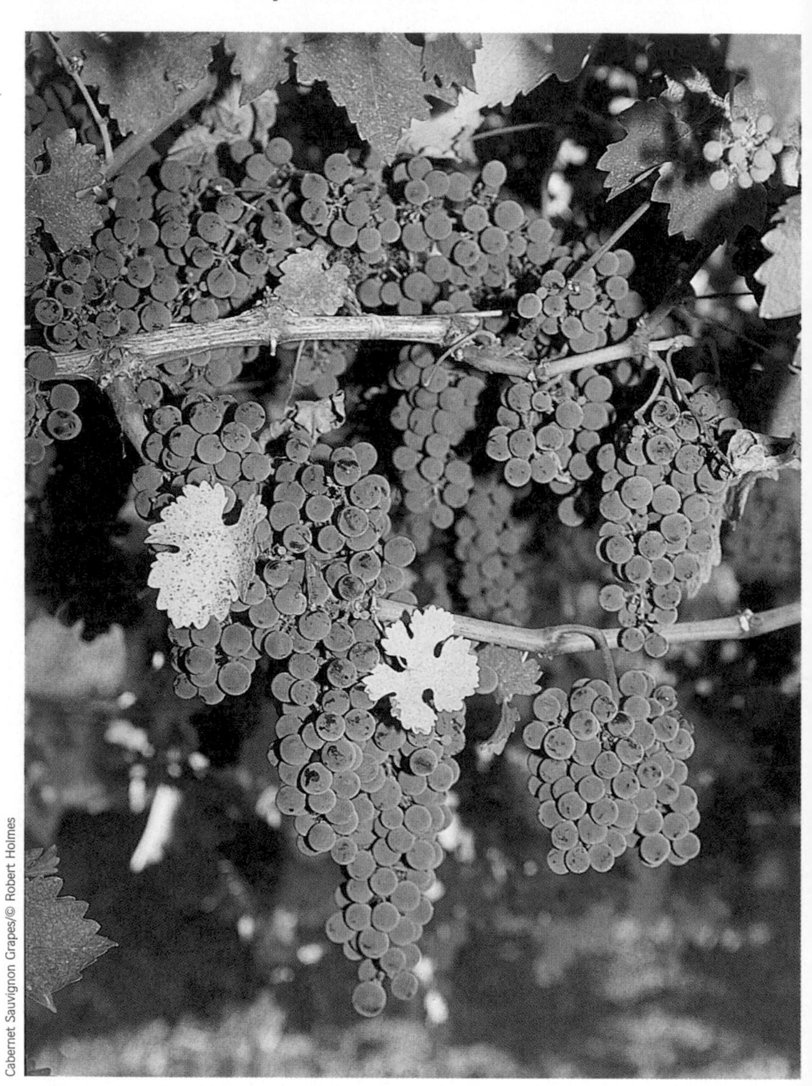

Cabernet Sauvignon Grapes/© Robert Holmes

Historical Notes

A Difficult Beginning – Cuttings of Criollas grapevines traveled north from the Baja Peninsula during the late 17C, transported by Franciscan padres as they established the mission chain in Alta California. Wines made from these "mission" grapes were used primarily for trade and for sacramental purposes; their quality would be considered poor by today's standards. In the early 1830s a French immigrant propitiously named Jean-Louis Vignes (*vigne* is French for "vine") established a large vineyard near Los Angeles using cuttings of European grapevines *(Vitis vinifera)*, and by the mid-19C winemaking had become one of southern California's principal industries.

In 1857 **Agoston Haraszthy** (1812-1869), a Hungarian immigrant, purchased a 400-acre estate in Sonoma County, named it Buena Vista *(p 207)*, and cultivated Tokay vine cuttings imported from his homeland. The grapes flourished, inspiring Haraszthy to visions of northern California as a mecca for the production of premium wines. In

Reading a Wine Label

Who made the wine and where was it bottled? Where and when were the grapes grown? How much alcohol is contained therein? The label on a bottle of wine says all of this and more. Labeling information is regulated by the US Treasury Department's Bureau of Alcohol, Tobacco and Firearms, and certain elements are required by law.

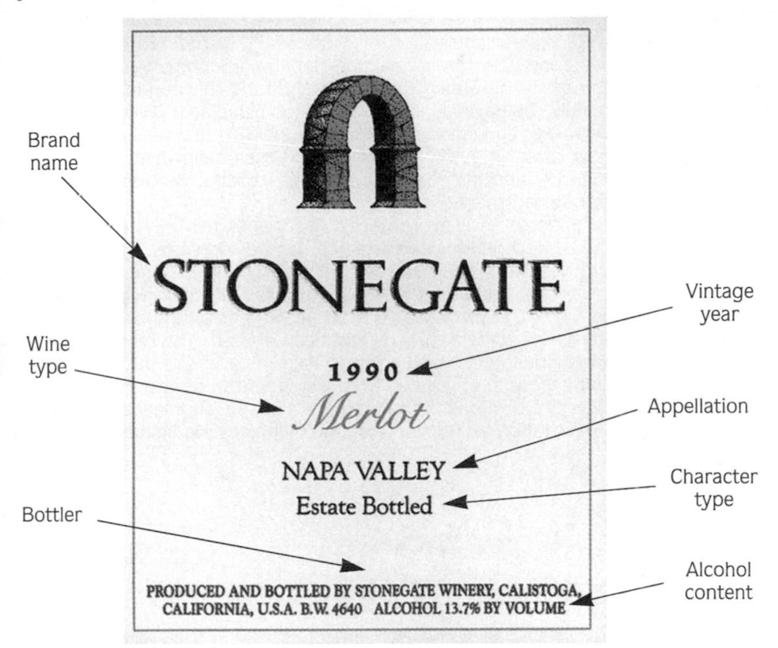

Required elements:

Brand name – May be the name of the producer, or a secondary or special brand name of the producer.

Wine type – If 75 percent of the grapes used in the wine are of one type, such as Chardonnay, Zinfandel or Pinot Noir, that name must appear on the label as the name of the wine. Otherwise the wine may be called "table wine" or take a generic name such as Burgundy or Chablis.

Appellation – This is the geographic origin of the grapes used in making the wine. In order for the name of an Approved Viticultural Area, such as Napa Valley, to appear on the label, 85 percent of the grapes used must come from that particular area. If the appellation is a county such as Napa or Sonoma, the grape content from that appellation must be 75 percent. If the appellation is the state of California, the wine must be produced entirely of California-grown grapes.

Bottler – The name of the bottling winery may be different from that of the brand name. "Produced and Bottled by" indicates that at least 75 percent of the wine was fermented by the bottler. "Made and Bottled by" indicates that at least 10 percent of the wine was fermented by the bottler.

Alcohol content – Table wines may contain 7 to 14 percent alcohol by volume; aperitif wines 15 to 24 percent; dessert wines 14 to 24 percent or greater. There is no requirement for sparkling wines.

Optional elements:

Vintage year – The year in which the grapes were grown may only appear on a label if 95 percent of the grapes used in the wine were harvested that year.

Character type – Additional information such as "Estate Bottled" indicates that the vineyard is managed by the winery, and that the vineyard and the winery are located within the stated appellation.

Vineyard – If the label indicates a specific vineyard, 95 percent of the grapes used must come from that vineyard.

1861, bolstered by promises of state funding from Governor John Downey, Haraszthy traveled to Europe to gather assorted varieties of *vinifera* cuttings for experimentation in California soil. Upon his return, the state legislature refused to uphold Downey's commitment, claiming that it was unfair for the state to favor any single industry. Undeterred, Haraszthy persisted in distributing (at his own expense) some 100,000 cuttings, training the area's grape growers (many of them European immigrants) and testing varieties with different soil types. The quality of California wines steadily improved, and areas around San Francisco began to supersede southern California as the state's principal viticultural region.

Boom and Bust – Successful application of Haraszthy's discoveries created a veritable boom in the wine industry throughout the Napa and Sonoma Valleys in the last decades of the 19C. Among the wineries established during this period were **Gundlach-Bundschu** (1858), founded by Bavarian immigrant Jacob Gundlach; **Charles Krug** (1861), first winery in Napa Valley; and **Schramsberg Vineyards** (1862), first of the region's hillside wineries to hew storage caves out of rock. Other renowned names of the present-day wine industry, including BERINGER BROTHERS WINERY, **Beaulieu** and **Inglenook**, also were established during this period.

As the 19C drew to a close, northern California grapevines fell prey to phylloxera, a root louse that attacks susceptible *vinifera* plants. Entire vineyards were decimated. Researchers at the University of California, in concert with French grapegrowers who had experienced similar devastation in the 1850s, discovered they could combat phylloxera by replanting vineyards with disease-resistant wild-grape rootstocks from the midwestern US, onto which *vinifera* cuttings had been grafted. The rebuilding process was slow, but the wine industry achieved a modicum of recovery by the early 20C only to find itself faced with growing opposition from the American temperance movement. On January 29, 1919, the US Congress ratified the 18th Amendment prohibiting the manufacture, sale, importation and transportation of intoxicating liquors in the US.

PRACTICAL INFORMATION. . . . . .Area Code: 707

Getting There

By Car – Consult individual entries for directions to the **Napa Valley** *(p 199)*, **Sonoma Valley** *(p 205)* and the **Upper Sonoma-Russian River Region** *(p 209)*.

By Bus – **Greyhound** service to Napa, Sonoma & Santa Rosa *(☎ 800-231-2222)*; **Golden Gate Transit** to most cities in Sonoma County *(☎ 415-923-2000)*.

General Information

When to Go – The best times to visit the Wine Country are in the spring, when yellow mustard plants blossom in the vineyards before the summer's heat sets in; and in the fall, when temperatures are comfortable, the sun shines without fail, and winemakers begin the harvest and crush (pressing of grapes). Advance reservations are recommended for lodging and attractions in summer and fall.

Visitor Information – Contact the following agencies to obtain maps and information on recreation, accommodation and seasonal events: **Napa Valley Tourist Bureau**, PO Box 3240, Yountville CA 94599, ☎ 944-1558 or **Napa Valley Conference & Visitors Bureau**, 1310 Napa Town Center, Napa CA 94559, ☎ 226-7459; **Sonoma Valley Visitors Bureau**, 453 1st St. E., Sonoma CA 95476, ☎ 996-1090; **Sonoma County Tourism Information**, 401 College Ave., Ste. D, Santa Rosa CA 95401 ☎ 524-7589 or 800-576-6662; **Sonoma County Wineries Association**, 5000 Roberts Lake Rd., Rohnert Park CA 94928, ☎ 586-3795 or 800-939-7666; **Russian River Wine Roads**, PO Box 46, Healdsburg CA 95448, ☎ 433-4335 or 800-723-6336. For a copy of the **Napa Valley Guide** or the **Sonoma County Guide** *($7)* which include complete information on accommodation, dining and shopping, call ☎ 538-8981.

Accommodations – Charming **Bed-and-breakfast inns** can be found in towns along Rte. 29 (Napa Valley) and US-101 (Russian River). Larger **hotels** are located in Napa, Sonoma and Santa Rosa. Bed-and-breakfast and hotel reservation services include: **B&B Style** ☎ 942-2888 or 800-995-8884, **Napa Valley's Finest Lodging** ☎ 257-1051, **Napa Valley Reservations Unlimited** ☎ 252-1985 or 800-251-6272, **Napa Valley Tourist Bureau Reservations** ☎ 258-1957. It is wise to reserve well in advance as the best accommodations fill up during peak tourist season. Year-round **camping** is available at Bothe-Napa Valley State Park ☎ 942-4575, Sugarloaf Ridge State Park ☎ 833-5712 and Lake Sonoma ☎ 433-9483.

Prohibition – Prohibition brought California's winemaking industry to a near-standstill as grapegrowers converted their vineyards to the cultivation of other crops. Licenses were granted to only seven California wineries (among them Christian Brothers, Beringer Vineyards, SEBASTIANI VINEYARDS and Beaulieu Vineyards) to produce wines for sacramental and medicinal use. Home production of "non-intoxicating" grape juice for private consumption was also permitted, though limited to 200 gallons a year per family.

In 1933, when Prohibition was repealed by the 21st Amendment, wine growers again were faced with the prospect of rebuilding their industry. The Great Depression slowed the reclamation of vineyards and the organization of related trades and distribution systems, and it was not until the early 1970s that the demand for fine table wines rose and California's wine industry was fully re-established.

Wine Country Today – In recent decades the Wine Country has experienced tremendous development. Besides significant increases in vineyard acreage, the 1970s and '80s witnessed an explosion of small-scale operations, some housed in old wineries updated with state-of-the-art equipment. Researchers at the University of California at Davis' renowned Department of Viticulture and Enology develop new methods of grape cultivation and winemaking, while advisory boards oversee quality control, and trade associations work to promote California wines throughout the world.

Today the Wine Country, moving beyond its traditional role, has become a center for fine art and gastronomy. Trendy restaurants evince a growing dedication to the joys of pairing food and wine, and in 1995 the renowned Culinary Institute of America installed a campus in the former Christian Brothers/Greystone Cellars winery *(p 202)*. Recent years have seen the rise of a new generation of showplace operations—among them OPUS ONE, CLOS PEGASE, CODORNIU NAPA and the HESS COLLECTION WINERY—that combine wine production with the display of fine art and innovative architecture.

Recreation

Ballooning – Balloon tours *(3-5hrs)* depart at sunrise and fly year-round. Prices range from $115–$195/person and may include a champagne brunch after the flight. Advance reservations required. Prices can vary with the number of passengers carried; inquire when booking. Napa Valley companies include **Bonaventura Balloon Company** ☎ 944-2822 or ☎ 800-358-6272 and **Napa Valley Balloons Inc.** ☎ 944-0228. Sonoma County companies include **Above the Wine Country Balloons and Tours** ☎ 829-7695 or 800-759-5638 and **Air Flambuoyant** ☎ 838-8500 or 800-456-4711.

Biking – A good way to enjoy the gentle, rolling terrain of the Wine Country is by bicycle. Rental shops offering trail information are located in Napa, Sonoma and Calistoga. Weekend and day **bicycle tours** of the area *(equipment provided; day trip $89;* **Get-Away Adventures** *www.getawayadventures.com* ☎ 763-3040 or 800-499-2453).

Farmers' Markets – These bustling markets offer local produce, poultry and other farm products (arrive early for the best selection): **Napa Valley Farmers' Market** *(Old Railroad Depot, St. Helena; May–Nov Fri 7:30am–noon; ☎ 252-2105)*, **Thursday Night Market** *(4th & East St., Santa Rosa; May–Sept Thu 5–8:30pm; ☎ 545-1414)*, **Sonoma Farmers Markets** *(Plaza; early Apr–Oct Tue 5:30pm–dusk; Depot Park; year-round Fri 9am–noon; ☎ 538-7023)*, **Healdsburg Farmers Market** *(North St. & Vine St.; late May–late Dec Sat 9am–noon; Plaza; Jun–Oct Tue 4pm–6pm; ☎ 431-1956)*.

Calistoga Mud Baths and Mineral Springs – A basic mud-bath package, including mud bath, herbal wrap and mineral whirlpool bath, lasts approximately one hour and costs $40-$55. Spas include **Calistoga Spa Hot Springs**, 1006 Washington St., ☎ 942-6269; **Dr. Wilkinson's**, 1507 Lincoln Ave., ☎ 942-4102; **Golden Haven Hot Springs**, 1713 Lake St., ☎ 942-6793; **Indian Springs**, 1712 Lincoln Ave., ☎ 942-4913; **Lincoln Avenue Spa**, 1339 Lincoln Ave., ☎ 942-5296; **Nance's Hot Springs**, 1614 Lincoln Ave., ☎ 942-6211; and **Mount View Spa**, 1457 Lincoln Ave., ☎ 942-5789.

Sightseeing – **California Wine Country Tours** take passengers by motor coach through Marin County and combine a stop in Calistoga with tours of one Napa and one Sonoma winery *(9hrs; depart San Francisco Transbay Terminal year-round daily 9am; $43; Red & White Fleet; ☎ 415-447-0597 or 800-229-2784)*. Hiking trips in Napa-Sonoma hills, and river canoeing and kayaking excursions, range from 1-6 days, $49-$1,589 (all inclusive); reservations recommended. **Get-Away Adventures** www.getawayadventures.com ☎ 763-3040 or 800-499-2453.

Viticulture and the Art of Winemaking

Fruit of the Vine – The Wine Country is organized into **Approved Viticultural Areas**, each suitable for the cultivation of certain types of grapes. Growing conditions vary among these areas, depending upon soil type and climate. Volcanic activity in the region has produced porous soils in which wine grapes thrive, but soil depth and moisture vary from region to region, as do mineral levels.

Weather is considered the most important factor affecting the cultivation of wine grapes, which require a long growing season of hot days and cool nights. In the Wine Country, grapes ripen slowly from April to October, giving flavors and acids plenty of time to develop. The average annual rainfall of 33in occurs mostly between November and May. Differences in elevation, proximity to the sea and exposure to sun, fog and wind create numerous microclimates, each affected by factors as seemingly slight as a dip in a mountain ridge or the tilt of a slope.

The Wine Country's current production is based primarily on descendants of the *vinifera* cuttings introduced by Agoston Haraszthy in the 19C. Best adapted to Wine Country growing conditions is the **Cabernet Sauvignon**, a small, blue-black grape from the Médoc district of France's Bordeaux region that produces a rich, full red wine. The Burgundy region's **Pinot Noir** grape is used for both table wine and California sparkling wine. Other red wine grapes from Europe include **Cabernet Franc**, **Petite Sirah**, **Napa Gamay** (derived from France's Gamay Beaujolais) and **Zinfandel**, now grown chiefly in California.

Some of California's finest white wines are made from **Chardonnay**, the premier white grape of France's Chablis and Burgundy regions. Chardonnay produces a dry, richly flavored wine. The **Sauvignon Blanc**, used in the making of French Sauternes and Pouilly-Fumé, grows well in the Wine Country's cooler areas. The **Pinot Blanc**, of the same family as the Burgundy's Pinot Noir, is an important ingredient in many sparkling wines. Other white European varieties include **Riesling** and **Chenin Blanc**.

From Vine to Barrel to Bottle – Once grapes have achieved desired levels of sugar and acid, they are picked by hand or machine and placed into a stemmer-crusher device. Here paddles remove the stems and break the skins to produce a soupy mixture of seeds, skins and juice called **must**. In the making of white wines, the must is pressed immediately, usually in a device known as a **bladder press**. The pressed juice is clarified, inoculated with yeast, transferred to tanks, and left to ferment. During **fermentation**, which can last from three days to six weeks, the yeast organisms consume the sugar in the grapes, creating ethyl alcohol, carbon dioxide and heat. If left unchecked, this heat can speed the fermentation process, completing it before desired flavors have had time to develop. To control the temperature, modern stainless-steel fermentation tanks are equipped with dimpled cooling sheaths or "jackets" that control the duration of fermentation. In the making of red wines, fermentation occurs before pressing; thus, skins and seeds are left in contact with the juice, imparting rich, dark colors and tannins to the fluid.

After fermentation the wine may be again clarified of impurities by filtration, centrifuging or **racking** (a process in which wine is transferred from tank to tank, leaving the settled sediments behind). In the last clarification, called **fining**, substances such as clay, gelatin or egg whites may be introduced; sediments and impurities adhere to these materials, which are then easily removed. Many wines are **barrel-aged** in white-oak barrels; aging can last from a few months to several years. Certain varieties require a blending stage in which various wines are mixed to achieve desired flavors. Some wines are bottled before the final aging period.

Visiting the Wine Country – To fully experience the region's relaxed pace and easy-going character, it's best to select no more than four wineries per day for tasting, and to limit guided tours to one or two per day. Many wineries offer self-guided tours. Auto traffic, especially during peak seasons, can be heavy. Travelers on tight schedules should bear in mind that although the Wine Country is blessed with lush vegetation, inspiring vistas and an enviable climate, tourist attractions other than wineries are few. Visitors for whom wines and winemaking hold limited appeal should plan less time to visit the region.

Picnicking is one of the joys of a visit to the Wine Country. Attractive picnic areas grace many wineries, and numerous delis and roadside markets offer abundant, often elegant takeout fare, wines and nonalcoholic beverages.

Wineries described in the following sections have been selected and rated on their historic, architectural and cultural merits. A comprehensive, updated listing of wineries is available in the *Wine Country Guide to California*, published annually by *Wine Spectator* magazine and available at bookstores, newsstands and visitor centers.

33 • NAPA VALLEY**

Time: 1-3 days.
Map p 203

Cradled between two elongated mountain ranges, this world-renowned valley extends roughly 35mi from San Pablo Bay northwest to Mt. St. Helena. The Napa Valley is home to some of California's most prestigious wineries, many of them clustered thickly along Route 29 as it passes through the towns of Napa, Yountville, Oakville, Rutherford, St. Helena and Calistoga. Others dot the more tranquil Silverado Trail *(p 205)* to the east and the intervening crossroads.

Access – From San Francisco (55mi), drive north on US-101; exit at Rte. 37 and drive east to Rte. 121. Turn left (north) on Rte. 121 and continue to Rte. 29 north. For a quicker if less scenic route, drive north on I-80 to Rte. 37 west and continue to Rte. 29 north.

SIGHTS *Sights are described from south to north.*

Napa – Population 65,030. Originally settled in 1832, this sprawling city on the banks of the Napa River serves as a gateway for the abundance of wines and agricultural goods produced in the verdant Napa Valley. The name is said to have been derived from a Native American word meaning "plenty." A pleasant business district centers on First, Second and Main Streets. Charming residential areas graced by elegant Victorian homes lie south and west of downtown in the vicinity of Jefferson, First, Third and Randolph streets.

★**Codorniu Napa** – *1345 Henry Rd. From downtown Napa take Rte. 29 south to Rte. 121. Turn right and drive west 4mi, turning right on Old Sonoma Rd. Turn left on Dealy Ln. then veer left on Henry Rd. Continue .3mi to driveway entrance. Open year-round daily 10am–5pm. Closed Jan 1, Thanksgiving Day, Dec 24–25. Guided tours (30min) available 11am & 2pm. $4-$6 (tasting fee).* ♿ 🅿 ☎ *707-224-1668.* In 1872 the Codorniu family of Barcelona became Spain's first producers of sparkling wine made in the *méthode champenoise* tradition *(p 200)*. Their Napa Valley operation occupies an innovative contemporary structure (1991, Domingo Triay) at the foot of Milliken Peak. Sloping, grass-covered earth berms bury the winery's walls, maintaining consistently cool temperatures in the storage and production areas within. From the entrance plaza a peaceful view extends eastward over the lower Napa Valley. Galleries surrounding a serene courtyard house 16C-17C European winemaking equipment and changing displays of works by local artists.

★**The Hess Collection Winery** – *4411 Redwood Rd. From Rte. 29 in Napa take the Redwood Rd./Trancas exit and drive west on Redwood Rd. 6mi to winery entrance. Open year-round daily 10am–4pm. Holidays 10am–2pm. Closed early Jan. $3 (tasting fee).* ♿ 🅿 *www.hesscollection.com* ☎ *707-255-1144.* Nestled in a remote southwestern corner of the Napa Valley on the slope of Mt. Veeder, this beautifully renovated structure contains one of the nation's largest and finest private art collections open to the public, as well as a state-of-the-art winemaking facility. The original stone structure (1903) was acquired by the Christian Brothers in the early 1930s to house their Mont LaSalle winery. In 1983, Swiss entrepreneur Donald Hess leased the property, transforming the upper floors into galleries to house his outstanding collection of works by contemporary American and European artists. Francis Bacon, Robert Motherwell and Frank Stella are among those represented, along with such lesser-known artists as Rolf Iseli, Theodoros Stamos, George Baselitz and Magdalena Abakanowicz. Through wide windows in the stairwells, visitors strolling through the sweeping galleries also can glimpse the steel tanks and ultramodern bottling rooms of the winery. A graceful audiovisual presentation *(12min)* focuses on the seasonal beauty of the vineyards and highlights the unique process of making wine in a mountain region.

Yountville – Population 3,375. This small community ranging along the east side of Route 29 was named for George C. Yount (1794-1865), a North Carolina frontiersman who established vineyards here in 1836 on a portion of the 11,814 acres granted to him by the Mexican government. Today Yountville's charming inns, trendy boutiques and excellent eateries make it a popular base for visitors to the southern Napa Valley. Of particular note is the historic brick Groezinger winery (1870), now restored as **Vintage 1870**, a center for specialty shops and boutiques.

★**Napa Valley Museum** – *55 Presidents Cir. From Rte. 29/Yountville exit, drive west .3mi toward Veterans Home. Museum is on right. Open year-round Wed–Mon 10am–5pm (8pm first Thu). Closed Jan 1, Thanksgiving Day, Dec 25. $4.50.* ♿ 🅿 ☎ *707-944-0500.* The highlight of this innovative new museum (1998, Fernau and Hartman)—which previously occupied a small space in the town of Napa—is an impressive multimedia display entitled **California Wine: The Science of an Art** **. By means of a computerized and interactive audiovisual program, visitors experience a full year in Napa Valley winemaking, along the way exploring soils, climates and microclimates, grape growth, rootstocks, pests, cloning, varietal characteristics, harvest, crushing, fermentation, racking, storage, blending and bottling.

An upper gallery houses the 300-item Johnson Collection of Minerals and Fossils, plus temporary exhibits ranging from history to art. Expansion—currently, only a quarter of the new facility's 40,000sq ft are occupied—is planned as funds become available.

****Domaine Chandon** – *1 California Dr. From Rte. 29/Yountville exit, drive west .2mi toward Veterans Home. Entrance is on right. Open May–mid-Sept daily 10am–8pm (Mon–Tue 6pm). Rest of the year Wed–Sun 10am–7pm. Closed Jan 1, Thanksgiving Day, Dec 25. Guided tours (45min) available. Tasting fee.* ✗ ♿ 🅿 *www.dchandon.com* ☎ *707-944-8844.* Visitors to this innovative winery complex (1973) are introduced to French winemaking tradition with a dash of California visual style and appeal. Commissioned by Moët-Hennessy, owners of France's famed Moët et Chandon, the modern structures of gray concrete harmonize with the sweeps and curves of the surrounding terrain; the arched ceilings are reminiscent of traditional wine caves in France's Champagne region. A small exhibit in the entrance hall describes the process of making sparkling wine according to the *méthode champenoise;* informative guided tours cover the principal stages involved.

■ Méthode champenoise

Most sparkling wines produced in the Wine Country are made according to the *méthode champenoise* developed in 17C France by Dom Perignon, a Benedictine monk. In this process, a still wine traditionally blended from Pinot Noir and Chardonnay grapes is inoculated with yeast and sugar, bottled, capped, and allowed to ferment a second time. The carbon dioxide gas retained in the bottle infuses the wine with bubbles, creating pressures of up to 110 pounds per sqare inch inside the bottle. The bottle is then stored on its side for as many as six years to let the wine age.
Following aging, the wine is clarified by "riddling," a painstaking process of turning and lifting the bottles daily, bit by bit, until they are nearly upside down, so that yeast and sediments gather in the neck. The wine must then be "disgorged": The neck of the bottle is immersed in a brine solution so that the sediments within it freeze; when the bottle is then uncapped, pressure from within forces out the plug of frozen sediment. A *dosage* of sugar and brandy or other wine is added to the bottle before final corking and labeling.

***Opus One** – *7900 St. Helena Hwy (Rte. 29). Visit by guided tour (1hr) only, year-round daily 10:30am–3:30pm. Closed Jan 1, Easter Sunday, Thanksgiving Day, Dec 25. Reservations required. $20 (tasting fee).* ♿ 🅿 ☎ *707-944-9442.* Every detail of this innovative structure (1991, Johnson Fain & Pereira)—from the French-style white limestone walls to the California redwood pergola crowning the building—testifies to the unique international collaboration that created Opus One, the first ultra-premium winery in the US. In 1970, Baron Philippe de Rothschild of Pauillac, France, approached Napa Valley vintner Robert Mondavi to discuss a joint winemaking venture based in California. Although the team produced its first vintage in 1979 from barrels in the Mondavi cellars, a decade passed before ground was broken for the innovative structure that houses the winery today. Visitors pass

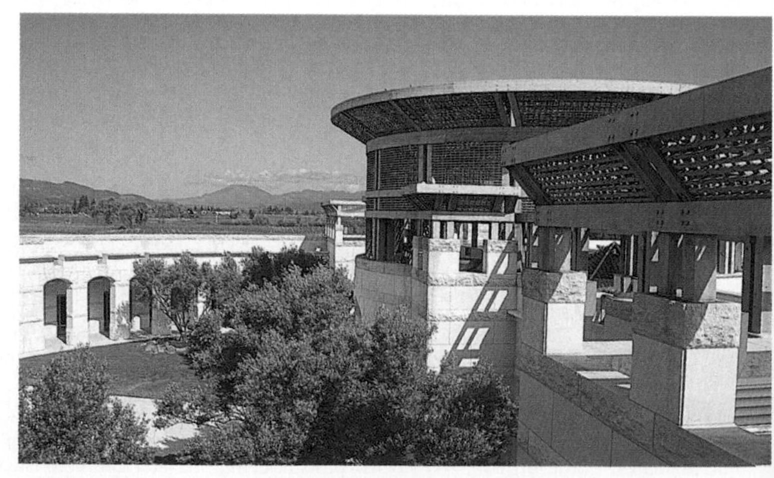

Opus One Winery

through an olive tree-studded courtyard before entering the dramatic reception hall. Works by well-known contemporary French and California artists grace the walls and open spaces, while in the comfortable Salon, Continental antiques blend seamlessly with luxurious contemporary furnishings and crafts. Descending a grand staircase shaped like the inside of a barrel, visitors enter an elegant tasting room and walk into the semicircular Grand Chai, or cellar, where row upon row of oak barrels stained with wine-colored bands curve into the distance on either side.

★**Robert Mondavi Winery** – *7801 St. Helena Hwy. (Rte. 29), Oakville. Open May–Oct daily 9am–5pm. Rest of the year daily 9:30am–4:30pm. Closed Jan 1, Easter Sunday, Thanksgiving Day, Dec 25. Guided tours (1hr) available. Reservations recommended. ♿ 🅿 www.robertmondaviwinery.com ☎ 707-259-9463 or 888-766-6328.* Constructed in 1966, this striking building anticipated a new generation of modern wineries designed to showcase art and architecture as well as wine. Sculptor Beniamino Bufano's figure of St. Francis with outstretched arms greets visitors beneath the monumental arched entry to the complex, and temporary exhibits of works by local artists are regular features at the winery. A popular Summer Music Festival and the Festival of Winter Classical Concerts are held here annually *(p 219)*.

1 Oakville Grocery

7856 St. Helena Hwy. (Rte. 29). ☎ 707-944-8802. French white-truffle oil, raspberry-peach-champagne jam, fresh crusty breads, more than a dozen types of olives and the best-stocked cheese counter in the Napa Valley lure visitors and locals to this tiny but deliciously crammed grocery for picnic or pantry supplies. Assemble a feast of meats, cheeses, breads and pâtés, and the friendly and knowledgeable staff will help you pick the perfect complementary wine from an impressive array of local vintages.

★★**St. Supéry** – *8440 St. Helena Hwy. (Rte. 29), Rutherford. Open May–Oct daily 9:30am–6pm. Rest of the year daily 9:30am–5pm. Closed Jan 1, Thanksgiving Day, Dec 25. Guided tours (1hr) available. $3 (tasting fee). ♿ 🅿 www.stsupery.com ☎ 707-963-4507 or 800-942-0809.* The modern winery structure houses a comprehensive **Wine Discovery Center**★, featuring in-depth displays on seasonal viticulture, the winemaking process, soil types and appellations. Especially interesting is the SmellaVision exhibit, a "nose-on" display where visitors can sniff eight characteristic aromas associated with Cabernet Sauvignon or Sauvignon Blanc varietals, and examine the color variations for each type of wine. Adjacent to the winery is a model vineyard with detailed panels and exhibits explaining how vines are trained, trellised and pruned according to the variety of grape. Also on the property is the charming Victorian home built by Joseph Atkinson, the first vintner to own the property. The house *(visit by guided tour only)* has been restored with period pieces to reflect the life and times of an 1880s winemaker.

★★**Niebaum-Coppola** – *1991 St. Helena Hwy. (Rte. 29), Rutherford. Open year-round daily 10am–5pm. Closed Jan 1, Easter Sunday, Thanksgiving Day & Dec 25. $7.50 tasting fee. Guided tours (1hr 30min) available daily 11am & 2pm. $20 (includes tasting fee). ♿ 🅿 ☎ 707-968-1161.* The imposing stone winery (1882) at the center of the Niebaum-Coppola estate was built for Gustave Niebaum, a Finnish sea captain and enterprising founder of Inglenook Wines (1879). Most of Niebaum's property, including his Victorian home and 1,600 acres of adjacent land, was purchased in 1975 by filmmaker Francis Ford Coppola and his wife Eleanor. The massive building, known as the "Inglenook Chateau," and a portion of the original vineyards remained in the hands of Heublein, Inc., until 1995, when the Coppola family acquired the entire estate, thus restoring the historic property to its original proportions.

A tree-lined courtyard surrounds a reflecting pool in front of the chateau, which is thought to have been constructed as the first gravity-flow winery in the valley. Upon entering the building, visitors can peek into the **Captain's Room** (1889) on the right, a replica of Niebaum's ship's quarters that includes 17C stained-glass windows, 16C Flemish wine cups and a 400-year-old lamp. To the left stands a set from Coppola's celebrated film *The Godfather*, a curious contrast that is echoed throughout the rest of the chateau. At the top of the breathtaking **grand stairway**, restored by Coppola with two-tone Belizean hardwoods, stands the Centennial Museum; this intriguing monument to film and winemaking reflects the careers of both of the winery's charismatic owners, Niebaum and Coppola. A retail emporium for gourmet foods occupies much of the main floor. Future plans for the chateau include a multimedia wine-tasting experience.

★**St. Helena** – Population 5,414. A picturesque main street graces this charming town at the heart of the Napa Valley. Plentiful and widely varied accommodations, intriguing and innovative restaurants, and a central location close to a number of popular wineries make St. Helena an excellent base for exploring the entire valley.

★ **Robert Louis Stevenson Silverado Museum** – *1490 Library Ln. From Main St. northbound, turn right on Adams St., cross the railroad tracks and turn left. Open year-round Tue–Sun noon–4pm. Closed major holidays. Contribution requested. ♿ 🅿 ☎ 707-963-3757.* Housed in a pleasant gallery within the town library building, this small, memorabilia-packed museum is devoted to the life and works of Robert Louis Stevenson (1850-1894), renowned and beloved author of such popular 19C stories as *Treasure Island, Kidnapped* and *A Child's Garden of Verses.* Stevenson honeymooned in a cabin on the slopes of Mt. St. Helena *(p 204)* in summer 1880 and immortalized this Napa experience in his story *The Silverado Squatters.* The museum's holdings, comprising photographs, books, manuscripts and the author's personal artifacts, are considered second in importance only to the Stevenson collections at Yale University's Beinecke Library.

★★ **Beringer Vineyards** – *2000 Main St. (Rte. 29), north of downtown St. Helena. Open year-round daily 9:30am–5pm. Closed Jan 1, Easter Sunday, Thanksgiving Day, Dec 25. Guided tours (45min) available. ♿ 🅿 ☎ 707-963-7115.* The Napa Valley's oldest continuously operating winery was established in 1876 by Jacob and Frederick Beringer, German immigrants who arrived in the US in the 1860s. The brothers' winery escaped the worst of the legislative strictures of Prohibition because they acquired a license to produce wine for religious and medicinal purposes. Extending into the sloping hillside behind the complex are over 1,000ft of tunnels where the temperature remains a constant 58°F, an ideal environment for aging wine.

The centerpiece of the property is the stately **Rhine House** (1883), constructed by Frederick Beringer as his residence. Modeled after the Beringer ancestral home in Germany, the 17-room mansion features elegant woodwork, inlaid floors and exceptional **stained-glass windows**★. The regal oleander trees about the property were planted at the turn of the century by Jacob Beringer.

The Culinary Institute of America at Greystone – *2555 Main St. (Rte. 29), north of downtown St. Helena. Campus Store & Marketplace open year-round daily 10am–6pm. Guided tours (40min) available year-round daily 10:30am, 1:30pm & 3:30pm, reservations suggested. $3 (Mon–Fri), $7.50 (weekends including cooking demonstration). Restaurant open year-round daily 11:30am–9pm (Fri–Sat 10pm). Closed major holidays. Reservations suggested. ✂ ♿ 🅿 www.ciachef.edu ☎ 707-967-2328 (tours), ☎ 707-967-1010 (restaurant).*

The massive stone **building**★ looming over Rte. 29 was erected in 1889 by William Bourn as Greystone Cellars, a cooperative effort by Napa Valley winegrowers in need of aging and storage facilities. The largest freestanding stone building in California when it was built, the winery changed hands several times before being purchased in the 1950s by the Christian Brothers, a Catholic teaching order. Today the building houses the West Coast campus of the renowned Culinary Institute of America, which is devoted to continuing education and career development for professionals in the food, wine, health and hospitality fields. Guided tours of the school take in the teaching kitchen. Visitors are welcome to explore the delightful herb gardens or browse through the Campus Store & Marketplace, a lively retail outlet. The structure also houses a whimsical **corkscrew collection** of more than 1,800 wine openers, some dating from the 18C. The collection was assembled over a period of 40 years by Brother Timothy, cellarmaster of the Christian Brothers. In the Wine Spectator Greystone Restaurant, CIA graduate chefs expertly prepare meals in an open kitchen.

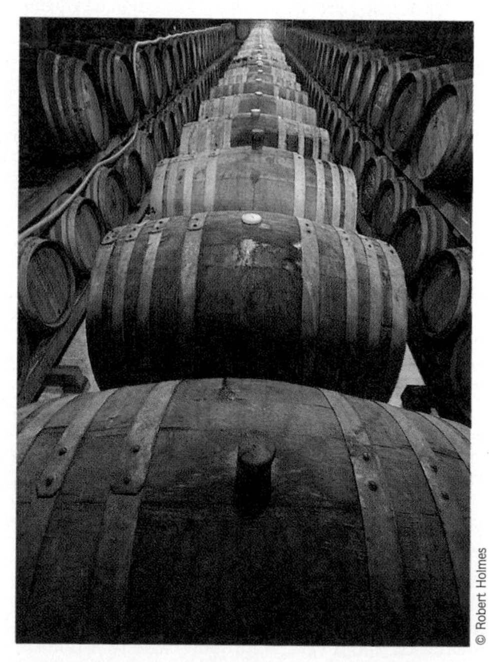

© Robert Holmes

Wine Cellar

Bale Grist Mill State Historic Park – Kids *3369 St. Helena Rte. (Rte. 29). 3mi north of downtown St. Helena. Open year-round daily 10am–5pm. Closed major holidays. $2. Guided tours (30min) available.* ♿ P ☎ *707-942-4575.* From the parking area, a pleasant, sylvan path leads to this charming historic **grist mill★**, powered by a 36ft waterwheel. Established in 1846 by Edward T. Bale, an English physician who married a niece of General Mariano Vallejo *(p 206)*, the mill ground into flour the grain harvested by Napa Valley farmers. The wooden mill and waterwheel, which ceased operation in the late 19C, have been partially restored. Docent tours and an audiovisual presentation provide a good introduction to the milling process, and weekend demonstrations allow a look at the mill in action *(call for demonstration schedule)*. Interpretive displays focus attention on the milling process and on local pioneer history. Visitors can purchase flour and cornmeal milled on site. *Note: Mill and granary closed for restoration; reopening scheduled spring 1999.*

★★**Sterling Vineyards** – *1111 Dunaweal Ln. From downtown St. Helena drive north 6.8mi on Rte. 29 to Dunaweal Ln. and turn right. Entrance is on the right. Open year-round daily 10:30am–4:30pm. Closed Jan 1, Thanksgiving Day & Dec 25. $6 (includes tramway and wine tasting).* ♿ P ☎ *707-942-3344.* Perched like a secluded Greek monastery on a 300ft knoll rising abruptly from the valley floor, this complex of pristine white buildings (1969, Martin J. Waterfield) is one of the Napa Valley's architectural grace notes. Visitors ascend to the winery from the parking area by a hushed ride *(5min)* on the vineyard's **aerial tramway** Kids, from which tranquil views extend over the surrounding area. At the summit, follow

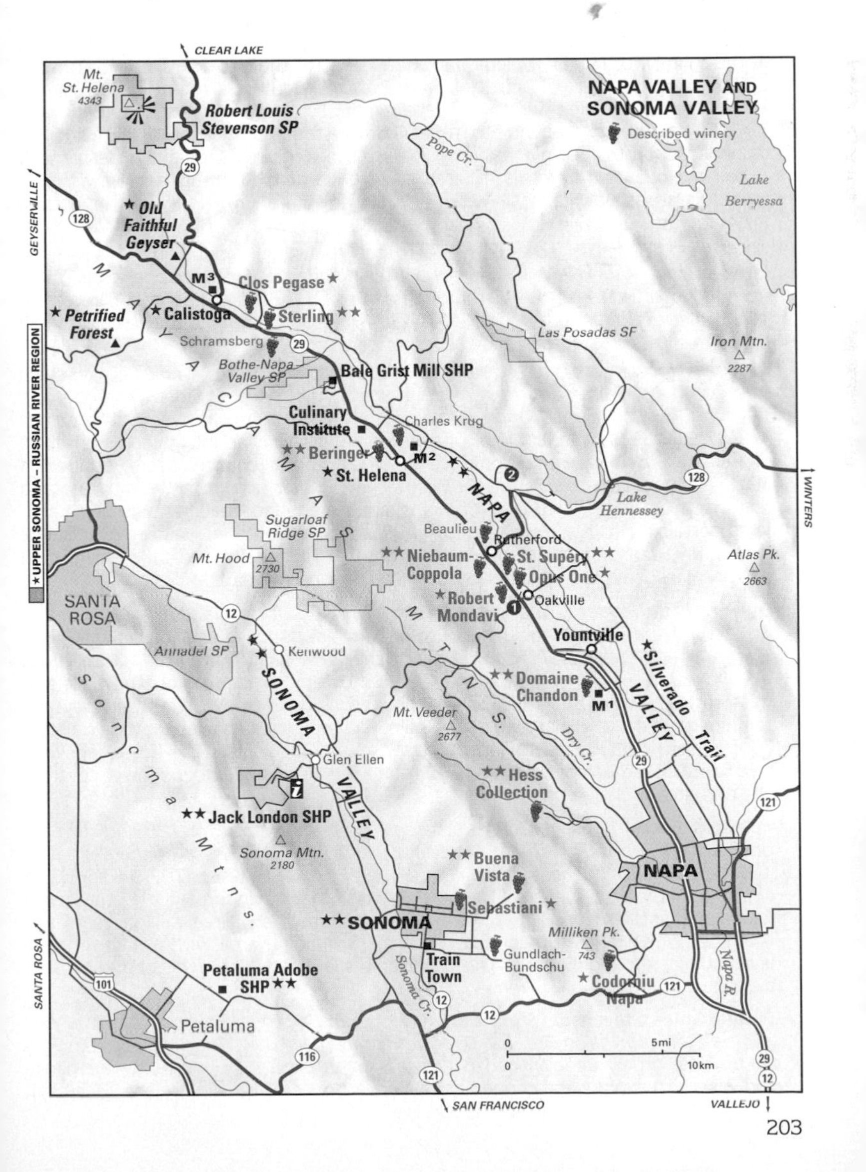

informative panels on a self-guided tour through the winery, past colorful examples of tile work, across terraces with **views★** of the northern Napa Valley, and under campaniles representing a contemporary take on traditional mission-style bell towers. The collection of eight bells dating from the early 18C was acquired for Sterling Vineyards in 1972 from London's church of St.-Dunstan-in-the-East.

★**Clos Pegase** – *1060 Dunaweal Ln. From downtown St. Helena drive north 6.8mi on Rte. 29 to Dunaweal Ln. and turn right. Entrance is on the left. Open year-round daily 10:30am–5pm. Closed Jan 1, Easter Sunday, Thanksgiving Day & Dec 25. $2.50 (tasting fee). Guided tours (30min) available daily 11am & 2pm.* ♿ 🅿 *www.clospegase.com* ☎ *707-942-4981.* Housed in a harmonious sprawl of terra-cotta and earth-toned structures at the base of a small volcanic knoll, Clos Pegase (1987, Michael Graves) is a striking example of the Napa Valley's variety of architectural styles. The winery is named for Pegasus, the famed winged horse of Greek mythology, who is said to have first created wine when he struck his hooves to the ground of Mt. Helicon, unleashing the Spring of the Muses and irrigating a vineyard below.

Conceived as a temple to wine and art, the monumental winery complex *(illustration p 24)* reveals architect Graves' signature view of themes from classical antiquity, reflected in oversized columns, triangular pediments and an open central atrium. Selections from owner Jan Shrem's private art collection appear throughout the winery, from the tasting room walls to niches in the 28,000sq ft of storage caves hewn into the knoll of volcanic tufa *(caves open to the public by guided tour only)*. Shrem's residence, also designed by Graves, crowns the knoll *(not open to the public)*.

★**Calistoga** – Population 4,680. Founded in 1859, this residential and resort town in the shadow of Mt. St. Helena unites the flavor of the late-19C frontier era with 20C modernity. Thermal activity in the area, released via a multitude of geysers and hot springs, fueled Calistoga's development as a resort where tourists flocked to "take the waters." Legend has it that Calistoga founder **Sam Brannan** (1819-1888) stumbled upon the town's name by confusedly (some say drunkenly) declaring it "The Calistoga of Sarafornia" (Saratoga of California) after upstate New York's famed Saratoga Hot Springs. Today, Calistoga is equally well-known for its bottled mineral water.

Numerous hot-spring spas continue to fuel Calistoga's popularity. False-front facades along **Lincoln Avenue**, the town's main thoroughfare, provide a charming frontier flavor, as does the historic **Railroad Depot** *(1458 Lincoln Ave.)*. Erected in 1868 to serve the long-defunct Napa Valley Railroad Company, the structure now houses shops, a restaurant and the visitor center.

★**Sharpsteen Museum** – Kids *1311 Washington St., 2 blocks north of Lincoln Ave. Open Apr–Oct daily 10am–4pm. Rest of the year daily noon–4pm. Closed Thanksgiving Day & Dec 25. Contribution requested.* ♿ 🅿 *www.napanet.net/vi/sharpsteen* ☎ *707-942-5911.* The highlight of this small museum is an intriguing assemblage of miniature **dioramas** re-creating scenes of Calistoga's colorful past. Founded in 1979 by Ben Sharpsteen, a former Walt Disney Studios producer, the museum also features a collection of early-19C photos, a restored stagecoach and assorted artifacts pertaining to the town's history. Adjoining the museum building is a **cottage** from Sam Brannan's resort, relocated from its original site and fully refurbished to appear as it would have during Calistoga's resort heyday.

★**Old Faithful Geyser** – Kids *From Calistoga drive east on Lincoln Ave.; bear left on Grant St. and continue 1mi. Turn left on Tubbs Ln. Entrance on the right. Open Apr–Oct daily 9am–6pm. Rest of the year daily 9am–5pm. $6.* ✂ ♿ 🅿 *www.oldfaithfulgeyser.com* ☎ *707-942-6463.* Located at the foot of Mt. St. Helena, this privately owned geyser is one of the world's three known "faithful" geysers, so named for their regular eruptions (the others are located at Yellowstone National Park and in New Zealand). Approximately every 40 minutes, the geyser spews a column of superheated water some 60ft into the air in a splendid shower of droplets and steam.

★**Petrified Forest** – Kids *6mi from Calistoga. Drive north on Rte. 128 and turn left on Petrified Forest Rd. Open Jun–Sept daily 10am–6pm. Rest of the year daily 10am–5pm. Closed Thanksgiving Day & Dec 25. $4.* ♿ 🅿 ☎ *707-942-6667.* A circuit trail through this small, privately owned forest winds past the stone remnants of giant redwoods that were petrified more than three million years ago when Mt. St. Helena erupted, covering the surrounding area with ash and molten lava. Among the highlights is The Giant, an ancient redwood 60ft long and 6ft in diameter.

Robert Louis Stevenson State Park – *7mi from Calistoga. Take Lincoln Ave. east and turn left (north) on Rte. 29. Open year-round daily dawn–dusk.* 🅿 ☎ *707-942-4575.* This largely undeveloped park provides an excellent opportunity for hikers and bikers to explore the rugged, picturesque slopes of Mt. St. Helena (4,343ft).

On its ascent to the summit, a trail passes the site (near an abandoned silver mine) where Robert Louis Stevenson *(p 202)* spent his honeymoon in 1880. After 1mi, the trail emerges from the forest to join an unpaved fire road to the summit; from the road, sweeping **views★★** extend over the northern Napa Valley.

★**Silverado Trail** – Ranging along the eastern edge of the Napa Valley between Napa and Calistoga, the scenic Silverado Trail offers a tranquil, relaxed alternative to the often traffic-choked Route 29. Its many dips and curves accommodate the rolling terrain at the base of the ridges bordering the valley, and acres of serene vineyards are punctuated by numerous wineries. Horseback riders and bikers are a common sight. Several crossroads link pastoral Silverado Trail with Route 29.

Auberge du Soleil

180 Rutherford Hill Rd., off the Silverado Trail. ☎ 707-963-1211. The breezy terrace of this elegant country inn offers the wine-weary traveler an unparalleled view across the Napa Valley. Select a meal from the inspired and highly acclaimed California-French menu in the dining room, or sip a fizzy lemonade *al fresco* while contemplating the silvery acres of olive trees that surround the inn.

34 • SONOMA VALLEY★★

Time: 1-2 days
Map p 203

The Sonoma Valley is agriculturally and topographically more diverse than the NAPA VALLEY. Anchored by the historic town of Sonoma, the valley dominates the southern portion of Sonoma County, where vineyards and wineries rub shoulders with orchards and fields. The region enjoys a reputation for excellent produce and other farm products, as well as for wines. Approved Viticultural Areas here include Los Carneros, Sonoma Valley and Sonoma Mountain. Most wineries lie in the vicinity of Sonoma and along or near Rte. 12 as it leads through the town to SANTA ROSA and to the UPPER SONOMA-RUSSIAN RIVER REGION.

Access – From San Francisco (49mi), take US-101 north; exit at Rte. 37, continue to Rte. 121 and turn left (north). Continue to Rte. 12 and turn left to Sonoma.

SIGHTS

★★**Sonoma** – *Map p 206.* Population 8,737. Site of the California mission chain's northernmost and final outpost, this charming community set amid the sun-soaked orchards and vineyards of the Sonoma Valley is the Wine Country's most historically significant town.

Sonoma was born in 1823 with the founding of the San Francisco Solano Mission *(p 206)*. Nearby, the Mexican government established a military outpost to guard against the threat of Russian encroachment from Fort Ross, 30mi to the north. After secularization of the mission chain in 1834, General Mariano Vallejo *(p 206)* was assigned to oversee distribution of the mission lands and to establish a pueblo at Sonoma. Sonoma's central plaza was the scene on June 14, 1846, of the **Bear Flag Revolt**, an uprising of American settlers disgruntled with Mexican control of California. Hoisting a white flag emblazoned with a brown bear and a star, the group proclaimed California an independent republic. A month later, American forces captured Monterey, declared California a US possession, and effectively ended the short-lived republic. Formally incorporated in 1850, Sonoma flourished as a supply and trade center for the area's farms and nascent winemaking industry. The town retains the charming flavor of that period, though today its historic adobe buildings, occupied by shops, restaurants and inns, stand beside contemporary structures. Several noteworthy examples of 19C residential architecture grace the streets south and west of the plaza, where attractive dwellings display elements of the Mission, Bungalow and Monterey Colonial styles. The **Sonoma State Historic Park★★**, headquartered near the Toscano Hotel, maintains and operates the town's important historic sites, including the San Francisco Solano Mission, the Sonoma Barracks, the Toscano Hotel, the Vallejo Home and Petaluma Adobe. *All sights are open year-round daily 10am–5pm. Closed Jan 1, Thanksgiving Day, Dec 25. Guided historical tours available weekends noon–2pm. $2 ticket includes all sights.* P ☎ *707-938-1519.*

★**Plaza** – *Bounded by Spain St., 1st St. W., Napa St., and 1st St. E.* Laid out by Mariano Vallejo in 1835, Sonoma's eight-acre plaza is the largest of its kind in California. Anchored at its center by the **City Hall** (1908), an eye-catching Mission Revival structure of roughly hewn basalt, the plaza today is attractively landscaped, laced with walkways and dotted with duck ponds, benches and play areas. On the east side of the Plaza, the **Sonoma Valley Visitor Center** *(453 1st St. E., ☎ 707-996-*

Sonoma Cheese Factory

2 Spain St. ☎ 707-996-1931. Step off the plaza to taste any of 11 varieties of Jack cheese made at this diminutive "factory," one of the area's largest cheese producers. A gloriously stocked gourmet deli offers a broad selection of local delicacies in addition to fine Sonoma Jack products, perfect for stocking a picnic basket or for sampling on the side terrace.

1090) is lodged in a restored Carnegie Library building (1913). A dramatic bronze **statue (1)** near the northeast corner depicts a soldier raising the Bear Flag, commemorating the 1846 revolt. Shady yews, sycamores and plane trees create a peaceful atmosphere amid the bustle of surrounding streets.

★**San Francisco Solano Mission** – *E. Spain St. & 1st St. E. ♿ ☎ 707-938-9560.* Founded in 1823 by Father José Altamíra, California's final mission was established as part of a Mexican government effort to strengthen its holdings against potential Russian invasion. The original wooden church and other structures, destroyed during an uprising in 1826, were replaced by adobe buildings the following year. The mission operated until secularization in 1834, when Mariano Vallejo dismantled the property and erected a parish chapel on the site of the original church. All that remain of the mission complex today are the chapel and part of the priests' quarters, restored around 1912. Displays of period furnishings and artifacts retell mission history. They precede an impressive collection of watercolor **paintings** depicting the California missions, executed by Norwegian artist Chris Jorgensen (1859-1935). In the restored chapel, the Stations of the Cross and framed paintings are authentic to the mission period.

Across Spain Street *(no. 217)* stands the **Blue Wing Inn** (1840), an attractive, symmetrical adobe structure that formerly served as a saloon and hotel. The enormous wisteria vine winding along its second-story balcony blooms luxuriantly in March and April.

★**Sonoma Barracks** – *Spain St. & 1st St. E.* This spacious, two-story adobe structure (1841), its wide balcony overlooking the plaza, housed Mexican troops stationed here to guard Sonoma. Following US occupation of California, the barracks served various American regiments during the Mexican-American War. Now a museum of the Sonoma State Historic Park, the barracks contain displays illustrating aspects of Sonoma's history, including artifacts from the various periods of Mexican and American settlement. To the right of the entrance, the re-created sleeping quarters appear as they might have during military occupation, with cots and bunks in neat rows. A video presentation *(22min)* highlights the northern frontier and the life of Mariano Vallejo.

Adjacent to the barracks sits the historic **Toscano Hotel** *(open year-round Sat–Mon 1pm–4pm; closed Jan 1, Thanksgiving Day, Dec 25; contribution requested; P ☎ 707-938-1519)*, built as a general store in the 1850s and converted to a boardinghouse in the 1880s for Italian immigrants working in nearby quarries. Today the wood-frame building's fancy Victorian furnishings belie its rough-and-tumble origins. Visitors can peek into cramped upstairs sleeping rooms, examine an intricate hair sculpture fashionable in the mid-19C, or explore the restored kitchen and dining room behind the main building.

★**Lachryma Montis** (Vallejo Home) – *North end of 3rd St. W., .5mi from the plaza. Leave the plaza by W. Spain St. and turn right on 3rd St. W. ☎ 707-938-9559.* The elegant Carpenter Gothic home, set amid attractively landscaped grounds, was named "tear of the mountain" in Latin for the mountain spring on the property. The lovely residence served as the final home of Mariano Vallejo, one of Mexican California's most powerful and colorful figures.

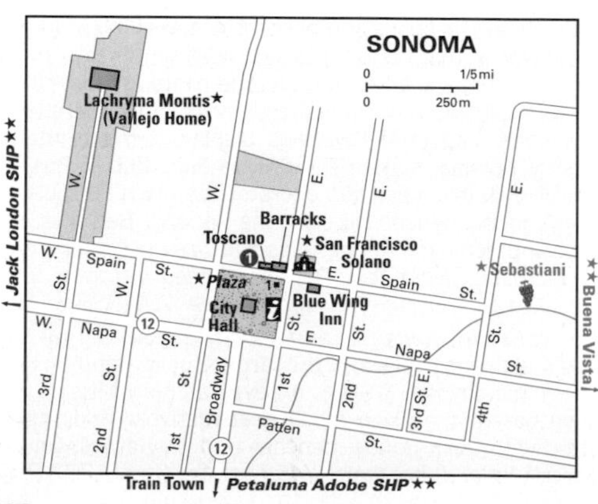

Born in Monterey, **Mariano Vallejo** (1807-1890) rose quickly through Mexican military ranks during the first part of his life, becoming commander of THE PRESIDIO at San Francisco at age 24. In 1834, Governor José Figueroa commissioned him to administer the secularization of the Sonoma mission and the founding of a pueblo and defense outpost. In return, Vallejo received 44,000 acres of land near Petaluma, which he developed as a private ranch *(p 208)*. Two years later he was appointed commander of all Mexican troops in California.

A supporter of American takeover of California, he was jailed briefly during the Bear Flag Revolt *(p 205)*. Vallejo was elected to California's first state senate in 1850 and served as mayor of Sonoma (1852-1860) before retiring at Lachryma Montis. The airy, spacious interior of the Gothic Victorian house is furnished to reflect the period when Vallejo lived there. It provides a delightful picture of his genteel lifestyle. Also on the property is a brick storehouse containing a small interpretive center and collection of artifacts from the 19C, among them a graceful French phaeton used by Vallejo and his family for excursions into town. A stroll through the well-tended grounds reveals a walkway around the spring, small outbuildings and guesthouses, and several orange trees that blossom in the spring and perfume the gardens with a delicious sweet scent.

★★ **Buena Vista Winery** – *18000 Old Winery Rd. From downtown Sonoma drive east on Napa St., turn left on 7th St. and right on Lovall Valley Rd., then left on eucalyptus-lined Old Winery Rd. for .5mi to the winery. Open year-round daily 10:30am–5pm. Closed Jan 1, Thanksgiving Day, Dec 25. Guided tours (30min) Jul–Sept 11am & 2pm, rest of the year 2pm. P www.buenavistawinery.com ☎ 707 938 1266 or 800-926-1266.* Sonoma County's first premium winery occupies a pleasantly rolling site amid eucalyptus, oak and bay laurel trees. It was founded in 1857 by Agoston Haraszthy *(p 194)*. Today, Buena Vista wines are made at another facility 5mi southeast of Sonoma.

Visitors may peer through an iron gate into Haraszthy's renowned **wine cellars**, dug into the limestone hill behind the winery by Chinese laborers in 1863. The stone **Press House** (1862), reputed to be California's oldest remaining winery building, today boasts a handsomely refurbished interior; the wooden beams are original. The second-floor gallery hosts an artist-in-residence program featuring works by local artists and craftspeople.

★ **Sebastiani Vineyards** – *From downtown Sonoma drive east on Spain St. and turn left on 4th St. E. Open year-round daily 10am–5pm. Winery visit by guided tour only (30min) 10:30am–4pm. Closed Jan 1 & Dec 25. ♿ P www.sebastiani.com ☎ 707-938-5532.* This sprawling winery incorporates sections of a livery stable purchased by Italian immigrant Samuele Sebastiani in 1904. Sebastiani transformed the stone structure into a wine cellar; construction of additional buildings progressed throughout the first half of the 20C. The winery's reception room displays rudimentary casks, crushers and other equipment from the early part of the century. On the guided tour, visitors see Sebastiani's two 60,000gal oak fermentation tanks, reputed to be the largest in the world outside of Heidelberg, Germany. Scattered throughout the winery are more than 300 wooden cask heads and doors embellished with whimsical **carvings** executed from 1967 to 1984 by local artist Earle Brown.

Train Town – Kids *20264 Broadway, 1mi south of the Plaza on Rte. 12. Open Jun–Labor Day daily 10am–5pm. Rest of the year Fri–Sun & holidays 10am–5pm. Train ride round-trip 20min. Closed during heavy rain. $3.75. ♿ P ☎ 707-938-3912.* An old-fashioned carousel and a working scale-model railroad make Train Town a fine destination for families with small children. Passengers big and little sit on benches in low, open-top train cars for a 20min ride through a landscaped countryside of bridges, tunnels, waterfalls and miniature buildings. The train stops midway at a petting zoo, where anyone so inclined can touch a goat or a pony. Train souvenirs and fairground snacks add to Train Town's old-time carnival atmosphere.

★★ **Jack London State Historic Park** – *10mi from Sonoma. 2400 London Ranch Rd., in Glen Ellen. From Sonoma, drive 5mi north on Rte. 12, turn left on Madrone Rd. and right on Arnold Dr. Continue into Glen Ellen and turn left on London Ranch Rd. Open Apr–Oct daily 9:30am–7pm. Rest of the year daily 9:30am–5pm. Closed Jan 1, Thanksgiving Day, Dec 25. $6/car. Guided tours (1-2hrs) available. P www.parks.sonoma.net ☎ 707-938-5216.* Sprawling among peaceful hills in the shadow of Sonoma Mountain is the 800-acre "Beauty Ranch," home of writer Jack London (1876-1916) during the last years of his life. Today a state park, the ranch commemorates this beloved American author of such adventure stories as *Call of the Wild* (1903) and *The Sea Wolf* (1904).

Sailor on Horseback – Born illegitimately in San Francisco in 1876, Jack London was raised in OAKLAND, where as a boy he labored in the city's canneries and mills. His huge capacity for hard work and his love of adventure were united with a voracious appetite for books. The poverty-stricken boy was encouraged in his reading at the Oakland Free Library by poet Ina Coolbrith. By age 16, London used his small savings to buy a sloop, the *Razzle Dazzle*. Living a reckless life on the Oakland docks, raiding oyster beds by night on San Francisco Bay, London was introduced to his lifelong nemesis of alcoholism in the waterfront bars, where he also began to nurse his socialist sympathies. He joined a sealing expedition to Siberia and joined the Klondike Gold Rush in 1897. Forced by scurvy to return to Oakland the following year, London directed his energies to writing stories of his adventures in the far north. His first short story, published by the *Overland Monthly*, earned him only $5 but launched a hugely successful career as a novelist, foreign correspondent, short-story writer and lecturer.

In 1905 London, by then renowned as an author and advocate of socialism, purchased a run-down ranch in the hills near Glen Ellen and settled there with his second wife, Charmian. In 1911 the Londons began construction of Wolf House, a massive four-story mansion of hand-hewn lava boulders and redwood logs. Its 26 rooms and nine fireplaces occupied 15,000sq ft. On the night of August 22, 1913, a month before the couple was to move in, a fire roared through the house, leaving only stone walls. Crushed, the Londons never rebuilt Wolf House, but continued to live in a small cottage on the ranch. Jack London died there in 1916 at the age of 40 of uremic poisoning.

Visit – *2hrs. Site plan available at park entrance.* Erected by Charmian London in 1919 as her residence, with the intention of making it a museum to honor her husband, the rustic stone **House of Happy Walls★** today serves as the park visitor center. The massive building contains memorabilia of both Londons, including artifacts from the author's life and work, letters, photographs, clothing and objects amassed during the couple's world travels, notably Pacific meanderings aboard their boat, the *Snark*.

A trail *(1.2mi round-trip; trailhead at House of Happy Walls)* winds through rolling meadows and forests to the ghostly ruins of **Wolf House★**, in the heart of a glade overlooking a peaceful valley. A short detour from this trail leads to the Londons' gravesite atop a peaceful hill.

The **Beauty Ranch Trail★** *(.5mi loop; accessible from the upper parking lot)* wanders about the property past stables, silos, a piggery and the Londons' modest cottage *(not open to the public)*. Other, more extensive hiking trails lead throughout the park and up the steep slope of Sonoma Mountain *(summit located on private property)*.

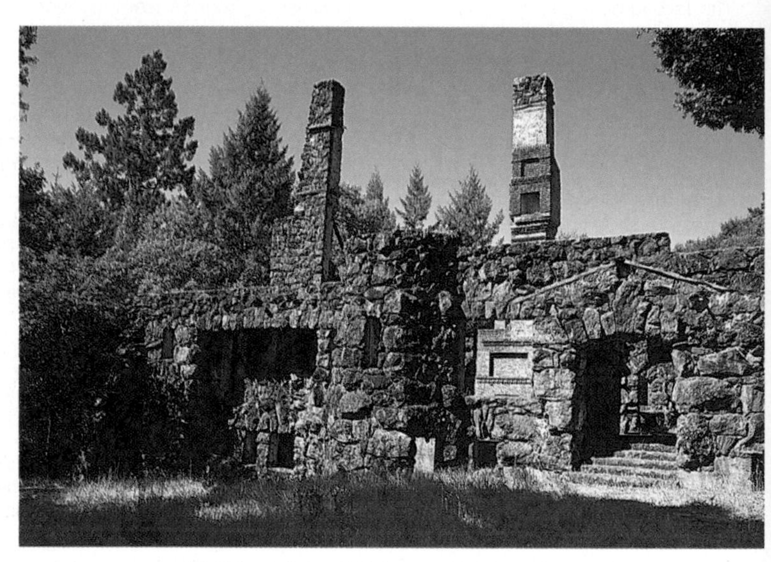

Wolf House Ruins, Jack London State Historic Park

★★ **Petaluma Adobe State Historic Park** – *3325 Adobe Rd., Petaluma, 10mi from Sonoma. Leave Sonoma by Rte. 12 south; turn right on Leveroni Rd. and left on Arnold Dr. Turn right on Rte. 116, continue 3mi and bear right on Adobe Rd. Continue 3.25mi to fork in road; turn sharply right and proceed another .25mi to park entrance on right. Open year-round daily 10am–5pm. Closed Jan 1, Thanksgiving Day & Dec 25. $2.* 🅿 ☎ *707-938-1519.* In 1834, Mexican commander Mariano Vallejo *(p 206)* established a 100sq mi ranch headquarters on this hilltop site overlooking the rolling Sonoma County countryside. Rancho Petaluma thrived, producing cattle, horses, sheep and voluminous crops of grain until Vallejo leased out the property in September 1850. The state of California took it over in 1951. Today the restored two-story dwelling, one-half its original size, re-creates the atmosphere of a prosperous 19C ranch with interpretive displays on history and especially the Californio lifestyle. Authentic period pieces decorate Vallejo's personal chambers and other rooms upstairs; ground-floor rooms are outfitted with looms, kitchen tools and candle-making equipment. In the courtyard stand hive-shaped ovens once used to prepare meals for the adobe's residents. Living history demonstrations are occasionally mounted in spring and summer *(call for dates and times)*.

35 • UPPER SONOMA-RUSSIAN RIVER REGION★

Time: 1-2 days
Map p 211

This region of northern Sonoma County comprises three principal viticultural areas: the Russian River Valley, the Dry Creek Valley and the Alexander Valley. Other smaller areas include Knight's Valley, Green Valley, Northern Sonoma and Chalk Hill. The city of Santa Rosa *(below)* serves as the principal commercial hub and center of government.

The lovely **Russian River Valley** follows the curving path of the Russian River as it meanders south through Healdsburg and veers west toward the coast, passing picturesque wineries, rolling vineyards and brooding stands of redwood trees. Swimming, canoeing and kayaking are popular sports on the river where it passes through the resort communities of Forestville, **Guerneville**, Monte Rio and Duncans Mills, and the surrounding forests offer ample opportunities for hiking and camping.

Hemmed by majestic mountain ridges, the **Alexander Valley** extends along the Russian River east and north of Healdsburg. Small, rustic wineries dot the curves and corners of Route 128 as it wanders across a pastoral landscape of vineyard-covered foothills. The 20mi-long valley was named for Cyrus Alexander, a Pennsylvania trapper who settled here in the 1840s.

The delightful **Dry Creek Valley★** extends from the Warm Springs Dam on Lake Sonoma to just south of Healdsburg. Approximately 12mi long, the narrow valley is laced with small, winding roads that meander among vineyards, beneath canopies of trees and across the valley floor. Zinfandel grapes have been grown here, and in the Alexander Valley, for more than a century.

Access – From San Francisco take US-101 north to Santa Rosa (49mi) or to Healdsburg (64mi).

SIGHTS

Santa Rosa – Population 121,879. Upper Sonoma's sprawling commercial hub is worth a visit for sights relating to three famed residents: horticulturalist Luther Burbank (1849-1926), collector Robert Ripley (1893-1949) and cartoonist Charles Schulz (b. 1922).

★**Luther Burbank Home & Gardens** – *Sonoma & Santa Rosa Aves. Home & carriage house visit by 30min guided tour only. Apr–Oct Tue–Sun 10am–4pm; $3; gardens open year-round daily;* ♿ *http://santarosachamber.com/membership/burbank* ☎ *707-524-5445.* Visitors can tour the renowned botanist's modest home or stroll among lush gardens. Burbank's extensive experiments in plant hybridization, resulting in such now-commonplace strains as the Russet Burbank potato, the Shasta daisy and the Santa Rosa plum, produced more than 800 new varieties of flowers, fruits and vegetables. The gardens at the site were beautifully redesigned in 1960 and renovated in 1992, and today feature many of his experimental hybrids, including some 100 varieties of roses.

Church of One Tree – *Juilliard Park, Santa Rosa Ave. Closed to the public.* ☎ *707-543-3282.* This Gothic Revival building is made of boards from a single redwood tree. It formerly housed a museum dedicated to Santa Rosa native Robert Ripley, creator of the famed *Believe It or Not!* cartoons.

Snoopy's Gallery and Gift Shop – Kids *1665 W. Steel Ln. Exit US-101 north at Steele Ln. and turn left; open year-round daily 10am–6pm; closed major holidays;* ✗ ♿ P *www.snoopygift.com* ☎ *707-546-3385 or 800-959-3385.* Lovers of the comic strip *Peanuts* will enjoy a visit to this gallery, where memorabilia, cartoons and original drawings are displayed on the mezzanine level. Charles Schulz, the strip's creator, lives and works in Santa Rosa.

★**Healdsburg** – Population 9,674. Founded in 1857 by Harmon Heald, a migrant farmer turned merchant, tranquil Healdsburg (pronounced HEELDS-burg) surrounds a picturesque central **plaza**, scene of numerous civic festivals and events. The charming community's location at the confluence of the Alexander, Dry Creek and Russian River valleys, and its several excellent restaurants and inns, make it an ideal starting point for forays into these areas. Visitors interested in learning more about northern Sonoma County can stop by the **Healdsburg Museum (M)** *(221 Matheson St., 2 blocks east of the plaza; open year-round Tue–Sun 11am–4pm; closed major holidays;* ♿ P ☎ *707-431-3325)*, housed in the beautifully preserved former Carnegie Library building. Half the museum is dedicated to a fine permanent collection of artifacts, including photographs, Pomo Indian baskets, grinding rocks and weapons, bringing to life the region's colorful history. The other half contains exhibits of regional historic interest that change quarterly.

Harvest at Jordan Vineyards, Alexander Valley

★**Simi Winery** – *16275 Healdsburg Ave., Healdsburg. Open year-round daily 10am–4:30pm. Closed Jan 1, Easter Sunday, Thanksgiving Day, Dec 25. Winery visit by guided tour (1hr) only, daily 11am, 1pm & 3pm. www.simiwinery.com 707-433-6981.* Founded in 1883 by Italian immigrants Guiseppe and Pietro Simi, this winery today boasts some of the oldest vines and stone cellars in California alongside an ultra-modern winemaking facility. The massive stone cellars were built in two phases, visible in the building's two types of stonework. Chinese workers constructed the original south side in the mid-1880s. They also built the railroad tracks that still run through the middle of the property and were once used to ship bottles directly from the cellars. The north side was constructed in 1904 by Italian masons under the direction of Isabel Simi, Guiseppe's daughter, who (according to local lore) took over management of the winery at age 14 when her father and uncle died of influenza. Legend has it that after Prohibition, with the winery all but bankrupt, Isabel rolled a barrel onto the old highway and offered free sips of wine, thereby establishing California's first tasting room.

An informative guided tour takes visitors through the historic stone cellars and into a high-tech fermentation center that is considered one of the finest in the state.

★**Lake Sonoma** – *11mi north of Healdsburg by Dry Creek Rd.* Nestled in the coastal foothills of northern Sonoma County, this elongated lake was created in 1983 when the Warm Springs Dam was constructed at the confluence of Warm Springs and Dry creeks. Now a popular recreation area, Lake Sonoma offers a plethora of activities including boating, swimming, fishing, picnicking, hiking and camping in and around its sapphire waters.

★★**Visitor Center and Fish Hatchery** – Kids *Open year-round daily 9:30am–4:30pm (hours may vary by season). www.spn.usace.army.mil 707-433-9483.* Displays of craftwork and artifacts exemplify the traditions and beliefs of the region's indigenous Pomo peoples, and the effects of the arrival of Hispanic and Caucasian settlers. Informative panels illustrate geological formations and thermal activity in the area. The adjacent hatchery building, created by the US Army Corps of Engineers to mitigate environmental disruption of Dry Creek caused by the Warm Springs Dam, offers a rare opportunity to observe the spawning and hatching of steelhead trout and silver salmon. Fish climb an inclined channel or "ladder" into the hatchery where they are held, sorted and spawned, activities visible from a mezzanine-level interpretive center. *Viewing times: Jan–Mar for steelhead trout; early Oct–Dec for salmon. Call ahead to verify.*

Lake Sonoma Overlook – *2.5mi from Visitor Center; follow signs.* Designed in harmony with its natural surroundings, the wood-timbered overlook offers soaring **views**★★ of the lake, dam and surrounding mountains, including Mt. St. Helena in neighboring Napa Valley.

★**Hop Kiln Winery** – *6050 Westside Rd., 5mi south of Healdsburg. Open year-round daily 10am–5pm. Closed Jan 1, Easter Sunday, Thanksgiving Day, Dec 25. 707-433-6491.* This historic **hop barn**★ (1905), one of the finest examples of its type, functioned as part of northern California's hop-growing industry. Hops were dried in three huge wooden kilns, resembling giant inverted funnels, before being pressed and baled for shipment to area breweries. The kiln was renovated as a winery in 1975.

★**Korbel Champagne Cellars** – *13250 River Rd., 2.5mi northeast of Guerneville. Visit by guided tour (50min) only, May–Sept daily 10am–3:45pm each hour. Rest of the year daily 10am–3pm. Closed Easter Sunday, Thanksgiving Day & Dec 25.*

✗ ♿ P ☎ *707-824-7000.* In the early 1870s, Czechoslovakian immigrants Anton, Francis and Joseph Korbel acquired a lumber mill at this site on the sloping banks of the Russian River. By the end of that decade, having largely denuded the surrounding hillsides of their redwoods, the Korbels planted grapevines among the stumps. Construction of a large, handmade-brick winery building was completed in 1886 for the production of brandy and sparkling wine.

The highlight of a visit to Korbel is an informative guided tour covering both historic and contemporary processes of *méthode champenoise* sparkling-wine production. Enjoy a wander through the 250-variety antique **rose garden** *(guided tours May–Sept Tue–Sun 11am, 1pm & 3pm)* on the slope below the Korbel family summer home. Stroll through the old train depot, formerly the terminus of the Fulton-Guerneville branch of the Northwest Pacific Railroad. After dining in the restaurant or picking up picnic food in the deli, you can take an impromptu tour of the Russian River Brewing Company—Korbel's response to visitors with champagne tastes but beer budgets.

★**Armstrong Redwoods State Reserve** – Kids *2mi north of Guerneville on Armstrong Woods Rd. Open year-round daily 8am–one hour past sunset. $5/car. Guided tours (30min) available by reservation.* △*(in adjacent Austin Creek State Recreation Area)* P ☎ *707-869-2015.* Lush, dense forests of varied species of trees surround a 500-acre grove of ancient redwoods that survived 19C logging operations thanks to the conservationist efforts of Colonel James Armstrong. Today the grove forms the heart of an 800-acre state park that boasts some of Sonoma County's finest surviving redwood trees. A self-guided nature trail *(.5mi)* passes through cool, fern-laced glades.

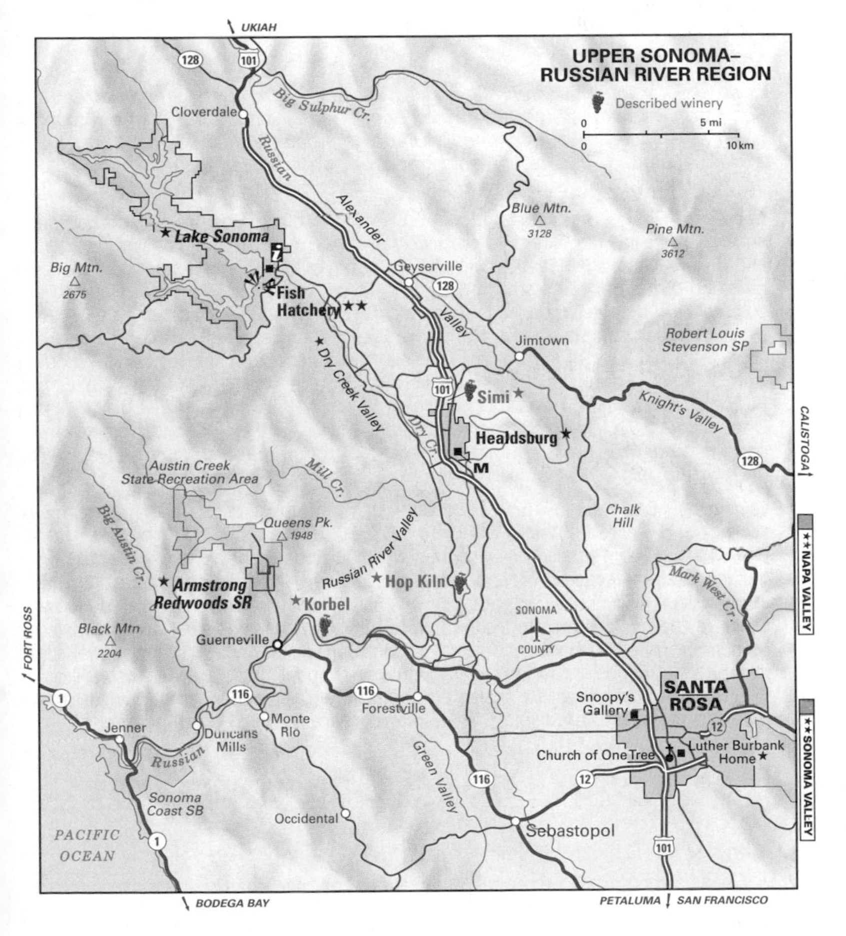

Admission prices and hours published in this guide are accurate at press time.

36 • FILOLI★★

Time: 1/2 day

Map of Principal Sights p 4

Nestled into the inland side of the Coast Range's heavily wooded foothills, this 654-acre estate is precariously situated almost directly astride the San Andreas Fault. Yet the elegance of the property exemplifies the gracious lifestyle made possible at the turn of the 20C by fortunes derived from several of California's great economic forces: mining, real-estate speculation, water development and agriculture.

Historical Notes

The property's formal gardens and U-shaped, "Modified" Georgian Revival mansion (1915-17, Willis Polk) were commissioned by William Bourn II (1857-1936), owner of the Empire Mine in Grass Valley; at the time, Empire was California's most productive hard-rock gold mine. Bourn was also president of the Spring Valley Water Company, consisting of Crystal Springs Lake and its adjacent lands, and it was here that he sited his 43-room country estate. Filoli (named for a favorite Bourn credo, *Fight for a just cause; Love your fellow man; Live a good life*), with its large, mature trees spreading shadows over acres of well-kept lawns, still expresses the confidence of settled rural wealth.

After the deaths of Bourn and his wife in 1936, Filoli was acquired by its only other owner, William P. Roth. Roth died in 1963. His widow, Lurline Roth, who expanded but did not redesign the gardens, donated Filoli to the National Trust for Historic Preservation in 1975.

VISIT

Located 30mi south of San Francisco on Cañada Rd. in Woodside. From downtown San Francisco, take I-280 south to the Edgewood Rd. exit and turn right; turn right again at Cañada Rd. and continue 1.3mi to the gate. Visit by guided tour (2hrs) mid-Feb–Oct Tue–Thu, reservations required. Visit by self-guided tour Thu–Sat 10am–3pm. $10. (Tea Room) www.filoli.org 650-364-8300 ext. 507.

★★ **Mansion** – The ground floor is appointed with furniture and art from both the Bourn and Roth families; an extensive collection of 17C-18C Irish and English furnishings and decorative arts bequeathed by Melvin Martin in 1998; and a smaller number of gifts and pieces on loan from the Fine Arts Museums of San Francisco. House tours commence in the Reception Room, where a 17ft-by-33ft Persian carpet (19C), woven over three generations, covers the floor. The kitchen features an impressive ship's stove acquired in 1942 from the Matson Navigation Company, owned by Lurline Roth's father. The grand ballroom, with its 22ft ceilings, is adorned with Ernest Peixotto murals (1925) depicting Ireland's Lakes of Killarney and nearby Muckross House, an 11,000-acre estate given by the Bourns to their daughter on her marriage in 1910. Muckross contains ruins of a Franciscan abbey destroyed by Oliver Cromwell in 1644—and preserved in distant imagery in the murals.

★★★ **Gardens** – Designed by Bruce Porter with continuing assistance from Isabella Worn, this 16-acre botanical wonder (1917-20) successfully combines the formal with the natural. Planned as a sequence of outdoor "rooms," each with its own horticultural and seasonal delights, the gardens are aligned along the same north-south axis as the house, extending the lines of the mansion's transverse hallway. Some of the most interesting plants were gifts or purchases from foreign governments that were disposing of display specimens after the 1915 Panama-Pacific International Exposition. Many of the column-shaped Irish yews, used as pillars in Filoli's garden "architecture," started as cuttings from the yews at Muckross. All floral arrangements on display in the mansion are supplied by the gardens.

37 • SAN MATEO COUNTY COAST

Time: 1 day

Map of Principal Sights p 4

Untouched by the sprawl of the city to its north or the urbanized peninsula area to its east, coastal San Mateo County is geographically isolated by the San Gregorio and Santa Cruz mountain ranges and protected against development by the lack of a practical commuter route. Route 1 narrows to two lanes as it wends its way south from Pacifica through the pastoral farming and fishing villages of Moss Beach, Princeton, San Gregorio and Pescadero. South of Half Moon Bay, the east side of the highway skirts a gently undulating landscape patterned with fields of flowers, wholesalers' greenhouses, and rows of artichoke and brussels sprout plants; pumpkin patches vividly dot the landscape in autumn. To the west extend ocean beaches, superb spots for strolling, picnicking, tidepooling and wildlife observation, though rip currents and frigid water temperatures make swimming inadvisable. From January to April, at many points along the drive, **gray whales** may be seen only a few hundred yards offshore, making their annual migration between summer feeding grounds in the Arctic and their winter home off the coast of Mexico's Baja Peninsula.

The notorious stretch of highway known as **Devil's Slide** forms a gateway to the coast from San Francisco. Just south of Point San Pedro, the highway narrows and swerves around steep cliffs dramatically striated with rock layers upthrust from ancient marine sediments. Rock slides have closed the road on several occasions in recent years, but conservationists fear that replacing it with a tunnel or inland route would encourage development of the delightfully rural coastal towns to the south.

Visiting San Mateo County Coast – From San Francisco drive south on Rte. 1 (19th Ave.) or Rte. 35 (Skyline Blvd.), which intersects Rte. 1 south of Daly City. To return to San Francisco, either retrace the route or take Rte. 92 east from Half Moon Bay, then continue north on I-280. Mileage to each sight is calculated from the preceding sight. The $5/car fee at some park entrances allows any same-day state park visit.

In summer, the coast is often cool and foggy; the weather clears in spring and fall. Reservations are necessary to visit the wildlife protection areas at Año Nuevo State Reserve *(below)* during the breeding season from December through March; the spectacle is well worth the effort of advance planning. Swimming is inadvisable along the San Mateo County Coast due to cold water and hazardous surf; beware of sneaker waves *(p 243)* when venturing close to shore. For information on camping and other parks amenities, contact the **California State Parks Bay Area District Office**, 250 Executive Park Blvd., Suite 4900, San Francisco CA 94134-3306, ☎ 415-330-6300.

DRIVING TOUR *distance: 50mi*

★**James V. Fitzgerald Marine Reserve** – Kids *16mi from San Francisco. In Moss Beach, turn right on California Ave. Open year-round daily dawn–dusk.* P *Tide information & reservations ☎ 650-728-3584.* Extensive shale reefs bridge the expanse between land and sea, creating tidepools richly populated with myriad marine life, including limpets, barnacles, mussels, sea urchins, starfish, anemones, chitons, hermit crabs, sponges and abalone. Rangers help visitors search the wonders of the pools and lead explorations during low tide. A small visitor center identifies specimens.

Pillar Point Harbor – *2.4mi.* A granitic headland extends from the coast here, creating a sheltered harbor that serves as an anchorage for local fishermen. Fresh fish is sold daily from boats and fish markets, and simple seafood restaurants serve up steaming chowder, seafood cocktails and fresh fish and chips. Whale-watching cruises depart from the wharf during the season *(depart Jan–Apr weekends & holidays 10am & 1:30pm; round-trip 3hrs; commentary; reservations required; $20;* P *Huck Finn Fishing Trips http://usafishing.com/halfmoon.html ☎ 650-726-7133 or 800-572-2934)*.

Francis State Beach – Kids *4.1mi. Foot of Kelly Ave. in Half Moon Bay. Open May–Oct daily 8am–9pm. Rest of the year 8am–5pm. $5/car (allows same-day entry for any state park).* ⚠ ♿ P *☎ 650-726-8819.* The Half Moon Bay state beach system extends 3mi to the north of this flat, sandy expanse, which provides a welcome departure from the coast's typically rocky beaches. Dune grasses fringing the shoreline provide habitat for snowy plovers. Picnic tables overlook the ocean from the day-use area, and a Coastside Trail *(3mi)* lures hikers and bikers. The skull of a blue whale entangled in a fisherman's net in 1988 is visible near the entry booth.

San Gregorio State Beach – *11mi. Open year-round daily 8am–sunset. $5/car* P *☎ 650-879-2170.* This broad, sandy beach lies at the mouth of San Gregorio Creek. Walk north at low tide to see dramatic, cavelike erosion at the base of the sandstone bluffs, or stroll atop to spot whales in season.

Pescadero State Beach – *4.4mi. Open year-round daily 8am–sunset. $5/car at north entrance only, free at south & central entrances.* P *☎ 650-879-2170.* From the bluffs that loom over this popular beach, views extend west over the Pacific and the San Mateo County coastline. East of Route 1, extensive walking trails penetrate the **Pescadero Marsh Natural Preserve**, a 510-acre freshwater/brackish coastal marsh. Migratory birds plying the Pacific Flyway stop here to rest, drawing flocks of birdwatchers, especially in late fall and early spring. Binoculars are helpful. *Guided walks of marsh year-round (weather permitting) Sat 10:30am & Sun 1pm. Meet in Central Pescadero parking lot, watch for signs off Rte. 1 just south of Pescadero Creek.*

Pebble Beach – Kids *2.1mi. Open year-round daily 8am–sunset. $5/car.* P ☎ *650-879-2170.* Waves breaking here deposit glistening, many-colored pebbles onto the beach from an offshore quartz reef *(note: it is illegal to remove pebbles)*. This part of the coast bears spectacular displays of **tafoni**—lacy, filigree-like formations wrought by erosion on the face of weathered stone. Pebble Beach forms the northernmost unit of **Bean Hollow State Beach**, accessible from here by car or via a 12-station clifftop nature trail *(1mi)*. Harbor seals occasionally may be seen sunning themselves on the wet rocks below the trail, or vying with swooping cormorants for fish.

★**Pigeon Point Lighthouse** – Kids *3mi. Visit by guided tour (50min) only. Sept–Jun weekends 11am–4pm. Jul–Aug Fri–Sun 11am–4pm (weather permitting). $2.* P ☎ *650-879-2120.* Built in 1871, this starkly graceful lighthouse tower was automated in 1926. The lantern room contains the original Fresnel lens, a device consisting of 1,008 glass prisms that shape light from a central lamp into a horizontal beam intense enough to be visible many miles out at sea. The point itself offers lovely views of the coast and surrounding landforms. A self-guided tour of the grounds explains the light station's past in vivid detail *(brochure available at entrance)*. The lighthouse outbuildings today house a unit of the American Youth Hostel Association.

★**Año Nuevo State Reserve** – Kids *6.6mi. Open year-round daily 8am–sunset. Elephant seal rookery open Apr–Nov daily 8:30am–3:30pm. Rest of the year by appointment only. Closed 1st 2 weeks in Dec.* P ☎ *650-879-0227. Seal Walks guided tours (2hr 30min) available Dec–Mar daily 8:45am–2:15pm every 15min. Closed Dec 25. Reservations recommended 8 weeks in advance. $4/walk & $5/car.* ☎ *800-444-4445.* This 4,000-acre coastal reserve encompasses a rocky offshore island *(not open to the public)* and a wildly beautiful promontory of bluffs and beaches. The promontory is the largest mainland rookery between Baja and northern California for **northern elephant seals**. From December through March, the seals gradually congregate here, the females coming ashore to give birth to single pups and joining "harems" dominated by massive, 2.5-ton alpha bulls. Violent clashes between males over harem control are common. In spring and summer, seals again come ashore to molt.

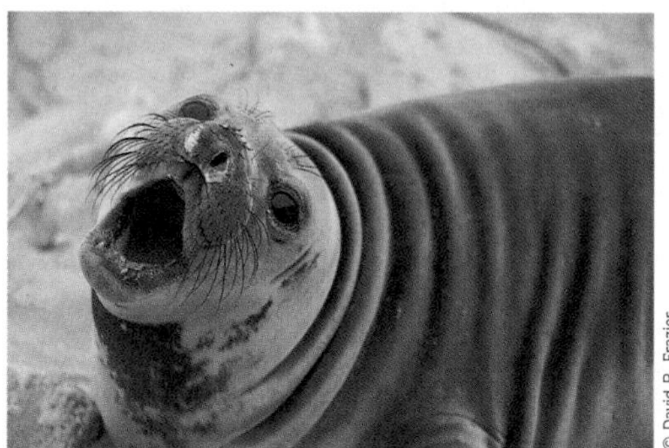

Elephant Seal Pup, Año Nuevo State Reserve

THE GOLDEN WHALES OF CALIFORNIA

Yes, I have walked in California,
And the rivers there are blue and white.
Thunderclouds of grapes hang on the mountains.
Bears in the meadows pitch and fight. ...
And flowers burst like bombs in California,
Exploding on tomb and tower,
And the panther-cats chase the red rabbits,
Scatter their young blood every hour.
And the cattle on the hills in California
And the very swine in the holes
Have ears of silk and velvet
And tusks like long white poles. ...
Goshawfuls are Burbanked with the grizzly bears.
At midnight their children come clanking up the stairs.
They wriggle up the canyons, nose into the caves,
And swallow the papooses and the Indian braves.
The trees climb so high the crows are dizzy
Flying to their nests at the top.
While the jazz-birds screech, and storm the brazen beach
And the sea-darts turn flip-flop.
The solid Golden Gate soars up to Heaven.
Perfumed cataracts are hurled
From the zones of silver snow
To the ripening rye below,
To the land of the lemon and the nut
And the biggest ocean in the world.
While the native sons, like lords tremendous,
Lift up their heads with chants sublime,
And the bandstands sound the trombone, the saxophone and xylophone
And the whales roar in perfect tune and time.
And the chanting of the whales in California
I have set my heart upon.
It is sometimes a play by Belasco,
Sometimes a tale of Prester John.

Vachel Lindsay, *Collected Poems*, 1923

Practical Information

Consult the main section of the guide for detailed practical information about **Golden Gate Park** *(p 108)*, **Point Reyes National Seashore** *(p 185)* and the **Wine Country** *(pp 196-197)*.

© David R. Frazier

Calendar of Events

Listed below is a selection of San Francisco's many popular annual events; some dates may vary annually. For more information about events in San Francisco, consult the periodicals listed on p 229, contact the San Francisco Convention and Visitors Bureau ☎ 415-391-2000, or access www.sfvisitor.org on the Internet.

Spring & Summer

mid- to late Apr	**Cherry Blossom Festival** *Japan Center*	415-563-2313
Easter Sunday	**Easter Parade & Hat Promenade** *Union St.*	415-885-1335
late Apr–early May	**San Francisco International Film Festival** *various locations*	415-929-5000
1st Sun in May	**Cinco de Mayo Festival** *Mission District*	415-826-1401
3rd Sun in May	**Bay to Breakers Race** *The Embarcadero to the Great Highway*	415-777-7770
Memorial Day Sun	**Carnaval San Francisco** *Mission District*	415-826-1401
1st weekend in Jun	**Union Street Spring Festival** *Union St. between Gough & Steiner Sts.*	415-346-9162
mid-Jun	**Dipsea Race** *Mill Valley to Stinson Beach*	415-331-3550
May–Oct	**Shakespeare at the Beach** *Stinson Beach*	415-868-9500
mid-Jun–mid-Aug	**Stern Grove Midsummer Music Festival**	415-252-6252
mid-Jun	**North Beach Festival** *Grant Ave. & Green St.*	415-989-6426

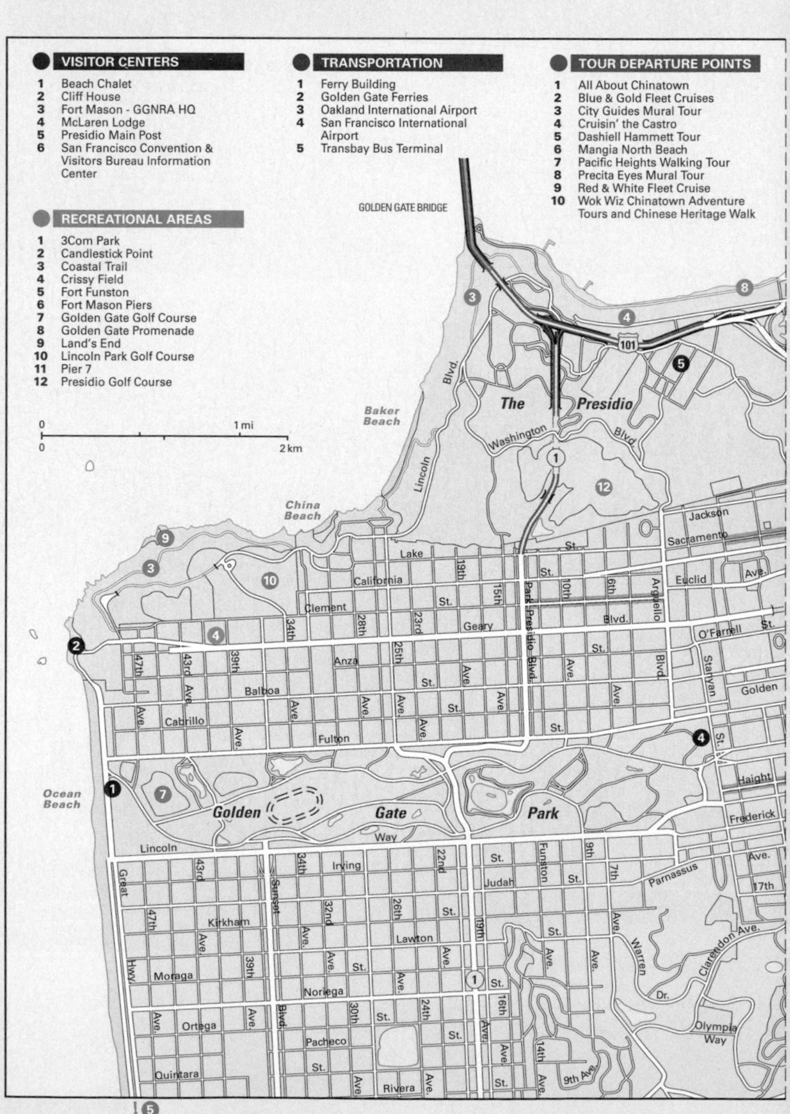

late Jun	**Lesbian, Gay, Bi-Sexual, Transgender Pride Celebration** *Castro District*	415-864-3733
Jul-Aug	**Summer Music Festival** *Robert Mondavi Winery, Napa Valley*	707-226-1395
3rd Thu in Jul	**Cable Car Bell-Ringing Championship** *Union Square*	415-923-6202
late Aug–late Sept	**Shakespeare in the Park** *Golden Gate Park*	415-831-5500
Labor Day weekend	**Sausalito Art Festival** *Marinship Park*	415-332-3555

Fall & Winter

last weekend in Sept	**San Francisco Blues Festival** *Great Meadow at Fort Mason*	415-979-5588
2nd Sat in Sept	**Latino Summer Fiesta** *Mission District*	415-826-1401
Oct	**San Francisco Open Studios** *various locations*	415-861-9838
1st Sun in Oct	**Castro Street Fair** *Castro & Market Sts.*	415-467-3354
late Oct–early Nov	**San Francisco Jazz Festival** *various locations*	415-398-5655
Oct 31	**Halloween San Francisco** *Civic Center*	415-826-1401
3rd Fri in Nov	**Embarcadero Center Holiday Lights Celebration** *Justin Herman Plaza*	415-788-1234
Dec	**Festival of Lights** *Fisherman's Wharf*	415-705-5500
Feb	**Festival of Winter Classical Concerts** *Robert Mondavi Winery, Napa Valley*	707-226-1395
late Feb	**Chinese New Year Parade** *Chinatown*	415-982-3000
last weekend in Feb	**Pacific Orchid Exposition** *Fort Mason*	415-546-9608

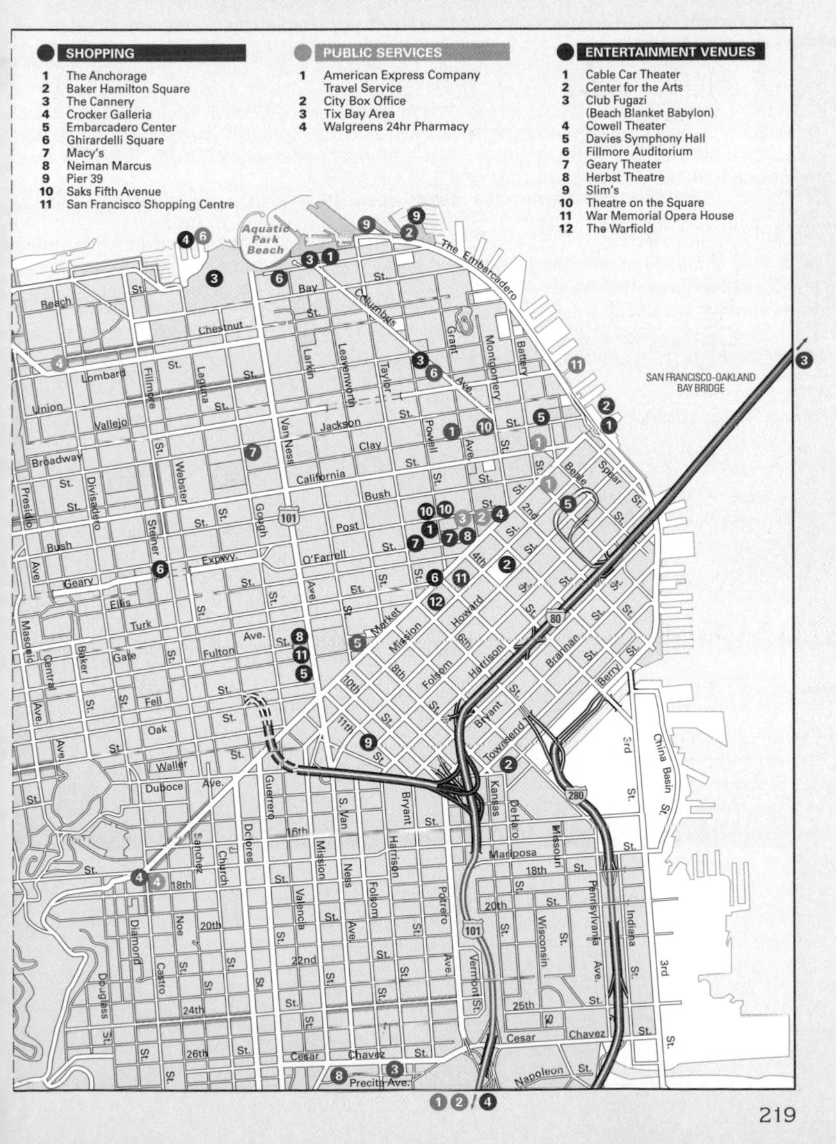

Planning a Trip to San Francisco

Visitors can contact the following agencies to obtain maps and information on points of interest, accommodations and seasonal events.

San Francisco Convention and Visitors Bureau .... ☎ 415-391-2000
P.O. Box 429097, San Francisco, CA 94142-9097 www.sfvisitor.org

Berkeley Convention and Visitors Bureau .... ☎ 510-549-7040
2015 Center St., Berkeley CA 94704 www.berkeleycvb.com

Visitor Marketing, City of Oakland .... ☎ 510-238-2935
250 Frank Ogawa Plaza, Ste. 3330, Oakland, CA 94612

Marin County Convention and Visitors Bureau .... ☎ 415-499-5000
1013 Larkspur Landing Circle, Larkspur, CA 94939 www.visitmarin.org

San Mateo County Convention and Visitors Bureau .... ☎ 650-348-7600
111 Anza Blvd., Suite 410, Burlingame CA 94010 www.sanmateocountycvb.com

San Francisco's Seasons

The San Francisco Bay Area enjoys a temperate climate year-round. Although temperature variation from season to season is slight, weather conditions can change quite suddenly in the course of a day, and from area to area. Inland temperatures are usually higher than those along the bayshore and especially the oceanfront. Nighttime lows tend to stay between 45°–55°F.

The key to comfort when visiting the region is dressing in layers. Shorts and other light clothing are rarely practical. In the **spring** and **summer**, daytime highs average in the 60s, although the infrequent fog-free day can bring sunny skies and temperatures in the 80s. The busiest tourist season is during July and August; visitors should make advance reservations whenever possible and expect long lines for the more popular attractions. The region's glorious views are at their finest during the clear days of **autumn**, when daytime temperatures in the 70s make exploring the area quite comfortable. Rain is the norm during the **winter** months; some 80 percent of the annual precipitation occurs between November and April, and temperatures fluctuate little throughout the day, hovering between 45° and 60°F.

Fog *(p 10)* is an important weather determinant: its presence causes temperatures to drop, making a sweater or jacket necessary. Spring fogs occur in the early morning and generally lift by mid-day. Fog persists throughout the day in coastal areas during summer, though it may burn off over inland areas before returning in the evening. Autumn days are relatively fog-free. Winter fogs usually occur inland, leaving coastal areas in the clear.

San Francisco Temperature Chart

(recorded at San Francisco International Airport)

	avg. high	avg. low	Precipitation
Jan	56°F (13°C)	41°F (5°C)	4.6in (11.7cm)
Apr	63°F (17°C)	47°F (8°C)	1.5in (3.8cm)
Jul	71°F (21°C)	53°F (12°C)	0.04in (0.1cm)
Oct	70°F (21°C)	51°F (10°C)	1.0in (2.5cm)

Getting to San Francisco

BY AIR

San Francisco International Airport (SFO) – *www.ci.sf.ca.us/sfo* ☎ *650-876-7809. 13.5mi south of San Francisco.* Most international and domestic flights arrive and depart from SFO. **Airport Information Booths** *(open year-round daily 8am–midnight)* are located on the upper and lower levels of all terminals. Computerized kiosks in baggage-claim areas, adjacent to the booths, provide information at all times. **Restaurants** are located on the upper levels of all terminals. Smoking is prohibited in the airport except in designated **smoking rooms**—located on the upper level of the North Terminal near Gates 64 and 80, in the South Terminal near Gate 21 and across from the Delta ticket counter, and on the lower level of the International Terminal near baggage claim. A **medical clinic** also is located on the lower level of the International Terminal *(open 24hrs daily)*. Most public transportation departs from the lower level of each terminal; for information call the **Ground Transportation Hotline** ☎ 800-736-2008 *(weekdays 7:30am–5pm)* or access the airport's website *(above)*. A $2.4 billion expansion is now proceeding; under construction are a new international terminal, a BART station (both by 2000) and an intra-airport rail-transit system *(by late 2001)*.

Taxis – Taxis depart near the yellow columns outside all terminals on the lower-level center island. Taxi service to downtown San Francisco takes approximately 20-30min and costs between $21 and $34.

Shuttles – ☎ *510-893-7665 or 800-736-2008.* Several companies offer transport between SFO and hotels in downtown San Francisco and surrounding areas. Shuttles depart near the center island outside all terminals on the upper level *(curbside service from airport 8am–midnight, $10-$14)*. Pre-arranged shuttle service departs from the lower level, courtyards 2 and 3 *(24hrs daily by reservation only, $9–$21)*.

Public Transit – **SamTrans, CalTrain-SFO Shuttle** *(free)* and **BART-SFO Express** depart from the upper-level roadway at the International and North Terminals. Follow "Public Transit" signs to bus stops, where schedules and fares are posted. Information may also be accessed at the **Airport Information Booths** or computerized kiosks located next to the booths in baggage-claim areas.

Rental Cars – *p 226.* Rental-car agency service counters are located on the lower level of each terminal. Conduct all business in the terminal before boarding shuttles for transport to rental car lots.

Oakland International Airport (OAK) – *http://oaklandairport.com* ☎ *510-577-4000. 7.5mi south of downtown Oakland; 17mi southeast of downtown San Francisco, allow 1hr transit time.* This smaller, easy-to-navigate airport handles both domestic and international flights. Information booths are located near main entrances *(open daily 8am–8pm)*.

Taxis and Shuttles – Taxi stands are located outside Terminals 1 and 2. Service to downtown San Francisco 35–40min, $40–$45; to downtown Oakland 15–20min, $22. Shuttles to hotels and to the surrounding area depart from the traffic island outside each terminal. Fares and transit time vary according to destination. Companies offering service to San Francisco include **A-1 Shuttle Services** *(☎ 925-676-0565)*, **Air-Transit Shuttle** *(☎ 510-568-3434)*, **BayPorter Express** *(☎ 415-467-1800)*, **RBJ Airporter** *(☎ 510-595-3000)* and **Super Shuttle** *(☎ 510-268-8700)*. Many companies require advance reservations.

Public Transit – **BART** *(p 225)* offers service from OAK to San Francisco and East Bay stations. Shuttle to Coliseum Station departs in front of Terminals 1 and 2. For information ☎ 510-465-2278. Local bus service is provided by **AC Transit** *(☎ 510-817-1717)* Line 58. Buses connect with BART and mainline bus routes.

Rental Cars – *p 226.* Service counters are located in each terminal near the baggage claim area. Rental cars are located in front of the terminals.

BY TRAIN

The **Amtrak** rail network offers a relaxing alternative for the traveler with time to spare. Advance reservations are recommended to ensure reduced fares and availability of desired accommodations. Passengers can choose from first-class, coach, sleeping cars and glass-domed cars allowing a panoramic view. Fares are comparable to air travel. Major long-distance routes to the Bay Area are the *California Zephyr* from Chicago via Denver and Salt Lake City (49hrs) and the *Coast Starlight* from Los Angeles (11hrs). Short-distance routes include the *Capitols* via Sacramento or San Jose and the *San Joaquins* via Bakerfield. The nearest **Amtrak station** to San Francisco is located across the bay at 5885 Landregan St. in Emeryville; a shuttle bus transports passengers from the station to four locations in San Francisco: the Ferry Building, Hyatt Embarcadero, Pier 39 and San Francisco Centre *(one-way 20min; free)*. Travelers from Canada should inquire with their local travel agents about Amtrak/VIARail connections. **All-Aboard Pass** allows up to 45 days travel nationwide (limited to three stops). **USA**

RailPass (not available to US or Canadian citizens or legal residents) offers unlimited travel within Amtrak-designated regions at discounted rates; 15- and 30-day passes are available. Schedule and route information: www.amtrak.com ☎ 800-872-7245 (toll-free in North America only; outside North America, contact your local travel agent).
CalTrain offers service between San Francisco and San Jose. Schedule and route information: ☎ 415-495-4546.

BY BUS

Greyhound provides access to San Francisco at a leisurely pace. Fares are generally lower than other forms of public transportation. **Ameripass** allows unlimited travel for 7, 15, 30 or 60 days. Some travelers may find long-distance bus travel uncomfortable due to the lack of sleeping accommodations. Advance reservations suggested. Schedule and route information: www.greyhound.com; ☎ 415-495-6789 or 800-231-2222.

BY CAR

Map p 4. San Francisco is easily accessible by major interstate highways. US-101 and I-280 enter the city from the south. I-80 crosses the Bay Bridge from Berkeley and Oakland ($1 bridge toll for westbound traffic only). US-101 provides access to San Francisco from the north, across the Golden Gate Bridge into San Francisco ($3 bridge toll for southbound traffic only).

International Visitors

PLANNING THE TRIP

In addition to the agencies listed on p 220, visitors from outside the US can contact the San Francisco Convention & Visitors Bureau's foreign language information lines (**Français** ☎ 415-391-2003; **Deutsch** ☎ 415-391-2004; **Español** ☎ 415-391-2122; **Japanese** ☎ 415-391-2101) or the US embassy in their country.

Foreign Consulates – In San Francisco, international visitors can contact the following consulates of their country of residence.

COUNTRY	Address	☎
Australia	1 Bush St.	415-362-6160
China	1450 Laguna St.	415-674-2900
France	540 Bush St.	415-397-4330
Germany	1960 Jackson St.	415-775-1061
Japan	50 Fremont St., 23rd Floor	415-777-3533
Mexico	870 Market St., Suite 528	415-392-5554
United Kingdom	1 Sansome St., Suite 850	415-981-3030

Entry Requirements – Citizens of countries participating in the Visa Waiver Pilot Program (VWPP) are not required to obtain a visa to enter the US for visits of fewer than 90 days. For more information contact the US consulate in your country of residence. Citizens of non-participating countries must have a visitor's visa. Upon entry, nonresident foreign visitors must present a valid passport and round-trip transportation ticket. Canadian citizens are not required to present a passport or visa to enter the US, although identification and proof of citizenship may be requested (a passport or Canadian birth certificate and photo identification are usually acceptable). Naturalized Canadian citizens should carry their citizenship papers. Inoculations are not generally required, but check with the US embassy or consulate before departing.

Health Insurance – The United States does not have a national health program. Before departing, visitors from abroad should check with their insurance company to determine if their medical insurance covers doctors' visits, medication and hospitalization in the US. Prescription drugs should be properly identified, and accompanied by a copy of the prescription.

US Customs – All articles brought into the US must be declared at the time of entry. **Prohibited items**: plant material; firearms and ammunition (if not intended for sporting purposes); meat or poultry products. For further information contact the US embassy or consulate before departing, or the US Customs Service, San Francisco Port Director, 555 Battery Street, San Francisco CA 94111 ☎ 415-782-9210 *(open Mon–Fri 8am–4:30pm)*.

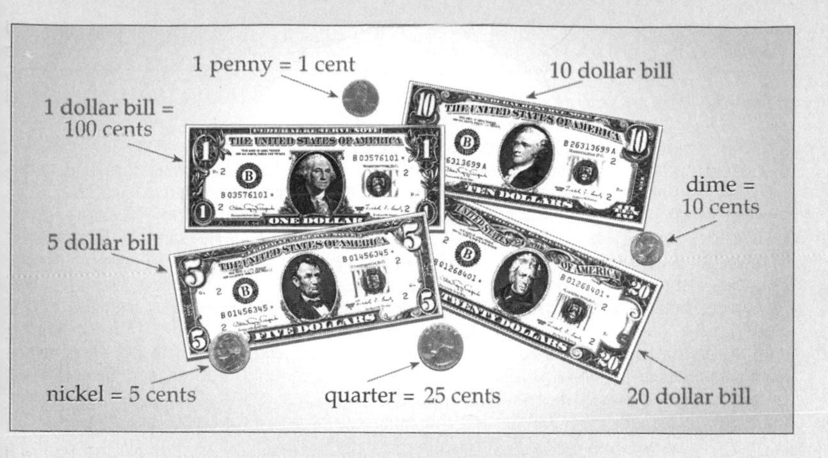

MONEY

Currency Exchange – Many banks located in the downtown area offer foreign currency exchange. Visitors can also exchange currency at San Francisco International Airport on the upper and lower levels of the International Terminal and in Area F, North Terminal.

Credit Cards and Travelers Checks – *p 229.*

Taxes and Tipping – *p 229.* Prices displayed or quoted in the US do not generally include **sales tax** (8.5% in San Francisco). Sales tax is not reimbursable. It is customary to give a small gift of money (a **tip**) for services rendered, to waiters, porters, chamber maids and cab drivers.

GENERAL INFORMATION

Driving in the US – *p 225.* Visitors bearing valid driver's licenses issued by their country of residence are not required to obtain an International Driver's License to drive in the US. Drivers must carry vehicle registration and/or rental contract, and proof of automobile insurance at all times. Rental cars *(p 226)* in the US are usually equipped with automatic transmission, and rental rates tend to be lower than those overseas. Gasoline is sold by the gallon (1 gal=3.8 liters) and is cheaper than in other countries. Most self-service gas stations do not offer car repair, although many sell standard maintenance items. Road regulations in the US require that vehicles be driven on the right-hand side of the road. Distances are posted in miles (1mi=1.6km).

Electricity – Voltage in the US is 120 volts AC, 60 Hz. Foreign-made appliances may need AC adapters (available at specialty travel and electronics stores) and North American flat-blade plugs.

Mail – *p 229.*

Temperature and Measurement – In the US temperatures are measured in degrees Fahrenheit and measurements are expressed according to the US Customary System of weights and measures.

Equivalents

Degrees Fahrenheit	95°	86°	77°	68°	59°	50°	41°	32°	23°	14°
Degrees Celsius	35°	30°	25°	20°	15°	10°	5°	0°	-5°	-10°

1 inch = 2.54 centimeters	1 foot = 30.48 centimeters
1 mile = 1.609 kilometers	1 pound = 0.454 kilograms
1 quart = 0.946 liters	1 gallon = 3.785 liters

Telephone – Instructions for using public telephones are listed on or near the phone. The cost for a local call from a pay phone is 35¢ (any combination of quarters, nickels or dimes). Some public telephones accept credit cards, and all will accept long-distance calling cards. Most hotels add surcharges for telephone calls. Unless otherwise indicated, most telephone numbers listed in this guide that start with "800", "888" or "877" are toll-free in the US only.

Planning a trip in the western United States?
Don't forget to take along the ***Michelin Road Map (No. 493)***

Getting Around San Francisco

PUBLIC TRANSPORTATION

The San Francisco Municipal Railway (Muni) *(below)* operates an extensive network of transportation lines using diesel and electric buses, light-rail streetcars and cable cars. Bus service to other areas is provided by **Golden Gate Transit** *(☎ 415-923-2000)*, serving Marin, Contra Costa and Sonoma Counties; **SamTrans** *(Mon–Fri 6am–10pm, weekends 8am–8pm, holidays 8am–3pm ☎ 650-508-6455)*, serving San Mateo County; and **AC Transit** *(☎ 510-817-1717)*, serving Alameda and Contra Costa Counties. All arrivals/departures in San Francisco occur at the Transbay Terminal. The Bay Area Rapid Transit (BART) *(p 225)* commuter rail line links San Francisco with cities in the East Bay including Oakland and Berkeley. **CalTrain** *(☎ 415-495-4546)* commuter rail service runs between San Francisco and San Jose. The **Bay Area Traveler Information System** provides information on traffic conditions, routes and fares for all transportation systems in the San Francisco Bay Area *(☎ 415-817-1717)*. Transit Information for all agencies serving the nine-county San Francisco Bay area may be accessed online at www.transitinfo.org.

San Francisco Municipal Railway (Muni)

949 Presidio Ave., Room 238, San Francisco CA 94115; ☎ 415-673-6864. System maps *($2)* are sold at newsstands, map shops, some bookstores and the Muni main office *(during the summer tourist season, route maps may be difficult to find and may be purchased by mail, $2.50)*. System timetables are available from the Muni main office. In this guide, recommended transit lines are indicated with the MUNI symbol.

Buses – Muni buses generally operate daily 5:30am–12:30am, every 4-20min; some routes on major corridors run 24hrs/day (**owl service** designates late-night schedule). Route number, name and destination are indicated on the front of the bus. Buses with the route name in black-and-white make all stops; green-and-white make limited stops, and red-and-white provide express service to destination only. Pickup points are recognizable by covered shelters and Muni signs (route numbers and names are clearly marked). Route maps are posted in bus shelters. More than half of the routes are accessible to riders with disabilities, and Muni is diligently expanding this service *(Muni Accessible Services ☎ 415-923-6142)*.

Metro Streetcars – Muni's five-line light-rail system runs underground below Market Street from The Embarcadero, and surfaces to provide street-level transportation along The Embarcadero, eastern bayshore and outlying neighborhoods. The J-Church, K-Ingleside and M-Oceanview lines operate daily 5:30am-12:30am. The L-Taraval and N-Judah lines operate 24hrs/day (buses provide owl service). All lines run every 5-15 minutes weekdays and every 10-20 minutes evenings and weekends.

Historic Streetcars – *p 54.*

Cable cars – *p 59.* As San Francisco's whimsical symbols, cable cars provide access to many attractions, including Chinatown and Fisherman's Wharf. Three lines operate daily 6am-12:30am, every 5-15min. The **Powell-Hyde** (PH) and **Powell-Mason** (PM) lines zigzag from Powell and Market Streets in the Union Square Area over Nob Hill to Fisherman's Wharf. The **California** (C) line runs along California Street through Chinatown from Market Street to Van Ness Avenue. Brown-and-white signs along the route indicate stops. Cable cars run in the middle of the streets, between the car lanes. Wait until the cable car comes to a complete stop before boarding or disembarking (on either side of the car). Watch out for oncoming traffic.

© LLEWELLYN

Nikolay Zurek/Tony Stone Images

ares – Bus and streetcar fares are $1 (exact fare required), cable cars $2 (change iven). Discounted fares available for children, senior citizens and disabled persons. ransfers *(free)*, valid for buses and streetcars only and good for two changes, are ssued when fare is paid. The Muni Passport allows unlimited travel on all systems for ne day *($6)*, three days *($10)* and seven days *($15)*. They also entitle holders to iscounts at many attractions. Muni Passports are sold at the Visitor Information enter *(p 230)*, Tix Bay Area *(p 71)* and Muni main office.

ay Area Rapid Transit (BART)

00 Madison St., Oakland CA 94607-2688; ☎ 510-464-6000. This fast, easy, comnuter rail line links San Francisco with cities in the East Bay including Oakland and erkeley. BART runs Mon–Fri 4am–1:30am, Sat 6am–1:30am and Sun 8am–1:30am. ree route maps and schedules are available at BART stations. Tickets are sold from nachines in each station; not all machines provide change. Fare is determined by desination; discounted fares available for children, senior citizens and disabled persons. irection of trains is indicated on video monitors above boarding platforms. All lines re accessible to riders with disabilities. In this guide, recommended stations are indiated with the symbol.

erries *p 231*

axis

ll San Francisco taxicab companies share the same rate schedule: $1.70 for the first nile and $1.80 for each additional mile. Taxis may not be readily available; it's best o call for a pickup. There are no extra fees for baggage handling or for assisting pasengers with physical disabilities. The major cab companies in San Francisco are **Yellow ab** ☎ 415-626-2345, **Pacific** ☎ 415-776-7755 and **National** ☎ 415-648-4444 (others nay be found in the Yellow Pages telephone directory).

RIVING IN SAN FRANCISCO

an Francisco Road Conditions: ☎ 415-557-3755. Given the efficiency of the public transortation system, and the ease with which many sights can by reached on foot, a car not necessary in San Francisco. However, a car is recommended for visiting other reas such as Marin County or the Wine Country. Keep in mind that roads are often ongested, public parking lots expensive and street parking difficult to find. In addiion, street parking requires strict attention to posted curb colors and correctly curbed res *(see "Parking" information below)*. **Rush hours**, the peak transit times for business ommuters, occur weekdays 7:30am–9am and 4pm–6pm. Visitors are encouraged to void driving during these times.

oad Regulations – The maximum **speed limit** on major expressways is 65mph in rural reas and 55mph in and around cities. Speed limits within the city range from 25mph residential areas to 35mph on major streets. Use of **seat belts** is mandatory for driver nd passengers. Child safety seats are required for children under 4 years old or weighg less than 40 pounds (seats available from most rental car agencies). Drivers must lways yield the **right of way** to cable cars and pedestrians.

Parking – When parking on a hill, drivers must block front wheels against the curb (facing downhill turn wheels *toward* curb, facing uphill turn wheels *away* from curb); use of parking brake is mandatory. Restricted parking is indicated by the color of curb: **red** (no standing or parking), **yellow** or **black** (loading zone), **white** (limited to 5min), **green** (limited to 10-30 min), **blue** (reserved for the disabled). Neighborhood parking is by permit only in many areas; check street signs carefully. Parking is prohibited during posted street-cleaning times.

Car Rental

Major rental-car agencies maintain locations downtown as well as at both San Francisco and Oakland airports. Most agencies will rent only to persons at least 25 years old, although some will rent to younger drivers for a daily surcharge. A major credit card and valid driver's license are required for rental (some agencies also require proof of insurance). The average daily rate for a car for 5–7 days ranges from $30 to $40. Car rental tax is 8.5%.

Rental Company	Reservations ☎
Dollar	415-771-5301
Alamo	800-327-9633
Avis	800-331-1212
Budget	800-527-0700
Dollar	800-421-6868
Enterprise	800-325-8007
Hertz	800-654-3131
National	800-227-7368
Thrifty	800-331-4200

(toll-free numbers may not be accessible outside of North America)

Accommodations

San Francisco offers a wide range of accommodations, from elegant hotels ($160–$300/night) to moderately priced motels ($50/night and up). The majority of hotels are clustered around the Union Square Area. Rates tend to be higher at Nob Hill, Financial District and Fisherman's Wharf establishments. Many motels can be found along Lombard Street in the Marina District. Amenities usually include television, restaurant and smoking/non-smoking rooms. The more elegant hotels also offer workout facilities, room service and valet service. Downtown hotels normally charge a substantial daily fee for parking; all room rates are subject to a 14 percent city hotel tax. Breakfast is not usually included. A similar variety of accommodations is available in the East Bay. For hotel listings, check the *San Francisco Lodging Guide*, available *($. with The San Francisco Book)* from the San Francisco Convention and Visitors Bureau *(p 220)* or consult the brief list below.

Hotels/Motels – Perhaps more than any other American city, San Francisco is known for its proliferation of small, often independently owned "boutique" hotels. These small luxury inns reflect the historic flavor of the city in ways that large, modern lodging cannot. Two local hotel groups that enjoy pairing their properties with personalities are the **Kimpton Group** *(222 Kearny St., Suite 200, San Francisco, CA 94108; ☎ 415-397-5572)* and **Joie de Vivre Hotels** *(567 Sutter St., San Francisco, CA 94102; ☎ 415-835-0300)*.

In addition, major national hotel chains are widely represented in the San Francisco Bay Area. Locations include:

Best Western	800-528-1234
Clarion, Comfort Inn & Quality Inn	800-228-5150
Hilton	800-445-8667
Holiday Inn	800-465-4329
Hyatt	800-233-1234
ITT Sheraton	800-325-353
Marriott	800-228-929
Ramada	800-228-282
Ritz-Carlton	800-241-333
Westin	800-228-300

We welcome corrections and suggestions that may assist us in preparing the next edition. Please send us your comments:

Michelin Travel Publications
Editorial Department
P. O. Box 19001
Greenville, SC 29602-9001

Reservation Services

Accommodations Express 800-444-7666
www.accommodationsexpress.com

California Reservations 800-576-0003
www.globalstore.com.au/cal-res.htm

Hotel Reservation Network 800-964-6835
www.hoteldiscount.com

SF Trips 800-738-7477
www.joiedevivre-sf.com

San Francisco Reservations 800-737-2060
www.hotelres.com

Central Reservation Service 800-548-3311
www.reservation-services.com

SF Convention & Visitors Bureau Leisure Reservation Service 888-782-9673
www.sfvisitor.org

(toll-free numbers may not be accessible outside of North America)

Bed and Breakfasts – Many privately owned historic homes located outside the downtown area are operated as B&Bs ($80–$150/day). Continental breakfast is customarily included. Private baths are not always available, and smoking indoors is not usually allowed. The following reservation services represent different properties throughout San Francisco and the Bay Area: **Bed & Breakfast San Francisco**, PO Box 420009, San Francisco CA 94142 ☎ 415-479-1913 or 800-452-8249; **American Property Exchange**, 2800 Van Ness Ave., San Francisco CA 94109 ☎ 415-447-2040 or 800-747-7784; **The Independent Innkeepers Association**, PO Box 150, Marshall, MI 49068; www.innbook.com ☎ 616-789-0393 or ☎ 800-344-5244.

Hostels and Apartments – A no-frills, economical option, **hostels** average $14–$25/night. Amenities include community living room, showers, laundry facilities, full-service kitchen and dining room, dormitory-style and private rooms (guests must bring their own towels). **Hostelling International** operates two facilities in San Francisco: Union Square Youth Hostel (downtown), 312 Mason St., San Francisco CA 94102 ☎ 415-788-5604; and Fisherman's Wharf Youth Hostel (Fort Mason), Building 240, Fort Mason, San Francisco CA 94123; www.hiayh.org ☎ 415-771-7277. **European Guest House** (member of American Association of International Hostels) also offers accommodations in the city at 761 Minna St., San Francisco CA 94103 ☎ 415-861-6634. Furnished apartment rentals (starting at $100/day) are available through **American Property Exchange** *(above)*.

Where to Stay in San Francisco

The accommodations listed below have been chosen for their location, character or value for money. Their appearance here does not constitute a recommendation. Lodgings are classified in five approximate price categories: **Ultra-Deluxe** (over $200), **Deluxe** ($150-$200), **Moderate** ($100-$150), **Budget** ($50-$100) and **Penny-Pincher** (under $50).

ULTRA-DELUXE ACCOMMODATIONS

Campton Place Hotel *(340 Stockton St., Union Square; ☎ 415-781-5555)*, a centrally located, mid-size inn renowned for service.

Dockside Boat & Bed *(Pier 39, Fisherman's Wharf; ☎ 415-392-5526)*, posh private yachts at the heart of the waterfront.

Fairmont Hotel & Tower *(950 Mason St., Nob Hill; ☎ 415-772-5000)*, grand hotel with rich history that includes 1906 earthquake and creation of the United Nations.

Mandarin Oriental San Francisco *(222 Sansome St., Financial District; ☎ 415-885-0999)*, beautifully decorated 38th- to 48th-story rooms atop 345 California Center.

Sheraton Palace Hotel *(2 New Montgomery St., Financial District; ☎ 415-392-8600)*, still regal after 124 years, located on Market Street at the edge of SoMa.

Westin St. Francis *(335 Powell St., Union Square; ☎ 415-397-7000)*, world-class 19th-century hotel whose rooms have a view from a 1972 tower.

DELUXE ACCOMMODATIONS

Hotel Diva *(440 Geary St., Union Square Area; ☎ 415-885-0200)*, polished Euro-tech hotel popular with the film-industry set.

Hotel Monaco *(501 Geary St., Union Square Area; ☎ 415-292-0100)*, Theater District boutique hotel, a remodeled 1910 Beaux Arts classic.

Hyatt Regency San Francisco *(5 Embarcadero Center, Financial District; ☎ 415-788-1234)*, architecturally acclaimed hotel with 17-story central atrium at foot of Market Street.

Prescott Hotel *(545 Post St., Union Square Area; ☎ 415-563-0303)*, elegant boutique hotel noted for handsome rooms and personal service.

Radisson Miyako Hotel *(1625 Post St., Japan Center; ☎ 415-922-3200)*, where visitors can request to sleep upon futons on tatami-matted floors.

Hotel Rex *(562 Sutter St., Union Square Area; ☎ 415-433-4434)*, historic boutique hotel with a literary theme.

MODERATE ACCOMMODATIONS

Hotel Boheme *(444 Columbus Ave., North Beach; ☎ 415-433-9111)*, quaint boutique hotel at the foot of Telegraph Hill.

Chancellor Hotel *(433 Powell St., Union Square; ☎ 415-362-2004)*, stately inn on the Powell-Hyde and Powell-Mason cable car lines.

Hotel Juliana *(590 Bush St., Union Square Area; ☎ 415-392-2540)*, brightly decorated boutique hotel at the foot of Nob Hill.

The Inn at the Opera *(333 Fulton St., Civic Center; ☎ 415-863-8400)*, elegant small hotel popular among musicians and stage performers.

The Maxwell *(386 Geary St., Union Square Area; ☎ 415-986-2000)*, chic boutique hotel adjacent to Theater District.

Phoenix Hotel *(601 Eddy St., Tenderloin; ☎ 415-776-1380)*, hippest hotel in town and a rockers' paradise with its swimming pool fringed by palm trees.

Hotel Triton *(342 Grant Ave. Union Square Area; ☎ 415-394-0500)*, colorful avant-garde boutique hotel at Chinatown Gate.

BUDGET ACCOMMODATIONS

Andrews Hotel *(624 Post St., Union Square Area; ☎ 415-563-6877)*, pleasant, classic Victorian inn near Theater District.

Hotel Beresford *(635 Sutter St., Union Square Area; ☎ 415-673-9900)*, basic small hotel that attracts British visitors with its English pub.

Commodore Hotel *(825 Sutter St., Union Square Area; ☎ 415-923-6800)*, refurbished building with hip design and popular avant-garde bar.

Grant Plaza *(465 Grant Ave., Chinatown; ☎ 415-434-3883)*, clean and bright bargain property, a good value.

"Minshuku" Suzume no Oyado *(8122 Geary Blvd., Richmond District; ☎ 415-752-3330)*, traditional Japanese-style bed-and-breakfast where dinner is also available.

24 Henry Guesthouse *(24 Henry St., Castro District; ☎ 415-864-5686)*, gay-oriented bed-and-breakfast in a handsome 19C Victorian home.

PENNY-PINCHER ACCOMMODATIONS

Central YMCA *(220 Golden Gate Ave., Tenderloin; ☎ 415-885-0460)*, offering private rooms with shared baths, plus light breakfast and swimming pool, near United Nations Plaza.

Green Tortoise Guest House *(494 Broadway, North Beach; ☎ 415-834-1000)*, pension with dorms and private rooms, operated by a long-distance budget bus service.

Hostel at Union Square *(312 Mason St., Union Square Area; ☎ 415-788-5604)*, five floors of dormitory rooms hard by the Theater District.

San Francisco International Hostel *(Bldg. 240, Fort Mason; ☎ 415-771-7277)*, dorm rooms with bayfront views in Golden Gate National Recreation Area.

General Information

Business Hours – Most businesses operate Monday to Friday 8am–5:30pm. Banks are usually open Monday to Friday 9am–3pm (some may have extended or Saturday hours). Department stores and shopping centers operate Monday to Saturday 9:30am–8pm, Sunday 11am–6pm; many extend their hours between Thanksgiving and Christmas. Smaller shops and stores (except those in Chinatown) are closed on Sunday.

Time Zone – San Francisco is on Pacific Standard Time (PST), 3 hours behind Eastern Standard Time (EST) and 8 hours behind Greenwich Mean Time (GMT). Daylight Savings Time (clocks advanced 1 hour) is in effect for most of the US from the first Sunday in April until the last Sunday in October.

Major Holidays – Most banks and government offices in the San Francisco area are closed on the following legal holidays *(many retail stores and restaurants remain open on days indicated with*)*:

New Year's Day	January 1
Martin Luther King, Jr.'s Birthday*	3rd Monday in January
Presidents' Day*	3rd Monday in February
Memorial Day*	Last Monday in May or May 30
Independence Day*	July 4
Labor Day*	1st Monday in September
Columbus Day*	2nd Monday in October
Veterans Day*	November 10 or 11
Thanksgiving Day	4th Thursday in November
Christmas Day	December 25

Money – Most banks are members of the network of Automatic Teller Machines (ATMs), which allows visitors from around the world to withdraw cash using bank cards and major credit cards 24hrs a day. ATMs can usually be found in banks, airports, grocery stores and shopping malls. Networks (Cirrus, Honor, Plus) serviced by the ATM are indicated on the machine. To inquire about ATM service, locations and transaction fees, contact your local bank, Cirrus ☎ 800-424-7787 or Plus ☎ 800-843-7587. For cash transfers, **Western Union** has agents throughout the Bay Area: www.westernunion.com ☎ 800-325-6000. Banks, most stores, restaurants and hotels accept **travelers checks** with picture identification. In San Francisco, **American Express Company Travel Service** offices are located at 560 California St., 455 Market St., 124 Geary St. and 333 Jefferson St. ☎ 415-536-2600. To report a lost or stolen **credit card**: American Express ☎ 800-528-4800; Diners Club ☎ 800-234-6377; MasterCard ☎ 800-627-8372; Visa ☎ 800-336-8472.

Taxes and Tipping – In San Francisco, the sales tax is 8.5%; cold food items are exempt. The hotel occupancy tax is 14% (not included in quoted hotel rates). Tax percentages in other areas (including Berkeley, Oakland, Marin County and the Wine Country) may vary. In restaurants, it is customary to tip the server 15-20% of the bill. At hotels, porters should be tipped $1 per suitcase and hotel maids $1 per day of occupancy. Taxi drivers are usually tipped 15% of the fare.

Liquor Law – The legal minimum age for purchase and consumption of alcoholic beverages is 21. Proof of age is normally required. Most bars stay open until 2am. Almost all packaged-goods stores sell beer, wine and liquor; legal hours of sale are 6am–2am.

TELEPHONE

Area Codes	☎
San Francisco (including Marin County)	415
Peninsula cities (south of Daly City, including San Mateo County)	650
East Bay (including Berkeley and Oakland)	510
East Bay (including Contra Costa County)	925
Wine Country	707

Important Numbers		☎
Police/Ambulance/Fire (emergency, *24hrs*)		**911**
Police (non-emergency, *24hrs*)		415-553-0123
Physician Referrals *(Mon–Fri 9am–5pm)*		415-353-6566
Dental Referrals *(24hrs)*		415-421-1435
Hotel Docs *(24hrs)*		800-468-3537
24hr Pharmacy		
Walgreens	3201 Divisadero St. (Marina District)	415-931-6417
	498 Castro St. (Castro District)	415-861-3136
	25 Point Lobos Ave. (Richmond District)	415-386-0736
Time		415-767-8900
Weather		415-936-1212

TELEVISION & RADIO

Major TV Networks

ABC	Channel 7	**FOX**	Channel 2
CBS	Channel 5	**NBC**	Channel 4
CNN	Channel 3	**PBS**	Channel 9

Major Radio Stations

88.5 FM	NPR	**102.1** FM	Classical	**680** AM	Sports/talk
93.3 FM	Country	**103.7** FM	Jazz	**810** AM	News/talk
97.3 FM	Rock	**104.5** FM	Alternative	**1550** AM	News/talk

Newspapers and Magazines – San Francisco's two main daily newspapers are the *San Francisco Chronicle* (morning) and the *San Francisco Examiner* (afternoon). The Sunday edition, the *Chronicle-Examiner* is published jointly and features an extensive arts & entertainment supplement. Two weekly alternative papers, *The San Francisco Bay Guardian* and the *SF Weekly*, both published on Wednesday, offer different perspectives of the city as well as diverse and comprehensive entertainment sections. These free publications are available in newspaper boxes and cafes. the *Bay Area Reporter* and the *San Francisco Bay Times* cater to the gay community. In addition, many neighborhood groups publish papers featuring upcoming events and social happenings in their areas.

Mail – Post offices located throughout the San Francisco Bay Area operate Monday–Friday 8am–5pm (some have extended weekday and Saturday hours). First-class rates within the US: letter 32¢ (1oz), postcard 20¢. Overseas: letter 60¢ (1/2oz), postcard 50¢. Letters and small packages can be mailed from most hotels. Stamps and packing material may be purchased at many convenience and drugstores, and at post offices. Businesses offering postal and express shipping services are located throughout the city *(see Yellow Pages of phone directory under Mailing Services)*. Postal Service Information Line *(Mon–Fri 8am–6pm)*: ☎ 800-725-2161.

Fax Services – Many hotels, and businesses that offer copying or mailing services, will send or receive faxes for a per-page fee.

Safety Tips – San Francisco is considered a relatively safe city, but visitors should heed the following common-sense tips to ensure a safe and enjoyable visit:

- Avoid carrying large sums of money, and don't let strangers see how much money you are carrying.
- Keep a firm hold of purses and knapsacks, carry your wallet in your front pocket, and avoid wearing expensive jewelry.
- Stay awake when riding on public transportation, and keep packages close by. Muni and BART vehicles are equipped with devices that enable riders to notify personnel of emergencies.
- Always park your car in a well-lit area. Close windows, lock doors and place valuables in the trunk.
- Exercise caution when visiting or traveling through the **Tenderloin** (roughly bounded by Golden Gate Ave., Van Ness Ave., O'Farrell St. and Mason St.), the **Western Addition** (the blocks immediately west of Civic Center and south of Japantown); and the **Mission District** (the blocks east of Valencia St. and north of 16th St.).

Earthquake Precautions – Although severe earthquakes are infrequent, they are also unpredictable, and earthquake preparedness is a fact of life in the San Francisco Bay Area. If an earthquake strikes when you are **outside**, move to an open area away from trees, buildings or power lines. If you are in a **vehicle**, decrease speed, pull to the side of the road and stop. Do not park on or under bridges; sit on the floor of the vehicle if possible. If you are in a **building**, stand within a doorway or sit under a sturdy table. Stay away from windows and outside walls. Remain in a safe place until shaking stops, and be prepared for aftershocks. If possible, listen to the radio or TV for advisories.

Sightseeing

VISITOR INFORMATION

Two free publications, *Key This Week* and *Where San Francisco*, offer information on events, attractions, shopping and dining. Both are available at hotels and visitor information kiosks. In addition, the **San Francisco Convention and Visitors Bureau** publishes *The San Francisco Book*. The SFCVB **Information Center** is located on the lower level of Hallidie Plaza at Market & Powell Sts. *(open year-round Mon–Fri 9am–5:30pm, Sat 9am–3pm, Sun 10am–2pm; ☎ 415-391-2000)*. The helpful, multilingual staff is well equipped to assist visitors. In addition, the center stocks brochures for area restaurants, hotels, clubs and attractions, and sells Muni maps and passes *(p 224)*. Access the San Francisco Convention and Visitors Bureau's website at: www.sfvisitor.org.

TOURS

Map pp 218-219. While in the San Francisco Bay Area, visitors may choose from a wide variety of guided tours. A selection appears below.

City and Bay Area Tours – Several tour operators offer overviews of the main attractions of San Francisco and the surrounding Bay Area. Conveyance is by mid-size coach. Packages may include a bay cruise or an excursion to Muir Woods National Monument, Sausalito, the Wine Country or other Bay Area attractions. Hotel pickup and foreign-language tours available.
Gray Line Deluxe City Tour: year-round daily 9am, 10am, 11am, 1:30pm, 2:30pm (May-Sept 3:30); 3hrs 30min; reservations required; $28; www.graylinesanfrancisco.com ☎ 415-558-7373.
Great Pacific Tour Co.: year-round daily 9am, 11am & 2pm (Jul–Aug 4pm); 3hrs 30min; reservations required; $29; ☎ 415-626-4499.
Tower Tours: depart from 77 Jefferson St., year-round daily 8:45, 11am & 2pm; 3hrs 30min; reservations suggested; $29; www.citysearch.com/sfo/towertours ☎ 415-434-8687.
Blue & Gold Fleet (www.blueandgoldfleet.com ☎ 415-773-1188) and **Red & White Fleet** (www.redandwhite.com ☎ 415-447-0597) also book city and Bay Area tours.

Chinatown – *p 36.* Several agencies offer in-depth walking tours examining the history, traditions and cuisine of this fascinating area. Several offer lunch for an additional fee.
All About Chinatown Walking Tours: depart from Jeanette's Travel Services, 812 Clay St.,

year-round daily 10am; 2hrs; reservations required; $25 or $37 (including dim sum luncheon noon–1pm); ♿ ☎ 415-982-8839.

Wok Wiz Chinatown Tours: depart from the Wok Wiz Cooking Center, 654 Commercial St., year-round daily 10am; 3hrs 15min; $25 or $37 (including lunch); reservations required; mim.com/wokwiz ☎ 415-981-8989.

Chinese Heritage Walk: depart from the Chinese Cultural Center, 750 Kearny St., 3rd floor, year-round Sat 2pm; 2hrs; reservations required; $15; (weekday luncheon walks also available, $30); ☎ 415-986-1822.

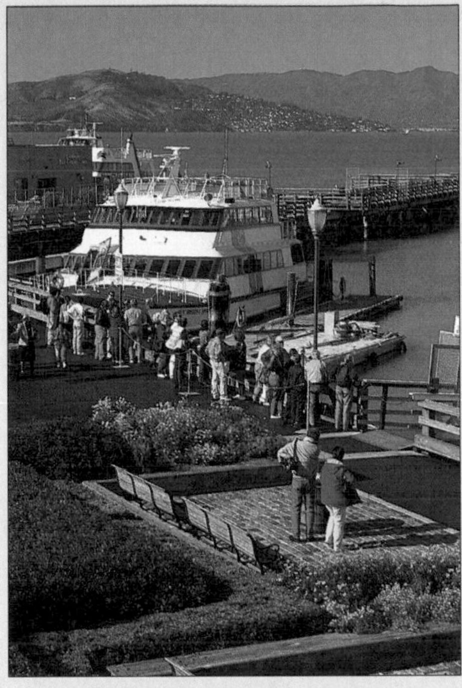

Scenic Cruises at Fisherman's Wharf

© Brenda Tharp

Culinary Tours – The following tours offer visitors the opportunity to explore local history while savoring some of San Francisco's legendary cuisine. **Mangia North Beach** tours depart from the Bank of America at Stockton & Columbus Sts. *(year-round Sat 10am; 4hrs; reservations required; $40; ☎ 415-397-8530)*. **Glorious Food Culinary Walktours** visit North Beach and Chinatown. *(North Beach: year-round daily 9:30am; 3hrs; $30. Chinatown: year-round daily 9:30am; 4hrs; $35. Combined tour: daily 9am; 6hrs; reservations required; $55; ☎ 415-441-5637.)*

Dashiell Hammett Tour – Visit Sam Spade's San Francisco in this popular literary walking tour, departing 100 Larkin St., near the San Francisco Public Library *(May–Aug Sat noon; 4hrs; $10; ☎ 510-287-9540)*.

History and Architecture – The following organizations offer tours exploring San Francisco's rollicking history and architectural highlights. **City Guides of San Francisco**, organized by the San Francisco Public Library, offers more than 20 free walking tours led by volunteer docents; tour quality may vary depending upon the proficiency of the docent *(tours operate year-round daily; no tours Jan 1, Thanksgiving Day, Dec 25; 1-2hrs; call for schedule & departure points www.hooked.net/users/jhum ☎ 415-557-4266)*.

Victorian Home Walk: unveils the city's past through its treasured "painted lady" architecture. Depart from Westin St. Francis hotel lobby, Union Square *(year-round daily 11am; 2hrs 30min; $20; www.victorianwalk.com ☎* 415-252-9485).

Pacific Heights Walking Tour: offered by the Foundation for San Francisco's Architectural Heritage. Depart from Haas-Lilienthal House, 2007 Franklin St. *(year-round Sun 12:30pm; 2hrs; $5; www.sfheritage.org ☎ 415-441-3000)*.

Cruisin' the Castro: highlights the fascinating past and lively present of the Castro District and San Francisco's gay community. Depart from Harvey Milk Plaza, Castro & Market Sts. *(year-round Tue–Sat 10am; 4hrs; reservations required; $35, brunch included; www.webcastro.com/castrotour ☎ 415-550-8110)*.

Mural Tours – *p 140.* Several organizations offer tours of the Mission District's powerful works of public art. **City Guides** *(see above; meets at Precita & Harrison Sts., behind Flynn Elementary School, year-round Sat 11am)*. **Precita Eyes Mural Arts Center** *(depart from 348 Precita Ave., year-round Sat 1:30pm; 1hr 30min; $5; www.precitaeyes.org ☎ 415-285-2287). Note that use of public transportation to this area is not recommended.*

Nightlife Tour – Enjoy a night on the town with **3 Babes and a Bus,** an adventurous tour of four unique San Francisco dance clubs *(depart from New Joe's, 357 Geary St., year-round Fri & Sat nights; reservations required, must be 21 or older; $30 includes cover charges; ☎ 415-552-2582)*.

Scenic Cruises & Ferries

Tours of San Francisco Bay offer panoramic views of the city's skyline, the Golden Gate Bridge, Alcatraz, and the hills of Marin County and the East Bay. Some companies offer evening and dinner/dance cruises. Following are some popular cruises and ferries; contact the individual companies for information on additional tours available.

Blue & Gold Fleet Bay Cruise: frequent departures from Pier 39 *(May–Sept daily 10am–6:45pm; rest of the year 10am–4pm; 1hr; $17; ✕ ♿ 🅿 www.blueandgoldfleet.com ☎ 415-705-5555)*.

Red & White Fleet Golden Gate Bridge Cruise: departs from Pier 43 1/2 *(Memorial Day–early Nov daily 10am–6:15pm; rest of the year daily 10am–5pm; round-trip 1hr; commentary; $16; www.redandwhite.com ☎ 415-447-0597).*
Alameda/Oakland Ferry: offers service between Jack London Square (Oakland), Alameda, Pier 39 and the Ferry Building as well as to Angel Island *(depart May–Sept Mon–Fri 6am–8:55pm, weekends & holidays 9:30am–10:30pm; rest of the year Mon–Fri 6am–8:50pm, weekends & holidays 10am–7:10pm; no service Jan 1, Thanksgiving Day, Dec 25; hours may vary according to destination; 20min one-way; $4.50; www.blueandgoldfleet.com ☎ 510-522-3300 or 415-705-5555).*
Golden Gate Ferry: access to Sausalito and Larkspur *(depart from the Ferry Building in San Francisco year-round Mon–Fri, hours vary according to destination; no service Jan 1, Thanksgiving Day, Dec 25; $2.75–$4.70; 30–45min; www.goldengate.org ☎ 415-923-2000).*

Whale watching – Whale sighting hotline: ☎ 415-474-0488. California gray whales can be seen from December through April along the California coast as they migrate from the Northern Pacific Ocean to Baja California. Sightings are most frequent at Muir Beach Overlook and Point Reyes Lighthouse. Oceanic Society Expeditions offers naturalist-led whale watching **cruises** *(departures from Fort Mason Center, Bldg. E; gray whales late Dec–Apr weekends, 3hrs or 6hrs 30min, $33 or $50, depending on excursion; humpback whales and blue whales Jun–Nov weekends, 8hrs, $65; 2-week advance reservations required, young children not permitted, food & beverages not provided; www.oceanic-society.org ☎ 415-474-3385).*

TIPS FOR SPECIAL VISITORS

Children

Throughout this guide, sights of particular interest to children are indicated with a **Kids** symbol. Many of these attractions offer special children's programs. Most attractions in San Francisco offer discounted admission to visitors under 18 years of age. In addition, many hotels offer family discount packages, and some restaurants provide a children's menu.

Travelers with Disabilities

Throughout this guide, full wheelchair accessibility is indicated in admission information accompanying sight descriptions by a ♿ symbol. All **BART** trains and stations and most **Muni** lines are wheelchair-accessible. The *Muni Access Guide* gives helpful hints for disabled persons using the system *(free from Muni Accessible Services, 949 Presidio Ave., San Francisco CA 94115; ☎ 415-923-6142 TTY 415-923-6366).* Both transit services offer discounts to persons with disabilities; contact telephone numbers listed on pp 224-225 for more information. Disabled visitors can obtain a temporary parking permit from the Department of Motor Vehicles *(1377 Fell St., San Francisco CA 94117; ☎ 415-557-1179).*
A Wheelchair Rider's Guide to San Francisco Bay and Nearby Shorelines provides a wealth of information about many sights in the Bay Area *(free from the California State Coastal Conservancy; ☎ 510-286-1015).*
Disabled travelers using **Amtrak** and **Greyhound** *(pp 221-222)* should contact these companies prior to their trip to make special arrangements and receive useful brochures. For information about travel for individuals or groups, contact the Society for the Advancement of Travel for the Handicapped, 347 5th Ave., Suite 610, New York NY 10016, www.sath.org ☎ 212-447-7284.

Senior Citizens

Most attractions, hotels and restaurants offer discounts to visitors age 62 and older (proof of age may be required). For information regarding events, policies and programs contact the "Senior Citizen Information Line," ☎ 415-626-1033. Additional information can be obtained from the American Association of Retired Persons (AARP), 601 E St. NW, Washington DC 20049 ☎ 202-434-2277.

Entertainment

PERFORMING ARTS

Visitors to the San Francisco Bay Area can pick from among the region's abundant and diverse performing-arts offerings. Nearly 100 live-performance theaters mount a variety of stage productions performed by traveling Broadway companies and respected regional and local groups. Acclaimed dance, symphony and opera companies perform at Civic Center venues. The main theater district is centered just west of Union Square, while stages at Yerba Buena Gardens and Fort Mason Center host a variety of music, film, theater and dance events. Popular rock and alternative music performers play at intimate and large-scale nightclubs as well as at stadiums and arenas throughout the Bay Area. A variety of public readings by both established and up-and-coming authors are held at bookstores, coffeehouses and other locations (check *The San Francisco Bay Guardian* or *SF Weekly* for current listings). *For a detailed listing of events, call the SFCVB's information line (☎ 415-391-2001) or consult the arts and entertainment sections of publications listed on* *p 229.*

Kathleen Mitchell in Balanchine's *Rubles*

Music & Dance

CLASSICAL MUSIC	Venue	Season	☎
Philharmonia Baroque	various locations	Sept–Apr	415-495-7445
Pocket Opera	various locations	Feb–Jun	415-575-1100
San Francisco Contemporary Music Players	Center for the Arts 701 Mission Street	Sept–Apr	415-252-6235
San Francisco Opera	War Memorial Opera House, 301 Van Ness Ave	Sept–Dec	415-864-3330
San Francisco Performances	various locations	Sept–May	415-398-6449
San Francisco Symphony	Davies Symphony Hall 201 Van Ness Ave.	Sept–Jul	415-552-8000

DANCE			
San Francisco Ballet	War Memorial Opera House	Feb–May	415-861-5600
Oakland Ballet	Paramount Theatre 2025 Broadway, Oakland	Sept–Dec	510-452-9288

ROCK/POP		
Cow Palace	Geneva & Santos Sts., Daly City	415-469-6065
Concord Pavilion	2000 Kirker Pass Rd., Concord	925-671-3123

Theaters, Companies and Performances

THEATERS	Address	☎
American Conservatory Theater Company	Geary Theater 415 Geary Blvd.	415-749-2228
Asian American Theatre	1840 Sutter	415-440-5545
Bayfront Theatre	Bldg. B, Fort Mason Center	415-776-8999
Berkeley Repertory Theater	2025 Addison St.	510-845-4700

Brava Theater Center	2789 24th St.	415-826-5773
Cable Car Theater	430 Mason St.	415-956-8497
Climate Theatre	252 Ninth St.	415-978-2345
Center for the Arts Theater	700 Howard St.	415-978-2787
Cowell Theater	Fort Mason Center	415-441-3687
Curran Theatre	445 Geary Blvd.	415-551-2000
Davies Symphony Hall	201 Van Ness Ave.	415-552-8000
Geary Theater	415 Geary Blvd.	415-749-2228
Golden Gate Theatre	1 Taylor St.	415-551-2000
Herbst Theatre	401 Van Ness Ave.	415-392-4400
Josie's Cabaret & Juice Joint	3583 16th St.	415-861-7933
Lorraine Hansberry Theatre	620 Sutter St.	415-474-8800
Magic Theatre	Bldg. D, Fort Mason Center	415-441-8822
New Conservatory Theater	25 Van Ness Ave.	415-861-8972
Paramount Theatre	2025 Broadway St., Oakland	510-465-6400
Stage Door Theatre	420 Mason St.	415-788-9453
Theater Artaud	450 Florida St.	415-621-7797
Theatre on the Square	450 Post St.	415-433-9500
Theatre Rhinoceros	2926 16th St.	415-861-5079
War Memorial Opera House	301 Van Ness Ave.	415-864-3330
Zellerbach Hall	University of California, Berkeley	510-642-9988

LONG-RUNNING PERFORMANCES		
Beach Blanket Babylon	Club Fugazi, 678 Green St.	415-421-4222
Shear Madness	Mason St. Theatre, 340 Mason St.	415-982-5463

THEATER FESTIVALS			
Shakespeare in the Park	Golden Gate Park	Labor Day–Oct	415-831-5500
California Shakespeare Festival	100 Gateway Rd., Orinda	Jun–Oct	510-548-3422
Mountain Theatre	Mount Tamalpais State Park	May–Jun	415-383-1100

Tickets

As some of the more popular events sell out months in advance, it is recommended to buy tickets early. Full-price tickets can be purchased directly from the venue's box office or from one of the brokers listed below; major credit cards are accepted (a service charge of $1-$7 may be added to the ticket price). Ticket brokers sometimes have tickets available when the box office is sold out, but expect to pay a substantial service fee (up to 25%). Hotel concierges may also be able to help secure tickets. **Tix Bay Area** offers half-price tickets for selected events on the day of the show. Purchases must be made in person from the box office in Union Square on Stockton St. between Post and Geary *(cash or travelers checks only, open year-round Tue–Thu 11am–6pm, Fri–Sat 11am–7pm)*, or by phone *(full price advance sale tickets only, VISA and MasterCard accepted; www.theatrebayarea.org ☎ 415-433-7827)*. **Bass Ticketmaster** *(☎ 510-762-2277)* outlets are operated at most locations of Tower Records and The Wherehouse. **City Box Office** offers tickets for classical performances and lectures held at smaller venues *(152 Kearny St., ☎ 415-392-4400)*.

NIGHTLIFE

San Francisco's nightlife is as diverse as its population, and ranges from elegant Nob Hill piano bars to North Beach coffeehouses to clubs offering alternative music and jazz in the Haight-Ashbury or South of Market areas. Consult the arts and entertainment sections of the publications listed on p 229 for detailed listings of events. Some establishments have a cover charge. Some clubs and coffeehouses serve food (menu may be scaled down to light appetizers after 10 or 11pm). Proof of age (21) is required to enter most clubs that serve alcoholic beverages. Nightlife tour: *(p 231)*.

San Francisco Nightclubs

COMEDY	Address	☎
Cobb's Comedy Club	2801 Leavenworth St. (Fisherman's Wharf)	415-928-4320
Finocchio's	506 Broadway (North Beach)	415-982-9388
Punch Line	444 Battery St (Financial Dist.)	415-397-7573

BLUES

Biscuits & Blues	401 Mason St. (Union Sq.)	415-292-2583
Blues	2125 Lombard St. (Marina Dist.)	415-771-2583
Boom Boom Boom	1601 Fillmore St. (Pacific Hts.)	415-673-8053
Eli's Mile High Club	3629 Martin Luther King Way (Oakland)	510-655-6661
Harry Denton's	161 Steuart St. (Embarcadero)	415-882-1333
The Saloon	1232 Grant Ave. (North Beach)	415-989-7666

JAZZ

Bruno's	2389 Mission St. (Mission Dist.)	415-550-7455
Cafe du Nord	2170 Market St. (near Castro Dist.)	415-861-5016
Cypress Club	500 Jackson St. (Jackson Sq.)	415-296-8555
Elbo Room	647 Valencia St. (Mission Dist.)	415-552-7788
Enrico's	504 Broadway (North Beach)	415-982-6223
Jazz at Pearl's	256 Columbus Ave. (North Beach)	415-291-8255
Kimball's East	5800 Shellmound St. (Emeryville/Berkeley)	510-658-2555
Storyville	1751 Fulton St. (Haight-Ashbury)	415-441-1751
Up & Down Club	1151 Folsom St. (SoMa)	415-626-2388
Yoshi's Nitespot	Jack London Square, Embarcadero West (Oakland)	510-238-9200

LATIN

Bahía Cabana	1600 Market St. (Civic Center)	415-626-3306
El Rio	3158 Mission St. (Mission Dist.)	415-282-3325
Sol y Luna	475 Sacramento St. (Financial Dist.)	415-296-8191

ROCK/FOLK

Bottom of the Hill	1233 17th St.(Potrero Hill)	415-621-4455
Fillmore Auditorium	1805 Geary Blvd. (Japantown)	415-346-6000
Freight & Salvage	1111 Addison St. (Berkeley)	510-548-1761
Great American Music Hall	859 O'Farrell St. (Tenderloin)	415-885-0750
Kilowatt	3160 16th St. (Mission Dist.)	415-861-2595
The Last Day Saloon	406 Clement St. (Richmond Dist.)	415-387-6343
Paradise Lounge	1501 Folsom St. (SoMa)	415-861-6906
Slim's	333 11th St.(SoMa)	415-522-0333
The Stork Club	380 12th St. (Oakland)	510-444-6174
The Warfield	982 Market St. (Theater Dist.)	415-775-7722

COCKTAIL DANCING

Coconut Grove	1415 Van Ness Ave.(Polk Gulch)	415-776-1616
Deluxe	1511 Haight St. (Haight-Ashbury)	415-552-6949
Hi-Ball Lounge	473 Broadway (North Beach)	415-397-9464
Julie's Supper Club	1123 Folsom St. (SoMa)	415-861-0707
Plush Room Cabaret	York Hotel, 940 Sutter St. (Union Sq.)	415-885-6800
Starlight Room	Sir Francis Drake Hotel, 450 Powell St. (Union Sq.)	415-395-8595
Tonga Room	Fairmont Hotel, 950 Mason St. (Nob Hill)	415-772-5278
Top of the Mark	Mark Hopkins Hotel, 999 California St. (Nob Hill)	415-616-6968

DANCE CLUBS

DNA Lounge	375 11th St. (SoMa)	415-626-1409
The Endup	401 Sixth St. (SoMa)	415-357-0827
Johnny Love's	1500 Broadway (Polk Gulch)	415-931-6053
Nickie's	460 Haight St. (Haight-Ashbury)	415-621-6508
Sound Factory	525 Harrison St. (SoMa)	415-979-8686
Ten 15 Folsom	1015 Folsom St. (SoMa)	415-431-1200
Townsend	177 Townsend St. (SoMa)	415-974-6020

Restaurants

The list below represents a sample of some of the city's more popular and well-frequented establishments, and does not constitute a recommendation. Most restaurants are open daily and accept major credit cards. The $ symbol under the price category indicates: $ = inexpensive (under $15); $$ = moderate ($15-$30); $$$ = expensive ($30-$50); $$$$ = deluxe (over $50). Prices indicate the average cost of an entree, an appetizer or dessert, and a beverage. *Reservations are highly recommended for $$$ and $$$$ restaurants.*

Where to Dine

SAN FRANCISCO

Castro District

La Méditerranée *(288 Noe St.; ☎ 415-431-7210)*. $. Mediterranean. North African falafel and Greek spanikopita are favorites; the 10-item *meza* offers greatest value.

Ma Tante Sumi *(4243 18th St.; ☎ 415-626-7864)*. $$. Japanese-French. Menu changes seasonally at this East-West eatery, whose chef and decorator deftly match contrasting cultures.

Chinatown

Brandy Ho's Hunan Food *(217 Columbus Ave.; ☎ 415-788-7527; and 450 Broadway; ☎ 415-362-6268)*. $$. Chinese-Hunanese. These popular, neon-lit restaurants are famed for spicy cooking.

Empress of China *(838 Grant Ave.; ☎ 415-434-1345)*. $$$. Chinese. Elegant decor of sixth-floor pavilion focuses around central pagoda.

Four Seas *(731 Grant Ave.; ☎ 415-989-8188)*. $$. Chinese. Wide choice of dim sum is served midday, traditional Chinese banquet foods at night.

House of Nanking *(919 Kearny St.; ☎ 415-421-1429)*. $. Chinese. Throngs queue to savor inventive dishes at loud, tiny, inexpensive hole in the wall.

Civic Center

California Culinary Academy *(625 Polk St.; ☎ 415-771-3500)*. $$$. French. Prix-fixe fare prepared by famous chefs-to-be.

Hayes Street Grill *(324 Hayes St.; ☎ 415-863-5545)*. $$$. Seafood. Fresh grilled fish, soups and salads are specialties of this restaurant near Davies Symphony Hall.

Jardinière *(300 Grove St.; ☎ 415-861-5555)*. $$$$. California. French-inspired cuisine served beneath amber domed skylight in elegant two-story restaurant.

Max's Opera Cafe *(601 Van Ness Ave.; ☎ 415-771-7300)*. $$. American. Highlight of New York-style deli is cast of singing waiters and waitresses.

Millennium *(246 McAllister St.; ☎ 415-487-9800)*. $$. Vegetarian. Gourmet eatery has menu changing weekly and "Full Moon Aphrodisiac" package that includes night at parent Abigail Hotel.

Stars *(555 Golden Gate Ave.; ☎ 415-861-7827)*. $$$. New American. Piano bar-bistro well-known for high-profile clientele and creative menu.

Tommy's Joynt *(1101 Geary Blvd.; ☎ 415-775-4216)*. $. American. Crowded sports bar's patrons love its big sandwiches and buffalo stew.

Zuni Café *(1658 Market St.; ☎ 415-552-2522)*. $$$. Mediterranean. California flavor pervades French and Italian dishes; copper bar and brick oven dominate decor.

Cow Hollow

Betelnut Pejiu Wu *(2030 Union St.; ☎ 415-929-8855)*. $$$. Pan-Asian. Upscale "street food" served in red-lacquered, bamboo-accented "beer house" atmosphere.

Plumpjack Cafe *(3127 Fillmore St.; ☎ 415-563-47055)*. $$. California. Popular Mediterranean-style bistro features intimate stage-set ambience.

Embarcadero

Boulevard *(1 Mission St.; ☎ 415-543-6084)*. $$$$. New American. Sumptuous restaurant with Belle Epoque accents occupies 19C building whose windows frame the Bay Bridge.

Fog City Diner *(1300 Battery St.; ☎ 415-982-2000)*. $$. American. Gourmet seafood and cheeseburgers with fries are standard fare at chrome-and-neon establishment beneath Telegraph Hill.

Gordon Biersch *(2 Harrison St.; ☎ 415-243-8246)*. $$. California. Eclectic variety of foods complement custom-brewed ales and pilsners at warehouse-style brewpub.

Il Fornaio *(1265 Battery St.; ☎ 415-986-0100)*. $$. Italian. Milanese pizzas, pastas, rotisserie meats and pastries served below eastern slope of Telegraph Hill.

One Market *(1 Market St.; ☎ 415-777-5577)*. $$$. New American. Hearty roots cuisine, served in cavernous dining room, draws folks to this popular restaurant.

Financial District

Aqua *(252 California St.; ☎ 415-956-9662)*. $$$$. Seafood. Imaginatively crafted dishes offered in opulent setting two blocks from Embarcadero Center.

Bix *(56 Gold St.; ☎ 415-433-6300)*. $$$. California. Art Deco-style supper club, tucked away in Jackson Square, appeals to after-business crowd.

Le Central *(453 Bush St.; ☎ 415-391-2233)*. $$$. French. Brasserie standbys like cassoulet and steaks, coupled with Left Bank ambience, draw power brokers to power lunches.

Rubicon *(558 Sacramento St.; ☎ 415-434-4100)*. $$$. California. Classic French-flavored cuisine served in loft-like restaurant owned by Hollywood film personalities.

Sam's Grill *(374 Bush St.; ☎* 415-421-0594). $$. Seafood. Founded in 1867 as open-air market, it is today a no-nonsense cafe serving fresh fish.

Splendido *(4 Embarcadero Center; ☎ 415-986-3222)*. $$$. Mediterranean. California influences dominate menu amid whimsical Italian seaside village atmosphere.

Tadich Grill *(240 California St.; ☎ 415-391-1849)*. $$$. Seafood. Gold Rush-era institution has long wooden bar, aproned waiters and popular menu of grilled fish.

Tommy Toy's *(655 Montgomery St.; ☎ 415-397-4888)*. $$$. French-Asian. Creative restaurant luxuriously decorated in 19C imperial Chinese fashion; known as a celebrity haunt.

Vertigo *(600 Montgomery St.; ☎ 415-433-7250)*. $$$$. Mediterranean-Asian. Windows looking into redwood grove at foot of Transamerica Pyramid, this creative restaurant keeps surprising diners—like Hitchcock movie for which it's named.

Yank Sing *(49 Stevenson St.; ☎ 415-541-4949; and 427 Battery St.; ☎ 415-781-1111)*. $. Chinese. Dozens of servers wheel heavily laden dim-sum carts past anxious lunchtime diners daily.

Fisherman's Wharf

Alioto's *(8 Fisherman's Wharf; ☎ 415-673-0183)*. $$. Seafood. Sidewalk frontage of Sicilian seafood restaurant features fastest crab-cracker on bay.

Chez Michel *(804 North Point St.; ☎ 415-775-7036)*. $$$. French. Set back from bustle of the Wharf, sophisticated restaurant offers contemporary takes on classic continental dishes.

Loongbar *(Ghirardelli Square; ☎ 415-771-6800)*. $$$. Asian Fusion. New in 1998, restaurant is elegant leap into innovative East-West cuisine by celebrity chef Mark Miller (of Coyote Cafe fame).

McCormick & Kuleto's *(Ghirardelli Square; ☎ 415-929-1730)*. $$$. Seafood. Spacious, attractive restaurant has oyster bar, grilled-fish menu and views toward Alcatraz.

Scoma's *(Pier 47; ☎ 415-771-4383)*. $$. Seafood. Rambling restaurant with broad waterfront views has been institution since the 1960s.

Tarantino's *(206 Jefferson St., ☎ 415-775-5600)*. $$. Seafood. Tiered seating has assured diners view of boat basin since 1946; steamed clams are specialty.

Haight-Ashbury

EOS *(901 Cole St.; ☎ 415-566-3063)*. $$$. Asian fusion. Artfully arranged experimental cuisine is presented in a minimalist setting.

Thep Phanom *(400 Waller St.; ☎ 415-431-2526)*. $$. Thai. Dishes like honey duck on spinach and seafood curry on banana leaves result in queues out the door.

Zazie *(941 Cole St.; ☎ 415-564-5332)*. $$. French. Cheery bistro with outdoor seating serves three meals daily.

Japantown

Café Kati *(1963 Sutter St.; ☎ 415-775-7313)*. $$$. Fusion. Creative blends of international cuisines draw patrons to this eatery, tucked away in a residential block.

Mifune *(1737 Post St.; ☎ 415-922-0337)*. $$. Japanese. Acclaimed noodle house serves 55 varieties of udon and soba in a stark red-and-black ambience.

Now and Zen Bistro *(1826 Buchanan St.; ☎ 415-922-9696)*. $$. Vegan. Small cafe makes case that meals with no meat, dairy, eggs nor sugar can still be gourmet.

Marina District

Ace Wasabi's Rock & Roll Sushi *(3339 Steiner St.; ☎ 415-567-4903)*. $$. Japanese. Cameras in Generation X hangout are wired to the internet.

Cafe Marimba *(2317 Chestnut St.; ☎ 415-776-1506)*. $$. Mexican. Diners come for dizzying displays of colorful folk art and stay for Oaxacan-style cuisine.

Green's *(Bldg. A, Fort Mason Center; ☎ 415-771-6222)*. $$$. Vegetarian. Innovative gourmet restaurant has award-winning wine list and view of Golden Gate Bridge.

Lhasa Moon *(2420 Lombard St.; ☎ 415-674-9898)*. $. Tibetan. Immigrant-run restaurant offers true adventure in dining with rarely sampled, Indian-influenced cuisine.

Mission District

Arabian Nights *(811 Valencia St.; ☎ 415-821-9747)*. $$. Middle Eastern. Belly dancers entertain diners who sit on floor eating off brass trays.

Fina Estampa *(2374 Mission St.; ☎ 415-824-4437)*. $$. Peruvian. Paellas, tapas and spicy South American specialties are served behind hard-to-find storefront.

Flying Saucer *(1000 Guerrero St.; ☎ 415-641-9955)*. $$$. California. Quirky restaurant's eclectic decor and cross-cultural cuisine could be from another world.

La Taqueria *(2889 Mission St.; ☎ 415-285-7117)*. $. Mexican. Fresh, basic tacos and burritos dished up with healthy fruit drinks at tiny neighborhood eatery.

Original Cuba Restaurant *(2886 16th St.; ☎ 415-255-0946)*. $$. Cuban. Authentic Caribbean-style spot boasts salsa music and ceiling fans.

Ti Couz *(3108 16th St.; ☎ 415-252-7373)*. $. French-Breton. Patrons queue up for savory and sweet crepes; also busy wine-and-cider bar.

Val 21 *(995 Valencia St.; ☎ 415-821-6622)*. $$. Fusion. Stylish restaurant, next door to natural-foods store, experiments with world of exotic ingredients.

Nob Hill

Hyde Street Bistro *(1521 Hyde St.; ☎ 415-292-4415)*. $$. Austrian. German and Italian influences on Viennese cuisine are evident at this intimate neighborhood restaurant.

Swan Oyster Depot *(1517 Polk St.; ☎ 415-673-1101)*. $$. Seafood. Lunch counter has been serving crab, shellfish, chowders and banter since 1912.

North Beach

Fior d'Italia *(601 Union St.; ☎ 415-986-1886)*. $$. Italian. Billed as America's oldest Italian restaurant, Washington Park institution opened in 1886.

Julius' Castle *(1541 Montgomery St.; ☎ 415-392-2222)*. $$$. Italian. Romantic hillside restaurant near Coit Tower persists as tourist draw with panoramic views.

Little City *(673 Union St.; ☎ 415-434-2900)*. $$. Italian. Noted for huge antipasti list and imported wines, this is favored place for people-watching.

Little Joe's *(523 Broadway; ☎ 415-433-4343)*. $$. Italian. Locals line up for huge plates of pasta at loud, traditional dining room.

Mario's Bohemian Cigar Store Cafe *(566 Columbus Ave.; ☎ 415-362-0536)*. $. Italian. Quaint corner cafe noted for toasted focaccia sandwiches.

Moose's *(1652 Stockton St.; ☎ 415-989-7800)*. $$$. California-Mediterranean. Blue neon moose over entrance lures civic leaders and wanna-bes to Washington Square.

Rose Pistola *(532 Columbus Ave.; ☎ 415-399-0499)*. $$. Italian. Lively family-style restaurant won 1997 James Beard award for best new restaurant in US.

San Francisco Brewing Company *(155 Columbus Ave.; ☎ 415-434-3344)*. $$. American. Former Andromeda Saloon of Barbary Coast notoriety now serves hearty food with award-winning beers.

The Stinking Rose *(325 Columbus Ave.; ☎ 415-781-7673)*. $$. Italian. Tourists flock for garlic-laden dishes guaranteed to repel vampires.

Washington Square Bar & Grill *(1707 Powell St.; ☎ 415-982-8123)*. $$$. Continental. Oldtime restaurant has noisy piano-and-martini bar and newly creative menu.

Pacific Heights

Baker Street Bistro *(2953 Baker St.; ☎ 415-931-1475)*. $$. French. Light bistro-style entrees and prix-fixe menu are offered at small neighborhood restaurant.

Leon's Bar-B-Q *(1911 Fillmore St.; ☎ 415-922-2436)*. $$. Barbecue. Long narrow "dive," contrast to ritzy neighborhood, is famous for pork ribs.

Rassellas *(2801 California St.; ☎ 415-567-5010)*. $. Ethiopian. Spicy African food served in dark, exotic atmosphere that doubles as jazz club after dark.

Richmond District

Angkor Wat *(4217 Geary Blvd.; ☎ 415-221-7887)*. $$. Cambodian. Classical Asian ballet is performed weekends amid exotic temple decor; Pope John Paul II ate here.

Formosa *(1125 Clement St.; ☎ 415-386-2198)*. $. Chinese-Taiwanese. Adventurous diners come for unusual dishes like pig ears and sea cucumber.

Katia's Russian Tea Room *(600 Fifth Ave.; ☎ 415-668-9292)*. $$. Russian. Cheery home-style cafe offers all the piroshki and stroganoff you might desire.

Kabuto Sushi *(5116 Geary Blvd.; ☎ 415-752-5652)*. $$. Japanese. Small sushi bar kept popular by fresh-fish preparations and highly entertaining chef-owner.

Lee's *(294 Eighth Ave.; ☎ 415-387-5883)*. $. Vietnamese. Deli and noodle house offers intriguing sandwiches and Asian fruit shakes.

Le Soleil *(133 Clement St.; ☎ 415-668-4848)*. $$. Vietnamese. French influence pervades Saigon cuisine at this thoughtfully decorated Asian eatery.

Restaurant Clémentine *(126 Clement St.; ☎ 415-387-0408)*. $$$. French. Formerly known as Alain Rondelli, this serene cafe blends California and continental elements.

Ton Kiang *(5821 Geary Blvd.; ☎ 415-386-8530)*. $$. Chinese-Hakka. Clay-pot casseroles and flavorful dim sum speak highly for Asian regional cuisines.

Russian Hill

Frascati *(1901 Hyde St.; ☎ 415-928-1406)*. $$. California. Fine artwork adorns Italian-style room with creative takes on American, Mediterranean and Asian dishes.

La Folie *(2316 Polk St.; ☎ 415-776-5577)*. $$$$. French. Fresh produce like avocadoes and huckleberries enhance classic dishes at romantic, family-run bistro.

Zarzuela *(2000 Hyde St.; ☎ 415-346-0800)*. $$. Spanish. Flamenco-style guitar music accents tapas and paellas served on hand-painted plates.

South of Market

Brain Wash Cafe & Laundromat *(1122 Folsom St.; ☎ 415-861-3663)*. $. American. Whacky diner boasts live bands, dance floor and, yes, a laundromat.

Hamburger Mary's *(1582 Folsom St.; ☎ 415-626-5767)*. $. American. Classic burger joint attracts many of the tattooed and pierced set.

Hawthorne Lane *(22 Hawthorne St., off Howard St.; ☎ 415-777-9779)*. $$$. Asian fusion. Bright, busy, innovative restaurant sits on small alley behind Museum of Modern Art.

Le Fringale *(570 Fourth St.; ☎ 415-543-0573)*. $$. French Basque. Stylish, authentic corner bistro, noted for mussels and pork dishes, is oasis in "multimedia gulch."

M&M Tavern & Grill *(198 Fifth St.; ☎ 415-362-6386)*. $. American. Smoky bar, popular with journalists, serves solid blue plates and sandwiches.

Restaurant LuLu *(816 Folsom St.; ☎ 415-495-5775)*. $$. Mediterranean. Bright and noisy converted warehouse specializes in rotisserie grills.

South Park Cafe *(108 South Park Ave.; ☎ 415-495-7275)*. $$. French. Casual sidewalk cafe, facing pretty park, evokes Latin Quarter ambience.

Sunset District

Casa Aguila *(1240 Noriega St.; ☎ 415-661-5593)*. $$. Mexican. Small neighborhood restaurant near Grand View Park offers wide choice of creative, authentic dishes.

PJ's Oysterbed *(767 Irving St.; ☎ 415-566-7775)*. $$. Cajun. New Orleans-style seafood served in Mardi Gras atmosphere with zydeco music playing in background, a block from Golden Gate Park.

YaYa Cuisine *(1220 Ninth Ave.; ☎ 415-566-6966)*. $$. Middle Eastern. Iraqi chef prepares exotic dishes amid ambience of ancient Babylon.

Sutro Heights

Beach Chalet Brewery & Restaurant *(1000 Great Hwy.; ☎ 415-386-8439)*. $$. American. Popular brewpub serves comfort food at west end of Golden Gate Park.

The Cliff House *(1090 Point Lobos Ave.; ☎ 415-386-3330)*. $$$. American. Romantic steak-and-seafood establishment overlooks Seal Rocks and the Pacific Ocean.

Union Square

Anjou *(44 Campton Pl.; ☎ 415-392-5373)*. $$. French. Hidden in small urban lane, restaurant offers traditional and creative cuisine.

Café de la Presse *(352 Grant Ave.; ☎ 415-398-2680)*. $$. French. Casual meals prepared early and late at international newsstand beside Chinatown Gate.

Dottie's True Blue Cafe *(522 Jones St.; ☎ 415-885-2767)*. $. American. Classic '50s-style diner doles out generous portions for breakfast and lunch.

Farallon *(450 Post St.; ☎ 415-956-6969)*. $$$$. Seafood. Decor of flamboyant and creative restaurant is characterized by blown-glass jellyfish hanging over tables.

Fleur de Lys *(777 Sutter St.; ☎ 415-673-7779)*. $$$$. French. Graciously elegant top-of-the-line restaurant adds contemporary California flair to classic recipes.

John's Grill *(63 Ellis St.; ☎ 415-986-3274)*. $$. American. The true Maltese Falcon, made famous by author-patron Dashiell Hammett and actor Humphrey Bogart, is at home behind the bar.

Masa's *(648 Bush St.; ☎ 415-989-7154)*. $$$$. French. Creative prix-fixe, special-occasion dinners served in luxurious and intimate setting.

Postrio *(545 Post St.; ☎ 415-776-7825)*. $$$. California. Wolfgang Puck's spacious and elegant Prescott Hotel eatery serves hybrid of American, Mediterranean and Asian dishes.

Scala's Bistro *(432 Powell St.; ☎ 415-395-8555)*. $$. Italian and French. Attractive regional-European bistro with arty decor, reliable service and lively bar scene.

Sears Fine Foods *(439 Powell St.; ☎ 415-986-1160)*. $. American. Campy diner in Chancellor Hotel known for frumpy waitresses and Swedish pancakes.

OTHER AREAS

East Bay

Bay Wolf *(3853 Piedmont Ave., Oakland; ☎ 510-655-6004)*. $$$. California. Mediterranean-influenced dishes served in romantic setting in refurbished Victorian home.

Chez Panisse *(1517 Shattuck Ave., Berkeley; ☎ 510-548-5525)*. $$$$. California. Craftsman-style restaurant begat California cuisine craze in 1971. Prix-fixe dinners are served downstairs; a more casual cafe is upstairs.

Oliveto *(5655 College Ave., Oakland; ☎ 510-547-5356)*. $$$. Italian. Simple seasonal Florentine cuisine served in country trattoria setting.

Santa Fe Bar & Grill *(1310 University Ave., Berkeley; ☎ 510-841-1110)*. $$. Southwestern. Remodeled train depot grows its own produce in adjoining garden.

Marin County

Buckeye Roadhouse *(15 Shoreline Hwy., Mill Valley; ☎ 415-331-2600)*. $$. American. Gourmet touch given to hearty home cooking in wilderness-lodge atmosphere.

Guaymas *(5 Main St., Tiburon; ☎ 415-435-6300)*. $$. Mexican. Diners sip margaritas and dine on Jaliscan-style tacos and tamales while enjoying panoramic view of Angel Island and San Francisco skyline.

Lark Creek Inn *(234 Magnolia Ave., Larkspur; ☎ 415-924-7766)*. $$$. New American. Chef Brad Ogden's culinary talents are showcased in spacious Victorian house surrounded by tall redwoods.

Wine Country

The French Laundry *(6640 Washington St., Yountville; ☎ 707-944-2380)*. $$$$. French. Lavish and creative prix-fixe restaurant indeed occupies an old stone laundry house.

Mustard's Grill *(7399 St. Helena Hwy., Yountville; ☎ 707-944-2424)*. $$. American. Winemakers and industry VIPs gather at casual, popular ranch-style restaurant.

Tra Vigne *(1050 Charter Oak Ave., St. Helena; ☎ 707-963-4444)*. $$$. Italian. Menu features home-processed grilled meats, pastas and pizzas; seating is outside among grape vines or inside spacious trattoria.

Wine Spectator Greystone Restaurant *(2555 Main St., St. Helena; ☎ 707-967-1010)*. $$$. New American. Open kitchen showcases student chefs and recent graduates from adjacent Culinary Institute of America.

Shopping

From large complexes incorporating national chains, restaurants and entertainment venues, to intimate rows of boutiques scattered throughout the city, San Francisco will satisfy the most ardent shopper. Most stores accept major credit cards and travelers checks, but not out-of-state checks. Many shops extend their hours during the holiday season (mid-November through December). *The San Francisco Book (p 220)* offers detailed information on types of shops, locations and hours of operation.

Union Square Area – *p 71*. Considered San Francisco's main shopping district, this area is home to most of the city's department stores. **Nordstrom** *(☎ 415-243-8500)* is located in the **San Francisco Shopping Centre** *(865 Market St., ☎ 415-495-5656)*, an enormous complex of more than 100 shops and restaurants. Other major department stores in this area include **Macy's** *(corner of Stockton & O'Farrell Sts., ☎ 415-397-3333)*, **Neiman Marcus** *(150 Stockton St., ☎ 415-362-3900)*, **Gump's** *(135 Post St. ☎ 415-982-1616)* and **Saks Fifth Avenue** *(384 Post St., The Men's Store at 220 Post St.; ☎ 415-986-4300)*. Designer boutiques and specialty shops such as **Emporio Armani** *(1 Grant Ave., ☎ 415-677-9400)* and **Burberry's** *(225 Post St., ☎ 415-392-2200)* can be found along and around Grant Avenue, Post Street, Sutter Street and Maiden Lane. San Francisco's largest concentration of art galleries is located along Geary, Sutter, Post and Powell Streets. The *San Francisco Gallery Guide*, published bimonthly, provides a comprehensive listing of exhibits and their locations *(available from SF Bay Area Gallery Guide, 1369 Fulton St., ☎ 415-921-1600)*.

Financial District – *p 47*. San Francisco's business district boasts the **Embarcadero Center** *(next to Justin Herman Plaza, ☎ 415-772-0550 or 800-733-6318)*, a 10-acre office and retail complex incorporating more than 125 shops and restaurants. The **Crocker Galleria** *(50 Post St., ☎ 415-393-1505)* contains nearly 50 designer and specialty shops. More than 25 fine **antique** shops are located in the Jackson Square Historic District near Jackson & Montgomery Streets *(Jackson Square Art & Antiques Dealers Association ☎ 415-397-6999)*.

Chinatown – *p 36*. Haggle at an open-air market or admire luxurious silks and jades in this colorful, bustling micro-city. Pharmacies sell traditional Asian herbal remedies and a plenitude of restaurants offer *dim sum* and other Chinese delicacies.

Fisherman's Wharf – *p 81*. Four major retail centers punctuate this festive strip of souvenir shops and novelty museums: the **Anchorage**, with more than 50 shops and restaurants *(☎ 415-775-6000)*; the **Cannery**, housing nearly 40 specialty shops and restaurants *(☎ 415-771-3112)*; **Ghirardelli Square**, featuring more than 70 shops including major retail chains *(☎ 415-775-5500)*; and **Pier 39**, boasting more than 100 specialty and gift shops *(☎ 415-981-7437)*.

Bob Thomason/Tony Stone Images

Ghirardelli Square

Haight Street – *p 124.* The erstwhile heart of San Francisco counterculture offers an eclectic assortment of boutiques, secondhand stores, record shops and bookstores.

South of Market – *p 141.* A bargain hunter's dream, this area incorporates dozens of outlet centers, resale shops and design showrooms. **Baker Hamilton Square** *(700 7th St., ☎ 415-861-3500)* incorporates a wide assortment of antique stores.

Mission District – *p 137.* This lively area abounds with shops selling Latin American imports, including jewelry and clothing; alternative art galleries; small grocery stores, and restaurants. **Valencia Street** is the hub of the shopping district.

Other Shopping Areas

In addition to the areas described above, charming neighborhood shopping areas can be found throughout San Francisco. Most harbor a pleasant mix of small boutiques, specialty shops, bookstores, restaurants and cafes.

Union Street (Cow Hollow)	*between Van Ness Ave. & Steiner St.*
Chestnut Street (Marina District)	*between Divisadero & Fillmore Sts.*
Fillmore Street (Pacific Heights)	*between Jackson & Bush Sts. & Union & Greenwich Sts.*
Hayes Street (Civic Center)	*between Franklin & Octavia Sts.*
24th Street (Noe Valley)	*between Church & Douglass Sts.*
Castro Street (Castro District)	*between 16th & 19th Sts.*
Sacramento Street (Richmond District)	*between Spruce & Baker Sts.*

Spectator Sports

Tickets for events can be purchased at the venue, or through Ticketmaster *(p 234)*. It's best to buy tickets well in advance.

Sport/Team	Season	Home Stadium	☎ Information
Major League Baseball	Apr–Oct		
San Francisco Giants (NL)		**3Com Park**	**415-467-8000**
			800-734-4268
Oakland A's (AL)		**Oakland Coliseum**	**510-568-5600**
National Football League	Sept–Dec		
San Francisco 49ers		**3Com Park**	**415-656-4949**
Oakland Raiders		**Oakland Coliseum**	**510-615-1888**
			800-949-2626
National Basketball Assn.	Nov–Apr		
Golden State Warriors		**Oakland Coliseum Arena**	**510-986-2200**

3Com Park (formerly Candlestick Park) is located south of San Francisco in the Candlestick Point State Recreation Area. By **car** take US-101 south to park exit. The "Ballpark Express" **bus** offers service between San Francisco and the stadium *($5 round-trip, Muni bus 9X, 28X & 47X, ☎ 415-673-6864). Note: the park is windy and chilly; bring a jacket or sweater.* **Oakland Coliseum** is located near Oakland International Airport. By **car** from San Francisco cross the Oakland Bay Bridge and take I-580 to I-980 to I-880 south to 66th Ave. exit. By rail, take the BART Fremont line to the Coliseum stop, where a walkway leads to the stadium.

Recreation

The mild climate of the San Francisco Bay Area promotes myriad recreational opportunities year-round, most located right in the city or within an hour's drive of its limits. Hikers, bikers and equestrians regularly avail themselves of the trails throughout Marin County, the East Bay and the San Francisco Peninsula. Lovers of water sports can take to the waves for surfing, windsurfing and sea kayaking, although swimming in most places is unsafe. Jogging, in-line skating, hang-gliding, kite-flying and sportfishing only begin to round out the recreational possibilities.
Golden Gate Park *(p 107)*, Marin County and the units of the Golden Gate National Recreation Area (GGNRA) are good places to start when seeking outdoor recreation information. Trail maps, facility hours and other information are available at the **San Francisco Recreation & Park Department** (McLaren Lodge, Golden Gate Park, San Francisco CA 94117 ☎ 415-831-2700) and the **GGNRA** (Fort Mason, Building 201, San Francisco CA 94123-1308, ☎ 415-556-0560). The **Marin County Convention & Visitors Bureau** (1013 Larkspur Landing Circle, Larkspur, CA 94939 ☎ 415-499-5000) provides maps and recreational information.

Hiking – The Bay Area is a hiker's paradise, with extensive trails exploring its valleys, scaling its peaks, tracing its coastlines and penetrating its forests. Contact the GGNRA or the San Francisco Recreation & Park Department *(above)* for trail maps and information. Within the city, the **Golden Gate Promenade** (4mi) from Aquatic Park to the Golden Gate Bridge, and the **Coastal Trail** (9mi) from the Golden Gate Bridge to Fort Funston, afford lovely ocean and cityscape views.

Biking – Mountain biking *(p 183)* is an especially popular sport among the hills and valleys of Marin County and in the Presidio and Land's End areas of San Francisco. Most trails are accessible to both hikers and bikers, though some are restricted to hikers only. Routes within San Francisco include the Golden Gate Promenade and the Coastal Trail *(above)*. In addition, many streets have designated bike lanes. Contact the SFCVB *(p 220)* for a book on biking in the area *($9)*. Shops offering rentals and trail information include:

Adventure Bike Company ....bikes, tandems
968 Columbus Ave., ☎ 415-771-8735

Blazing Saddles Bike Rentals ....bikes, tandems
1095 Columbus Ave., ☎ 415-202-8888

Park Cyclery ....bikes, tandems, skates
1749 Waller St., ☎ 415-221-3777

Golden Gate Park Skate & Bike ....bikes, tandems, skates
3038 Fulton St., ☎ 415-668-1117

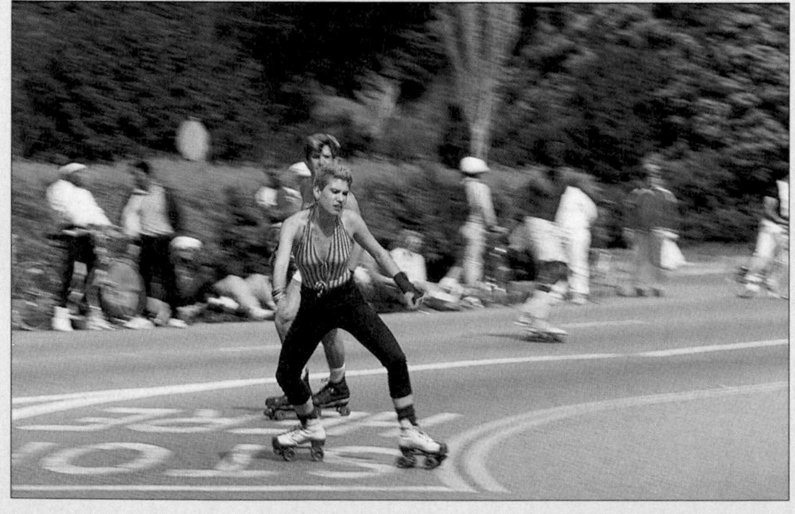
© Robert Holmes

Fishing – The most common fishes found in the bay are striped bass, halibut and rock cod. Sport fishing charters specializing in salmon (Jun–Oct) and giant sturgeon depart for the ocean from Fisherman's Wharf. Public fishing piers include Aquatic Park Municipal Pier, Fort Mason Piers, Fort Point/Crissy Field Pier, Baker Beach and Pier 7 at the Embarcadero. A fishing license is required to take fish and crustaceans (except for persons angling from a public pier); one-day nonresident licenses are available in fishing supply stores.

Swimming and Beachwalking – The waters along the Pacific shore and the Golden Gate can be dangerous. Tides sweep in suddenly and powerfully and "sneaker waves" can appear without warning. Never turn your back to the ocean and avoid walking along coastal cliffs; keep to established trails. Riptides (strong, narrow, seaward flows), sudden dropoffs and strong currents make most areas dangerous for swimming and even wading. In addition, water temperatures average a chilly 55°F (13°C) year-round. Exercise caution when swimming at all times, and obey posted warnings.

Selected Bay Area Beaches

	$	swimming	lifeguard	camping	disabled facilities	surfing
Aquatic Park Beach *(p 87)*		●			●	
Baker Beach *(p 102)*						●
Bean Hollow State Beach *(p 214)*						
Bolinas Beach *(p 185)*		●				●
China Beach *(p 159)*		●	●	●		●
Crissy Field *(p 101)*						
Drakes Beach *(p 187)*		●			●	
Fort Funston *(p 150)*		●				●
Francis State Beach *(p 213)*	●	●		●	●	●
Kehoe Beach		●				●
Land's End *(p 155)*		●				
Lighthouse Field State Beach					●	●
Limantour Beach *(p 187)*		●			●	
McClures Beach *(p 188)*		●				
Montara State Beach		●				
Muir Beach *(p 184)*		●			●	
North Beach & South Beach *(p 187)*	●			●		
Ocean Beach *(p 149)*					●	●
Pebble Beach *(p 214)*						
Pescadero State Beach *(p 213)*						●
Rodeo Beach *(p 181)*					●	●
San Gregorio State Beach *(p 213)*	●				●	
Stinson Beach *(p 184)*		●	●		●	●
Tomales Bay State Park *(p 188)*	●	●		●	●	

Symbols on the above chart indicate: $ admission/parking fee; swimming; lifeguard; camping; disabled facilities; surfing.

Golf – There are three public courses in San Francisco; all rent out clubs and other equipment.

Lincoln Park .... *open daily dawn–dusk*
34th Ave. & Clement St., ☎ 415-221-9911

Golden Gate Golf Course .... *open daily dawn–dusk*
47th Ave. & Fulton St., ☎ 415-751-8987

Presidio Golf Course .... *open daily 7am–7pm*
West Pacific Ave., The Presidio, ☎ 415-561-4653

Windsurfing – Consistent westerly winds from March to October make San Francisco Bay a prime spot for windsurfing, particularly at Crissy Field, Candlestick Point and Lake Merced. Many organizations offer instruction and rental equipment, including **San Francisco School of Windsurfing** (Candlestick Point & Lake Merced, ☎ 415-753-3235) and **City Fun Sailboards** (Crissy Field, ☎ 415-929-7873). Note that certification is required to rent windsurfing equipment; contact the **San Francisco Boardsailing Association** (1592 Union St., P.O. Box 301, San Francisco CA 94123, www.sfba.org) for additional information.

Hang-gliding – The cliffs of Fort Funston rank among the finest hang-gliding sites in the US *(main season Mar–Oct)*. Several hang-gliding shops, located near the fort, offer rentals and instruction. Contact the **Bay Area Paragliding Association** for a list of shops, current conditions and hang-gliding events (BAPA, P.O. Box 1809, Pacifica, CA 94044, www.igi.org/bapa ☎ 415-864-6359).

Working Out – Many clubs allow non-members to utilize their facilities for a daily fee *($10-$15)*.

Club One	☎
Two Embarcadero Center *(Financial District)*	415-398-1111
950 California St. *(Nob Hill)*	415-398-1111
24-Hour Fitness	
350 Bay St. *(North Beach)*	415-395-9595
100 California St. *(Financial District)*	415-434-5080
1200 Van Ness Ave. *(Japantown)*	415-776-2200
303 2nd St. at Folsom St. *(SoMa)*	415-543-7808
Marina Fitness Club	
3333 Fillmore St. *(Marina District)*	415-563-3333
Pinnacle Fitness Club	
345 Spear St. *(SoMa)*	415-495-1939
61 New Montgomery St. *(Union Square)*	415-543-1110
465 California St. *(Financial District)*	415-982-9800

Some hotels offer guest access to private fitness centers; check with the concierge.

YMCA memberships are valid worldwide; call for closest recreation center and available facilities ☎ 415-391-9622.

Index

Transamerica Pyramid .... Point of interest, city, building
Hopkins, Mark .... Person, historical event, subject, Practical Information
Museums and Parks are also grouped separately under those headings.

A

B

C

D

E

F

G

H

I

J

K

L

M

N

O

P

Q – R

S